Lecture Notes in Artificial Intelligence   2752

Edited by J. G. Carbonell and J. Siekmann

Subseries of Lecture Notes in Computer Science

Springer
Berlin
Heidelberg
New York
Hong Kong
London
Milan
Paris
Tokyo

Gal A. Kaminka   Pedro U. Lima
Raul Rojas (Eds.)

RoboCup 2002:
Robot Soccer
World Cup VI

Springer

Series Editors

Jaime G. Carbonell, Carnegie Mellon University, Pittsburgh, PA, USA
Jörg Siekmann, University of Saarland, Saarbrücken, Germany

Volume Editors

Gal A. Kaminka
Bar Ilan University, Computer Science Department
Ramat Gan, 52900 Israel
E-mail: galk@cs.biu.ac.il

Pedro U. Lima
Instituto Superior Tecnico, Instituto de Sistemas e Robotica
Av. Rovisco Pais, 1, 1049-001 Lisbon, Portugal
E-mail: pal@isr.ist.utl.pt

Raul Rojas
Freie Universität Berlin, Fachbereich Mathematik und Informatik
Takustr. 9, 14195 Berlin, Germany
E-mail: rojas@inf.fu-berlin.de

Cataloging-in-Publication Data applied for

A catalog record for this book is available from the Library of Congress

Bibliographic information published by Die Deutsche Bibliothek
Die Deutsche Bibliothek lists this publication in the Deutsche Nationalbibliographie;
detailed bibliographic data is available in the Internet at <http://dnd.ddb.de>.

CR Subject Classification (1998): I.2, C.2.4, D.2.7, H.5, I.5.4, J.4

ISSN 0302-9743
ISBN 3-540-40666-2 Springer-Verlag Berlin Heidelberg New York

Springer-Verlag Berlin Heidelberg New York,
a member of BertelsmannSpringer Science+Business Media GmbH

http://www.springer.de

© Springer-Verlag Berlin Heidelberg 2003
Printed in Germany

Typesetting: Camera-ready by author, data conversion by Olgun Computergrafik
Printed on acid-free paper   SPIN: 10930656   06/3142   5 4 3 2 1 0

Preface

RoboCup 2002, the 6th Robot World Cup Soccer and Rescue Competitions and Conference, took place during June 19–25, 2002, at the Fukuoka Dome (main venue) in Fukuoka, Japan. It was, by far, the RoboCup event with the largest number of registered participants (1004 persons, distributed in 188 teams from 29 countries) and visitors (around 120,000 persons). As was done in its previous editions since 1997, the event included several robotic competitions and an international symposium. The papers and posters presented at the symposium constitute the main part of this book. League reports in the final section describe significant advances in each league and the results.

The symposium organizers received 76 submissions, among which 17 papers (22%) were accepted for oral presentation at the symposium (first section of the book), and 21 papers (29%) were accepted as posters (second section of the book). Most papers were evaluated by three reviewers each, chosen from the members of the International Program Committee (IPC). The IPC consisted of a balanced combination of regular RoboCup participants and researchers from outside this community. The reviewers worked hard to guarantee a fair review process – the result of their work was a high-quality symposium with very interesting presentations.

From the papers accepted for oral presentation, the IPC and the symposium chairs selected three finalists for the symposium prizes. The Scientific Challenge Award was given to the paper "RoboCupJunior: Learning with Educational Robotics," by Elizabeth Sklar, Amy Eguchi, and Jeffrey Johnson. The Engineering Challenge Award was given to two papers: "MPADES: Middleware for Parallel Agent Discrete Event Simulation," by Patrick Riley, and "Towards RoboCup Without Color Labeling," by Robert Hanek, Thorsten Schmitt, Sebastian Buck, and Michael Beetz.

Five internationally renowned researchers accepted our invitation to give special talks at the symposium:

- "Humanoid Robots as Research Tools of Neuroscience," by Mitsuo Kawato (ATR, Japan).
- "A Small Humanoid Robot SDR-4X for Entertainment Based on OPEN-R," by Masahiro Fujita (DCL, SONY, Japan).
- "Cooperation by Observation," by Yasuo Kuniyoshi (University of Tokyo, Japan).
- "A Research and Development Vision for Robot-Assisted Search and Rescue," by John Blitch (CRASAR, USA).
- "Multi-robot Systems: Where We've Been and Where We're Going," by Lynne Parker (Oak Ridge National Laboratory and University of Tennessee, USA).

The last talk was delivered at a joint session with DARS-2002, the 6th International Symposium on Distributed Autonomous Robotic Systems.

The competitions were organized into seven leagues, the Rescue leagues (Simulation and Real Robots), the Soccer leagues (Simulation, Humanoids, Middle-Size, Small-Size, and 4-Legged), and the RoboCup Junior soccer and dance competitions for children, roughly in the age range 10–18 years old. The overview article at the beginning of the book summarizes all the competitions.

The editors of this book are grateful to the RoboCup Federation for all the logistic and financial assistance provided for the realization of the symposium. Minoru Asada carried the burden of organizing the printed edition of the preproceedings and the production of the respective CD. He did a great job organizing RoboCup 2002 and making the symposium possible. We are also grateful to our families who had to cope with our strange working hours, while we were sending e-mails and files back and forth across three time zones and three continents.

The next international RoboCup events will be held in Padua, Italy, in 2003, and in Lisbon, Portugal, in 2004.

May 2003   Gal Kaminka
Pedro U. Lima
Raul Rojas

RoboCup Federation

Thomas Christaller (observer), Fraunhofer Institute
for Autonomous Intelligent Systems – AiS, Germany

Education
Daniele Nardi, University of Rome "La Sapienza," Italy
Paul Levi, University of Stuttgart, Germany

RoboCup Rescue
Satoshi Tadokoro, Kobe University, Japan
Adam Jacoff (observer), National Institute of Standards and Technology
– Intelligent Systems Division, USA

RoboCup Junior
Henrik Hautop Lund, University of Southern Denmark, Denmark
Elizabeth Sklar, Columbia University, USA

RoboCup 2002 Organization and Support

General Chair

Minoru Asada, Osaka University, Japan

Associate Chairs

Hitoshi Matsubara (Organizing Chair), Future University-Hakodate, Japan
Sho'ji Suzuki (Robotics Chair), Future University-Hakodate, Japan
Itsuki Noda (Simulation Chair), National Institute of Advanced Industrial
Science and Technology, Japan

Simulator League Committee

Daniel Polani (Chair), University of Hertfordshire, UK
Masayuki Ohta (Local Chair), National Institute of Advanced Industrial Science
and Technology, Japan
Patrick Riley, Carnegie Mellon University, USA
Oliver Obst, University of Koblenz, Germany

Small-Size Robot League (F180) Committee

Brett Browning (Chair), Carnegie Mellon University, USA
Yuki Nakagawa (Local Chair), National Museum of Emerging Science and
Innovation, Japan
Paulo Costa, FEUP, Portugal

Middle-Size Robot League (F2000) Committee

Andrea Bonarini (Chair), Politecnico di Milano, Italy
Takayuki Nakamura (Local Chair), Wakayama University, Japan
Yasutake Takahashi (Local Chair), Osaka University, Japan
Mansour Jamzad, Sharif University of Technology, Iran
Pedro Lima, Instituto Superior Técnico, Portugal

Four-Legged Robot League Committee

Masahiro Fujita (Chair), Sony, Inc., Japan
Takeshi Ohashi, Kyushu Institute of Technology, Japan

RoboCup Junior Committee

Elizabeth Sklar (Chair), Columbia University, USA
Tairo Nomura (Local Chair), Saitama University, Japan
Emi Ami Eguchi, University of Cambridge, UK

Humanoid League Committee

Thomas Christaller (Chair), Fraunhofer Institute
for Autonomous Intelligent Systems – AiS, Germany

RoboCup Rescue Simulation League Committee

Tomoichi Takahashi (Chair), Chubu University, Japan

RoboCup Rescue Robot League Committee

Adam Jacoff (Chair), NIST, USA
Satoshi Tadokoro (Local Chair), Kobe University, Japan
Robin Murphy, USF, USA

Symposium Program Committee

Giovanni Adorni, Italy
Richard Alami, France
Tamio Arai, Japan
Minoru Asada, Japan
Ronald Arkin, USA
Minoru Asada, Japan
Tucker Balch, USA
Suzanne Barber, USA
Mike Bowling, USA
Henrik Christensen, Sweden
Brad Clement, USA
Jorge Dias, Portugal
Ian Frank, Japan
Dani Goldberg, USA
Claudia Goldman, Israel
Steffen Gutmann, Germany
Joao Hespanha, USA
Adele Howe, USA
Huosheng Hu, UK
Mansour Jamzad, Iran
Jeffrey Johnson, UK
Pieter Jonker, The Netherlands
Hyuckchul Jung, USA
Gerhard Kraetzschmar, Germany
Pradeep Khosla, USA
Sarit Kraus, Israel

Sanjeev Kumar, USA
Kostas Kyriakopoulos, Greece
Stacy Marsella, USA
Robin Murphy, USA
Ranjit Nair, USA
Daniele Nardi, Italy
Itsuki Noda, Japan
Masayuki Ohta, Japan
Daniel Polani, Germany
David Pynadath, USA
Martin Riedmiller, Germany
Alessandro Saffiotti, Denmark
Paul Scerri, USA
Sandeep Sen, USA
Onn Shehory, Israel
Roland Siegwart, Switzerland
Elisabeth Sklar, USA
Elizabeth Sonenberg, Australia
Peter Stone, USA
Katya Sycara, USA
Satoshi Tadokoro, Japan
Will Uther, USA
Tom Wagner, USA
Marco Wiering, The Netherlands
Laura Winer, Canada

Table of Contents

Introduction

Technical Papers

Posters

League Reports

An Overview of RoboCup 2002 Fukuoka/Busan

Minoru Asada[1] and Gal A. Kaminka[2]

[1] Emergent Robotics Area, Dept. of Adaptive Machine Systems
Graduate School of Engineering, Osaka University
Yamadaoka 2-1, Suita, Osaka 565-0871, Japan
asada@ams.eng.osaka-u.ac.jp
[2] Computer Science Dept. Bar Ilan University
galk@macs.biu.ac.il

1 Introduction

The sixth Robot World Cup Competition and Conference (RoboCup 2002) Fukuoka/Busan took place between June 19th and 25th in Fukuoka: competitions were held at Fukuoka Dome Baseball Stadium from June 19th to 23rd, 2002, followed by the International RoboCup Symposium on June 24th and 25th, 2002.

RoboCup is an attempt to foster research on intelligent robotics by providing a standard problem with the ultimate goal of building a team of eleven humanoid robots that can beat the human World Cup champion soccer team by 2050. It is obvious that building a robot to play soccer is an immense challenge; readers might therefore wonder why we even bother to organize RoboCup. Our answer is: It is our intention to use RoboCup as a vehicle to promote robotics and AI research, by offering a publicly appealing but formidable challenge [1, 2].

A unique feature of RoboCup is that it is a systematic attempt to promote research using a common domain, mainly soccer. Also, it is perhaps the first benchmark to explicitly claim that the ultimate goal is to beat a human World Cup champion team. One of the more effective ways to promote engineering research, appart from specific application developments, is to define a significant long term goal. When the accomplishment of such a goal has significant social impact, we call it a *grand challenge project*. Building a robot to play soccer is not such a project. But its accomplishment would certainly be considered a major achievement in the field of robotics, and numerous technology spin-offs can be expected during the course of the project. We call this kind of project a *landmark project*, and RoboCup definitely falls into this category.

Since the first RoboCup in 1997 [3], the event has grown into an international joint-research project in which about 3000 scientists from 30 nations around the world participate (see Table 1 and Figure 1). It is one the most ambitious landmark projects of the 21st century. RoboCup currently consists of three divisions: RoboCupSoccer, aiming towards the final goal stated above, RoboCupRescue, a serious social application to rescue activities for any kinds of disasters, and RoboCupJunior, an international education-based initiative designed to introduce young students to robotics. The RoboCup 2002 competition was the largest

G.A. Kaminka, P.U. Lima, and R. Rojas (Eds.): RoboCup 2002, LNAI 2752, pp. 1–7, 2003.
© Springer-Verlag Berlin Heidelberg 2003

Table 1. Evolution of RoboCup Initiatives

Leagues/years	1997	1998	1999	2000	2001	2002
RoboCupSoccer						
Simulation	official	$\Longrightarrow$	$\Longrightarrow$	$\Longrightarrow$	$\Longrightarrow$	$\Longrightarrow$
Small-size	official	$\Longrightarrow$	$\Longrightarrow$	$\Longrightarrow$	$\Longrightarrow$	$\Longrightarrow$
Middle-size	official	$\Longrightarrow$	$\Longrightarrow$	$\Longrightarrow$	$\Longrightarrow$	$\Longrightarrow$
Legged		exhibition	official	$\Longrightarrow$	$\Longrightarrow$	$\Longrightarrow$
Humanoid				exhibition	exhibition	official
RoboCupRescue						
Simulation				official	$\Longrightarrow$	$\Longrightarrow$
Real robot				exhibition	official	$\Longrightarrow$
RoboCupJunior			exhibition	official	$\Longrightarrow$	$\Longrightarrow$

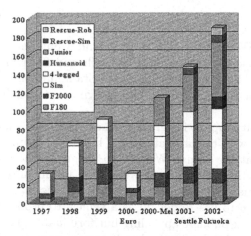

Fig. 1. The number of teams

since 1997, and set epoch-making new standards for future RoboCups. 1004 team members of 188 teams from 30 nations around the world participated. The first humanoid league competition was held, with participation from 13 teams from 5 nations. Further, the first ROBOTREX (robot trade and exhibition) was held with about 50 companies, universities, and institutes. A total of 117,000 spectators witnessed this marvelous event. To the best of our knowledge, this was the largest robotics event in history. Figs. 2 (a) and (b) show the dome and competition site.

This article presents the summary of the RoboCup 2002 (for more details, refer to [4]). The reports and symposium proceedings of past RoboCups are available [5–13].

2   RoboCupSoccer

RoboCup Soccer has the largest number of leagues: the simulation league, the small-size robot league, and the middle-size robot league (since the first RoboCup

(a) The RoboCup 2002 flag and the dome

(b) Inside the dome

Fig. 2. The competition site

Fig. 3. All participating members

in 1997); also the four-legged league (which was introduced at the exhibition in 1998 and became an official league in 1999). From this year on, there is also a humanoid league, a big challenge with a long term and high impact goal, which could generate major spill-over effects. The expected industrial, scientific and educational impacts will be enormous [14].

Table 2 summarizes each league's settings and challenges.

3 RoboCupRescue

Simulation League

A rescue team is composed of heterogeneous agents - fire brigades, ambulances, police, and their control centers. The agents cooperate each other in order to

Table 2. RoboCupSoccer Leagues and Challenges in 2002

Items Leagues	robot size	On-board sensing	Off-board sensing	# of players	filed size	Challenges & Issues
Simulation	N/A	YES	coach agent	11	N/A	coach competition visualization
Small-size	[diameter] < 18cm	allowed but almost not used	TV camera from ceiling color markers on the players	5	2.4m x 2.9m	navigation shooting passing
Middle-size	[diameter] < 50cm	YES color uniform & color corner poles	NO	4	5m x 8m	dribbling cooperation
Legged	AIBO	YES color uniform six color poles & wireless comm.	NO	4	3m x 4.5m	pattern recognition collaboration ball collection
Humanoid	[Height] ≈ 40cm ≈ 80cm ≈ 120cm ≈ 180cm	YES	YES	1	7.2m x 10.4m	one-leg standing walking PK free performance

save buried victims, to extinguish fires, to repair roads, etc., in a virtual disaster field. Programming rescue agents provides a concrete platform for multi-agents research issues such as: handling incomplete information, no global system control, decentralized data and asynchronous computation. The teams are ranked based on the total points of their rescue operations.

Real Robot League

Ten teams from five countries participated in the RoboCupRescue Robot League in 2002. Most robots were remotely teleoperated and had limited autonomy. Due to the complexity of the problem, fully autonomous robots cannot be practical, yet. Adjusted autonomy, shared autonomy, and autonomy for human interfaces are suitable to apply AI to real disaster problems.

4   RoboCupJunior

In 2002 the third international RoboCupJunior tournament was held. As indicated by the number and range of registrations, the initiative has exploded in popularity. Fifty-nine teams from twelve countries participated. For the first time, the event attracted teams from a wide geographical region. Three challenges were offered: *dance*, *1-on-1 soccer* and *2-on-2 soccer*. In total, 240 students and mentors were involved.

Fig. 4. Robovie is playing with kids at ROBOTREX 2002

5   ROBOTREX

To promote the robot technologies necessary to achieve the final goal of
RoboCup, we organized the first ROBOTREX (Robot Trade and Exhibition) at
the same site of the sixth RoboCup. A wide range of the most advanced robot
technologies for perception, action, and intelligence should be evolved toward
our final goal. Therefore, it has been said that robotics is the main industry in
this century. The main aim of ROBOTREX is to promote robotics research and
development by providing the space for researchers and industry to meet each
other. It also allows ordinary people to be informed about the current technology
and to think about its future, through experiences with robots.

In spite of being the first event of this kind, fifty companies, institutes, universities, and local governments participated. A variety of exhibitions covering
a wide range of applications, such as factory automation, security, care, and
entertainment were shown and many people enjoyed the exhibitions.

6   Symposium and RoboCup Milestones Panel

The International RoboCup Symposium, an annual event at RoboCup, was held
on June 24 and 25, 2002, immediately following the RoboCup competition events.
The symposium attracted approximately 300 researchers, some who participate
in RoboCup and others who came for the symposium itself. The symposium was
multi-disciplinary, sporting research results in areas such as learning, planning
and plan-recognition, vision, robot localization and navigation, education, and
simulation. 17 oral presentations were given, marking an acceptance rate of 22%.
In addition, 21 short papers were presented in two poster sessions.

The 2002 RoboCup Symposium held a number of special events. Three papers
were selected for awards signifying science and engineering excellence (see the

Preface). A long-term milestone road-map for RoboCup was discussed in a panel including all league-chairs (see below). Finally, there were five invited talks, two of which took place in a joint session with DARS 2002, the 6th International Symposium on Distributed Autonomous Robotic Systems, which was also held in Fukuoka.

The RoboCup road-map panel was held to discuss recent and future work from the perspective of the year 2050 goal: develop a team of fully autonomous humanoid robots that can win against the human world soccer champion team. The RoboCup leagues started the discussion about the Roadmap in 2001 ([15]). The panelists from the different leagues were asked to think about milestones in the following way: What do we need in 2040 to reach the 2050 goal? To reach this milestone in 2040, what do we need in 2030? Then the milestones for 2020 and 2010 can be defined with the view to 2030.

Many of the milestones discussed require progress in fields very different from AI, including material engineering, power supply, mechanics, artificial muscles and sensors, etc. Other milestones pose significant, but more familiar challenges, including integrated perception, planning, and learning, vision, action-selection, multi-agent collaboration and coordination, etc. Combined efforts in all these fields will lead to new scientific and technological issues and new results. In addition, The panel touched on the educational challenges facing the RoboCup Junior league in teaching children to build and work with robotic technology.

7   Conclusion

The RoboCup 2002 competitions, the exhibitions, and the conference were a great success. Many people, not only researchers but also ordinary people, especially children, participated and enjoyed the whole event. RoboCup 2003 will be held in July 2003 in Padva, Italy.

Acknowledgement

We thank all participating team members, the organizing committee members, and the local arrangement committee members for their efforts. Special thanks should go to the Fukuoka City people for their tremendous efforts to make RoboCup 2002 possible. Two photos in Fig.2 were taken by Dr. Kaori Yoshida, CS, Kyushu Institute of Technology.

References

1. H. Kitano, M. Asada, Y. Kuniyoshi, I. Noda, E. Osawa, and H. Matsubara. "robocup: A challenge problem of ai". *AI magazine*, 18(1):73–85, 1997.
2. Minoru Asada, Hiroaki Kitano, Itsuki Noda, and Manuela Veloso. Robocup: Today and tomorrow – what we have learned. *Artificial Intelligence*, 110:193–214, 1999.
3. Hiroaki Kitano, editor. *RoboCup-97: Robot Soccer World Cup I*. Springer, Lecture Note in Artificail Intelligence 1395, 1998.

4. Gal Kaminka, Pedro U. Lima, and Raul Rojas, editors. *RoboCup 2002: Robot Soccer World Cup VI*. Springer, Lecture Note in Artificail Intelligence, 2003 (to appear).

5. I. Noda, S. Suzuki, H. Matsubara, M. Asada, and H. Kitano. Robocup-97 the first robot world cup soccer games and conferences. *AI magazine*, 19(3):49–59, 1998.

6. Minoru Asada, Manuela M. Veloso, Milind Tambe, Itsuki Noda, , Hiroaki Kitano, and Gerhard K. Kraetzschmar. Overview of robocup-98. *AI magazine*, 21(1):9–19, 2000.

7. Silvia Coradeschi, Lars Karlsson, Peter Stone, Tucker Balch, Gerhard Kraetzschmar, and Minoru Asada. Overview of robocup-99. *AI magazine*, 21(3):11–18, 2000.

8. Peter Stone, Minoru Asada, Tucker Balch, Raffaello D'Andrea, Masahiro Fujita, Bernhard Hengst, Gerhard Kraetzschmar, Pedro Lima, Nuno Lau, Henrik Lund, Daniel Polani, Paul Scerri, Satoshi Tadokoro, Thilo Weigel, and Gordon Wyeth. Robocup-2000: The fourth robotic soccer world championships. *AI magazine*, 22(1):11–38, 2001.

9. Manuela Veloso, Tucker Balch, Peter Stone, Hiroaki Kitano, Fuminori Yamasaki, Ken Endo, Minoru Asada, M. Jamzad, B. S. Sadjad, V. S. Mirrokni, M. Kazemi, H. Chitsaz, A. Heydarnoori, M. T. Hajiaghai, and E. Chiniforooshan. Robocup-2001: The fifth robotic soccer world championships. *AI magazine*, 23(1):55–68, 2002.

10. Minoru Asada and Hiroaki Kitano, editors. *RoboCup-98: Robot Soccer World Cup II*. Springer, Lecture Note in Artificail Intelligence 1604, 1999.

11. Manuela Veloso, Enrico Pagello, and Hiroaki Kitano, editors. *RoboCup-99: Robot Soccer World Cup III*. Springer, Lecture Note in Artificail Intelligence 1856, 2000.

12. Peter Stone, Tucker Balch, and Gerhard Kraetzschmar, editors. *RoboCup-2000: Robot Soccer World Cup IV*. Springer, Lecture Note in Artificail Intelligence 2019, 2001.

13. Andreas Birk, Silvia Coradeschi, and Satoshi Tadokoro, editors. *RoboCup 2001: Robot Soccer World Cup V*. Springer, Lecture Note in Artificail Intelligence 2377, 2002.

14. H. Kitano and M. Asada. The robocup humanoid challenge as the millennium challenge for advanced robotics. *Advanced Robotics The international Journal of the Robotics Society of Japan*, 13, 2000.

15. H.-D. Burkhard, D. Duhaut, M. Fujita, P. Lima, R. Murphy, and R. Rojas. The road to robocup 2050. *IEEE Robotics and Automation Magazine*, 9(2):31 – 38, June 2002.

Constraint-Based Landmark Localization

Ashley W. Stroupe[1], Kevin Sikorski[2], and Tucker Balch[3]

[1] The Robotics Institute
Carnegie Mellon University, Pittsburgh, Pennsylvania, USA
ashley@ri.cmu.edu
[2] Computer Science Department
University of Washington, Seattle, Washington, USA
kws@cs.washington.edu
[3] College of Computing,
Georgia Institute of Technology, Atlanta, Georgia, USA
tucker@cc.gatech.edu

Abstract. We present an approach to the landmark-based robot localization problem for environments, such as RoboCup middle-size soccer, that provide limited or low-quality information for localization. This approach allows use of different types of measurements on potential landmarks in order to increase landmark availability. Some sensors or landmarks might provide only range (such as field walls) or only bearing measurements (such as goals). The approach makes use of inexpensive sensors (color vision) using fast, simple updates robust to low landmark visibility and high noise. This localization method has been demonstrated in laboratory experiments and RoboCup 2001. Experimental analysis of the relative benefits of the approach is provided.

1 Introduction

Localization is an essential component of many mobile robot systems. One of the most common approaches uses landmarks distributed throughout the environment to make estimates of position that are combined with a model of the robot's motion. Typically, sensing and odometry are combined using a Kalman-Bucy filter or a Monte Carlo approach. The popularity of landmark-based localization is due to its potential applicability to a large range of environments: indoor and outdoor, natural and artificial landmarks. Applying landmark localization to some environments because a challenge when few landmarks are available, when landmarks provide limited information, and when sensor measurements are noisy. It may also be difficult for dynamic environments when updates must occur quickly, as many approaches require complex updates. RoboCup middle-size soccer is an example of this type of environment.

The success of landmark-based localization relies on accurate sensing and adequate availability of landmarks. Traditional landmark navigation uses range and bearing to any sensed landmark [1]. In indoor environments like RoboCup, walls can provide distance information without bearing in some cases. Examples include sonar and vision. In some vision systems, like ours, it may be impossible

G.A. Kaminka, P.U. Lima, and R. Rojas (Eds.): RoboCup 2002, LNAI 2752, pp. 8–24, 2003.
© Springer-Verlag Berlin Heidelberg 2003

or impractical to determine bearing to the surface or identify specific points on the surface in order for a bearing to be useful. Goals, due to their large size and complex geometry, can provide useful bearing measurements but may produce unreliable distances. In outdoor environments, landmarks may be at large distances that cannot be measured accurately, yet they can still provide accurate bearing information. Bearing may also be available without accurate range in the event of partial occlusion of the landmark or oddly shaped landmarks. Some approaches have attempted to solve the problem of partial measurement availability by reducing the available measurements (such as always using only bearing) [2]. However, to make use of all available information, different types of landmarks must be accommodated.

The goal of this work is to provide a method of localization that is fast, mathematically simple, and takes advantage of different types of measurements on landmarks. We have attempted to expand the number of landmarks available to a robot by using only those measurements that are reliable for each landmark: range and bearing, range only, or bearing only. We have implemented the general method described here. Additionally, we applied our approach in our RoboCup 2001 middle-size team by developing a method for reliably using goals as bearing landmarks.

2   Background and Related Work

There are several possible approaches to landmark-based navigation. Prominent among these are triangulation, Kalman-Bucy filters, and Monte Carlo Localization (MCL) [1].

Triangulation depends on the range and bearing to landmarks and uses geometry to compute a single point that is most consistent with the current location [3]. This method is prevalent in human navigation approaches. Triangulation may be done with no weight given to previous positions, such as systems that use GPS, or may be incorporated with odometric information. Many robotic systems use approaches based on triangulation [4].

Kalman-Bucy filter approaches represent positions and measurements (odometry and sensing) probabilistically as Gaussian distributions. Position estimates are updated by odometry and sensing alternately using the property that Gaussian distributions can be combined using multiplication [5], [6]. Typical implementations require range and bearing to landmarks and use geometry to determine the means of sensor-based position estimate distributions, though some implementations using only bearing exist [2]. While Kalman-Bucy filters are quite efficient, the additional computation of coefficients and covariance add to computation time; in some applications and on some platforms, reducing even this small time may be desirable.

Monte Carlo Localization is similar to Kalman-Bucy filter approaches, but represents the probabilistic distribution as a series of samples [7], [8]. The density of samples represents the probability estimate that the robot is in a particular location. Distributions are updated by moving samples according to a probabilistic model of odometry and then adding samples to regions consistent with sensing and dropping samples highly inconsistent with sensing. In one implementation, called Sensor Resetting Localization, the robot can reinitialize its position based on sensors when samples become highly improbable [9].

To resolve the difficulty in range measurements for outdoor environments, some work has been done using only bearing to localize [2]. In order to achieve pose estimates from bearing only, that work relies on a shape-from-motion type of formulation. This requires several frames and many simultaneously visible landmarks, and does not make use of range information when available. The SPmap approach allows use of different sets of measurements from different sensors, using all information from single sensors together, and takes into account landmark orientation [10]. This approach is based on Kalman-Bucy filters and thus requires covariance computation for position (and for landmarks for the mapping phase).

Our work has the mathematical simplicity of triangulation and uses all available landmark information, both bearing and range. Unlike many other approaches, landmarks that do not provide both range and bearing can be included without discarding useful information (as is range in bearing-only approaches). Bearing-only landmarks are incorporated in a single frame, rather than over several. Current implementation provides no estimate of position uncertainty, though the approach can be easily expanded to include it if computational demands permit.

3   Summary of Approach

The localization problem involves the use of odometry and measurements on landmarks to determine a robot's position and heading within an environment. Potential measurements on landmarks include range and bearing. The determination of a new estimate (position, heading, or pose) can be summarized as follows:

1. The robot estimate is updated after each movement based on the odometry model.
2. The robot senses available landmarks and computes an estimate consistent with sensing.
3. The estimates resulting from the movement update and from sensing are combined to produce a final estimate result.

Each type of measurement, bearing or range, provides an independent constraint on the position or heading of the robot. These constraints can either be a single-value constraint or a curve constraint. With single-value constraints, only one value of the position/heading is consistent with the constraint. With curve constraints, heading or position must be on a curve. Curves are typically circles or lines, but can be arbitrary.

For each sensor measurement of a landmark, a constraint is determined. A landmark may have multiple measurements, each of which will provide a separate constraint. For each measurement, the point consistent with the constraint that

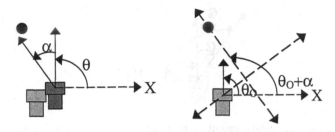

Fig. 1. A noisy bearing α is taken by a robot (true pose dark, estimate light). Right: Bearing and heading estimate create a line of possible consistent positions.

lies closest to the current estimate (position or heading) is assigned as the estimate for that measurement. Each constraint-based estimate is determined based on the original pose estimate; thus they are independent and can be combined in any order. The final estimate (position or heading) is determined by combining the previous estimate and the estimate(s) from the sensor measurements.

In this work, uncertainty estimates are not required and all updates are performed using simple weighted averages. All sensor results are combined first and then this result is combined with the original estimate. In this way, order becomes irrelevant. Estimates in position and heading are alternately updated with a minimum time required between updates of the same type. This ensures independence of updates.

If uncertainty estimates are required, estimates can be expressed as probability distributions and integrated using probabilistic approaches.

4   Landmark Measurement Types

Three landmark measurement types are considered here: bearing to point, range to point, and range to surface. Each landmark provides one or more of these types. In each example, the robot has a pose estimate (light gray) (X_O, Y_O, Θ_O) with actual pose (X, Y, Θ) (dark gray). The landmark is at or passes through (X_L, Y_L). Range and bearing measurements are r and α, respectively. Sensor-based estimates are x', y', Θ'.

4.1   Bearing to Point

A bearing to point measurement provides a linear constraint on position when heading is assumed known (Figure 1). This line passes through the landmark at (X_L, Y_L) at an angle of $\alpha + \Theta_0$ (line slope is the tangent of this angle).

The point closest to the pose estimate is the intersection of the constraint line,

$$y = \tan(\alpha + \Theta_0)x + Y_L - \tan(\alpha + \Theta_0)X_L \qquad (1)$$

and the line perpendicular to the constraint through the current position estimate:

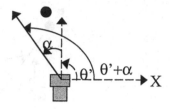

Fig. 2. Using bearing measurement α and the angle determined by robot position estimate and landmark position, heading estimate Θ' can be computed by subtraction.

$$y = \frac{-1}{\tan(\alpha + \Theta_0)} x + Y_0 + \frac{1}{\tan(\alpha + \Theta_0)} X_0 \qquad (2)$$

This point can be computed as:

$$x' = \cos^2(\alpha + \Theta_0)X_0 + \sin^2(\alpha + \Theta_0)X_L$$
$$+ \cos(\alpha + \Theta_0)\sin(\alpha + \Theta_0)(Y_0 - Y_L) \qquad (3a)$$
$$y' = \tan(\alpha + \Theta_0)(x' - X_L) + Y_L \qquad (3b)$$

with $y' = Y_0$ in the special case then $\alpha + \Theta = \pm 90°$.

A single-value constraint on heading, when position is known, is also provided by bearing measurements (Figure 2).

Using position estimate, landmark position, and bearing measurement, the heading estimate can be determined as:

$$\Theta' = \tan^{-1}\left(\frac{Y_L - Y_0}{X_L - X_0}\right) - \alpha \qquad (4)$$

4.2   Range to Point

Range to a point provides a circular constraint on position (Figure 3). The constraint is centered at the landmark and is of radius r. Heading need not be known.

The closest point on the constraint is at the intersection of the circle and the line between landmark and position estimate. This is determined using similar triangles:

$$\frac{X_L - x'}{r} = \frac{X_L - X_0}{d} \Rightarrow \quad x' = \frac{(X_0 - X_L)r}{\sqrt{(X_L - X_0)^2 + (X_L - X_0)^2}} + X_L \qquad (5a)$$

$$\frac{Y_L - y'}{r} = \frac{Y_L - Y_0}{d} \Rightarrow \quad y' = \frac{(Y_0 - Y_L)r}{\sqrt{(X_L - X_0)^2 + (Y_L - Y_0)^2}} + Y_L \qquad (5b)$$

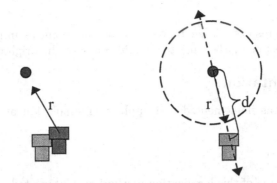

Fig. 3. Left: A noisy range (r) is taken by robot (true pose dark, estimate light). Right: The range places the robot on a circle, radius r, around the landmark. The closest point on he constraint lies on the line from landmark to position estimate.

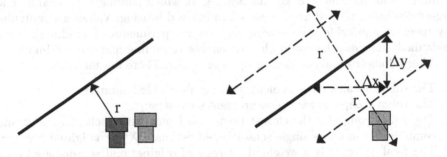

Fig. 4. Left: The robot (true pose dark, pose estimate light) makes a noisy range measurement r on a wall. Right: The range places the robot on one of two lines parallel to the wall at that range (r, Δx, Δy), at the point closest to the estimate.

4.3   Range to Surface

Range to a surface provides two-dimensional position constraints parallel to and on either side of the surface for position (Figure 4). Heading need not be known.

Given a wall projecting into the plane as a line through (X_L, Y_L) with slope m, two possible line constraints (on each side of the wall) are provided. These lines are shifted from the original by:

$$\Delta y = m\Delta x = \pm m \frac{r}{\sin(\tan^{-1}(m))} \tag{6}$$

$$y = mx + Y_L - mX_L \pm \frac{mr}{\sin(\tan^{-1}(m))} \tag{7}$$

The closest point on this constraint are computed as:

$$x' = mY_0 + X_0 - mY_L + m^2 X_L \pm \frac{mr}{\sin(\tan^{-1}(m))} \tag{8a}$$

$$y' = mx' + Y_L - mX_L \pm \frac{mr}{\sin(\tan^{-1}(m))} \tag{8b}$$

Ambiguity is resolved either by eliminating one point as impossible (off the field, for example) or by choosing the result closer to the original estimate.

5   Implementation

The algorithm was implemented and applied in simulation and teams of real robots.

5.1   Software

The implementation of this localization method was integrated as part of *Team-Bots* [13]. *CMVision* performs color analysis and color blob detection and merging on raw camera images [14].

A landmark is represented by position, color, type of available measurements, minimum and maximum range and bearing at which landmark is reliable, and largest deviation allowed from expected range and bearing. Values are individually specified a priori for each landmark. In our experiments, all landmarks were predefined; however, the approach is amenable to adding mapped landmarks.

After odometry updates, sensor updates occur. There are four steps:

1. The robot obtains measurement data on all visible landmarks.
2. The robot computes each measurement's constraint.
3. The robot computes the closest point consistent with each constraint and combines these into a single sensor-based estimate X' by weighted average.
4. The final estimate is a weighted average of original and sensor-based estimates: $X_{k+1} = wX' + (1 - w)X_k$.

Sensor updates are here illustrated in Figure 5 by a position update example. Position updates alternate with heading updates, which are computed similarly.

5.2   Hardware Platform

The Minnow robot [15] is based on the Cye robot, an inexpensive and commercially available platform (Figure 6). The Cye consists of a drive section, with two-wheel differential drive, and a passive trailer. On the Minnow, a 700 MHz laptop communicates with the Cye's on-board processor via a serial link. High-level commands and image processing are implemented in C and Java on the laptop using *TeamBots*. Robots communicate using wireless Ethernet.

A commercial USB camera provides images at 240 by 360 resolution. The camera is calibrated so that, at run-time, a selected image pixel is used to compute the ray from the camera to the point in space. Landmark ranges are determined from this ray by providing an intersection height, z; the point at which the ray intersects the given z value is the object's three-dimensional location (x, y, z). This provides range. Bearing is determined using the yaw angle of the ray directly or the angle produced by the position coordinates, $\text{atan}(y/x)$. After color region processing using *CMVision*, pixels representing each region are chosen on which to compute range and bearing. Vision has not been implemented

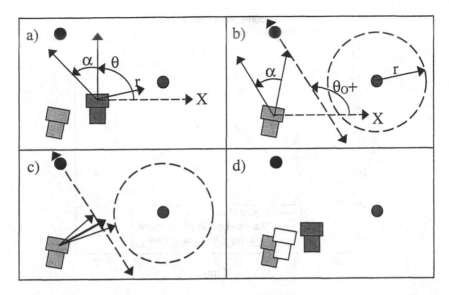

Fig. 5. Position example. a) A robot (dark) with pose estimate (light) makes landmark measurements (one bearing, one range). b) Constraints matching sensors are computed. c) Closest constraint points are determined (thin arrows) and combined (wide). The final estimate (white) is a combination of former and sensor estimates.

Fig. 6. Two Minnow robots with colored block landmarks for localization.

to determine distance to walls, but minimum distance obtained during a scan could be used (as the robot turns the camera, different sections of the wall would be visible, and a closest point could be found for each section). Vision cannot compute lines in the image, making bearing to walls unusable.

6   Quantitative Experimental Validation

To quantitatively evaluate this approach, a series of lab experiments were conducted.

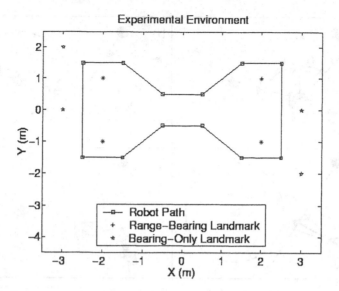

Fig. 7. Experimental environment. Waypoints are shown along the robot's path. Landmarks differ by type of measurements available for position updates.

6.1 Experimental Setup

Several small block-shaped objects were placed throughout an indoor environment that measures 7 by 5 meters (Figure 7). Each block was a different color that the robot's vision system was calibrated to recognize. Three experiments were conducted in which landmark measurements varied. Some landmarks were defined to provide range and bearing information while others were defined to provide only bearing.

A. Four landmarks providing range for position estimation and bearing for heading estimation;
B. Four landmarks providing range and bearing for position estimation and bearing for heading estimation;
C. Landmarks from B with four additional landmarks providing bearing for position and heading estimation.

Within the environment, the robot was commanded to follow a looping, piece-wise-linear path defined by 12 waypoints (Figure 7). At each waypoint, the robot paused and reported its pose estimates from localization and from on-board odometry. During a pause, ground truth for pose was measured (position within 0.5 cm, heading within 1°). Each experimental run consisted of five loops (60 data points).

This experiment is intended to evaluate:

− The ability of this approach to localize a robot;
− The impact on performance resulting from the use of additional landmarks or measurements on landmarks that would not be available to approaches that rely on the same measurement(s) being available for all landmarks.

6.2   Parameters

Sensor models and weights for combining estimates through averaging were determined experimentally. After calibration, it was empirically determined that range measurements produce errors on the order of $10 - 15\%$ and bearing measurements produce errors on the order of $2°$.

To update position or heading, first all sensor information is combined. If more than one measurement is used for a single landmark, the estimate from each measurement is weighted equally to determine that landmark's final estimate; in a more general approach, these could be weighted by individual measurement certainty. For combining all estimates from all landmarks, individual estimates are weighted (w) by an estimate of landmark quality ($1/\sigma$), where $\sigma^2 = 10\%$ of range).

The final result is a weighted average of previous estimate (updated for movement) and the sensor-based estimate.

For position updates, the sensor-based estimate is weighted based on the best (closest) landmark; if the closest landmark falls below a threshold, $w = 0.2$ is used and otherwise $w = 0.05$ is used. The threshold of 3.75 meters was experimentally determined based on range accuracy across distances. For heading estimates, which are less affected by changes in range to landmarks, $w = 0.5$ if more than half of the landmarks were visible and $w = 0.2$ otherwise.

6.3   Experimental Results

In each experiment, the total error in position, $\sqrt{\Delta x^2 + \Delta y^2}$, and heading was computed at each waypoint. From this the maximum and mean errors were obtained. Additionally, the standard deviation of absolute error in x and y were found. In Figure 8, the total error at each waypoint is plotted for the best odometry result and the worst localization test (4 landmarks with range only for position estimation). While position estimation initially has error greater than odometry, the magnitude of these errors does not increase unbounded over time as it does for odometry.

Peaks in localization error occur when landmarks are furthest away from the robot. The cyclical nature of odometry error, with minima at loop ends, is most likely due to predominance of heading drift. Such errors may temporarily cancel, producing artificially accurate data.

The results for pose estimation in all experiments are shown in Table 1. Mean and maximum errors are shown with standard deviation in x and y position error.

This method of localization reduces absolute position error (mean, maximum, and standard deviation) and eliminates odometry drift. While the method for updating heading did not vary (except by number of landmarks for C) heading results improved as a result of better position estimates: heading updates use position (Equation 4), thus position improvement leads to heading improvement. In these experiments, each addition of landmarks or measurement types to existing landmarks further improves performance.

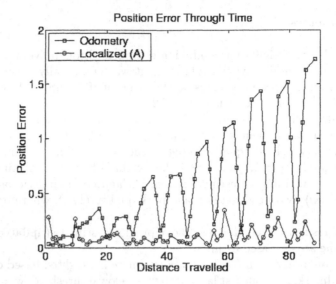

Fig. 8. Experimental results for best odometry run a nd worst localization run. Total position error (m) as a function of distance (at each waypoint) is shown. Odometry errors grow with time while localization errors remain roughly constant.

Table 1. Pose Estimation Experimental Results.

	Odometry (Best)	Localization (Range Only)	Localization (Range-Bearing)	Localization (Range-Bearing + Bearing Only)
Mean Position Error	0.5592m	0.0994m	0.0719m	0.0627m
$\sigma_{\Delta x}$	0.4378m	0.0822m	0.0578m	0.0562m
$\sigma_{\Delta y}$	0.5624m	0.0920m	0.0620m	0.0482m
Max Position Error	1.7275m	0.3459m	0.2326m	0.1652m
Mean Heading Error	29.6°	5.1°	2.3°	1.7°
Max Heading Error	42°	11°	5°	4°

7   RoboCup Middle-Size Soccer Implementation

A bearing-only approach was used to localize the robots for our middle-size RoboCup 2001 team, the CMU-Hammerheads. The most critical aspect of applying this approach to RoboCup is the accurate sensing of field landmarks.

7.1   Landmark Sensing

For robots with only visual sensing, the RoboCup middle-size environment provides a challenge in accurately measuring landmark position and ranges. Features available on the field consist of:

- Small black squares on the walls. Walls may not be present in the future. The small squares are not visible from many points on the field.

Fig. 9. RoboCup middle-size field. Note that left side of goal is occluded by field walls and goal wall. The right side is visible but partially occluded by the goalie.

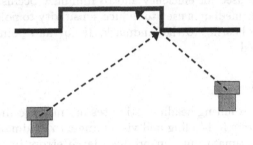

Fig. 10. The angle from robot to visible edge of the goal is measured to the same point on the goal from all robot positions, despite the concavity. Range varies.

- Field walls. Ambiguous landmarks which (as a surface) cannot alone provide accurate pose.
- Field lines. Complex methods of line fitting are required to accurately position the robot with respect to field lines.
- Goals. Goals are large and brightly colored and thus easy to sense (Figure 9). However, it is difficult to get a range to a large and concave object, as some parts may be closer than others or may be occluded.

Field goals, easily identified visually from any distance, are the obvious landmark choice. Due to the size and concavity of the goal, it is often difficult to determine which point on the goal is being observed or to get an accurate range measurement. In the example shown in Figure 10, the edge of the detected goal represents the front edge of the goal (left robot) or a variable point on the back of the goal (right robot), resulting in inconsistent ranges and inconsistent landmark reference position. However, the angle to the front corners can be reliably determined, even when not directly observable. As shown, even in the instance when the back of the goal is detected, this angle is coincident with the angle to the front corner.

As goal corner angles can be reliably detected, they are amenable to use as bearing-only landmarks. The angles to each edge of the goal can be independently determined, providing four landmarks on the field.

A second difficulty that arises frequently in RoboCup middle-size soccer is occlusion (Figure 9). With up to 8 robots on the field, two of which are specifically tasked with blocking the goals, occlusion of part of the goal is common. It was necessary to determine when the edge of the goal was visible in order to known when the landmark was measured accurately.

In order to deal with occlusion, we took advantage of the color-coded aspects of the RoboCup world. When the sensed goal is observed adjacent to another color (such as robot, robot marker, ball, etc), occlusion is present. Points on the edge of the goal that are adjacent to the occlusion are thrown out. Once valid edge points have been selected, the median bearing is computed. Only the top ten valid points are used for efficiency and to minimize occlusion, which occurs at ground level. The median is used to reduce sensitivity to noise. It is this value that is used as the bearing to the landmark. If no valid points are found, the landmark is not used.

7.2   Parameters

Using bearing only, resulting heading estimates are more accurate than position estimates. Small errors in heading and visual angle to landmarks produce small errors in heading estimate but can produce large errors in position at larger distances from the landmark. Thus, a smaller weight, a, is assigned to sensor estimates for position than for heading when combining with the previous estimate. For both heading and position, a larger weight was used when more landmarks were visible (2 or more). For heading, w = 0.5 or 0.2. For position, w = 0.2 or 0.1.

7.3   Performance

It is difficult to quantify performance at RoboCup, as ground truth data cannot be obtained during play. Qualitatively, the use of this localization method greatly improved performance during practice and play, as observed primarily in the "go home" behavior. Without localization, the robots would achieve greater than 1-meter error in position and 20-degree error in heading within a few minutes of play. With localization, pose was typically maintained with less than 0.5m and a few degrees error. Occasionally, greater errors would arise briefly due to the high percentage of time when landmarks were occluded by the many robots on the field. Accuracy of 0.5m is adequate for the soccer application, which is highly reactive and large-scale.

7.4   Simulation Experiments

Difficulties in generating quantitative results on the soccer field, including not having a real field in our lab, necessitated simulation. The TeamBots simulator

Table 2. Pose Estimation Simulation Results: Soccer Field.

	Odometry	Localization (Bearing)	Localization (Range-Bearing)
Mean Position Error	0.2536m	0.1714m	0.1068m
$\sigma_{\Delta x}$	0.1057m	0.0929m	0.0500m
$\sigma_{\Delta x}$	0.1852m	0.0886m	0.0558m
Max Position Error	1.0353m	0.5500m	0.2613m
Mean Heading Error	4.0262°	2.2328°	2.0938°
$\sigma_{\Delta t}$	2.9382°	1.8450°	1.6631°
Max Heading Error	15.7897°	8.5425°	8.4449°

was used with block landmarks positioned at goal corner locations. To simulate reduced landmark visibility (occlusion), field of view was limited to 5 meters (about half the field). Simulation parameters for noise standard deviations were: right and left wheel velocities = 5%, vision range = 5%, vision angle = 5o (slightly higher than actual). Robots followed the path of Figure 7 for five 5-loop trials. Table 2 shows results comparing performance using only landmark bearing to that using range and bearing.

Results indicate that even with only bearing information, the robot is consistently able to remain relatively well localized with frequent (though not constant) landmark observations; errors do not continuously grow over time as in odometry. Eliminating range information slightly reduces performance in position (increasing magnitude of the largest outliers) and does not adversely affect heading estimation. The magnitude of errors agrees with the qualitative results obtained by observing the robot on the real mid-size field over the short time represented by the 5-loop simulation.

8 Discussion

This localization method, using a weighted average, keeps robot navigational error bounded within the limits of sensor accuracy when provided with adequate landmarks. Initial position estimates may show slightly higher error than pure odometry. Noise in sensing leads to immediate small estimate errors while odometry errors accumulate over time. However, the localization method presented prevents drift evident in odometry and maintains a consistent, bounded level of error.

The ability to use different types of measurements on landmarks may expand the number of landmarks available to a robot and thereby improve localization performance, as shown in these experiments. Successful bearing-only approaches require several frames and many landmarks to compute pose. Our approach incorporates bearing-only landmarks in a single-frame update. Range information is accommodated when available and few concurrently visible landmarks are required.

If only range measurements are used, no corrections can be made on robot heading. If only bearing measurements are used, this approach cannot solve all

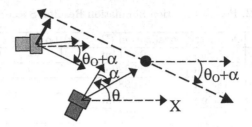

Fig. 11. A robot measures landmark bearing from its actual location (dark). The robot's erroneous pose estimate (light) with a correct bearing produces an erroneous constraint line which pulls the position estimate further away from truth (wide arrow).

"lost robot" problems. The linear constraints on position can only provide corrections to position within limits. When heading estimates are highly incorrect, the line constraint falls far from truth and provides very erroneous results. An example is in Figure 11; the constraint pulls the robot's estimate further from the actual position.

If both bearing and range measurements are available, from the same or different landmarks, this approach can converge to the correct answer from any initial condition. While no formal proof is offered, it has been experimentally determined (in simulation and on real robots) that if three landmarks can provide each type of measurement, the robot is able to eventually recover from any errors. If fewer measurements are available, the ability to recover may be limited.

This simple approach to localization is useful when computational time is extremely limited. In some applications with some platforms, such as the Minnow in RoboCup, saving even the small amount of additional time required to compute covariance and proper Kalman-Bucy updates might be desirable. However, when computational constraints are relaxed, this approach may provide a useful method for generating probabilistic distributions for Bayesian or Monte Carlo updates even with noisy and limited information.

9   Conclusions

We provide a fast, efficient, method of mobile robot localization that takes advantage of the different types of measurements made on landmarks to improve landmark availability. This method prevents odometry drift. With adequate landmarks, it can recover from being lost. While performance improves with additional measurements, few simultaneously visible landmarks are required for reasonable updates.

This method takes advantage of different types of measurements that may be available with different types of landmarks. Unlike approaches that preclude use of valid measurements to eliminate noisy measurements, we use all viable data and complete updates in a single frame. Cooperative localization may be performed by using teammates as landmarks or updating with measurements made by teammates.

Our approach can be used in the simple manner described, using weighted averages, or can be used to provide input for generating samples for Monte Carlo localization or a Gaussian distribution for Kalman-Bucy filter localization. We recognize that a statistical approach such as these may provide more accurate pose estimates. However, combination by weighted average is extremely simple and fast computationally, which is an important feature for real-time, dynamic domains such as RoboCup.

The described method provides a simple method of localization that is applicable to RoboCup middle-size soccer, despite many difficulties in achieving accurate measurements on visual landmarks in the RoboCup middle-size environment. This is accomplished by determining a means by which the angles to goal corners can be reliably measured and used as bearing landmarks.

A probabilistic implementation with collaboration (based on [11] and [16]) has been implemented in simulation and will be applied to our RoboCup legged team in 2002. For curve constraints, Gaussian distributions are aligned tangent to the curve with means computed in the same manner as the approach described here. For single value constraints, Gaussian distributions are centered at this value. The sensor model determines variances of these Gaussian distributions. The probabilistic updates use Gaussian multiplication [12] to compute mean and covariance. This type of approach was used for the CMU 2001 legged team [11]. Updates could also be done using Kalman-Bucy filter updates, (also approximating estimates with Gaussian distributions). Similarly, samples representing arbitrary distributions can be generated for Monte Carlo Localization using the constraint and sensor models.

References

1. Borenstein, J. Everett, H. R., Feng, L.: Where am I? Sensors and Methods for Autonomous Mobile Robot Positioning. Technical Report, U Michigan (1996).
2. Deans, M., Hebert, M.: Experimental Comparison of Techniques for Localization and Mapping using a Bearings Only Sensor. Proc ISER '00. IEEE (2000).
3. Graydon, D., Hanson, K. (eds.): Mountaineering: The Freedom of the Hills. 6th ed, (1997).
4. Rekleitis, I., Dudek, G., Milios, E.: Multi-Robot Collaboration for Robust Exploration. Proc. 2000 IEEE ICRA (2000).
5. Smith, R.C., Cheeseman, P.: On the Representation and Estimation of Spatial Uncertainty. International Journal of Robotics Research. 5 (1998) 5:56-68.
6. Leonard, J., Durrant-Whyte, H.: Mobile Robot Localization by Tracking Geometric Beacons. IEEE Transactions on Robotics and Automation, 7 (1991) 3:376-382.
7. Dellaert, F., Fox, D., Burgard, W., Thrun, S.: Monte Carlo Localization for Mobile Robots. Proc. IEEE ICRA. IEEE (1999).
8. Fox, D., Burgard, W., Thrun, S.: Markov Localization for Mobile Robots in Dynamic Environments. Journal of Artificial Intelligence Research. 11 (1999).
9. Lenser, S., Veloso, M.: Sensor Resetting Localization for Poorly Modeled Mobile Robots. Proc. IEEE ICRA, 2000. IEEE (2000).
10. Castellanos, J., Montiel, J., Neira, J., Tards, J.: The SPmap: A probabilistic Framework for Simultaneous Localization and Map Building. IEEE Transactions on Robotics and Automation. 15 (1999) 5:948-952.

11. Uther, W., Lenser, S., Bruce, J., Hock, M., Veloso, M.: CM-Pack'01: Fast Legged Robot Walking, Robust Localization, and Team Behaviors. In: RoboCup-2001: Robot Soccer World Cup V, A. Birk, S. Coradeschi, S. Takodoro (eds.), Springer-Verlag (2002).
12. Stroupe, A.W., Martin, M.C., Balch, T.: Distributed Sensor Fusion for Object Position Estimation by Multi-Robot Systems. Proc. IEEE ICRA, 2001. IEEE (2001).
13. Balch, T.: TeamBots. http:// www.cs.cmu.edu/~trb/TeamBots.
14. Bruce, J.: CMVision Realtime Color Vision. http://www-2.cs.cmu.edu/~jbruce.
15. Balch, T.: The Minnow Project. http://www-2.cs.cmu.edu/~coral/minnow.
16. Stroupe, A., Balch, T.: Collaborative Probabilistic Constraint-Based Landmark Localization. Submitted to Proc IROS 2002.

Improving Vision-Based Self-localization

Hans Utz, Alexander Neubeck, Gerd Mayer, and Gerhard Kraetzschmar

University of Ulm, Neuroinformatics, D-89069 Ulm, Germany

Abstract. After removing the walls around the field, vision-based localization has become an even more interesting approach for robotic soccer. The paper discusses how removal of the wall affects the localization task in ROBOCUP, both for vision-based and non-visual approaches, and argues that vision-based Monte Carlo localization based on landmark features seems to cope well with the changed field setup. An innovative approach for landmark feature detection for vision-based Monte Carlo Localization is presented. Experimental results indicate that the approach is robust and reliable.

1 Introduction

Knowing the position and orientation in the operating environment is an essential capability for any robot exhibiting coherent, goal-oriented behavior [23, 15]. The basic principle of self-localization is to compare perceptual information derived from sensor readings with a priori or previously acquired knowledge about the environment. The self-localization problem has been studied intensively in the mobile robot community, and a wide variety of approaches with distinct methods and capabilities have been developed [3, 8, 15, 7, 14, 17].

Several localization approaches have been successfully adopted and applied to ROBOCUP, where the perceptual input included laser scans [16], omnidirectional vision [21], and directional vision [20, 19, 18, 10, 11]. However, in late 2001, the ROBOCUP middle-size league adopted major changes to the environment, the most challenging of which is the removal of the walls around the playground. The field is now limited simply by line markings. While formerly all green area could safely assumed to be playground, we now have substantial green-colored regions outside of the field. As a temporary measure, there will be a number of poles of 10cm diameter about 1m outside of the field. The distance between pole center points has been fixed at 40cm for 2002, but this may change already in the very near future. People are allowed everywhere outside of the poles; referees and some team members will also be allowed inside the area surrounded by the poles. In addition, a new corner post was defined, which consists of a 40cm diameter pole with specific coloring. Within the next few years, a significant enlargement of the field up to 20m x 30m is one of the changes teams should expect.

It is an interesting and open question, how the known approaches will perform under the new environmental conditions. In this paper, we first analyze, how the adopted changes to the field will affect various localization approaches. We argue that Monte Carlo Localization based on visual features is sufficiently flexible, so

G.A. Kaminka, P.U. Lima, and R. Rojas (Eds.): RoboCup 2002, LNAI 2752, pp. 25–40, 2003.

that it can be easily adapted to the new challenges. We improve the approach presented in [10], including the set of visual features used, and an innovative approach to perform subsymbolic line matching. Experimental results both on simulated and real environments indicate that the improvements significantly increase robustness and precision of self-localization.

2   Self-Localization in RoboCup

For the analysis of self-localization methods in ROBOCUP, a useful distinction to make is the sensor modality used and the type of information it can deliver. The most reliable and successful approach so far was CS Freiburg's self-localization, which relies on scans of angular distance readings obtained by a laser range finder (LRF) mounted on the robot [16]. Two contributing factors for its success were that the LRF provides rather precise and reliable measurements of the distance to the wall surrounding the field and that the scans are dense (361 readings in a half-circle). The density allows to throw away readings that are suspected to be noisy without loosing the ability to localize. The precision results in high localization accuracy by matching the sensor scans against a precise yet simple geometric model of the field. Like any other self-localization approach that is based on distance measurements, CS Freiburg must significantly revise its localization procedure to cope with the new situation. The set of poles around the field can be viewed as making up a different kind of "wall", with many holes in it. It should still be possible to detect these "walls" with LRFs, although data will be much more noisy and require more computational effort for extracting "wall" hypotheses. The potential presence of people inside the pole-surrounded area adds additional noise. Sonar-based approaches seem to be of little use for self-localization in the future, although they can still be used for obstacle avoidance and opponent detection. In both cases, the ranges of the distances sensors used may have to be given more consideration. Currently, the range of typically 8m for LRFs seems still sufficient for current field size, but significantly larger field sizes may render the sensor almost useless for localization purposes in large portions of the field. Summarizing, we can infer that self-localization based on distance sensor readings is still possible, but of decreasing importance for the foreseeable future.

Another popular localization method in ROBOCUP is based on omnidirectional vision [21, 1] A camera looking at a specially-shaped mirror (conic, spheric, or with custom geometries) provides the robot with visual information in all directions simultaneously. Resolution of particular objects in the scene is usually less than for directional cameras, and both resolution and camera range depend on the mirror geometry. In ROBOCUP, several examples of custom-designed omnidirectional cameras exist where the robot could see the complete field with goals and surrounding walls in all locations on the field. Thus, these robots had more or less a global view of the field [5]. The wall height of 50cm was sufficient to reliably detect the field boundaries for localization purposes despite the lower resolution of objects at farther distances. In the modified playground, this will be much more difficult, because field lines will be just 12cm wide and flat, instead of 50cm high and upright. If the robot sees field lines (or other landmark features) in its vicinity, nothing much will change. However, field lines farther away may be hard or impossible to detect. Taking into account the geometry of the robot on the field, mirror geometry and camera resolution, detecting the field boundaries can be expected to be noisier, less accurate and reliable, with a higher likelihood of not detecting the boundary at all. This problem will get more serious if field size will be further enlarged in the future. A possible solution could be to localize against larger visual landmarks found in the environment, like cardboards with large sponsor logos, doors, supporting poles of the building structure, and so forth. However, these features are different in every environment, and consequently the localization algorithm must be adopted on-site. Furthermore, such landmark features may temporarily or permanently (on the time scale of a match) be obstructed by spectators or media people. Altogether, self-localization based on omnidirectional vision is bound to be more difficult, but methods for fast on-site adaptation and improved algorithms coping with temporary obstruction of landmarks can render this approach very valuable for the forseeable future. Note, that the method presented below could be easily adapted to omnidirectional vision.

Self-localization methods based on perceptual input from directional cameras seem to be the least-affected by the environmental changes [2, 19]. However, this is a premature conclusion. Despite of the usually higher per-object resolution available on directional cameras, using them to detect 12cm wide field lines instead of 50cm high walls is significantly more difficult and less robust, especially at farther distances. Thus, even self-localization methods using directional cameras will have to be improved, especially if they relied on detecting the walls. One example for self-localization that should need comparatively little change are the Agilo RoboCuppers, who use directional cameras to extract walls and field lines and match these against a geometric model [18].

What follows for the future? One consequence is that vision-based localization based on landmark features seems to be a good idea. Another one is that methods that can quickly adapt on-site to the available landmarks, cope with temporary or permanent obstruction of particular landmarks, and are robust even when landmarks can be detected only sparsely seem to hold the best promises for the future. Monte Carlo localization based on visual landmark features seems to offer all the required characteristics.

3   Feature-Based Monte Carlo Localization

In the past few years, Monte-Carlo localization (MCL) has become a very popular framework for solving the self-localization problem in mobile robots [12, 13]. This method is very reliable and robust against noise, especially if the robots are equipped with laser range finders or sonar sensors. In ROBOCUP, however, using a laser scanner on each robot may be difficult, or impossible, or too costly, and sonar data is extremely noisy due to the highly dynamic environment. Thus, localization methods that use other sensory channels, like uni- or omni-directional vision systems, are highly desirable. In previous work [11], we already presented a vision-based MCL approach based on landmark features that were very simple and easy to detect. For the modified ROBOCUP environment, feature detection needs to be significantly more sophisticated, and the remainder of the paper is dedicated to present an enhanced approach for detecting visual features in ROBOCUP. This section recaps some essentials of MCL needed for further discussion.

3.1 Markov Localization

In Markov lokalization [12], the position $l = \langle x, y, \theta \rangle$ of a robot is estimated by computing the probability distribution $Bel(l)$ over all possible positions in the environment. During robot operation, two kinds of update steps are iteratively applied to incrementally refine $Bel(l)$:

- *Belief Projection across Robot Motion:* A *motion model* $P(l|l', m)$ is used to predict the likelihood of the robot being in position l assuming that it executed a motion command m and was previously in position l'. It is assumed that the new position depends only on the previous position and the movement (Markov property). The robot's position belief $Bel(l)$ is updated according to the formula for Markov chains [4]:

$$Bel(l) = \int P(l|l', m)\, Bel(l')\, dl' \qquad (1)$$

- *Integration of Sensor Input:* Data obtained from the robot's sensors are used to update the belief $Bel(l)$. An *observation model* $P(o|l')$ models the likelihood of making an observation o given the robot is at position l'. $Bel(l)$ is then updated by applying Bayes' rule as follows:

$$Bel(l) = \alpha\, P(o|l')\, Bel(l') \qquad (2)$$

where α is a normalization factor ensuring that $Bel(l)$ integrates to 1.

Markov localization method provides a mathematical framework for solving the localization problem. Unlike methods based on Kalman filtering [22], it is easy to use multimodal distributions. However, implementing Markov localization on a mobile robot in a tractable and efficient way is a non-trivial task.

3.2 Monte Carlo Localization

The Monte Carlo localization (MCL) approach [13] solves the implementation problem by representing the infinite probability distribution $Bel(l)$ by a set of N samples $S = \{s_i | i = 1 \ldots N\}$. Each sample $s_i = \langle l_i, p_i \rangle$ consists of a robot *location* l_i and *weight* p_i. The weight corresponds to the likelihood of l_i being the robots correct position, i.e. $p_i \approx Bel(l_i)$ [24]. Furthermore, as the weights are interpreted as probabilities, we assume $\sum_{i=1}^{N} p_i = 1$.

The algorithm for Monte Carlo localization is adopted from the general Markov localization framework described above. During robot operation, the following two kinds of update steps are iteratively executed:

- *Sample Projection across Robot Motion:* A new sample set S is generated from a previous set S' by applying the motion model $P(l|l', m)$ as follows: For each sample $\langle l', p' \rangle \in S'$ a new sample $\langle l, p' \rangle$ is added to S, where l is randomly drawn from the density $P(l|l', m)$. The motion model takes into account robot properties like drift and translational and rotational errors.
- *Belief Update and Weighted Resampling:* Sensor inputs are used to update the robot's beliefs about its position. According to Equation 2, all samples are re-weighted by incorporating the sensor data o and applying the observation model $P(o|l')$. Most commonly, sensors such as laser range finders or sonars, which yield distance data, are used. In this case, ideal sensor readings can be computed a priori, if a map of the environment is given. An observation model is then obtained by noisifying the ideal sensor readings, often simply using Gaussian noise distributions. Given a sample $\langle l', p' \rangle$, the new weight p for this sample is given by $p = \alpha \, P(o|l') \, p'$, where α is again a normalization factor which ensures that all beliefs sum up to 1. These new weights for the samples in S' provide a probability distribution over S', which is then used to construct a new sample set S. This is done by randomly drawing samples from S' using the distribution given by the weights, i.e. for any sample $s_i = \langle l_i, p_i \rangle \in S'$, $Prob(s_i \in S) \approx p_i$. The relationship is approximate only, because after each update step we add a small number of uniformly distributed samples, which ensure that the robot can re-localize in cases where it lost track of its position, i.e. where the sample set contains no sample close to the correct robot position.

The Monte Carlo localization approach has several interesting properties; for instance, it can be implemented as an anytime algorithm [6], and it is possible to dynamically adapt the sample size[13].

3.3   Visual Feature-Based Monte Carlo Localization (VMCL)

An example for using visual information for MCL has been provided by Dellaert et al. [7]. On their indoor robot MINERVA, they successfully used the distribution of light intensity in images obtained from a camera facing the ceiling. Due to the rather uniform lighting structure above a RoboCup field, this approach is not applicable in RoboCup.

Feature-Based Modeling. The MCL sensor update mechanism needs a sensor model $P(o|l)$ which describes how probable a sensor reading o is at a given robot location l. This probability is often computed by estimating the sensor reading $\tilde{o}$ at location l and determine a similarity measure between the given measurement o and the estimation $\tilde{o}$. If sensor readings o_i are camera images two problems arise: (i) Estimating complete images $\tilde{o}_i$ for each sample's location is computationally very expensive. (ii) Finding and computing a similarity measure between images is quite difficult. A better idea is to lift the similarity test to work on processed, more aggregated, and lower-dimensional data, such a feature vectors. The selection of the visual features is guided by several criteria: (i) uniqueness of the feature in the environment, (ii) computational effort needed to detect the feature in images, and (iii) reliability of the feature detection mechanism.

In our previous visual feature-based MCL implementation for ROBOCUP [11], only few environment features could be detected: goal posts and field corners as landmark features, and distances to walls as distance features. The corner detector yielded ambiguous landmarks, because corners were indistinguishable from each other, while the four goal post features were unique landmarks. At most eight landmark features could be detected in any particular pose. Despite feature detection being sparse and sporadic, we could show that VMCL is still able to provide reasonably reliable and accurate self-localization. However, the accepted changes to the environment now necessitate a different approach to feature detection and the weighting of position samples.

4   VMCL Using RoboCup Field Markings

Field markings like lines and the center circle are visible at many positions on the field even within the limited viewing field of a directional vision system. At least in the vicinity of the robot, they can often be perceived with high accuracy and can therefore be used as landmark features for robot self-localization. The following processing steps are executed to utilize field markings for VMCL:

1. Image pixels belonging to field markings are extracted from the image by a green/white edge detector. As this edge detector relies on two color features, it provides some robustness against noise (false positives) originating from the field surroundings, like white or green clothes.
2. Taking the camera distortion into account, the edge pixels are then mapped to spatial representations. Two shape-based representations – egocentric Hough spaces for lines and circles – are used as shape detectors in our approach.
3. By applying a Gaussian filter on the Hough representations of field lines and circles, sensor inaccuracies and noise are taken into account and a heuristic distance metric is defined.
4. For each position hypothesis (sample), the expected positions of visible lines and circles in the respective Hough spaces are computed.
5. A matching of visually detected and expected line and circle features is performed for each position hypothesis. By combining the distances of all detected lines and circles, a weight for the correctness of a given position hypothesis is obtained.

4.1   Hough Transformed Feature Lookup

Two Hough space representations [9] serve as shape detectors for the observed edges. One for field lines $\mathcal{H}^L$ and one for the center circle $\mathcal{H}^C$. A similar approach was taken by Iocchi and Nardi[19]. They *explicitly* extract *symbolic* field

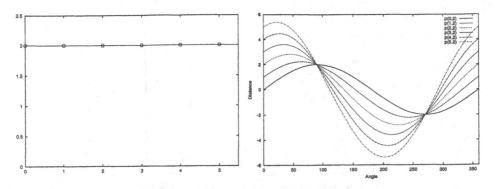

Fig. 1. Mapping of line point into the line Hough space.

markings by thresholding and searching for local maxima in the Hough spaces. A matching process is then performed which associates detected line and circle features with expected ones. If a consistent correspondence can be found, a position difference can be directly computed from the Hough representations and used for position correction.

Applying Iocchi and Nardi's approach in VMCL encounters some problems. First, searching for the local maxima is non-trivial, because the absolute values in the Hough spaces of lines and circles at various distances can vary widely due to camera resolution. In some situations it is even possible to mistake circles as lines and vice versa, especially if they are partially occluded or only partially visible. Second, symbolically finding consistent matchings of detected and expected features can be very expensive, especially if it must be done for large number of position estimates (samples).

Instead of explicitly extracting symbolic representations of field markings, we suggest to perform *subsymbolic feature matching*. A distance metric is defined in the Hough spaces by applying a Gaussian filter operation to the representation of detected features. Matching of feature sets is then done *implicitly* by lookup of expected features directly in the Hough spaces and computation of the distance metric for each position sample. Thus, an *explicit* symbolic feature extraction is omitted.

4.2 Hough Transformation

The Hough space representation for lines is their distance to the origin and the angle of the orthogonal vector. A single edge point is represented in line Hough space by all lines to which the point can belong, resulting in a sinusoid in the Hough space. All sinusoids representing points belonging to the same line cross themselves within the two points in the Hough space representing that line. In Figure 1 this is the line $(90^\circ, 2)$, or $(270^\circ, -2)$ respectively. The angular axis of the Hough space can therefore be restricted to $[0^\circ, 180^\circ)$. The Hough representation of the center circle is similar. As the radius of the circle is fixed, only the Cartesian coordinates of the circle center need to be modeled within

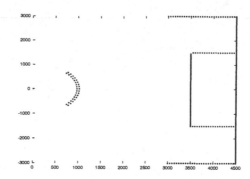

Fig. 2. Edges visible for the robot at p(0,0,0°).

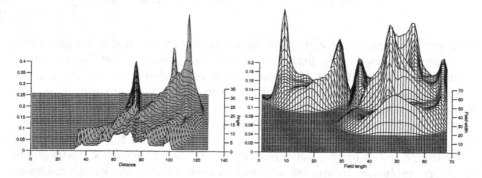

Fig. 3. The resulting line (left) and circle (right) Hough spaces.

that space. A point is then represented as all the circles it can belong to, resulting in a circle of possible circle centers within the Hough space.

4.3　Discretized Hough Spaces

By using discretized Hough spaces, the value of each coordinate lying on the sinusoid/circle of the added point is increased. Thereby every cell of the discretized Hough space becomes a feature detector for the set of lines it represents. The n observed field markings then result in the n highest local maxima within the Hough spaces, or the n feature detectors with the highest activation levels. As pointed out above, searching for those maxima can difficult in practice due to potentially high noise within the observed edges. Also, as it is not a priori known, whether an edge belongs to a field line or the center circle, they are entered into both Hough spaces. Field corners get then mismatched as a circle and a partially visible center circle can be well misinterpreted as a line, making the matching of observed local maxima infeasible.

4.4　Feature Representation

The left plot in Figure 3 shows the results of mapping the edge samples shown in Figure 2 into the line Hough space. The robot is positioned at the field center and looking at the goal. The camera apex angle is $90°$. In this simulated edge sample set, there is no inaccuracy in the detected edges. As the edge sample set in this position is symmetric, only a section of $90°$ is plotted. The axis of the line Hough space is scaled from $-5m$ (index 0) to $5m$ (index 127). The angle column 0 represents the lines parallel to the viewing axis (field and penalty area side lines) the column 63 represents the field markings, orthogonal to the robots viewing angle. Note, that the first local maximum, which is blurred along the angular axis, is actually not a field line, but the artefact produced by the center circle. The right plot in Figure 3 illustrates the circle Hough space for the same sample set. The field center lies at (8,63) and the lower edge post would be located at (56, 32). The sharp peak represents the actual circle. The rest of the Hough space is obfuscated by the artefacts of the field lines.

4.5 Subsymbolic Feature Mapping

Although the extraction of the actual field markings from the Hough representations is possible, it needs some analysis even for a simulated edge scan without noise. Instead, we suggest to look up the activation of each feature detector for each expected visible field marking. For the sum of activations to be an accurate measure for the correctness of the position hypothesis, the following characteristics of the Hough representations have to be explored.

Directly matching the expected features to the observed edges within the Hough transformation avoids the previously described problems and is much more computationally efficient. A measure for the fitting of the observed features to the expected ones is the percentage of observed edges that match with the expected field markings. This measure can be obtained as follows:

As the total number t of edge pixels mapped into the Hough spaces is known, the activation value for a cell can be scaled accordingly. The activation value for each potential circle center is increased just once for each edge mapped to the circle Hough space. Therefore $\mathcal{H}^C(x,y)/t$ always is within $[0...1]$, representing the percentage of edges observed in the image that match a circle at a certain position. For the line Hough space, a similar measure can be constructed by summing up the activation of each visible line.

For each type of feature, a quality measure for rating the matching of an observed feature to an expected one is needed. Usually, a distance metric is used to determine the difference between an observed feature and its expected position. As we do not have an explicit representation of the field marking, this is again infeasible. Instead we model this function by applying a Gaussian filter on the Hough spaces. Note, that as long as width of the filter is smaller than half of the minimum distance between two parallel lines, each visual edge can still be matched to only one expected field marking.

A Gauss filter is applied for each angle column in the line Hough space to model the distance metric. Care must be taken to avoid, that after the filter operation a mapped edge is counted multiple times for a single cell. Therefore, the activation of only one cell per column and sinusoid of the line Hough space is increased. Additionally, all activated cells should be connected in an 8-connectedness, which results in the following connectedness constraint:

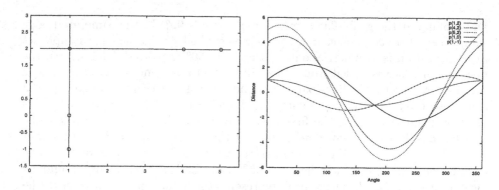

Fig. 4. Points belonging to two lines.

$$\max_{\alpha_0, |d| \le d_{max}} \left[rnd \left(\frac{d * \sin \alpha_0}{\Delta d} \right) - rnd \left(\frac{r * \sin(\alpha_0 + \Delta \alpha)}{\Delta d} \right) \right] \le 1$$

where Δd denotes the discretization step size for the distance, $\Delta \alpha$ the angular discretization step size accordingly and d_{max} the maximum viewing distance of the camera. That is, for all possible sinusoids, successive column indices may only differ by one. By abandoning the rounding step the above constraint can be tightened and formulated as:

$$\frac{d_{max}}{\Delta d} * 2 \sin \left(\frac{\Delta \alpha}{2} \right) \le 1$$

By approximating $\sin x$ as x, this results in the following maximum angular step size: $\Delta \alpha \le \Delta d / d_{max}$. This ensures, that the summed activation of the line feature detectors for each angle is t.

Crossings of orthogonal field lines result in edges, that belong to two lines in the line Hough space. This is exemplified in Figure 4. Those edges are counted twice and therefore introduce an error that can be dealt with in different ways: One is to ignore this effect and to apply clipping of high values in order to ensure that weight values are at most 1. The alternative is trying to factor out line crossings in order to not overweigh position hypotheses with visible line crossings. This can be done by substracting edge pixels counted twice. Due to the distance-variant camera resolution, the effect is correlated with the distance of the crossing point. Empirically, a constant factor e is sufficient to ensure adequate results. In order to avoid negatives weights, clipping of values lower than 0 should be applied. Experimentation with both alternatives turned out to produce good results. The first alternative results in higher ambiguity, while the latter underestimates the correct values of positions, especially in situations with partial occlusions of line features. Summing up the above analysis, the weight of the correctness of a position hypothesis $p(x, y, \theta)$ can be calculated as $w(p) = \max(0, \min(1, \hat{w}(p)))$ with

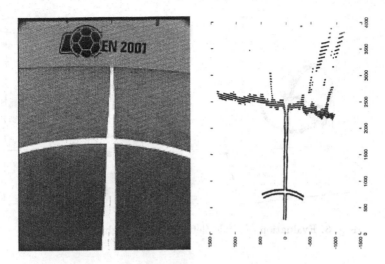

Fig. 5. The camera image and the detected edges.

$$\hat{w}(p) = \frac{1}{t}\left(\mathcal{H}^C(-p) + \sum_{l \in V_p^l(L)} \mathcal{H}^L(l-p) - c(p) * e\right),$$

where L is the set of field lines, $V_p^L(L)$ the set of visible lines at position p, $c(p)$ is the number of crossings visible at the proposed position.

5 Evaluation

The Hough space feature lookup is implemented and first empirical results could be obtained, both in lab experiments and during the RoboCup German Open 2002.

5.1 Experiments

In the first real world example, the robot is standing in the middle of the center circle facing the side wall. Figure 5 shows the image obtained by the camera of the robot and the resulting edge feature set, after projection to the floor. The camera apex angle is 45° and as we do not have enough room in our lab, the side wall is only $2.2m$ away and the radius of the center circle is $0.80m$. There is also some noise, as dark parts of the wall are partially interpreted as green.

To give an impression of the quality of the position estimation based on the above edge feature set, we evaluated one million samples uniformly distributed over all of the robot's three dimensional configuration space. To account for the removed walls, positions up to $1m$ off the field along both axis are also part of the configuration space. To visualize the results of the position estimation, the iso surface for the weight of 80% is plotted into a 3-dimensional plot. The x axis

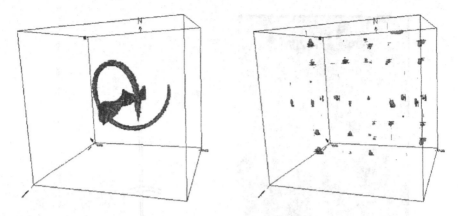

Fig. 6. Evaluation of circle (left) and line (right) edges only.

is aligned with the field sides and the y axis with the goals. The z axis represents the orientation of the robot, scaled from $-180°$ to $180°$. That is, looking at the plot, the center of the cube matches with the center of the football field looking at the opponents goal. The actual robots position in the plot is in the center of the x and y axis. On the z axis there exist two possible positions, due to the symmetry of the field. Either at one quarter, or at three quarters of the range of the z axis.

The left plot in Figure 6 shows the position estimation based on just the circle. For this estimation, an edited version of the image in Figure 5 was used, showing just the circle part of the image. The thick spiral around the z axis shows, that the robot can clearly map its position but is not able to tell its orientation from the circle. The thin spiral is the maximum weight of those position hypotheses that try to match the circle samples to a circle with its center located at $1.6m$ distance directly in front of the robot. For this matching there is significantly less evidence available.

For the distribution estimation of only the line Hough space evaluation, an edge feature set without the circle edges was used. The noise was not eliminated. The result is shown in Figure 6. All positions on the field at which the robot is standing on a line facing an orthogonal line at about $2.2m$ distance have a high rating. Using both Hough spaces together for evaluating the original edge feature set, the iso surface plotted in Figure 7 is obtained. Due to the symmetry of the field, two possible positions remain.

In a further laboratory experiment, the robot's task was to move along a virtual square in a RoboCup field half the original size. The experiment lasted 15 hours and showed that line feature lookup is sufficient for robust position tracking even over very long periods.

The method was also successfully evaluated during the recent RoboCup GermanOpen 2000 in Paderborn. The features used there included field lines, center circle, goal and corner posts. The accuracy is typically within the Hough discretizations used ($\approx$ 12cm translational and $3°$ rotational). Image processing typically required 35ms, while the VMCL typically required 100ms.

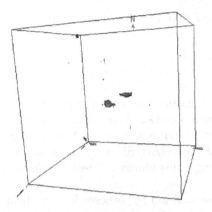

Fig. 7. Evaluation of line and circle edges.

5.2   Weighting of False Positives and False Negatives

For the Hough tranformed feature lookup to be a reliable position estimator, it has to be able to cope with visual noise as especially prominent in the RoboCup F-2000 league scenario. One source of error is the occlusion of features by other robots on the field (false negatives). The other source is a direct consequence of the latest rule changes, the removal of the walls around the field, which makes the spectators visible for the robots. This can introduce false positives, as green/white edges can be visible, that do not belong to field markings. Unfortunately, the indifference of a feature detector to unmapped (potential false positives) or missing features (potential false negatives) also hinders its ability to detect mislocalization.

The Hough transformed feature lookup is quite indifferent to false negatives in the feature set. The weight for a matching of a feature is directly related to the evidence available for this feature. The only exception is the elimination of edge pixels at line crossings, which are counted twice. If a line crossing is occluded by other robots, this indeed decreases the weight for this position. This effect can cause position hypothesis with many crossings to be assigned a negative weight, if there are very little edges available, that support this hypothesis. This requires a low default weight to be assigned for such a hypothesis, to keep the weight scaled correctly. But since this obviously is, according to the sensory information available, a bad position estimation anyway, it should be discarded. Additionally, this effect prevents positions at which many lines are visible to be erroneously weighted as good hypothesis.

Even though hardly anything is done to actively suppress false positives by the edge detection operator, this method is fairly robust against it. White noise, that is, randomly observed edges have very little effect on the method, since it inhibits all position hypotheses equally. Falsely detected lines only give false positives if they are aligned with the field axis. As vertical lines vary in angle after the floor projection step for every viewing angle, they only sporadically introduce false positives that can be filtered out by the Markov localization process.

5.3 Efficiency

The Hough transformed feature lookup is computationally cheap. The most expensive part is the creation of the Hough spaces. The cost scales linearly with the resolution of discretization as well as the the number of the observed edges ($|E|$): $O(d_{max}/d_\Delta * 180°/\alpha_\Delta * |E|)$. Since all those factors increase the accuracy of mapping field markings, this allows a direct trading of speed against quality of the feature detector.

The weighting of the position hypotheses is very cheap and has almost constant cost. For each field marking, there is one lookup within the Hough spaces the indices of which are also cheap to calculate since all field lines are axis aligned and orthogonal to each other. For each field marking a visibility check is required to increase the robustness against white noise. The visibility of the field markings from a given position can be precomputed and stored in a lookup table for discrete positions. The calculation of actual coordinates is again very cheap. The discretization introduces little error, since the number of edges observed for a field marking decays as it leaves the field of view of the camera. Thus it contributes little to the weight of a position hypothesis, either if erroneously ignored or looked up.

6   Conclusion

Recent changes to the ROBOCUP environment necessitate major revisions of the self-localization methods used on most robots. Vision-based MCL seems to be able to cope well with the recent and some expected future changes. The performance of the VMCL method depends mainly on the quality of the available feature detectors. We presented a subsymbolic shape-based feature detector and its usage for the weighting of position hypotheses as used within the VMCL process. It is robust against noise, as introduced by the latest rule changes, and computationally efficient especially in terms of per-sample evaluation time.

References

1. Giovanni Adorni, Stefano Cagnoni, Stefan Enderle, Gerhard Kraetzschmar, Monica Mordonini, Michael Plagge, Marcus Ritter, Stefan Sablatnög, and Andreas Zell. Vision-based localization for mobile robots. *Robotics and Autonomous Systems*, 36(2/3):103–118, August 2001.
2. Thorsten Bandlow, Michael Klupsch, Robert Hanek, and Thorsten Schmitt. Fast image segmentation, object recognition and localization in a robocup scenario. In Manuela Veloso, Enrico Pagello, and Hiroaki Kitano, editors, *RoboCup-99: Robot Soccer World Cup III*, number 1856 in Lecture Notes in Artificial Intelligence, pages 174–185. Springer-Verlag, Berlin, 2000.

3. Wolfram Burgard, Dieter Fox, and Sebastian Thrun. Active mobile robot localization. *Proceedings of the Fifteenth International Joint Conference on Artificial Intelligence (IJCAI-97)*, February 1997. Nagoya, Japan.

4. K. Chung. *Markov chains with stationary transition probabilitites.* Springer, 1960.

5. Paolo de Pascalis, Massimo Ferraresso, Mattia Lorenzetti, Alessandro Modolo, Matteo Peluso, Roberto Polesel, Robert Rosati, Nikita Scattolin, Alberto Speranzon, and Walter Zanette. Golem team in middle size robotics league. In Peter Stone, Tucker Balch, and Gerhard Kraetzschmar, editors, *RoboCup 2000: Robot Soccer World Cup IV*, number 2109 in Lecture Notes in Artificial Intelligence, pages 603–606. Springer-Verlag, Berlin, 2001.

6. T. Dean and M. Boddy. An analysis of time-dependent planning. In *Proceedings of AAAI-88*, pages 49–54, 1988.

7. F. Dellaert, W. Burgard, D. Fox, and S. Thrun. Using the condensation algorithm for robust, vision-based mobile robot localization. In *Proc. of the IEEE Computer Society Conference on Computer Vision and Pattern Recognition*, pages 588–94, 1999.

8. F. Dellaert, D. Fox, W. Burgard, and S. Thrun. Monte carlo localization for mobile robots. In *Proc. of the IEEE International Conference on Robotics & Automation*, 1998.

9. Richard Duda and Peter Hart. Use of the hough transformation to detect lines and curves in the pictures. *Communications of the ACM*, 15(1), 1972.

10. S. Enderle, M. Ritter, D. Fox, S. Sablatnög, G. Kraetzschmar, and G. Palm. Soccer-robot locatization using sporadic visual features. In *Proceedings of the IAS-6 International Conference on Intelligent Autonomous Systems*, pages 959–66, 2000.

11. Stefan Enderle, Marcus Ritter, Dieter Fox, Stefan Sablatnög, Gerhard Kraetzschmar, and Günther Palm. Vision-based localization in robocup environments. In Peter Stone, Tucker Balch, and Gerhard Kraetzschmar, editors, *RoboCup 2000: Robot Soccer World Cup IV*, number 2109 in Lecture Notes in Artificial Intelligence, pages 291–296. Springer-Verlag, Berlin, 2001.

12. D. Fox. *Markov Localization: A Probabilistic Framework for Mobile Robot Localization and Navigation.* PhD thesis, University of Bonn, Bonn, Germany, December 1998.

13. D. Fox, W. Burgard, F. Dellaert, and S. Thrun. Monte Carlo localization: Efficient position estimation for mobile robots. In *Proc. AAAI99*, pages 343–9. AAAI, 1999.

14. Dieter Fox, Wolfram Burgard, Frank Dellaert, and Sebastian Thrun. Markov localization for mobile robots in dynamic environments. *Journal of Artificial Intelligence Research*, 11:391–427, 1999.

15. J.-S. Gutmann, W. Burgard, D. Fox, , and K. Konolige. An experimental comparison of localization methods. In *Proceedings of the International Conference on Intelligent Robots and Systems (IROS'98)*, Victoria, Canada, October 1998.

16. J.-S. Gutmann, T. Weigel, and B. Nebel. Fast, accurate, and robust self-localization in polygonal environments. In *Proceedings of the International Conference on Intelligent Robots and Systems (IROS-99)*. IEEE/RSJ, 1999.

17. Jens-Steffen. Gutmann and Kurt Konolige. Incremental mapping of large cyclic environments. In *International Symposium on Computational Intelligence in Robotics and Automation (CIRA'99)*, Monterey, November 1999.

18. Robert Hanek and Thorsten Schmitt. Vision-Based Localization and Data Fusion in a System of Cooperating Mobile Robots. In *Proc. of the IEEE Intl. Conf. on Intelligent Robots and Systems (IROS-2000)*, pages 1199–1204. IEEE/RSJ, 2000.

19. Luca Iocchi and Daniele Nardi. Self-localization in the robocup environment. In Manuela Veloso, Enrico Pagello, and Hiroaki Kitano, editors, *RoboCup-99: Robot Soccer World Cup III*, number 1856 in Lecture Notes in Artificial Intelligence, pages 318–330. Springer-Verlag, Berlin, 2000.
20. Scott Lenser and Manuela Veloso. Sensor resetting localization for poorly modelled mobile robots. In *Proceedings of the IEEE International Conference on Robotics and Automation*, 2000.
21. Carlos F. Marques and Pedro U. Lima. A localization method for a soccer robot using a vision-based omni-directional sensor. In Peter Stone, Tucker Balch, and Gerhard Kraetzschmar, editors, *RoboCup 2000: Robot Soccer World Cup IV*, number 2109 in Lecture Notes in Artificial Intelligence, pages 96–107. Springer-Verlag, Berlin, 2001.
22. P.S. Maybeck. The Kalman filter: An introduction to concepts. pages 194–204. Springer, 1990.
23. Bernt Schiele and James L. Crowley. A comparison of position estimation techniques using occupancy grids. In *Proceedings of the 1994 IEEE International Conference on Robotics and Automation*, pages 1628–1634, San Diego, CA, May 1994.
24. A.F.M. Smith and A.E. Gelfand. Bayesian statistics without tears: a sampling-resampling perspective. *American Statistician*, 46(2):84–88, 1992.

Evaluation of Self-localization Performance for a Local Vision Robot in the Small Size League

Daisuke Sekimori[1], Tomoya Usui[2], Yasuhiro Masutani[2], and Fumio Miyasaki[2]

[1] Akashi College of Technology, Akashi, Hyougo 674-8501, Japan
sekimori@akashi.ac.jp
[2] Osaka University, Toyonaka, Osaka 560-8531, Japan
{usui,masutani,miyazaki}@robotics.me.es.osaka-u.ac.jp

Abstract. The main purpose of this paper is to examine the upper limits of self-localization ability using a local-vision system in the RoboCup Small Size League. Using an omni-directional vision system on a mobile robot, we originally developed a self-localization method based on imaging of the floor region. However, we could not explore its full potential because of a quantization error in the images. Therefore, we developed a self-localization method that allowed for better estimates of values than by individual methods, by integrating omni-directional vision and dead reckoning with the Kalman filter. This paper describes the algorithms and experimental results with an actual robot. In addition, we examine error recovery when the robot position changes due to collision with other objects and human intervention in the RoboCup competition.

1 Introduction

It is important for a mobile robot to estimate self-position in the environment when the robot moves around in a wide-range area and works with other robots cooperatively. In the RoboCup, especially, a high level of self-localization is required because advanced tasks executed in cooperation with several robots are demanded. Methods of matching observed range data with the field model [1, 2], of finding and tracking goals and walls [3], of relative constraints between robots [4], and other self-localization techniques have been proposed.

We, as the Team OMNI, have developed a mobile robot equipped with a local vision system, and have participated in the RoboCup Small Size League [5]. Although a global vision system overlooking the whole field is allowed in the Small Size League, we have adopted a local vision system, taking the position that a distributed autonomous robot system is significant. Inevitably, thus, self-localization is carried out based solely on on-board vision.

In general, landmarks are used for self-localization. In the Small Size League, however, there are no exclusive landmarks, unlike the Sony 4-Legged League. The objects that can be used as landmarks are only the goal and the wall. The dimensional ratio of such landmarks to the field is smaller than in the Middle Size League. Furthermore, self-localization is thwarted when the landmarks are hidden by other robots. In other words, in the Small Size League the self-localization method based on local vision, is more difficult than in other leagues.

G.A. Kaminka, P.U. Lima, and R. Rojas (Eds.): RoboCup 2002, LNAI 2752, pp. 41–52, 2003.
© Springer-Verlag Berlin Heidelberg 2003

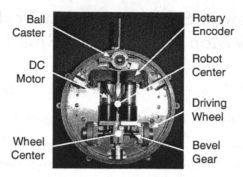

Fig. 1. Overall view of the robot

We previously utilized imaging of the whole floor region provided by the omni-directional vision on the mobile robot as a landmark, and developed a method of estimating self-position by matching the image with the shape of the known floor region [6]. In this method, even if a part of the floor region is hidden by obstacles, this can be compensated for by computing the convex hull of a boundary point set of the floor region in the omni-directional image. As a result, self-position can be estimated in a field where a lot of robots exist. Then we applied this method to the RoboCup competition and confirmed its effectiveness. However, we found that it is sensitive to quantization errors and noise in the images. In this paper, to overcome the problem, we examine a sensor fusion method, which integrates estimation based on omni-directional imaging of the floor region and dead reckoning based on incremental rotation of wheels with the Kalman filter. The main purpose of this paper is to explore the upper limits of self-localization ability using the local vision system allowed in the RoboCup Small Size League. In addition, we examine error when the robot position changes due to collision with other objects and human intervention in the RoboCup competition.

The rest of the paper is organized as follows. In section 2, outlines of a method of estimating robot position based on omni-directional imaging of the floor region are described. The integration of this vision-based estimation and dead reckoning is explained in section 3. In section 4, the results of benchmark tests to evaluate the accuracy of self-localization for robots are given. Finally, in section 5 conclusions are provided.

2   Self-localization Based on Omni-directional Imaging of the Floor Region

Our proposed method is based on an omni-directional, vertical-axis visual sensor model mounted on a mobile robot. The robot we developed for the RoboCup Small Size League is shown in Fig. 1. Based upon the floor region as seen by the omni-directional vision on the robot, position x_c, y_c and orientation θ_c of the camera center in the floor coordinate system are estimated. Fig. 2 shows

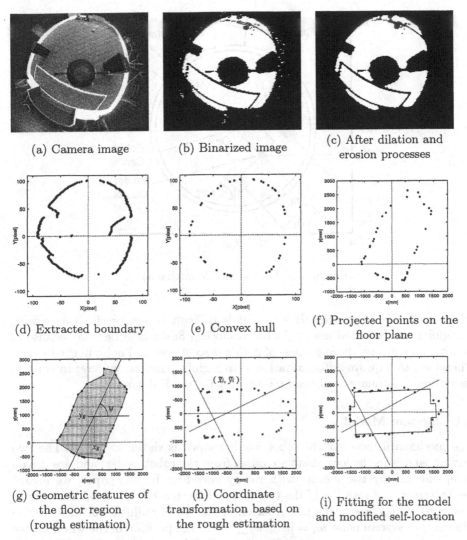

(a) Camera image   (b) Binarized image   (c) After dilation and erosion processes

(d) Extracted boundary   (e) Convex hull   (f) Projected points on the floor plane

(g) Geometric features of the floor region (rough estimation)   (h) Coordinate transformation based on the rough estimation   (i) Fitting for the model and modified self-location

Fig. 2. Example of the method of self-localization based on an omni-directional image

a typical procedure of this self-localization method. Details are provided in the literature [6]. Although this algorithm is meant for the RoboCup field, it is widely applicable for floor regions surrounded by several lines.

3 Integration of Vision-Based Estimation and Dead Reckoning

By using our self-localization method, based on omni-directional imaging of the floor region, moderate estimation can be computed in the RoboCup environment,

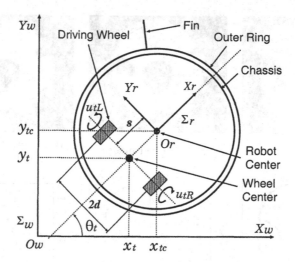

Fig. 3. Model of the mobile mechanism

where some obstacles exist. However, it is difficult to get precise values with the global camera used mainly in the RoboCup Small Size League because of quantization errors, the vagueness of multiple solutions, and noise in the images. Therefore, to improve self-localization with a global camera, we have integrated vision-based estimates and dead reckoning with the Kalman filter.

3.1   System Model

The mechanical model of the robot we developed is shown in Fig. 3. The two driving wheels in the lower part are offset from the robot center, and are driven independently by two motors with rotary encoders. In this paper, we regard the increments of rotation of the two wheels detected by the encoders as input vector $u_t = [u_{tR}, u_{tL}]^T$, the perturbation of the wheel radius (equivalent to the slip rate) as system noise $w_t = [w_{tR}, w_{tL}]^T$, and the position of the wheel center as state vector $x_t = [x_t, y_t, \theta_t]^T$. The state equation of this model is described as:

$$x_{t+1} = f_t(x_t, u_t, w_t), \tag{1}$$

$$\begin{bmatrix} x_{t+1} \\ y_{t+1} \\ \theta_{t+1} \end{bmatrix} = \begin{bmatrix} x_t + \frac{(r+w_{tR})u_{tR}+(r+w_{tL})u_{tL}}{2} \cos\theta_t \\ y_t + \frac{(r+w_{tR})u_{tR}+(r+w_{tL})u_{tL}}{2} \sin\theta_t \\ \theta_t + \frac{(r+w_{tR})u_{tR}-(r+w_{tL})u_{tL}}{2d} \end{bmatrix}, \tag{2}$$

where r and d represent wheel radius and half of the distance between wheels, respectively. Since the robot can easily slip as the speed difference between the right and left wheels increases, covariance matrix Q of system noise w_t is modeled as:

$$Q_t = \mathrm{E}[\boldsymbol{w}_t \boldsymbol{w}_t^T] = \begin{bmatrix} \sigma_{tR}^2 & 0 \\ 0 & \sigma_{tL}^2 \end{bmatrix}, \tag{3}$$

$$\sigma_{tR}, \sigma_{tL} = \sigma_{\min} + \frac{k}{\Delta t} |u_{tR} - u_{tL}|, \tag{4}$$

where σ_{tR} and σ_{tL} represent the standard deviation of the change in the radius of the right and left wheels respectively, $\sigma_{\min}$ represents the minimum values of σ_{tR}, σ_{tL}, k represents the coefficient of influence of the speed difference, and Δt represents the difference of time from t to $t+1$.

3.2 Observation Model

The center of the omni-directional vision system mounted on the robot coincides with the center of the robot body, which is distance s away from the center of the two wheels (Fig. 3). The observation equation of the robot's center position $\boldsymbol{z}_t = [x_{tc}, y_{tc}, \theta_{tc}]^T$ is calculated as:

$$\boldsymbol{z}_t = \boldsymbol{h}_t(\boldsymbol{x}_t) + \boldsymbol{v}_t, \tag{5}$$

$$\begin{bmatrix} x_{tc} \\ y_{tc} \\ \theta_{tc} \end{bmatrix} = \begin{bmatrix} x_t + s \cos \theta_t \\ y_t + s \sin \theta_t \\ \theta_t \end{bmatrix} + \begin{bmatrix} v_{tx} \\ v_{ty} \\ v_{t\theta} \end{bmatrix}, \tag{6}$$

where $\boldsymbol{v}_t$ is the observation noise caused by quantization errors and other noises in the image. Furthermore, covariance matrix $\boldsymbol{R}_t$ of observation noise $\boldsymbol{v}_t = [v_{tx}, v_{ty}, v_{t\theta}]^T$ is modeled as:

$$\boldsymbol{R}_t = \mathrm{E}[\boldsymbol{v}_t \boldsymbol{v}_t^T] = \begin{bmatrix} \sigma_{tx}^2 & 0 & 0 \\ 0 & \sigma_{ty}^2 & 0 \\ 0 & 0 & \sigma_{t\theta}^2 \end{bmatrix}, \tag{7}$$

where σ_{tx}, σ_{ty}, and $\sigma_{t\theta}$ represent the standard deviation of observation errors from the robot's center position, respectively.

3.3 Integration of Two Value Estimates with the Kalman Filter

Because the Kalman filter is fundamental for linear systems, Eqs.(2) and (6) need to be linearized. Eq. (2) is linearized around the measured value u_t. Eq. (6) is linearized around $\hat{\boldsymbol{x}}_{t|t-1}$, which is the estimated value of $\boldsymbol{x}_t$ at time $t-1$. Furthermore, by assuming that system noise $\boldsymbol{w}_t$ and observation noise $\boldsymbol{v}_t$ have mean values of 0, covariance matrices $\boldsymbol{Q}_t$ of $\boldsymbol{w}_t$ and $\boldsymbol{R}_t$ of $\boldsymbol{v}_t$ are normal white noise and have no correlation to each other, respectively. Then, the Kalman filter is derived as:

$$\hat{x}_{t+1|t} = f_t(\hat{x}_{t|t}, u_t, 0), \tag{8}$$

$$P_{t+1|t} = F_t P_{t|t} F_t^T + G_t Q_t G_t^T, \tag{9}$$

$$K_t = P_{t|t-1} H_t^T [H_t P_{t|t-1} H_t^T + R_t]^{-1}, \tag{10}$$

$$\hat{x}_{t|t} = \hat{x}_{t|t-1} + K_t[z_t - h_t(\hat{x}_{t|t-1})], \tag{11}$$

$$P_{t|t} = P_{t|t-1} - K_t H_t P_{t|t-1}, \tag{12}$$

where

$$F_t = \begin{bmatrix} 1 & 0 & -\frac{r}{2}(u_{tR} + u_{tL})\sin\theta_t \\ 0 & 1 & \frac{r}{2}(u_{tR} + u_{tL})\cos\theta_t \\ 0 & 0 & 1 \end{bmatrix},$$

$$G_t = \begin{bmatrix} \frac{u_{Rt}}{2}\cos\theta_t & \frac{u_{Lt}}{2}\cos\theta_t \\ \frac{u_{Rt}}{2}\sin\theta_t & \frac{u_{Lt}}{2}\sin\theta_t \\ \frac{u_{Rt}}{2d} & -\frac{u_{Lt}}{2d} \end{bmatrix},$$

$$H_t = \begin{bmatrix} 1 & 0 & -s\sin\theta_t \\ 0 & 1 & s\cos\theta_t \\ 0 & 0 & 1 \end{bmatrix},$$

$$\hat{x}_{0|-1} = x_0$$

$$P_{0|-1} = P_0.$$

Using these equations, self-localization of the robot is executed with the following algorithm. The robot measures the left and right rotational increments of the wheels during every time cycle, and estimates self-position by dead reckoning Eqs.(8) and (9). Next, the self-position information, estimated with dead reckoning using Eq. (10)~Eq. (12), is improved, based on the self-position observations using omni-directional vision. In the RoboCup field, because the shape of the floor region is a rectangle, two possible solutions always exist based on visually estimated values. The first is based on the position of the goal. If it is not selected, the solution is based on the most recent values estimated.

In the RoboCup competition, there are many cases in which the robot must be moved by human intervention. When the robot position is changed dramatically, the precision of self-localization estimates falls greatly for a while. In order to avoid such a situation, $\hat{x}_{t|t-1}$ and $P_{t|t-1}$ are re-initialized, when the Mahalanobis distance d_{tm} between observed and estimated values satisfies the following condition:

$$d_{tm} = d_{tz}^T P_{t|t-1}^{-1} d_{tz}, \tag{13}$$

$$d_{tz} = z_t - h(\hat{x}_{t|t-1}), \tag{14}$$

$$\begin{cases} \text{if}(d_{tm} > D_{th})\ c \leftarrow c+1,\ \hat{x}_{t|t} \leftarrow \hat{x}_{t|t-1},\ P_{t|t} \leftarrow P_{t|t-1}, \\ \text{else} \qquad\qquad c \leftarrow 0 \end{cases} \tag{15}$$

$$\text{if}(c > n)\ \hat{x}_{t|t-1} \leftarrow z_t,\ P_{t|t-1} \leftarrow P_{0|-1}, \tag{16}$$

where n and D_{th} represent temporal numbers, in the past and to the threshold, respectively.

4   Experiments

We equipped the robot (Fig. 1) with omni-directional vision, using a wireless CCD camera (RF Systems, PRO-5) and hyperboloidal mirror (Accowle, small). The omni-directional image is provided at the lens center, 165[mm] above the floor. Image processing is executed in a main computer unit separated from the robot unit. The video signal transmitted from the camera on the robot unit is processed with a simple frame grabber and the CPU in the main computer unit. To extract colors and label regions, modified CMVision [7] is employed. The resolution of captured images is $320 \times 240[\text{pixel}^2]$. In order to evaluate our method, experiments using a benchmark test were executed with the above-mentioned system configurations. First of all, we show the results of self-localization using only omni-directional image information, and these using only for dead reckoning information. After that, we report on integrated position estimate values using the Kalman filter. Finally, we show the results of self-localization when the position of the robot changes greatly.

4.1   Vision-Based Estimation

First, we executed experiments for self-localization using an algorithm based on omni-directional imaging of the floor region. The shape of the field used for the experiments was the same as for the field of the RoboCup Small Size League, and the material was a green felt mat. The test motion for evaluation was a crank-shaped movement at a speed of 400[mm/s]. Robot positions were estimated using only local omni-directional vision and measured by a camera mounted on the ceiling, as shown in Fig. 4. Although the estimates do not differ much from the actual position, image quantization and shaking of the robot due to a bumpy floor caused estimation errors.

4.2   Dead Reckoning

Next, we executed experiments for self-localization using only dead reckoning. The conditions were the same as stated above. Robot position estimates and measures using only dead reckoning are shown in Fig. 5. The results show that differences between actual position and estimates were small in the beginning and get bigger as time elapsed.

4.3   Integrated Estimation

By using the Kalman filter introduced in section 3, we carried out self-localization experiments using integrated estimate values based on omni-directional vision

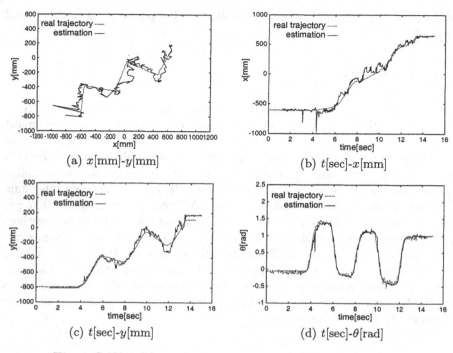

Fig. 4. Self-localization based only on an omni-directional image

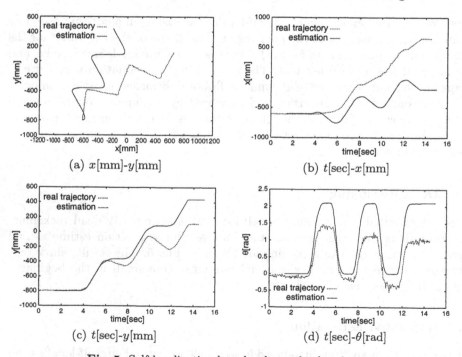

Fig. 5. Self-localization based only on dead reckoning

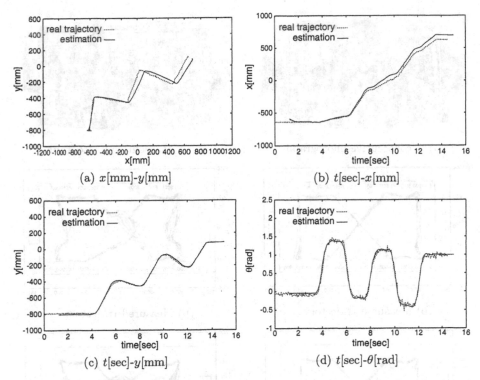

(a) $x[\mathrm{mm}]$-$y[\mathrm{mm}]$ 　　　　　　　　　(b) $t[\mathrm{sec}]$-$x[\mathrm{mm}]$

(c) $t[\mathrm{sec}]$-$y[\mathrm{mm}]$ 　　　　　　　　　(d) $t[\mathrm{sec}]$-$\theta[\mathrm{rad}]$

Fig. 6. Self-localization based on omni-directional imaging and dead reckoning

and dead reckoning. We chose experimental parameters to use with the Kalman filter as follows:

$$\sigma_{\min} = 1[\mathrm{mm}],$$

$$k = 0.5[\mathrm{mm} \cdot \mathrm{s/rad}],$$

$$\sigma_x = 80[\mathrm{mm}],$$

$$\sigma_y = 50[\mathrm{mm}],$$

$$\sigma_\theta = 0.05[\mathrm{rad}],$$

$$\hat{x}_{0|-1} = [0[\mathrm{mm}], 0[\mathrm{mm}], 0[\mathrm{rad}]]^T,$$

$$P_{0|-1} = \begin{bmatrix} 1.0[\mathrm{mm}^2] & 0 & 0 \\ 0 & 1.0[\mathrm{mm}^2] & 0 \\ 0 & 0 & 0.01[\mathrm{rad}^2] \end{bmatrix}.$$

The same conditions as in the two previous experiments were applied, as shown in Fig. 6. The results show that precision was better than when estimated only by vision or by dead reckoning. Estimates were almost the same as measured values, as observed by the ceiling camera.

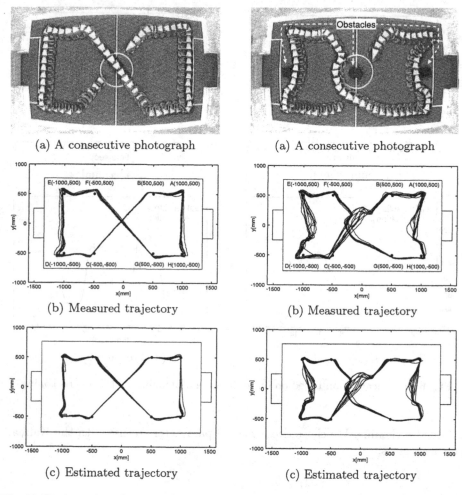

(a) A consecutive photograph   (a) A consecutive photograph

(b) Measured trajectory   (b) Measured trajectory

(c) Estimated trajectory   (c) Estimated trajectory

Fig. 7. Trajectories when no obstacle is present

Fig. 8. Trajectories when obstacles are present

4.4   Long-Term Positioning

In order to confirm of the effectiveness of on-line estimates using the proposed method, a long-term positioning experiment was executed in the RoboCup field. In this experiment, the robot determines velocity and direction based on the difference between estimated self-position and the goal position. After arriving at one goal, it switches to the next. Then it repeats the process many times. The points that the robot passes sequentially are as follows: A(1000,500), B(500,500), C(−500,−500), D(−1000,−500), E(−1000,500), F(−500,500), G(500,−500), and H(1000,−500), where the field center is origin of the floor coordinate system and the blue goal direction is positive, on the RoboCup field. Under two conditions, with/without obstacles in the field, we show as consecutive photographs of 1

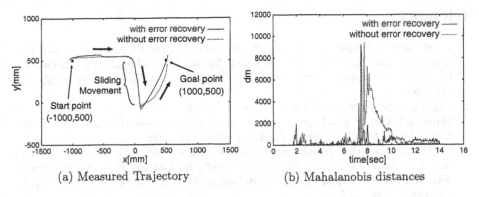

(a) Measured Trajectory   (b) Mahalanobis distances

Fig. 9. An example movement after interruption

cycle, tracing the robot's center position after 10 cycles as measured by the ceiling camera and estimated using the Kalman filter, as shown in Fig. 7 and Fig. 8. In this experiment the robot's speed was 200mm/s. The results show that even in the presence of an obstacle, the robot can move robustly according to orders. In addition, the time required for 10 cycles was about 500[sec], and the mean estimated cycle time was about 50[msec].

4.5 Error Recovery

Finally, we examined error recovery when robot position changed due to collisions with other objects or human intervention. A green vinyl sheet was put in the center of the field, a surface which caused the robot to move at high speed During the experiments, if the Mahalanobis distances between observed values and estimated values were satisfied in Eqs.(13) and (16), we re-initialized estimated values $\hat{x}_{t|t-1}$ and covariance matrix $P_{t|t-1}$. The experimental results given $n=1$ and $D_{th}=1000$ are shown in Fig. 9. The results show that the method using re-initializing $\hat{x}_{t|t-1}$ and $P_{t|t-1}$ achieved the best self-position estimates.

5 Conclusion

In this paper, we have presented a self-localization method that allows much better value estimates than individual methods, by integrating omni-directional image information and dead reckoning information using the Kalman filter. This is an attempt to improve self-localization accuracy with a local-vision robot in the RoboCup Small Size League. In addition, in the same context, we have suggested that effective self-localization can be achieved when robot position differs dramatically due to collisions with other obstacles or to human intervention. Furthermore, we have carried out several experiments using benchmark tests on a real robot, and have proved the effectiveness of these methods. Future work will focus on the implementation of advanced tasks and cooperation play using these methods.

References

1. J.Gutmann, T.Weigel, and B.Nebel: "Fast, Accurate, and Robust Self-Localization in the RoboCup Environment", In Manuela Veloso, Enrico Pagello, and Hiroaki Kitano, editors, Robocup 1999: Robot Soccer World Cup III. Springer-Verlag, pp.304-317, 2000.
2. L.Iocchi, and D.Nardi: "Self-Localization in the RoboCup Environment", In Manuela Veloso, Enrico Pagello, and Hiroaki Kitano, editors, Robocup 1999: Robot Soccer World Cup III. Springer-Verlag, pp.318-330, 2000.
3. F.v.Hundelshausen, S.Behnke, and R.Rojas: "An Omnidirectional Vision System that finds and tracks color edges and blobs", In Andreas Birk, Silvia Coradeschi, and Satoshi Tadokoro, editors, Robocup 2001: Robot Soccer World Cup V. Springer-Verlag, 2002.
4. T.Nakamura, M.Oohara, A.Ebina, M.Imai, T.Ogasawara, and H.Ishiguro: "Real-Time Estimating Spatial Configuration Between Multiple Robots by Triangle and Enumeration Constraints", Peter Stone, Tucker Balch, and Gerhard Kraetzscmar editors, Robocup 2000: Robot Soccer World Cup IV. Springer-Verlag, pp.219-228, 2000.
5. D.Sekimori, et al.: "The Team Description of the Team OMNI", In Andreas Birk, Silvia Coradeschi, and Satoshi Tadokoro, editors, Robocup 2001: Robot Soccer World Cup V. Springer-Verlag, 2002.
6. D.Sekimori, T.Usui, Y.Masutani, and F.Miyazaki: "High-speed obstacle avoidance and self-localization for mobile robots based on omni-directional imaging of floor region", In Andreas Birk, Silvia Coradeschi, and Satoshi Tadokoro, editors, Robocup 2001: Robot Soccer World Cup V. Springer-Verlag, 2002.
7. CMVision web site: http://www-2.cs.cmu.edu/~jbruce/cmvision/

Fast Image Processing
and Flexible Path Generation System
for RoboCup Small Size League

Shinya Hibino[1], Yukiharu Kodama[1], Yasunori Nagasaka[2],
Tomoichi Takahashi[2], Kazuhito Murakami[1], and Tadashi Naruse[1]

[1] Aichi Prefectural University, Nagakute-cho, Aichi, 480-1198 Japan
[2] Chubu University, Kasugai, Aichi, 487-8501 Japan

Abstract. Two key features of successful multi-robot systems in RoboCup are robustness of a vision system and optimization of feedback control in order to reach the goal point and generate the action under the team strategy. This paper proposes two new methods. One is a fast image processing method, which is coped with the spatial variance of color parameters in the field, to extract the positions of robots and ball in 1/30 sec. The separation problem in the interlaced format image is solved. Another one is a path generation method in which the robot approaches the goal by changing its direction convergently. With these two algorithms, the real time processing system is realized by generating a stable path under a low quality input image.

1 Introduction

In the physical multi-robot systems in RoboCup[1],[2], it is important to raise the robustness of vision system and to give an optimal feedback in order to control a robot to reach the goal point. There are several technical problems to be solved from the viewpoints of image processing; for example,

- R-, G-, B-values are not constant by shading in the region of the ball in the image, since a golf-ball used in small-size league is a sphere with dimples.
- Lighting is not always uniform in the game field.
- It is difficult to recognize an object moving at high speed, because the object would appear as split patterns in an interlaced format image.

On the other hand, from the viewpoints of processing time to control robots,

- Calculation time should be short because all objects such as a ball and robots move at high speed.
- A small size input image is desirable, however, the quality of image is getting low.

This paper proposes two new methods. One is a fast image processing method, which is coped with the spatial variance of color parameters in the field,

G.A. Kaminka, P.U. Lima, and R. Rojas (Eds.): RoboCup 2002, LNAI 2752, pp. 53–64, 2003.

to extract the positions of robots and ball in 1/30 sec. Although many labeling methods for the connected component have been reported [7–10], our method is focused on the separation problem in the interlaced format image. This problem is solved with a small overhead for real time image processing. Another one is a path generation method in which the robot approaches the goal by changing its direction convergently. With these two algorithms, the real time processing system is realized by generating a stable path under a low quality input image.

2   Image Processing System

In the small size robot league, an image obtained from a camera installed on ceiling is usually processed to get the position and the direction of each robot and the position of a ball. We also use such images. It is necessary to develop an image processing algorithm which works well for low quality images, since an off-the-shelf camera and frame grabber are used in our system. In this section, we discuss such an algorithm. Throughout this section, a word 'ID' and an 'object' are used for the identification number of each robot and an object region such as a ball, color markers and team markers in the image, respectively.

2.1   System Configuration

Figure 1 shows a configuration of our image processing system. The Video4Linux was used as a driver of frame grabber. The processing is as follows. The frame grabber gives the yuv-image (YUV422). Then, search range is calculated by using history information. For the search range, the segmentation algorithm is applied in order to extract the segments of the object, where the segment is a connected component of pixels which have the color value of specified range. The extracted segments are merged to make a candidate of object by using a labeling algorithm. Finally, the true objects are selected by calculating the size and the location of each object.

It is difficult to get sharp images, since an off-the-shelf camera and frame grabber are used in our system. An example of grabbed image is shown in figure 2. In the figure, a boundary of the object area is blurred and an unexpected scan line is contained. For such an image, the above system should work well. To make a system be robust, we developed a new labeling algorithm which is discussed in sec. 2.3

2.2   Color Image Segmentation for Object Extraction

6 colors should be detected to identify objects, i.e. 1 color for ball (C_1), 2 for team markers(C_2,C_3), and 3 for ID markers (C_4,C_5,C_6). The system classifies each pixel into one of 6 color clusters $C_i(i = 1, 2, ..., 6)$ or the other in the color segmentation process,.

This process utilizes a color image segmentation algorithm developed by CMU[3]. In the algorithm, 32 different colors can be segmented simultaneously.

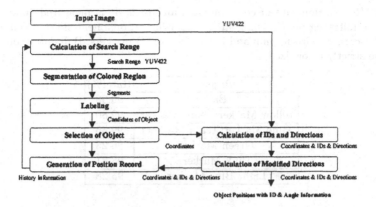

Fig. 1. Image processing system

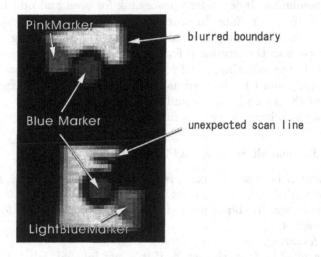

Fig. 2. Example of grabbed image

Thus, we assigned 5 different colors for 1 color cluster, which can compensate the subtle color variations of the object caused by the lighting condition. The image is segmented in this way.

An experimental result under the lighting condition, 700-1500 luxs (which is specified in the regulation of RoboCup small size league), is shown in Table 1. Very high recognition rate is achieved, especially for the ball and team markers (over 99%).

2.3   Labeling Algorithm for Object Extraction

Next step is the labeling process for the segmented image to extract a candidate of the object. Conventional labeling algorithms or methods do not work well for interlaced format image[7–10], since robots and ball move at high speed. Even

Table 1. Recognition rate of color markers and balls. It is measured 1000 times at each of the following points; the goals of the own and opponent sides, a center of the field and 4 corners. Green, pink and light blue are ID markers. Ball and team markers should be strictly recognized

Object	Rate(%)
Ball	99.98
Yellow Marker(Team Marker)	99.80
Blue Marker(Team Marker)	99.35
Green Marker	96.23
Pink Marker	98.31
Light Blue Marker	95.28

though there is a method which processes either even or odd field of an image, it sacrifices the resolution. Independent processing for even and odd fields makes it difficult to unify the results. In order to overcome these difficulties, a new labeling algorithm called **diagonal alternate spread labeling** was developed. It can cope with the interlaced format image which has blurred objects of moving robots. In the following, i and k denote the scanning parameters for the x coordinate and j and l for y coordinate. For the simplicity of explanation, it is assumed that the image is binary and an object is black.

Our labeling algorithm is given as follows.

Algorithm. diagonal alternate spread labeling

Step0 Let A and B be a set of pixels, respectively, and put $A = \phi, B = \phi$. Let *num* be a label number, and put *num* = 0.

Step1 Scan the image. If a black pixel (i, j) which is not labeled is found, put it into the set A.

Step2 Do the following.

1) For a pixel (i, j) in the set A, if it is not labeled, label it with *num*. Then, search the following 8 pixels.

$$(i + 2, j + 2), (i + 2, j - 2), (i - 2, j + 2), (i - 2, j - 2),$$
$$(i + 1, j + 1), (i + 1, j - 1), (i - 1, j + 1), (i - 1, j - 1)$$

For each pixel, if it is black, put it into the set B.

2) For a pixel (k, l) in the set B, if it is not labeled, label it with *num*. Then, search the following 4 pixels.

$$(k, l + 1), (k, l - 1), (k - 1, l), (k + 1, l)$$

For each pixel, if it is black, put it into the set A.

3) Repeat *Step2* while new black pixels are gotten.

Step3 Increment *num* and repeat *Step1* and *2* while there are unlabeled black pixels.

Figure 3 shows a labeling example.

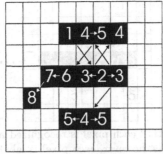

This is an example of segments recognized as one object. The number added to the pixel is a processing order in Step 2 of the labeling algorithm. Since the scan is sequential, the first pixel of an object is always the upper left pixel which is numbered 1

Fig. 3. An example of labeling

Effectiveness of the Proposed Labeling Algorithm. This algorithm can detect line segments, where each of them appears by every two lines, as one object as shown in figure 3. This solves the interlace problem of alternate appearance of black and white lines when the object moves. This algorithm can detect moving objects up to speeds of $v_{max}[cm/sec] = d[cm]/(1/60[sec]) = 60d[cm/sec]$, where, d is the size of an object (ex. $240cm/sec$ for a $4cm$ ball). If the object moves over the maximum speed v_{max}, it is completely separated into 2 objects in the image.

This algorithm has another unique characteristics that a vertical or horizontal line segment of length n and width 1 (pixel) would be divided into n pieces of different objects of size 1 (pixel), because the search to the horizontal and vertical directions occurs after the search to the diagonal directions in Step 2. An example is shown in figure 4. This algorithm works well for such straight line segments that are unexpectedly generated around the boundary of the field or objects shown in figure 5, because the system would delete small size(pixel size) objects as noises by a simple thresholding.

2.4 ID Recognition

ID Recognition Method. The image processing module recognizes the ID and the direction of each robot in our system. Each robot has a black and white plate on its top as shown in figure 6. In the image, the plate region is detected as an object by the image processing module. The ID of robot can be decided by measuring the sector of white region. To do so, we prepared the reference table. The size of the table is 40 or 44 entries[1], that is suited for the size of the robot in an image. The reference table consists of entry number, angle, x and y distance from the center of the plate as shown in table 2.

---

[1] The size of a table is changed according to the situation, because the field size in the image changes with the camera arrangement in the hall.

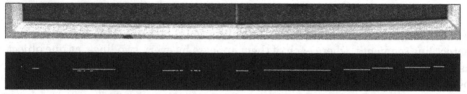

This is an example of object that each pixel is recognized as a different object. Black pixels are candidates of objects, however, each pixel is labeled with different alphabet (a,b,...,i). White pixels with an alphabet show that they are searched in step 2 in conjunction with the black pixel with the same alphabet (Labels d,..,i are omitted here)

Fig. 4. An example of labeling to a straight line

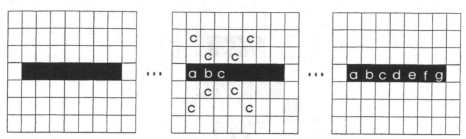

Blue color regions appear near a field boundary by the characteristics of frame grabber. The color segmentation algorithm detects them as the candidate segments

Fig. 5. An example of straight lines caused by color blur

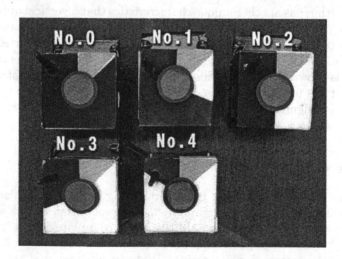

Fig. 6. ID plate

This table is applied to the robot region as shown in figure 7. The image processing module detects a center of the object and refers the pixel values which are pointed by the table entries. The module saves the entry number

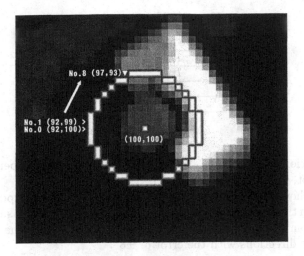

Fig. 7. Applying the reference table to the robot region

Table 2. ID reference table

Entry No.	Angle	X distance	Y distance
0	0	-8	0
1	7	-8	-1
2	14	-8	-2
3	24	-7	-3
4	30	-7	-4
5	38	-6	-5
6	50	-5	-6
7	58	-4	-7
8	65	-3	-7
9	75	-2	-8
10	83	-1	-8

First 11 entries of the 44 entries table are shown

corresponding to the point that the pixel value changes from white to black(it is No.8 in fig.7), and saves the number of pixels whose color is white. In addition, as RoboCup rule allows ID plate to attach other color markers other than black and white, we have set up all markers other than black to be recognized as white by thresholding. It is not difficult to decide this threshold.

This processing is applied to each robot. The ID is obtained by counting the number of pixels judged to be white, and the direction of the robot is given by the table entry corresponding to the pixel whose value changes from black to white.

Resolution and Verification. The ID decision does not depend on the direction of the robot, since the reference points are arranged around the circle. The

Table 3. Measured direction

Measured direction	Frequency
172	165
180	731
188	96
196	8

Measured 1000 times

angle resolution is about $8°(= 360°/44)$. This processing is operated only once to each robot, so the processing time is negligible.

Table 3 shows the accuracy of measured direction. In the experiment, a robot was placed in the horizontal direction and the direction was measured 1000 times. It is clear from the table that 73% of the measurements give the right direction, 26% give the directions with the error of $\pm 8°$.

3   Path Generation

Although we have designed the image processing system with angle resolution of 8° so far, the accuracy is not enough to control the direction of the robot. Inaccuracy of the direction should be compensated in the path generation system.

The path generation system generates and evaluates a path from a current position to a target position, where the target position is given by the strategy system[4]. Moreover, there is a constraint to control the direction, since our robot has only 2 wheels.

For the robot with 2 wheels, Cornell Big Red [5] generated the path by using polynomials in RoboCup '99. CMUnited-99 [6], also in RoboCup '99, proposed a method to control the direction of robot depending on the difference between the direction of the target point and the forward direction of the robot at the target point. We propose, in this section, a method to control the direction of robot depending on the curvature of a geometric path and the difference between the direction of the target point and the robot's orientation. With this method, curved paths shown in figure 9 are generated.

3.1   System Configuration

A path generation system consists of a path generator, a path evaluator, an auxiliary target point generator, a simple predictor and a velocity generator, as shown in figure 8. This system works as follows;

1. The path generation system receives the target position, the robot direction and the action (stop, shoot, etc.) at the target position from a strategy system.
2. The path generator generates a working path by using a curvature control variable and sends it to the path evaluator. The path evaluator estimates the required time to arrive at the target position and finds out the path not to violate the RoboCup soccer rules.

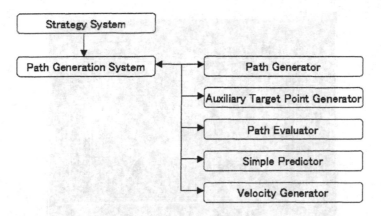

Fig. 8. Path generation system

3. Determine an advancing direction of a robot based on an evaluation result.
4. If there is an obstacle on the path or if robot direction at the target does not satisfy the given direction, the auxiliary target point is added for avoiding collision or for satisfying the direction at the target. Then, a new path is calculated again.
5. The new path is evaluated again.
6. Iterate step 3 - 5 by modifying the value of curvature control variable, and get an optimal path.
7. The velocity generator generates the velocities of wheels which move on the optimal path.
8. The simple predictor corrects the velocities of wheels to compensate the delay of processing time of image processing system. The corrected velocities are sent to the robot through a radio system.

3.2   Path Generator

The degree of control freedom is two and the control of direction is limited, because our robot has two wheels. Considering this and the fact that the target position where each robot should go changes from hour to hour, it is realistic to generate a path which the robot approaches the target position by asymptotically changing its direction. We call this a **direction converging path generation**. Figure 9 shows the paths generated by this method. In the figure, paths are superimposed on the field image. Each double circle with a number is a current position of our robot and the end point of each path is a target position. A triple circle at the target position is a ball. The dotted circles are opponent robots. If opponent robots stand on the generated path, subtargets are put near the opponents to avoid collision. In the case, the robot goes to the subtargets at first and then goes to the target. The robots number 2 and 3 have a subtarget and the robots number 0 and 1 do not. The goal keeper (number 4) does not move

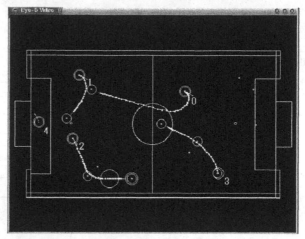

This figure shows generated paths in a certain time slice of a real game. Each dotted circle is an opponent robot. Each double circle with a number is our robot and each solid circle is a target point. A triple circle is a ball. For robot 3, the strategy system gives a subtarget point in order to avoid an enemy. So is for robot 2. In case of robot 2, one more subtarget point is generated (a large solid circle in front of the ball) to adjust a robot direction as facing the ball

Fig. 9. Planned paths in a real game

in this figure. Note that the path is generated only to determine the velocity for next Δt time step[2]. The path is newly generated every Δt time step.

Our path generation algorithm is given as follows.

Algorithm. direction converging path generation

Step1 Let $p(= (x, y)), (v_l, v_r), \mathbf{u}$ be position, velocity (of left and right wheels) and forward direction vector of a robot, respectively. Let t be the current time. Calculate the curvature κ and robot velocity $v = \frac{v_l + v_r}{2}$. See literature [5] for detail.

Step2 Get a goal position $p' = (ox, oy)$. This is given by the strategy algorithm.

Step3 Let $\overrightarrow{pp'}$ be a vector directed from the current position to the goal position and let θ be an angle between vectors $\overrightarrow{pp'}$ and $\mathbf{u}$.

Step4 Give a curvature at the time $t + \Delta t$ by $\kappa_{new} = \theta \times n_a/R_A$, where R_A is a constant and n_a is a variable depending on subgoal(s). (This equation generates a path which has a large curvature at first and a small as approaching to the goal. See fig. 9.)

Step5 Putting $dr = 1/\kappa - 1/\kappa_{new}$, calculate a velocity variation of robot $|dv| = |S/dr|$, where S is a constant. Let $v_m(\kappa)$ be a maximum robot speed when a curvature κ is given. Give new velocity by $v_{new} = v + dv$ if $v_{new} < v_m(\kappa_{new})$, otherwise by $v_{new} = v - dv$. Then, calculate a new position at the time $t + \Delta t$.

---

[2] Image processing speed determines the Δt. In our system, $\Delta t = 33 msec$.

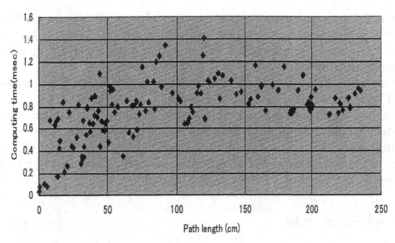

Each plot shows generated path length and its runtime for a robot (Processor is Pentium III 800 MHz. Operating system is Linux)

Fig. 10. Runtime for randomly selected generated-path in a real game

Step6 Calculate repeatedly the steps from *step1* to *step5* and check whether the path reaches the given goal or not. (Fig. 9 shows the result of this calculation in a real game.) If the path reaches the goal, it is OK. If not (if over M times repeated), recalculate these steps by changing the constant R_A until the path reaches the goal. This computation gives the robot velocity of next Δt time period.

3.3 Runtime Evaluation

Figure 10 shows the performance of our path generation system. In the figure, each plot shows generated path length and its runtime for a robot in a real game. The path generator runs on the Pentium III 800 MHz processor under the Linux operation system.

The runtime for typical path with length of 100 cm takes about 1 msec from the figure. This is short enough to make the image processing, strategy and path generation computation within 1/30 sec on the host processor.

The runtime disperses over the vertical axis, since the path generation time, for the same length paths, depends on the curvature of the geometrical path, i.e. the computation time of the path with large curvature takes long time and the small takes short time.

4 Concluding Remarks

In this paper, we proposed a fast and robust image processing method which is coped with the variance of color parameters in the field and a new labeling algorithm, "diagonal alternate spread labeling algorithm". It was clarified experimentally that these method and algorithm are highly effective and robust to extract moving objects up to 240 cm/sec without any condition that it is an interlaced format image or not.

We also show the path generation algorithm in which the robot approaches the goal by changing its direction convergently.

These two algorithms realized the fast and robust robot system. Although our system installed these algorithms works well in real time, there are some remaining issues. As the robustness of the image processing under the spatial variance of lighting is improved, it still remains the problem for improving the robustness under the time variance of lighting.

Acknowledgements

This paper was partially supported by Grant-in-Aid for General Scientific Research (C) of Ministry of Education, Culture, Sports, Science and Technology, and the Tatematsu Foundation and AI Research Promotion Foundation.

References

1. M. Veloso et al eds. "Lecture Notes in Artificial Intelligence 1856, RoboCup-99: Robot Soccer World Cup III", Springer, 2000.
2. P. Stone et al eds. "Lecture Note in Artificial Intelligence 2019, RoboCup 2000: Robot Soccer World Cup IV", Springer, 2001.
3. J. Bruce, T. Balch, M. Veloso "Fast and Inexpensive Color Image Segmentation for Interactive Robots", Proc. 2000 IEEE/RSJ Int. Conf. on Intelligent Robots and Systems, pp. 2061 - 2066, 2000.
4. Y.Nagasaka, K.Murakami, T.Naruse, T. Takahashi and Y.Mori: "Potential Field Approach to Short Team Action Planning in RoboCup F180 League", in P. Stone et al eds., Lecture Note in Artificial Intelligence 2019, RoboCup 2000: Robot Soccer World Cup IV, pp.345-350, Springer, 2001.
5. R. D'Andrea and J. Lee "Cornell Big Red Small-Size-League Winner", AI magazine, Vol. 21, No. 3, pp. 41 - 44, 2000.
6. M. Veloso, M. Bowling, S. Achim "The CMUnited-99 Small Robot Team", Team Descriptions Small and Middle Leagues, Linköping University Electronic Press, 1999.
7. A.Rosenfeld and A.C.Kak, "Digital Picture Processing", 2nd ed., Vol.2, Chap.10, Academic Press, 1982.
8. R.M.Haralick, "Some neighborhood operations", in Real Time/Parallel Computing Image Analysis, M.Onoe, K.Preston,Jr., and A.Rosenfeld Eds., Plenum Press, New York, pp.11-35, 1981.
9. Y.Shirai, "Labeling connected regions", in Three-Dimensional Computer Vision, Springer-Verlag, pp.86-89, 1987.
10. K.Suzuki et al., "Fast Connected-Component Labeling Based on Sequential Local Operations in the Course of Forward Raster Scan Followed by Backward Raster Scan", Proc. of ICPR2000, Vol.2, pp.434-437, Barcelona(Spain), 2000.

A Modified Potential Fields Method
for Robot Navigation Applied to Dribbling
in Robotic Soccer

Bruno D. Damas, Pedro U. Lima, and Luis M. Custódio

Instituto de Sistemas e Robótica
Instituto Superior Técnico, Av. Rovisco Pais, 1, 1049-001, Lisboa, Portugal ·
bdamas@math.ist.utl.pt, {pal,lmmc}@isr.ist.utl.pt
http://socrob.isr.ist.utl.pt

Abstract. This paper describes a modified potential fields method for robot navigation, especially suited for unicycle-type non-holonomic mobile robots. The potential field is modified so as to enhance the relevance of obstacles in the direction of the robot motion. The relative weight assigned to front and side obstacles can be modified by the adjustment of one physically interpretable parameter. The resulting angular speed and linear acceleration of the robot can be expressed as functions of the linear speed, distance and relative orientation to the obstacles. For soccer robots, moving to a desired posture with and without the ball are relevant issues. To enable a soccer robot to dribble a ball, i.e., to move while avoiding obstacles and pushing the ball without losing it, under severe restrictions to ball holding capabilities, a further constraint among the angular speed, linear speed and linear acceleration is introduced. This dribbling behavior has been used successfully in the robots of the RoboCup Middle-Size League ISocRob team.

1 Introduction

The navigation problem for a mobile robot in an environment cluttered with obstacles is a traditional problem in Robotics. Some variations, such as dynamics *vs.* static obstacles or non-holonomic *vs.* holonomic robots make it harder to solve [5]. Other issues such as a car with a trailer moving backwards or pushing an object can also be of practical interest. In the latter case, constraints must be imposed on the robot linear and angular velocities so as to ensure that the pushed object is not lost.

An algorithm (Freezone) to solve the navigation problem for a mobile robot endowed with omni-directional vision, sonars and odometry, with a particularization for soccer robots, has been introduced in previous work [6]. The algorithm was designed to move the robot towards a desired posture while avoiding obstacles, using omni-directional vision-based self-localization to reset the odometry after some relevant events, and a sonar ring to detect the obstacles. The application of this algorithm to robotic soccer was mainly focused on moving the robot, without the ball, towards a desired posture. However, nothing is said on how

G.A. Kaminka, P.U. Lima, and R. Rojas (Eds.): RoboCup 2002, LNAI 2752, pp. 65–77, 2003.

to move the robot *with* the ball and simultaneously avoiding other robots (e.g., dribbling). Only a few teams of the RoboCup Middle-Size league are capable of dribbling the ball. Dribbling is accomplished either by a suitable mechanical design of the robot [2] or by path planning [7]. In the latter work, problems may be experienced in the presence of fast moving robots. Furthermore, it is not clear how the constraints on angular and linear speeds are specified.

Some of the design features of the Freezone algorithm were conceived to avoid problems displayed by other navigation methods available in the literature (see [6] and the references therein). Among those is the well-known potential fields algorithm [3]. The original potential fields algorithm was designed to drive holonomic vehicles. Nevertheless, it can be modified in different ways to handle nonholonomic constraints such as by projecting the resulting field on the possible acceleration vectors, as in the generalized potential fields method [4].

This paper introduces an alternative approach where the generalized potential field is modified so as to enhance the relevance of obstacles in the direction of the robot motion. The relative weight assigned to front and side obstacles can be modified by the adjustment of one physically interpretable parameter. Furthermore, the resulting angular speed and linear acceleration of the robot, obtained under the modified potential field method, can be expressed as functions of the linear speed, distance and relative orientation to the obstacles. This formulation enables the assignment of angular and linear velocities for the robot in a natural fashion, physically interpretable. Moreover, it leads to an elegant formulation of the constraints on angular speed, linear speed and acceleration that enable a soccer robot to dribble a ball, i.e., to move while avoiding obstacles and pushing the ball without losing it, under severe restrictions to ball holding capabilities. It is shown that, under reasonable physical considerations, the angular speed must be less than a non-linear function of the linear speed and acceleration, which reduces to an affine function of the acceleration/speed ratio when a simplified model of the friction forces on the ball is used and the curvature of the robot trajectory is small. This dribbling behavior has been used successfully in the robots of the RoboCup Middle-Size League ISocRob team.

This paper is organized as follows: in Section 2, the generalized potential fields method, its virtues and shortcomings, are revisited. Section 3 describes the modified potential fields method introduced in this paper. The application of the method to dribbling a ball in robotic soccer is introduced in Section 4, by determining physical constraints on the expressions for angular and linear acceleration obtained in the previous section. In Section 5 some experimental results are presented and Section 6 concludes the paper.

2   Generalized Potential Fields Method

The traditional potential fields method of avoiding obstacles consists of evaluating a repulsive force for each obstacle. That evaluation is made taking into account the distance to the obstacle and the relative velocity between the robot and the obstacle(s). An attractive force that tends to drive the robot to its target is also calculated. Each of these forces has the direction of the object that gave rise to it. The attractive force accelerates the robot towards its target while the repulsive forces accelerate in the opposite direction of the obstacles.

In the generalized potential fields method [4] the absolute value of each repulsive vector is obtained using

$$|a| = \frac{\alpha v}{2d\alpha - v^2} \, , \tag{1}$$

where α is the maximum acceleration available to the robot and v and d are respectively the velocity component in the obstacle direction and the distance to that obstacle. Expression (1) arises when the repulsive potential is defined as the inverse of the critical time interval until a collision happens. This potential is infinite when the estimated time until a collision takes place equals the time needed to stop the robot using full backward acceleration.

This method has some serious drawbacks: it is not always possible for non-holonomic vehicles to accelerate in the direction given by the resulting force vector, and so the potential fields concept is not fully applicable; also, when an obstacle is close enough, the singularity of (1) is reached due to errors caused by the sensors sampling time and the unavoidable noise contained in the sensors measures, leading the robot to an undesirably unstable behavior.

Despite not being well suited for non-holonomic vehicles, the potential fields method is very appealing, since it allows the use of other several navigation methods within the framework of a behavior-based architecture [1], using an independent potential fields module for obstacles avoidance and other modules such as path planning or pose stabilization to drive the robot to its target. In fact, the potential fields method implicitly defines such a behavior-based architecture, where the evaluation of the sum of repulsive forces acts as one module and the evaluation of the attractive vector acts as another module, the robot actuations being simply a result of the vectorial sum of the output of each module.

Therefore, a solution more suitable than just replacing, in the navigation system, the potential fields method by a different method, is to modify it for non-holonomic vehicles in such a way that the method modularity is preserved.

3   Modified Potential Fields Method – The Unicycle Case

The kinematic model of the unicycle vehicle represented in Fig. 1 is given by

$$\begin{bmatrix} v \\ w \end{bmatrix} = \begin{bmatrix} r/2 & r/2 \\ r/2L & -r/2L \end{bmatrix} \begin{bmatrix} w_R \\ w_L \end{bmatrix} \tag{2}$$

where v is the speed of the robot, $w = \dot{\theta}$ is the angular velocity of the robot, w_R and w_L are the rotating speeds of the right and left wheels, r is the wheels radius and L is half of the distance between the contact points of each wheel.

The non-holonomic nature of a unicycle vehicle does not allow movements in arbitrary directions. The instantaneous velocity of the robot has always the same direction as the robot heading (the vehicle body frame is depicted in Fig. 1). So

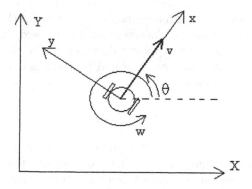

Fig. 1. Kinematics model

it is much more natural to state the repulsion acceleration in two independent components: the first component is the normal acceleration (along the y-axis) and is given by $a_y = vw$; the second component, the tangential acceleration of the robot (along its direction of motion, the x-axis), is equal to the time derivative of the instant velocity. The key point here is that the vectorial sum of these two acceleration components does not necessarily need to have the direction of the fictitious line that connects the obstacle and the robot, as was the case when using the generalized method. In fact it can be a better approach to design the robot behavior separately in terms of its angular and linear speed in the presence of obstacles.

3.1   Potential Fields

The idea behind the potential fields method is the analogy with the movement of electrically charged particles in free space: each one is repelled by the particles with equal signs and attracted to the particles with opposite signs. The force exerted by one particle on another has always the direction of that particle, with an orientation opposite to the particle if the particles have the same sign and the opposite orientation when the particles have different signs. The intensity of the electrostatic force does not depend on the velocity of the particles: since the field is radial it is sufficient to know the distances between them to completely define the potential function. This is a natural consequence of the absence of restrictions on the movement. Nevertheless it is not much useful to act regarding a repulsive force generated by an obstacle whose position can hardly be reached due to the robot kinematics restrictions. Instead of using a Euclidean distance, one can "shape" the potential field to the non-holonomic nature of the robot. In the unicycle case, in the absence of slippage, there is a restriction of movement along the y-axis: v_y is necessarily equal to zero for all times, and so it is convenient to increase the repulsive force along the x-axis since the velocity has only a component along that axis. There are many different possible potential field shapes: the triangular potential field and the elliptic potential field are only two examples. The former is described by the equation

$$|y| = -\frac{|x|}{m} + d \tag{3}$$

while the latter is given by

$$\frac{y^2}{d^2} + \frac{x^2}{(md)^2} = 1 \ . \tag{4}$$

In both cases x and y are the obstacle coordinates in the vehicle referential, d is the potential value for that particular obstacle and m is a constant that defines the potential field "stretch" along the feasible direction of movement (the x-axis in the unicycle case). The constant m usually has a value greater than 1, meaning that the potential value of an obstacle placed along the y-axis equals the potential value of the same obstacle placed at a distance m times larger along the x-axis. If the potential value is expressed in terms of x and y, then

$$d = \frac{|x|}{m} + |y| \tag{5}$$

and

$$d = \sqrt{y^2 + \frac{x^2}{m^2}} \tag{6}$$

for the triangular and elliptic potential fields, respectively. It can also be useful to express these potential fields in polar coordinates, respectively,

$$d = r \left(\frac{1}{m} |\cos \varphi| + |\sin \varphi| \right) \tag{7}$$

and

$$d = r \sqrt{\frac{1}{m^2} \cos^2 \varphi + \sin^2 \varphi} \ , \tag{8}$$

where φ, the orientation of the obstacle relative to the robot, and r, the obstacle distance, are obtained by the usual transformations, $r = \sqrt{x^2 + y^2}$ and $\varphi = \arctan(y/x)$. The contour lines for both potential fields can be seen in Fig. 2. Note that, in the generalized potential fields method [4], the potential fields are described by $d = r/\cos \varphi$, since only the velocity component in the obstacle direction is taken into account. Note that generally the potential value corresponds to a distance to the robot using a different, non-Euclidian metric. The generalized potential fields method also leads to a "stretch" of the potential field in the direction of movement (see Fig. 3), as is the case of the triangular and elliptic potential fields when $m > 1$. Also note that if we set $m = 1$ in the elliptic case a circular potential field is obtained and the distance in terms of potential becomes an Euclidean distance.

Up to now nothing has been said about the navigation through the obstacles and the repulsive forces themselves; in fact, the only purpose of this section was to conceive the idea of a non-Euclidean distance that can prove itself more useful when taking into consideration the non-holonomic restrictions of the robot. The navigation algorithms will be presented in the next sub-sections.

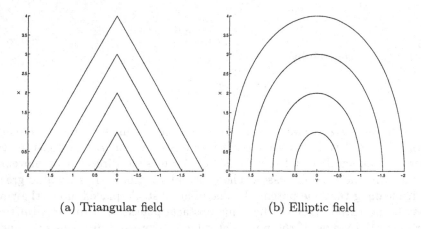

(a) Triangular field   (b) Elliptic field

Fig. 2. Field countour lines, with $m = 2$

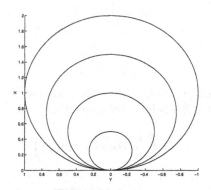

Fig. 3. Potential fields used in (1)

3.2   Normal Repulsive Acceleration

The total applied acceleration in the direction perpendicular to the movement is simply equal to the sum of individual normal accelerations, $a_y = a_{y1} + a_{y2} + a_{y3} + \cdots$. Since $a_y = vw$, where v is the robot linear speed, the last expression can be written as

$$w = w_1 + w_2 + w_3 + \cdots . \tag{9}$$

This means that the total normal acceleration of the robot is given by the sum of individual angular velocities applied to that robot, apart a scale factor.

Should the robot generate the same path independently of its linear speed, given an obstacle configuration and the initial conditions, one must ensure that its curvature function C for those obstacles is independent of the linear speed. Noting that $C = w/v$, if, for each obstacle i,

$$w_i = c(d_i) \cdot v , \tag{10}$$

where $c(d_i)$ is a function of the distance d_i to the obstacle (measured using the chosen potential field), then $C = c(d_i)$ and the curvature function becomes dependent only on the position of that obstacle. Generally that function is assumed to decrease with distance: once again there are several candidates for the curvature function. $c(d)$ could be any of the following:

$$|c(d)| = \frac{G}{d - D} , \tag{11}$$

$$|c(d)| = \frac{G}{(d - D)^2} , \tag{12}$$

$$|c(d)| = \begin{cases} G(1 - d/D) & \text{if } d < D \\ 0 & \text{otherwise} \end{cases} . \tag{13}$$

G is an overall gain and D is a parameter that controls the derivative of the curvature function with respect to d, the distance of the target to the center of the robot. D has distance units and in the case of (11) and (12) must be dimensioned in order to guarantee that $D < R$, where R is the robot radius (if it were not so the curvature function could reach a singularity). A careful choice of values of D and G is critical in what concerns to the robot performance.

The signal of the curvature function is given by

$$\frac{c(d)}{|c(d)|} = \begin{cases} 1 & -\frac{\pi}{2} \leq \varphi < 0 \\ -1 & 0 < \varphi \leq \frac{\pi}{2} \end{cases} . \tag{14}$$

For $\varphi = 0$ the signal is undefined: it can be randomly assigned, but when multiple obstacles exist there are other possible approaches (see Section 3.5).

3.3   Tangential Repulsive Acceleration

The total tangential acceleration is also given by the sum of the individual tangential components, $a_x = a_{x1} + a_{x2} + a_{x3} + \cdots$, which can be transformed to

$$\dot{v} = \dot{v}_1 + \dot{v}_2 + \dot{v}_3 + \cdots . \tag{15}$$

For each obstacle, the tangential repulsive acceleration can be projected in several ways: usually it should increase when the obstacle gets closer and should decrease when the robot goes slower. This acceleration depends on the speed of the robot and the distance to the target as well,

$$\dot{v} = F(d, v, \ldots) , \tag{16}$$

although it can also depend on the time derivatives of v and d when a dynamic relation is used instead of a static one (e.g., a PID controller).

There is no need to use the same parameters, not even the same potential field shapes, when modeling the normal and the tangential repulsive accelerations: those two components are actually independent.

3.4   Attractive Acceleration

To drive the robot to its desired final posture an attractive module is needed. This module can consist of a path-follower or a posture stabilizer by state feedback. For example, a simple controller one can design is

$$\begin{cases} w_c = K_w(\theta_{ref} - \theta) \\ \dot{v}_c = K_v(v_{ref} - v) \end{cases} , \qquad (17)$$

where θ_{ref} and v_{ref} are respectively the desired angle and velocity and K_v and K_w are controller parameters to be tuned. θ_{ref} is defined as

$$\theta_{ref} = \arctan\left(\frac{y_{ref} - y}{x_{ref} - x}\right) , \qquad (18)$$

where (x_{ref}, y_{ref}) is the robot target position and (x, y) its current position. The control algorithm is simple and the study of its stabilization properties is out of the scope of this work: the goal is simply to achieve the target position with a simple controller. Nevertheless, despite its simplicity, these controllers have proven to be quite satisfactory when conjugated with the obstacle avoidance modules.

Equations (9) and (15) simply state that after the obstacle avoidance modules are designed the modules responsible for getting the robot to its target posture can be added by simply summing the respective acceleration components.

3.5   Multiple Obstacles

Although (9) and (15) are extremely attractive, suggesting a natural sum of the tangential and normal components relative to the respective obstacles, such an approach has serious drawbacks: two small obstacles placed side by side would give rise to a repulsive force much more stronger than the repulsive force caused by an obstacle with an equivalent size and placed at the same position. Moreover in many cases an autonomous robot has access only to measurements provided by, e.g., a sonar or infrared ring placed around it, and has no clue on whether the reading of two contiguous sensors belongs to distinct obstacles or to the same object. A possible solution is to consider only the most critical obstacle at each side of the robot, determining the nearest left and right obstacles and discarding all the others. In the tangential repulsion case it suffices to get the nearest front obstacle, and so the repulsive accelerations become defined as

$$w_{obs} = c(d_{LMax}) \cdot v + c(d_{RMax}) \cdot v \qquad (19)$$

and

$$\dot{v}_{obs} = F(d_{FMax}, v, \cdots) , \qquad (20)$$

where d_{LMax}, d_{RMax} and d_{FMax} are respectively the minimum obstacle distance at the left side, right side and front side of the robot, and F is a suitable function. When the nearest obstacle is located precisely in front of the robot, (19)

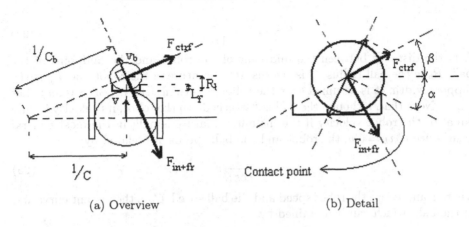

(a) Overview   (b) Detail

Fig. 4. Forces acting on the ball

becomes undefined; it is not recommended then to choose randomly the side to which assign that obstacle, since such an approach can be a cause of undesirable unstability. One can calculate the second nearest obstacle and then assign the nearest obstacle to the second nearest obstacle side, creating a kind of hysteresis that prevents the robot "hesitation". The robot actuations are finally given by

$$w = w_c + w_{obs}$$
$$\dot{v} = \dot{v}_c + \dot{v}_{obs} \quad , \tag{21}$$

where $\dot{w}_c$ and $\dot{v}_c$ are the attractive accelerations that try to drive the robot to its final target and w_{obs} and $\dot{v}_{obs}$ are the repulsive accelerations due to the obstacles, defined in (19) and (20).

4   Dribbling

To keep the ball controlled near the robot while the robot moves is a crucial and a challenging problem under the RoboCup Middle-Size League rules. ISocRob and other teams developed a flipper mechanism in order to dribble a ball better.

It is only possible to keep the ball between the flippers while navigating through obstacles if the inertial and the friction forces exerted on the ball are able to balance or overcome the torque originated by the centrifugal force at the contact point (see Fig. 4). This means that

$$\sin(\alpha + \beta)F_{ctrf} \leq \cos(\alpha + \beta)(F_{fr} + F_{in}) \ , \tag{22}$$

where F_{ctrf}, F_{fr} and F_{in} are respectively the centrifugal, the friction and the inertial forces, and where the angles are given by

$$\alpha = \arcsin \frac{R_b - L_f}{R_b} \tag{23}$$

and

$$\beta = \arctan \frac{L}{1/C} \ . \tag{24}$$

L is the distance between the midpoint of the robot and the midpoint of the ball, R_b is the ball radius, C is the instant curvature of the robot and L_f is the flippers width. It is assumed that the robot is turning left, i.e., $w > 0$ and that $v > 0$. Note that, although the ball is "attached" to the robot, its velocity is only equal to the robot velocity if the instant curvature is null; in the most general case, since $C_b v_b = Cv$, the robot and the ball speeds are related by

$$v_b = \frac{1}{\cos \beta} v \ , \tag{25}$$

where v and v_b are the robot speed and the ball speed. C_b is the instant curvature of the ball, which can be obtained by

$$\frac{1}{C_b} \approx \sqrt{\left(\frac{1}{C}\right)^2 + L^2} \ . \tag{26}$$

The inertial, centrifugal and friction forces can be replaced, according to their definitions, by

$$F_{ctrf} = m_b C_b v_b^2 = m_b \frac{C}{\cos \beta} v^2 \ , \tag{27}$$

$$F_{in} = m_b \dot{v}_b = m_b \frac{\dot{v}}{\cos \beta} \tag{28}$$

and

$$F_{fr} = m_b a_{fr} \ , \tag{29}$$

where m_b is the mass of the ball and a_{fr} is acceleration caused by the friction force. Expression (22) consequently becomes $Cv^2 \le \cot(\alpha + \beta)[\cos(\beta)a_{fr} + \dot{v}]$, leading to

$$w \le \cot(\alpha + \beta) \left[\frac{\cos(\beta)}{v} a_{fr} + \frac{\dot{v}}{v} \right] \ . \tag{30}$$

The friction between the ball, the robot and the floor is usually very hard to model accurately, as it usually does not depend exclusively on the ball speed and its derivatives. If, for the sake of simplicity, only the term proportional to the ball speed is taken into account when evaluating the friction force, e.g.,

$$a_{fr} = \mu_{fr} v_b = \mu_{fr} \frac{v}{\cos \beta} \ , \tag{31}$$

where μ_{fr} is the friction coefficient, then (30) becomes

$$w \le \cot(\alpha + \beta) \left[\mu_{fr} + \frac{\dot{v}}{v} \right] \ . \tag{32}$$

Finally, when the curvature C of the robot is small enough, corresponding to a large curved path, (32) simplifies to

$$w \le \cot(\alpha) \left[\mu_{fr} + \frac{\dot{v}}{v} \right] \ . \tag{33}$$

Since α is constant, (33) can be written as

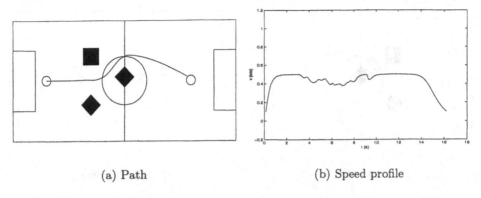

(a) Path   (b) Speed profile

Fig. 5. Obstacle avoidance ($v_{ref} = 0.5m/s$)

$$w \leq A + B\frac{\dot{v}}{v} \, , \tag{34}$$

where $A = \cot(\alpha)\mu_{fr}$ and $B = \cot(\alpha)$.

The constant B is easily obtained since it depends only on the geometry of the robot and the size of the ball. Constant A must be determined empirically. Note that (34) is only a valid expression when the curvature is small enough; in the most general case one should use (32). This model assumes that the robot is always turning to the same side. When this is not the case and the robot curvature function changes the ball goes from one flipper to another. Usually that leads to some bouncing, which can actually be a serious problem. Note also that a more sophisticated friction model may be needed to get better results.

Expression (34) states the dribbling fundamental restriction on the robot movement. Usually the angular velocity is bounded in order to meet condition (34), although other more complex schemes may be found, restricting both w and $\dot{v}$, that meet that condition.

5   Experimental Results

The attractive acceleration components were obtained using very simple controllers, namely those referred on (17), with $K_w = 3$ and $K_v = 0.4$. The repulsive normal acceleration was based on (13), while the tangential acceleration was based on a PD controller whose error is a function of distance also given by (13). Both normal and tangential repulsions use an elliptic field with $m \approx 2$. All the experiments were performed using the robots of the ISocRob team. The start point was $(-3.5, 0)$ — left side of the camp — and the target position was $(3.0, 0)$ — in the right side of the camp.

Note that, as pointed out in Section 3.2, theoretically (10) makes the curvature function independent of the robot speed. However the robot dynamics effectively contribute to a degradation of the robot performance, especially at high speeds. To take that effect into account, the parameter D of equation (13) is a linear function of v, providing the robot with a faster response to obstacles at high speeds. Fig. 5 presents the robot path in the presence of obstacles and

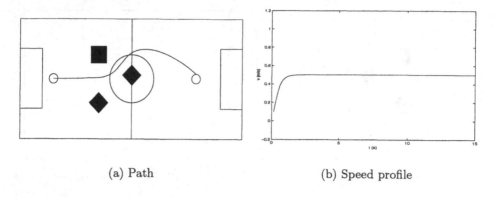

(a) Path   (b) Speed profile

Fig. 6. Obstacle avoidance with dribbling restrictions ($v_{ref} = 0.5m/s$)

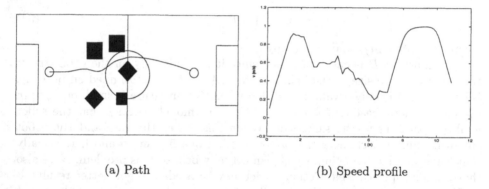

(a) Path   (b) Speed profile

Fig. 7. Obstacle avoidance in a highly cluttered environment ($v_{ref} = 1.0m/s$)

the correspondent speed profile. Fig. 6 shows how the behaviour of the robot changes when the dribbling restriction is active, with $A = 0.3$ and $B' = 0.19$. The value $B' = B/T$, where T is the sampling time, is referred because a discrete time version of equation (34) was used.

In Fig. 6(a), after the mid-field obstacle, the robot follows a wider path to keep ball. It is also visible in Fig. 6(b) that the speed never decreases, since this would leed to a ball loss.

Finally, Fig. 7 shows the robot response in a cluttered environment. The dribbling limitations presented in Section 4 create considerable difficulties to the task of traversing such a cluttered environment, unless the reference speed of equation (17) is a very low one, decreasing the normal acceleration obtained from the obstacle avoidance module (see equation (10)).

6   Conclusions

This paper introduced a modified version of the generalized potential fields method. The modification allows different potential field shapes "stretchable" by changes in one parameter. It also allows a decoupled specification of the tangential and normal components of the acceleration caused by an obstacle. These accelerations can be seen as disturbances acting on the robot efforts to go to its target posture, based on a suitable closed loop guidance controller. This algorithm, such as all the other potential field based methods, can lead to situations where the robot becomes trapped in a local minima situation, in particular in highly cluttered environments. This does not pose too much of a problem since that is precisely the underlying philosophy of that kind of method: to provide a simple and fast, although non-optimal, way of moving to a desired posture while avoiding collisions with other objects (this method is computationally unexpensive, since it only needs to perform some simple calculations for each obstacle distance measured). The independence of the normal and tangential components of repulsive acceleration formulated in Section 3 can nevertheless provide a better way of avoiding those local minima if the normal acceleration is preferred over the tangential acceleration, leading to a behavior where the robot only brakes when it has no place to turn. The escape from local minima should be left to a path-planner, embebbed in the attractive module.

The method enables an elegant formulation of the required constraints for a soccer robot to keep the ball while moving towards a given posture, also known as dribbling. The general case and a simplified version, affine on the ratio between the linear acceleration and velocities, are presented. These results have been successfully applied to the RoboCup Middle-Size League robots of the IsocRob team, leading to goals after a dribble, or 180 degrees turns with the ball.

References

1. R. Arkin, *Behavior-Based Robotics*, The MIT Press, 1998
2. M. Jamzad, A. Foroughnassiraei, E. Chiniforooshan, R. Ghorbani, M. Kazemi, H. Chitsaz, F. Mobasser, S. B. Sadjad, "Design and Construction of a Soccer Player Robot ARVAND", in *RoboCup 1999: Robot Soccer World Cup III*, pp 745–749, M. Veloso, E. Pagello, H. Kitano, Editors, 2000
3. O. Khatib, "Real-Time Obstacle Avoidance for Manipulators and Mobile Robot", 1985 IEEE Int. Conf. On Robotics and Automation, St. Louis, Missouri, pp. 500–505, March 25–28, 1985
4. B. H. Krogh, "A Generalized Potential Field Approach to Obstacle Avoidance Control", Proc. of Intern. Robotics Research Conference, Bethlehem, Pennsylvania, August, 1984
5. J. C. Latombe, *Robot Motion Planning*, Kluwer Academic Publ., 1991
6. C. Marques, P. Lima, "Multi-Sensor Navigation for Soccer Robots", in *RoboCup 2001 Book*, A. Birk, S. Coradeschi, S. Tadokoro, Editors, Springer-Verlag, Berlin, to be published soon.
7. T. Weigel, W. Auerbach, M. Dietl, B. Dumler, J. S. Gutmann, K. Marko, K. Muller, B. Nebel, B. Szerbakowski, M. Thiel, "CS Freiburg: Doing the Right Thing in a Group", in *RoboCup 2000: Robot Soccer World Cup IV*, pp 52–63, P. Stone, T. Balch, G. Kraezschmar, Editors, 2001

Using Online Learning
to Analyze the Opponent's Behavior

Ubbo Visser and Hans-Georg Weland

TZI - Center for Computing Technologies, University of Bremen
Universitätsallee 21-23, D-28334 Bremen, Germany
{visser,weland}@tzi.de
http://www.virtualwerder.de/

Abstract. Analyzing opponent teams has been established within the simulation league for a number of years. However, most of the analyzing methods are only available off-line. Last year we introduced a new idea which uses a time series-based decision tree induction to generate rules on-line. This paper follows that idea and introduces the approach in detail. We implemented this approach as a library function and are therefore able to use on-line coaches of various teams in order to test the method. The tests are based on two 'models': (a) the behavior of a goal-keeper, and (b) the pass behavior of the opponent players. The approach generates propositional rules (first rules after 1000 cycles) which have to be pruned and interpreted in order to use this new knowledge for one's own team. We discuss the outcome of the tests in detail and conclude that on-line learning despite of the lack of time is not only possible but can become an effective method for one's own team.

1 Introduction

The standard coach language provides the on-line coaches in the RoboCup soccer simulation league with a possibility to rapidly change the behavior of his team. In addition, its existence allows a competition between coaches. In order to achieve a successful coaching, a lot of information about the opponent has to be collected, to which the coach can react and change his own team according to the opponent. For this reason several methods have been introduced in the past to analyze on-line and to adapt to the opponents. These papers demonstrated how to recognize team formation [Visser et al., 2001] or how to adapt to play situations [Riley and Veloso, 2002]. [Drücker et al., 2002] showed the idea and a first prototype of the method presented in this paper.

Very important aspects of the behavior of a soccer team are the goalkeeper and the pass behavior.

A pass is a frequent event within a soccer game. It allows the team passing to move the ball across a great distance in a short time and to defeat the opposing defenders. Thus, successful passing can be a great advantage. On the other hand, a pass is always a risk. When the ball is passing it moves without being guarded by a team member who could change the direction of the ball, if necessary. This

G.A. Kaminka, P.U. Lima, and R. Rojas (Eds.): RoboCup 2002, LNAI 2752, pp. 78–93, 2003.

gives the opposing players the possibility to intercept the pass. These intercepted passes are a certain disadvantage. When a team is passing less successful in certain situations than in others, it makes sense for the opposing team to try to create these situations as often as possible. However, in order to do this, it must be known which factors lead to these mistakes.

Therefore, analyzing the goalkeeper the moment when he leaves the goal is of special interest. A possibility to play around him or to reach a point near the goal while he does not attack the forwards, produces great chances to score. It is important to know which factors have led to the players' decision. Also, it is important to know the threshold where they react in a certain way. Thus, it is crucial to use a method that is not hampered by pre-discreeted values but does the discreetization itself. As the outcome of such a method should directly be used by the on-line coach, the results require a certain form. They should be employed to generate instructions for the players. For these constraints the time series-based decision tree induction described in [Boronowsky, 2001] seems suitable. As this method operates with continuous-valued time series, a pre-discreetization of the data is not required. The method finds the split points and therefore the thresholds where the analyzed player act.

2   Time Series-Based Decision Tree Induction

This method consists of a entropy minimization heuristic that only has to be calculated for certain points as opposed to C4.5[Quinlan, 1993] where all possible split points are calculated. This is an important advantage to other decision tree algorithms. Due to the great amount of possible split points, the calculation effort can be very high with continuous data.

The basic ideas for the optimization of the method we use are similar to those of ID3 and C4.5 described in [Fayyad and Irani, 1992]. It shows that the entropy minimization heuristic can only be minimal at the so-called boundary points. A boundary point is a point within the range of a certain attribute whose neighbors belong to two different classes. Thus, the range of an attribute holds for a boundary point T, and

$$A(e_1) < T < A(e_2). \tag{1}$$

$E_1, e_2 \in S$ belong to the set of all samples S, $A(e)$ is the attribute value of e and

$$\neg \exists e_3 \in S : A(e_1) < A(e_3) < A(e_2) \tag{2}$$

where e_1 and e_2 belong to disjunctive classes.

This approach already leads to a noticeable increase in efficiency given appropriate samples. If the samples include overlapping classes the increase of efficiency ends. There are boundary points in the overlapping area in such cases. The calculation then has to be done for all these points because the entropy minimization heuristic can be minimal for all of them. In RoboCup environments such overlapping areas cannot be ruled out.

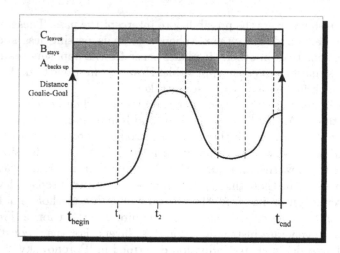

Fig. 1. Qualitative abstraction of the behavior of a goalkeeper

It can be shown though that for continuous equal distributions the entropy minimization heuristic can only be minimal at so-called true boundary points. True boundary points are those boundary points that are located at the boundaries of the interval of one class assignment. When a continuous equal distribution can be reached, the number of interesting points can be reduced and therefore the calculations. This leads to an significant increase in efficiency.

Since this decision tree induction does not work on a set of examples but on time series, the calculation of the optimal split point does not depend on the amount of examples belonging to a certain class. Instead, it depends on the time interval of such an assignment. Instead of $freq(C_j, S)$ and $|S|$ the interesting issues are

- the duration of the assignment of the time series smaller than the split point y to a class C_j $time_{C_j}(y)$,
- the duration of the assignment of the time series above the split point $\overline{time_{C_j}}(y)$, and
- the total duration of the assignment to one class $tmax_{C_j}$.

Thus, there isn't an assignment to a class for every single sample, but there is a qualitative abstraction to one or a combination of multiple time series. This defines which time intervals are assigned to which class. Figure 1 shows an example of a qualitative abstraction of a time series. It shows the behavior of a goalkeeper. At time t_{begin} the distance between the keeper and the goal remains stable. At time t_1 the distance increases which means that he leaves the goal. This state holds until time t_2. The function will be abstracted to class B_{stays} and C_{leaves} accordingly.

For partial linear measured value gradients it can be shown that the entropy minimization heuristic can be calculated efficiently [Boronowsky, 2001]. This is based on the characteristic that the duration of a class assignment $time_c(y)$ for partial linear measured value gradients can be described by linear functions. Such linear durations of class assignments are continuously equally distributed. Thus, the correlation between a continuous equal distribution and an entropy minimization heuristic, as described above, can be used.

It is therefore possible to perform an efficient decision tree induction for continuous valued time series, if these time series consist of partial linear functions. As it cannot be assumed that such partial linear measured value gradients are found, they must be adapted in an appropriate way. This is done by an approximation of the continuous measured values by partial linear functions. As an approximation does not exactly equal the original function an approximation error occurs. This error should be as small as possible, especially at the split points. In general, one can achieve a better approximation by increasing the number of linear functions. On the other hand, this leads to a higher number of potential split points. Thus, the reduction of the approximation error leads to a loss of efficiency. Although, certain points seems to be very important and should therefore be used as boundary points for the linear functions. These are

- the start and end of the used time series
- the times of a change in the class assignment
- the extreme values of the measurement course

It makes sense to use the start and end of the time series because this is the only way to represent the whole series. By using the points where the class assignment changes as boundary point for the linear approximations, a linear function is always assigned to exactly one class. This makes the calculations of the duration of class assignments easier. The extreme values are interesting because they give the option to find a split point, which separates the time series in such a way that the complete series assigned to one class is under or above this split point.

With these partial linear functions the entropy minimization heuristic only need to be calculated for the boundary points of the linear functions because it can only be minimal at these points. Fig.2 shows an approximation with four boundary points (1-4) and the according four points for potential horizontal splitting (y1-y4). To calculate the entropy, the information contents of the duration of class assignments and $(info(y))$ an above $(\overline{info}(y))$ the potential split point has to be calculated.

$$info(y) = - \sum_{i \in C} \frac{time_i(y)}{\sum_{k \in C} time_k(y)} ln \left(\frac{time_i(y)}{\sum_{k \in C} time_k(y)} \right) \tag{3}$$

$\overline{info}(y)$ has to be calculated in the analogue, by changing $time(y)$ to $\overline{time}(y)$. The entropy can be calculated by

$$entropy = \frac{\sum_{i \in C} time_i(y) info(y) + \sum_{i \in C} \overline{time}_i(y) \overline{info}(y)}{\sum_{i \in C} tmax_i} \tag{4}$$

This calculation must be done for all boundary points in all time series. At the point where the results are minimal the according time series is split horizontally. All the others are split vertically at certain points. These points are those where the horizontally splitted time series crosses the value by which it is split. The result is that two new time series are created for every existing time series. One consists of those time intervals in which the horizontal splitted series is greater than the split threshold and the other of those where it is not. This process is then repeated with the two new sets until a certain end criterion is reached.

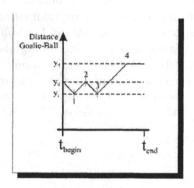

Fig. 2. Partial linear approximation with potential points for horizontal splitting

The ending criterion cannot be the number of correct classified examples as used in regular supervised symbolic machine learning techniques. As it is a time series-based method the ending criterion should be the correct classified time intervals.

At the splitting of the time series the approximation error has to be considered. If the splitting is only calculated by the approximations and not on the basis of real functions there can be errors in the horizontal as well as in the vertical splitting. At the horizontal splitting the approximation can be different from the real value on the time axis and at the vertical there can occur an error on the ordinate. This can be prevented by adapting the approximation in a suitable way. Therefore, all points are added to the approximation that should be split horizontally where the real functions crosses the threshold y. To the other approximations new points are added at all vertical split points.

3   Preprocessing of the Used Data

In order to use the method in an online-coach it has to be defined what should be analyzed and which data should be used for it. In this paper we focus on two scenarios:

1. We analyze the moment when the goalkeeper leaves the goal.
2. We analyze the pass behavior of opponent players

In order to do this a suitable qualitative abstraction must be found. It defines which time intervals are assigned to which class, e.g. if the goalkeeper leaves the goal or if he stays on the line. This leads to the problem that the things that should be learned are not always directly included in the data provided by the soccer server. Therefore, the given data have to be combined or even an element of guessing has to be included. It is important to note that we can only analyze what is happening and that we cannot recognize the player's intention.

The result of this method always depends on the abstraction. If the abstraction is not correct something different is learned. A slight error in the abstraction of the goalkeeper could lead to a tree that has learned the movement of the goalkeeper rather than when he is leaving the goal. These results cannot be used correctly to improve the behavior of a team.

In order to use a decision tree algorithm it is necessary to choose suitable attributes from which the tree is built. It is essential that these attributes represent those values that are important for the decisions of the opponent player. If they are not represented in the attributes the behavior cannot be learned.

3.1   Analysing Goalkeeper Behavior

In the analysis of the goalkeeper's behavior the moment when he leaves the goal is of special interest, because this is when the goal becomes vacant. Thus, a qualitative abstraction is chosen which represents this behavior. The movements of the goalkeeper are represented in three classes, *(a) goalkeeper stays in goal, (b) goalkeeper leaves goal and (c) goalkeeper returns to goal.* This calculation is based upon the movement of the goalkeeper towards the ball. If he moves towards the ball he leaves the goal, and if he goes away from the ball he returns to the goal. In all other cases he stays in the goal. This is not always correct in relation to the goal, but it represents what should be learned. The movement vector of the goalkeeper and the position of the ball are used to compute the abstraction. The length of the movement vector gives the speed, and the angle between the movement vector and a vector from the goalie to the ball are used for the direction.

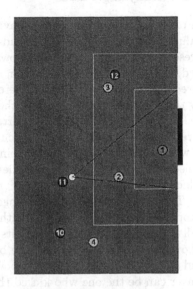

Fig. 3. Cone from ball to both sides of the goal and some positions of opponent players (1-3) as attributes for the learning process

As described above, suitable attributes must be chosen. These attributes should include those that are used by the analyzed goalkeeper to make his decisions. The position of the ball seems to be very important. It will be the major aspect in the goalkeeper's decisions. Murray [Murray, 1999] even describes a goalkeeper whose decisions are totally based upon the ball position. Because of the relative view of the goalie and the abilities of our own players, the relative distance of the ball to the goal and the goalkeeper seems more interesting than its absolute position. Another interesting fact are the positions of the other players (see figure 3). Especially those who can directly interfere in a possible shot at the goal. Particularly the players within the penalty area are relevant to the goalkeeper because of his ability to catch the ball. This is why he may react differently to players in this area. Thus, the number of forwards and defenders in the penalty area is used to analyze the goalkeeper.

Very important for a goalkeeper is the question whether the opposing ball carrier can run and shoot at the goal without being attacked by a defender. In these cases a goalkeeper should leave the goal and run towards the ball carrier to prevent him from shooting into a free corner of the goal. Hence, the defenders within a cone from the ball to the sides of the goal (figure 3), which are likely to intercept the ball, are used as an attribute for the decision tree.

3.2   Analysing Passes

In order to analyze the pass behavior, a qualitative abstraction and some input values have to be found. This leads to some problems owing to the kind of the present data. The coach only knows the positions and movements of all players and of the ball, but not whether a player kicks the ball or not and in which direction the ball was kicked. Therefore, it is impossible to see in the data given by the soccer server who kicked the ball or even if the ball was passed at all.

However, because there are certain rules describing the changes in speed and direction of the ball, it can be calculated from the movement of the ball whether it was kicked or not. Without being kicked by a player the ball cannot gather speed. The same applies to a sudden stop. In both cases a player must have sent a kick command.

This does not apply to a change of direction. A direction change could also happen as a result of a collision with a player. Thus, it cannot be verified that the ball was kicked when it changes its direction. A bigger problem is the question who kicked the ball. Suppose the ball is within the kickable area of one player and one of the events described above happens at the same time. Then, only that player can be the one who kicked the ball. But if the ball is in the kickable area of several players it cannot be determined who kicked it. It also is not possible to tell which intention the player had when he kicked the not be told. On the other hand, it makes no difference to a team whether it gets the ball by intercepting a pass, by dribbling, or by a goal shot. If a team can provoke situations that lead to an interception always has an advantage.

These considerations lead to a qualitative abstraction based upon two kick events. Every kick event is compared with the prior one. It is important which players did the two kicks. The qualitative abstraction assigns these events into four classes:

— pass between two opponents,
— opponent dribbles,
— pass of an opponent was intercepted, and
— team-mate kicked the ball.

A kick command is supposed to have happened if the ball gathers speed or is suddenly stopped. The player who is next to the ball is assumed to have kicked.

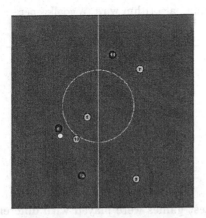

Fig. 4. A passing situation, attributes are positions of the opponent players, surrounding of the ball carrier (e.g. distance and directions of nearest player)

When defining which data should be used as attributes for the learning method one has to take into account that the method has to find out what the player does. Therefore, it is important to use the values used by the player while making decisions. The surroundings of the ball carrier are of special significance for the analysis of pass behavior, especially the distances and directions of the nearest players (see figure 4). It makes no sense to use absolute positions because the player only gets local information and is likely to make his decisions based on relative values, as given to him by the server. Also, players far away from the ball carrier are of no importance. The ball carrier does not see them well, maybe not at all, and a pass across a very long distance is a high risk. Thus it is unlikely that such players play an important part in the decisions of the passer.

While calculating the angles to the other players, it has to be taken into account that in soccer it is more important whether a player is located towards the middle of the field or towards the sideline than to the right or to the left. If e.g. the ball carrier is attacked from his left side it has a different meaning to him whether he is on the right or on the left side of the field. If he is on the right the defender blocks his way to the goal and pushes him towards the sideline. On the other hand, if he is on the left side the defender attacks him from the sideline and the way towards the goal is free. This applies even more in the simulation league because there are only physical differences between the players if a team uses the optional heterogeneous players. And all players can kick the ball to the left as well as to the right. This is why all angles on one half of the field are flipped horizontally. As a result, all passes to the middle have a similar angle and can be represented by the decision tree in the same branch.

Another aspect is the horizontal position of the passing player. The pass behavior may change depending on how far the ball carrier is away from his goal line. E.g. a pass played directly in front of the own goal carries a high risk of being intercepted, thus leading to a good scoring position for the opponent, while a pass in front of the opposing goal may give team-mates the chance to score. Additionally, some parts of a team may pass with a higher risk than others. VirtualWerder 00/01 does take this differences into account. The defenders play as securely as possible while the forwards sometimes even pass into the penalty area without knowing whether anybody is there.

In both cases, goalkeeper and pass behavior, the decision tree algorithm is used every 1000 cycles to generate rules about the opponent's behavior.

Table 1. Typical input data for the learning algorithm w.r.t. a goalkeeper

	Series 0	Series 1	Series 2	Series 3	Series 4	Series 5	Class
1	50	0	52.5	1	0	3	0
2	50	0	52.5	1	0	3	0
3	50	0	52.5	1	0	3	0
⋮	⋮	⋮	⋮	⋮	⋮	⋮	⋮
1000	88.1415	0.487918	90.3164	1	0	0	1

4   Results

To test the quality of the method several test games were played with different teams of last year's competition. VirtualWerder, Robolog Koblenz and Karlsruhe Brainstormers were used to evaluate the implemented algorithm. Robolog was used because, in contrary to most other teams, it is logic- based. The were chosen because they represent a reactive team and because they finished second in the last competition.For technical reasons, Tsinghuaeolus, the world champion, could not be used. It is a Windows-based team while the computers available for the tests where Linux computers. The binaries of FC Portugal were not available at the time of the tests.

4.1   Goalkeeper

To analyze the goalkeeper a qualitative abstraction was used based upon the movement of the goalkeeper, as described above, and six time series. Here are the time series:

- Series 0 - distance ball goalkeeper
- Series 1 - speed of the ball
- Series 2 - distance ball goal
- Series 3 - number of defenders within the penalty area
- Series 4 - number of forwards within the penalty area
- Series 5 - number of defenders that may intercept a direct shot at the goal

After 1000 cycles the decision tree is computed for the first time, based on data shown in table 1.

For the tests with respect to the analysis of the goalkeeper ten test games where played with

- Robolog vs Brainstormers
- Robolog vs VirtualWerder

In the first constellation, both goalkeepers were analyzed, and in the second, for technical reasons, only the one from Virtual Werder.

```
if    series 4 < 2.000000
and   series 0 < 20.105579
then  0(1) 1(0) 2(0)

if    series 4 < 2.000000
and   series 0 > 20.105579
then  0(0.71219) 1(0.245547) 2(0.0422634)

if    series 4 > 2.000000
and   series 0 < 0.385009
then  2(0.950617) 0(0.0493827) 1(0)

if    series 4 > 2.000000
and   series 0 > 0.385009
then  2(0.48) 0(0.34) 1(0.18)
```

Fig. 5. The Brainstormers goalkeeper in a game against Robolog

```
(1) if    series 3 < 1.000000
    then  0(1) 1(0) 2(0)

(2) if    series 3 > 1.000000
    and   series 3 < 4.000000
    and   series 1 < 0.031605
    and   series 0 < 6.774502
    and   series 0 < 5.984714
    then  0(1) 1(0) 2(0)

(3) if    series 3 > 1.000000
    and   series 3 < 4.000000
    and   series 1 < 0.031605
    and   series 0 < 6.774502
    and   series 0 > 5.984714
    then  1(0.8) 0(0.2) 2(0)

(...)

(4) if    series 3 > 1.000000
    and   series 3 > 4.000000
    and   series 2 < 7.680346
    then  1(0.75) 0(0.25) 2(0)

(5) if    series 3 > 1.000000
    and   series 3 > 4.000000
    and   series 2 > 7.680346
    and   series 0 < 6.799984
    then  1(1) 0(0) 2(0)

(...)
```

Fig. 6. The VirtualWerder goalkeeper in a game against Robolog

The rules concerning the Brainstormers' goalkeeper are shown in figure 5. We see that the goalkeeper reacts at different distances to the ball (series 0) depending on the number of attackers in the penalty area (series 4). This change in the distance was often noticed but sometimes it depended on the number of defenders in the penalty area. However, this might be the same because both sounds like a breakaway.

The tests with the VirtualWerder goalkeeper revealed noticeable longer rules than with the two other goalkeepers. One possible explanation is that the VirtualWerder field players cannot keep the ball out of their penalty area and therefore the goalkeeper needs often to react. As this leads to more changes between the classes, he can be better analyzed or he may have a more complex behavior than the others. The rules in figure 6 reflect a part of the behavior of the VirtualWerder goalkeeper in a game against Robolog. The rules show that the goalkeeper changes his behavior depending on the number of defenders in the penalty area (series 3). The first rule reveals that he stays in the goal if there are no defenders present. While the second and third shows that if there are one to four defenders (rules 2 and 3,) he makes his decision based on the speed of the ball (series 1) and the distance from the ball to him. Having more than four defenders within the penalty area (rules 4 and 5,) the decision is based on the distance of the ball to the goal (series 2).

The decision tree method does not produce interesting results about the goalkeeper if there are not enough scenes where he reacts. This can happen if

Table 2. Typical input data for the learning algorithm w.r.t a pass

	Series 0	Series 1	Series 2	Series 3	Series 4	...	Series 9	Class
1	9.01388	-2.33172	10.5	-1.5708	10.1623	...	0	0
2	9.01388	-2.33172	10.5	-1.5708	10.1623	...	0	3
3	9.01388	-2.33172	10.5	-1.5708	10.1623	...	0	3
⋮	⋮	⋮	⋮	⋮	⋮	...	⋮	⋮
1000	7.93404	0.904754	8.04407	1.64693	8.92419	...	-35.3793	1

the opponent is too strong for the team of the coach. It may happen that one team is not able to bring the ball into the opposing penalty area. Sometimes teams even have problems to cross the middle line. In these cases the goalkeeper does not have to act often enough to be analyzed, or maybe he doesn't act at all. In such cases the method only delivers one rule saying that the goalie doesn't move at all. But this is no problem, because if the goalkeeper needs not to act it is not an advantage to know what he would do if he had to. At first the other parts of the play have to be improved. If this is possible fast enough there might be enough information to analyze the goalkeeper later on when there is a possibility to draw an advantage out of this knowledge. This problem was revealed by the tests with VirtualWerder. This team was not able to produce enough pressure on the other two teams to produce enough goalkeeper-scenes. Thus, there were no sensible results about the other teams from these games.

4.2 Pass

According to the reflections in 3.2 ten time series had been chosen as attributes to analyze the pass behavior.

- Series 0 - distance to the next opponent
- Series 1 - angle to the next opponent
- Series 2 - distance to the second next opponent
- Series 3 - angle to the second next opponent
- Series 4 - distance to the next team-mate
- Series 5 - angle to the next team-mate
- Series 6 - distance to the second next team-mate
- Series 7 - angle to the second next team-mate
- Series 8 - side of the passer
- Series 9 - x-position of the ball

The distances and angles are always relative to the ball carrier because he makes his decisions based on his own perceptions. Because of the reasons described above, the angles are horizontally flipped in one half of the field, hence, the angles towards the middle of the field are always negative while the angles towards the sidelines are positive. After 1000 cycles the rules are generated from data shown in table 2.

The first tests showed that a pass is a frequent event, but owing to the short period of time of the actual passing, the total duration of the 'passing classes' is too short. In less than 10% of the time an actual pass is happening. But this is not sufficient to produce good results.

To get rules about the behavior of the opponent from such a rare event with the described decision tree method no error-based pruning can be done. Splitting the samples into the two not-passing classes dribbling and ball with the other team, leads to rules which are in more than 90% correct. With these values the error used to end the decision tree algorithm must be noticeably smaller than 10%.

```
(...)

(1)  if    series 8 > 1.000000
     and   series 0 < 1.530345
     and   series 0 < 0.862784
     and   series 2 < 3.559328
     then  0(1) 1(0) 2(0)

(2)  if    series 8 > 1.000000
     and   series 0 < 1.530345
     and   series 0 < 0.862784
     and   series 2 > 3.559328
     then  2(0.589744) 1(0.282051) 0(0.128205)

(3)  if    series 8 > 1.000000
     and   series 0 < 1.530345
     and   series 0 > 0.862784
     then  1(0.489796) 0(0.346939) 2(0.142857)

(4)  if    series 8 > 1.000000
     and   series 0 > 1.530345
     then  1(0.797297) 0(0.13964) 2(0.05630063)
```

Fig. 7. The passing behavior of the Brainstormers in a game against Robolog

However, if the according threshold is set to such a low value problems of overfitting occur. This means that the necessary generalization is lost and the tree exactly learns the samples given to the algorithm. But this is not what we want because the results should be used to adapt the own team to the opponent. Overfitted rules describe how the opponent has acted in special situations but not how his general behavior operates. This cannot be used to predict the future behavior of the opponent. Thus, another way to improve the results must be found.

The results of a learning algorithm can also be changed by modifying the input values. In this case the problem is obviously the qualitative abstraction. It does not assign enough pass classes. This is a result of the shortness of the pass event. So if there would be a possibility to increase the duration of such an event this should improve the results noticeably. A close look at the game reveals that the positions of the players does not change much between two cycles, thus the environment short before and after the pass is very similar to the one at the pass itself. Hence, they can also be assigned to the same pass class. As a result the pass event is not longer analyzed, but the situation leading to a pass. If the two cycles before and after the actual event are also assigned to the class, the decision tree can be built without the overfitting problem.

To test the method on passes again Robolog Koblenz, Karlsruhe Brainstormers and VirtualWerder were used. Again, ten games were played between Robolog and Brainstormers, VirtualWerder and Robolog and VirtualWerder and Brainstormers. The game Robolog against Brainstormers revealed for the pass behavior of the Brainstormers rules as in figure 7. The first rule showed that the Brainstormers had problems if they were attacked by two players (series 0 < 0.9, series 2 < 3.6). In this case they always lost the ball. But if the second opponent was more than 3.6m away they only lost the ball 12% of the time. The small value used to split series 0 shows that the Brainstormers react very late. The ball is already in the kickable area of the attacker.

In the ten games between Robolog and Brainstormers there were always similar values in the rules, but not all at all times and not in the same order. Although very similar rules to those above could be found in the half of all games, the values just differed slightly .

While analyzing the passing behavior of Robolog, the coach found rules like in figure 8. These rules reveal that Robolog tends to lose the ball if one of their own players is near to the ball carrier (series 4 < 0.5m) except if the attacker is coming from behind (series 1 < -1.36), in this case they are passing very successfully to a team mate. The problem of two Robolog player close to each other was revealed in nearly every game. It was found in the games against VirtualWerder as well.

```
if    series 8 < 1.000000
and   series 4 < 0.462778
and   series 1 < -1.356436
then 2(1) 0(0) 1(0)

if    series 8 < 1.000000
and   series 4 < 0.462778
and   series 1 > -1.356436
then 0(1) 1(0) 2(0)

if    series 8 < 1.000000
and   series 4 > 0.462778
then 1(0.613426) 0(0.208333) 2(0.157407)

(...)
```

Fig. 8. The passing behavior of Robolog in a game against Brainstormers

The tests with analyzing passes also showed that the difference in the quality of the teams influences the results. It is, however, not nearly as great as with the goalkeeper where it could happen that a goalkeeper did not have to move during a whole game which made an analysis of his behavior impossible. It is not as obvious with the passes because even with a weak opponent all teams still passed. Though VirtualWerder could not put much pressure on the Brainstormers there were only few interceptions and thus they have only seldom appeared in the results.

4.3   Related Work

Similar work has be done by Raines and colleagues (1999). They describe a program called ISAAC for off-line analysis that uses C5.0 and pattern matching to generate rules about the success of individual players and team cooperation in certain key events. Key events are events which directly effect the result of the game. The only one used in ISAAC is a shot at the goal. These events are analyzed, similar to the approach in this paper, with a decision tree algorithm. However, ISAAC has to be is used off-line, thus the program is not able to support real-time conditions. The team cooperation is analyzed by a pattern matching algorithm. This patterns are kicks of the ball by certain players which lead to a goal. The rules produced by ISAAC are intended support the development of the analyzed team. Therefore, they show how successful the team is in certain situations but not in which situations the players show which reaction.

An other off-line approach is described in [Wünstel et al., 2000], it uses self organizing maps to analyze the players movement and the players movement in relation to the ball. The trained map can be used to determine which kind of movement is done how often in a game. The results of this method show which kind of movements a player performs, but not in which situations he is doing so.

In the RoboCup 2000 the VirtualWerder coach [Visser et al., 2001] analyzed the opponent with an artificial neuronal network. The network was trained from log-files, from past competitions, to recognize 16 different team formations. To react on the opposing formation the coach was able to change the behavior of his own players.

Riley and Veloso (2002) use a set of pre-defined movement models and compare these with the actual movement of the players in set play situation. In new set play situations the coach uses the gathered information to predict the opponent agent's behavior and to generate a plan for his own players. The main difference to the approach described in this paper is that they analyze the movement of all players in set play situations, while the decision tree approach analyzes certain behaviors of single players and how successful they are in these situations.

5   Conclusion and Future Work

We showed that on-line learning is possible in time-critical environments as demonstrated in the simulation league. The idea is to see an object in the game as a time series. We applied a qualitative abstraction of those time series and used a new approach which is able to discreetize the time series in a way that the results are useable for symbolic learning algorithms. We implemented the approach and ran various tests in real games. We were using two scenarios to analyze the behavior of the goalkeeper and the pass behavior of opponent players. The discussion indicated that the knowledge derived from our approach is valuable and can be used for further instructions to players of the analyzed team. At present, results are generated every 1000 cycles, however, this depends on the situation to be analyzed.

At the moment we are developing our on-line coach in a way that he can use the results of the described approach and give instructions to his players. In order to use the collected rules and get advantage from them they still need to be processed in order to generate advice and to transmit it through the standard coach language to the players. For this purpose the rules should be refined. This process should e.g. reduce the number of attributes in a rule. One attribute should occur in one rule more than twice to mark a range of a value. Additionally, rules which cannot be transformed into advice for the own team can be deleted. The approach is very promising and we hope that first results can be seen on-line at the competitions in June.

If we try to generalize our approach the following statements can be made. Firstly, the proposed minimization heuristic has been successfully applied in a scenario for a qualitative substitution of sensors [Boronowsky, 2001]. It has been shown that qualitative cohesions between measurement-value time series are generally valid and that these cohesions can be discovered by automatic knowledge extraction procedures. The heuristic was also employed with respect to a qualitative analysis of a technical system. The scenario is purification of sewage water under experimental conditions dealing with two regulation circuits. They are regulating the pH value and the oxygen content. The results show that the regulation of both the pH value and the oxygen content can be modelled qualitatively.

Secondly, the method can be used to generate more rules skipping pruning techniques. Usually the amount of generated rules have to be decreased in order to derive comprehensible rules. This can done with the help of pruning methods while creating the decision tree. There are also ideas of how to automatically reduce the number of rules after being generated. This is investigated currently in a project and is subject of a masters thesis. However, sometimes pruning is not an option at all, e.g. if the number of generated rules are to small. In this case, we would be able to skip the pruning methods and therefore generate more rules. These rules should then enable a domain expert to either verify given hypothesis or producing hypothesis about a certain domain.

References

[Boronowsky, 2001] Boronowsky, M. (2001). *Diskretisierung reellwertiger Attribute mit gemischten kontinuierlichen Gleichverteilungen und ihre Anwendung bei der zeitreihenbasierten Entscheidungsbauminduktion.* PhD thesis, Department of Mathematics and Computer Science, University of Bremen, St. Augustin.

[Drücker et al., 2002] Drücker, C., Hübner, S., Visser, U., and Weland, H.-G. (2002). "as time goes by" - using time series based decision tree induction to analyze the behaviour of opponent players. In *RoboCup-01, Robot Soccer World Cup V*, Lecture Notes in Computer Science, Seattle, Washington. Springer-Verlag. in print.

[Fayyad and Irani, 1992] Fayyad, U. and Irani, K. (1992). On the handling of continuous-valued attributes in decision tree generation. In *Machine Learning*, volume 8, pages 87–102.

[Murray, 1999] Murray, J. (1999). My goal is my castle – die höheren fähigkeiten eines robocup-agenten am beispiel des torwarts. http://www.uni-koblenz.de/ag-ki/ROBOCUP/PAPER/papers.html.

[Quinlan, 1993] Quinlan, J. (1993). *C4.5 Programs for Machine Learning.* Morgan Kaufmann.

[Raines et al., 1999] Raines, T., Tambe, M., and Marsella, S. (1999). Automated assistants to aid humans in understanding team behabiors. In Veloso, M., Pagello, E., and Kitano, H., editors, *Proceedings of the Third International Workshop on Robocup 2000, Robot Soccer World Cup IV*, volume 1856 of *Lecture Notes in Computer Science*, pages 85–102, Stockholm, Sweden. Springer-Verlag.

[Riley and Veloso, 2002] Riley, P. and Veloso, M. (2002). Recognizing probabilistic opponent movement models. In *RoboCup-01, Robot Soccer World Cup V*, Lecture Notes in Computer Science, Seattle, Washington. Springer-Verlag. in print.

[Visser et al., 2001] Visser, U., Drücker, C., Hübner, S., Schmidt, E., and Weland, H.-G. (2001). Recognizing formations in opponent teams. In Stone, P., Balch, T., and Kraetschmar, G., editors, *RoboCup 2000, Robot Soccer World Cup IV*, volume 2019 of *Lecture Notes in Computer Science*, pages 391 – 396, Melbourne, Australia. Springer-Verlag.

[Wünstel et al., 2000] Wünstel, M., Polani, D., Uthmann, T., and Perl, J. (2000). Behavior classification with self-organizing maps. In Stone, P., Balch, T., and Kraetschmar, G., editors, *RoboCup 2000, Robot Soccer World Cup IV*, volume 2019 of *Lecture Notes in Computer Science*, pages 108–118, Melbourne, Australia. Springer-Verlag.

Hidden Markov Modeling of Multi-agent Systems and Its Learning Method

Itsuki Noda[1,2]

[1] Cyber Assist Reseach Center National Institute
of Advanced Industrial Science and Technology
[2] PRESTO, Japan Science and Technology Corporation (JST)

Abstract. Two frameworks of hidden Markov modeling for multi-agent systems and its learning procedure are proposed. Although a couple of variations of HMMs have been proposed to model agents and their interactions, these models have not handled changes of environments, so that it is hard to simulate behaviors of agents that act in dynamic environments like soccer. The proposed frameworks enables HMMs to represent environments directly inside of state transitions. I first propose a model that handles the dynamics of the environments in the same state transition of the agent itself. In this model, the derived learning procedure can segment the environments according to the tasks and behaviors the agent is performing. I also investigate a more structured model in which the dynamics of the environments and agents are treated as separated state transitions and coupled each other. For this model, in order to reduce the number of parameters, I introduce "symmetricity" among agents. Furthermore, I discuss relation between reducing dependency in transitions and assumption of cooperative behaviors among multiple agents.

1 Introduction

When we train an agent or a team of agents (learners) to imitate behaviors of another agent or team (demonstrators), we must determine a framework to model agents or teams. Hidden Markov Model (HMM) is a popular candidate for this purpose. Because the behaviors of intelligent agents are complicated and structured, however, we should apply HMM carefully.

Suppose that we write a code of a reactive soccer agent by hands. We may write the following code for it:

```
while(true) {
  if ((⟨is my role a passer ?⟩) {
    if ((⟨is a receiver near ?⟩) {
      ⟨kick the ball to the receiver !⟩; ...
      ⟨change my role to receiver !⟩; }
    else if ((⟨found dribbling course ?⟩...
  }
  else if ((⟨is my role a receiver ?⟩) {
    if ((⟨find an open space ?⟩) {
      ⟨move to the space !⟩ }... }
  else ... }
```

G.A. Kaminka, P.U. Lima, and R. Rojas (Eds.): RoboCup 2002, LNAI 2752, pp. 94–110, 2003.

As shown in this example, situations (combinations of states of the environment and the agent) are segmented into finite states like *"is a receiver near?"* and *"found dribbling course?"*. These segmentations are vary according to agent's role or intention. In this example, *"is a receiver near?"* is not used when the agent's role is *"receiver"*. In the context of the imitation learning, it is important to estimate what kind of segmentation of environment a demonstrator is using. The difficulty of the segmentation of environment is that the segmentation should change according to agent's current intentions that are usually invisible. This means that segmentation of environment should be acquired in the same time of learning intentions in the context of imitation learning.

In addition to it, when agents interact with each other, it is necessary to assume a kind of structure of states in HMM. In the above example, whole situations are classified into states based on roles of agents (*"passer"* and *"receiver"*) and conditions of the environment (*"is a receiver near?"* and so on). Because it is difficult to acquire such structure through learning, it is better to use HMM in which states are structured suitably. In this case, we must pay attention the learning performance and reasonabilities of the structure.

In this article, I propose frameworks of HMM that can segment environment interaction between agents effectively through learning. In the following sections, I introduce a integrated HMM of agents and environment for learning of segmentation of environment in Section 2, and framework of HMM to represent interaction of agents in Section 3.

2 HMM for Agents in Dynamic Environment

2.1 Agent Model

In general, an autonomous agent is modeled as a Mealy-type HMM (shown in Figure 1(a)), in which the agent's behaviors are decided by the following manner:

- The agent has finite internal states.
- The internal state is transfered in a discrete time step.
- The next state ($s^{\langle t+1 \rangle}$) is determined only by the previous state ($s^{\langle t \rangle}$).
- The agent' action ($a^{\langle t+1 \rangle}$) is selected by the current state transition ($s^{\langle t \rangle} \rightarrow s^{\langle t+1 \rangle}$).

Moreover, in order to represent agent's behavior in a dynamic environment, we need take effect of interaction between the agent and the environment in account. Strait forward implementation of the effect is using input-output-type HMM [BF95,JGS97a], in which the data from the environments are treated as input for the HMM. However, using the such HMM has the following drawbacks:

- If an HMM handles the environment as input, the HMM may not include world model by which agent can predict changes of the environments.
- When the data from the environment consists of continuous values, we need additional mechanisms to handle the continuous values to bridge them to HMM's behaviors.

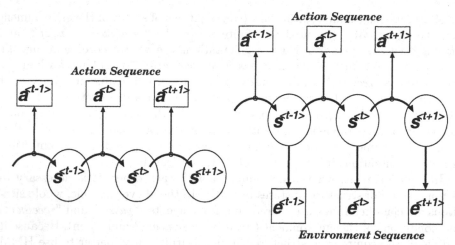

(a) Agent Model by Mealy-type HMM.   (b) Agent Model by Moore-Mealy-type
HMM.

Fig. 1. Agent HMM.

In order to overcome these drawbacks, we introduce the following assumption:

– The internal state and the environment has a probabilistic relation.

This means that the environment $(e^{\langle t \rangle})$ can be determined by the internal state $(s^{\langle t \rangle})$ under the probabilistic relation $(Pr(e^{\langle t \rangle}|s^{\langle t \rangle}))$. In other words, the changes of the environment can be handled as a Moore-type HMM (Figure 1(b)).

In summary, an agent and its environment can be defined as a combination of Moore- and Mealy-type HMM (MM-HMM) as follows:

$$\text{Agent} = \langle S, A, E, P, Q, R, \pi \rangle,$$

where $S = \{s_i\}$ is a set of internal states, $A = \{a_i\}$ is a set of action symbols, $E = \{e_i\}$ is a set of environment symbols, $P = \{p_{ij} = Pr(j^{\langle t+1 \rangle}|i^{\langle t \rangle})|i, j \in S, \forall t\}$ is a probability matrix of state transitions, $Q = \{q_{ij}(a) = Pr(a^{\langle t+1 \rangle}|i^{\langle t \rangle}, j^{\langle t+1 \rangle})|i, j \in S, a \in A, \forall t\}$ is a set of probability functions of actions for each transition, $R = \{r_i(e) = Pr(e^{\langle t \rangle}|i^{\langle t \rangle})|i \in S, e \in E, \forall t\}$ is a set of probability functions of environment for each state, $\pi = \{\pi_i = Pr(i^{\langle 0 \rangle})\}$ is a set of probability functions of initial states, and $\langle t \rangle$ on the right shoulder of each variable indicates time t.

2.2   Learning Algorithm

Suppose that a learner can observe a sequence of demonstrator's actions $\{a^{\langle 1 \rangle} \ldots a^{\langle T \rangle}\}$ and changes of an environment $\{e^{\langle 0 \rangle} \ldots e^{\langle T \rangle}\}$. The purpose of the learner is estimate an HMM that can explain the given action and environment sequences most likely. We can derive a learning procedure based on the combination of Baum-Welch algorithms for Moore-type and Mealy-type HMM as follows:

For given a set of sequences $\langle\{a^{\langle 1\rangle}\dots a^{\langle T\rangle}\}, \{e^{\langle 0\rangle}\dots e^{\langle T\rangle}\}\rangle$, the forward $(\alpha^{\langle t\rangle}(j))$ and backward $(beta^{\langle t\rangle}(i))$ probabilities are given by the following recursive formulas.

$$\alpha^{\langle t\rangle}(j) = \begin{cases} \pi_j r_j(e^{\langle 0\rangle}) & ; t = 0 \\ \displaystyle\sum_{i \in S} \alpha^{\langle t-1\rangle}(i) p_{ij} q_{ij}(a^{\langle t\rangle}) r_j(e^{\langle t\rangle}) & ; otherwise \end{cases}$$

$$\beta^{\langle t\rangle}(i) = \begin{cases} 1 & ; t = 0 \\ \displaystyle\sum_{j \in S} p_{ij} q_{ij}(a^{\langle t+1\rangle}) r_j(e^{\langle t+1\rangle}) \beta^{\langle t+1\rangle}(j) & ; otherwise \end{cases}$$

Using these probabilities, p_{ij}, $q_{ij}(a)$, $r_i(e)$ and π_i are adjusted by the following formulas:

$$p_{ij} \leftarrow \frac{\displaystyle\sum_t \xi^{\langle t\rangle}(i,j)}{\displaystyle\sum_t \gamma^{\langle t-1\rangle}(i)} \qquad q_{ij}(a) \leftarrow \frac{\displaystyle\sum_{t|a^{\langle t\rangle}=a} \xi^{\langle t\rangle}(i,j)}{\displaystyle\sum_t \xi^{\langle t-1\rangle}(i,j)}$$

$$r_i(e) \leftarrow \frac{\displaystyle\sum_{t|e^{\langle t\rangle}=e} \gamma^{\langle t\rangle}(i)}{\displaystyle\sum_t \gamma^{\langle t\rangle}(i)} \qquad \pi_i \leftarrow \gamma^{\langle 0\rangle}(i)$$

where

$$\xi^{\langle t\rangle}(i,j) = \frac{\alpha^{\langle t-1\rangle}(i) p_{ij} q_{ij}(a^{\langle t\rangle}) r_j(e^{\langle t\rangle}) \beta^{\langle t\rangle}(j)}{P(a^{\langle *\rangle}, e^{\langle *\rangle}|\text{Agent})}$$

$$\gamma^{\langle t\rangle}(j) = \frac{\alpha^{\langle t\rangle}(j) \beta^{\langle t\rangle}(j)}{P(a^{\langle *\rangle}, e^{\langle *\rangle}|\text{Agent})}$$

2.3 Segmentation of Environments

When the above learning succeeds, the learner gets a suitable HMM, each of whose states corresponds a combination of internal intentions of the demonstrator and fragments of the environment. In other words, the representation of the intention and the segmentation are mixed in a set of states. While such representation is enough to imitate demonstrator's behavior, it will be still useful to know how the HMM segments the environment.

In the MM-HMM context, the segmentation of the environment means how each data of the environments is mapped to the states of the HMM. Therefore, the segmentation is represented by a probability function $Pr(s|e)$ where e is an environment data and s is an internal state of HMM. This probability can be calculated by the following equation:

$$Pr(s|e) = \frac{Pr(e|s)Pr(s)}{Pr(e)} = \frac{r_s(e)Pr(s)}{Pr(e)} \tag{1}$$

Using this equation, we can illustrate the mapping from the environments to the states.

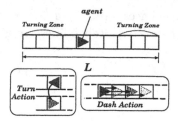

Fig. 2. Setting of Ex.1: Discrete World.

2.4   Experimental Result

In order to show the performance of the proposed model to acquire segmentation of environments, I conducted the following experiments.

Ex.1: Discrete World. In the first experiment, we use a linear block world shown in Figure 2. An agent is moving in the world using *dash* and *turn* actions. When the agent *turns*, the agent's direction flips between left and right. When the agent *dashes*, the agent's position moves forward. The step size of a dash action varies 1 to 3 randomly.

The task of a learner is to acquire the rule of another agent (demonstrator) who behaves as described below. A learner can observe the demonstrator's position (= environment, $\{e^{(t)}\}$) and action ($\{a^{(t)}\}$) in each time t. We suppose that the demonstrator behaves according to the following rules:

- If the position is in the left(or right) turning zone (margin of the zone is 3) and the direction is left (or right), then *turn*.
- Otherwise, *dash*.

The main point of this experiment is that whether the learner can acquire the correct segmentation by which the turning zone will be represented explicitly in the state transition, because the concept of the turning zone is unobservable to the learner. Also, estimation of the dash step size is also important, because it defines how the world (environment) should be segmented in order to simulate it by an HMM. Note that demonstrator's direction is not observable. This means that the learner needs to acquire the representation of the direction through the learning.

In the experiments, we executed the above learning procedure using different initial parameters 100 times, calculated the average of the likelihood of given example sequences, and select the best one as the result. This is because the learning of general HMMs is not guaranteed to reach the global optimal solution: the adaptation may fall down to a local optimum.

Figure 3 shows the result of the experiment. In this figure, (a) shows possibilities of environment symbols ($e_0 \ldots e_9$) for each state ($s_0 \ldots s_7$). Each box corresponds to $Pr(e_i|s_j)$ whose value is denoted the size of black area in the box. For example, in the s_0 line of boxes, columns of e_5 and e_6 have significant values

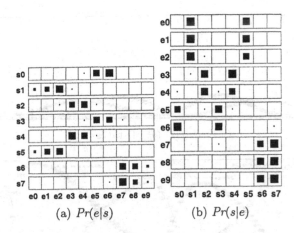

(a) $Pr(e|s)$ (b) $Pr(s|e)$

Fig. 3. Result of Ex.1: Discrete World (L=10).

and both values are relatively equal. This can be interpreted that e_5 and e_6 are grouped in the same state s_0, because the environment is estimated e_5 or e_6 equally when the HMM is in state s_0. Similarly, Figure 3-(b) shows possibilities of states for each environment symbol calculated by Eq. 1, whose value $Pr(s_j|e_i)$ is denoted black area of each box. For example, the e_0 line has two columns of s_1 and s_5 who have relatively the same significant possibilities. This can be interpreted that e_0 can correspond to two states, s_1 and s_5, equally.

From these figures, we found that the acquired HMM segments the environment into 4 regions, $\{e_0, e_1, e_2\}$, $\{e_7, e_8, e_9\}$, $\{e_3, e_4\}$, and $\{e_5, e_6\}$. The first two regions correspond the "turning zone" defined inside of the demonstrator. Rest of the two regions have the same length, 2. This value correspond the average step size of dash commands. These results means that the acquired HMM represents both of the rules of agent behavior and dynamics of the environment. In addition to it, each environment symbol corresponds two states. This means that the HMM recognizes the (unobservable) direction of the demonstrator by doubled states for each environment.

Ex.2: Continuous World. The second experiment is a continuous version of the previous experiment, in which the demonstrator's position (e) is a continuous value instead of a discrete symbol. The rule of the demonstrator's behavior is the same as the previous one. The length of the world L is 25.0 and step size of a dash varies 5.0 to 15.0 randomly.

Figure 4 shows the acquired probabilities, $Pr(e|s)$ and $Pr(s|e)$. In these graphs, the probabilities are plotted as follows:

- $Pr(e|s)$ is plotted as a set of probability density functions of environment value, $g_s(e) = Pr(e|s)$, for each state s.
- $Pr(s|e)$ is plotted as a set of changes of probability of each state, $f_s(e) = Pr(s|e)$, according to environment value.

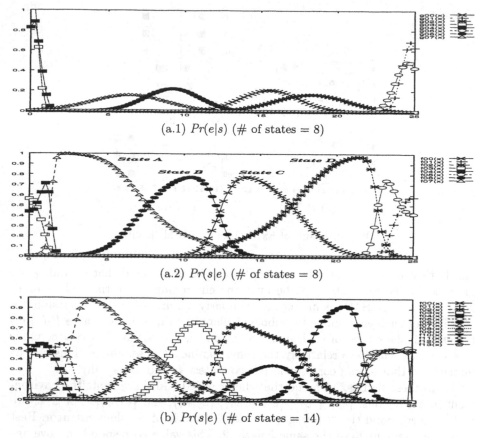

(a.1) $Pr(e|s)$ (# of states = 8)

(a.2) $Pr(s|e)$ (# of states = 8)

(b) $Pr(s|e)$ (# of states = 14)

Fig. 4. Result of Ex.2.

In the figure, (a.1) and (a.2) show the result when the number of HMM's states is 8, and (b) shows the result in the case of 14. From (a.1) and (a.2), we can find that the HMM segments the environment in the similar way as the discrete case.

- Two turning zones at the both ends of the world are segmented clearly.
- There are two corresponding states for the most of the environment value. This means that the HMM represents the direction of movement.

We can also find an additional features from these graphs: There are 4 peaks (State A–D in (a.2)) in the middle of the environment in the graph, and, A and B (or C and D) are relatively overlapped with each other. As same as the first experience, this means that the two states A and B (or C and D) indicate difference of the direction of the movement. On the other hand, while two states share the same part of the environment in the first experiment, peaks of A and B (or C and D) are shifted. As a result, the segment point of the environment in each direction are different. For example, the segment point[1] is at about 13.0 in

---

[1] A crossing point of probabilities of two states in the graph of Figure 4-(a.2).

the case of the rightward transition (B →D), and it is at about 11.0 in the case of leftward (C →A)[2] This means that the segmentation of the environment is not fixed for every agent's internal state, but varies depend on them. The structure of the segmentation are stable when we use more states in the learning. For example, when we use 14 states to learn the same task, the HMM can acquire the similar segmentation of the environment (Figure 4-(b)).

In order to show that the proposed method can acquire segmentation of environment flexibly, we conducted the following experiment. We introduce an additional *half turning zone* in the middle of the world, where the demonstrator turns in the probability 0.5 . The detailed rule in this turning zone is as follows:

- If the demonstrator faces rightward (leftward)and the position is in the left (right) hand side of the *half turning zone*, then turn in the probability 0.5.

Figure 5 shows how the segmentation of the environment ($Pr(s|e)$) changes according to the various numbers of states. As shown in this result, many states are used to represent turning zones, especially the half turning zone (the middle area of the world). We can see when the number of state increases, the HMM assigns many states to segment the half turning zone. This is because that the conditions to decide demonstrator's behaviors are complicated so that the HMM needs to represent detailed information about the environment.

2.5   Discussion: Environment as Output

The proposed method looks little bit strange because it handles environment as output from states rather than as input to state transitions. As mentioned above, input-output HMMs seems more reasonable to model relations between agents and environments, in which the environment is treated as input to state-transitions [BF95,JGS97a]. There are the following different points between these two methods:

- When we handle the environment as input, we can apply the HMM for planning. Suppose that initial and goal situations of environment ($e^{(0)}$ and $e^{(T)}$) are given. Then, the planning can be formalized as follows:
    To get the most likely path of state transitions that maximizes the probability $Pr(e^{(0)}, e^{(T)}|\text{Agent})$.
  When the environment is handled as output like the proposed method, we can seek the most likely path simply using well-known algorithm like Viterbi's one. On the other hand, we need an additional simulator or inverse model of environment when the environment is handled as input.
- When we use continuous value for input of HMM, we need to use gradient ascent methods like neural networks to learn the parameters in a cycle, which requires more computation power. On the other hand, in the proposed method, we can apply the one-shot adaptation algorithm derived in Section 2.2.

---

[2] The transitions B →D and C →A are extracted from the probability matrix of state transitions of the trained HMM.

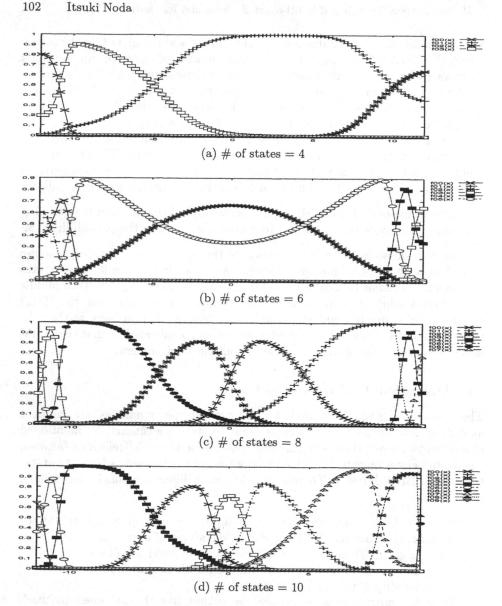

(a) # of states = 4

(b) # of states = 6

(c) # of states = 8

(d) # of states = 10

Fig. 5. Changes of Segmentation ($Pr(s|e)$) by the Number of States (in Ex.2).

3   Symmetrically Coupled HMM

3.1   Symmetricity Assumption

In Section 2, we handle environment and agent's intention by a single HMM. However, the number of states increases exponentially when the agent has more complex intentions. This is significant when HMM handles interactions among agents in multi-agent systems(MAS). In this case, we will face *generalization performance problem*. As the number of states or learning parameters increases,

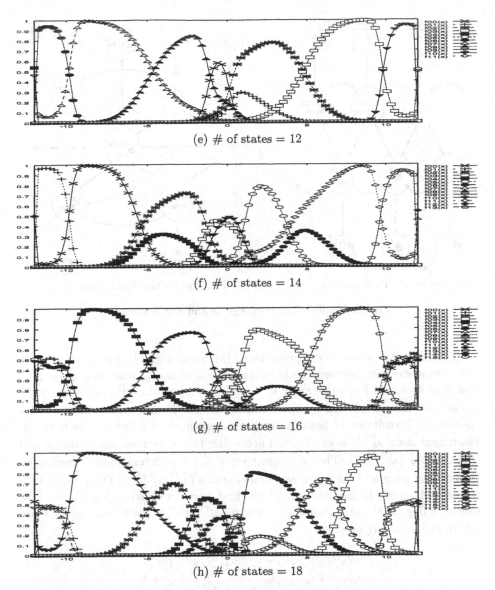

(e) # of states = 12

(f) # of states = 14

(g) # of states = 16

(h) # of states = 18

Fig. 5. (Continued).

the huge number of examples are required to guarantee the generalization performance. In order to avoid this problem, I introduce *symmetricity assumption* among agents as follows:

symmetricity assumption
Agents in a MAS are *symmetric*, that is, every agent has the same rules of behavior. In the HMM context, every agent shares the same state transition rules with each other.

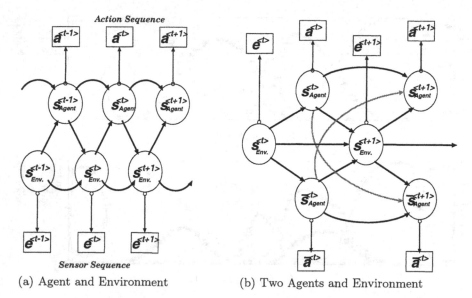

(a) Agent and Environment   (b) Two Agents and Environment

Fig. 6. Coupled HMMs of Agents and Environment.

To reflect the above assumption in HMM, first, I divide the internal state into two states, environment state s_e and agent state s_a, and form a coupled HMM as shown in Figure 6-(a). In this model, sensor data $e^{\langle t \rangle}$ and action commands $a^{\langle t \rangle}$ are determined by environment states $s_e^{\langle t \rangle}$ and agent states $s_a^{\langle t \rangle}$ respectively. Transitions of both states are determined as follows: The next environment state $s_e^{\langle t+1 \rangle}$ is determined according to the current environment and agent states $\{s_e^{\langle t \rangle}, s_a^{\langle t \rangle}\}$. The next agent state $s_a^{\langle t+1 \rangle}$ is determined according to the current agent and the new environment states $\{s_a^{\langle t \rangle}, s_e^{\langle t+1 \rangle}\}$. Then I introduce the second agent who cooperates with the first agent as shown in Figure 6-(b). In this coupling, both state transitions become affected by the second agent state $\bar{s}_a^{\langle t \rangle}$ in the following manner:

$$Pr(s_e^{\langle t+1 \rangle}|*) = Pr(s_e^{\langle t+1 \rangle}|s_e^{\langle t \rangle}, s_a^{\langle t \rangle}, \bar{s}_a^{\langle t \rangle})$$
$$Pr(s_a^{\langle t+1 \rangle}|*) = Pr(s_a^{\langle t+1 \rangle}|s_a^{\langle t \rangle}, \bar{s}_a^{\langle t \rangle}, s_e^{\langle t+1 \rangle})$$

In order to complete the state transition for Figure 6-(b), we must consider about transitions of the second agent state $\bar{s}_a$. Here, I apply *symmetricity assumption* for the second state transition, that is, the probabilities of state transitions of the second agent are determined by the same one of the first agent. The most naive implementation of this assumption is that the probabilities are described as follows:

$$Pr(\bar{s}_a^{\langle t+1 \rangle}|*) = Pr(\bar{s}_a^{\langle t+1 \rangle}|\bar{s}_a^{\langle t \rangle}, s_a^{\langle t \rangle}, s_e^{\langle t+1 \rangle})$$
$$= Pr(s_a^{\langle t+1 \rangle} = \bar{s}_a^{\langle t+1 \rangle}|s_a^{\langle t \rangle} = \bar{s}_a^{\langle t \rangle}, \bar{s}_a^{\langle t \rangle} = s_a^{\langle t \rangle}, s_e^{\langle t+1 \rangle})$$

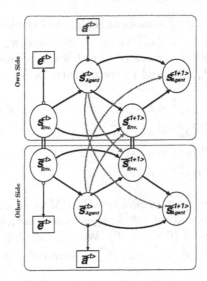

Fig. 7. Symmetrically Coupled HMM. s_{Agent} and s_{Env} correspond to $s_\mathbf{a}$ and $s_\mathbf{e}$ in the agent definition respectively.

This formulation is valid when both agents share the same environment state. In general, however, two agents may have different environment state inside of them, because the environment state in this formalization is a kind of internal world state that each agent has. Such a situation is not avoidable especially when the sensor data $e^{\langle t \rangle}$ is represented from the viewpoint of each agent. In order to overcome this problem, I propose a *symmetrically coupled HMM* (sCHMM) shown in Figure 7. In this model, the second agent has its own environment state $\bar{s}^{\langle t \rangle}$. Using this, the transition of $\bar{s}_\mathbf{a}^{\langle t \rangle}$ are represented as follows:

$$Pr(\bar{s}_\mathbf{a}^{\langle t+1 \rangle}|*) = Pr(s_\mathbf{a}^{\langle t+1 \rangle} = \bar{s}_\mathbf{a}^{\langle t+1 \rangle}|s_\mathbf{a}^{\langle t \rangle} = \bar{s}_\mathbf{a}^{\langle t \rangle}, \bar{s}_\mathbf{a}^{\langle t \rangle} = s_\mathbf{a}^{\langle t \rangle}, s_\mathbf{e}^{\langle t+1 \rangle} = \bar{s}_\mathbf{e}^{\langle t+1 \rangle}),$$

where the transition of the second environment state $\bar{s}^{\langle t \rangle}$ follows:

$$Pr(\bar{s}_\mathbf{e}^{\langle t+1 \rangle}|*) = Pr(s_\mathbf{e}^{\langle t+1 \rangle} = \bar{s}_\mathbf{e}^{\langle t+1 \rangle}|s_\mathbf{e}^{\langle t \rangle} = \bar{s}_\mathbf{e}^{\langle t \rangle}, s_\mathbf{a}^{\langle t \rangle} = \bar{s}_\mathbf{a}^{\langle t \rangle}, \bar{s}_\mathbf{a}^{\langle t \rangle} = s_\mathbf{a}^{\langle t \rangle})$$

3.2   Formalization and Learning Procedure

I summarize the sCHMM agent as the following tuple:

$$\text{Agent} = \langle S_\mathbf{e}, S_\mathbf{a}, E, A, P_\mathbf{e}, P_\mathbf{a}, Q_\mathbf{e}, Q_\mathbf{a}, \pi_\mathbf{e}, \pi_\mathbf{a} \rangle,$$

where $S_\mathbf{a} = \{s_{\mathbf{a}i}\}$ and $S_\mathbf{e} = \{s_{\mathbf{e}i}\}$ are sets of states for agent and environment respectively, $E = \{e_i\}$ is a set of sensor data of environment, and $A = \{a_i\}$ is a set of agent action symbols. $P_\mathbf{e} = \{p_{\mathbf{e}ijkl}|i \in S_\mathbf{e}, j, k \in S_\mathbf{a}, \forall t\}$ and $P_\mathbf{a} = \{p_{\mathbf{a}jklm}|j, k \in S_\mathbf{a}, m \in S_\mathbf{e}, \forall t\}$ are probability tensors of state transitions of environment and agent, $Q_\mathbf{e} = \{q_{\mathbf{e}i}(e)|i \in S_\mathbf{e}, e \in E, \forall t\}$ and $Q_\mathbf{a} = \{q_{\mathbf{a}j}(a)|j \in$

$S_a, a \in A, \forall t\}$ are probability tensors of is observed symbols of environment and actions, and $\pi_e = \{\pi_{ei} = Pr(s_e^{\langle 0 \rangle} = i) | i \in S_e\}$ and $\pi_a = \{\pi_{aj} = Pr(s_a^{\langle 0 \rangle} = j) | j \in S_a\}$ are probability vectors of initial states of environment and agent. Each element of P_e, P_a, Q_e, and Q_a represents the following probability.

$$p_{eijkl} = Pr(s_e^{\langle t \rangle} = l \mid s_e^{\langle t-1 \rangle} = i, s_{a0}^{\langle t-1 \rangle} = j, s_{a1}^{\langle t-1 \rangle} = k)$$
$$p_{ajklm} = Pr(s_a^{\langle t \rangle} = m \mid s_{a0}^{\langle t-1 \rangle} = j, s_{a1}^{\langle t-1 \rangle} = k, s_e^{\langle t \rangle} = l)$$
$$q_{ei}(e) = Pr(e^{\langle t \rangle} = e \mid s_e^{\langle t \rangle} = i)$$
$$q_{aj}(a) = Pr(a^{\langle t \rangle} = a \mid s_a^{\langle t \rangle} = i)$$

We can derive a learning procedure for sCHMM as shown below. Suppose that sequences of sensor information $\{e^{\langle t \rangle}\}$, agent's own actions $\{a^{\langle t \rangle}\}$, and other's actions $\{\bar{a}^{\langle t \rangle}\}$ are observed $(0 \le t < T)$. We can calculate agent's own forward and backward probabilities, $\alpha_{lmn}^{\langle t \rangle}$ and $\beta_{ijk}^{\langle t \rangle}$ respectively, as follows:

$$\alpha_{lmn}^{\langle t \rangle} = \begin{cases} \pi_{el}\pi_{am}\pi_{an}Q_{(lmn)}(W^{\langle 0 \rangle}) & ; t = 0 \\ \sum_{(ijk)} \alpha_{ijk}^{\langle t-1 \rangle} P_{(ijk)(lmn)}Q_{(lmn)}(W^{\langle t \rangle}) & ; otherwise \end{cases}$$

$$\beta_{ijk}^{\langle t \rangle} = \begin{cases} 1 & ; t = T-1 \\ \sum_{(lmn)} P_{(ijk)(lmn)}Q_{(lmn)}(W^{\langle t+1 \rangle})\beta_{lmn}^{\langle t+1 \rangle} & ; otherwise \end{cases},$$

where

$$P_{(ijk)(lmn)} = p_{eijkl} \cdot p_{ajklm} \cdot p_{akjln}$$
$$Q_{(ijk)}(W^{\langle t \rangle}) = Q_{(ijk)}(e^{\langle t \rangle}, a^{\langle t \rangle}, \bar{a}^{\langle t \rangle})$$
$$= q_{ei}(e^{\langle t \rangle}) \cdot q_{aj}(a^{\langle t \rangle}) \cdot q_{ak}(\bar{a}^{\langle t \rangle})$$

In the same way, other's forward and backward probabilities, $\bar{\alpha}_{lnm}^{\langle t \rangle}$ and $\bar{\beta}_{ikj}^{\langle t \rangle}$ respectively, can be calculated:

$$\bar{\alpha}_{lnm}^{\langle t \rangle} = \begin{cases} \pi_{el}\pi_{am}\pi_{an}Q_{(lnm)}(\bar{W}^{\langle 0 \rangle}) & ; t = 0 \\ \sum_{(ikj)} \bar{\alpha}_{ikj}^{\langle t-1 \rangle} P_{(ikj)(lnm)}Q_{(lnm)}(\bar{W}^{\langle t \rangle}) & ; otherwise \end{cases}$$

$$\bar{\beta}_{ikj}^{\langle t \rangle} = \begin{cases} 1 & ; t = T-1 \\ \sum_{(lnm)} P_{(ikj)(lnm)}Q_{(lnm)}(\bar{W}^{\langle t+1 \rangle})\beta_{lnm}^{\langle t+1 \rangle} & ; otherwise \end{cases},$$

where $\bar{W}^{\langle t \rangle} = \{\bar{e}^{\langle t \rangle}, \bar{a}^{\langle t \rangle}, a^{\langle t \rangle}\}$, and $\bar{e}^{\langle t \rangle}$ is the sensor data received by the second agent. Using these probabilities, we can adapt transition and output probabilities $p_{eijkl}, p_{ajklm}, q_{ei}, q_{ej}$ as follows:

$$p_{eijkl} \leftarrow \sum_m \sum_n \hat{P}_{(ijk)(lmn)}$$

$$p_{ajklm} \leftarrow \frac{\sum_i \sum_n \hat{P}_{(ijk)(lmn)}}{\sum_i p_{eijkl}}$$

$$q_{ei}(e) \leftarrow \sum_j \sum_k \sum_a \sum_{\bar{a}} \hat{Q}_{(ijk)}(e, a, \bar{a})$$

$$q_{aj}(a) \leftarrow \sum_i \sum_k \sum_e \sum_{\bar{a}} \hat{Q}_{(ijk)}(e, a, \bar{a}),$$

where

$$\hat{P}_{(ijk)(lmn)} = \frac{\sum_t \xi_{(ijk)(lmn)}^{\langle t \rangle} + \sum_t \bar{\xi}_{(ikj)(lnm)}^{\langle t \rangle}}{\sum_t \gamma_{ijk}^{\langle t-1 \rangle} + \sum_t \bar{\gamma}_{ikj}^{\langle t-1 \rangle}} \tag{2}$$

$$\hat{Q}_{(ijk)}(W) = \frac{\sum_{t, W^{\langle t \rangle} = W} \gamma_{(ijk)^{\langle t \rangle}} + \sum_{t, W^{\langle t \rangle} = W} \bar{\gamma}_{ikj}^{\langle t \rangle}}{\sum_t \gamma_{(ijk)^{\langle t \rangle}} + \sum_t \bar{\gamma}_{ikj}^{\langle t \rangle}} \tag{3}$$

$$\xi_{(ijk)(lmn)}^{\langle t \rangle} = \alpha_{(ijk)}^{\langle t-1 \rangle} P_{(ijk)(lmn)} Q_{(lmn)}(W^{\langle t \rangle}) \beta_{(lmn)}^{\langle t \rangle}$$

$$\bar{\xi}_{(ikj)(lnm)}^{\langle t \rangle} = \bar{\alpha}_{(ikj)}^{\langle t-1 \rangle} P_{(ikj)(lnm)} Q_{(lnm)}(\bar{W}^{\langle t \rangle}) \bar{\beta}_{(lnm)}^{\langle t \rangle}$$

$$\gamma_{(lmn)}^{\langle t \rangle} = \alpha_{(lmn)}^{\langle t \rangle} \beta_{(lmn)}^{\langle t \rangle}$$

$$\bar{\gamma}_{(lnm)}^{\langle t \rangle} = \bar{\alpha}_{(lnm)}^{\langle t \rangle} \bar{\beta}_{(lnm)}^{\langle t \rangle}$$

3.3   Discussion: The Number of Parameters in the Model

As mentioned before, the number of parameters in HMM is an important factor for generalization performance of learning. In the case of the coupled HMM, especially, the number of parameters increases exponentially. Actually, if we use the model shown in Figure 6-(b) without the symmetricity assumption, the number of parameters in the state transition is

$$|S_e|^2 |S_a|^N + N |S_e| |S_a|^{N+1}$$

where N is the number of agents. This is already reduced from $(|S_e| |S_a|^N)^2$, the number of parameters in the case we represent the same model using single HMM. Compared with this, symmetrically coupled HMM has fewer parameters as follows:

$$|S_e|^2 |S_a|^N + |S_e| |S_a|^{N+1}$$

In addition to it, the symmetricity assumption can increase the virtual number of examples. Eq. 2 and Eq. 3 mean that the same HMM is trained by using both pairs of $\{e^{\langle t \rangle}, a^{\langle t \rangle}\}$ and $\{\bar{e}^{\langle t \rangle}, \bar{a}^{\langle t \rangle}\}$ for a given observation $\{e^{\langle t \rangle}, a^{\langle t \rangle}, \bar{a}^{\langle t \rangle}\}$. As a result, the generalization performance is improved by the virtually doubled examples.

It is, however, true that an sCHMM still has too many parameters for real applications. Therefore, it is meaningful to introduce additional assumptions to reduce the number of parameter. Fortunately, in the case of cooperative interaction in the MAS, we can pick-up reasonable assumptions as follows:

- *"no explicit communication"* assumption: In the formalization of sCHMM, the transition of the agent state is affected by the previous states of other agents. This corresponds the case that agents use explicit communication with each other in every action cycle. In the case of human cooperative behaviors like soccer, on the other hand, we do not use so much explicit communication, but model others via sensor information instead. In such case, the transition of the agent state can be represented as follows:

$$Pr(s_a^{\langle t+1 \rangle}|*) = Pr(s_a^{\langle t+1 \rangle}|s_a^{\langle t \rangle}, s_e^{\langle t+1 \rangle})$$

In this case, the total number of the parameters is reduced to:

$$|S_e|^2 |S_a|^N + |S_e| |S_a|^2$$

- *"filtering"* assumption: Usually, when we write a code of agent behavior, we classify states systematically. For example, in the code shown in Section 1 states are grouped by agent's roles (agent states) first then branched by world status (environment states) second. This can be represented by the following manner in the transition of HMM:

$$Pr(s_a^{\langle t+1 \rangle}|*) = Pr(s_a^{\langle t+1 \rangle}|s_e^{\langle t+1 \rangle}) \cdot Pr(s_a^{\langle t+1 \rangle}|s_a^{\langle t \rangle})$$

In this case, the number of parameters are reduced to:

$$|S_e|^2 |S_a|^N + |S_e| |S_a| + |S_a|^{N+1}$$

- *"shared joint intention"* assumption: During a cooperation of multiple agents each agent believes that all agents share the joint intention. This means that each agent thinks that all other agents will behave as the agent wants. In this case, the transition of environment states can be represented as follows:

$$Pr(s_e^{\langle t+1 \rangle}|*) = Pr(s_e^{\langle t+1 \rangle}|s_e^{\langle t \rangle}, s_a^{\langle t \rangle})$$

This reduces the number of parameters to:

$$|S_e|^2 |S_a| + |S_e| |S_a|^{N+1}$$

Note that this assumption can not be applied with the *"no explicit communication"* assumption, because the sCHMM is reduced into a simple CHMM like Figure 6-(a) that does not reflect cooperation among agents.

3.4   Related Works

Uther and Veloso [UV98] have been attacked the problem of segmentation of the continuous environment and proposed Continuous U Tree algorithm. Although the algorithm is a powerful tool for segmenting a given continuous data space, it is hard to apply for the purpose to find unobservable features like direction feature in the experiments shown in Section 2.4. Han and Veloso [HV99] showed a framework to recognize behaviors of robots by HMM in which the environment is handled as output. In this work, they did not focused on acquiring state transitions, but method to find an HMM from multiple pre-defined HMMs for seen data.

Brand Et al. [Bra97,hMmfcar96] proposed coupled HMM and its learning method, in which several HMMs are coupled via inter-HMM dependencies. Jordan Et al. [JGS97b,GJ97,JGJS99] proposed factorial HMM and hidden Markov decision trees. Both of works mainly focused on reducing the complexity in EM processes. Even using these HMMs, the complexity of calculation of a naive implementation increase exponentially, so that it is hard to handle the large number of states. They use mean field approximation or N-heads dynamic programming to reduce the cost of the approximation of posterior probabilities. However, they does not focused on symmetricity in agent-interactions and generalization performance problem.

These methods can be applicable to our model. Actually, a naive implementation of learning method derived in the previous section costs $O(TN^4M^2)$, which is too huge for dynamical application like soccer. Above methods will reduce the cost into $O(TN^2M)$, which is reasonable cost for real application.

4   Concluding Remarks

In this article, we proposed two frameworks to learn behaviors of multiple agents in dynamic environment using HMM. The first framework handles agent's environments as output of HMM rather than as input. As the result, the acquired HMM represents suitable segmentation of environment explicitly in the states. The explicit segmentation is expected to leads the following features to the HMM:

- HMM can be used planning of agent's behavior working in a dynamic environment.
- Flexible segmentation can improve generalization performance of the learning.

The second framework is conducted to represent interactions among multiple agents and environments. In order to avoid the explosion of the number of parameters, I introduced symmetricity assumptions among agents, and propose symmetrically coupled HMM (sCHMM) and its learning procedure.

There are the following open issues on the proposed model and method:

- The cost of calculation increase exponentially when structures of agents and environments become complicated. In order to reduce the complexity, several techniques like mean field approximation and N-head dynamic programming should be applied to these models.
- The incremental learning will suit to acquire high-level cooperative behaviors. We may be able to realize the step-by-step learning using dependency of the initial parameters.

References

[BF95]   Yoshua Bengio and Paolo Frasconi. An input output hmm architecuture. In G. Tesauro, D. Touretzky, and T. Leen, editors, *Advances in Neural Information Processing Systems*, pages 427–434. The MIT Press, 1995.

[Bra97]   Matthew Brand. Coupled hideen markov models for modeling interacting processes. Perceptual Computing/Learning and Common Sense Technical Report 405, MIT Lab, jun 1997.

[GJ97]   Zoubin Ghahramani and Michael I. Jordan. Factorial hidden markov models. *Machine Learning*, 29:245–275, 1997.

[hMmfcar96] Coupled hidden Markov models for complex action recognition. Matthew brand and nuria oliver and alex pentland. Perceptual Computing/Learning and Common Sense Technical Report 407, MIT Media Lab, 20 1996.

[HV99]   Kwun Han and Manuela Veloso. Automated robot behavior recognition applied to robotic soccer. In *Proceedings of IJCAI-99 Workshop on Team Behaviors and Plan Recognition*, 1999.

[JGJS99]   Michael I. Jordan, Zoubin Ghahramani, Tommi Jaakkola, and Lawrence K. Saul. An introduction to variational methods for graphical models. *Machine Learning*, 37(2):183–233, 1999.

[JGS97a]   Michael I. Jordan, Zoubin Ghahramani, and Lawrence K. Saul. Hidden markov decision trees. In Michael C. Mozer, Michael I. Jordan, and Thomas Petsche, editors, *Advances in Neural Information Processing Systems*, volume 9, page 501. The MIT Press, 1997.

[JGS97b]   Michael I. Jordan, Zoubin Ghahramani, and Lawrence K. Saul. Hidden markov decision trees. In Michael C. Mozer, Michael I. Jordan, and Thomas Petsche, editors, *Advances in Neural Information Processing Systems 9*, page 501. The MIT Press, 1997.

[UV98]   William T. B. Uther and Manuela M. Veloso. Tree based discretization for continuous state space reinforcement learning. In *AAAI/IAAI*, pages 769–774, 1998.

Learning the Sequential Coordinated Behavior of Teams from Observations

Gal A. Kaminka*, Mehmet Fidanboylu, Allen Chang, and Manuela M. Veloso

Computer Science Department, Carnegie Mellon University
Pittsburgh PA 15213, USA
{galk,veloso}@cs.cmu.edu, {mehmetf,allenc}@andrew.cmu.edu

Abstract. The area of agent modeling deals with the task of observing other agents and modeling their behavior, in order to predict their future behavior, coordinate with them, assist them, or counter their actions. Typically, agent modeling techniques assume the availability of a plan- or behavior-library, which encodes the full repertoire of expected observed behavior. However, recent applications areas of agent modeling raise challenges to the assumption of such a library, as agent modeling systems are increasingly used in *open* and/or *adversarial* settings, where the behavioral repertoire of the observed agents is unknown at design time. This paper focuses on the challenge of the unsupervised autonomous learning of the sequential behaviors of agents, from observations of their behavior. The techniques we present translate observations of the dynamic, complex, continuous multi-variate world state into a time-series of recognized atomic behaviors. This time-series is then analyzed to find repeating subsequences characterizing each team. We compare two alternative approaches to extracting such characteristic sequences, based on frequency counts and statistical dependencies. Our results indicate that both techniques are able to extract meaningful sequences, and do significantly better than random predictions. However, the statistical dependency approach is able to correctly reject sequences that are frequent, but are due to random co-occurrence of behaviors, rather than to a true sequential dependency between them.

1 Introduction

The area of agent modeling deals with the task of observing other agents and modeling their behavior, in order to predict their future behavior, coordinate with them, assist them, or counter their actions. For instance, agent modeling techniques have been used in intelligent user interfaces [1, 2], in virtual environments for training [3, 4], and in coaching and team-training [5]. Typically, agent modeling techniques assume the availability of a plan- or behavior- library, which encodes the complete repertoire of expected observed behavior. The agent

---

* As of July 2002, Gal Kaminka's new contact information is galk@cs.biu.ac.il, Computer Science Department, Bar Ilan University, Israel.

G.A. Kaminka, P.U. Lima, and R. Rojas (Eds.): RoboCup 2002, LNAI 2752, pp. 111–125, 2003.
© Springer-Verlag Berlin Heidelberg 2003

modeling techniques typically focus on matching the observations with library prototypes, and drawing inferences based on successful matches.

Recent applications areas of agent modeling raise challenges to the assumption of an available complete and correct behavior library. Agent observers are increasingly used in *open* and/or *adversarial* settings, where the behavioral repertoire of the observed agents are unknown at design time. Thus agents that are engaged in modeling must be able to autonomously acquire the models used in agent-modeling prior to using them in the agent modeling tasks. While there have been reports on successful techniques that begin to address of the task of constructing the behavior library (e.g., [6, 2]), key challenges remain open.

In particular, this paper focuses on the challenge of autonomous unsupervised learning of the sequential behavior of agents and teams from observations of their behavior. Our approach combines plan-recognition techniques and symbolic time-series sequence identification to translate raw multi-agent, multi-variate observations of a dynamic, complex environment, into a set of sequential behaviors that are characteristic of the team in question. Our approach is appropriate for domains in which recognizing the basic behaviors of agents and/or teams is a tractable task, but the space of sequential combinations of these behaviors is practically unexploreable.

In our approach, the observing agent first uses a set of simple basic-behavior recognizers to parse the stream of raw observations and translate it into a stream of recognized behaviors, which we call *events*. Unlike previous approaches, the construction of such recognizers does not attempt to cover the entire multi-agent behavioral repertoire of the team. Instead, the behavior recognizers focus on recognizing only the most basic, atomic behaviors, without addressing how they are combined together.

The stream of raw multi-variate, multi-agent observations is therefore turned into a stream of labeled events. The recognized behavior stream is first broken into segments, each containing the uninterrupted consecutive events of only one team. Multiple segment are collected together in a *trie*-based data structure [7], that allows for on-line, incremental identification of important and predictive sequences (this data-structure is explained in Section 3.2).

For instance, given a stream of raw observations about soccer players' position and orientation, and the position of the ball, the behavior recognizers may produce a stream of recognized passes, dribbles, and other soccer-playing behaviors, for instance

$$Pass(Player_1, Player_2) \rightarrow Pass(Player_2, Player_3) \rightarrow Dribble(Player_3) \rightarrow \ldots$$

Identification of important (sub)sequences in this resulting stream can be difficult in dynamic settings. Ideally, the segments contain examples of *coordinated* sequential behavior, where the execution of one atomic behavior is dependent on the prior execution of another behavior, possibly by a different agent. However, such coordinated sequences are sometimes disrupted by the need to respond to dynamic changes in the environment or the behavior of other agents. Thus the resulting segments are often noisy, containing only portions of the true sequences, intermixed with possibly frequent observations of reactive behaviors that are not part of any sequence. For example, in the sequence above, the *Dribble* event may have not been planned part of the team's sequence, and may have been independent of the coordinated two-pass sequence that preceded it. In other words, the *Dribble* was possibly executed by $Player_3$ to respond dynamically to the situation that it faced, independently of whom passed the ball to it. In this case, a subsequence $Pass(Player_2, Player_3) \leftarrow Dribble(Player_3)$ would not have been a useful sequence to discover—it reveals nothing about the coordinated behavior of the team.

We present a technique for processing such a stream of events, building on earlier work by Howe and Cohen [8], and extending it in novel ways. The technique we present rejects such false sequences, by uncovering sequential statistical dependencies between atomic observed behaviors of agents. We demonstrate the efficacy of our approach in learning sequential behavior of several RoboCup simulation teams from observations, and compare the results of using frequency counts [9] and statistical dependency detection [8], two important sequence-mining techniques, in identifying important sequences. We show that while the two techniques are both significantly better than random selection, statistical dependency detection has important benefits in being able to distinguish causal dependencies between observed behaviors, from frequent co-occurrence, due to chance, of independent behaviors.

This paper is organized as follows. Section 2 presents the motivation for our approach, and related work. Section 3 presents the behavior recognizers and the trie-based data structure used in determining subsequences. Section 4 presents the dependency-detection method and frequency counts. Section 5 discusses results of experiments, validating our approach. Section 6 presents conclusions and directions for future work.

2 Learning Coordinated Sequential Behavior in Open, Adversarial Settings

Most agent modeling techniques assume that an accurate behavior library is available to the observing agent such that it has to match its observations with the library, identify successful matches, and possibly select between them. As noted, recent applications of agent modeling raise challenges to this assumption, as agents are increasingly applied in settings that are *open* and/or *adversarial*. In such settings, the behavioral repertoire of observed agents is unknown to the observer. Indeed, such is the case in our application area in robotic soccer. We are developing a coach that is able to improve the performance of a team by analyzing its behavior, and that of the opponent [5]. Since both the coached team and the opponent are unknown at the time of the design, an accurate behavior library describing their expected behavior is unavailable to the coach agent. In particular, a key challenge here is to determine what sequential behaviors best characterize a team, and best serve for predicting its goals and its future behaviors.

Unfortunately, this challenge of constructing an agent-modeling library from observed sequences has only partially been addressed. Bauer [6] presents an approach using clustering to find clusters of similar sequences which are then fed into a specialized supervised plan-acquisition algorithm that determines abstract plans from these clusters. This approach does not attempt to rank sequences by frequency or discover statistical dependencies. Also it has not been applied in multi-variate continuous domains: It assumes that actions are discrete and are executed by a single agent. In addition, Bauer's method depends on the manual selection of a *clustering factor* parameter (in the range $[0, 1]$), a process which we seek to avoid.

Davidson and Hirsh present the IPAM algorithm [2] that successfully predicts a user's next shell command from prior commands, and accumulates such predictions from unsupervised training data. However, IPAM focuses solely on prediction of the next command, and is unable to support modeling in service of more sophisticated tasks that requires analysis. Such analysis, however, is very much needed in the coaching application which motivates our research. Zaki et al. [9] use an efficient sequence clustering algorithm to determine causes for failures in plan execution, by analyzing sequences of plans ending with failure and success. Their approach focuses on labeled examples, and assumes that spurious or irrelevant details may be observed, and must therefore be filtered out from the result. Their approach relies heavily on frequency counts to assess the significance of discovered sequences, and on the user manually fine-tuning frequency and support thresholds. In contrast, we seek sequence detection with unlabeled data, and wish to avoid any manual threshold settings.

Howe and Somlo [10] present an approach, called dependency-detection, to identifying sequences in an incoming data stream, which ignores frequency counts in favor of statistical dependency checks. They thus discover sub-sequences which are statistically significant, in that they appear too often compared to random chance. However, their approach is only applicable to categorical time-series, and cannot be used as is to discover sequential patterns in multi-variate, multi-agent, continuous domains.

To address multi-variate, multi-agent, continuous data, we investigate an approach whereby the basic behaviors of a team are recognized by manually-constructed set of recognizer, which parses a stream of multi-variate, multi-agent observations and translates it to a stream of recognized *atomic* behaviors, annotated by the agents taking part in them. We note that in many domains, the different basic behaviors of agents and teams are often easily described by domain experts, and are often easily recognizable. For instance, in the soccer domain, behaviors such as passing, shooting to the goal, intercepting the ball, etc. are all easily recognized. However, teams differ in how they sequence these basic behaviors, to form coordinated activities which attempt to achieve the team's goals.

This stream of annotated behaviors provides a symbolic abstraction of the raw observations. It is a categorical time-series, amenable to sequence learning of the type investigated by Howe and Somlo [10]. However, while they focused on extracting patterns limited by length, our algorithm extracts all sequences of any length, and facilitates prediction and analysis based on either statistical dependency checks, or on frequency counts. Indeed, one of the contribution of this paper is its comparison of these two techniques and their relative performance.

3 Discovering Sequences of Behavior

This section provides a detailed description of the approach we present in this paper. Our approach takes several stages. First, the raw multi-variate observation stream is turned into a stream of recognized atomic behaviors. This is achieved by utilizing a set of atomic behavior recognizers that parse the observations, and determine what behavior is being executed by players at any given moment. This process is described in Section 3.1. The resulting event stream is segmented to distinguish one team's behaviors from its opponent, and these segments are stored in a trie for analysis (Section 3.2). The next section will describe methods for identifying important sequences using this representation (Section 4).

3.1 Atomic Behavior Recognition

The incoming observation stream is a multi-variate time-series of sensor readings. Each observation is a snapshot of the sensors. In our application, these report state of the soccer field including the coordinate position and orientation of each player and its identification (team and uniform number), the position of the ball, and the state of the game (e.g., goal scored, normal play, free kick, off-side). As such, these sensor snapshots do not offer any information about actions taken by agents, only about the state of the environment and agents embodied in it. However, by contrasting consecutive snapshots one can estimate the movement and rotation velocity of the players and ball, and from those, infer (with some uncertainty) what actions have been taken. For instance, the observer may be able to infer that a player had kicked the ball, based on observations of the changes to the ball's velocity vector that had occurred when the ball was in proximity to the player.

The multi-variate stream is fed, one raw observation after another, into a set of independent atomic-behavior recognizers, working in parallel. These opportunistically parse the observed world-state snapshots and extract from them a summary: a series of recognized atomic behaviors, that each summarizes the team activity during a time interval.

Each recognizer is built as a logical combination of quantifiers and predicates, indexed by time, testing spatial relationships between the ball and player, and organizational relationships between players. Here are a few of the ones we used:

- $Possessor(p, t)$ true if, as of time t, player p is able to kick the ball, i.e., it is within its kicking range. Note this may be true of several players at time t.
- $Owner(p, t)$ true if, as of time t, player p was the last player to kick the ball. This will hold true after the ball leaves the control of the player, until it is

either kickable by another player (i.e., another player becomes a possessor), or the game mode changes (e.g., a goal is scored or the ball goes outside of the field).

- $Receiver(p,t)$ true if, as of time t, player p was within the region defined by an angle of $10°$ centered around the ray defined by the velocity vector of the ball. In other words, true if the ball was possibly aimed at the player. A receiver may be of any team.
- $Teammate(p,q,T)$ true if players p,q are both on team T.
- $Moved(p,t_1,t_2)$ is true if the player p has moved more than 2 meters between time t_1 and time t_2.

For instance, a pass between two members of team T is recognized as occurring between times $t - k$ and t (where k is a positive integer) if the ball has been kicked by one player p at time $t - k$, and then the ball came into the control of *another* player q at time t, where p,q are on the same team. A final condition is that during the interval $[t - k + 1, t - 1]$ the ball should not have been under the control of any player, nor the game play interrupted. Thus a pass would be recognized if the following holds: (1) the ball possessor at time $t - k$ and the ball possessor at time t are teammates in T, but (2) are not the same player; (3) the ball possessor at time $t - k$ is was the ball owner during the interval $[t - k + 1, t - 1]$, but was no longer in control of the ball:

$$Possessor(q,t) \wedge Possessor(p,t - k)$$
$$\wedge \qquad \neg Possessor(q,t - k) \wedge Teammate(p,q,T)$$
$$\wedge \forall i \in [t - k + 1, t - 1] \Rightarrow (Owner(p,i) \wedge \neg Possessor(p,i))$$

Here is another example. An atomic dribble is recognized when a player runs while maintaining the ball under its control, or when it shoots the ball a bit forward and then runs up to catch it. Thus the following conditions must hold: (1) a player d was a possessor at time $t - k$, and is a possessor at time t; (2) d moved more than a specified minimum distance between $t - k$ and t; and either (3a) d remained possessor during $[t - k, t - 1]$, or (3b) d was owner during $[t - k, t - 1]$:

$$Possessor(d,t - k) \wedge Possessor(d,t)$$
$$\wedge \qquad Moved(d,t - k,t)$$
$$\wedge \forall i \in [t - k, t - 1] \Rightarrow (Owner(d,i) \vee Possessor(d,i))$$

Each such behavior recognizer is essentially a rule that captures an atomic behavior, typically of only one or two teammates, and ignores most of what is happening in the world. Its design obviously builds much on the expertise of the domain experts, and their ability to describe the behavior and differentiate it from others using the predicates.

As is commonly recognized in the literature, observations can often lead to ambiguous interpretations. For instance, the ball velocity vector may be a complex function of the kick actions taken by several players, environmental noise, and the timing of agents' actions. Thus the actual kicker or kickers may not be known with certainty: The observer may only be able to narrow it down to three possible players, for instance. It is therefore possible that recognized behaviors may have overlapping times.

However, we believe that in many domains, much like in the soccer domain, simple atomic behaviors are easily describable by domain experts, and would be easily recognizable with little uncertainty. Our hypothesis is that in these domains, it is the sequential combinations of such behaviors that gives rise to the complexity of the recognition task, and the uncertainty that associates it. Indeed, these sequential combinations of these atomic behaviors by a team of agents that are difficult to describe in advance, since the open nature of the applications causes a variety of sequences to appear. For instance, the basic Unix shell commands are common to all users. However, users differ in how they interact with the shell using these commands [2].

Furthermore, since behaviors typically span over several actions and game states taken in aggregate, uncertainty can often be reduced by looking at the results of an hypothesized action several time-steps after it has taken place. For instance, suppose two players of opposing teams were both within a kicking range of the ball just before it changed its velocity. Though it cannot be decided from this observation snapshot which one (if any) has kicked the ball, if the ball is observed to be headed towards a teammate, than a pass could be recognized despite the uncertainty about the kicker. While it is possible that this interpretation is wrong, our results have shown that this is only rarely the case[1]. Our system treats any ambiguity in recognized behaviors using a set of domain-dependent heuristic rules, that prefer specific interpretations over other, and preprocess the stream of recognized behaviors. For instance, an uninterrupted sequence of atomic dribbles is combined together into a longer-duration recognized dribble.

Using the recognizers and these heuristic rules, the stream of world state observation is to turned into a steam of symbols called *events*, each denoting a recognized atomic behavior. For instance, a resulting event stream may look like:

$$Pass(Player_1, Player_2) \rightarrow Pass(Player_2, Player_3) \rightarrow \ldots$$
$$\ldots \rightarrow Dribble(Player_3) \rightarrow Pass(Player_3, Player_4) \rightarrow \ldots$$
$$\ldots \rightarrow Intercept(Player_{16}) \rightarrow Pass(Player_{16}, Player_{20}) \rightarrow \ldots$$

3.2   Storing Sequences in a Trie

The event stream is processed in several stages to discover sequences of behaviors that characterize the observed teams. First, the event stream is segmented by team, such that the event sequence of one team is separated from the events of its opponent team. This creates multiple segments for each team, each segment composed of an uninterrupted sequence of recognized behaviors that were

---

[1] We point the reader to [11] for a more systematic method of recognizing such coordinated activities, and to [12] for an approach dealing explicitly with uncertainty in recognizing behaviors.

Team 1   Team 2

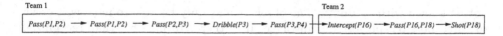

Fig. 1. A sample segmentation of a stream of events, based on agent team membership.

executed by the team in question. The next stage stores these segments in a trie (one for each team), such that all possible subsequences are easily accessible and explicitly represented. Finally, the trie is traversed to calculate statistical dependencies between events and extract useful subsequences.

We begin by describing the segmentation process. Every event—recognized atomic behavior—is annotated by the agents that take part in the recognized activity. Based on the agents that are involved, the events can be categorized as describing one of three parties to the game: the two teams and the referee. All consecutive events belonging to one party are grouped together, in order, into a segment. Each segment is therefore made from a series of uninterrupted activities of only one team (or the referee).

For instance, Figure 1 presents the segmentation of a portion of an event stream. The resulting segments are stored and processed separately, to focus the learning on examples of only one team at a time. In other words, separate models are learned for each team. From this point on, our description will focus on the learning task as it is carried out for one team. The learner is therefore presented with multiple segments, each composed of a number of events, in order, describing an uninterrupted sequence of behavior. Ideally, each such sequence is an example of a well-executed pre-planned coordinated activity leading to a goal. However, though agents may try to carry out pre-planned coordinated activities, their behavior in the simulated environment has to address the dynamic, complex nature of the game, the autonomy of their teammates (each with its own limited sensing and noisy actions) and the behavior of the opponents. Thus, the segments are very rarely the same.

Each segment represents the emergent results of complex interactions between teammates, opponents, and the dynamic, noisy environment in which all of them are embodied. Thus each segment may contain examples of coordinated sequential behavior, but also examples of independent responses to dynamic situations, which are not sequentially dependent on prior decisions by the agents. With sufficient examples, one hopes to uncover repeating patterns of behavior, and capture significant pieces of the team's coordinated plans.

To find such repeating sequences, the learner stores all segments in a trie [7], inserting each segment, and each of its suffixes. A trie is a tree-like data structure, which efficiently stores sequences such that duplicated sub-sequences are stored only once, but in a way that allows keeping a count of how many times they had appeared. In the trie, every node represents an event, and the node's children represent events that have appeared following this event. Thus a path from the root to a node represents a (sub)sequence that has appeared in at least one, but possibly more, segments. An entire segment would therefore be represented as a complete path through the trie, root node to leaf. Each node

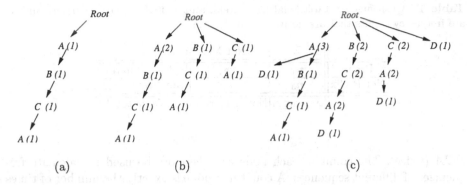

(a)   (b)   (c)

Fig. 2. A trie in construction. Numbers in parentheses are the node counts.

keeps track of the number of times an event has been inserted on to it, and the number of times a segment ended with this node. These two values are called the node's *count* and the node's *end-count*, and are marked $C(x)$ and $N(x)$ for a node x.

For example, suppose the learner has seen two segments, $ABCA$ and $BCAD$, where A, B, C, D stand for different events. Suppose that it is starting with an empty trie. It would first insert $ABCA$ into it, resulting in a trie in Figure 2-a. It would then insert the three remaining suffixes of $ABCA$: $\{BCA, CA, A\}$, resulting in the trie in Figure 2-b. Note that the insertion of the suffix A does not entail creating a new node. Instead, the count in the top node representing A is updated to 2. Next, the learner would insert the next segment and its suffixes, $\{BCAD, CAD, AD, D\}$, into the trie, resulting in the trie in Figure 2-c. Note that in this final trie, the most common single-event sequence is A, the most common two-event sequence is CA and the most common three-event sequence is BCA.

4   Sequential Behavior Identification

Two methods have been discussed in the literature for evaluating the significance of subsequences. The first one, frequency counting, determines the significance of sub-sequences from their frequency in the data [9]. The second method uses statistical dependency checks to determine sequences whose constituent events are deemed statistically dependent on each other; that is, their co-appearance is not due to chance [10]. While the frequency-count method has the benefit of simplicity and intuitive appeal, and the second method has better filtering of sequences that appear common, but in fact are not characteristic of a team. We describe these two methods in detail below, and show how the trie representation can be used efficiently for either method.

We begin by describing how the trie representation can be used for frequency counting. As previously discussed (Figure 2), the simple insertion of the two segments $ABCA$ and $BCAD$ (with their suffixes) almost immediately reveals frequent sub-sequences of different lengths: A (three times), CA (twice), and

Table 1. A contingency table relating a prefix and a single event. n_1, n_2, n_3 and n_4 are frequency counts that are derived from the trie.

	X	Not X	
Prefix	n_1	n_2	Prefix margin
Not Prefix	n_3	n_4	Not-Prefix margin
	X margin	Not-X margin	Table total

BCA (twice). The count in each node can therefore be used to calculate frequencies of different sequences: A count in a node is exactly the number of times the sequence beginning with the root and ending with the node has appeared in the data. A simple traversal through the trie can determine all high-frequency sequences at any given length. However, there is a difficulty with this method, in that it may incorrectly determine that sequences are significant even when in fact they are due to common, but independent, co-occurrence of two highly-frequent events (see a detailed example in Section 5).

Fortunately, a second method for evaluating the significance of sequences exists. This method is called *Dependency Detection*, and was first used by Howe and Cohen in analyzing how plan failures were effected by recovery actions in the Phoenix planner [8]. This method works by statistically testing for the a dependency between a prefix (a sequence containing at least one event) and an event that follows it. In other words, it tests whether the co-occurrence of the prefix and the event is due to chance.

This is achieved by constructing a 2×2 contingency table, relating four different frequency counts (Table 1): (a) the number of times the prefix was followed by the event (n_1); (b) the number of times the prefix was followed by a different event (n_2); (c) the number of times a different prefix (of the same length) was followed by the event (n_3); and (d) the number of times a different prefix was followed by a different event (n_4).

The prefix margin is simply the number of times the prefix was seen (that is, it is equal to $n_1 + n_2$). The not-prefix margin is similarly $n_3 + n_4$. The X margin stands for the number of times X was seen, independently of the prefix, and is $n_1 + n_3$, the not-x margin is $n_2 + n_4$. The table total is $\sum_{i=1}^{4} n_i$. Once the counts are known for a given prefix and an event X, a statistical test can be applied to determine the likelihood that X depends on its prefix, i.e., that a sequence composed of a prefix followed by X is unlikely to be due to a random co-occurrence of the prefix and of X. One such test is the G statistic test, which is calculated as follows

$$G = 2 \sum_{i=1}^{4} n_i log(\frac{n_i}{E_i})$$

where E_i is the *expected frequency* in each cell. These expected frequencies are calculated by multiplying the margins and dividing by the table total:

$$E_1 = \quad (Prefix\,margin) * (X\,margin)/(Table\,Total)$$
$$E_2 = \quad (Prefix\,margin) * (not\,X\,margin)/(Table\,Total)$$
$$E_3 = \quad (not\,Prefix\,margin) * (X\,margin)/(Table\,Total)$$
$$E_4 = (not\,Prefix\,margin) * (not\,X\,margin)/(Table\,Total)$$

The G statistic test is a well-known statistical dependency test, similar in nature to the familiar chi-square test. The result of the computation is a positive number, and the greater it is, the greater the likelihood that the prefix and X are dependent on each other. That is, X is more likely to appear after the prefix, compared to random chance[2]. One can establish the significance of this dependency, by consulting statistical tables, however, in general, we use it to rank hypothesized sequences, and thus simply take greater values to signify stronger dependencies.

With the addition of one data-structure, the trie-based representation supports calculation of the G statistic for each node, i.e., for any sub-sequence. This additional data structure is a two-dimensional table that records, for each sequence length and event, how many events of the given length ended with this event. This table can be updated during the insertion of each event into the trie, with access time $O(1)$. For a given event e and sequence length l, we denote this number by $\alpha(e, l)$.

Given a node x, representing a subsequence ending with the event e, we use the node's count $C(x)$ and end-count $N(x)$ and the event-length entries $\alpha(e, l)$, to calculate its associated G statistic, which is the G rank for the sequence beginning with the root and ending with the node. The following algorithm recursively calculates this for all nodes in a trie, when called with the root node and depth 0. Once the algorithm has calculated a G value for every node, a traversal of the trie can sort sub-sequences by their G value, thus ranking hypothesized sequences, and highlighting those that are likely to be indicative of coordinated sequential behavior.

Algorithm 1 CALCG(TRIENODE T, DEPTH D)

1: $s \leftarrow \sum_e \alpha(e, D)$ {Calculate the total number of strings of the depth D}
2: **for all** children X of T **do**
3: $\quad n_1 \leftarrow C(X),\ smargin \leftarrow C(T) - N(T)$
4: $\quad n_2 \leftarrow smargin - n_1$
5: $\quad n_3 \leftarrow \alpha(X, D) - n_1$
6: $\quad n_4 \leftarrow s - smargin - n_3$
7: $\quad$ Calculate margins and expected frequencies E_i

8: $\quad G \leftarrow 2\sum_{i=1}^{4} n_i log(\frac{n_i}{E_i})$ {This is child X's G}
9: $\quad$ CALCG($X, D+1$)
10: **end for**

---

[2] Negative dependencies (where X is less likely to appear after the prefix) are also discovered, but are filtered out in our approach.

5   Experiments and Results

To evaluate our approach, we have fully implemented a system that observes recordings (logs) of RoboCup soccer simulation games, and is able to identify and extract important sequences of coordinated team behaviors, for the two opposing teams. The system is able to identify 16 different events, corresponding to basic behaviors by agents and game-state changes (such as referee decisions or goals scored). It is able to learn and identify sequences from only a single game or from a number of games, and outputs all the sequences found for each team, together with their frequency counts and with their G statistic ranks.

We have conducted several experiments using this system, intended to test the ability of the different techniques to identify sequences that were characteristic of the team. This was evaluated by using each technique to pick the top 10, 25, 50 and 100 sequences for an observed team, on training data. Then, each technique was used to pick the top 10, 25, 50, and 100 sequences out of test data, for the same observed team. Finally, the size of the overlap in these selections was computed. The hypothesis underlying this test was that greater overlap between the selections based on the training data and the test data, would indicate greater ability to pick sequences that were characteristic of the team, rather than arbitrary. To provide a baseline for this task, random selection of sequences was also used.

This set of experiments used a 5-fold cross-validation design, conducted on a series of 75 games conducted between the Andhill97 team [13] and itself, all using the exact same settings, down to machines and network settings. Andhill was chosen because of its simplicity—we believed that its game play will indeed contain repeating patterns. The games were arbitrarily divided into 5 groups, each containing 15 games. In each experiment, 4 groups (60 games) were used as a training set, and the remaining group (15 games) used as a test set. Five experiments were run, each one using a different training and test groups. In each experiment, a trie for the *left* team was built and maintained, using all observed behavior segments from the games in the training set. Frequency counts and G statistics were then calculated for all nodes in the trie. On average, 4600 different sub-sequences were found for each of the training sets (left team only), and 1200 sub-sequences were found for each test set.

The results of this first set of experiments were very surprising, with frequency counts having an accuracy of 90%-100% in all ranges, and the G statistic method having only a 30%, 51%, 70% and 86% success rate in the top 10, top 25, top 50 and top 100 tests, respectively. However, we quickly found out that the high accuracy for the frequency counts was mostly due to it picking, as the most frequent, sequences containing only a single event. Since single events often occur much more frequently than any sequences they are part of, they were likely to be present in the test set as well. In contrast the G statistic technique flagged two-event and three-event sequences as being representative of the team.

This initial result of course made us reconsider the usefulness of the frequency-count technique, since it was obvious that its result were simply not indicative of any real sequential behavior in the observed team. To make it comparable

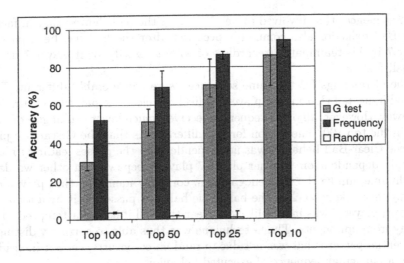

Fig. 3. Prediction accuracy using random selection, G statistics, and frequency counts.

to the G statistic technique, we restricted the considered length to two events and above, and re-ran the test. The results of this second set of experiments are presented in Figure 3. The Y-axis in Figure 3 shows the percentage of sequences picked by each technique, that were included both in the training set and the test set. The X-axis shows the three different ranges of prediction that were tested: Top 10 sequences, top 25, top 50, and top 100. For each of these categories, three bars are shown, contrasting the performance of the frequency counts with that of G statistic and random selection. The error bars on each column show the minimum and maximum results across the 5 test.

The figure shows that both frequency counts and G do significantly better than random selection at predicting what sequences will be picked in the test set. Indeed, random selection success is almost nil. Frequency counts do better than G. However, the advantage for frequency counts grows weaker with narrower selection ranges, i.e., with the selection becoming more critical for evaluation. Furthermore, as the error bars show, the range of performance for frequency counts is well within the range of performance for G for the top-10 selection.

Building on our experience with misleading results with frequency counts, we examined closely the sequences selected by the two techniques, and found interesting discrepancies. In particular, highly frequent two-event sequences found by frequency counts sometimes had relatively low G rankings. Closer examination showed that indeed, the events in these sequences were not always dependent on each other. For instance, player 7 in the observed team sometimes chose the *Clear-Ball* behavior (kicking it outside or to a free location on the field, essentially giving it up). Since it was an active player in many of the games, sequences involving its recognized behavior of clearing the ball were all fairly frequent. Some of the training sets showed that when player number 7 plays *Keepaway* (i.e., keeps the ball to itself, away from opponents, but not moving forward), then the next behavior it is likely to display is clearing of the ball.

Other sequences that involved player 7 clearing the ball showed that in fact this Clear-Ball behavior also commonly occurred after the ball has been passed to player 7 by his teammates (regardless of whom passed), or if player 7 dribbled the ball first.

The G rankings for the same sequences were considerably different. The G method indicated that indeed player 7 is likely to clear the ball when it first plays keepaway. However, all other sequences received much lower rankings—often not even in the top 100. The reason for this difference is that the G statistic judged that the Clear-Ball behavior was not dependent on the passes leading to it, but was only dependent on whether player 7 played keepaway. In other words, the G technique, unlike the frequency counts, correctly identified that player 7 was *not* any more likely to clear the ball if the ball was passed to it by a teammate. However, player 7 was indeed likely to clear the ball if it first attempted to keep it away from opponents. The G technique was thus able to correctly distinguish a sequential pattern that was not due to random co-occurrence, but instead was due to a particular sequence of executed behaviors.

6   Conclusions and Future Work

We presented a hybrid approach to learning the coordinated sequential behavior of teams, from a time-series of continuous multi-variate observations, of multiple interacting agents. The hypothesis underlying this approach is that such a complex time-series can be parsed and transformed into a single-variable categorical time-series, using a set of behavior recognizers that focus only on recognizing simple, basic, behaviors of the agents. Once the categorical time-series is available, it is segmented and stored in a trie, an efficient representation amenable to statistical analysis of the data.

We demonstrated the usefulness of the trie representation in supporting two important methods of statistical analysis—frequency counting and statistical dependency detection—in service of discovering important sequences of behaviors. We evaluated these two techniques in a rigorous set of experiments, and concluded that statistical dependency detection may be more suitable to discovering coordinated sequential behavior, since it is able to reject frequently observed sequences whose constituent behaviors have co-occurred due to chance.

We are currently investigating ways to build on our approach in several directions. First, we are investigating ways of using both frequency counts and the G rankings on-line, such that predictions of the next k events can be made, based on an observed prefix. Second, we are investigating a method for transforming the discovered sequences into a graphical model, essentially a probabilistic finite state automata, that can be used for deeper analysis of team behavior. In this task, we are aided by prior work by Howe and Somlo [10].

Acknowledgements

This research was sponsored by grants Nos. F30602-98-2-0135, F30602-97-2-0250, and NBCHC010059. The views and conclusions contained in this document are those of the authors and should not be interpreted as necessarily representing the official policies or endorsements, either expressed or implied, of the Defense Advanced Research Projects Agency (DARPA), the US Army, the US Air Force, or the US Government.

References

1. Lesh, N., Rich, C., Sidner, C.L.: Using plan recognition in human-computer collaboration. In: Proceedings of the International Conference on User Modelling (UM-99), Banff, Canada (1999)
2. Davidson, B., Hirsh, H.: Probabilistic online action prediction. In: Proceedings of the 1998 AAAI Spring Symposium on Intelligent Environments. (1998)
3. Rickel, J., Johnson, W.L.: Animated agents for procedural training in virtual reality: Perception, cognition, and motor control. Applied Artificial Intelligence **13** (1999) 343–382
4. Tambe, M., Rosenbloom, P.S.: RESC: An approach to agent tracking in a real-time, dynamic environment. In: Proceedings of the International Joint Conference on Artificial Intelligence. (1995)
5. Riley, P., Veloso, M., Kaminka, G.: An empirical study of coaching. In: Proceedings of Distributed Autonomous Robotic Systems 6, Springer-Verlag (2002) (to appear).
6. Bauer, M.: From interaction data to plan libraries: A clustering approach. In: Proceedings of the International Joint Conference on Artificial Intelligence. Volume 2., Stockholm, Sweden, Morgan-Kaufman Publishers, Inc (1999) 962–967
7. Knuth, D.E.: Sorting and Searching. Volume 3 of The art of computer programming. Addison-Wesley (1973)
8. Howe, A.E., Cohen, P.R.: Understanding planner behavior. Artificial Intelligence **76** (1995) 125–166
9. Zaki, M., Lesh, N., Ogihara, M.: Planmine: Sequence mining for plan failures. In: Proceedings of the 4th International Conference on Knowledge Discovery and Data Mining, AAAI Press (1998) 369–374
10. Howe, A.E., Somlo, G.L.: Modeling intelligent system execution as state-transition diagrams to support debugging. In: Proceedings of the Second International Workshop on Automated Debugging. (1997)
11. Wendler, J., Kaminka, G.A., Veloso, M.: Automatically improving team cooperation by applying coordination models. In: The AAAI Fall symposium on Intent Inference for Collaborative Tasks, AAAI Press (2001)
12. Han, K., Veloso, M.: Automated robot behavior recognition applied to robotic soccer. In: Proceedings of the IJCAI-99 Workshop on Team Behavior and Plan-Recognition. (1999) Also appears in Proceedings of the 9th International Symposium of Robotics Research (ISSR-99).
13. Ando, T.: Refinement of soccer agents' positions using reinforcement learning. In Kitano, H., ed.: RoboCup-97: Robot soccer world cup I. Volume 1395 of LNAI. Springer-verlag (1998) 373–388

Towards a Life-Long Learning Soccer Agent*

Alexander Kleiner, Markus Dietl, and Bernhard Nebel

Institut für Informatik
Universität Freiburg
79110 Freiburg, Germany
{kleiner,dietl,nebel}@informatik.uni-freiburg.de

Abstract. One problem in robotic soccer (and in robotics in general)
is to adapt skills and the overall behavior to a changing environment
and to hardware improvements. We applied hierarchical reinforcement
learning in an SMDP framework learning on all levels simultaneously.
As our experiments show, learning simultaneously on the skill level and
on the skill selection level is advantageous since it allows for a smooth
adaption to a changing environment. Furthermore, the skills we trained
turn also out to be quite competitive when run on the real robotic players
of the players of our *CS Freiburg* team.

1 Introduction

The *RoboCup* context provides us with problems similar to those encountered by
robots in real world tasks. The agents have to cope with a continuously changing
environment, noisy perception and a huge state space [6]. Mid size robots are
additionally confronted with a complex motion model and non-trivial ball handling problems. Programming robots overcoming all these difficulties is a tedious
task. Furthermore, with changes in the environment or hardware improvements,
previous solutions may not work any longer and it is necessary to reprogram
the robots. *Reinforcement Learning (RL)* offers a rich set of adaptive solutions
which have also proven to be applicable to complex domains [4]. However, before
one can apply *RL*, it is necessary to reduce the state space. In particular, often
one uses generalization techniques on the input space. We reduce the size of the
state space by *tile coding* [1, 2] which is a widely used method for linear function
approximation in RL.

In addition, it is advantageous to decompose the task into *skills* that are
selected on a higher level, instead of trying to learn a "universal" control strategy.
For example, *dribbling*, *shooting*, and *taking the ball* are three different skills that
can be learned individually. Once the robots have learned these skills, the robots
can learn when to apply them – similar to *layered learning* [12].

While decomposing a task might simplify the learning problem, it can lead
to problems when we want to adapt to new environmental conditions. Using a

---

* This work has been partially supported by *Deutsche Forschungsgemeinschaft* (DFG)
and by *SICK AG.*

G.A. Kaminka, P.U. Lima, and R. Rojas (Eds.): RoboCup 2002, LNAI 2752, pp. 126–134, 2003.
© Springer-Verlag Berlin Heidelberg 2003

"layered" approach and assuming that a new kicking device is used or that the carpet has changed, one would be forced to first adapt the basic skills to the new situation and then to adapt the selection strategy. However, it is not clear what the best setting would be to re-train the lower level skills in this case. As a matter of fact, we would like to confront our robots with the new situation and train both levels simultaneously. In other words, we want them to adapt their low level skills to the new environments as well as learning to decide which skill to apply in which situation [5]. The ultimate goal in this context is to build robotic soccer agents that improve their skills during their whole life and doing this as efficiently and quickly as possible.

In order to address these problems we decided to apply hierarchical RL based on Semi Markov Decision Processes (SMDPs), as introduced by Bradtke and Duff [3, 7] and further developed by Sutton [13]. In contrast to Markov Decision Processes (MDPs), which are defined for an action execution at discrete time steps, SMDPs are providing a basis for learning to choose among *temporally abstract actions*. Temporally abstract actions are considered in standard SMDPs as *black box skills*, which execute a sequence of actions in a defined partition of the state space for an arbritrary amount of time.

RL methods have already successfully been applied to the simulation league in the *Karlsruhe Brainstormers* [8] and CMUnited [10] teams. This work is different from ours since both teams are focusing mainly on the multi-agent problem of robotic soccer and use different techniques for state space generalization. Stone and Sutton [11] have shown how RL trained agents can beat even hand-coded opponents in the *keepaway* scenario. Their skill selection has also been learned by SMDP techniques. However, their skills are hand-coded.

One team applying RL in the mid size league are *Osaka Trackies*, which use a method building self-organized hierarchical structures [14]. In contrast to other approaches which favor the decomposition to "standard" soccer skills, the resulting hierarchy consists of small, but very flexible skills. In contrast to our work that is build upon a world model, their system can be considered as behavior-based, because the state space is defined by uninterpreted images from the vision system.

The rest of the paper is structured as follows. In the next section we specify the SMDP learning model. In Section 3, we sketch how to apply our hierarchical RL approach to robotic soccer. In Section 4, we describe our experimental results, and in Section 5 we conclude.

2   Learning in (S)MDPs

The framework of MDPs provides a formal description for time discrete interactions between an agent and its environment. It is assumed that the agent chooses at discrete time steps t an action a_t according to the state s_t previously received from the world. An MDP is defined by the tuple (S, A, T, R), where S is the set of world states, A is the set of actions, $T : S \times A \times S' \Rightarrow [0, 1]$ is the transition model and $R : S \times A \Rightarrow \Re$ is the reward function. The transition model T is defined by $p(s_{t+1}|a_t, s_t)$ which returns for every world state s_t and action a_t the probability distribution over world states s_{t+1}. Furthermore, the reward function $R(s, a)$ defines real valued rewards returned by the environment according to the agent's last state and action taken.

An MDP is solved when the agent has identified a policy π which maximizes rewards received over time. By RL methods this can be achieved by identifying the optimal value function $V^*(s)$, indicating the maximal future (discounted) rewards to be expected from state s. Once the optimal value function is found, the agent can behave optimally by selecting actions greedily according to $V^*(s)$.

There are well known methods to approximate the optimal value function by successive steps through the state space. One widely used method is known as *Q-Learning* [16] which allows learning without the transition model T. Rather than learning a mapping from states to values, this method learns an approximation for $Q^*(s, a)$ which maps from state-action pairs to values. The update rule for one-step Q-Learning is defined as

$$Q_{k+1}\left(s_t, a_t\right) := (1 - \alpha)\, Q_k\left(s_t, a_t\right) + \alpha \left[R\left(s_t, a_t\right) + \gamma \max_{a \in A} Q_k\left(s_{t+1}, a_{t+1}\right) \right], \quad (1)$$

where α denotes the *learning rate*, and γ a *discount factor*.

Convergence speed of Q-Learning and other RL methods can be improved by considering eligibility traces [2]. The idea is, roughly speaking, to keep track of previously visited states and update their value when visiting states in the future. This yields the effect that a whole trace can be updated from the effect of one step. The influence of states on the past can be controlled by the parameter λ. Q-Learning with eligibility traces is denoted by $Q(\lambda)$.

In Q-Learning the value $Q^\pi(s, a)$ of a state s is the approximated utility for selecting a in s and following the greedy policy afterwards. Therefore the traces have to be cut off when selecting a non-greedy-action for execution (e.g. for exploration). However, when replacing $max_a Q_k(s_{t+1}, a_{t+1})$ by $Q_k(s_{t+1}, a_{t+1})$ in equation 1 and selecting a_{t+1} according to the policy selecting actions, we get the update for an on-policy method, known as *Sarsa* [9] that allows updates of the whole trace.

In SMDPs, actions are allowed to continue for more than one time step. An SMDP is an extension to the definition for MDPs and defined by the tuple *(S,A,T,R,F)*. F is defined by $p(t|s, a)$ and returns the probability of reaching the next SMDP state at time t when the *temporally abstract action a* is taken in state s. Q-Learning has been extended for learning in SMDPs [3]. The method is guaranteed to converge [7] when similar conditions as for standard Q-Learning are met.

The update rule for *SMDP Q-Learning* is defined as

$$Q_{k+1}\left(s_t, a_t\right) := (1 - \alpha)\, Q_k\left(s_t, a_t\right) + \alpha \left[r + \gamma^t \max_{a \in A} Q_k\left(s_{t+1}, a_{t+1}\right) \right], \quad (2)$$

where t denotes the sampled time of execution and r the accumulated discounted reward received during the execution. Like the transition model T, the time model F is sampled by experience and has not to be known in advance.

In recent work, a unification of MDPs and SMDPs has been proposed [13]. It also has been shown that there is a clear advantage of interrupting temporally abstract actions during their execution and switch among them if the change is profitable. Our work, however, is based on the standard framework for SMDPs.

3 Applying Hierarchical Reinforcement Learning to Robotic Soccer

The learner's state space is based on the world model of a *CS Freiburg* player [17]. The world model is continuously updated in 100 msec intervals and consists basically of positions and velocities of the ball and robots on the field. Each sensor has a specific field of view which means that the world model can be incomplete.

The robot's trajectory is controlled by a differential drive. Furthermore, the robot is equipped with a custom manufactured kicking device for handling the ball. This device consists of a kicker to shoot and two "fingers" mounted on the left and righthand side of the kicker to control the ball. We noticed that effects of the kicking device and differential drive might vary on different robots of our team. It is one of the goals of our work to cope with these differences.

Experimental results presented in this paper have firstly been achieved using a simulation of our robots. The simulation is implemented as a client-server architecture and executes asynchronously to world model updates. Since the world models generated on the real robots and generated from the simulation are the same, the learner can switch between them on the fly.

Given a constant cycle time, the interface can be used for learning in MDPs. Within cycle c_t the learner receives the current world state s_t, and consequently returns the selected action a_t which causes s_{t+1} to be emitted in the successive cycle c_{t+1}. Since the world model provides reliable "high-level" features of the robot's perception, simulated and real perception can be considered as almost equivalent.

The application of RL to our players has been carried out in a straight-forward manner, similar to the way humans would train soccer. Firstly, basic skills, namely *shootGoal, shootAway, dribbleBall, searchBall, turnBall, approach-Ball* and *freeFromStall* [18, 17] have been trained in simple, static scenarios. Secondly, the appropriate selection of these skills and their embedding into the task has been trained in a realistic scenario which was a game against a *CS Freiburg* player from 2001. Finally, the simulation-trained soccer player has been executed on one of our real robots.

Early experiments have shown that $Sarsa(\lambda)$ performs better than $Q(\lambda)$ when learning the skills above. We assume that this is mainly caused by the necessary cuts of eligibility traces after non-greedy actions when applying the off-policy method. Therefore, skills have been trained by $Sarsa(\lambda)$. We set $\gamma = 1.0$ (due to the presence of an absorbing state), $\alpha = 0.1$ (small, due to the non-determinism of the environment), $\epsilon = 0.05$ (small, since high exploration could lead to failures) and $\lambda = 0.8$ (a common value when learning with n-step updates).

The *state space* of each skill consists of features extracted from the world model, e.g. *distance* and *angle* to the *ball* or to the *opponent*. These features were chosen according to their relevance for the behavior to be learned. The automation of this selection will be subject of future work. The *action space* of each skill is given by two discretized scalar values for the translational and rotational velocity and one binary value for kicking. For each skill, terminal states have been defined depending on the skill's natural goal. The skill *approachBall*, for example, terminates when either the ball has been approached successfully or could not be seen by the robot anymore. We defined a reward of 100 when the goal state was reached, a reward of −100 when the robot failed its task and a reward of −1 for each action taken.

For the learning of the skill-selection SMDP we decided to allow a high degree of exploration to guarantee the recurrent selection of all skills. Exploration on the skill selection level supports the selection of skills with low expectation of future rewards. This leads to more training of those skills and therefore to their improvement which might lead to higher expectations. Hence, we applied $Q(\lambda)$, since it is an off-policy method that learns the optimal policy, regardless of performing explorative actions[1]. During learning, goals made by the learner were rewarded with 100, goals made by the opponent with −100 and steps taken in a skill with −1. The state space of the SMDP was defined by the scalars *angle* and *distance* to ball, *angle* and *distance* to opponent, *angle* and *distance* to goal, and the binary values *ball is visible* and *opponent is visible*.

4   Experimental Results

The results presented in this section are selected from a series of experiments and are representative. Each experiment has been carried out with a learner that was equipped with previously trained skills that had been learned in simple scenarios. All graphs shown in this section are smoothed by averaging over 100 episodes.

In the first series of experiments the task of the learner was to learn the selection of skills when playing against a static goalkeeper. We intentionally chose a simple scenario in order to give a first impression of the learner's performance. During each episode the goalkeeper was placed on an arbitrary position in front of the goal, whereas learner and ball were placed anywhere on the field. We compared two learners, one and that was focusing on the learning of skill selection, and a second that was additionally allowed to improve its skills further. Figure 1 shows the progress of the two learners.

The baseline indicates the average of the accumulated rewards a CS Freiburg Player achieves during one episode. In both settings a good action selection strategy was learned after 500 episodes. Learning within skills, however, leads to a noticeably better performance. Although the scenario in the experiment was similar to the one used to pre-learn the skills, the learning within the skills enables the learner to adapt more flexibly to the game-playing situation.

---

[1] Note, due to the much smaller number of steps during an SMDP episode, the negative effect of Q-Learning on eligibility traces is of minor importance.

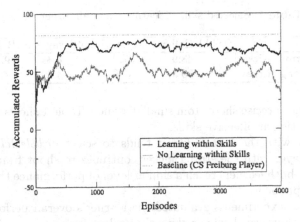

Fig. 1. Learner versus static goalkeeper with and without learning within skills

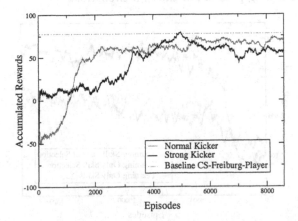

Fig. 2. Learner versus a *CS Freiburg* player with a normal and with a strong kicker. The initial skills were trained with a strong kicker. Both players reach an adequate level of play after some time of training

The results presented in Figure 2 demonstrate how the system reacts on a significant change of the environment. We compared learners with a normal and a strong kicker. The strong kicker was able to accelerate the ball much faster, but less precise. The task now was to compete against a *CS Freiburg* player that was slowed down to a third of its normal velocity. At the beginning of each episode the learner and ball were placed randomly into one half, facing the opponent.

Again, the baseline indicates the average of the accumulated rewards a CS Freiburg Player with normal velocity achieves during one episode. Due to the fact that skills were pre-trained with a strong kicker the learner using the normal kicker reaches less reward during the first 1000 episodes. After 6000 episodes, however, playing with a normal kicker turns out to be more successful than playing with the strong one. The learner with the normal kicker develops a different way of playing: He is dribbling more often to the front of the goal and

Table 1. Selected skills if learner was ball owner (in %)

	DribbleBall	ShootGoal	ShootAway	TurnBall
Normal Kicker	48.9	37.0	4.8	9.3
Strong Kicker	30.3	57.6	4.5	7.7

performs a rather precise shoot from small distance. Table 1 shows the frequency of selecting particular offensive skills.

The learner with the normal kicker tends to select *dribbleBall* more often, whereas the player with the strong kicker continues to shoot from further distances. Finally, both learners reach a similar level of performance that is winning against their opponent.

The previous experiments evaluated the learner's overall performance. It is also important, however, how the skills themselves improve over time. Figure 3 documents the learning progress of the skill *shootGoal*.

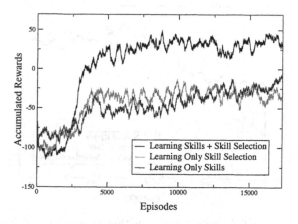

Fig. 3. Learning of the skill *shootGoal* while playing against a *CS Freiburg* player

The result shows that the simultanous learning of skills and their selection leads to higher rewards. The learner improving skills and skill selection reached an accumulated reward of nearly 50, whereas the other learners could not reach more than −25. Without learning the skill selection, skills are executed randomly, and thus also in inadequate situations. For example, *ShootGoal* could be chosen when facing the own goal. Certainly, it is possible that *ShootGoal* learns to handle such situations as well, but this could take a very long time of learning. In fact, the slowly improving curve for learning without skill selection indicates this learning process. On the other hand, without learning inside the skills, skills are executed as they were trained for static scenarios. Figure 3 shows that adaption of skills to the task at hand benefits the overall result.

Finally, we started a first experiment with our best learned skills and skill-selection on a real robot. The task was, as also evaluated in the simulation, a static scenario with a goalkeeper in front of the goal. The learner started an episode from the center of the field, whereas the ball was placed randomly. As we expected, the learner started to chose reasonable skills, such as *searchBall* to locate the ball on the field, *approachBall* to get close to it and *turnBall* to get the right direction. To our surprise, most skills executed impressively well. The learner was robustly playing the ball without losing quality in skill selection or execution.

While playing for one hour the learner was able to score 0.75 goals per minute. In contrast, the hand-coded CS Freiburg player scores 0.94 goals per minute when limited to one third of its maximal velocity and 1.37 goals per minute when playing with maximal velocity. Although the performance of the player is superior, the result is remarkable, since the learner was completely trained in the simulation. Note that the learners result was achieved by far less time for design and parametrization.

In order to evaluate how the total performance improves over time, more than one hour of playing will be necessary. A long-term evaluation will be presented in future work.

5   Conclusion and Discussion

We studied the applicability of hierarchical reinforcement learning to robots in the mid size league. For our particular setting, RL methods perform remarkably well. Our learner was able to compete with one of our hand-coded players, even when environmental conditions were changed. Additionally, the low amount of learning time indicates that there is still potential for learning in hierarchies with more than two levels.

The experiments show that learning inside skills improves the overall performance significantly. Thus, the results lead to two important conclusions: Firstly, the whole system achieves higher adaptivity to changes in the environment while acting stable without tending to aimless behavior. Secondly, based on the fact that skills adapt themselves to the global task, it seems to be possible to reuse these skills for a different task, such as ball passing or general team cooperation.

Our final experiment on a real soccer robot has shown that knowledge learned in our simulation can be reused for a real-world task. It can be assumed that the hierarchical structure supports the stable behavior of the robots.

In future work we will investigate how the process of adaption can be accelerated further by using more flexible hierarchies. Furthermore it will be interesting, whether our implementation can be scaled-up to the game of more than one robot, particularly, in which way single players are able to adapt their skill selection when they are exposed to the multi-agent problem.

References

1. J. S. Albus. A theory of cerebellar function. In *Mathematical Biosciences*, volume 10, pages 25–61.
2. A. Barto and R.S. Sutton. *Reinforcement Learning – An Introduction*. MIT Press, Cambridge, 1998.

3. S. J. Bradtke and M. O. Duff. Reinforcement learning methods for continuous-time Markov decision problems. In G. Tesauro, D. Touretzky, and T. Leen, editors, *Advances in Neural Information Processing Systems*, volume 7, pages 393–400. The MIT Press, 1995.
4. R. H. Crites and A. G. Barto. Improving elevator performance using reinforcement learning. In David S. Touretzky, Michael C. Mozer, and Michael E. Hasselmo, editors, *Advances in Neural Information Processing Systems*, volume 8, pages 1017–1023. The MIT Press, 1996.
5. Thomas G. Dietterich. The MAXQ method for hierarchical reinforcement learning. In *Fifteenth International Conference on Machine Learning*. Morgan Kaufmann, 1998.
6. H. Kitano, M. Tambe, P. Stone, M. Veloso, S. Coradeschi, E. Osawa, H. Matsubara, I. Noda, and M. Asada. The RoboCup synthetic agent challenge,97. In *International Joint Conference on Artificial Intelligence (IJCAI97)*, 1997.
7. R. Parr. *Hierarchical Control and Learning for Markov decision processes*. Ph.d. thesis, University of California at Berkeley, 1998.
8. M. Riedmiller and A. Merke. Karlsruhe Brainstormers – a reinforcement learning approach to robotic soccer ii. In Veloso et al. [15]. To appear.
9. G. Rummery and M. Niranjan. On-line q-learning using connectionist systems. Technical Report CUED/F-INFENG/TR, Cambridge University Engineering Department, 1996.
10. P. Stone, P. Riley, and M. Veloso. The CMUnited-99 champion simulator team. In M. Veloso, E. Pagello, and H. Kitano, editors, *RoboCup-99: Robot Soccer World Cup III*, Berlin, Heidelberg, New York, 2000. Springer-Verlag.
11. P. Stone and R.S. Sutton. Scaling reinforcement learning toward RoboCup soccer. In *Proceedings of the 18th International Conference on Machine Learning*, 2001.
12. Peter Stone and Manuela Veloso. Layered learning. In R. Lopez de Mantaras and E. Plaza, editors, *Eleventh European Conference on Machine Learning (ECML-2000)*. Springer-Verlag, 2000.
13. R. Sutton, D. Precup, and S. Singh. Between MDPs and semi-MDPs: A framework for temporal abstraction in reinforcement learning. In *Artificial Intelligence*, volume 112, pages 181–211, 1999.
14. Y. Takahashi and M. Asada. Vision-guided behavior acquisition of a mobile robot by multi-layered reinforcement learning. In *IEEE/RSJ International Conference on Intelligent Robots and Systems*, volume 1, pages 395–402, 2000.
15. M. Veloso, T. Balch, and P. Stone, editors. *International RoboCup Symposium 2001*, 2002. To appear.
16. C. J. C. H. Watkins. *Learning with Delayed Rewards*. Ph.d. thesis, Cambridge University., 1989.
17. T. Weigel, A. Kleiner, F. Diesch, M. Dietl, J. S. Gutmann, B. Nebel, P. Stiegeler, and B. Szerbakowski. CS Freiburg 2001. In Veloso et al. [15]. To appear.
18. Thilo Weigel, Willi Auerbach, Markus Dietl, Burkhard Dümler, Jens-Steffen Gutmann, Kornel Marko, Klaus Müller, Bernhard Nebel, Boris Szerbakowski, and Maximilian Thiel. CS Freiburg: Doing the right thing in a group. In P. Stone, G. Kraetzschmar, and T. Balch, editors, *RoboCup-2000: Robot Soccer World Cup IV*, pages 52–63. Springer-Verlag, Berlin, Heidelberg, New York, 2001.

Adaptive Synchronisation for a RoboCup Agent

Jefferson D. Montgomery and Alan K. Mackworth

Computer Science Department of the University of British Columbia
Vancouver, B.C., Canada, V6T 1Z4
{jdm,mack}@cs.ubc.ca

Abstract. We describe an algorithm that adaptively synchronises an agent with its environment enabling maximal deliberation time and improved action success rates. The method balances its reliance upon noisy evidence with internal representations, making it robust to interaction faults caused by both communication and timing. The notion of action correctness is developed and used to analyse the new method as well as two special cases: Internal and External synchronisation. Action correctness is determined online by a novel action accounting procedure that determines the outcome of commanded actions. In conjunction, these elements provide online analysis of agent activity, action confirmation for model prediction, and a coarse measure of the agent's coherence with the environment that is used to adapt its performance.

1 Introduction

Distributed systems, with relevant coordination, can be more efficient and productive than independent entities. This fact has not escaped those in search of a computational model of intelligence where intelligent, distributed agents also promise more efficient and productive solutions. Accordingly, multi-agent systems have become an important and widely researched topic. For example, robot soccer was presented as a suitable domain for exploring the properties of situated, multi-agent systems [9] and has since been developed into a popular yearly competition between artificial soccer teams [7].

However, distributed systems are subject to problems such as partial failure, incomplete observability, and unreliable communication. Therefore, it is an important property for successful distributed systems to be able to efficiently coordinate between individuals, including the environment. Unified operation — a *synchronised* system — can be achieved using accurate system specification [4] or through sufficient communication [6, 12]. Asynchronous operation can result in irrelevant sensing, inconsistent representations, and delayed or failed action; problems which can affect event the most sophisticated skills and plans [2, 5, 10, 14].

Considerable research has been done in the related areas of clock skew detection and distributed system monitoring [6, 8], particularly given recent interest in streaming multimedia. In the RoboCup Simulation league, however, the communication protocol is too restrictive to support the standard solutions developed

G.A. Kaminka, P.U. Lima, and R. Rojas (Eds.): RoboCup 2002, LNAI 2752, pp. 135–149, 2003.

in these efforts. Accordingly, simple solutions have been adopted often entailing unjustified assumptions. In this paper, we describe a new adaptive algorithm for synchronising the agent with its environment that is robust to communication delays, lost messages, and timing faults.

In Section 2, we develop the notion of correct action, which defines criteria for a solution and forms the basis of our evaluation and analysis. Section 3 presents a taxonomy of practical issues which is used to motivate and compare typical synchronisation techniques in Section 4. Sections 5 and 6 present a novel, adaptive synchronisation algorithm based on an online accounting procedure for action commands. Finally, the results of an empirical comparison of the presented techniques are included and discussed in Section 7.

2   Robots that Act Correctly

In general, a *robotic system* is the coupling of a *robot* with its *environment*. Further, a robot can be viewed as a *controller* embedded in a *plant*, through which the robot senses and acts in the environment. A general robotic system is shown in Fig. 1. In the RoboCup Simulation league, two distinct software programs (the *agent* and `SoccerServer`) interact through a lossy communication channel. This can be viewed as a robotic system where the `SoccerServer` is the environment, the communication channel is the plant, and the agent is the controller.

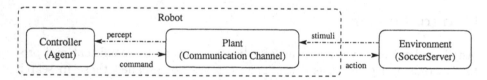

Fig. 1. A general robotic system showing the interactions between the robot's controller and plant as well as with the environment.

The environment effects action and provides stimuli to the robot. `SoccerServer`, shown in Fig. 2, simulates real-life robotic soccer and disseminates stimulus to each of the competing agents [11]. The simulation cycles with a period of 100 milliseconds and can be described by four states. Each cycle begins in the SB state (where `sense_body` stimulus describing the agent's condition is provided) and ends in the E state (where the domain dynamics are simulated). `SoccerServer` accepts actions in the R state and enters the SE state every one and a half cycles to provide visual sensor data in the `see` stimulus. Because of the inherent frequency mismatch, state-space is traversed sequentially through three distinct cycle types: type 1 (SB → SE → R → E), type 2 (SB → R → SE → R → E), and type 3 (SB → R → E).

The controller supplies a command trace to the plant to achieve the desired system behaviour. For simplicity, we assume an agent capable of rational thought

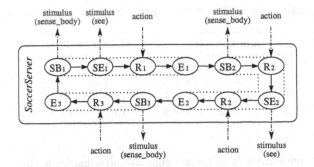

Fig. 2. States and state transitions for the `SoccerServer` environment. To emphasize the three cycle types, state transitions are multiplied out and the cycle type is denoted by a subscript to the state label.

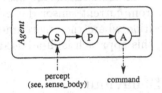

Fig. 3. States and state transitions for the agent.

based on a sense-plan-act architecture, as shown in Fig. 3. This agent receives percepts while in state S, then deliberates in state P, and finally commands the desired action in state A.

Successful agents must generate action that is consistent with the current environment. To achieve this coherence, an agent must make decisions based on sensor data and command action in such a way that it is effected while the relevant sensor data is still valid. We call this *correct action*.

Definition 1 (Correct action). In the RoboCup Simulation domain, an agent's actions are *correct* when the following temporal precedence constraints are satisfied, where $X \prec Y$ constrains state X to happen before state Y.

$$1)\ A \prec E$$
$$2)\ SB \prec P \wedge SE \prec P^1$$

The first constraint is strict: `SoccerServer` *must* receive one action command before it begins simulating the dynamics. If $A \not\prec E$, the agent will remain idle until the next simulation cycle. If `SoccerServer` receives more than one command in a single cycle, the second and any subsequent command is ignored. Therefore, whether action is effected on time is determined not only by the command reception time, but also by that of the previous cycle as described in Table 1.

---

[1] In cycle type 3, which does not include the SE state, the second term of the conjunction is ignored. Otherwise, where $SB \prec SE$ is considered a tautology, the first term can be ignored.

Table 1. SoccerServer rules for effecting action based on command reception times.

Command reception	Current action
$A_{prev} \prec E_{prev} \wedge A \prec E$	Effected on time
$A_{prev} \not\prec E_{prev} \wedge A \prec E$	Failed
$A_{prev} \prec E_{prev} \wedge A \not\prec E$	Effected late
$A_{prev} \not\prec E_{prev} \wedge A \not\prec E$	Effected late

The second constraint is soft: the agent *should* consider action only after sufficient sensing. If this constraint is violated then the agent is basing its action on possibly inconsistent sensor data. For example, the CMUnited98 agent acts at the beginning of each simulation cycle [13]. This virtually ensures the first constraint by abandoning the second: all decisions are based on dead-reckoning from the previous cycle and not from current sensor data. Though this method has proven successful in competition where the environmental dynamics are structured and easy to simulate, this approach is ill-advised in general.

3   Desired System Behaviour

Given the required computation for sensor processing, deliberation, and simulation, the constraints in Definition 1 imply that there is an optimal time, t^*, within the simulation cycle when actions should be commanded. If commanding at the optimal time, the agent will receive relevant stimuli, have the maximum amount of time to deliberate, and have all action occur as expected. This ideal behaviour is shown in Fig. 4.

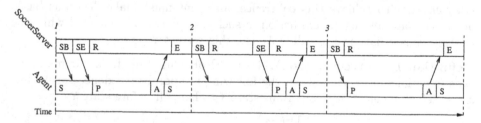

Fig. 4. An event timing diagram depicting ideal, coherent behaviour for each of the three cycle types: all three actions are correct.

In practice, however, there are several factors that disrupt the ideal behaviour. The simulation cycle is not observable by the agent and appears to fluctuate in its periodicity. These fluctuations are the result of one or more of the following practical considerations which make acting correctly difficult. For example, see Fig. 5.

Clock inaccuracies. The quartz oscillations that computers use to keep time are inaccurate. Typically, a clock can deviate from real time by as much as 30 milliseconds over a 10 minute period [12]. Also, since the system is typically not run over a real-time operating system, interval timers tend to overrun when the processor is overly taxed. These anomalies occur independently across the system which, over the course of a full game, can incur timing deviations that constitute significant portions of the simulation cycle period.

Varying communication reliability. Varying network traffic causes unobservable and unpredictable communication delays. Further, since the system uses a lossy communication protocol, messages can arrive out of order or be lost entirely in the transport layer. Therefore, the sensitivity of a synchronisation method to such communication faults is extremely relevant.

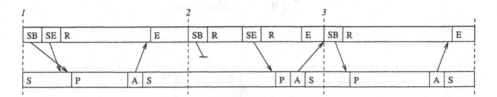

Fig. 5. An example showing possible faults associated with clock inaccuracies and varying network reliability. In the first cycle, the sense_body is delayed, arriving out of order with the see stimulus. Also, the SoccerServer's interval timer overruns causing the next sense_body (which ends up being lost in transit) to be delayed. In the second cycle, the action command is delayed and not effected until the third cycle. Since this action arrives late, the agent remains idle and the action commanded in the third cycle is ignored by SoccerServer.

4   Synchronisation Algorithms

In order to synchronise with the environment, each agent must determine its best estimate of the environment's state, which is not directly observable. This section presents two estimation techniques based on internal and external evidence and compares them based on their likelihood of producing correct aciton.

4.1   Synchronisation Using Internal Evidence

Internal synchronisation uses internal evidence to coordinate with the environment. The evidence commonly used is the expiration of an interval timer that mimics the simulation periodicity: the agent assumes a new simulation cycle upon the timer's expiry every 100 milliseconds [3]. The agent then commands an action at some fixed *internal* time, t^*. An example is shown in Fig. 6.

Due to the internal nature of this algorithm, there are no observed fluctuations due to network variation. However, there will always exist a temporal offset, δ, between the true simulation cycle and the agent's internal representation:

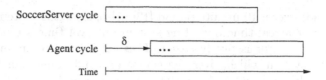

The fundamental assumption behind Internal synchronisation is that the internal and external cycles are in phase (i.e., $\delta = 0$ [2]). If this assumption holds the internal method produces excellent results, but assuming correlation is unjustified. In general, δ is uniformly distributed depending on when the agent is initiated and varies dynamically due to clock inaccuracies.

$$P(\delta = t) \equiv \begin{cases} \frac{1}{100} & \text{if } t \in [-50, 50] \\ 0 & \text{otherwise} \end{cases} \qquad (1)$$

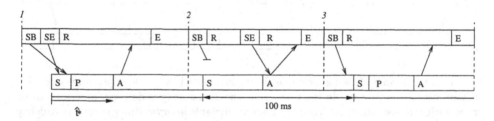

Fig. 6. An example of Internal synchronisation where an internal cycle is initiated upon expiration of an interval timer. The first and third cycles show correct action, although the agent is not fully utilizing the available deliberation time. In the second cycle, the action is scheduled before the **see** stimulus. Therefore, the action decision is based on previous (possibly inconsistent) sensor data.

In order to determine how violation of this fundamental assumption effects action correctness, we consider how likely it is that Definition 1 will hold under these conditions. Taking Table 1 into consideration, the probability of correct action is

$$P(\text{Correct action}) \equiv P((A_{prev} \prec E_{prev} \wedge A \prec E) \wedge (SB \prec P \wedge SE \prec P)) \qquad (2)$$

To proceed, we assume that the communication channel introduces a transmission delay, T_{delay}, that is exponentially distributed with expected delay τ, and independent of time [1].

$$P(T_{delay} = t) \equiv \begin{cases} \frac{1}{\tau} e^{-\frac{t}{\tau}} & \text{if } t \geq 0 \\ 0 & \text{if } t < 0 \end{cases} \qquad (3)$$

---

[2] Unless otherwise specified, this paper describes time in integer milliseconds. Units will be omitted for the remainder of the paper.

If T_{see} is the external cycle time that the see stimulus is provided (or the sense_body stimulus during cycle type 3), then

$$P\left(T_{see} = t\right) \equiv \begin{cases} \frac{2}{3} & \text{if } t = 0 \\ \frac{1}{3} & \text{if } t = 50 \\ 0 & \text{otherwise} \end{cases} \tag{4}$$

Finally, if T_{delib} and T_{sim} are the time required to decide on and to simulate an action respectively (both of which are assumed constant) then the probability of correct action using Internal synchronisation follows directly from Equation 2:

$$P\left(\begin{array}{c} \text{Correct} \\ \text{action} \end{array} \middle| \begin{array}{c} \text{Internal} \\ \text{synchronisation} \end{array}\right) = P\left(\begin{array}{c} \left(\delta - 100 + \hat{t^*} + T_{delay}^{(1)} + T_{sim} \leq 0\right) \\ \wedge \left(\delta + \hat{t^*} + T_{delay}^{(2)} + T_{sim} \leq 100\right) \\ \wedge \left(T_{see} + T_{delay}^{(3)} + T_{delib} \leq \delta + \hat{t^*}\right) \end{array}\right) \tag{5}$$

Equation 5 can be computed analytically, and a partial elevation plot is shown in Fig. 7. It shows that Internal synchronisation is not very sensitive to network variation, but that the probability of correct action is low because δ is unlikely to fall in the desired range.

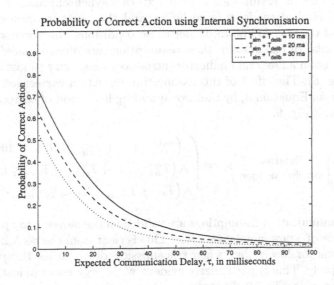

Fig. 7. The probability of correct action using Internal synchronisation.

4.2   Synchronisation Using External Evidence

As demonstrated in Section 4.1, the probability of correct action is directly related to the validity of the internal representation. External synchronisation abandons the internal timer and uses an external indicator to achieve a more favourable δ distribution. Perception of a sense_body stimulus is used as evidence of the SB state and of a new SoccerServer cycle. As shown in Fig. 8, this evidence triggers a new internal cycle and action commands are scheduled after a fixed internal time, $\hat{t}^*$ [3, 10].

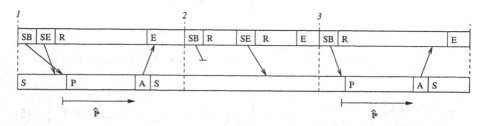

Fig. 8. An example of External synchronisation where action is commanded a fixed time, $\hat{t}^*$, after sense_body perception. In the first cycle, the action command is not received in time and the agent remains idle. In the second cycle, the sense_body message is lost: no internal cycle is initiated, and no action is commanded. The second action (in the third cycle) is correct.

The fundamental assumption behind External synchronisation is that variation in communication delay is negligible and that an appropriate value for the command time, $\hat{t}^*$, is known. Under these conditions, this method produces excellent results. In real systems these assumptions are often violated, however, and reliance upon an external indicator introduces sensitivity to lost stimuli (as shown in Fig. 8). The effect of this assumption on action correctness is shown, continuing from Equation 2, by the corresponding likelihood of correct action in Equation 6 and Fig. 9.

$$
P\left(\begin{array}{c} \text{Correct} \\ \text{action} \end{array}\middle|\begin{array}{c} \text{External} \\ \text{synchronisation} \end{array}\right) = P\left(\begin{array}{c} \left(T^{(1)}_{delay} + \hat{t}^* + T^{(2)}_{delay} + T_{sim} \le 100\right) \\ \wedge \left(T^{(3)}_{delay} + \hat{t}^* + T^{(4)}_{delay} + T_{sim} \le 100\right) \\ \wedge \left(T_{see} + T^{(5)}_{delay} + T_{delib} \le T^{(3)}_{delay} + \hat{t}^*\right) \end{array}\right) \quad (6)
$$

If the communication assumptions are valid then the sense_body percept is a good indicator of a new simulation cycle. This is clear from the peak in probable correct actions for low τ, but when transmission delay varies the probability decreases rapidly. This is particularly evident with large communication delays where, as shown in Fig. 10, External synchronisation can perform worse than the naive Internal synchronisation.

5   Adaptive Synchronisation

The analysis in Section 4 (specificly Fig. 10) motivates a more robust synchronisation algorithm. Ideally, such an algorithm would combine the reliability of

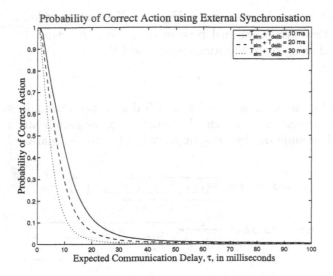

Fig. 9. The probability of correct action using External synchronisation.

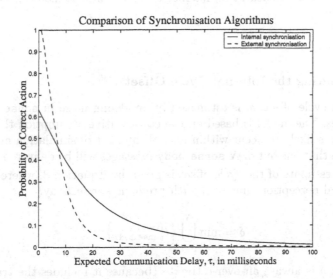

Fig. 10. A comparison of the Internal and External synchronisation algorithms when $T_{sim} + T_{delib} = 10$. As communication delays increase, External synchronisation performance degrades more rapidly. In this case, Internal synchronisation becomes favourable when $\tau \geq 7.3$.

Internal synchronisation with external information to improves the δ distribution.

The proposed *Dynamic Action Index* algorithm uses an interval timer as the internal representation of the simulation cycle, and schedules action commands at the *action index*, I, as shown in Fig. 11. The action index is the agent's estimate of the optimal internal time to command an action, $\widehat{t^* - \delta}$, which is approximated using separate estimates of δ and t^*:

$$I \equiv \hat{t}^* - \hat{\delta} \tag{7}$$

As described in Sections 5.1, 5.2, and Table 3, the Dynamic Action Index algorithm generalises Internal and External synchronisation and relaxes their fundamental assumptions by using improved, adaptive estimates.

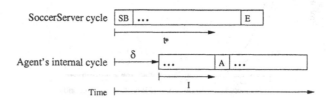

Fig. 11. Synchronisation using a Dynamic Action Index (showing correct estimates), where action is commanded at an internal time, I, which is modified based on its inferred validity.

5.1   Estimating the Internal Cycle Offset

The internal cycle offset, δ, is estimated by modeling noise in `sense_body` perception times. The model is based on the conservative assumption that a quick transmission is likely to occur within a small number of simulation cycles [4, 1]. If we assume that one out of N `sense_body` messages will be delivered promptly, then a good estimate of the cycle offset is given by Equation 8, where $t^{(i)}_{\text{sense\_body}}$ is the internal perception time of the ith previous `sense_body`.

$$\hat{\delta} = \min \bigcup_{i=1}^{N} \left\{ t^{(i-1)}_{\text{sense\_body}} \right\} \tag{8}$$

Although $\hat{\delta}$ is always an over-estimate (because it includes the transit time of the quickest message), the bias can be neglected by considering necessary communication delays while estimating the optimal time to command action, i.e., by assuming known cycle offset.

5.2   Estimating the Optimal Time to Command Action

Because both network delays and processor strain vary over time, so too does the optimal time, t^*, to command action. Therefore, it is beneficial to adapt the estimate of the optimal command time, $\hat{t}^*$, during operation. The validity of the current estimate can be inferred if the agent can confirm how action is being

Table 2. Inferring the validity of the optimal command time estimate assuming known cycle offset.

Action	Cause	Inference
Effected on time	$I \leq t^* - \delta$	$\hat{t}^* \leq t^*$
Effected late	$I > t^* - \delta$	$\hat{t}^* > t^*$
Failed	$(I + \delta) \bmod 100 \simeq 0$	$\hat{t}^* \bmod 100 \simeq 0$

Table 3. The internal cycle offset and optimal command time estimates used in the Internal, External, and Dynamic Action Index synchronisation algorithms.

Algorithm	Estimates	
	Internal cycle offset ($\hat{\delta}$)	Optimal command time ($\hat{t}^*$)
Internal	0	constant (e.g., 70)
External	$t^0_{\text{sense\_body}}$	constant (e.g., 70)
Dynamic Action Index	$\min \bigcup_{i=0}^{N-1} \left\{ t^i_{\text{sense\_body}} \right\}$	inferred and modified online

effected. This inference is summarised in Table 2 and because it operates on the timescale of cycles (where communication delay can be deemed negligible) and does not depend on **sense_body** perception times, reliance upon network responsiveness is minimal.

If the action was effected on time, then the action index was not too large. However, if the estimate is less than optimal then it can be increased (thereby increasing sensing and deliberation) while still commanding action on time. Because the optimal time is not observable, there is little indication of how much to increase the estimate where there is risk of commanding future actions late.

If the action was effected late, then the action index was too large and should be decreased. Because the true amount is unknown, the estimate is decreased by some fixed amount for each late action.

If the action failed, then the command was either lost in transport (which has no implication on synchronisation), or it was ignored by SoccerServer. The latter case occurs often if the estimate is on the simulation cycle boundary (in which case the estimate can be reset to its initial value) or intermittently when a single command is excessively delayed (which does not imply an incorrect estimate).

Each inference case can be adversely affected by periodic communication delays. This side effect can be avoided by assuming that each delay is independent and identically distributed and by requiring successive evidence of any inference.

6   Confirming Commanded Action

The validity of the optimal command time estimate is inferred based on the outcome of commanded action. Each action is classified by assigning it to one of two disjoint sets: P is an ordered set of pending action, and C is a set of confirmed action. Actions initially belong to P and only become members of C if they obey a specific causal relationship between time and the count of effected actions, n_e [3].

Definition 2 (Action age). The *age* of a commanded action is the number of sense_body's perceived while waiting for its confirmation.

Definition 3 (Confirmed action). The ith pending action is *confirmed*, if $n_e \geq \|C\| + i$.

If a pending action of age 1 is confirmed, that action was effected on time. Otherwise, it can be difficult to distinguish between late and failed action. The distinction can be made by imposing a bound, τ_{max}, on communication delays, above which unaccounted messages are assumed lost. The confirmation relationship is made explicit in Table 4.

Table 4. Inferring the outcome of an unambiguous action from the count of effected actions.

Count of effected actions	ith pending action Age	Confirmed outcome
$n_e \geq i$	1	Effected on time
$n_e \geq i$	$[2, 1 + 2\lceil\frac{\tau_{max}}{100}\rceil)$	Effected late
$n_e < i$	$[1 + 2\lceil\frac{\tau_{max}}{100}\rceil, \infty)$	Failed

However, ambiguities arise if a new action is commanded before a previous action has been confirmed, which often occurs while waiting to distinguish between late and failed action. The ith pending action is *ambiguous* if $i < \|P\|$. In such circumstances, all hypotheses are maintained until the ambiguity can be resolved or can be proven to be undecidable[4].

The basis of the disambiguation procedure are the strict rules that govern how an action command is handled by SoccerServer, based on when it is received (see Table 1). In particular, we exploit the fact that an action cannot be effected on time following late action. The procedure is outlined in Table 5.

7   Comparing of Synchronisation Algorithms

Synchronisation algorithms can be compared in a number of ways. Butler *et al.* develop a system for automatically extracting team activity as well as idle and

---

[3] A count of effected actions is included as part of the sense_body stimulus. Any two stimuli can be used to determine the number of actions effected between them.

[4] Ambiguities are only undecidable when a failed action cannot be assigned to a specific pending command. For the purpose of $\hat{t}^*$ estimation, this does not matter because failure is certain, but this does effect model prediction and activity analysis since the agent does not know which action failed.

Table 5. A procedure for disambiguating the set of pending actions, $P = \{p_1, ...\}$ based on the property that late-on time action pairs can not exists in P.

```
if pᵢ effected on time then
    ∀j ≤ i action pⱼ effected on time
else if pᵢ effected late ∨nₑ = ‖C ∪ P‖ then
    ∀j ≥ i action pⱼ effected late
else if pᵢ lost then
    if pᵢ₋₁ effected on time then
        ∀j ≤ i − 1 action pⱼ effected on time
    else if pᵢ₋₁ effected late then
        for each j in 1 up to i − 2 do
            if pⱼ effected late then
                ∀k ≥ j action pₖ effected late
    else if i = ‖P‖ then
        ∀j ≤ i action pⱼ ambiguous, ‖C ∪ P‖ − nₑ of which are lost
```

---

failure ratios from game log files [3]. However, these measures do not encode the notion of action correctness (for example, late and failed actions increase activity). The online procedure described in Section 6 provides information that is more expressive. In fact, the measures used in [3] can be directly calculated using counts of correct, late, and failed actions. The ability is a special feature of the online algorithm, which combines the intended action time with its inferred outcome.

The three synchronisation methods described in this paper were tested in competition against previous RoboCup competitors [15]. All algorithms were implemented using the Dynamic Action Index framework (i.e., action commands were scheduled $\hat{t}^* - \hat{\delta}$ after internal cycle initiation) using the parameters specified in Table 3. The outcome of approximately ten thousand commanded actions was recorded throughout several partial games played using a network that introduced varying transmission delays of approximately 20 ± 15 milliseconds. The fraction of correct action varied with synchronisation algorithm as shown in Fig. 12.

The higher variance observed using Internal synchronisation is significant. It corresponds to the uniform distribution of possible cycle offsets. If the internal cycle happens to be synchronised with the external cycle the agent is able to perform a high fraction of correct action. However, poor synchronisation is just as likely.

External synchronisation was observed to produce fewer correct actions than the other algorithms on average. For External synchronisation, variance from the average is a result of sensitivity to sense_body perception times: small changes in communication delay can cause a large change in the fraction of actions that are correct.

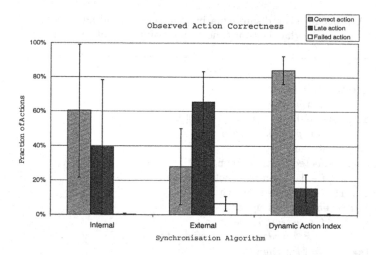

Fig. 12. Experimentally observed distributions of correct, late, and failed action for agents using the Internal, External, and Dynamic Action Index synchronisation algorithms.

The Dynamic Action Index synchronisation algorithm produces the most correct actions on average. Also, the observed variance is low because the δ and t^* estimates continually converge on optimal values making the algorithm robust to varying conditions.

8   Conclusion

This paper introduces the Dynamic Action Index synchronisation algorithm that estimates internal cycle offset and optimal action command times online. We have shown that the Internal and External synchronisation algorithms are each extremal special cases of the new algorithm, providing a satisfying theoretical framework. Moreover, our experimental results show that our new algorithm outperforms the other two approaches under varying network delays. We have shown that combining an internal synchronisation algorithm with estimates derived from the external SoccerServer performs better than either alone. In general, any agent must weight and integrate its internal representation with external evidence for optimal performance. Our results demonstrate how this can be achieved for even the low-level task of synchronisation. Practically, agents using the algorithm can choose the optimal time to act and make good decisions, approaching the rational ideal.

References

1. Jean-Chrysostome Bolot. Characterizing End-to-End Packet Delay and Loss in the Internet. *Journal of High-Speed Networks* **2**(3):305–323, December 1993.

2. Hans-Dieter Burkhard, Joscha Bach, Kay Schrter, Jan Wendler , Michael Gollin, Thomas Meinert, and Gerd Sander. AT Humboldt 2000 (Team Description). In P. Stone, T. Balch, and G. Kraetzschmar, editors, RoboCup 2000: Robot Soccer. World Cup IV (LNAI No. 2019), pages 405–408, Springer-Verlag, Berlin, 2000.

3. Marc Butler, Mikhail Prokopenko, and Thomas Howard. Flexible Synchronisation within RoboCup Environment: a Comparative Analysis. In P. Stone, T. Balch, and G. Kraetzschmar, editors, RoboCup 2000: Robot Soccer. World Cup IV (LNAI No. 2019), pages 119–128, Springer-Verlag, Berlin, 2000.

4. F. Cristian. Probabilistic Clock Synchronization. *Distributed Computing* 3:146–158. 1989.

5. Klaus Dorer. Improved Agents of the magmaFreiburg2000 Team. In P. Stone, T. Balch, and G. Kraetzschmar, editors, RoboCup 2000: Robot Soccer. World Cup IV (LNAI No. 2019), pages 417–420, Springer-Verlag, Berlin, 2000.

6. Orion Hodson, Colin Perkins, and Vicky Hardman. Skew Detection and Compensation for Internet Audio Applications. Proceedings of the IEEE International Conference on Multimedia and Expo, New York, NY, July 2000.

7. Hiroaki Kitano, Minoru Asada, Yasuo Kuniyoshi, Itsuki Noda and Eiichi Osawa. RoboCup: The Robot World Cup Initiative. In W. Lewis Johnson and Barbara Hayes-Roth, editors, Proceedings of the First International Conference on Autonomous Agents (Agents'97), pages 340–347. ACM Press, New York, 1997.

8. J. L. Lamport. Time, Clocks and the Ordering of Events in a Distributed System. *Communications of the ACM* **21**(7):558–565, 1978.

9. Alan K. Mackworth. On Seeing Robots. In A. Basu and X. Li, editors, Computer Vision: Systems, Theory, and Applications, pages 1–13, World Scientific Press, Singapore, 1993.

10. Birgit Schappel and Frank Schulz. Mainz Rolling Brains 2000. In P. Stone, T. Balch, and G. Kraetzschmar, editors, RoboCup 2000: Robot Soccer. World Cup IV (LNAI No. 2019), pages 497–500, Springer-Verlag, Berlin, 2000.

11. Itsuki Noda. Soccer Server: a Simulator for RoboCup. JSAI AI-Symposium 95: Special Session on RoboCup, Dec. 1995

12. Rafail Ostrovsky and Boaz Patt-Shamir. Optimal and Efficient Clock Synchronization Under Drifting Clocks. In Proceedings of ACM Symposium on PODC '99. Atlanta, GA, 1999.

13. Peter Stone, Manuela Veloso, and Patrick Riley. The CMUnited-98 Champion Simulator Team. (extended version) In M. Asada and H. Kitano, editors, RoboCup-98: Robot Soccer World Cup II (LNAI No. 2019), Springer-Verlag, Berlin, 2000.

14. Shahriar Pourazin. Pardis. In Manuela M. Veloso, Enrico Pagello and Hiroaki Kitano, editors, RoboCup-99: Robot Soccer World Cup III. (LNCS No. 1856), pages 614–617, Springer-Verlag, Berlin, 2000.

15. The RoboCup Simulator Team Repository, http://medialab.di.unipi.it/Project/Robocup/pub/, January 31, 2002.

Team Formation for Reformation
in Multiagent Domains Like RoboCupRescue

Ranjit Nair[1], Milind Tambe[1,2], and Stacy Marsella[2]

[1] Computer Science Department, University of Southern California
Los Angeles CA 90089, USA
{nair,tambe}@usc.edu
[2] University of Southern California's Information Sciences Institute
Marina del Rey, CA 90292, USA
marsella@isi.edu

Abstract. Team formation, i.e., allocating agents to roles within a team or subteams of a team, and the reorganization of a team upon team member failure or arrival of new tasks are critical aspects of teamwork. They are very important issues in RoboCupRescue where many tasks need to be done jointly. While empirical comparisons (e.g., in a competition setting as in RoboCup) are useful, we need a quantitative analysis beyond the competition — to understand the strengths and limitations of different approaches, and their tradeoffs as we scale up the domain or change domain properties. To this end, we need to provide complexity-optimality tradeoffs, which have been lacking not only in RoboCup but in the multiagent field in general.

To alleviate these difficulties, this paper presents *R-COM-MTDP*, a formal model based on decentralized communicating POMDPs, where agents explicitly take on and change roles to (re)form teams. R-COM-MTDP significantly extends an earlier COM-MTDP model, by introducing roles and local states to better model domains like RoboCupRescue where agents can take on different roles and each agent has a local state consisting of the objects in its vicinity. R-COM-MTDP tells us where the problem is highly intractable (NEXP-complete) and where it can be tractable (P-complete), and thus understand where algorithms may need to tradeoff optimality and where they could strive for near optimal behaviors. R-COM-MTDP model could enable comparison of various team formation and reformation strategies — including the strategies used by our own teams that came in the top three in 2001 — in the RoboCup Rescue domain and beyond.

1 Introduction

The utility of the multi-agent team approach for coordination of distributed agents has been demonstrated in a number of large-scale systems for sensing and acting like disaster rescue simulation domains, such as RoboCupRescue Simulation Domain [5, 10] and sensor networks for real-time tracking of moving targets [7]. These domains contain tasks that can be performed only by collaborative

G.A. Kaminka, P.U. Lima, and R. Rojas (Eds.): RoboCup 2002, LNAI 2752, pp. 150–161, 2003.

actions of the agents. Incomplete or incorrect knowledge owing to constrained sensing and uncertainty of the environment further motivate the need for these agents to explicitly work in teams. A key precursor to teamwork is team formation, the problem of how best to organize the agents into collaborating teams that perform the tasks that arise. For instance, in RoboCupRescue, injured civilians in a burning building may require teaming of two ambulances and three nearby fire-brigades to extinguish the fire and quickly rescue the civilians. If there are several such fires and injured civilians, the teams must be carefully formed to optimize performance.

Our work in team formation focuses on dynamic, multiagent environments, such as RoboCupRescue Simulation Domain [5, 10] and sensor networks [7]. In such domains teams must be formed rapidly so tasks are performed within given deadlines, and teams must be reformed in response to the dynamic appearance or disappearance of tasks. The problems with the current team formation work for such dynamic real-time domains are two-fold. First, most team formation algorithms [12, 4, 2, 3, 7] are static. In order to adapt to the changing environment the static algorithm would have to be run repeatedly.

Second, much of the work in RoboCupRescue has largely relied on experimental work and the competitions have been very useful in comparing various algorithms. A complementary technique is theoretical analysis. However, there has been a lack of theoretical analysis of algorithms, such as their worst-case complexity. This is especially important in understanding how algorithms work if domain parameters change, how they will scale up, etc.

In this paper we take initial steps to attack both these problems. As the tasks change and members of the team fail, the current team needs to evolve to handle the changes. In RoboCupRescue [5, 10], each re-organization of the team requires time (e.g., fire-brigades may need to drive to a new location) and is hence expensive because of the need for quick response. Clearly, the current configuration of agents is relevant to how quickly and well they can be re-organized in the future. Each re-organization of the teams should be such that the resulting team is effective at performing the existing tasks but also flexible enough to adapt to new scenarios quickly. We refer to this reorganization of the team as "Team Formation for Reformation". In order to solve the "Team Formation for Reformation" problem, we present *R-COM-MTDPs* (**R**oles and **Com**munication in a **M**arkov **T**eam **D**ecision **P**rocess), a formal model based on communicating decentralized POMDPs, to address the above shortcomings. R-COM-MTDP significantly extends an earlier model called COM-MTDP [9], by making important additions of roles and agents' local states, to more closely model current complex multiagent teams. Thus, R-COM-MTDP provides decentralized optimal policies to take up and change roles in a team (planning ahead to minimize reorganization costs), and to execute such roles.

We use the disaster rescue domain to motivate the "Team Formation for Reformation" problem. We present real world scenarios where such an approach would be useful and use the RoboCup Rescue Simulation Environment [5, 10] to explain the working of our model. We show that the generation of optimal policies in R-COM-MTDPs is NEXP-complete although different communication and observability conditions significantly reduce such complexity. The nature of observability and communication in the RoboCupRescue domain makes it computationally intractable thus motivating the study of optimality-complexity tradeoffs in approximation algorithms are necessary. R-COM-MTDPs provide a general tool for analysis of role-taking and role-executing policies in multiagent teams and for comparison of various approximate approaches. This will allow us to model the agents we developed for this domain [8] (which finished third at RoboCup 2001 and second at Robofesta, 2001) as an R-COM-MTDP and determine how changes in the agents' behavior could result in an improved performance. It is important that we develop tools in RoboCup that are relevant beyond RoboCup and contribute to the wider community. This work is aimed at meeting that objective.

2   Domain and Motivation

The RoboCupRescue Simulation Domain [5, 10], provides an environment where large-scale earthquakes can be simulated and heterogeneous agents can collaborate in the task of disaster mitigation. Currently, the environment is a simulation of an earthquake in the Nagata ward in Kobe, Japan. As a result of the quake many buildings collapse, civilians get trapped, roads get damaged and gas leaks cause fires which spread to neighboring buildings. There are different kinds of agents that participate in the task of disaster mitigation viz. fire brigades, ambulances, police forces, fire stations, ambulance centers and police stations. In addition to having a large number of heterogeneous agents, the state of the environment is rapidly changing – buried civilians die, fires spread to neighboring buildings, buildings get burnt down, rescue agents run out of stamina, etc. There is uncertainty in the system on account of incorrect information or information not reaching agents.

In such a hostile, uncertain and dynamically changing environment teams need to continually form and reform. We wish to understand the properties of such team formation and reformation algorithms. For instance, as new fires start up or fire engines get trapped under buried collapsing buildings, teams once formed may need to reform. While current algorithms in RoboCup Rescue for such reformation (and outside) react to such circumstances based solely on current information, in general, such reactive techniques may not perform well. In fact, methods that plan ahead taking future tasks and failures into account may be needed to minimize reformation, given that reformations take time. While we can perform useful empirical comparisons of current algorithms within the current competition settings,the field needs to analyze the performance of such algorithms for a wide variety of settings of agent failure rates, new task arrival rate, reformation costs, domain scale-up, and other factors. Theoretical analysis can aid in such analysis, providing us techniques to understand general properties of the algorithms proposed.

We focus in particular on a technique called "Team Formation for Reformation", i.e.., teams formed with lookahead to minimize costs of reformation.

The following real-world scenarios illustrate the need for such team formation for reformation.

1. A factory B catches fire at night. Since it is known that the factory is empty no casualties are likely. Without looking ahead at the possible outcomes of this fire, one would not give too much importance to this fire and might assign just one or two fire brigades to it. However, if by looking ahead, there is a high probability that the fire would spread to a nearby hospital, then more fire brigades and ambulances could be assigned to the factory and the surrounding area to reduce the response time. Moving fire brigades and ambulances to this area might leave other areas where new tasks could arise empty. Thus, other ambulances and fire brigades could be moved to strategic locations within these areas.
2. There are two neighborhoods, one with small wooden houses close together and the other with houses of more fire resistant material. Both these neighborhoods have a fire in each of them with the fire in the wooden neighborhood being smaller at this time. Without looking ahead to how these fires might spread, more fire brigades may be assigned to the larger fire. But the fire in the wooden neighborhood might soon get larger and may require more fire brigades. Since we are strapped for resources, the response time to get more fire brigades from the first neighborhood to the second would be long and possibly critical.
3. There is an unexplored region of the world from which no reports of any incident have come in. This could be because nothing untoward has happened in that region or more likely, considering that a major earthquake has just taken place, that there has been a communication breakdown in that area. By considering both possibilities, it might be best if police agents take on the role of exploration to discover new tasks and ambulances and fire brigades ready themselves to perform the new tasks that may be discovered.

Each of these scenarios demonstrate that looking ahead at what events may arise in the future is critical to knowing what teams will need to be formed. The time to form these future teams from the current teams could be greatly reduced if the current teams were formed keeping this future reformation in mind.

3   From COM-MTDP to R-COM-MTDP

The COM-MTDP model[9] has two main advantages. First, COM-MTDP provides complexity analysis of team coordination given different communication assumptions. Even though it does not focus on team formation or reformation (which are topics of this paper), it serves as a basis for developing a new computational framework called R-COM-MTDP that provides such an analysis. Second, COM-MTDP was used to analyze different general team coordination algorithms based on the joint intentions theory, including the STEAM algorithm, part of the ISIS teams that participated in RoboCup soccer [11]. COM-MTDP analysis revealed the types of domains where the team coordination behaved optimally, and specific domains where the algorithm communicated too much or too little — and the complexity of optimal communication strategies. Such analysis may in turn provide guidance in developing a new generation of team coordination algorithms which can intelligently engage in optimality-complexity tradeoffs. We attempt to do something similar with R-COM-MTDP.

3.1   COM-MTDP

Given a team of selfless agents, α, a COM-MTDP [9] is a tuple, $\langle S, A_\alpha, \Sigma_\alpha, P, \Omega_\alpha, O_\alpha, B_\alpha, R \rangle$. S is a set of world states. $A_\alpha = \prod_{i \in \alpha} A_i$ is a set of combined domain-level actions, where A_i is the set of actions available to agent i. $\Sigma_\alpha = \prod_{i \in \alpha} \Sigma_i$ is a set of combined communicative actions, where Σ_i is the set of messages that agent i can broadcast to the other team members. The effects of domain-level actions obey the specified transition probability function, $P(s_b, \mathbf{a}, s_e) = Pr(S^{t+1} = s_e | S^t = s_b, A_\alpha^t = \mathbf{a})$.

$\Omega_\alpha = \prod_{i \in \alpha} \Omega_i$ is a set of combined observations, where Ω_i is the set of observations that agent i may receive. The observation function (or *information structure*), O_α, specifies a probability distribution over the joint observations that the agents may make, conditioned on the current state and combined actions of the agents: $O_\alpha(s, \mathbf{a}, \omega) = Pr(\Omega_\alpha^t = \omega | S^t = s, A_\alpha^{t-1} = \mathbf{a})$. We can define classes of information structures as in [9]:

Collective Partial Observability: We make no assumptions about the observability of the world state.

Collective Observability: There is a unique world state for the combined observations of the team: $\forall \omega \in \Omega, \exists s \in S$ such that $\forall s' \neq s, \Pr(\Omega^t = \omega | S^t = s') = 0$.

Individual Observability: Each individual's observation uniquely determines the world state: $\forall \omega \in \Omega_i, \exists s \in S$ such that $\forall s' \neq s, \Pr(\Omega_i^t = \omega | S^t = s') = 0$.

In domains that are not individually observable, agent i chooses its actions and communication based on its belief state, $b_i^t \in B_i$, based on the observations and communication it has received through time t. $B_\alpha = \prod_{i \in \alpha} B_i$ is the set of possible combined belief states. Agent i updates its belief state at time t when it receives its observation, $\omega_i^t \in \Omega_i$, and when it receives communication from its teammates, Σ_α^t. We use separate state-estimator functions to update the belief states in each case: initial belief state, $b_i^0 = SE_i^0()$; pre-communication belief state, $b_{i\Sigma_\bullet}^t = SE_{i\bullet\Sigma}(b_{i\Sigma_\bullet}^{t-1}, \omega_i^t)$; and post-communication belief state, $b_{i\Sigma_\bullet}^t = SE_{i\Sigma_\bullet}(b_{i\bullet\Sigma}^t, \Sigma_\alpha^t)$.

Finally, the COM-MTDP reward function represents the team's joint utility (shared by all members) over states, as well as both domain and communicative actions, $R : S \times \Sigma_\alpha \times A_\alpha \rightarrow \mathbb{R}$. We can express this overall reward as the sum of two rewards: a domain-action-level reward, $R_A : S \times A_\alpha \rightarrow \mathbb{R}$, and a communication-level reward, $R_\Sigma : S \times \Sigma_\alpha \rightarrow \mathbb{R}$. We can classify COM-MTDP (and likewise R-COM-MTDP) domains according to the allowed communication and its reward:

General Communication: no assumptions on Σ_α nor R_Σ.
No Communication: $\Sigma_\alpha = \emptyset$.
Free Communication: $\forall \sigma \in \Sigma_\alpha, R_\Sigma(\sigma) = 0$.

Analyzing the extreme cases, like free communication (and others in this paper) helps to understand the computational impact of the extremes. In addition, we can approximate some real-world domains with such assumptions.

3.2 R-COM-MTDP Extensions to COM-MTDP Model

We define a R-COM-MTDP as an extended tuple, $\langle S, A_\alpha, \Sigma_\alpha, P, \Omega_\alpha, O_\alpha, B_\alpha, R, \mathcal{PL} \rangle$. The key extension over the COM-MTDP is the addition of subplans, $\mathcal{PL}$, and the individual roles associated with those plans.

Extension for Explicit Sub-plans. $\mathcal{PL}$ is a set of all possible sub-plans that α can perform. We express a sub-plan $p_k \in \mathcal{PL}$ as a tuple of roles $\langle r_1, \ldots, r_s \rangle$. r_{jk} represents a *role instance* of role r_j for a plan p_k and requires some agent $i \in \alpha$ to fulfill it. Roles enable better modeling of real systems, where each agent's role restricts its domain-level actions [13]. Agents' domain-level actions are now distinguished between two types:

Role-Taking actions: $\Upsilon_\alpha = \prod_{i \in \alpha} \Upsilon_i$ is a set of combined role taking actions, where $\Upsilon_i = \{\upsilon_{ir_{jk}}\}$ contains the role-taking actions for agent i. $\upsilon_{ir_{jk}} \in \Upsilon_i$ means that agent i takes on the role r_j as part of plan p_k. An agent's role can be uniquely determined from its belief state.

Role-Execution Actions: $\Phi_{ir_{jk}}$ is the set of agent i's actions for executing role r_j for plan p_k [13]. $\Phi_i = \bigcup_{\forall r_{jk}} \Phi_{ir_{jk}}$. This defines the set of combined execution actions $\Phi_\alpha = \prod_{i \in \alpha} \Phi_i$.

The distinction between role-taking and role-execution actions ($A_\alpha = \Upsilon_\alpha \cup \Phi_\alpha$) enables us to separate their costs. Within this model, we can represent the specialized behaviors associated with each role, and also any possible differences among the agents' capabilities for these roles. While filling a particular role, r_{jk}, agent i can perform only those role-execution actions, $\phi \in \Phi_{ir_{jk}}$, which may not contain all of its available actions in Φ_i. Another agent ℓ may have a different set of available actions, $\Phi_{\ell r_{jk}}$, allowing us to model the different methods by which agents i and ℓ may fill role r_{jk}. These different methods can produce varied effects on the world state (as modeled by the transition probabilities, P) and the team's utility (as modeled by the reward function, R_Φ). Thus, the policies must ensure that agents for each role have the capabilities that benefit the team the most.

In R-COM-MTDPs (as in COM-MTDPs), each decision epoch consists of two stages, a communication stage and an action stage. In each successive epoch, the agents alternate between role-taking and role-execution epochs. Thus, the agents are in the role-taking epoch if the time index is divisible by 2, and are in the role execution epoch otherwise. Although, this sequencing of role-taking and role-execution epochs restricts different agents from running role-taking and role-execution actions in the same epoch, it is conceptually simple and synchronization is automatically enforced. As with COM-MTDP, the total reward is a sum of communication and action rewards, but the action reward is further separated into role-taking action vs. role-execution action: $R_A(s, \mathbf{a}) = R_T(s, \mathbf{a}) + R_\Phi(s, \mathbf{a})$. By definition, $R_T(s, \phi) = 0$ for all $\phi \in \Phi_\alpha$, and $R_\Phi(s, v) = 0$ for all $v \in T_\alpha$. We view the role taking reward as the cost (negative reward) for taking up different roles in different teams. Such costs may represent preparation or training or traveling time for new members, e.g., if a sensor agent changes its role to join a new sub-team tracking a new target, there is a few seconds delay in tracking. However, change of roles may potentially provide significant future rewards.

We can define a role-taking policy, $\pi_{iT} : B_i \to T_i$ for each agent's role-taking action, a role-execution policy, $\pi_{i\Phi} : B_i \to \Phi_i$ for each agent's role-execution action, and a communication policy $\pi_{i\Sigma} : B_i \to \Sigma_i$ for each agent's communication action. The goal is to come up with joint policies π_T, π_Φ and π_Σ that will maximize the total reward.

Extension for Explicit Local States: S_i. In considering distinct roles within a team, it is useful to consider distinct subspaces of S relevant for each individual agent. If we consider the world state to be made up of orthogonal features (i.e., $S = \Xi_1 \times \Xi_2 \times \cdots \times \Xi_n$), then we can identify the subset of features that agent i may observe. We denote this subset as its *local state*, $S_i = \Xi_{k_{i1}} \times \Xi_{k_{i2}} \times \cdots \times \Xi_{k_{im_i}}$. By definition, the observation that agent i receives is independent of any features not covered by S_i: $\Pr(\Omega_i^t = \omega | S^t = \langle \xi_1, \xi_2, \ldots, \xi_n \rangle, A_\alpha^{t-1} = \mathbf{a}) = \Pr(\Omega_i^t = \omega | S_i^t = \langle \xi_{k_{i1}}, \ldots, \xi_{k_{im_i}} \rangle, A_\alpha^{t-1} = \mathbf{a})$.

4   Applying R-COM-MTDP in RoboCupRescue

The notation described above can be applied easily to the RoboCup Rescue domain as follows:

1. α consists of three types of agents: ambulances, police forces, fire brigades.
2. Injured civilians, buildings on fire and blocked roads can be grouped together to form tasks. The designer can choose how to form tasks, e.g. the world could be broken into fixed regions and all fires, hurt civilians and blocked roads within a region comprise a task. We specify sub-plans for each task type. These plans consist of roles that can be fulfilled by agents whose capabilities match those of the role.
3. We specify sub-plans, $\mathcal{PL}$, for each task type. Each sub-plan, $p \in \mathcal{PL}$ comprises of a number of roles that need to be fulfilled by agents whose capabilities match those of the role in order to accomplish a task. For example, the task of rescuing a civilian from a burning building can be accomplished by a plan where fire-brigades first extinguish the fire, then ambulances free the buried civilian and one ambulance takes the civilian to a hospital. Each task can have multiple plans which represent multiple ways of achieving the task.

4. Each agent receives observations about the objects within its visible range. But there may be parts of the world that are not observable because there are no agents there. Thus, RoboCupRescue is a *collectively partially observable domain*. Therefore each agent, needs to maintain a belief state of what it believes the true world state is.
5. The reward function, R can be chosen to consider the capabilities of the agents to perform particular roles, e.g., police agents may be more adept at performing the "search" role than ambulances and fire-brigades. This would be reflected in a higher value for choosing a police agent to take on the "search" role than an ambulance or a fire-brigade. In addition, the reward function takes into consideration the number of civilians rescued, the number of fires put out and the health of agents.

The R-COM-MTDP model works as follows: Initially, the global world state is S^0, where each agent $i \in \alpha$ has local state S_i^0 and belief state $b_i^0 = SE_i^0()$ and no role. Each agent i receives an observation, ω_i^0, according to probability distribution $O_\alpha(S^0, null, \omega^0)$ (there are no actions yet) and updates its belief state, $b_{i\bullet\Sigma}^0 = SE_{i\bullet\Sigma}(b_i^0, \omega_i^0)$ to incorporate this new evidence. In RoboCupRescue, each agent receives the complete world state before the earthquake as its first observation. Each agent then decides on what to broadcast based on its communication policy, $\pi_{i\Sigma}$, and updates its belief state according to $b_{i\Sigma\bullet}^0 = SE_{i\Sigma\bullet}(b_{i\bullet\Sigma}^0, \Sigma_\alpha^0)$. Each agent, based on its belief state then executes the role-taking action according to its role-taking policy, $\pi_{i\Upsilon}$. Thus, some police agents may decide on performing the "search role", while others may decide to "clear roads", fire-brigades decide on which fires "to put out". By the central assumption of teamwork, all of the agents receive the same joint reward, $R^0 = R(S^0, \Sigma_\alpha^0, A_\alpha^0)$. The world then moves into a new state, S^1, according to the distribution, $P(S^0, A_\alpha^0)$. Each agent then receives the next observation about its new local state based on its position and its visual range and updates its belief state using $b_{i\bullet\Sigma}^1 = SE_{i\bullet\Sigma}(b_{i\Sigma\bullet}^0, \omega_i^1)$. This is followed by another communication action resulting in the belief state, $b_{i\Sigma\bullet}^1 = SE_{i\Sigma\bullet}(b_{i\bullet\Sigma}^1, \Sigma_\alpha^1)$. The agent then decides on a role-execution action based on its policy $\pi_{i\Phi}$. It then receives new observations about its local state and the cycle of observation, communication, role-taking action, observation, communication and role-execution action continues.

5   Complexity of R-COM-MTDPs

R-COM-MTDP supports a range of complexity analysis for generating optimal policies under different communication and observability conditions.

Theorem 1. *We can reduce a COM-MTDP to an equivalent R-COM-MTDP.*

Proof. Given a COM-MTDP, $\langle S, A_\alpha, \Sigma_\alpha, P, \Omega_\alpha, O_\alpha, B_\alpha, R \rangle$, we can generate an equivalent R-COM-MTDP, $\langle S, A'_\alpha, \Sigma_\alpha, P', \Omega_\alpha, O_\alpha, B_\alpha, R' \rangle$. Within the R-COM-MTDP actions, A'_α, we define $\Upsilon_\alpha = \{null\}$ and $\Phi_\alpha = A_\alpha$. In other words, all of the original COM-MTDP actions become role-execution actions in the R-COM-MTDP, where we add a single role-taking action that has no effect (i.e.,

$P'(s, null, s) = 1$). The new reward function borrows the same role-execution and communication-level components: $R'_{\Phi}(s, \mathbf{a}) = R_A(s, \mathbf{a})$ and $R'_{\Sigma}(s, \sigma)$. We also add the new role-taking component: $R'_{\Upsilon}(s, null) = 0$. Thus, the only role-taking policy possible for this R-COM-MTDP is $\pi'_{i\Upsilon}(b) = null$, and any role-execution and communication policies (π'_{Φ} and π'_{Σ}, respectively) will have an identical expected reward as the identical domain-level and communication policies (π_A and π_{Σ}, respectively) in the original COM-MTDP. $\square$

Theorem 2. *We can reduce a R-COM-MTDP to an equivalent COM-MTDP[1].*

Proof. Given a R-COM-MTDP, $\langle S, A_{\alpha}, \Sigma_{\alpha}, P, \Omega_{\alpha}, O_{\alpha}, B_{\alpha}, R, \mathcal{PL}\rangle$, we can generate an equivalent COM-MTDP, $\langle S', A_{\alpha}, \Sigma_{\alpha}, P', \Omega_{\alpha}, O_{\alpha}, B_{\alpha}, R'\rangle$. The COM-MTDP state space, S', includes all of the features, Ξ_i, in the original R-COM-MTDP state space, $S = \Xi_1 \times \cdots \times \Xi_n$, as well as an additional feature, $\Xi_{\text{phase}} = \{\text{taking}, \text{executing}\}$. This new feature indicates whether the current state corresponds to a role-taking or -executing stage of the R-COM-MTDP. The new transition probability function, P', augments the original function with an alternating behavior for this new feature: $P'(\langle \xi_{1b}, \ldots, \xi_{nb}, \text{taking}\rangle, v, \langle \xi_{1e}, \ldots, \xi_{ne}, \text{executing}\rangle) = P(\langle \xi_{1b}, \ldots, \xi_{nb}\rangle, v, \langle \xi_{1e}, \ldots, \xi_{ne}\rangle)$ and $P'(\langle \xi_{1b}, \ldots, \xi_{nb}, \text{executing}\rangle, \phi, \langle \xi_{1e}, \ldots, \xi_{ne}, \text{taking}\rangle) = P(\langle \xi_{1b}, \ldots, \xi_{nb}\rangle, \phi, \langle \xi_{1e}, \ldots, \xi_{ne}\rangle)$. Within the COM-MTDP, we restrict the actions that agents can take in each stage by assigning illegal actions an excessively negative reward (denoted $-r_{max}$): $\forall v \in \Upsilon_{\alpha}$, $R'_A(\langle \xi_{1b}, \ldots, \xi_{nb}, \text{executing}\rangle, v) = -r_{max}$ and $\forall \phi \in \Phi_{\alpha}$, $R'_A(\langle \xi_{1b}, \ldots, \xi_{nb}, \text{taking}\rangle, \phi) = -r_{max}$. Thus, for a COM-MTDP domain-level policy, π'_A, we can extract role-taking and -executing policies, π_{Υ} and π_{Φ}, respectively, that generate identical behavior in the R-COM-MTDP when used in conjunction with identical communication-level policies, $\pi_{\Sigma} = \pi'_{\Sigma}$. $\square$

Thus, the problem of finding optimal policies for R-COM-MTDPs has the same complexity as the problem of finding optimal policies for COM-MTDPs. Table 1 shows the computational complexity results for various classes of R-COM-MTDP domains, where the results for individual, collective, and collective partial observability follow from COM-MTDPs [9] (Proof of COM-MTDP results are available at *http://www.isi.edu/teamcore/COM-MTDP/*). In the individual observability and collective observability under free communication cases, each agent knows exactly what the global state is. The P-Complete result is from a reduction from and to MDPs. The collectively partial observable case with free communication can be treated as a single agent POMDP, where the actions correspond to the joint actions of the R-COM-MTDP. The reduction from and to a single agent POMDP gives the PSPACE-Complete result. In the general case, by a reduction from and to decentralized POMDPs, the worst-case computational complexity of finding the optimal policy is NEXP-Complete.

Table 1 shows us that the task of finding the optimal policy is extremely hard, in general. However, reducing the cost of communication so it can be treated as if it were free has a potentially big payoff in complexity reduction. As can be

---

[1] The proof of this theorem was contributed by Dr. David Pynadath

Table 1. Computational complexity of R-COM-MTDPs.

	Ind. Obs.	Coll. Obs.	Coll. Part. Obs.
No Comm.	P-Comp.	NEXP-Comp.	NEXP-Comp.
Gen. Comm.	P-Comp.	NEXP-Comp.	NEXP-Comp.
Free Comm.	P-Comp.	P-Comp.	PSPACE-Comp.

seen from table 1, when communication changes from no communication to free communication, in collectively partially observable domains, the computational complexity changes from NEXP-Complete to PSPACE-Complete. In collectively observable domains, like the sensor domain, the computational savings are even greater, from NEXP-Complete to P-Complete. This emphasizes the importance of communication in reducing the worst case complexity. Table 1 suggests that if we were designers of a domain, we would increase the observability of the domain so as to reduce the computational complexity. However, in using existing domains, we don't have this freedom. The following section describes how R-COM-MTDPs could be useful in combating the computational complexity of "Team Formation for Reformation" in RoboCupRescue.

6   Analysis of RoboCupRescue

In RoboCupRescue, agents receive visual information of only the region in its surroundings. Thus no agent has complete knowledge of the global state of the world. Therefore the RoboCupRescue domain is in general *Collectively Partially Observable*. The number of communication messages that each agent can send or receive is restricted and in addition, communication takes up network bandwidth and so we cannot assume a communication policy where the agents communicate everything they see. Hence, RoboCupRescue comes under the *General Communication* case. Thus, the computational complexity of finding the optimal communication, role-taking and role-execution policies in RoboCupRescue is NEXP-Complete (see Table 1).

However the observability conditions are in our control— because we can devise agents that can try to provide collective observability. Thus what our results provide is guidance on "How to Design Teams" in Rescue, and what types of tradeoffs may be necessary based on the types of teams. What our results show is stunning – if we do collective observability and free communication then the complexity of our planning drops substantially. Now, as we know, this is not going to be possible — we can only approximate collective obesrvability and free communication. However, we could then treat our result as an approximation – the resulting policy would be near-optimal but may be not optimal.

But, one of the biggest problems with developing agents for RoboCupRescue is not being able to compare different strategies easily. Owing to external factors like the packet loss and non-determinism internal to the simulation, a large number of simulations would be necessary to determine for certain if one strategy dominates another. However, just as in COM-MTDPs[9], where different approximate strategies for communication were analysed, RoboCupRescue can be modeled as an R-COM-MTDP. We could then treat alternative strategies as alternative policies and evaluate these. This would be very useful in making improvements to existing agents as well. For example, we could evaluate the policies specified by our agents[8], and evaluate their performance in the RoboCupRescue R-COM-MTDP. This would allow us to make changes to this policy and determine relatively quickly if this change resulted in an improvement. Such kind of incremental improvements could greatly improve the performance of our agents which finished in third place in RoboCup 2001 at Seattle and in second place in Robofesta 2001.

7   Summary and Related Work

This work addresses two shortcomings of the current work in team formation for dynamic multiagent domains: i) most algorithms are static in the sense that they don't anticipate for changes that will be required in the configuration of the teams, ii) complexity analysis of the problem is lacking. We addressed the first shortcoming by presenting *R-COM-MTDP*, a formal model based on decentralized communicating POMDPs, to determine the team configuration that takes into account how the team will have to be restructured in the future. *R-COM-MTDP* enables a rigorous analysis of complexity-optimality tradeoffs in team formation and reorganization approaches. The second shortcoming was addressed by presenting an analysis of the worst-case computational complexity of team formation and reformation under various types of communication.

While there are related multiagent models based on MDPs, they have focused on coordination after team formation on a subset of domain types we consider, and they do *not* address team formation and reformation. For instance, the *decentralized partially observable Markov decision process* (DEC-POMDP) [1] model focuses on generating decentralized policies in *collectively partially observable* domains with *no communication*; while the Xuan-Lesser model [14] focuses only on a subset of collectively observable environments.

Modi *et al.[7]* provide an initial complexity analysis of distributed sensor team formation, their analysis is limited to static environments (no reorganizations) — in fact, illustrating the need for R-COM-MTDP type analysis tools. Our complexity analysis illustrate where the problem is tractable and where it is not. Thus, telling us where algorithms could strive for optimality and where they should not. We intend to use the *R-COM-MTDP* model to compare the various team formation approaches for RoboCupRescue which were used by our agents in RoboCup-2001 and Robofesta 2001, where our agents finished in third place and second place respectively. It is important that tools be developed in RoboCup that step beyond RoboCup and contribute to the wider community. This work is a step in that direction.

Acknowledgments

We would like to thank David Pynadath for his discussions on extending the COM-MTDP model to R-COM-MTDP and Takayuki Ito for his invaluable contribution to the development of our Rescue agents, and the Intel Corporation for their generous gift that made this research possible.

References

1. Bernstein, D. S., Zilberstein, S., Immerman, N.: The Complexity of Decentralized Control of MDPs. Proceedings of the Sixteenth Conference on Uncertainty in Artificial Intelligence (2000)
2. Fatima, S. S., Wooldridge, M.: Adaptive Task and Resource Allocation in Multiagent Systems. Proceedings of the Fifth International Conference on Autonomous Agents (2001)
3. Horling, B., Benyo, B., Lesser, V.: Using Self-Diagnosis to Adapt Organizational Structures. Proceedings of the Fifth International Conference on Autonomous Agents (2001)
4. Hunsberger, L., Grosz, B.: A Combinatorial Auction for Collaborative Planning. Proceedings of the Fourth International Conference on Multiagent Systems (2000)
5. Kitano, H., Tadokoro, S., Noda, I., Matsubara, H., Takahashi, T., Shinjoh, A., Shimada, S.: RoboCupRescue: Search and Rescue for Large Scale Disasters as a Domain for Multi-agent Research. Proceedings of IEEE International Conference on Systems, Man and Cybernetics (1999)
6. Marsella, S., Adibi, J., Alonaizon, Y., Kaminka, G., Muslea, I., Tambe, M.: On being a teammate: Experiences acquired in the design of robocup teams. Proceedings of the Third International Conference on Autonomous Agents(1999)
7. Modi, P. J., Jung, H., Tambe, M., Shen, W.-M., Kulkarni, S.: A Dynamic Distributed Constraint Satisfaction Approach to Resource Allocation. Proceedings of Seventh International Conference on Principles and Practice of Constraint Programming (2001)
8. Nair,R., Ito, T., Tambe, M., Marsella, S.: Task Allocation in the Rescue Simulation Domain. RoboCup-2001: The Fifth Robot World Cup Games and Conferences, *Eds. Coradeschi, S., Tadokoro, S., Andreas Birk*, Springer-Verlag (2001)
9. Pynadath, D., Tambe, M.: Multiagent Teamwork: Analyzing the Optimality Complexity of Key Theories and Models. Proceedings of First International Joint Conference on Autonomous Agents and Multi-Agent Systems (2002)
10. Tadokoro, S., Kitano, H., Tomoichi, T., Noda, I., Matsubara, H., Shinjoh, A., Koto, T., Takeuchi, I., Takahashi, H., Matsuno, F., Hatayama, M., Nobe, J., Shimada, S.: The RoboCup-Rescue: An International Cooperative Research Project of Robotics and AI for the Disaster Mitigation Problem. Proceedings of SPIE 14th Annual International Symposium on Aerospace/Defense Sensing, Simulation, and Controls (AeroSense), Conference on Unmanned Ground Vehicle Technology II (2000)
11. Tambe, M.: Towards Flexible Teamwork. Journal of Artificial Intelligence Research, 7, 83-124 (1997)
12. Tidhar, G., Rao, A. S., Sonenberg, E.: Guided Team Selection. Proceedings of the Second International Conference on Multi-Agent Systems (1996)
13. Wooldridge, M., Jennings, N., Kinny, D.: A Methodology for Agent Oriented Analysis and Design. Proceedings of the Third International Conference on Autonomous Agents (1999)
14. Xuan, P., Lesser, V., Zilberstein, S.: Communication Decisions in Multiagent Cooperation. Proceedings of the Fifth International Conference on Autonomous Agents (2001)

MPADES: Middleware for Parallel Agent Discrete Event Simulation

Patrick Riley*

Carnegie Mellon University, Computer Science Dept., Pittsburgh, PA 15213-3891
pfr@cs.cmu.edu
http://www.cs.cmu.edu/~pfr

Abstract. Simulations are an excellent tool for studying artificial intelligence. However, the simulation technology in use by and designed for the artificial intelligence community often fails to take advantage of much of the work by the larger simulation community to produce stable, repeatable, and efficient simulations. We present the new system Middleware for Parallel Agent Discrete Event Simulation (MPADES) as a simulation substrate for the artificial intelligence community. MPADES focuses on the agent as a fundamental simulation component. The "thinking time" of an agent is tracked and reflected in the results of the agents' actions. MPADES supports and manages the distribution of agents across machines while being robust to variations in network performance and machine load. We present the system in detail and give experimental results for a simple world model and set of agents. MPADES is not tied to any particular simulation, and is a powerful new tool for creating simulations for the study of artificial intelligence.

1 Introduction

Simulations are an excellent tool for studying artificial intelligence. They can allow the systematic modification of parameters of the environment, execute the large number of trials often required for machine learning, and facilitate the interaction of agents created by different research groups. However, many general simulation environments do not address the special concerns of the artificial intelligence community, such as the computation time of the agent being an integral part of its behavior. On the other hand, many simulators created in the artificial intelligence community fail to take advantage of the vast work in the simulation community for designing stable, repeatable, and efficient simulations.

This paper covers the MPADES (Middleware for Parallel Agent Discrete Event Simulation) system. The system is designed to support simulations for the AI community without being tied to any particular simulated world. MPADES

---

* I would like to thank Emil Talpes of the Carnegie Mellon ECE department for his contributions to the design and initial implementation of the MPADES system. This research was sponsored by Grants Nos. F30602-98-2-0135 and F30602-00-2-0549 and by an NSF Fellowship. The content of this publication reflects only the position of the authors.

G.A. Kaminka, P.U. Lima, and R. Rojas (Eds.): RoboCup 2002, LNAI 2752, pp. 162–178, 2003.

provides support for simulations with agents running in parallel across multiple machines, and for tracking the computation time used by those agents. By taking advantage of work in discrete event simulation, the middleware eases the design of a simulation by taking care of many of the system details required to handle distribution in an efficient and reproducible way.

The system is implemented and is described in detail in this paper. In order to test the efficiency of the system, a simulation of a simple world and agents was created. Experimental results with this world model are given, but it should be emphasized that MPADES is not tied to any particular world model.

2 Related Work

The problem of creating efficient simulations has attracted diverse attention from a wide range of sources, including the AI community, scientific computing, industry, and government.

A division in the simulation literature is between discrete event and continuous simulations. A discrete event simulation is one in which every system change takes place in the form of events which occur at a particular time. Continuous simulations simulate worlds which evolve continuously over time, typically by using a small time step and advancing all components of the simulation step by step. MPADES is a hybrid of the two. The agents' interactions with the world are through discrete events, but the underlying world model can be a continuous simulation. When an event is ready to be realized (that is cause a state change in the simulation), the world is first stepped forward to the appropriate time. However, all the reasoning about distributed messages and timing is done in the discrete event framework.

MPADES is a conservative simulator (such as [1]); events are not realized until it can be guaranteed that casual event ordering will not be violated. Optimistic simulations [2], on the other hand, support a back up mechanism in case events are executed out of order. Debates over the merits of conservative and optimistic simulation are common and several surveys discuss the issues [3, 4].

Agent-based or agent-oriented simulation seems to be a relatively new idea for the simulation community. There are still differing ideas about what "agent-based" simulation actually means. MPADES reflects ideas similar to Uhrmacher [5], where the deliberation (i.e. thinking) time of the agent is considered to be part of the simulation events. Uhrmacher also provides an overview of the current state of agent-oriented simulation [6].

Agent simulation has existed for much longer in the AI community. Perhaps the most comprehensive work on simulations that track the thinking time of the agents is the MESS system by Anderson [7, 8]. MESS allows the computation of the agents to be tracked at a level as low as primitive LISP instructions, as well as providing perfectly reproducible results. However, MESS requires that all agents are written in LISP and provides no support for distributed, parallel simulation.

One widely used agent simulation from the AI community is the SoccerServer [9], which provides a simulation of a soccer game among agents. While the SoccerServer supports distribution of agents and effectively limits the computation time that the agents have, there are a myriad of problems with the structure of the SoccerServer.

The SoccerServer operates in fairly large discrete time steps (100ms by default), commonly called a cycle, and all agents take actions simultaneously. Discretizing what is fundamentally a continuous problem is always a difficult task and large discrete steps cause problems with action and interaction modelling. MPADES allows agent actions to take place over many cycles, helping to create a more realistic simulation. The SoccerServer could run at smaller time steps to achieve better simulation. However, the smaller the time step, the more random effects like network performance and machine load can affect the result of the simulation (see below). In addition, the SoccerServer rigidly requires that all agent actions begin at synchronized discrete cycles.

In order to limit the computation time of the agents, the SoccerServer relies on a hard limit of wall clock time. Each discrete cycle, the SoccerServer sends sensations in the form of network packets to the agents based on a fixed wall clock time schedule. The agents send actions as network packets, and if the actions do not arrive before the specified wall clock time in the server, the actions are not applied. Thus, any change to the network configuration, network load, or machine load can cause the outcome of the simulation to vary considerably. This makes it extremely difficult to run reproducible simulations unless every aspect of the network can be carefully controlled. Even then, it is not clear whether the results from a simulation in one network and machine configuration are directly comparable to a simulation in another configuration. One of the major goals of MPADES is to avoid this dependency on the network and machine configurations.

Also, the SoccerServer performs very poorly in terms of efficiency of CPU usage. Because of the many wall clock timings in the server, it is difficult to avoid having the CPU idle for lengthy times. When running all components on a single machine, MPADES always achieves 100% CPU usage.

TeamBots (previously known as JavaBots) is another simulation environment which comes from the robotics community [10]. The primary focus of TeamBots is in creating control algorithms which can then be applied directly to robots without rewriting. Similar to the SoccerServer, the world advances in time steps with all agent actions synchronized. TeamBots requires all agents to be written in Java, and while agents could be distributed across machine with Java remote method calls, there is no mechanism for achieving a parallel speedup by distributing the agents. However, the TeamBots interface provides a mechanism for creating reusable control and learning algorithms, which is an issue not addressed with MPADES.

The High-Level Architecture (HLA) [11] is one example of a general architecture for creating distributed simulations. Rather than dealing with specific simulation algorithms, HLA and similar architectures provide interface and mechanism specifications to support reusable and inter-operable simulations. MPADES supports a smaller set of simulations, but provides more structure to aid in the construction of any particular world model. In essence, MPADES makes it easier to write agent based simulation of the sort described here, while HLA is designed to support a broader class of simulations. The algorithms of MPADES could be implemented using an HLA interface.

3   System Features

This section covers the major features of the MPADES simulation system. Briefly, these relevant features:

- Agent based execution, including explicit support for modelling latencies in sensation, thinking, and acting.
- Agents can be distributed among multiple machines.
- The result of the simulation is unaffected by network delays or load variations among the machines.
- The architecture for the agents is unconstrained, and does not require that the agents are written in a particular programming language.
- The agents' actions do not have to be synchronized in the domain.

Before discussing these features, an important point of terminology must be clarified. When we use the term "simulation time" or simply "time", we will be referring to the time in the simulated world. For example, if we say that event A occurs 5 seconds after event B, we mean 5 seconds in the simulated world, not 5 seconds to a person outside watching the simulation run. If we want to refer the latter time, we will explicitly say "wall clock" or "real world" time.

MPADES supports agent-based *execution*, as opposed to agent-based modelling or implementation [6]. In this context, agent-based execution means that the system explicitly models the sensing, thinking, and acting components (and their latencies) which are the core of any agent. Figure 1 represents a time line of executions of this cycle. Consider the topmost cycle. Time point A represents the point at which a sensation is generated, such as the frame of video from a robot's camera or a snapshot of stock market prices. The time between points A and B represents the time to transfer/process a sensation to be used by the thinking component starting at point B. Between points B and C, some computation is done to determine which actions to take. Between points C and D, the messages are sent to the effectors and those actions begin to take effect at point D. Note that we are not claiming that there is a fundamental difference between the computation that happens in the sense and act components of the cycle and the think component. A simulation system must necessarily create an abstraction over whatever world is being modelled. Since the simulation provides information and receives actions in a processed form, the use of an explicit latency allows the simulation to account for the time that that would be needed in the real world to convert to and from that processed form. Note that MPADES does *not* require that all sensations and actions have the same latency.

In many agents, the sense, think, and act components can be overlapped in time as depicted in Figure 1. MPADES explicitly allows all overlaps except that

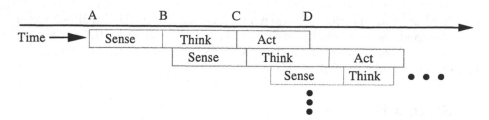

Fig. 1. Example timeline for the sense-think-act loop of an agent

think cycles may not overlap in time because it is assumed that each agent has a single processing unit.

Another important feature of the agent-based execution of the MPADES system is that the computation resources used by the agent are tracked in order to determine the latency of the thinking of the agent. This provides an incentive for agents to use as little computation as possible in the same way that the real world does: if an agent takes a long time to think, the world will have evolved while it was thinking. Thinking faster leads to a tighter control loop and generally better execution.

Unlike many other simulators which support the tracking of an agent's thinking latency (see Section 2 for a brief discussion), MPADES supports the distribution of agents across machines. Creating efficient parallel simulations is notoriously hard [3], and MPADES provides efficient distributed simulation for environments with the right properties (see Sections 6 and 7 for more details).

In spite of distributing the simulation across machines and in contrast to other AI simulation systems (notably the SoccerServer [9]) MPADES provides a reproducibility property: changes in network topology, network traffic, or machine loads does not affect the *result* of the simulation, only the *efficiency*.

In order to provide maximum inter-operability, MPADES makes no requirements on the agent architecture (except that it supports the sense-think-act cycle) or the language in which agents are written (except that they can write to and from Unix pipes). In the same spirit as the SoccerServer [9], MPADES helps provide an environment where agents built with different architectures or languages can inter-operate and interact in the simulated world.

As discussed in Section 2, MPADES is a discrete event simulator in the interaction with the agents, and a continuous simulator for the world model. This means that all of the distributed reasoning is done in the discrete event framework, while the world model works in small time steps. This notably means that the agents' actions are not necessarily synchronized; any subset of the agents can have actions take effect at a given time step. Many simulations, especially in the AI community, require that all agents choose an action, then the global effect of those actions is then applied, then the agents choose again.

4   System Architecture

Figure 2 gives an overview of the entire MPADES system, along with the components users of the system must supply (shaded in the diagram). The simulation

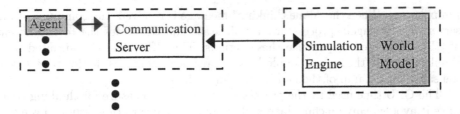

Fig. 2. Overview of the architecture of the MPADES system. The shaded components are provided by the users of the system, not by the middleware itself. The dotted lines denote machine boundaries

engine and the communication server are supplied as part of MPADES. The world model and the agents are created by a user to simulate a particular environment.

The simulation engine is the heart of the discrete event simulator. All pending events are queued here, and the engine manages all network communication. A communication server must be run on each machine on which agents run. The communication server manages all communication with the agents (through a Unix pipe interface) as well as tracking the CPU usage of the agents to calculate the thinking latency. The communication server and simulation engine communicate over a TCP/IP connection[1].

The world model is created by a user of the middleware to create a simulation of a particular environment. The simulation engine is a library to which the world model must link, so the simulation engine and world model exist in the same process. The world model must provide such functionality as advancing the state of the world to a particular time and realizing an event (changing the state of the world in response to an event occurring). MPADES provides a collection of C++ classes from which objects in the world model can inherit in order to interact with the simulation engine.

The agents communicate with the communication server via pipes, so the agents are free to use any programming language and any architecture as long as they can read and write to pipes. From the agent's perspective, the interaction with the simulation is fairly simple:

1. Wait for a sensation to be received
2. Decide on a set of actions and send them to the communication server
3. Send a "done thinking" message to indicate that all actions were sent

One of the communication server's primary jobs is to track the thinking time of the agent. When sending a sensation to an agent, the communication server begins tracking the CPU time used by the agent, information provided by the

---

[1] Since the simulation needs the lowest latency traffic possible in order to achieve efficient simulation, Nagle's algorithm is turned off on the TCP sockets (using the TCP_NODELAY socket option in the Linux socket interface). Manual bundling of messages is done to avoid sending an excessive number of small packets.

Linux kernel. When the "done thinking" message is received, the communication server puts the agent process into a wait state and calculates the total amount of CPU time used to produce these actions. The CPU time is translated into simulation time through a simple linear transformation[2]. All actions are given the same time stamp of the end of the think phase.

The CPU time used by the process is a reasonable measure for thinking time since it avoids many machine load and memory usage variation issues. However, there may still be slight effects of machine load based on, for example, the number of interrupts and cache performance. Also, the current time slice reported by the Linux kernel is in 10ms increments, a fairly large amount of computation on today's computers. With the randomness in interrupts and other system activity, CPU usage numbers are unfortunately not perfectly reproducible, in contrast to a more language specific time tracking system like [8, 7]. However, tracking the CPU time via kernel-provided information allows much more flexibility in the implementation of the agents and provides a better substrate for interoperability of agents designed by separate groups.

The agents have one special action which MPADES understands: a "request time notify." The agent's only opportunity to act is upon the receipt of a sensation. Therefore if an agent wants to send an action at a particular time (such as a stop turning command for a robot), it can request a time notify. A time notify is an empty sensation. On the receipt of the time notify, the agent can send actions as normal. In order to give maximum flexibility to the agents, MPADES does not enforce a minimum time in the future that time notifies can be requested. However, all actions, whether resulting from a regular sensation or a time notify, are still constrained by the action latency.

While the world model may create new events to be used in the simulation, there are several special kinds of events which the simulation engine understands:

Sense Event. When a sense event is realized, a message is sent to the communication server representing that agent. The communication server forwards this message to the agent and begins tracking agent computation time.

Time Notify. This event is an empty sensation event, and can be inserted in the queue by the special action "request time notify" of the agent.

Act Event. When actions are received from the agents, an act event is inserted into the queue. The simulation event does nothing on the realization of the event, expecting the world model to handle the effects.

5   Discrete Event Simulator

This section describes the simulation algorithm used by MPADES. This algorithm is a modification of a basic discrete event simulator.

---

[2] The parameters of this linear transformation are a user controllable parameter. The bogoMIPS value of the processor as reported by the Linux kernel is also used. However, if different types of machines are to be used in the same simulation, some benchmarking would need to be done to determine what an equitable setting of these CPU time to simulation time parameters would be.

Table 1. Inner loop for basic conservative discrete event simulator

```
repeat forever
    receive messages
    next_event = pending_event_queue.head
    while (no event will be received for time less than next_event.time)
        advanceWorldTime (next_event.time)
        pending_event_queue.remove(next_event)
        realize (next_event)
        next_event = pending_event_queue.head
```

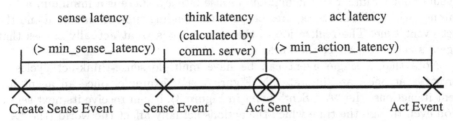

Fig. 3. The events in the sense-think-act cycle of an agent. The "Act Sent" time is circled because unlike the other marks that represent events in the queue, "Act Sent" is just a message from the communication server to the engine and not an event in the event queue

The inner loop of a basic discrete event simulator is shown in Table 1. The one primary difference is the "advanceWorldTime" call. This supports the one continuous aspect of the simulation, the world model. This function advances the simulated world to the time of the discrete event. The realization of the event causes changes in the world, and notably can cause other events to be enqueued into the pending_events_queue.

The key decision in parallel discrete event simulation is whether any event will be received in the future which has a time less than that of the next event. Typically, a "lookahead" value is determined such that the current time plus the lookahead is the smallest time stamp of a message that can be received. This problem is well studied (see [3] for a survey). This section is devoted to the lookahead algorithm of MPADES. We will first cover a simple version which covers some of the fundamental ideas and then describe the MPADES algorithm in full.

An explanation of the events that occur in the normal think-sense-act cycle of the agents must first be given. The nature of this cycle illustrated in Figure 3. First, an event is put into the queue to create a sensation. Typically, the realization of this event reads the state of the world and converts this to some string of information to be sent to the agent. This string is encapsulated in a sense event and put into the event queue. MPADES requires that the time between the create sense event and the sense event is at least some minimum sense latency, which is specified by the world model. When the sense event is realized, this string will be sent to the agent to begin the thinking process. Notice that the realization of a sense event does not require the reading of any of the current world state since the string of information is fixed at the time of the realization of the create sense event. Upon the receipt of the sensation, the communication server begins timing the agent's computation. When all of the agent's actions have been received by the communication server, the computation time taken by the agent to produce those actions is converted to simulation time. All the actions and the think latency are sent to the simulation engine (shown as "Act Sent" in Figure 3). Upon receipt, the simulation engine adds the action latency (determined by querying the world model) and puts an act event in the pending events queue. Similar to the minimum sense latency, there is a minimum action latency which MPADES requires between the sending time of an action and the act event time. The realization of that act event is what actually causes that agent's actions to affect the world.

Note that a single agent can be have multiple sense-think-act cycles in progress at once, as illustrated in Figure 1. For example, once an agent has sent its actions (the "Act Sent" point in Figure 3), it can receive its next sensation even though the time which the actions actually affect the world (the "Act Event" point in Figure 3) has not yet occurred. The only overlap MPADES forbids is the overlapping of two think phases.

Note also that all actions have an effect at a discrete time. Therefore there is no explicit support by MPADES for supporting the modelling of the interaction of parallel actions. For example, the actions of two simulated robots may be to start driving forward. It is the world model's job to recognize when these actions interact (such as in a collision) and respond appropriately. Similarly, communication among agents is handled as any other action. The world model is responsible for providing whatever restrictions on communication desired.

The sensation and action latencies provide a lookahead value for that agents and allows the agents to think in parallel. When a sense event is realized for agent 1, it cannot cause any event to be enqueued before the current time plus the minimum action latency. Therefore it is safe (at least when only considering agent 1) to realize all events up till that time without violating event ordering.

The quantity we call the "minimum agent time" determines the maximum safe time over all agents. The minimum agent time is the earliest time which an agent can cause an event which affects other agents or the world to be put into the queue. This is similar to the Lower Bound on Timestamp (LBTS) concept used in the simulation literature. The calculation of the minimum agent time is shown in Table 2. The agent status is either "thinking," which means that a sensation has been sent to the agent and a reply has not yet been received, or "waiting," which means that the agent is waiting to hear from the simulation engine. Besides initialization, the agent status will always be thinking or waiting. The current time of an agent is the time of the last communication with the agent (sensation sent or action received). The receipt of a message from a communication server cannot cause the minimum agent time to decrease. However, the realization of

Table 2. Code to determine the minimum time that an agent can affect the simulation

```
calculateMinAgentTime()
    ∀i ∈ set_of_all_agents
        if (agentᵢ.status = Waiting) agent_timeᵢ = ∞
        else agent_timeᵢ = agentᵢ.currenttime + min_action_latency
    return minᵢ agent_timeᵢ
```

Table 3. Main code for parallel agent discrete event simulator

```
repeat forever
    receive messages
    next_event = pending_event_queue.head
    min_agent_time = calculateMinAgentTime()
    while (next_event.time < min_agent_time)
        advanceWorldTime (next_event.time)
        pending_event_queue.remove(next_event)
        realizeEvent (next_event)
        next_event = pending_event_queue.head
        min_agent_time = calculateMinAgentTime()
```

an event can cause an increase or a decrease. Therefore, the minimum agent time must be recalculated after each event realization.

Based on the calculation of the minimum agent time, we can now describe a simple version of parallel agent discrete event simulator, which is shown in Table 3. The value min_agent_time is used to determine whether any further events can appear before the time of the next event in the queue.

While this algorithm produces correct results (all events are realized in order) and achieves some parallelism, it does not achieve the maximum amount of possible parallelism. Figure 4 illustrates an example with two agents. When the sense event for agent 1 is realized, the minimum agent time becomes A. This allows the create sense event for agent 2 to be realized and the sense event for agent 2 to be enqueued. However, the sense event for agent 2 will not be realized until the response from agent 1 is received. However, as discussed above, the effect of the realization of a sense event does not depend on the current state of the world. If agent 2 is currently waiting, there is no reason not to realize the sense event and allow both agents to be thinking simultaneously.

However, this allows the realization of events out of order; agent 1 can send an event which has a time less the time of the sense event for agent 2. Certain kinds of out of order realizations are acceptable (as the example illustrates). In particular, we need to verify that out of order events are not causally related. The key insight is that sensations received by agents are casually independent of

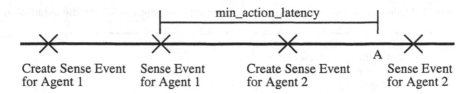

Fig. 4. An example illustrating possible parallelism that the simple parallel agent algorithm fails to exploit

sensation received by other agents. In order to state our correctness guarantees, we will define a new sub-class of events "fixed agent events" which have the following properties:

1. They do not depend on the current state of the world.
2. They affect only a single agent, possibly by sending a message to the agent.
3. Sense events and time notify events are both fixed agent events.
4. Fixed agent events are the only events which can cause the agent to start a thinking cycle, but they do *not* necessarily start a thinking cycle.

The correctness guarantees that MPADES provides are:

1. All events which are not fixed agent events are realized in time order.
2. All events which send sensations to the agents are fixed agent events.
3. The set of fixed agent events for a particular agent are realized in time order.

In order to achieve this, several new concepts are introduced. The first is the notion of the "minimum sensation time." This is the earliest time that a *new* sensation (i.e. fixed agent event) *other than a time notify* can be generated and enqueued. The current implementation of MPADES requires that the world model provide a minimum time between the create sense event and the sense event (see Figure 3), so the minimum sensation time is the current simulation time plus that time.

The time notifies are privileged events. They are handled specially because they affect no agent other than the one requesting the time notification. MPADES also allows time notifies to be requested an arbitrarily small time in the future, before even the minimum sensation time. This means that while an agent is thinking, the simulation engine cannot send any more fixed agent events to that agent without possibly causing a violation of correctness condition 3. However, if an agent is waiting (i.e. not thinking), then the first fixed agent event in the pending event queue can be sent as long as its time is before the minimum sensation time.

To insure proper event ordering, one queue of fixed agent events per agent is maintained. All fixed agent events enter this queue before being sent to the agent, and an event is put into the agent's queue only when the event's time is less than the minimum sensation time.

Table 4. Code for maintaining the per agent fixed agent event queues

```
checkForReadyEvents(a: Agent)
    while (true)
        if (agent_a.status = thinking)
            return
        if (agent_a.pending_agent_events.empty())
            return
        next_event = agent_a.pending_agent_events.pop()
        realizeEvent(next_event)
```

```
enqueueAgentEvent(e:Event)
    a = e.agent
    agent_a.pending_agent_events.insert(e)
    checkForReadyEvents(a)
```

```
doneThinking(a: Agent, t:time)
    agent_a.currenttime = t
    checkForReadyEvents(a)
```

There are two primary functions for the agent queue. First, enqueueAgentEvent puts a fixed agent event into the queue. The doneThinking function is called when an agent finishes its think cycle. Both functions call a third function checkForReadyEvents. Psuedo-code for these functions is shown in Table 4. Note that in checkForReadyEvents, the realization of an event can cause the agent status to change from waiting to thinking.

Using these functions, we describe in Table 5 the main loop that MPADES uses. This is a modification of the algorithm given in Table 3. The two key changes are that in the first while loop, fixed agent events are not realized, but are put in the agent queue instead. The second loop (the "foreach" loop) scans ahead in the event queue and moves all fixed agent events less that the minimum sensation time into the agent queues. Note that in both cases, moving events to the agent queue can cause the events to be realized (see Table 4).

6 Empirical Validation

In order to test the efficiency of the simulation and to understand the effects of the various parameters on the performance of the system, we implemented a simple world model and agents and ran a series of experiments. We tracked the wall clock time required to finish a simulation as a measure of the efficiency.

The simulated world is a two dimensional rectangle where opposite sides are connected (i.e. "wrap-around"). Each agent is a "ball" in this world. Each sensation the agent receives contains the positions of all agents in the simulation, and the only action of each agent is to request a particular velocity vector. The dynamics and movement properties are reasonable if not exactly correct for

Table 5. Code for efficient parallel agent discrete event simulator as used by MPADES

```
repeat forever
    receive messages
    next_event = pending_event_queue.head
    min_agent_time = calculateMinAgentTime()
    while (next_event.time < min_agent_time)
        advanceWorldTime (next_event.time)
        pending_event_queue.remove(next_event)
        if (next_event is a fixed agent event)
            enqueueAgentEvent(next_event)
        else
            realizeEvent (next_event)
        next_event = pending_event_queue.head
        min_agent_time = calculateMinAgentTime()
    min_sense_time = current_time + min_sense_latency
    foreach e (pending_event_queue) /* in time order */
        if (e.time > min_sense_time)
            break
        if (e is a fixed agent event)
            pending_event_queue.remove(e)
            enqueueAgentEvent(e)
```

small omni-directional robots moving on carpet, except that collisions are not modelled. The world model advanced in 1ms increments.

We varied three parameters of the simulation:

- The number of machines. We used five similar Linux machines with varying speeds. While this variation in machines is undesirable, we did not have a uniform cluster available for testing. The machines were behind a firewall to control the network traffic, but the use and processing of the machines was not totally controlled. The machines used were all running Linux RedHat 5.2 with the following processors: Pentium II 450MHz, Pentium Pro 200MHz, Pentium Pro 200MHz, Pentium II 233MHz, and Pentium II 233MHz.
- The number of agents, varying from 2 to 14.
- Computation requirements of the agents. To simulate agents that do more or less processing, we put in simple delay loops (not sleeps, since we need the processes to actually require CPU time) to change the amount of computation required by the agents. We used 3 simple conditions of fast, medium, and slow agents. Fast agents simply parse the sensations and compute their new desired velocity with a some simple vector calculations. The time this takes is smaller than the resolution of CPU time reported by the Linux kernel. The medium and slow agents add a simple loop that counts to 500,000 and 5,000,000 respectively. On a 1GHz Pentium III, this translates to approximately 1.2ms and 10.6ms average response time.

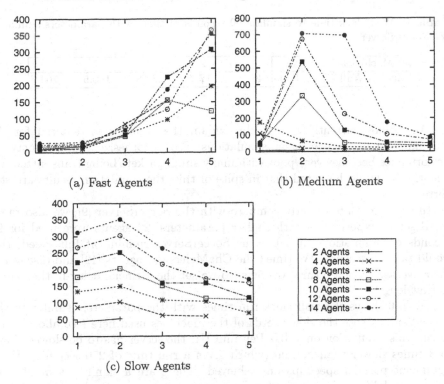

Fig. 5. Timing results with the sample world model and agents. The x-axis is the number of machines, the y-axis is the median wall clock time required to run the simulation

Every experimental condition was run five times and the median of those five times is reported. Each simulation was run for 90 seconds of simulation time. In all experiments, the agents received sensations every 95–105 milliseconds (actual value chosen uniformly randomly after each sensation). The sensation latency and action latency was chosen uniformly randomly between 30 and 40 milliseconds for each sensation and action.

Figure 5 shows the wall clock time required to finish the simulations with various parameters. First, note that the speed of the agent gives fundamentally different trends in the parallel performance. With fast agents, distribution actually slows down the overall simulation. By distributing agents, the round trip times between the world model and the agents increase. This latency increase slows the simulation, and that effect will only be outweighed if a significant amount of computation is done in parallel on the machines. The medium speed agents clearly express this trend. With two machines, the simulation slows (usually quite significantly), only improving once the number of machines becomes large enough to balance the increased latency. The slow agents exhibit the same trend, except that parallel speedups are finally achieved with the larger amount of computation distributed.

Table 6. Wall clock time to simulate 90 seconds of time, with parameters similar to the SoccerServer

# Machines	1	2	3	4	5
Median Wall Clock Time	446.8	317.7	231.8	190.5	164.3

We cannot currently adequately explain the large times required for the medium and fast speed agent simulations. We hypothesize that the network performance becomes very poor with many small packets being transmitted frequently. It should be noted that in spite of this, the simulation results are still correct.

In order to more directly compare with the SoccerServer [9], we also ran a small set of experiments with similar parameters. 22 agents were used for 90 seconds on simulation time. For the SoccerServer running at full speed, this would take 90 seconds. We timed the ChaMeleons01 agents [12] and discovered their average response time was 5ms, so we set the artificial delay in the agents to that length.

Table 6 shows the wall clock run times with the parameters similar to the SoccerServer. Note the slow speeds of the machines used here (see above), and to run this simulation on 1GHz Pentium III, the server has to be slowed down to 3 times slower than normal (which gives a run time of 270 seconds). Here, significant parallel speedups are achieved. There are a significant number of agents available to be distributed, and each one has reasonable computation requirements.

Even though the parameters were set similarly, there are a few important differences in these simulations. The MPADES based simulation has a step size of 1ms, where the SoccerServer has a step size of 100ms. The MPADES based simulation has a simpler world model. The agents have fewer actions (just a velocity request), where the SoccerServer has movement, ball control, communication, and internal state updating actions. The SoccerServer likely sends more data across the network because of the larger action set and especially the broadcast communication. Therefore, while these results are suggestive about the comparison in efficiency, no hard conclusions can be made.

7   Conclusion

We have presented the design of and experimental results for the MPADES system to support efficient simulation. The system supports the tracking of computation time of the agents in order to model the thinking time as part of the simulation. Unlike other AI simulators, this is accomplished in a distributed environment while being tolerant of network and machine load variations, and without requiring the agents to be implemented in a particular programming architecture or language. This provides an open agent environment where agents designed by different groups can interact.

Further, MPADES supports simulation where the smallest time step of the simulation is much smaller than the typical sensation and action latencies of the world being modelled. Agent actions do not have to be synchronized. These features allow a much closer approximation to the continuous time frame underlying most simulations.

With the implementation of a sample world model, we empirically tested the system. The results show that good parallel speedups can be achieved when the computation time of the agents is significant. Otherwise, the price paid by the network latency can slow down the overall simulation. However, we have not yet fully explored the issue of how the sensation and action latencies affect the parallel speedups.

The system does suffer from several drawbacks. The simulation engine is a centralized component and the system provides no direct support for the distribution of the simulation of the world model, only the distribution of the agents themselves. This makes it unlikely that the simulation will scale well to a large number of agents in its current form. Support for such distribution could draw on the extensive experience of other simulations, but has the potential to considerably complicate the system.

MPADES provides no structure for the design of the agents other than interface requirements. While this is a benefit in allowing a greater degree of inter-operability, it does place more of a burden on the agent designers. Also, the current implementation uses the CPU usage reported reported by the Linux kernel. Since those reports are fairly coarse and can vary with the other activity on the system, MPADES does not exhibit perfect reproducibility. There is a degree of uncontrolled randomness in the tracking of the thinking latencies of the agents. However, better tracking and reporting from the kernel could potentially alleviate these problems.

MPADES provides a solid foundation for producing high-quality agent based simulations. It handles many system and distribution details so that they can be largely ignored by the world model and agent designers, while still maintaining efficient and largely reproducible results. MPADES is a powerful new tool for creating simulations for the study of artificial intelligence.

References

1. Misra, J.: Distributed discrete-event simulation. ACM Computing Surveys **18** (1986) 39–65
2. Jefferson, D.: Virtual time. ACM Trans. Prog. Lang. and Syst. **7** (1985)
3. Ferscha, A., Tripathi, S.: Parallel and distributed simulation of discrete event systems. In Zomaya, A.Y., ed.: Parallel and Distributed Computing Handbook. McGraw-Hill (1996) 1003 – 1041
4. Fujimoto, R.M.: Parallel discrete event simulation. Communications of the ACM **33** (1990) 30–53
5. Uhrmacher, A., Gugler, K.: Distributed, parallel simulation of multiple, deliberative agents. In Bruce, D., Donatiello, L., Turner, S., eds.: Proceedings of the 14th Workshop on Parallel and Distributed Simulation (PADS 2000). (2000) 101–108

6. Uhrmacher, A.M.: Concepts of object- and agent-oriented simulation. Transactions of SCS **14** (1997) 59–67
7. Anderson, S.D.: Simulation of multiple time-pressured agents. In Andradóttir, S., Healy, K.J., Withers, D.H., Nelson, B.L., eds.: Proceedings of the 1997 Winter Simulation Conference. (1997) 397–404
8. Anderson, S.D.: A simulation substrate for real-time planning. Technical Report 95-80, University of Massachusetts at Amherst Computer Science Department (1995) (Ph.D. thesis).
9. Noda, I., Matsubara, H., Hiraki, K., Frank, I.: Soccer server: A tool for research on multiagent systems. Applied Artificial Intelligence **12** (1998) 233–250
10. Balch, T.: Behavioral Diversity in Learning Robot Teams. PhD thesis, College of Computing, Georgia Institute of Technology (1998) (available as tech report GIT-CC-98-25).
11. U.S. Department of Defense: High level architecture interface specification, version 1.3 (1998)
12. Riley, P., Carpenter, P., Kaminka, G., Veloso, M., Thayer, I., Wang, R.: ChaMeleons-01 team description. In Birk, A., Coradeschi, S., Tadokoro, S., eds.: RoboCup-2001: Robot Soccer World Cup V. Springer, Berlin (2002) (forthcoming).

Towards RoboCup without Color Labeling

Robert Hanek, Thorsten Schmitt, Sebastian Buck, and Michael Beetz

Munich University of Technology
Department of Computer Science IX
Orleanstr. 34, D-81667 Munich, Germany
http://www9.in.tum.de/agilo/

Abstract. Object recognition and localization methods in RoboCup work on color segmented camera images. Unfortunately, color labeling can be applied to object recognition tasks only in very restricted environments, where different kinds of objects have different colors. To overcome these limitations we propose an algorithm named the Contracting Curve Density (CCD) algorithm for fitting parametric curves to image data. The method neither assumes object specific color distributions, nor specific edge profiles, nor does it need threshold parameters. Hence, no training phase is needed. In order to separate adjacent regions we use local criteria which are based on local image statistics. We apply the method to the problem of localizing the ball and show that the CCD algorithm reliably localizes the ball even in the presence of heavily changing illumination, strong clutter, specularity, partial occlusion, and texture.

1 Introduction

Currently in all three real robot soccer leagues (small-size, middle-size, and Sony four-legged league) the task of visual perception is considerably simplified by two restrictions: 1.) all objects on the pitch have a distinct color, 2.) the illumination is constant and roughly homogeneous. Due to this restrictions classes of objects (e.g. robots, ball, lines, color markers, goals) can roughly be identified by their color. To the best of our knowledge, all robot soccer teams using cameras apply a color labeling step to the sensed image data, e.g. [29, 32, 15, 17, 6, 3]. In this labeling or classification step the color value of a pixel is mapped to one of the distinct colors. Labeling provides the advantage of a fast and substantial reduction of the image data while maintaining the major part of the relevant information. However even in the restricted RoboCup scenario for all color spaces the color histograms, i.e. probability density functions (pdf), of different object classes do overlap. Furthermore the pdf of an object class varies spatially. This causes an uncertainty in the labeling process. Obviously in a less restricted environment the uncertainty would be much higher.

To avoid this difficulty we use raw image data (in RGB space). Our method refines iteratively a vague interpretation of the scene by alternating two steps[1]:

---

[1] An initial vague interpretation may be obtained for example by a Monte Carlo method or by prediction over time.

G.A. Kaminka, P.U. Lima, and R. Rojas (Eds.): RoboCup 2002, LNAI 2752, pp. 179–194, 2003.
© Springer-Verlag Berlin Heidelberg 2003

Fig. 1. The CCD algorithm is able to localize the ball in natural environments (red: initial ball contour, blue: estimated ball contour).

1.) based on a vague interpretation (e.g. the ball has the 3-D position X) local pdfs are learned from the image data. These pdfs describe the local color distributions of different objects. 2.) in the second step the local pdfs are used in order to refine the interpretation of the scene. The method naturally takes the uncertainty into account caused by the overlapping pdfs. Model knowledge such as the shape of the ball is used in order to reduce the uncertainty. Pixels are not interpreted independently but based on the context and the model knowledge.

The CCD algorithm fits parametric curve models, also known as active contours, deformable models, or snakes [5, 18] into the image. Problems such as the self-localization / pose estimation problem can be addressed by curve fitting [12]. Here the position of the ball with respect to the observing robot is estimated. With our labeling-based approach [12] we experienced substantial inaccuracies under some circumstances, especially if temporal derivatives, e.g. the ball speed, are computed. The CCD algorithm achieves a substantially higher accuracy. Even more important, we think that this work could be an important contribution towards the goal of playing robot soccer in natural environments, see Fig. 1.

The reminder of this paper is organized as follows: in section 2 the contour of the ball is modeled as a function of the ball position. In section 3 an overview of the Contracting Curve Density (CCD) algorithm is given. Sections 4 describe the two main steps of the CCD algorithm. Section 5 contains an experimental evaluation. In section 6 the body of related work is briefly summarized and finally section 7 concludes the paper.

2   Modeling the Ball Contour

In this section the contour of the ball is described (modeled) as a function of the ball position. In this modeling process knowledge of the ball (the object of inter-

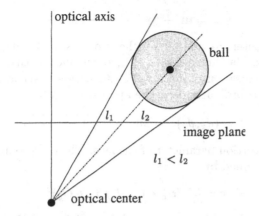

optical axis

ball

l_1 l_2

image plane

$l_1 < l_2$

optical center

Fig. 2. Projection of the ball into the image plane: the projection of the ball's center point does not yield the center of the ball contour.

est) and the imaging device is incorporated. Here the ball is modeled as a sphere with known radius. We use a camera with known internal and external camera parameters. The method proposed here is developed for our non-omnidirectional vision system. However, the method can easily be adapted to omnidirectional vision systems which are quite popular in robotic soccer, e.g. [14, 24, 25].

We denote the center point of the ball in the coordinate system of the observing robot by M_r. We distinguish two cases: 1.) in the first case the ball is assumed to lay on the floor. Hence the center point $M_r = (x, y, r)^T$ of the ball has two degrees of freedom, namely x and y. The z-coordinate is given by the radius r of the ball. 2.) in the second case we assume that the ball may fly, i.e. not lay on the floor, which sometimes happens in robotic soccer. In this case the ball position has three unknown coordinates: $M_r = (x, y, z)^T$. While the second case is more general, it requires an optimization for more parameters and tends to be less precise, if the ball is on the floor. By Φ we denote the unknown parameters of the ball position M_r (for the first case $\Phi = (x, y)^T$, for the second case $\Phi = (x, y, z)^T$).

In the following the relation between Φ and the pixel coordinates of the ball contour is derived. First the center point of the ball is expressed in camera coordinates M_c by

$$M_c = R \cdot (M_r - t) \tag{1}$$

where R and t specify the orientation and location of the camera with respect to the robot coordinate system. The set of tangent lines to the sphere (the ball) passing through the optical center of the camera define a cone, see Fig. 2. As known, the intersection of the cone with the image plane yields an ellipse [28]. Note the intersection is a circle only if the center point of the sphere lies on the optical axis of the camera. In all other cases the projection of the center point is not the center point of the ball contour, see Fig. 2. The set of contour points can be described in undistorted image coordinates u by

$$\mathbf{u}(s) = \mathbf{m}_i + \cos(s) \cdot \mathbf{a}_1 + \sin(s) \cdot \mathbf{a}_2 \tag{2}$$

where $\mathbf{m}$ is the center, $\mathbf{a}_1$ and $\mathbf{a}_2$ are the two axis of the ellipse in undistorted image coordinates. The angle $s \in [-\pi, ..., \pi[$ specifies a particular point on the ellipse. Our lens causes substantial radial distortions. According to Lenz et al. [19] the distorted coordinates $\mathbf{d}$ can be approximated by

$$\mathbf{d} = (d_x, d_y)^T = 2\mathbf{u}/(1 + \sqrt{1 - 4\kappa |\mathbf{u}|^2}) \tag{3}$$

where κ is the distortion parameter of the lens. The corresponding pixel coordinates $\mathbf{c}$ can be obtained by

$$\mathbf{c} = (d_x/S_x + C_x, d_y/S_y + C_y)^T \tag{4}$$

where S_x and S_y define the pixel size and C_x and C_y specify the center point of the camera.

3   Overview of the Contracting Curve Density (CCD) Algorithm

The CCD algorithm fits parametric curve models to image data [11]. The algorithm can roughly be characterized as an extension of the EM algorithm [10] using additional knowledge. The additional knowledge consists of: (i) a curve model, which describes the set of possible boundaries between adjacent regions, and (ii) a model of the image generation process. The CCD algorithm, depicted in Fig. 3, performs an iteration of two steps, which roughly correspond to the two steps of the EM algorithm: **1. Local statistics of image data are learned** from the vicinity of the curve. These statistics locally characterize the two sides of the edge curve. **2.** From these statistics, the **estimation of the model parameters is refined** by optimizing the separation of the two sides. This refinement in turn leads in the next iteration step to an improved statistical characterization of the two sides. During the process, the uncertainty of the model parameters decreases and the probability density of the curve in the image contracts to a single edge estimate. We therefore call the algorithm Contracting Curve Density (CCD) algorithm.

Input: The input of the CCD algorithm consists of the image data $\mathbf{I}^*$ and the curve model. The image data are local features, e.g. RGB values, given for each pixel of the image. The curve model consists of two parts: 1.) a differentiable curve function c describing the model edge curve in the image as a function of the model parameters $\mathbf{\Phi}$, 2.) a Gaussian a priori distribution $p(\mathbf{\Phi}) = p(\mathbf{\Phi} \mid \mathbf{m}_\Phi^*, \mathbf{\Sigma}_\Phi^*)$ of the model parameters $\mathbf{\Phi}$, defined by the mean $\mathbf{m}_\Phi^*$ and the covariance $\mathbf{\Sigma}_\Phi^*$. (The superscript $*$ indicates input data.)

Output: The output of the algorithm consists of the estimate $\mathbf{m}_\Phi$ of the model parameters $\mathbf{\Phi}$ and the covariance $\mathbf{\Sigma}_\Phi$ describing the uncertainty of the estimate. The estimate $\mathbf{m}_\Phi$ and the covariance $\mathbf{\Sigma}_\Phi$ define a Gaussian approximation $p(\mathbf{\Phi} \mid \mathbf{m}_\Phi, \mathbf{\Sigma}_\Phi)$ of the posterior density $p(\mathbf{\Phi} \mid \mathbf{I}^*)$.

Contracting Curve Density (CCD) algorithm

Input: image data $\mathbf{I}^*$, differentiable curve function c, mean $\mathbf{m}_\Phi^*$ and covariance $\mathbf{\Sigma}_\Phi^*$
Output: estimate $\mathbf{m}_\Phi$ of model parameters and associated covariance $\mathbf{\Sigma}_\Phi$

Initialization: mean $\mathbf{m}_\Phi = \mathbf{m}_\Phi^*$, covariance $\mathbf{\Sigma}_\Phi = c_1 \cdot \mathbf{\Sigma}_\Phi^*$
repeat

1. **learn local statistics** of image data from the vicinity of the curve
   (a) compute pixels v in vicinity $\mathcal{V}$ of the image curve from c, $\mathbf{m}_\Phi$ and $\mathbf{\Sigma}_\Phi$
       $\forall v \in \mathcal{V}$ compute vague assignment $\mathbf{a}_v(\mathbf{m}_\Phi, \mathbf{\Sigma}_\Phi)$ to the sides of the curve
   (b) $\forall v \in \mathcal{V}$ compute local statistics $\mathbf{S}_v$ of image data $\mathbf{I}_\mathcal{V}^*$
2. **refine estimation** of model parameters
   (a) update mean $\mathbf{m}_\Phi$ by performing one iteration step of MAP estimation:

$$\mathbf{m}_\Phi = \arg\min_{\mathbf{m}_\Phi} \chi^2(\mathbf{m}_\Phi) \quad \text{with}$$

$$\chi^2(\mathbf{m}_\Phi) = -2\ln[p(\mathbf{I}_\mathcal{V} = \mathbf{I}_\mathcal{V}^* \mid \mathbf{a}_\mathcal{V}(\mathbf{m}_\Phi, \mathbf{\Sigma}_\Phi), \mathbf{S}_\mathcal{V}) \cdot p(\mathbf{m}_\Phi \mid \mathbf{m}_\Phi^*, \mathbf{\Sigma}_\Phi^*)]$$

   (b) updated covariance $\mathbf{\Sigma}_\Phi$ from Hessian of $\chi^2(\mathbf{m}_\Phi)$

until changes of $\mathbf{m}_\Phi$ and $\mathbf{\Sigma}_\Phi$ are small enough

Post-processing: estimate covariance $\mathbf{\Sigma}_\Phi$ from Hessian of $\chi^2(\mathbf{m}_\Phi)$
return mean $\mathbf{m}_\Phi$ and covariance $\mathbf{\Sigma}_\Phi$

Fig. 3. The CCD algorithm iteratively refines a Gaussian a priori density $p(\Phi) = p(\Phi \mid \mathbf{m}_\Phi^*, \mathbf{\Sigma}_\Phi^*)$ of model parameters to a Gaussian approximation $p(\Phi \mid \mathbf{m}_\Phi, \mathbf{\Sigma}_\Phi)$ of the posterior density $p(\Phi \mid \mathbf{I}^*)$.

Initialization: The estimate $\mathbf{m}_\Phi$ of the model parameters and the associated covariance $\mathbf{\Sigma}_\Phi$ are initialized using the mean $\mathbf{m}_\Phi^*$ and covariance $\mathbf{\Sigma}_\Phi^*$ of the a priori distribution. The factor c_1 (e.g. $c_1 = 9$) increases the initial uncertainty and thereby enlarges the capture range of the CCD algorithm.

4 Steps of the CCD Algorithm

The two basic steps of the CCD algorithm, depicted in Fig. 3, are briefly summarized in this section. A more detailed description is given in [11].

4.1 Learn Local Statistics (Step 1)

The Gaussian distribution of model parameters $p(\Phi \mid \mathbf{m}_\Phi, \mathbf{\Sigma}_\Phi)$ and the model curve function c define a probability distribution of the edge curve in the image. This curve distribution vaguely assigns each pixel in the vicinity of the surmised curve to one side of the curve. In **step 1a** the set $\mathcal{V}$ of pixels v in the vicinity of the surmised curve is determined and for the pixels $v \in \mathcal{V}$ the vague side assignments $\mathbf{a}_v(\mathbf{m}_\Phi, \mathbf{\Sigma}_\Phi)$ are computed. The components of the assignments $\mathbf{a}_v$ specify to which extent pixel v is expected to belong to the corresponding side. Fig. 4 row b.) depicts for pixels $v \in \mathcal{V}$ the assignments to the ball region. White pixels indicate a quite certain assignment to the ball region.

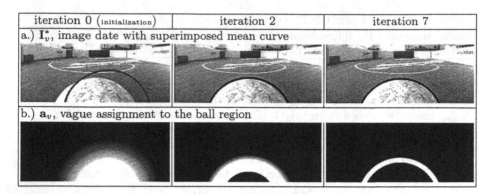

iteration 0 (initialization)	iteration 2	iteration 7
a.) $\mathbf{I}_v^*$, image date with superimposed mean curve		
b.) $\mathbf{a}_v$, vague assignment to the ball region		

Fig. 4. a.) The initial error is iteratively reduced. **b.)** During the process also the uncertainty of the curve is reduced and the vague side assignments $\mathbf{a}_v$ become certain.

In **step 1b** local statistics $\mathbf{S}_v$, i.e. first and second order moments, of the image feature vectors $\mathbf{I}_v^*$ are learned from pixels which are assigned to one side with high certainty. This is done for each of the two sides separated by the curve. In order to obtain the statistics locally adapted windows (weights) are used. The windows are chosen such that the local statistics $\mathbf{S}_v$ can be computed recursively. The resulting time complexity of computing $\mathbf{S}_v$ for all pixels $v \in \mathcal{V}$ is $O(|\mathcal{V}|)$, where $|\mathcal{V}|$ is the number of pixels in the vicinity $\mathcal{V}$. Note that the time complexity is independent of the window size along the curve.

4.2 Refine the Estimation of Model Parameters (Step 2)

In the second step, the estimation of the model parameters is refined based on a MAP optimization. **Step 2a** updates the estimate $\mathbf{m}_\Phi$ such that the vague assignments $\mathbf{a}_v(\mathbf{m}_\Phi, \boldsymbol{\Sigma}_\Phi)$ of the pixels $v \in \mathcal{V}$ fit best to the local statistics $\mathbf{S}_v$. The feature vectors $\mathbf{I}_v^*$ of pixels $v \in \mathcal{V}$ are modeled as Gaussian random variables. The mean vectors and covariances are estimated from the local statistics $\mathbf{S}_v$ obtained from the corresponding side of pixel v. The feature vectors of edge pixels are modeled as weighted linear combinations of both sides of the edge. In step 2a, only one iteration step of the resulting MAP optimization is performed. Since the vague assignments $\mathbf{a}_v(\mathbf{m}_\Phi, \boldsymbol{\Sigma}_\Phi)$ explicitly take the uncertainty (the covariance $\boldsymbol{\Sigma}_\Phi$) of the estimate into account the capture range is enlarged according to the local uncertainty in the image. This leads to an individually adapted scale selection for each pixel and thereby to a big area of convergence, see [11]. In **step 2b**, the covariance $\boldsymbol{\Sigma}_\Phi$ of the estimate $\mathbf{m}_\Phi$ is updated based on the Hessian of the resulting χ^2 objective function.

5   Experiments

In our experiments we apply the proposed method to several scenes. Fig. 5 shows a mainly white non-RoboCup ball in front of a white and grey, partially textured background. Despite the lack of color the method precisely segments the ball.

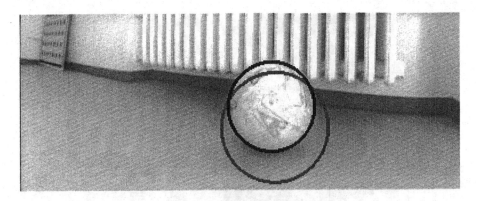

Fig. 5. The white non-RoboCup ball is precisely segmented in front of a white-grey background. This is hardly possible with color labeling. (red: initialization, black: estimated ball contour).

Fig. 6 shows several images where the ball is just partially in the image. But this is enough in order to estimate the ball position. For close up views such as the first three images in Fig. 6 the average error is just a few millimeters, depending on the accuracy of the camera calibration.

In the next experiment we varied the background of the ball and the illumination, see Fig. 7. For the five investigated images the standard deviation of the ball estimates is 0.43 cm which is 0.62% of the estimated distance. Unfortunately, we do not have a sufficiently precise ground truth to compare our results with.

In order to evaluate the performance for a partially occluded ball, we took two images with the same ball position, one with partial occlusion and one without occlusion, see Fig. 8. The ball estimates of the two images differ by 2.0 cm, which is just 2.5% of the ball distance. However, the number of necessary iterations is about 3 times higher in the partially occluded case. The CCD algorithm not only yields an estimate of the ball position, but also a covariance matrix describing the expected uncertainty of the estimate. For the partially occluded ball the expected uncertainty is about three times higher than for the not occluded case. This allows a reasonable data fusion with other sensors data. For a partially occluded ball the area of convergence is significantly reduced, compare Fig. 9 with Fig. 1.

The next example shows that the CCD algorithm can also be successfully applied to objects of a non-spherical shapes. In Fig. 10 the 3-D pose of a cylindrical mug is estimated by fitting the cylinder contour to the image data. Such a cylindrical model could also be used for the corner posts. Examples for radially distorted straight edges are given in [11]. Straight edges could be used for polyhedral models (e.g. goals).

Finally the accuracy of the CCD algorithm is investigated. Semi-synthetic images with a known ground truth are constructed as follows: from two images one combined image is obtained by taking for one side of the curve the content

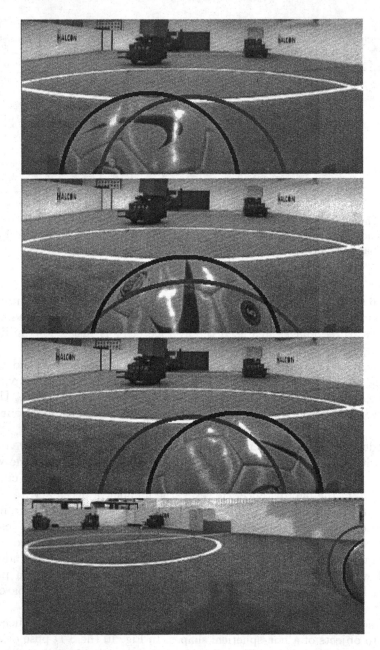

Fig. 6. Refinement of the ball position: initial ball contour (red) and estimated ball contour (black) after 7 iterations. The ball is just partially in the image. Furthermore, the ball has strong specularity and black elements. Nevertheless, the CCD algorithm reliably estimates the ball position.

Fig. 7. The strong variations of background and illumination cause just small variations of the ball estimates. For these five images the standard deviation of the ball estimates is 0.43 cm which is 0.62% of the estimated distance.

Fig. 8. The same ball position with and without occlusion: the estimates of the ball position differ by 2.0 cm which is just 2.5% of the estimated ball distance.

of image one and for the other side of the curve the content of image two. For pixels on the curve the pixel data are interpolated. In Fig. 11 a circle is fitted to two semi-synthetic images. In both cases the errors for all three quantities (x-coordinate, y-coordinate, radius) are less than 5% of a pixel. In both cases the initial error is reduced by more than 99.8%.

The CCD algorithm as used in this paper is designed to achieve high accuracy. The method is not optimized for speed. Hence, the runtime per image is several seconds or even minutes, depending on the resolution and the initial uncertainty. In order to apply the CCD algorithm to real-time object tracking we propose a fast version of the CCD algorithm [13]. This version does not use all pixels in the vicinity of the curve. Instead it uses just a few carefully selected pixels. This method works within frame rate for simple objects such as a ball.

6   Related Work

In this section we first characterize image segmentation methods applied outside RoboCup. Afterwards we discuss briefly related work applied in RoboCup. The

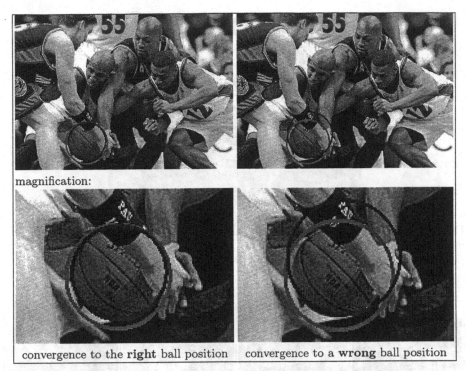

convergence to the **right** ball position   convergence to a **wrong** ball position

Fig. 9. Due to the partial occlusion of the ball and the very heterogeneous non-ball region, the area of convergence is strongly reduced. (red: initial ball contour, blue: estimated ball contour).

body of work on image segmentation methods (developed outside RoboCup) can be roughly classified into three categories: (i) **edge-based segmentation**, (ii) **region-based segmentation**, and (iii) **methods integrating edge-based and region-based segmentation**.

(i) **Edge-based segmentation** (which is also referred as boundary-based segmentation) relies on discontinuities of image data. Methods for different edge-profiles, i.e. types of discontinuities, exist (e.g. step-edge [2, 26, 7], roof-edge [2, 26], others [2, 26]). The problem of edge-based segmentation is that in practice usually the edge-profile is not known. Furthermore, the profile often varies heavily along the edge caused by e.g. shading and texture. Due to these difficulties usually a simple step-edge is assumed and the edge detection is performed based on a maximum image gradient. However, methods maximizing the image gradient have difficulties to separate regions with internal structure or texture.

(ii) **Region-based segmentation** methods such as [34, 9] rely on the homogeneity of spatially localized features (e.g. RGB values). The underlying homogeneity assumption is that the features of all pixels within one region are statistically independently distributed according to the same probability density function. Contrary to edge-based methods region-based methods do not require

Fig. 10. An example of a cylindrical mug: the cylinder contour fitted to the image data matches the mug's contour. The estimated parameters of the contour are the five pose parameters of the cylinder. (red: initial contour, black: estimated contour).

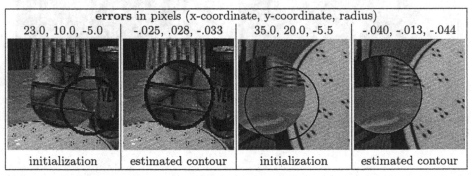

errors in pixels (x-coordinate, y-coordinate, radius)			
23.0, 10.0, -5.0	-.025, .028, -.033	35.0, 20.0, -5.5	-.040, -.013, -.044
initialization	estimated contour	initialization	estimated contour

Fig. 11. Despite the inhomogeneity of the foreground and the background in both cases the final error is less than 5% of a pixel for all three coordinates.

an edge-profile. Furthermore, they are able to exploit higher statistical moments of the distributions. Hence, regions which have the same mean feature but different covariances (e.g. caused by texture) can be separated. However often the underlying assumption of a spatially constant probability density function per region does not hold.

(iii) **Integrating methods:** especially in recent years methods have been published which aim to overcome the individual shortcomings of edge-based and region-based segmentation by integrating both segmentation principles [30, 27, 8, 16]. These methods seek a tradeoff between an edge-based criterion, e.g. the magnitude of the image gradient, and a region-based criterion evaluating the homogeneity of the regions. However, it is questionable whether a tradeoff between the two criteria yields reasonable results when both the homogeneity assumption and the assumption regarding the edge profile do not hold. Due to these difficulties we use local criteria in order to separate adjacent regions. These separation criteria are iteratively obtained from local image statistics.

Model-based methods optimize the fit between the model and the image data. **Global optimization** methods like dynamic programming [1] and Monte Carlo optimization (particle filters, condensation algorithm [5]) are very successfully used (e.g., for tracking). However, dynamic programming requires a discretization of the search space[2], which leads to a limited accuracy, and particle filters show a very slow convergence especially if the sensor noise is low [31].

Local optimization methods may achieve a fast, i.e. quadratic, convergence. Approaches aiming to increase the area of convergence such as [21, 33] are edge-based. For methods maximizing the gradient, the area of convergence depends on the window size used to compute the spatial derivatives. Scale-space theory provides means for automatic scale selection [20]. However, blurring the image data eliminates useful high frequency information. The CCD algorithm does not blur the image data but the curve model. This yields a local and fast optimization with an enlarged area of convergence. Furthermore, high frequency information of the image data is not lost. Several segmentation methods integrate different image cues such as texture and color or brightness [4, 22, 23, 30].

To the best of our knowledge all RoboCup teams use color labeling [29, 32, 15, 17, 6, 3] which belongs to the category of region-based methods. Used color spaces are for example YUV [32, 17, 6, 3] and HSY [15]. The boundaries between the classes are usually defined as rectangles, boxes, or 'pizza-slices'. Simon et al. [29] propose spatially adapted thresholds. In order to infer the ball position from the labeled image data Jonker et al. [17] use a circular Hough Transform. This method is reported to be robust against partial occlusions. Weigel et al. [32] perform a blob analysis and an inverse projection. Contrary to methods based on color labeling, our method does not need known object specific color distributions. Furthermore, knowledge on the ball contour is explicitly modeled and exploited.

7   Conclusion

We have proposed a novel method, called CCD algorithm, for fitting parametric curve models to image data and we applied this method to the problem of localizing the ball. The CCD algorithm does not depend on prior knowledge of object specific color distributions or properly adjusted threshold parameters. Instead the method starts with a vague object model that can be used to infer the expected object contour. The CCD algorithm alternately performs two steps: local statistics of RGB values are computed describing the two sides of the expected contour. Based on these statistics the model parameters are refined in a MAP step by optimizing the separation of the adjacent regions.

We have shown that the method achieves high robustness and accuracy even in the presence of heavy changes in illumination, strong texture, clutter, and specularity. Knowledge of the object of interest and the imaging sensor is explicitly modeled and exploited. This allows a straightforward adaption to other

---

[2] Often the contour is approximated by pixel coordinates, i.e. integers. Hence subpixel positions cannot be obtained.

imaging devices and other problems. Since the CCD algorithm provides a confidence region for the estimates and a likelihood, a fusion with other sources of uncertain information (e.g. multiple observer) can easily be accomplished.

While other methods applied in RoboCup use color information in order to identify objects, in this paper we use shape information. However, vague knowledge on object specific (local or global) color distributions can easily be exploited and subsequently updated by the CCD algorithm. When applied to tracking this could gain additional robustness and accuracy.

Acknowledgments

The authors would like to thank Wiebke Bracht for carefully proof-reading this paper.

References

1. AMINI, A., WEYMOUTH, T., AND JAIN, R. Using dynamic programming for solving variational problems in vision. *IEEE Transactions on Pattern Analysis and Machine Intelligence 12*, 9 (September 1990), 855–867.

2. BAKER, S., NAYAR, S., AND MURASE, H. Parametric feature detection. *International Journal of Computer Vision 27*, 1 (March 1998), 27–50.

3. BANDLOW, T., KLUPSCH, M., HANEK, R., AND SCHMITT, T. Fast image segmentation, object recognition and localization in a robocup scenario. In *Third International Workshop on RoboCup (Robot World Cup Soccer Games and Conferences)* (1999), Lecture Notes in Computer Science, Springer-Verlag.

4. BELONGIE, S., CARSON, C., GREENSPAN, H., AND MALIK, J. Color- and texture-based image segmentation using the expectation-maximization algorithm and its application to content-based image retrieval. In *Proc. International Conference on Computer Vision* (1998), pp. 675–682.

5. BLAKE, A., AND ISARD, M. *Active Contours*. Springer-Verlag, Berlin Heidelberg New York, 1998.

6. BRUCE, J., BALCH, T., AND VELOSO, M. Fast and inexpensive color image segmentation for interactive robots. In *International Conference on Intelligent Robots and Systems (IROS)* (2000).

7. CANNY, J. A computational approach to edge detection. *IEEE Transactions on Pattern Analysis and Machine Intelligence 8*, 6 (November 1986), 679–698.

8. CHAKRABORTY, A., AND DUNCAN, J. Game-theoretic integration for image segmentation. *IEEE Transactions on Pattern Analysis and Machine Intelligence 21*, 1 (January 1999), 12–30.

9. CHESNAUD, C., REFREGIER, P., AND BOULET, V. Statistical region snake-based segmentation adapted to different physical noise models. *IEEE Transactions on Pattern Analysis and Machine Intelligence 21*, 11 (November 1999), 1145–1157.

10. DEMPSTER, A., LAIRD, N., AND RUBIN, D. Maximum likelihood from incomplete data via the EM algorithm. *J. R. Statist. Soc. B 39* (1977), 1–38.

11. HANEK, R. The Contracting Curve Density Algorithm and its Application to Model-based Image Segmentation. In *Proc. Conf. Computer Vision and Pattern Recognition* (2001), pp. I:797–804.

12. HANEK, R., AND SCHMITT, T. Vision-Based Localization and Data Fusion in a System of Cooperating Mobile Robots. In *Proc. of the IEEE Intl. Conf. on Intelligent Robots and Systems* (2000), IEEE/RSJ, pp. 1199–1204.

13. HANEK, R., SCHMITT, T., BUCK, S., AND BEETZ, M. Fast Image-based Object Localization in Natural Scenes. In *Proc. of the IEEE Intl. Conf. on Intelligent Robots and Systems (submitted)* (2002), IEEE/RSJ.

14. HUNDELSHAUSEN, F., BEHNKE, S., AND ROJAS, R. An omnidirectional vision system that finds and tracks color edges and blobs. In *5th International Workshop on RoboCup (Robot World Cup Soccer Games and Conferences)* (2001), Lecture Notes in Computer Science, Springer-Verlag.

15. JAMZAD, M., SADJAD, B., MIRROKNI, V., KAZEMI, M., CHITSAZ, H., HEYDARNOORI, A., HAJIAGHAI, M., AND CHINIFOROOSHAN, E. A fast vision system for middle size robots in RoboCup. In *5th International Workshop on RoboCup (Robot World Cup Soccer Games and Conferences)* (2001), Lecture Notes in Computer Science, Springer-Verlag.

16. JONES, T., AND METAXAS, D. Image segmentation based on the integration of pixel affinity and deformable models. In *Proc. Conf. Computer Vision and Pattern Recognition* (1998), pp. 330–337.

17. JONKER, P., CAARLS, J., AND BOKHOVE, W. Fast and Accurate Robot Vision for Vision based Motion. In *4th International Workshop on RoboCup (Robot World Cup Soccer Games and Conferences)* (2000), P. Stone, T. Balch, and G. Kraetzschmar, Eds., Lecture Notes in Computer Science, Springer-Verlag, pp. 72–82.

18. KASS, M., WITKIN, A., AND TERZOPOULOS, D. Snakes: Active contour models. *International Journal of Computer Vision 1*, 4 (January 1988), 321–331.

19. LENZ, R., AND TSAI, R. Y. Techniques for Calibration of the Scale Factor and Image Center for High Accuracy 3-D Machine Vision Metrology. *IEEE Trans. on Pattern Analysis and Machine Intelligence 10*, 5 (Sept. 1988), 713–720.

20. LINDEBERG, T. Feature detection with automatic scale selection. *International Journal of Computer Vision 30*, 2 (November 1998), 79–116.

21. LUO, H., LU, Q., ACHARYA, R., AND GABORSKI, R. Robust snake model. In *Proc. Conf. Computer Vision and Pattern Recognition* (2000), pp. I:452–457.

22. MALIK, J., BELONGIE, S., SHI, J., AND LEUNG, T. Textons, contours and regions: Cue integration in image segmentation. In *Proc. International Conference on Computer Vision* (1999), pp. 918–925.

23. MANDUCHI, R. Bayesian fusion of color and texture segmentations. In *Proc. International Conference on Computer Vision* (1999), pp. 956–962.

24. MARQUES, C., AND LIMA, P. Vision-Based Self-Localization for Soccer Robots. In *International Conference on Intelligent Robots and Systems (IROS)* (2000).

25. NAKAMURA, T., EBINA, A., IMAI, M., OGASAWARA, T., AND ISHIGURO, H. Real-time Estimating Spatial Configurations between Multiple Robots by Trinagle and Enumeration Constraints. In *International Conference on Intelligent Robots and Systems (IROS)* (2000).

26. NALWA, V., AND BINFORD, T. On detecting edges. *IEEE Transactions on Pattern Analysis and Machine Intelligence 8*, 6 (November 1986), 699–714.

27. PARAGIOS, N., AND DERICHE, R. Coupled geodesic active regions for image segmentation: A level set approach. In *Proc. European Conference on Computer Vision* (2000), pp. 224–240.

28. SEMPLE, J., AND KNEEBONE, G. *Algebraic projective geometry.* Oxford University Press, 1952.

29. SIMON, M., BEHNKE, S., AND ROJAS, R. Robust real time color tracking. In *4th International Workshop on RoboCup (Robot World Cup Soccer Games and Conferences)* (2000), P. Stone, T. Balch, and G. Kraetzschmar, Eds., Lecture Notes in Computer Science, Springer-Verlag, pp. 239–248.

30. THIRION, B., BASCLE, B., RAMESH, V., AND NAVAB, N. Fusion of color, shading and boundary information for factory pipe segmentation. In *Proc. Conf. Computer Vision and Pattern Recognition* (2000), pp. II:349–356.

31. THRUN, S., FOX, D., AND BURGARD, W. Monte carlo localization with mixture proposal distribution. In *Proc. of the AAAI National Conference on Artificial Intelligence* (2000), pp. 859–865.

32. WEIGEL, T., KLEINER, A., DIESCH, F., DIETL, M., GUTMANN, J.-S., NEBEL, B., STIEGELER, P., AND SZERBAKOWSKI, B. Cs freiburg 2001. In *5th International Workshop on RoboCup (Robot World Cup Soccer Games and Conferences)* (2001), Lecture Notes in Computer Science, Springer-Verlag.

33. XU, C., AND PRINCE, J. Snakes, shapes, and gradient vector flow. *IEEE Transactions on Image Processing 7*, 3 (March 1998), 359–369.

34. ZHU, S., AND YUILLE, A. Region competition: Unifying snakes, region growing, and bayes/mdl for multiband image segmentation. *IEEE Transactions on Pattern Analysis and Machine Intelligence 18*, 9 (September 1996), 884–900.

Integration of Advice
in an Action-Selection Architecture

Paul Carpenter, Patrick Riley, Manuela M. Veloso, and Gal A. Kaminka

Department of Computer Science
Carnegie Mellon University
Pittsburgh, PA 15213-3891, USA
{carpep,pfr,mmv,galk}@cs.cmu.edu

Abstract. The introduction of a coach competition in the RoboCup-2001 simulation league raised many questions concerning the development of a "coachable" team. This paper addresses the issues of dealing with conflicting advice and knowing when to listen to advice. An action-selection architecture is proposed to support the integration of advice into an agent's set of beliefs. The results from the coach competition are discussed and provide a basis for experiments. Results are provided to support the claim that the architecture is well-suited for such a task.

1 Introduction

In the future, the complexity of the tasks agents will be expected to perform will dramatically increase. It is not feasible to think one could hand-code execution plans for agents to utilize in all situations. Instead, it is likely that agents will employ a generalized architecture capable of integrating advice from external agents tailored to its current goal. Advice is not necessarily a plan to reach a goal, but rather hints or directions that will likely aid in the agent's planning.

In the simulated robotic soccer domain, an online coach acts as an advice-giving agent [11] [15]. The coach receives a global view of the world but it has limited opportunities to communicate with the team. Therefore, it is impossible for the coach to act as a centralized agent controlling the actions of the other agents. However, a coach has the ability to periodically offer general advice or suggest changes in the team's strategy. It is clear that the coach has the potential to greatly impact the performance of a team; whether it is for better or for worse depends on how the team chooses to use the advice.

This work describes the issues one must consider while implementing a "coachable" team. In addition, this work describes how coach advice is integrated into the ChaMeleons-2001 action-selection architecture as well as how advice from other agents (e.g., a "team captain", others teammates, or even humans) can be used [2].

A specific issue of consideration is whether to blindly follow all advice that is given. For example, the ChaMeleon's online coach, OWL, offers advice in the form of passing rules [14] [13]. Consider the situation when an agent has a

G.A. Kaminka, P.U. Lima, and R. Rojas (Eds.): RoboCup 2002, LNAI 2752, pp. 195–205, 2003.
© Springer-Verlag Berlin Heidelberg 2003

clear shot on goal but one of the coach's passing rules is applicable - should the agent follow the advice and pass the ball or should it attempt to score on the open goal? In the same situation, a human is able to quickly reason about the choices and realize that an open shot on goal must be an exception to one of the coach's rules. How does an agent know when to ignore the coach however? The coach agent could attempt to make its advice rules more strict, incorporating exceptions in the rules; however, this is not feasible. Instead, the players need a mechanism to recognize exceptions to the advice given to them.

An agent should also be allowed to ignore pieces of advice in order to resolve conflicting rules. As in the example above, a coach gives a rule for player one to pass to player two given a specific state of the world. Later, the coach observes that player one should shoot on goal in that very same state. Player one now has two conflicting pieces of advice and cannot execute both actions simultaneously. If it chooses to follow the advice of the coach, it must resolve this conflict and choose only one rule to follow.

A third issue that must be considered is how to handle advice in such a way that facilitates the inclusion of advice from several sources. The advice could be weighted differently or organized as a hierarchical mixture of experts similar to [6].

The design of the ChaMeleons-2001 addresses each one of these issues.

2   Related Work

There has been little research involving online coaches in the RoboCup simulation community. Before RoboCup-2001, the most common uses of a coach were to communicate formation/role information [1] [3] [4] and setplay information [4] [12] [16]. Robocup-2001 introduced a standard coach language in which information is communicated to the players via condition-action rules [15]. With the introduction of the coach competition in 2001, it is likely that more will concentrate on developing "coachable" teams.

The idea of integrating advice from an external source is not new though; McCarthy made the suggestion nearly 45 years ago [9]. However, the number of systems that have done just this are limited and usually specific to a particular problem, e.g., integrating advice in Q-learning to increase an agent's overall reward [7].

There has also been work that attempts to address how to handle conflicting advice [5]. This is one of the very same issues soccer agents must address when accepting advice from other agents. [5] offers four criteria to determine how to resolve conflicts:

- Specificity - more constraining rules followed first
- Freshness - more recent advice followed first
- Authority - one agent has the ability to over rule another agent's advice
- Reliability - follow the advice that has the highest probability of success

This technique is much different than how conflicts are resolved in ChaMeleons-2001. Depending on the type of conflict, advice may be ignored or prioritized based on what type of advice is given. Modifications to the architecture to support other types of complex conflict resolution, e.g., the ones proposed by [5], would require implementing only a new behavior arbitrator.

One of the techniques used by the ChaMeleons-2001 to solve conflicts is very similar to the soft enforcement method introduced by [10]. Soft enforcement gives preference towards plans consistent with pieces of advice. Advice that introduces conflicts however are ignored. In the ChaMeleons-2001, before advice is attached as a child, it is verified as being both recommended and not discouraged by the coach.

3   Architecture Overview

The ChaMeleons-2001 utilize a hierarchical, behavior-based architecture. Action-selection for the agents presents itself in the three primary components of the architecture:

- Individual Behaviors
- Behavior Manager
- Behavior Arbitrator

An agent executes the root behavior each cycle. The root behavior selects which actions to consider depending on the current world state. The Behavior Manager is responsible for actually instantiating the behaviors to consider as well as including other considerations based on the coach's advice. A Behavior Arbitrator is used to ultimately determine which choice is executed. The relationship between each component is shown in Figure 1.

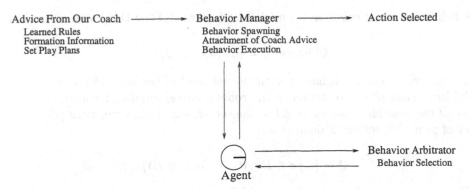

Fig. 1. Action Selection Architecture

3.1   Behaviors

A behavior is a means to achieve a goal. The goal is reached through the execution of a behavior and a chain of child behaviors. A child behavior is a way to achieve the goal of its parent and it too may have children of its own. Every child of a behavior is an alternative way to achieve the goal of its parent. For example, the *passBall* behavior may have many *passToPlayer* children corresponding to the different passing options it has. Every behavior also possesses the following properties:

- **Applicability Conditions** - Determines whether or not it is appropriate for the behavior to execute given the current state of the world
- **Probability of Success** - The likelihood that the behavior will execute successfully
- **Value** - The value of the future world state assuming its execution is successful
- **Class** - Used when integrating advice by adding those behaviors recommended by the coach that match one of the classes of its children. Therefore, a *passToPlayer* behavior recommended by the coach is added as a child of *passBall* because its class matches one of *passBall*'s children.
- **Source** - A behavior is generated by its parent or as a result from advice. A behavior's source marks its origin, i.e., parent or coach

Behavior Organization. The behaviors are organized in a hierarchical fashion with the most primitive actions being at the bottom and the root behavior at the top. The hierarchy is organized as a directed acyclic graph with vertices and edges (B, E) where:

$$B = \{b : b \text{ is a behavior}\}$$
$$E = \{(b_1, b_2) : b_2 \text{ is a child of } b_1\}$$

A behavior's set of children can be defined in terms of the DAG as:

$$\text{Children}(b) = \{c : (b, c) \in E\}$$

A primitive action is a behavior at the lowest level of the hierarchy as it has no children. Each primitive action in the robotic soccer simulator corresponds to one of the possible actions to send to the server, e.g., kick, turn, dash [15]. The set of primitive actions is defined as:

$$A = \{a : a \in B \wedge (\neg \exists b)((a, b) \in E)\}$$

Given a set of primitive actions, the DAG has the property that there exists a path from every behavior to at least one primitive action:

$$(\forall b \in B)(\exists a \in A)(\exists p)(p \text{ is a path from } b \text{ to } a)$$

Because there exists a path from every behavior to one of the primitive actions, it is guaranteed that at every simulation cycle, an action will be selected to execute.

3.2   Behavior Manager

The Behavior Manager (BM) is the component responsible for all things related to a behavior's creation and execution, including the integration of advice. The BM maintains a pool of fresh behaviors so that they do not have to be repeatedly instantiated throughout the action-selection process or even across cycles. Stale behaviors are periodically flushed from the pool in such a way to balance the time needed to search for behaviors in the pool and the time required to instantiate new behaviors.

Behaviors are also executed through the BM. The BM logs the execution state of each behavior and if no action is selected, it may attempt to execute another behavior [17]. The bookkeeping the BM maintains makes it possible to trace the complete chain of behaviors considered and executed. As a result, the architecture used to implement a "coachable" team is also convenient in tracing and debugging behaviors during development.

Integration of Advice. The BM is also responsible for integrating advice from the coach. Advice generates new behaviors to be added to a behavior's set of children. Given a set B_{advice} of coach recommended behaviors, the advice integration is done as follows:

$$\forall b \in B \exists b_c \in \text{Children}(b) \exists b_a \in B_{\text{advice}} b_c.\text{class} = b_a.\text{class} \Rightarrow E \leftarrow E \cup \{(b, b_a)\}$$

A behavior recommended by the coach is inserted into the set of children of all behaviors for which it matches one of the behaviors' classes of children. The integration of advice from other sources would be done in the same fashion. Because all behaviors maintain its source as one of its properties, different arbitration methods, e.g. a hierarchical mixture of experts, could potentially be developed to decide among the children [6].

3.3   Behavior Arbitrator

A Behavior Arbitrator (Arb) is a function that chooses a single behavior to execute among a behavior's set of children. More specifically, given a set of children a behavior is considering for execution, an arbitrator determines which child to actually execute. In general, an arbitrator selects the argument c that maximizes some function $f(c)$:

$$\text{Arb}(b) = \text{argmax}_c \ c \in \text{Children}(b) \wedge f(c)$$

The type of arbitrator used depends highly on the class of the behavior, however they all maximize some function that "scores" each child. Three arbitrators are described below:

1. **Value-Based** - The child that maximizes the future state of the world:

$$\text{Arb}_{\text{value}}(b) = \text{argmax}_c \ c \in \text{Children}(b) \wedge c.\text{value}$$

2. **Probability of Success** - The child with the highest probability of success:

$$\text{Arb}_{\text{prob}}(b) = \text{argmax}_c \; c \in \text{Children}(b) \wedge c.\text{probabilityOfSuccess}$$

3. **Coach-Based** - If there exists children recommended by the coach, arbitrate among those choices. Otherwise, choose an alternative arbitration method:

$$\text{Arb}_{\text{coach}}(b) = \left\{ \begin{array}{ll} \text{argmax}_c \begin{array}{l} c \in \text{Children}(b) \wedge \\ c.\text{src} = COACH \wedge \\ f(c) \end{array} , \{c : c.\text{src} = COACH\} \neq \emptyset \\ \text{Arb}(b) \qquad\qquad\qquad , \text{otherwise} \end{array} \right\}$$

The example arbitrators are all fairly straightforward. The complexity of the arbitration depends highly on the scoring function, $f(c)$. One could potentially use decision trees to arbitrate among passing options [17] or neural networks to determine when and where to shoot on goal [8]. One of the more complex arbitrators used by the ChaMeleons-2001 is the *handleBall* BA.

handleBall Arbitrator. The *handleBall* arbitrator provides a way for the players to choose what behavior to execute while having possession of the ball, including when, and when not, to follow the advice of the coach. There exists a set, P, of priority levels each having a behavior descriptor. Associated with each priority level is a threshold for the behavior's probability of success. The probability threshold, currently hand-coded, must be met in order for the behavior to execute. When given a set of choices, the behavior with the highest priority that meets its threshold is executed. A subset of the priority levels and thresholds is shown in Table 1. Please note that it is possible for the same descriptor to appear with different priorities and thresholds. This allows a behavior to be considered for execution at more than one priority level based on its threshold of success. For example, if a shot on goal has a .6 probability of success, it has a fairly low priority, however, it still might have a higher priority than simply clearing the ball down the field. A shot with a .8 probability of success has a much higher priority and therefore would be one of the first behaviors considered for execution.

There exists a relation, R, from *handleBall*'s set of children, C, to the set of priority levels, P. It is possible for a behavior to be described by more than one priority level. For example, *pass_forward* and *pass_to_less_congested* could potentially describe the same behavior. The relation has the property that the set of behaviors a priority level describes all have the same type:

$$\forall p \in P \exists b_1 \in B \exists b_2 \in B$$
$$(b_1, p) \in R \wedge (b_2, p) \in R \wedge b_1 \neq b_2 \Rightarrow b_1.\text{class} = b_2.\text{class}$$

In order to choose a single child to execute, the elements in the set of priority levels are sorted based on the priority of each descriptor:

$$(\forall p_i \in P)(p_i < p_{i+1})$$

Table 1. One Possible Priority Level Ordering

Priority	Descriptor	Success Probability Threshold
1	*shoot_on_goal*	.8
2	*coach_pass_for_shot*	.7
3	*pass_for_shot*	.8
4	*pass_forward*	.75
5	*dribble_to_goal*	.75
6	*dribble_to_corner*	.8
7	*pass_to_less_congested*	.7
8	*coach_pass_forward*	.8
9	*pass_to_closer_to_goal*	.75
10	*pass_to_better_path_to_goal*	.8
11	*shoot_on_goal*	.6

This allows the arbitrator to be defined as a function of a behavior's probability of success (probSucc) and its threshold:

$$\text{Arb}_{handleBall} = \text{argmax}_{i,b} \quad \begin{aligned} &b \in \{b : (b, p_i) \in R\} \wedge \\ &p_i \wedge b.\text{probSucc} \wedge \\ &b.\text{probSucc} > p_i.\text{Threshold} \end{aligned}$$

The *handleBall* arbitrator maximizes both the priority level and the probability of success for all behaviors at that level, given the constraint that the threshold is met. The ordering of the priority levels makes it possible to ignore the coach when it is possible to execute a behavior that is given a higher priority. For example, an agent should always choose to shoot when the probability of success is high as opposed to making a coach-recommended pass.

4   Coach Advice

This section gives an overview of the type of advice given by the OWL coach, which was also created at Carnegie Mellon [14] [13].

There are five main types of advice. The first four are given at the beginning the game. The first gives a home position for each member of the team to define a team formation. Next, static marking advice assigns defenders to mark the opponent forwards, based on the expected opponent formation. Passing advice is based on trying to imitate another team. Rules are learned about passing behavior of a team by observing them. Those rules are then sent as advice to try and mimic the observed team's behavior. Similarly, rules are learned about the opponent's passing, and the advice the agents receive predicts the opponent's passes. Finally, during the game play, the coach makes short passing and movement plans for "set-play" situations, where our team has a free kick. For information concerning how the advice is generated, please refer to [14] [13].

Table 2. Results of the 2001 RoboCup Coach Competition

		Coach Used			
	No Coach	Wright Eagle	Helli Respina	Dirty Dozen	ChaMeleons-2001
Wright Eagle	8:0	-	0:0	0:0	2:0
Helli-Respina	5:0	2:11	-	0:14	0:0
Dirty Dozen	0:10	0:28	0:29	-	0:20
ChaMeleons-01	0:4	0:6	0:6	0:9	-

5   Experimental Results

The RoboCup simulation league had its first coach competition in 2001. The competition was open only to teams that supported the standard coach language [15]. Teams played a baseline game without a coach against a fixed opponent. A team's coach is used with all the other teams against the same opponent, Gemini, and the winner is determined based on a ranking of goal differentials. The teams were not tested using their own coaches since the competition was geared towards developing a coach capable of improving the performance of any team. The goal differentials were determined by differences in goals scored, e.g., the goal differential for the Helli-Respina game using the Wright Eagle coach is -14 (3 fewer goals scored, and 11 more goals allowed).

The results of the coach competition, given in Table 2, were very surprising. It appeared as if using a coach hindered the performance of every team in every game throughout the competition. It was believed that due to slight differences in the interpretation of the coach language semantics, it was very difficult to support another team's coach.

What is also interesting is that, in addition to winning the competition with its coach OWL, the ChaMeleon-2001 appeared to be the most coachable team in the competition - the team with the largest overall goal differential. This raised many questions, but statistically significant results cannot be inferred from such a few number of games. It became obvious that in order to reach any conclusions about the effects a coach has on a team, many experiments would need to be conducted.

After RoboCup, hundreds of games were played using different coaches as well as different advice taking strategies in an attempt to better understand exactly what happened during the coach competition at RoboCup-2001 and determine exactly how much impact a coach has on a team. For each experiment, a different coach or advice-taking strategy was used during thirty regulation length games. The goal differentials were based on a separate set of games using no coach - the same as in the coach competition. The fixed opponent remained the same as in the coach competition, Gemini.

Figure 2 shows the resulting goal differentials using the ChaMeleons-2001 with each of the coaches from that entered the coach competition with the exception of Wright Eagle. Wright Eagle's coach was implemented in Windows and the testing environment set up could not support its inclusion. A statistically significant improvement in performance is shown by the ChaMeleons-2001 using

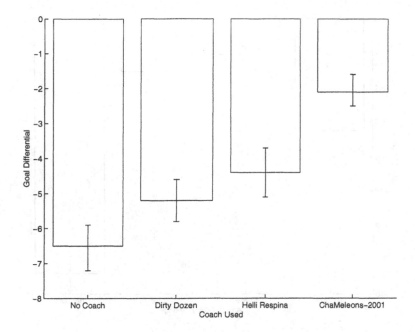

Fig. 2. Goal Differentials Using Several Coaches

every coach tested. Using its own coach, OWL, the ChaMeleons-2001 experienced a three times improvement over the baseline goal differential.

Figure 3 shows the results of the experiments using different advice taking strategies with a single coach, OWL. The normal coach is the same coach used above (with the same results). The strict strategy blindly follows all advice that is given to the agents. As shown, it performs slightly worse though statistically significant at a level $p < .05$ with a two-tailed t-test. The random strategy is one in which truly random advice is sent to the agents. As expected, it performs far worse than any of the other strategies including not listening to the coach at all.

6   Conclusion

The action-selection architecture for the ChaMeleons-2001 simulated robotic soccer team was designed to integrate advice from many sources. This year, advice from only the coach agent was used. It was shown experimentally that the architecture is successful in its integration of advice and choosing when, and when not, to listen to the coach agent's advice. The team saw improvement while using every coach tested with. The success of the ChaMeleons is due to the agents ability to ignore the coach when the agents believe they are able to execute a higher priority action. It can also be concluded that a coach agent does indeed have the potential to greatly impact the performance of a team.

Although it has been shown that the ChaMeleon's are indeed a highly coachable team, other possibilities for the architecture lie ahead. For example, it is

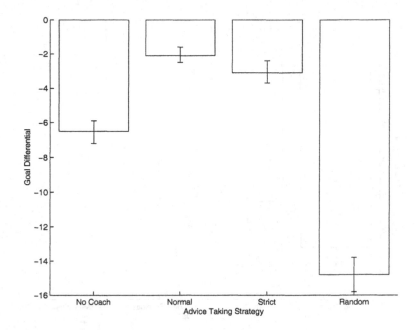

Fig. 3. Goal Differentials Using Different Advice-Taking Strategies

possible for the behavior descriptors used by the *handleBall* to also describe the sequence of actions performed by an opponent. Given these sequences, rules can be inferred to describe when an opponent performs an action or an opponent's equivalent ordering of priority levels can be learned. A team receiving this advice from a coach could learn how to mimic the playing style of its opponents - hence the name ChaMeleons.

Another possibility for the ChaMeleons is the inclusion of several advice sources. Players could potentially receive advice from other players on the team, including a "captain." This raises many questions including which piece of advice does an agent follow when more than one rule matches from different sources or how to handle conflicting advice from multiple sources.

The action-selection architecture for the ChaMeleons-2001 was designed to facilitate both the integration of advice into the agents set of beliefs as well as other future learning tasks. An attempt was made to ensure that the architecture was not domain-dependent and could easily be adapted to other problems as well. As agent research shifts from learning to learning from other agents, the architecture proposed will provide a framework for others considering some of the issues involved with the integration of advice.

References

1. Ciprian Candea and Marius Staicu. AIRG Sibiu. In Peter Stone, Tucker Balch, and Gerhard Kraetszchmar, editors, *RoboCup-2000: Robot Soccer World Cup IV*, pages 409–412. Springer Verlag, Berlin, 2001.

2. Paul Carpenter, Patrick Riley, Gal Kaminka, Manuela Veloso, Ignacio Thayer, and Robert Wang. ChaMeleons-2001 team description. In *RoboCup-2000: Robot Soccer World Cup V*. Springer Verlag, Berlin, 2002.

3. Christian Drucker, Sebastian Hubner, Esko Schmidt, Ubbo Visser, and Hans-Georg Weland. Virtual werder. In Peter Stone, Tucker Balch, and Gerhard Kraetszchmar, editors, *RoboCup-2000: Robot Soccer World Cup IV*, pages 421–424. Springer Verlag, Berlin, 2001.

4. Tetsuya Esaki, Taku Sakushima, Shinji Futamase, Nobuhiro Ito, Tomoichi Takahashi, Wei Chen, and Koichi Wada. Kakitsubata team description. In Peter Stone, Tucker Balch, and Gerhard Kraetszchmar, editors, *RoboCup-2000: Robot Soccer World Cup IV*, pages 425–428. Springer Verlag, Berlin, 2001.

5. B. Grosof. Conflict handling in advice taking and instruction. Technical report, IBM Research Report 20123, 1995.

6. M.I. Jordan and R.a. Jacobs. Hierarchical mixture of experts and the em algorithm. In *Neural Computation*, 1993.

7. R. Maclin and J.W. Shavlik. Incorporating advice into agents that learn from reinforcements. In *Proc. of AAAI-1994*, pages 694–699, 1994.

8. Frederic Maire and Doug Taylor. A quadratic programming formulation of a moving ball interception and shooting behaviour, and its application to neural network control. In Peter Stone, Tucker Balch, and Gerhard Kraetszchmar, editors, *RoboCup-2000: Robot Soccer World Cup IV*, pages 327–332. Springer Verlag, Berlin, 2001.

9. J. McCarthy. Programs with common sense. In *Proc. Symp. on the Mechanization of Thought Processes*, pages 77–81, 1958.

10. Karen L. Myers. Planning with conflicting advice. In *Artificial Intelligence Planning Systems*, pages 355–362, 2000.

11. Itsuki Noda, Hitoshi Matsubara, Kazuo Hiraki, and Ian Frank. Soccer server: A tool for research on multiagent systems. *Applied Artificial Intelligence*, 12:233–250, 1998.

12. Patrick Riley, Peter Stone, David McAllester, and Manuela Veloso. Att-cmunited-2000: Third place finisher in the robocup-2000 simulator league. In Peter Stone, Tucker Balch, and Gerhard Kraetszchmar, editors, *RoboCup-2000: Robot Soccer World Cup IV*, pages 489–492. Springer Verlag, Berlin, 2001.

13. Patrick Riley, Manuela Veloso, and Gal Kaminka. An empirical study of coaching. In *Distributed Autonomous Robotic Systems 6*. Springer-Verlag, 2002. (to appear).

14. Patrick Riley, Manuela Veloso, and Gal Kaminka. Towards any-team coaching in adversarial domains. In *AAMAS-02*, 2002. (poster paper) (to appear).

15. RoboCup Federation, http://sserver.sourceforge.net/. *Soccer Server Manual*, 2001.

16. Birgit Schappel and Frank Schulz. Mainz rolling brains 2000. In Peter Stone, Tucker Balch, and Gerhard Kraetszchmar, editors, *RoboCup-2000: Robot Soccer World Cup IV*, pages 497–500. Springer Verlag, Berlin, 2001.

17. Peter Stone, Patrick Riley, and Manuela Veloso. The cmunited-99 champion simulator team. In *RoboCup-99: Robot Soccer World Cup III*. Springer Verlag, Berlin, 2000.

The Role of Motion Dynamics in the Design, Control and Stability of Bipedal and Quadrupedal Robots

Michael Hardt and Oskar von Stryk

Department of Computer Science, Technische Universität Darmstadt
Alexanderstr. 10, 64283 Darmstadt, Germany
{hardt,stryk}@sim.tu-darmstadt.de
www.sim.informatik.tu-darmstadt.de

Abstract. Fundamental principles and recent methods for investigating the nonlinear dynamics of legged robot motions with respect to control, stability and design are discussed. One of them is the still challenging problem of producing dynamically stable gaits. The generation of fast walking or running motions require methods and algorithms adept at handling the nonlinear dynamical effects and stability issues which arise. Reduced, recursive multibody algorithms, a numerical optimal control package, and new stability and energy performance indices are presented which are well-suited for this purpose. Difficulties and open problems are discussed along with numerical investigations into the proposed gait generation scheme. Our analysis considers both biped and quadrupedal gaits with particular reference to the problems arising in soccer-playing tasks encountered at the RoboCup where our team, the Darmstadt Dribbling Dackels, participates as part of the German Team in the Sony Legged Robot League.

1 Introduction

RoboCup and Dynamics of Legged Robot Motion. The RoboCup scenario of soccer playing legged robots represents an extraordinary challenge for the design, control and stability of bipedal and quadrupedal robots. In a game, fast motions are desired which preserve the robot's stability and can be adapted in real-time to the quickly changing enviroment. Existing design and control strategies for bipedal and quadrupedal robots can only meet these challenges to a small extent.

During the nineties, both trajectory planning methods relying on nonlinear robot dynamics and model-based control methods have evolved into the state-of-the-art for developing and implementing fast and accurate motions for industrial manipulators. Successful control of the nonlinear robot dynamics is also the key to fast and stable motions of bipedal and quadrupedal robots. Many subproblems remain unsolved in fulfilling this objective. This paper contributes to this ambitious goal by discussing fundamental principles and recent methods in the modeling, simulation, optimization and control of legged robot dynamics.

G.A. Kaminka, P.U. Lima, and R. Rojas (Eds.): RoboCup 2002, LNAI 2752, pp. 206–223, 2003.
© Springer-Verlag Berlin Heidelberg 2003

Nonlinear Dynamics of Legged Robot Motion. A precise modeling of fast moving legged locomotion systems requires high dimensional nonlinear multibody dynamics which can accurately describe the nonlinear relationships existing between all linear and rotational forces acting at each joint and the feet on the one hand and the position, velocity and acceleration of each link in the kinematic tree-structure on the other hand. It is thus a complex task to generate and control stable motions for such systems. Biped and quadruped constructions generally consist of a minimum of five bodies with two to six degrees of freedom (DoF) per leg in addition to the six DoF corresponding to the base body in order to give the necessary amount of motion dexterity necessary for a wide range of movement. Dynamic model simplifications in previous work, however, have generally ranged from pendulum models [22] to multi-link planar models [5, 6, 14, 16] for bipeds and for quadrupeds [17] or to multi-link spatial models [20, 27]. Though these simplifications allow one to analyze certain predominant behaviors of the dynamic system, many other important features are lost. A complete and complex dynamical system description will contain much more of the significant dynamical effects, yet a control solution for these models based on an analytical approach is usually not possible and results must be sought for numerically.

The dynamic effects characterizing bipedal and quadrupedal motion may be further complicated by external disturbance factors and forces, quickly changing system goals, low friction conditions, a limited power source, and inexact sensor information resulting from fast movements and a highly dynamic environment. These are all characteristics of the difficulties encountered in the Four-Legged and Humanoid Leagues of the RoboCup soccer challenge.

Solutions for Multibody Dynamics of Legged Robot Models. Multibody dynamical models for real legged systems are typically characterized by a high number of DoF, relatively few contact constraints or collision events, and a variety of potential ground contact models, actuator models, and mass-inertial parameter settings due to changing load conditions. Such detailed multibody dynamical models are generally required for the realistic reproduction of legged system behavior in gait optimization (Sect. 4.2), tuning of construction design parameters (Sect. 6), or in simulation and feedback control (Sect. 5). Closed-form dynamical expressions are the most efficient form of evaluating the dynamics, but are not well-suited to legged systems due to the many changing kinematic and kinetic parameters. Recursive, numerical algorithms are also highly efficient for large systems and permit the easy interchangeability of parameters and the introduction of external forces without repeated extensive preprocessing (Sect. 2.2). This approach has been used here. Reduced dynamical approaches appropriate for legged robots are additionally presented in Sect. 2.2.

Dynamical Stability of Legged Robot Motion. There exists a wide spectrum of previously presented approaches for generating dynamically stable motions in bipeds and quadrupeds. Analytical methods [14, 19, 22] usually rely on simplified models and are not yet at a stage where the many influencing dynamical effects previously mentioned can be considered. More complete 3-D modeling approaches [20, 27] for bipeds generally rely on heuristic schemes to construct dynamically stable motions. The dynamic stability criterion is usually based on the Zero-Moment-Point [35] yet this criterion is limited in its ability to classify stability [12] during, for example, periods of rolling motion of the feet, which for fast-moving systems can be considerable. In the case of quadrupeds with point contacts, a similar problem occurs. Such gait planning techniques also rarely consider the stabilizing potential of the torso sway motion or that of arm swinging which can be advantageous for increasing robustness and reducing power consumption. Nonetheless, 3-D bipeds and quadrupeds have been constructed which perform dynamically stable walking and running [18, 34, 37]. Though due to excessive power consumption they were either not autonomous or required a substantial battery supply for only a short operational period. In Sect. 3, alternative stability as well as energy-based performance measures suited for bipedal and quadrupedal gait generation are presented.

Numerical Optimization and Feedback Control of Bipedal and Quadrupedal Robot Motions. Algebraic control strategies for legged systems cannot yet handle the high dimension and many modeling constraints present in the locomotion problem. Heuristic control methods, on the other hand, tend to have poor performance with respect to power efficiency and stability and require much hand-tuning to acquire an acceptable implementation in a fast-moving legged system. The remaining proven approach is the use of sophisticated numerical optimization schemes to generate optimal trajectories subject to the numerous modeling constraints. The resulting trajectories may later be tracked or used to approximate a feedback controller in the portion of state space of interest.

In our efforts to achieve dynamically stable and efficient gaits for the Sony RoboCup quadruped (Figure1) and our own competition biped currently under construction, we explore in this work a numerical optimization approach which minimize performance or stability objectives in the gait generation problem. Numerical optimization tools have advanced sufficiently [2, 11, 32] such that all the above-mentioned modeling and stability constraints can be incorporated into the problem formulation together with a relatively complete dynamical model so as to obtain truly realistic energy-efficient, stable and fast motions. The optimization approach described in Sect. 4.1 has been developed during the last decade and has already been successfully applied for gait planning in bipeds in two dimensions [16] and for quadrupeds [17].

2   Dynamic Modeling of Legged Locomotion

2.1   Two Case Studies for Biped and Quadruped Dynamics

Two models of a bipedal and a quadrupedal robot are treated here. The presented approach, however, is applicable to any other legged robot design.

Our model for the Sony quadruped (see Fig. 1) consists of a 9-link tree-structured multibody system with a central torso attached to a relatively heavy head at a fixed position and four two-link legs. Each leg contains a 2 DoF universal joint in the hip and a 1 DoF rotational joint in the knee. A (almost) minimum

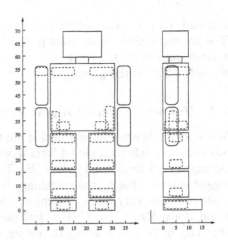

Fig. 1. Four-legged Sony robots

Fig. 2. Design of humanoid robot prototype

set of coordinates consists of 19 position and 19 velocity states $(\mathbf{q}(t), \dot{\mathbf{q}}(t))$ which include a four-parameter unit quaternion vector for the orientation, a three-dimensional global position vector, and their time derivatives for the torso, and additionally three angles and their velocities for each leg. The 12 control variables $\mathbf{u}(t)$ correspond to the applied torques in the legs. The required kinematic and kinetic data for each link (length, mass, center of mass, moments of inertia) have been provided by Sony. A refined model will be used in further investigations which also includes the three motion DoF for the head.

The physical dimensions for our biped protype fall under the specifications set for the 80 *cm* category of the RoboCup competition[1]. The biped (Fig. 2) has six DoF (hip 3, knee, 1, foot 2) in each leg and 2 DoF in the shoulder so that a coordinate set consists of 23 position and 23 velocity states $(\mathbf{q}(t), \dot{\mathbf{q}}(t))$ including 7 position states with a quaternion and position vector to describe the torso orientation and position. There are 16 actuated joints whose input torques are represented in the control vector $\mathbf{u}(t)$. Different to quadruped gaits where in many cases a foot contact model may be sufficient, a foot contact area must be considered for a biped.

In both cases, the structure of the equations of motion are those for a rigid, multibody system experiencing contact forces,

$$\ddot{\mathbf{q}} = \mathcal{M}(\mathbf{q})^{-1}\Big(B\mathbf{u} - \mathcal{C}(\mathbf{q}, \dot{\mathbf{q}}) - \mathcal{G}(\mathbf{q}) + J_c(\mathbf{q})^T \mathbf{f}_c\Big)$$
$$0 = \mathbf{g}_c(\mathbf{q}) \, , \tag{1}$$

where N equals the number of links, $\mathcal{M} \in \mathbb{R}^{N \times N}$ is the positive-definite mass-inertia matrix, $\mathcal{C} \in \mathbb{R}^N$ contains the Coriolis and centrifugal forces, $\mathcal{G} \in \mathbb{R}^N$ the gravitational forces, and $\mathbf{u}(t) \in \mathbb{R}^m$ are the control input functions which are

---

[1] http://www.robocup.org/regulations/humanoid/rule_humanoid.htm

mapped with the constant matrix $B \in \mathbb{R}^{N \times m}$ to the actively controlled joints. The ground contact constraints $\mathbf{g_c} \in \mathbb{R}^{n_c}$ represent holonomic constraints on the system from which the constraint Jacobian may be obtained $J_c = \frac{\partial \mathbf{g_c}}{\partial \mathbf{q}} \in \mathbb{R}^{n_c \times N}$, while $\mathbf{f}_c \in \mathbb{R}^{n_c}$ is the ground constraint force.

2.2 Robotic Dynamic Algorithms

Many methods exist for evaluating multibody robot dynamics. Symbolic methods construct efficient, closed form dynamics for the *specific* multibody systems through symbolic simplifications [28]. This approach is not well-suited though to legged systems due to the switching characteristic of the dynamics in different contact states, varying parameter and exterior load conditions. The Composite Rigid Body Algorithm (CRBA) [36] numerically solves the equations of motion efficently by first assembling the entire mass matrix $\mathcal{M}$ and then solving the resulting system. It is used in many commercial packages, and it permits an easy change of parameters or the introduction of additional external forces directly. These solution methods are, in general, superceded in modularity and in efficiency for systems with more than 7–8 links by the articulated body algorithm (ABA) of $\mathcal{O}(N)$ complexity [9].

The ABA [8, 31] is a very exact and numerically stable multibody algorithm superior to the CRBA as it introduces less cancellations [29]. It exploits the linear relationship between accelerations and applied forces in a rigid-body system. The definition of the articulated body inertia, the inertia of the 'floppy' outboard chain of rigid bodies not subject to applied forces, permitted the construction of a recursive forward dynamics algorithm [8]. Similarities to the Kalman filtering algorithm then led to an alternative decomposition of the mass-inertia matrix and, consequently, to an $\mathcal{O}(N)$ recursive algorithm for calculating the inverse mass matrix $\mathcal{M}^{-1}$ [31]. A description of the original algorithms may be found in [8, 31] with improvements found in [15, 25, 29].

For numerical reasons, it is often convenient to work with a dynamical system free of contact constraints. Many standard discretization or integration schemes found in optimization or simulation software can then be applied. It is generally possible to convert the contact dynamics in legged systems into a reduced-dimensional, unconstrained equation by projecting (1) onto a set of independent states. The resulting ODE can be evaluated efficiently using a recursive multibody algorithm [16]. The approach requires solving the inverse kinematics problem for the dependent states. A closed-form solution exists for common leg constructions with knowledge of the relative hip and foot contact locations by defining the contact leg states as the dependent states.

The position state vector $\mathbf{q}$ may be partitioned into independent position states $\mathbf{q}_1$ and dependent position states $\mathbf{q}_2$ obtained from $\mathbf{q}$ via a linear transformation, $\mathbf{q}_1 = Z\mathbf{q}$. The transformation $Z \in \mathbb{R}^{(N-n_c) \times N}$ is in the case of legged systems a constant full-rank matrix consisting of unit vectors or $\mathbf{0}$. The dependent position states $\mathbf{q}_2$ are calculated from $\mathbf{q}_1$ with the inverse kinematics function $i(\cdot)$, $\mathbf{q}_2 = i(\mathbf{q}_1)$, which for legged systems can generally be expressed in closed-form [15]. One may partition the constraint velocity equation

$J_c\dot{\mathbf{q}} = 0$ with respect to the independent $\dot{\mathbf{q}}_1$ and dependent velocity states $\dot{\mathbf{q}}_2$, $J_{c,1}\dot{\mathbf{q}}_1 + J_{c,2}\dot{\mathbf{q}}_2 = 0$. This similarly provides a change of variables for the velocity states,

$$\dot{\mathbf{q}}_1 = Z\dot{\mathbf{q}}, \quad \dot{\mathbf{q}}_2 = -J_{c,2}^{-1}J_{c,1}\dot{\mathbf{q}}_1 \ . \tag{2}$$

Substituting $\mathbf{q}_1$, $\mathbf{q}_2$, $\dot{\mathbf{q}}_1$, and $\dot{\mathbf{q}}_2$ into (1) and multiplying (1) by Z then gives an ODE of size $(N - n_c)$

$$\ddot{\mathbf{q}}_1 = Z\mathcal{M}(\mathbf{q}_1, i(\mathbf{q}_1))^{-1}$$
$$\times \left(B\mathbf{u} - \mathcal{C}(\mathbf{q}_1, i(\mathbf{q}_1), \dot{\mathbf{q}}_1, -J_{c,2}^{-1}J_{c,1}\dot{\mathbf{q}}_1) - \mathcal{G}(\mathbf{q}_1, i(\mathbf{q}_1)) + J_c^T\mathbf{f}_c \right). \tag{3}$$

The principal advantage of this approach is that one need only perform the optimization on the reduced dimensional state. The state must then be monitored such that it remain within a well-defined region of the state space. In Sect. 4.2, where the optimal amble gait is investigated for a quadruped, there are always two legs in contact. As a result, instead of the full 36 states $(\mathbf{q}, \dot{\mathbf{q}})$, 24 states can describe the system.

2.3   Constraints

An important aspect of formulating a gait optimization problem is establishing the many constraints on the problem. Legged systems are examples of general hybrid dynamical systems [17] as they periodically enter different discrete states with each new contact state which (discontinuously) switch the dynamical model. The numerical solution of hybrid optimal control problems is in its early stages [3, 33], yet when the discrete trajectory (contact events) is previously specified, current numerical solution techniques have been shown to work well [5, 16].

Specifying the order of contact events for a biped is easy as one need only distinguish between walking and running. The range of different quadruped gaits, however, can be quite large. The problem of searching over all possible gaits in a gait optimization problem has not yet been completely solved [17]. Biological studies, however, can provide a good indication as to which quadrupedal gaits are the most efficient at different speeds [1]. A numerical advantage for considering gaits with the left and right legs of a pair with equal duty factors is that the problem can be completely formulated within half a gait cycle. This is not a severe restriction as both symmetric and asymmetric gaits fit within this framework; the relative phases of each leg are free.

Summary of the modeling constraints for a *complete* gait cycle in $[0, t_f]$:

Periodic gait constraints (enforced during gait optimization):

1. Periodicity of continuous state and control variables: $\mathbf{q}(t_f) = \mathbf{q}(0)$, $\dot{\mathbf{q}}(t_f^+) = \dot{\mathbf{q}}(0)$, where $\dot{\mathbf{q}}(t_f^+) := \lim_{\epsilon > 0, \epsilon \to 0} \dot{\mathbf{q}}(t_f + \epsilon)$.
2. Periodicity of ground contact forces: $\mathbf{f}_c(t_f^+) = \mathbf{f}_c(0)$.

Exterior environmental constraints:

1. Kinematic constraints on the height (z-coordinate) of the swing leg tips. The leg tip height $q_{tip,z}$ is calculated from a forward kinematics function $FK(\cdot)$ of the position states $\mathbf{q}$:

$$q_{tip,z} = FK(\mathbf{q}(t)) \geq 0. \tag{4}$$

In the case of unlevel ground, the 0 may be replaced by a ground height function of the horizontal position of the swing leg tips. We consider here only level ground.

2. Ground contact forces lie within the friction cone and unilateral contact constraints are not violated [10, 30]. In the case of point contact, ground linear contact forces $\mathbf{F} = [F_x \ F_y \ F_z]^T$ must satisfy (otherwise a slipping contact state is entered)

$$\sqrt{F_x^2 + F_y^2} \leq \mu_t F_z, \qquad F_z \geq 0 \tag{5}$$

with friction coefficient μ_t. The contact force vector $\mathbf{f_c}$ which appears in (1) is composed of all the contact linear force vectors $\{\mathbf{F}_j\}$ from each contact leg j.

In the case of multiple contact, such as a foot lying flat on the ground, the rotational contact force vector $\mathbf{T}_j = [T_{j,x} \ T_{j,y} \ T_{j,z}]^T$ is additionally constrained

$$|T_x| \leq 0.5 F_z l_y, \qquad |T_y| \leq 0.5 F_z l_x, \qquad |T_z| \leq \mu_d F_z \tag{6}$$

where μ_d is a friction coefficient, and l_x and l_y are the length and width of the foot.

Interior modeling constraints:

1. Jump conditions in the system velocities due to inelastic collisions of the legs with the ground. If the exterior constraint (4) is violated, a collision occurs. The resulting instantaneous jump in the state velocities at the k-th such collision event is

$$\dot{\mathbf{q}}(t_{S,k}^+) = Jump_{q,q'}(\mathbf{q}(t_{S,k}^-), \dot{\mathbf{q}}(t_{S,k}^-)) \tag{7}$$

where $\mathbf{q}(t_{S,k}^-)$ and $\dot{\mathbf{q}}(t_{S,k}^+)$ indicate the values of $\mathbf{q}$ just before and after the collision event respectively. The function *Jump* calculates the jump in the state velocities resulting from the point of collision instantaneously reaching a zero velocity. The jump is physically modeled as the consequence of an impulsive force propagating throughout the system which may be calculated using the law of conservation of angular momentum. This form is an approximation to real collision phenomena and is better tractable numerically than using mixed elastic-inelastic collision models.

2. Magnitude constraints on states, controls and control rates:
$$L_q \leq q \leq U_q, \qquad L_{\dot{q}} \leq \dot{q} \leq U_{\dot{q}}, \qquad L_u \leq u \leq U_u, \qquad L_{\dot{u}} \leq \dot{u} \leq U_{\dot{u}} \quad .$$
$L_{(\cdot)}$ and $U_{(\cdot)}$ are constant vectors of length equal to their arguments.

3. Actuator torque-speed limitations. The applied torque at the actuated joint i is constrained by the characteristic line of the motor-gear train: $|u_i| \leq (\dot{\theta}_{max,i} - |\dot{\theta}_i|) \frac{G_i^2 \eta_i}{m_i}$, where u_i is the applied torque at joint i, $\dot{\theta}_i$ and $\dot{\theta}_{max,i}$ are the joint i velocity and maximum absolute joint velocity respectively, G_i is the gear ratio, η_i is the gear efficiency, and m_i is the slope of the motor characteristic line.

Numerical simulation of legged locomotion must not only enforce the interior constraints and robot dynamics but must also supervise the environmental constraints. When the latter can no longer be enforced, the system enters a new discrete state often leading to a switch in the system's state and dynamics, which in turn must reflect the interior modeling constraints.

3   Dynamic Stability and Performance

3.1   Measures of Stability

There exists a general agreement on the definition of static stability for legged systems: the ground projection of the center of mass (GCoM) lies within the convex hull of its foot-support area. Various forms of static stability margins have been defined usually concerning the minimum distance between the GCoM and the support boundary which have served to develop statically stable walking motions in all types of legged systems. There exists, however, no general consensus on a mathematical description for dynamic stability other than "its negation implies a lack of static stability and an unsustainable gait" [12]. In [19], dynamic stability was categorized into postural stability and gait stability. Postural stability is maintained when the posture (torso orientation and position) remains within a bounded range of values. Gait stability refers to the dynamical system definition of stability for limit cycles in periodic gaits. Numerical methods for classifying or acquiring stable gait trajectories are presented in [21] and [26] respectively. Due to the nonconvexity of the problem and the high dimensional nonlinear dynamics, direct optimization methods cannot be readily applied to the full-dimensional dynamical model and, thus, we do not consider this problem here.

The zero-moment-point (ZMP) and its relationship with the support polygon is often used for measuring postural stability [18–20, 27, 35]. The ZMP is that point on the ground where the total moment generated due to gravity and inertia equals zero or equivalently the point where the net vertical ground reaction force acts. As pointed out in [12], this point cannot leave the support polygon and, in the case when the foot is rotating about a point, it lies directly on the edge of the support polygon. That is during periods of single foot support in biped walking when the foot is rotating about the heel or the toe, the ZMP does not provide information as to the amount of instability in the system. This period can amount to up to 80% of a normal human walking gait. Evidently, fast dynamically stable biped walking and running requires foot rotation for stability and efficiency. The alternative measure proposed in [12], the foot-rotation-indicator (FRI), coincides with the ZMP during periods of static equilibrium of the foot and otherwise provides information as to the foot's rotational instability. Foot rotation instability measured by the FRI is a more complete measure of postural instability, but it still does not provide any information as to gait stability/instability.

Within all possible quadrupedal gaits [1] (pace, gallop, amble, etc.), there exist many configurations where the ZMP provides little useful information. The FRI can also be extended to the quadrupedal case though other similar measures specialized to quadrupeds have been introduced. In [24], the angular momentum about the support edges was used to define a postural stability index. Like the FRI, this method provides both directional information and a reference stability quantity that can be used to quantify system instability. Though postural stability measures are not rigorous dynamical system stability measures, these measures provide a means to monitor the stability or instability present in legged systems. Another advantage is that these measures may be directly incorporated into controllers for *on-line* use and, additionally, they can treat aperiodic gaits, a necessity in an environment containing obstacles.

3.2   Performance Specifications

The minimization of several, alternative performance functions measuring (in-)stability and/or efficiency of the periodic motion enables (at least locally) optimal and unique trajectories for the states $\mathbf{q}, \dot{\mathbf{q}}$ and controls $\mathbf{u}$.

Stability Performance 1: The FRI point may be computed as that point $\mathbf{S}$ for which the net ground tangential impressed forces (FI_x, FI_y) acting on the foot are zero. These forces are the acting forces and may differ from the constraint forces $\mathbf{F} = [F_x \; F_y \; F_z]^T$ [12]. If N_f feet/leg-tips are in contact with the ground, $\mathbf{S}$ may be considered as the net point of action for all ground impressed forces resulting from the robot gravity and inertial forces. It may be computed using the rotational static equilibrium equation for the feet,

$$\sum_{j=1}^{N_f} \left(\mathbf{n}_j + \mathbf{SO}_j \times \mathbf{f}_j - \mathbf{SG}_j \times m_j \mathbf{g} \right)_T = 0 \, , \qquad (8)$$

where $\mathbf{n}_j$ and $\mathbf{f}_j$ are the moment and linear force vectors from contact foot j acting on its connecting point $\mathbf{O}_j$ to the remainder of the robot, $\mathbf{SO}_j$ and $\mathbf{SG}_j$ are the vectors from $\mathbf{S}$ to $\mathbf{O}_j$ and the foot center of mass $\mathbf{G}_j$ respectively, m_j is the foot mass, and $\mathbf{g}$ is the gravity vector. The subscript T indicates that only the ground tangential x- and y-coordinates must satisfy the equation. A stability performance index which may be used for maximizing postural stability is the average distance in the ground plane between the point $\mathbf{P}$ and the ground projected center of mass GCoM.

$$\mathbf{J}_{s1}[\mathbf{q}, \dot{\mathbf{q}}, \mathbf{u}] = \int_0^{t_f} \left((\text{GCoM}_x - S_x)^2 + (\text{GCoM}_y - S_y)^2 \right) dt \qquad (9)$$

Stability Performance 2: The measure proposed in [24] is an alternative measure based on the angular momentum and it takes into consideration the momentum of the swing legs. It is however limited to gaits with at least two legs in contact with the ground. The stability/instability margin is equal to:

$$S_H(t) = \min\{S_H^l(t), \; l = 1, \ldots, n_l\}, \quad t \in [0, t_f], \tag{10}$$

where n_l is the number of edges in the support polygon. The stability values S_H^l for each edge depend on whether the edge is a diagonal or non-diagonal edge.

In the case of a non-diagonal support edge, $S_H^l = H_l^{ref} - H_l$ where the reference angular momentum H_l^{ref} about edge l is defined as the minimum angular momentum to tip over the edge if the system were an inverted pendulum $H_l^{ref} = (\mathbf{r}_{l,CM} \times m_{total}\mathbf{v}_{ref}) \cdot \hat{\mathbf{e}}_l$ and H_l is the rotational tendency about that edge $H_l = \mathbf{H}_P \cdot \hat{\mathbf{e}}_l$. Here, $\mathbf{r}_{l,CM}$ is the orthogonal vector from edge l to the system center of mass **CoM**, m_{total} is the total system mass, $\mathbf{v}_{ref}$ is the reference velocity vector computed from the kinetic energy required to attain the higher potential energy at which the system **CoM** would lie above edge l, $\mathbf{H}_P$ is the angular momentum about a point P on the support edge, and $\hat{\mathbf{e}}_l$ is a unit vector along the edge.

In the case of a diagonal support edge, $S_H^l = \{\min(H_l - H_l^{ref}, H_l^{max} - H_l) :$ two legs in contact & **GCoM** before diagonal edge, $S_H^l = H_l^{max} - H_l :$ two legs in contact & **GCoM** past diagonal edge, $S_H^l = H_l^{max} - H_l :$ third support leg behind diagonal support edge, $S_H^l = H_l^{ref} - H_l :$ third support leg in front of diagonal support edge$\}$, where the maximum angular momentum about $\hat{\mathbf{e}}_l$ is defined as $H_l^{max} = (\mathbf{r}_{l,CM} \times m_{total}\mathbf{v}_{tip}^{max}) \cdot \hat{\mathbf{e}}_l$ and $\mathbf{v}_{tip}^{max}$ is the maximum velocity vector of the swing leg's tip.

A worst-case stability measure is defined as the minimum value of S_H over the entire gait cycle which should be maximized to find the best worst-case performance. Introducing an additional control parameter p_1, the min-max objective may be transformed to a standard Mayer-type, $p_1 := \min_{0 \le t \le t_f} S_H(t)$, where an additional inequality constraint is needed, $S_H(t) - p_1 \ge 0$ $(0 \le t \le t_f)$, and the performance index becomes

$$\mathbf{J}_{s2}[\mathbf{p}] = -p_1. \tag{11}$$

Energy Performance 1: In the case of robots where a high torque is generated by a large current in the motor, the primary form of energy loss is called the Joule thermal loss [23]. Define R_i, G_i, and K_i as the armature resistance, gear ratio, and torque factor for link i respectively. Also let d_S be the forward distance traveled during one gait cycle, then the normalized average energy loss to be minimized is

$$\mathbf{J}_{e1}[\mathbf{u}] = \frac{1}{d_S} \int_0^{t_f} \sum_{i=1}^{N} R_i \left(\frac{u_i}{G_i K_i}\right)^2 \, \mathrm{d}t \, . \tag{12}$$

Energy Performance 2: In [13], the specific resistance ϵ was used to measure efficiency or more precisely an average power consumption normalized over distance traveled. It is a dimensionless quantity, and by minimizing its integral over the gait cycle, a normalized form of the kinetic energy is minimized. Let

mg be the system weight of the system, $\dot{\theta}_i(t)$ is the joint i angle velocity contained within the velocity state vector $\dot{q}(t)$, and $v(t)$ is the forward velocity. The performance index to be minimized is

$$\mathbf{J}_{e2}[\mathbf{q}, \dot{\mathbf{q}}, \mathbf{u}] = \int_0^{t_f} \frac{\sum_{i=1}^{N} |u_i \dot{\theta}_i|}{mgv}. \tag{13}$$

Summary: Stability performance 1 delivers a solution with a minimum average level of postural instability during the gait while stability measure 2 is intended towards improving the worst-case unstable configuration occurring in a gait. Energy performance 1 is a direct measure of energy loss in the joints normalized over the distance traveled, and energy performance 2 measures average power consumption.

4 Trajectory Optimization and Numerical Investigations

The optimization of the stability or energy performance functions of Sect. 3.2 with respect to the controls $\mathbf{u}(t)$ over a period of time $[0, t_f]$ and subject to the system dynamics and constraints of Sect. 2 leads to optimal control problems. Although the computation of the optimal, state feedback control is the ultimate goal where the control is a function of the system state vector $\mathbf{x}$, $\mathbf{u}^*(\mathbf{x})$, it cannot be computed directly because of the system's high dimension, nonlinearity and constraints. However, with the help of numerical optimization methods developed during the last decade, optimal open loop trajectories $\mathbf{x}^*(t)$, $\mathbf{u}^*(t)$, $0 \leq t \leq t_f$, can nowadays be computed efficiently [2, 32].

4.1 Trajectory Optimization Framework

The optimization we are faced with is to find the unknown open-loop state and control trajectories $(\mathbf{x}(t), \mathbf{u}(t))$ which minimize a performance function $\mathbf{J}$ (Sect. 3.2) subject to a set of possibly switching differential equations f^k (resulting from the legged robot dynamics of Sects. 2.1–2.3, i.e., $\mathbf{x} = (\mathbf{q}, \dot{\mathbf{q}})$), nonlinear inequality g_i^k and equality h_i^k constraints, and boundary conditions r_i^k (resulting from the constraints and conditions of Sect. 2.3). All constraints of the dynamic optimization problem are formulated in the general first order form

$$\dot{\mathbf{x}}(t) = \begin{cases} f^1(\mathbf{x}(t), \mathbf{u}(t), \mathbf{d}(t), \mathbf{p}, t), & t \in [0, t_{S,1}], \\ f^k(\mathbf{x}(t), \mathbf{u}(t), \mathbf{d}(t), \mathbf{p}, t), & t \in [t_{S,k-1}, t_{S,k}], \ k = 2, \ldots, m-1 \\ f^m(\mathbf{x}(t), \mathbf{u}(t), \mathbf{d}(t), \mathbf{p}, t), & t \in [t_{S,m-1}, t_f], \end{cases}$$

$$g_i^k(\mathbf{x}(t), \mathbf{u}(t), \mathbf{d}(t), \mathbf{p}, t) \geq 0, \ t \in [t_{S,k-1}, t_{S,k}], \ i = 1, \ldots, n_{g_m^k}, \ k = 1, \ldots, m,$$
$$h_i^k(\mathbf{x}(t), \mathbf{u}(t), \mathbf{d}(t), \mathbf{p}, t) = 0, \ t \in [t_{S,k-1}, t_{S,k}], \ i = 1, \ldots, n_{h_m^k}, \ k = 1, \ldots, m,$$

$$r_i^1(\mathbf{x}(0), \mathbf{u}(0), \mathbf{d}_0, \mathbf{p}, 0, \mathbf{x}(t_f), \mathbf{u}(t_f), \mathbf{d}_f, t_f) = 0, \ i = 1, \ldots, r_m^k,$$
$$r_i^k(\mathbf{x}(t_{S,k}^-), \mathbf{u}(t_{S,k}^-), \mathbf{d}(t_{S,k}^-), \mathbf{p}, t_{S,k}, \mathbf{x}(t_{S,k}^+), \mathbf{u}(t_{S,k}^+), \mathbf{d}(t_{S,k}^+)) = 0, \ k = 2, \ldots, m-1.$$

The integer-valued discrete state trajectory $\mathbf{d}(t)$ is assumed to be constant in each phase $[t_{S,j-1}, t_{S,j}]$ and describes the sequence of switches of the system dynamics, i.e., a quadrupedal gait, and must generally be provided. The program DIRCOL [32] uses the method of sparse direct collocation to approximate the piecewise continuous states $\mathbf{x}$, controls $\mathbf{u}$, and constant parameters $\mathbf{p}$ of the optimal control problem. This leads to a multiphase optimal control problem to be solved in all phases $[t_{S,j-1}, t_{S,j}]$ through adaptively selected grids $t_{S,j-1} = t_1^j < t_2^j < \cdots < t_{n_{G,j}}^j = t_{S,j}$ in each subinterval $t \in [t_k^j, t_{k+1}^j]$ by the approximation

$$\begin{aligned} \tilde{\mathbf{u}}_{app}(t) &= \beta(\hat{\mathbf{u}}(t_k^j), \hat{\mathbf{u}}(t_k^{j+1})), & \beta &- \text{linear} \\ \tilde{\mathbf{x}}_{app}(t) &= \alpha(\hat{\mathbf{x}}(t_k^j), \hat{\mathbf{x}}(t_k^{j+1}), f_k^j, f_{k+1}^j), & \alpha &- \text{cubic} \end{aligned} \tag{14}$$

where $f_k^j = f^j(\hat{\mathbf{x}}(t_k^j), \hat{\mathbf{u}}(t_k^j), \mathbf{p}, t_k^j)$ [32]. The infinite-dimensional optimal control problem is thereby converted to a finite dimensional, but large-scale and sparse, nonlinearly constrained optimization problem containing the unknown values for $\mathbf{x}, \mathbf{u}$ at the discretization grid as well as $\mathbf{p}, t_{S,i}, t_f$. The problem is then solved using an SQP method for sparse systems SNOPT [11]. The resulting optimal control method is thus equipped to handle the complexities of the walking problem: unknown liftoff times $t_{S,i}$, different ground contact combinations for the legs $\mathbf{d}(t)$, discontinuous states at collision times $t_{S,k}$ of the legs with the ground, switching dynamics, and actuation limits.

This method of generating optimal reference trajectories was also used in [7, 16, 17]. It may be applied to much higher dimensional systems than finite-element approaches as used for example in [4], and the numerical package is more general than that for example used in [5].

4.2   Numerical Investigations for the Quadruped

The goal in our numerical investigations is to plan and implement efficient, stable, and rapid periodic motions for our test platforms of the Sony four-legged robot and our humanoid robot currently under construction (Sect. 6). To obtain starting values when setting up the iterative optimization procedure from scratch, a series of optimal solutions for subproblems was computed. First the problem was solved in two dimensions with most parameters fixed, then all constraints were gradually relaxed using the previous solution to start the subsequent problem. Optimization run times for a single subproblem ranged from 5 to 20 minutes on a Pentium III, 900 MHz PC.

In our investigations, dynamically stable quadruped gaits were investigated with *Stability Performance 2*. Energy efficiency is not as important for the quadruped in RoboCup competition (Fig. 1) since the robot's battery provides sufficient power for the duration of half a regulation match. An optimization over this min-max performance will optimize the worst-case configuration, thereby facilitating a more robust closed-loop implementation.

The solution displayed in Fig. 3 is for a desired forward velocity of 40 m/min or 0.67 m/s. The optimal gait stride is 0.416 m and the gait period is 1.25

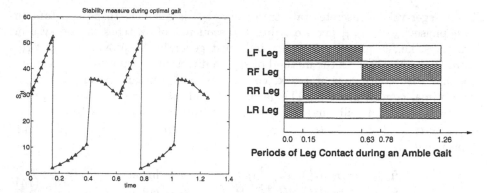

Fig. 3. Stability index S_H for an optimized amble gait of a quadruped moving forward at 0.67 m/s and duty factor $\beta = 0.5$ based on a full, spatial dynamical model. The first sharp drop in the stability index occurs at the instant when the RR (right rear) leg initially makes contact and the (left rear) leg breaks contact. At that time the diagonally opposed legs support the body and a minimally sufficient amount of forward momentum exists to bring the system **CoG** over the support edge. As the **CoG** approaches the support edge, the stability index increases then falls again once this point has been passed. The second half of the gait is symmetric to the first half

seconds. Fig. 3 shows the evolution of the optimized stability index S_H over one gait period. A negative value of S_H indicates an unstable configuration while the more positive S_H is, the more stable the system. The large variations in the index are caused by the changing of support legs in the robot. The gait displayed is an amble gait between walking and running with the legs having a duty factor of $\beta = 0.5$ which is a demanding, fast-moving gait. The order of support leg order is (LF-LB, LR-RR, RF-RR, RF-LR: LF=left front, RR=right rear) so that the system alternates between having two support legs on one side and diagonal support legs. The steepest drop in S_H occurs when the system switches from a side pair of support legs to a diagonal pair. At that point the angular momentum of the system about the diagonal edge is slightly greater than the required angular momentum for the **CoM** to "roll over" the diagonal edge and not fall backward. A conservative value of 2 m/sec was chosen for the attainable velocity of the swing leg tip $\mathbf{v}_{tip}^{max}$.

Our investigations are continuing with a thorough investigation and comparison of the stability/energy performances and their combinations as presented in Section 3.2. Furthermore, they will be evaluated using gait stability tools, tested with a real-time legged system simulator currently under development in our group. At RoboCup 2002 we plan to present optimized motion primitives implemented on the actual quadruped using trajectory-following controllers.

5   Control of Bipedal and Quadrupedal Robot Motions

Today, most all feedback walking control strategies that have been implemented successfully in three-dimensional humanoid robots or quadrupeds are based on

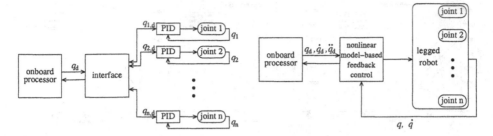

Fig. 4. Structure of a decentralized trajectory tracking control scheme: The local feedback control loops operate within milliseconds and are implemented using a microprocessor for each joint. The reference trajectories are provided or generated by an onboard processor, usually a mobile PC or similar, and are updated within seconds or tenths of a second

Fig. 5. Structure of a centralized, nonlinear model-based feedback control scheme: Its implementation requires the solution of the full nonlinear dynamic model described in Sect. 2 in real-time. Thus, strict requirements are imposed on the computational power and on the efficient coding of the dynamic equations. The reference trajectories are updated by an onboard processor (mobile PC) and are updated within seconds or tenths of a second for each new step while considering constraints and performance specifications

trajectory following control. Reference trajectories for the body posture, ZMP, or foot flight paths are developed off-line (e.g. through extensive simulations) and implemented on the bipedal robot using standard controllers such as PID to follow the reference trajectories which have been transformed to desired position (and velocity) information for each of the leg and foot joints (Fig. 4). This control strategy cannot easily nor automatically be adapted to a changing environment and can only handle relatively small changes to the reference data. However, it can be realized using decoupled, decentralized conventional control strategies in each of the joint motors. This strategy has been applied, e.g., to the Honda humanoid robot [18], the Humanoid H6 [27], [20], or [37] for a quadruped.

Feedback linearization techniques (computed torque) are also based on trajectory tracking techniques yet it takes full advantage of a nonlinear dynamical model to arrive at asymptotically stable closed-loop controllers. In contrast to simpler trajectory tracking schemes, these controllers are not decentralized nor decoupled. An example of this type of implementation may be found with Johnnie at the TU Munich [10].

In order to meet the challenge of producing fast and stable motions for bipedal and quadrupedal robots that can quickly adapt to a changing environment, nonlinear, model-based feedback control methods must be developed which can generate completely new motion trajectories through adaptation within a few seconds and ensure stability within milliseconds (Fig. 5). To achieve this goal, fast and robust modeling and simulation methods for legged robot dynamics are needed. Contributions have been described in this paper. Furthermore, a more centralized control scheme is needed. Decentralized joint controllers with standard control schemes, as provided with the often used servos, cannot satisfy these requirements.

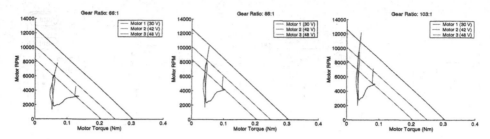

Fig. 6. Motor torque vs. rpm from an 18 kg biped with different motor/gear combinations

6   Robot Design and Dynamics of Legged Locomotion

To achieve optimal motion performance of an autonomous legged robot, especially a humanoid robot, a full dynamical study should ideally be made already in the design phase of the robot. The selection of motors and gears for the hip, knee or foot joints of a humanoid must be based on the expected applied force at each joint if the robot is walking or running while further considering the onboard energy supply and other hardware. These forces depend not only on the geometry of the robot links and joints but also on the distribution of masses in each part of the robot's body. The faster the robot moves, the stronger the motors and gears that are required. However, stronger motors and gears are also heavier and require more electrical power and, thus, more and heavier batteries. The heavier weight, though, will counteract the ability of fast walking. Thus, the design of a fast walking humanoid must find a good compromise between the different, counteracting objectives!

A design study was performed for the prototype of a fast walking humanoid (Fig. 2) using detailed numerical investigations with a nonlinear dynamical model. Numerical optimizations of *Energy Performance 1* in combination with maximum input power constraints were used to determine the minimum required energy needed while moving at walking motions with speeds of up to 1.8 *km/h*. This preliminary analysis served to identify the most suitable class of motors. The final selection was based on graphing the torque-rpm workspace of interest for the respective joints during locomotion for a selection of different gear ratios and motors with different voltage ratings in combination with each motor's maximum operational characteristic line. The example displayed in Fig. 6 led to the choice of 42 *V* motors with 66:1 gear ratios. Minimum power requirements is a vital property for rapid locomotion and its autonomous functionality.

Ongoing joint work with the Control Systems Group of M. Buss at the Technische Universität Berlin is directed towards the completion of the construction, controller design, and remaining components such that this new humanoid robot may be presented in the 80 *cm* humanoid league at RoboCup.

7   Conclusion and Extensions

In this paper, the modeling, simulation and optimization of nonlinear dynamics and its role in the development and control of bipedal and quadrupedal robots is investigated. A discussion is provided explaining the choice of robotic dynamics algorithms that are well-suited to legged systems together with efficient reduced dynamics algorithms to be used for increased numerical stability. A powerful and efficient numerical optimization framework is also presented which has been thoroughly tested in previous work in optimal gait planning. Several performance criteria have been presented which serve to either optimize energy or stability in legged systems. Much of this work has been geared towards the demanding setting of RoboCup where many external factors influence the robot's movement in a fast-changing dynamic environment. A minimax performance stability criteria is used for generating maximally stable quadruped gaits. The investigated dynamic stability criterion is well-suited to a changing environment and on-line stability assessment for closed-loop control design. The results must then be combined with trajectory tracking controllers which may additionally incorporate the stability index. At other times energy concerns are equally important such as in autonomous humanoid biped design. Efficient multibody algorithms combined with powerful numerical optimal control software solve energy-based performance criteria to aid in the humanoid construction design.

Acknowledgement

The authors thankfully acknowledge the information and help in using the Sony quadrupeds provided by Sony Corporation and its Open-R Support Team for this research.

References

1. Alexander, R.: The Gaits of Bipedal and Quadrupedal Animals. International Journal of Robotics Research **3**(2) (1984) 49–59
2. Betts, J.T.: Survey of numerical methods for trajectory optimization. AIAA J. Guidance, Control, and Dynamics **21**(2) (1998) 193–207
3. Buss, M., Glocker, M., Hardt, M., von Stryk, O., Bulirsch, R. Schmidt, G.: Nonlinear Hybrid Dynamical Systems: Modeling, Optimal Control, and Applications. Submitted to Lectures in Computer Science (2002)
4. Channon, P.H.; Pham, D.T.; Hopkins, S.H.: Variational Approach to the Optimization of Gait for a Bipedal Robot. Journal of Mechanical Engineering Science **210** (1996) 177–186
5. Chevallereau, C.; Aoustin, Y.: Optimal reference trajectories for walking and running of a biped robot. Robotica **19**(5) (2001) 557–569
6. Chow, C.K.; Jacobson, D.H.: Studies of human locomotion via optimal programming. Mathematical Biosciences **10** (1971) 239–306
7. Denk, J.; Schmidt, G.: Walking primitive synthesis for an anthropomorphic biped using optimal control techniques. CLAWAR: Int. Conf. on Climbing and Walking Robots (2001)
8. Featherstone, R.: Robot Dynamics Algorithms. Kluwer Academic Publishers (1987)
9. Featherstone, R.; Orin, D.: Robot Dynamics: Equations and Algorithms. IEEE Int. Conf. on Robotics and Automation (2000) 826–34

10. Gienger, M.; Löffler, K.; Pfeiffer, F.: Towards the Design of a Biped Jogging Robot. IEEE Int. Conf. on Robotics and Automation (2001) 4140–45
11. Gill, P.E.; Murray, W.; Saunders, M.A.: User's Guide for SNOPT 5.3: a Fortran Package for Large-Scale Nonlinear Programming, Math. Dept., Univ. of California, San Diego (1997)
12. Goswami, A.: Postural Stability of Biped Robots and the Foot-Rotation Indicator (FRI) Point. International Journal of Robotics Research 18(6) (1999) 523–533
13. Gregorio, P.; Ahmadi, M.; Buehler, M.: Design, Control, and Energetics of an Electrically Actuated Legged Robot. IEEE Systems, Man and Cybernetics, Part B 27(4) (1997) 626–634
14. Grizzle, J.W.; Abba, G.; Plestan, F.: Asymptotically stable walking for biped robots: Analysis via systems with impulse effects. IEEE Trans. Automatic Control 46 (2001) 51–64
15. M. Hardt, Multibody Dynamical Algorithms, Numerical Optimal Control, with Detailed Studies in the Control of Jet Engine Compressors and Biped Walking. Ph.D. Thesis, Electrical Engineering, University of California San Diego, U.S.A. (1999)
16. Hardt, M.; Helton, J.W.; Kreutz-Delgado, K.: Optimal Biped Walking with a Complete Dynamical Model. IEEE Conference on Decision and Control (1999) 2999–3004
17. Hardt, M.; von Stryk, O.: Towards Optimal Hybrid Control Solutions for Gait Patterns of a Quadruped. CLAWAR: Int. Conf. on Climbing and Walking Robots (2000) 385–392
18. Hirai, K.; Hirose, M.; Haikawa, Y.; Takenaka, T.: The Development of Honda Humanoid Robot. IEEE Int. Conf. on Robotics and Automation (1998) 1321–26
19. Hu, J.; Pratt, G.: Nonlinear Switching Control of Bipedal Walking Robots with Provable Stability. Humanoid conference, Boston, U.S.A. (2000)
20. Huang, Q.; Yokoi, K.; Kajita, S.; Kaneko, K.; Arai, H.; Koyachi, N.; Tanie, K.: Planning Walking Patterns for a Biped Robot. IEEE Trans. Robotics and Automation 116 (1994)30-36
21. Hurmuzlu, Y.; Basdogan, C.: On the Measurement of Dynamic Stability of Human Locomotion. ASME Journal Biomechanical Engineering 116 (1994) 30–36
22. Kajita, S.; Tanie, K.: Experimental study of biped dynamic walking. IEEE Control Systems Magazine 16(1) (1996) 13–19
23. Kimura, H.; Shimoyama, I.; Miura, H.: Dynamics in the Dynamic Walk of a Quadruped Robot. Advanced Robotics 4(3) (1990) 283–301
24. Koo, T.W.; Yoon, Y.S.: Dynamic instant gait stability measure for quadruped walking robot. Robotica 17 (1999) 59–71
25. McMillan, S.; Orin, D.E.: Efficient Computation of Articulated-Body Inertias Using Successive Axial Screws. IEEE Trans. on Robotics and Automation 11(4) (1995) 606–11
26. Mombaur, K.D.; Bock, H.G.; Schlöder, J.P.; Longman, R.W.: Human-like actuated walking that is asymptotically stable without feedback. IEEE Int. Conf. on Robotics and Automation (2001) 4128–33
27. Nishiwaki, K.; Sugihara, T.; Kagami, S.; Inaba, M.; Inoue, H.: Online Mixture and Connection of Basic Motions for Humanoid Walking Control by Footprint Specification. IEEE Int. Conf. on Robotics and Automation (2001) 4110–15
28. Otter, M.; Elmqvist, H.; Cellier, F.E.: Modeling of Multibody Systems with the Object-Oriented Modeling Language Dymola. Nonlinear Dynamics 9 (1996) 91–112

29. Pai, D.K.; Ascher, U.M.; Kry, P.G.: Forward Dynamics Algorithms for Multibody Chains and Contact. IEEE Int. Conf. on Robotics and Automation (2000) 857–63
30. Pfeiffer, F.; Glocker, C.: Multibody Dynamics with Unilateral Contacts. Wiley Series Nonlinear Science, New York (1996)
31. Rodriguez, G.; Kreutz-Delgado, K.; Jain, A.: A Spatial Operator Algebra for Manipulator Modeling and Control. International Journal of Robotics Research **40** (1991) 21–50
32. von Stryk, O.: DIRCOL: A direct collocation method for the numerical solution of optimal control problems. Technische Universität Darmstadt, World Wide Web: `http://www.sim.informatik.tu-darmstadt.de/sw/dircol` (2001)
33. von Stryk, O.; Glocker, M.: Numerical mixed-integer optimal control and motorized travelling salesmen problems. APII-JESA – European Journal of Control **35**(4) (2001) 519–533
34. Yamamoto, Y.; Fujita, M.; de Lasa, M.; Talebi, S.; Jewell, D.; Playter, R.; Raibert, M.: Development of dynamic locomotion for the entertainment robot – teaching a new dog old tricks. CLAWAR: Int. Conf. on Climbing and Walking Robots (2001) 695–702
35. Vukobratović, M.; Borovac, B.; Surla, D.; Stokić, D.: Biped Locomotion. Dynamics, Stability, Control, and Application. Springer-Verlag, Berlin (1990)
36. Walker, M.W.; Orin, D.E.: Efficient Dynamic Computer Simulation of Robotic Mechanisms. Trans. ASME Journal of Dynamic Systems, Measurement, & Control **104** (1982) 205–211
37. Yoneda, K.; Iiyama, H.; Hirose, S.: Intermittent trot gait of a quadruped walking machine dynamic stability control of an omnidirectional walk. IEEE Int. Conf. on Robotics and Automation (1996) 3002–7

Multiagent Competitions and Research:
Lessons from RoboCup and TAC

Peter Stone

Department of Computer Sciences
The University of Texas at Austin
pstone@cs.utexas.edu
http://www.cs.utexas.edu/~pstone

Abstract. This paper compares and contrasts two recent series of competitions in which multiple agents compete directly against one another: the robot soccer world cup (RoboCup) and the trading agent competition (TAC). Both of these competitions have attracted large numbers of competitors and have motivated important research results in artificial intelligence. Based on extensive personal experiences, both as a participant and as an organizer, this paper reflects upon and characterizes both the benefits and the hazards of competitions with respect to academic research.

1 Introduction

Competitions are becoming increasingly prevalent in the research world. For one example, the annual Loebner competition [13] challenges entrants to create a computer program whose verbal responses in conversation are judged to be most "human." For another example, the recent planning systems competition [15] compared the performance of AI planning systems in a variety of planning domains.

In both the Loebner and planning competitions, the judging and/or scoring is done independently for each program: an entrant's score does not depend on the behavior of the other entrants. However, there have also been several competitions in which the agents *do* interact directly. Examples include Axelrod's iterated prisoner's dilemma (IPD) tournament from the late 1970's [3]; the Santa Fe double auction tournament in the late 1980's [16]; and the recent RoShamBo (rock-paper-scissors) programming competition [4]. All three of these competitions led to interesting results despite the fact that entered programs faced very limited sensation and action spaces in domains that have been well-studied and understood in isolation (non-iterated).

This paper compares and contrasts two recent series of competitions in which—like IPD, double auctions, and RoShamBo—agents must interact directly with one another, and in which the substrate domains are much more complicated and difficult to analyze in isolation: the robot soccer world cup (RoboCup) and the trading agent competition (TAC). In both cases, the agents face complex sensations with a good deal of hidden state and, for all intents and

G.A. Kaminka, P.U. Lima, and R. Rojas (Eds.): RoboCup 2002, LNAI 2752, pp. 224–237, 2003.

purposes, continuous action spaces. The success of agent strategies depends a great deal on the strategies of the other competitors.

Both of these competitions have attracted large numbers of competitors and motivated important research results in artificial intelligence and robotics. However, along with the many benefits, competitions also bring with them some potential hazards. Based on extensive personal experiences within RoboCup and TAC, both as a successful participant and as an organizer, this paper reflects upon and characterizes the benefits and hazards of competitions with respect to the research world.

The remainder of the paper is organized as follows. Section 2 gives a brief overview of the RoboCup domain. Section 3 gives a more detailed introduction to TAC. Section 4 compares the relevant features of these two domains and Section 5 lays out the potential benefits and hazards of these and other competitions. Section 6 concludes.

2 RoboCup

RoboCup is an international initiative designed to encourage research in the fields of robotics and artificial intelligence, with a particular focus on developing cooperation between autonomous agents in dynamic multiagent environments. It uses the game of soccer as the main underlying testbed. A long-term grand challenge posed by RoboCup is the creation of a team of humanoid robots that can beat the best human soccer team by the year 2050.

The first international RoboCup competition was held from August 23–29, 1997 in Nagoya, Japan. It involved 35 teams from 12 countries. By the 3rd RoboCup in 1999, there were 90 teams from 30 countries and RoboCup continues to grow in popularity, now including many regional events as well as the annual international championships.

Currently, RoboCup includes four robotic soccer competitions (simulation, small-size, mid-size, and legged), and two disaster rescue competitions (simulation and real-robot). A humanoid robotic soccer competition is also planned for the near future. Each of these competitions has its own format, but generally they are run over the course of about a week, beginning with round-robins and culminating with elimination tournaments. Competitors are all responsible for bringing their own robots and/or software to the competition site.

Some commonalities across the different soccer leagues are that they are run in *dynamic, real-time, distributed, multiagent* environments with both *teammates* and *adversaries*. In general, there is *hidden state*, meaning that each agent has only a partial world view at any given moment. The agents also have *noisy sensors and actuators*, meaning that they do not perceive the world exactly as it is, nor can they affect the world exactly as intended. In addition, the perception and action cycles are *asynchronous*, prohibiting the traditional AI paradigm of using perceptual input to trigger actions. *Communication* opportunities are limited; and the agents must make their decisions in *real-time*. These italicized domain characteristics combine to make robotic soccer a realistic and challenging domain.

For the purposes of this forum, I assume a general familiarity with RoboCup. For complete details on the competitions in the different leagues, see the continuing series of RoboCup books [11, 2, 23, 19].

3   Trading Agent Competition

The first Trading Agent Competition (TAC) was held from June 22nd to July 8th, 2000, organized by a group of researchers and developers from the University of Michigan and North Carolina State University [26]. Their goals included providing a benchmark problem in the complex and rapidly advancing domain of e-marketplaces [7] and motivating researchers to apply unique approaches to a common task. TAC-00 included 16 agents from 6 countries. Building on the success of TAC-00, TAC-01 included 19 agents from 9 countries. The precise rules and tournament structures changed slightly from TAC-00 to TAC-01. The details in this section reflect the state of affairs as of TAC-01.

TAC has been motivated in some ways by RoboCup. Although it is based on a fundamentally different problem—auction bidding as opposed to playing soccer, it is also a multiagent competition. The organizers explicitly took some cues from RoboCup in planning out the competition [25]. This section gives a detailed overview of the TAC domain.

One key feature of TAC is that it requires *autonomous bidding agents* to buy and sell *multiple interacting goods* in auctions of different types. Another key feature is that participating agents compete against each other in preliminary rounds consisting of many games leading up to the finals. Thus, developers change strategies in response to each others' agents in a sort of escalating arms race. Leading into the day of the finals, a wide variety of scenarios are generally possible. A successful agent needs to be able to perform well in any of these possible circumstances.

A TAC game instance pits 8 autonomous bidding agents against one another. Each TAC agent is a simulated travel agent with 8 clients, each of whom would like to travel from TACtown to Tampa and back again during a 5-day period. Each client is characterized by a random set of preferences for the possible arrival and departure dates; hotel rooms (Tampa Towers and Shoreline Shanties); and entertainment tickets (alligator wrestling, amusement park, and museum). In order to obtain utility for a client, an agent must construct a travel package for that client by purchasing airline tickets to and from TACtown and securing hotel reservations; it is possible to obtain additional utility by providing entertainment tickets as well. A TAC agent's score in a game instance is the difference between the sum of its clients' utilities for the packages they receive and the agent's total expenditure.

TAC agents buy flights, hotel rooms and entertainment tickets in different types of *auctions*. The TAC server, running at the University of Michigan, maintains the markets and sends price *quotes* to the agents. The agents connect over the Internet and send bids to the server that update the markets accordingly and execute transactions.

Each game instance lasts 12 minutes and includes a total of 28 auctions of 3 different types.

Flights (8 auctions): There is a separate auction for each type of airline ticket: flights to Tampa (*inflights*) on days 1–4 and flights from Tampa (*outflights*) on days 2–5. There is an *unlimited* supply of airline tickets, and their *ask price* changes every 24–32 seconds by from $ − 10$ to x. x increases linearly over the course of a game from $10–y$, where $y \in [10, 90]$. y is independent for each auction, and is unknown to the bidders. In all cases, tickets are priced between \$150 and \$800. When the server receives a bid at or above the ask price, the transaction is *cleared immediately* at the ask price. *No resale* of airline tickets is allowed.

Hotel Rooms (8): There are two different types of hotel rooms—the Tampa Towers (TT) and the Shoreline Shanties (SS)—each of which has 16 rooms available on days 1–4. The rooms are sold in a 16th-price *ascending* (English) auction, meaning that for each of the 8 types of hotel rooms, the 16 highest bidders get the rooms at the 16th highest price. For example, if there are 15 bids for TT on day 2 at \$300, 2 bids at \$150, and any number of lower bids, the rooms are sold for \$150 to the 15 high bidders plus one of the \$150 bidders (earliest received bid). The ask price is the current 16th-highest bid. Thus, agents have no knowledge of, for example, the current highest bid. New bids must be higher than the current ask price. *No bid withdrawal* and *no resale* is allowed, though the price of bids may be lowered provided the agent does not reduce the number of rooms it would win were the auction to close. Transactions only *clear when the auction closes*. One randomly-chosen hotel auction closes at minutes 4–11 of the 12-minute game. Quotes are only changed on the minute.

Entertainment Tickets (12): Alligator wrestling, amusement park, and museum tickets are each sold for days 1–4 in *continuous double auctions*. Here, agents can *buy and sell* tickets, with transactions *clearing immediately* when one agent places a buy bid at a price at least as high as another agent's sell price. Unlike the other auction types in which the goods are sold from a centralized stock, each agent starts with a (skewed) random endowment of entertainment tickets. The prices sent to agents are the *bid-ask spreads*, i.e., the highest current bid price and the lowest current ask price (due to immediate clears ask price is always greater than bid price). In this case, *bid withdrawal* and *ticket resale* are both permitted. Each agent gets blocks of 4 tickets of 2 types, 2 tickets of another 2 types, and no tickets of the other 8 types.

In addition to unpredictable market prices, other sources of variability from game instance to game instance are the client profiles assigned to the agents and the random initial allotment of entertainment tickets. Each TAC agent has 8 clients with randomly assigned travel preferences. Clients have parameters for ideal arrival day, *IAD* (1–4); ideal departure day, *IDD* (2–5); hotel premium, *HP* (\$50–\$150); and entertainment values, *EV* (\$0–\$200) for each type of entertainment ticket.

The utility obtained by a client is determined by the travel package that it is given in combination with its preferences. To obtain a non-zero utility, the client must be assigned a *feasible* travel package consisting of an arrival day AD with the corresponding inflight, departure day DD with the corresponding outflight, and hotel rooms of the *same type* (TT or SS) for each day d such that $AD \leq d < DD$. At most one entertainment ticket can be assigned for each day $AD \leq d < DD$, and no client can be given more than one of the same entertainment ticket type. Given a feasible package, the client's utility is defined as

$$1000 - travelPenalty + hotelBonus + funBonus$$

where

- $travelPenalty = 100(|AD - IAD| + |DD - IDD|)$
- $hotelBonus = HP$ if the client is in the TT, 0 otherwise.
- $funBonus = $ sum of relevant EV's for each entertainment ticket type assigned to the client.

A TAC agent's final score is simply the sum of its clients' utilities minus the agent's expenditures. Throughout the game instance, it must decide what bids to place in each of the 28 auctions. At the end of the game, it must submit a final allocation of purchased goods to its clients.

The client preferences, allocations, and resulting utilities from an example game are shown in Tables 1 and 2.

Table 1. One agent's preferences from a sample game. *AW, AP,* and *MU* are *EV*s for alligator wrestling, amusement park, and museum respectively.

Client	IAD	IDD	HP	AW	AP	MU
1	Day 2	Day 5	73	175	34	24
2	Day 1	Day 3	125	113	124	57
3	Day 4	Day 5	73	157	12	177
4	Day 1	Day 2	102	50	67	49
5	Day 1	Day 3	75	12	135	110
6	Day 2	Day 4	86	197	8	59
7	Day 1	Day 5	90	56	197	162
8	Day 1	Day 3	50	79	92	136

For full details on the design and mechanisms of the TAC server and TAC game, see http://tac.eecs.umich.edu.

TAC-01 was organized as a series of four competition phases, starting on September 10, 2001 and culminating with the semifinals and finals on October 14, 2001 at the EC-01 conference in Tampa, Florida. First, the qualifying round, consisting of about 270 games per agent, served to select the 16 agents that would participate in the semifinals. Second, the seeding round, consisting of about 315 games per agent, was used to divide these agents into two groups of eight. After

Table 2. The client allocations and utilities from the agent and game shown in Table 1. Client 1's "MU4" under "Entertainment" indicates museum on day 4.

Client	AD	DD	Hotel	Entertainment	Utility
1	Day 2	Day 5	SS	MU4	1175
2	Day 1	Day 2	TT	AW1	1138
3	Day 3	Day 5	SS	MU3, AW4	1234
4	Day 1	Day 2	TT	None	1102
5	Day 1	Day 2	TT	AP1	1110
6	Day 2	Day 3	TT	AW2	1183
7	Day 1	Day 5	SS	AP2, AW3, MU4	1415
8	Day 1	Day 2	TT	MU1	1086

the semifinals, consisting of 11 games per agent, on the morning of October 14th, four teams from each group were selected to compete in the 24-game finals during that same afternoon.

4   Comparisons

The RoboCup and TAC domains have many similarities when considered from a research perspective. For example, agents in both domains must deal with a dynamic, real-time environment with hidden state and unpredictable adversaries. In most RoboCup leagues, the team must be distributed among several agents[1], and in TAC, some of the agents have used a distributed approach (for example using one agent to bid on hotels and another to bid on entertainment tickets).

Another key similarity between the two domains is that they are complex enough to prohibit any realistic attempt to solve them from a game theoretic perspective, and there is very little chance that strategies will emerge that can be described as in "equilibrium" in any sense. Rather, to be successful in TAC or RoboCup, an agent must be robust to a wide variety of opponents or economies. Ideally, an agent should be able to adapt on-line as opponents and environments change.

There are also many differences between the two domains. In many ways, RoboCup introduces additional research challenges that are not present in TAC, such as sensor and actuator noise, communication among teammates, and asynchronous sensing and acting: TAC agents can operate by choosing a set of actions (bids) every time they receive a new set of sensations (prices).

On the other hand, One feature of TAC not present in RoboCup is that the agents play against each other over an extended period leading up to the finals. In both TAC-00 and TAC-01, the competitors learned about each others' strategies in the weeks leading up to the finals, and made many adjustments as a result. For example, in TAC-00, only 14% of the agents were using a particularly effective (in isolation) high-bidding strategy during the qualifying round; by the finals 58% of the agents were using this strategy [21]. In RoboCup there is a

---

[1] The small-size robot league allows for centralized control of all 5 robots.

Table 3. Some comparisons between the TAC and RoboCup domains.

	TAC	RoboCup
Dynamic	+	+
Real-time	+	+
Multiagent	+	+
Hidden state	+	+
Adversaries	+	+
Teammates	—	+
Noisy sensors	—	+
Noisy actuators	—	+
Noisy actuators	—	+
Asynchronous	—	+
Communication	—	+
Distributed	(+)	+
Repeated play	+	—

good deal of technology exchange from year to year. But within a single year, teams tend to meet each other for the first time during the actual competition. Table 3 summarizes some of the characteristics of TAC and RoboCup.

Another interesting relationship between TAC and RoboCup is that they have proven to be attractive as research domains to many of the same people. In TAC-01, at least 6 of the 19 entries either involved the same institution or some of the same people as previous RoboCup entries[2]. In fact, the top two teams from the RoboCup-99 simulator competition and from TAC-01 involved two of the same people on opposing teams[3].

5   Lessons Learned from Competitions

Competitions have the potential to accelerate scientific progress within specific domains. However, there are also many potential hazards that can render them detrimental to progress.

Both RoboCup and TAC are primarily research initiatives. As such, their primary goals are to help advance the state of the art. They have certainly done so by providing new and challenging domains for studying issues within robotics and AI, such as "design principles of autonomous agents, multiagent collaboration, strategy acquisition, real-time reasoning and planning, intelligent robotics, sensor-fusion, and so forth" [12].

However, the domains exist without the competitions. In this section, I examine the potential hazards and potential benefits of having periodic large-scale

---

[2] The teams from AT&T Labs - Research, Carnegie Mellon University, Cornell University, Swedish Institute of Computer Science, and the University of Essex.

[3] Klaus Dorer from magmaFreiburg (RoboCup-99) [6] and livingagents (TAC-01) [9]; and Peter Stone from CMUnited-99 (RoboCup-99) [22] and ATTac (TAC-01) [17].

competitions, drawing on my experiences as a participant and organizer. I operate under the premise that scientific progress (as opposed to, for example, entertainment) is the primary goal.

I start by examining the potential hazards of competitions; then I point out the potential benefits. As many potential hazards and benefits are quite similar, it is up to the participants and organizers to sway the balance towards the benefits.

5.1 Hazards

There are many potential hazards to scientific progress involved in holding organized competitions. However, many can be avoided through careful organization of the competitions along with an engineered social climate within the community. Here, I list the possible hazards while, where possible, indicating how RoboCup and TAC have tried to avoid them.

Obsession with winning. One of the most obvious potential hazards of competitions is that people try to win them at the expense of all else, including science. Especially if there are monetary prizes involved, many people will focus only on winning and there is a potential incentive to keep successful techniques secret from year to year. RoboCup and TAC both do their best to avoid this hazard by not awarding any monetary prizes. Instead, the winners are rewarded with opportunities to disseminate their research via invited publications. In addition, in RoboCup, "scientific challenge" awards are given to teams who, in the opinions of the organizers, have demonstrated the best scientific contributions in their teams. In comparison with the competition winners, winners of these scientific challenge awards are given equal, if not greater, status at the awards ceremonies and within the community. Thus, there is explicit incentive given to deemphasize winning in favor of focusing on scientific contributions. Nonetheless, competitive spirit can easily take over.

Domain-dependent solutions. Another potential hazard of competitions, particularly within complex domains, is that it can be difficult to avoid getting bogged down in the low-level details of the domain. If the competition is to serve scientific interests, the winning solutions should be ones that are generally applicable beyond the particular domain in question. Of course, it is impossible to avoid requiring some domain-dependent solutions. However, while necessary, they should not be sufficient to produce a winning team. One way to encourage an emphasis on high-level, generalizable solutions is to repeat the same competition several times. While the first iteration is likely to be won by the best domain-dependent solution, subsequent events are more likely to find several teams using the same low-level approach that has already been proven effective. Then the difference among the teams will be more at the general levels. For example, at RoboCup-97, the winning teams in both the simulator and small-robot competitions were the ones that had the best low-level sensing and acting capabilities. However at RoboCup-98, there were several teams with similar low-level capabilities. Similarly, the biggest differences among agents in TAC-00 were their approaches to the TAC-specific allocation sub-problem [20], while in TAC-01 many of the agents were solving it optimally by building upon the previous year's published approaches. Instead, the crucial differences were at the level of strategic reasoning using techniques that are not limited to the specific domains.

Cost escalation. Especially in the robot competitions, there is the potential to have increasingly expensive solutions. If an expensive technology provides a significant advantage at one competition, then it might become a prerequisite for success in future years. If the expense is prohibitive to academic researchers, then the competition could die out. This issue has not yet been addressed in RoboCup. One possible solution would be to require that all teams use a common hardware platform, restricting the differences to the software. In fact, the RoboCup legged robot competition uses this approach as the only robots meeting the competition specifications were the Sony legged robots [24]. However, in general, this is not a satisfactory approach for RoboCup given that some of the interesting research issues are in the creation of the hardware itself. Another possible solution would be to enforce cost limits on entrants. However, such a restriction would be very difficult to define and enforce adequately. Cost escalation may become a serious issue for RoboCup in the near future.

Barrier to entry. As a competition repeats from year to year, it is natural that the people who have been involved in the past have an advantage over newcomers. As time goes on, this effect can magnify to the point that new-comers can never hope to compete meaningfully: the barrier to entry becomes too high. For example, in the world of computer chess, the leaders in the field invested large amounts of time and money building specialized hardware expressly for the purpose. It became virtually impossible for a new-comer to get up to speed in a reasonable amount of time. One reason for this effect was that the rules of chess are well-defined and unchanging: a successful approach in one competition is likely to remain successful even if left unchanged. One way around this effect is to gradually change the rules from year to year in order to make them slightly more challenging. For example, from the first year to the second year, the TAC competition changed from having all of the hotel auctions close at the end of the game to having them close randomly over the course of the game. Thus the previous year's competitors had to address an important new challenge at the same time as the new-comers. The barrier to entry can also be lowered considerably if competitors make portions of their code available as has happened consistently in the RoboCup simulation league.

Restrictive rules. While it is important to have well-defined rules for competitions, there is a potential to discourage research innovations via these rules. Especially for competitions involving robots, it is difficult to create rules that have no loopholes but are not overly restrictive. Over the years, RoboCup competitions have been run with varying degrees of specificity in the rules. Since the first year, the simulator league has always included a general "unsportsmanlike" clause, generally prohibiting anything that is not "in the spirit of the competition." Similarly, the TAC organizers reserved "the right to disqualify agents violating the spirit of fair play." The RoboCup small-robot league, on the other hand, has tended towards precise, completely-specified rules. While the former approach has the potential to lead to some heated arguments, my experience is that it is the best from a research perspective since it discourages participants from focusing on exploiting minute aspects of the rules.

Invalid evaluation conclusions. There is the potential at competitions to conclude that if agent (or team) A beats team B, then all of the techniques used by team A are more successful than those used by team B. However, this conclusion is invalid. Unless the agents are identical except in one respect, no individual aspect of either agent can conclusively be credited with or blamed for the result. Indeed, I have been involved on teams that won several of the competitions described above, but we do not present the results of these competitions as evaluations of any of the contributions of our research other than the agents as a whole. Instead, we conduct extensive controlled experiments to validate our research contributions [18, 21, 17].

5.2 Benefits

While there are many potential hazards to holding competitions, there are also many potential benefits. Here I list the possible benefits, again illustrating them with specific examples from RoboCup and TAC whenever possible.

Research Inspiration. While one potential hazard of competitions stemming from peoples' competitive spirit is an obsession with winning, a related benefit is that competitions are a great source of research inspiration. Several research innovations have been the direct result of preparations for one of the above competitions. While they started as innovative solutions to challenging specific problems, participants were then able to abstract their contributions into general frameworks. The natural desire to win is a strong motivation to create a good team by solving the challenging aspects of the domain.

Deadlines for creating complete agents. Competitions create hard deadlines for the creation of *complete* working systems. In order to compete, it is not sufficient for any one component of the system to be operational. Therefore, entrants must confront the challenging issues of "closing the loop," i.e. getting all components working from sensing, to acting, to strategic reasoning. They must create complete agents. No matter how sophisticated a team's high-level strategic reasoning, if it does not solve the low-level issues, some other team will easily win. Our experience has been that these deadlines have forced us to solve difficult holistic problems that we might have otherwise overlooked: these problems have been a source of research inspiration for us.

Common platform for exchanging ideas. Competitions can bring together a group of people who have all tried to solve the same problems in the same domain. Unlike in many research communities, there is a common substrate system and a common language among participants. For example, in the planning community, researchers use a wide variety of planning systems, each with its own properties and idiosyncrasies, sometimes making it difficult to directly compare approaches and technique. Indeed, in a recent planning competition one main challenge was finding the commonalities and compatibilities among different planning representations [15]. In RoboCup and TAC, on the other hand, everyone implements their ideas in the same underlying architecture. Consequently, it is relatively easy to compare the various systems.

Continually improving solutions. When holding repeated competitions with the same platform, there is likely to be a continual improvement in solutions from event to event. All entrants know that in order to have a chance of winning a competition, they must be able to outperform the previous champion. Therefore, they are motivated to find some method of improving over the previous solutions. Of course, this benefit only applies if the same, or similar, rules are used as the basis for competition year after year. For example, in the AAAI robot competitions [1], there are some new tasks to be solved every year (in recent years there have also been some repeated tasks). While the new tasks encourage new entrants, there is no basis for directly measuring improvement from year to year.

Excitement for students at all levels. The inherent excitement of the RoboCup and TAC competitions encourages students at all levels to become involved in serious research. Competition entries often come from large teams of professors, graduate students, and undergraduates working together. By encouraging more people to become involved in research, the competitions can speed up progress. In addition, the competitions are ideal for undergraduate and graduate classes. There have been several courses around the world that have culminated in either simulated robotic soccer or trading agent competitions[4]. From all accounts, students in these classes have genuinely *enjoyed* putting in a good deal of time and effort to create their agents, and have learned a lot in the process.

Wide pool of teams created. After each competition, all of the entrants have created agents capable of performing in the given domain. If these agents are made available in some way, they can subsequently be used for controlled testing of research contributions. For example, in order to test technique x that is a single aspect of one's agent (or team), one could play the agent against another agent first with technique x active, and then without, thus establishing the effects of technique x. While such testing could be done against any agent, it is often up to the researchers themselves to

---

[4] For instance, I recently taught a course using the RoboCup simulator (http://cs.nyu.edu/courses/fall01/G22.3033-012/index.htm). For a recent class that used TAC, see http://ecommerce.ncsu.edu/csc513/.

create the team against which to test. As a result the comparison is often done against a trivial or simple team: a "straw-man." The competition can provide several teams against which to test, each of which is the result of serious effort by an independent group of researchers.

Generate realistic economies. Another related benefit of competitions is that realistic pools of teams, or economies in the case of TAC, can be studied. Presumably there are many groups in the financial industry who have created or are creating automatic trading agents. However they generally do not share any information about their techniques, or often even let on that they are using agents at all. Therefore, there may be significant innovations that are hidden from the public domain. Research competitions provide the incentive for people to develop similar innovations, and give us the ability to study their properties in an open forum.

Encourage flexible software and hardware. Taking a system out of one's own lab and into a new setting, whether it be a software system that is to be run on different computers or a robotic system that is to be run under different environmental conditions, requires a certain degree of flexibility in the system's creation. For example, rather than creating a vision system that works only in the lighting conditions in one's own lab, researchers must create a system that is easily adaptable to new conditions. Thus, the competition encourages general solutions that are more likely to apply in a wide variety of circumstances. In addition, since it is expected that rules of the competition may change slightly from year to year, it is always beneficial to create software that can be easily adapted to these changes.

It has been our experience so far that the benefits of RoboCup and TAC competitions outweigh the hazards. Most significantly as a strong source of inspiration, these competitions have played an important role in my own research [18, 21, 17]. Numerous other participants from both competitions have also published articles based on research originally motivated by RoboCup and TAC competitions (e.g [5, 14, 8, 10]). Again, the competition results themselves are not scientifically conclusive. But the process of competition, including the lessons learned, can be scientifically valuable.

6   Conclusion

RoboCup and TAC are both the focal points for large and growing research communities. The competitions play a large role in concentrating peoples' energies around consistent, challenging problems as well as providing them with concrete deadlines for producing complete working systems. Although there are significant potential pitfalls that need to be avoided when trying to facilitate research via competitions, the evidence from both RoboCup and TAC is that the benefits outweigh the hazards. From all indications, RoboCup, TAC, and perhaps other competitions that they will inspire will continue to play important roles within the research community in the foreseeable future.

Acknowledgments

Thanks to my collaborators on entries in the RoboCup and TAC competitions including Sorin Achim, Michael Bowling, János Csirik, Kwun Han, Michael Kearns, Michael Littman, David McAllester, Patrick Riley, Robert Schapire, Satinder Singh, and Manuela Veloso. Also thanks to the countless organizers of these competitions over the years.

References

1. Ronald C. Arkin. The 1997 AAAI mobile robot competition and exhibition. *AI Magazine*, 19(3):13–17, 1998.
2. Minoru Asada and Hiroaki Kitano, editors. *RoboCup-98: Robot Soccer World Cup II*. Lecture Notes in Artificial Intelligence 1604. Springer Verlag, Berlin, 1999.
3. Robert Axelrod. *The Evolution of Cooperation*. Basic Books, 1984.
4. Darse Billings. The first international RoShamBo programming competition. *International computer Games Association Journal*, 23(1):42–50.
5. Simon Ch'ng and Lin Padgham. From roles to teamwork: a framework and architecture. *Applied Artificial Intelligence*, 12:211–232, 1998.
6. Klaus Dorer. The magmaFreiburg soccer team. In M. Veloso, E. Pagello, and H. Kitano, editors, *RoboCup-99: Robot Soccer World Cup III*, pages 600–603. Springer Verlag, Berlin, 2000.
7. Anne Eisenberg. In online auctions of the future, it'll be bot vs. bot vs. bot. *The New York Times*, 2000. August 17th.
8. Nicoletta Fornara and Luca Maria Gambardella. An autonomous bidding agent for simultaneous auctions. In *Fifth International Workshop on Cooperative Information Agents*, number 2182 in Lecture Notes on Artificial Intelligence, pages 130–141, 2001.
9. Clemens Fritschi and Klaus Dorer. Agent-oriented software engineering for successful TAC participation. In *First International Joint Conference on Autonomous Agents and Multi-Agent Systems*, Bologna, 2002.
10. Amy Greenwald and Justing Boyan. Bidding algorithms for simultaneous auctions. In *Proceedings of Third ACM Conference on E-Commerce*, pages 115–124, Tampa, FL, 2001.
11. Hiroaki Kitano, editor. *RoboCup-97: Robot Soccer World Cup I*. Springer Verlag, Berlin, 1998.
12. Hiroaki Kitano, Milind Tambe, Peter Stone, Manuela Veloso, Silvia Coradeschi, Eiichi Osawa, Hitoshi Matsubara, Itsuki Noda, and Minoru Asada. The RoboCup synthetic agent challenge 97. In *Proceedings of the Fifteenth International Joint Conference on Artificial Intelligence*, pages 24–29, San Francisco, CA, 1997. Morgan Kaufmann.
13. Hugh Loebner. Home page of the Loebner prize. At http://www.loebner.net/Prizef/loebner-prize.html.
14. Stacy Marsella, Milind Tambe, Jafar Adibi, Yaser Al-Onaizan, Gal A. Kaminka, and Ion Muslea. Experiences acquired in the design of RoboCup teams: a comparison of two fielded teams. *Autonomous Agents and Multi-Agent Systems*, 4(2):115–129, June 2001.
15. Drew McDermott. The 1998 AI planning systems competition. *AI Magazine*, 21(2):35–55, 2000.

16. J. Rust, J. Miller, and R. Palmer. Behavior of trading automata in a computerized double auction market. Addison-Wesley, Redwood City, CA, 1992.
17. Robert E. Schapire, Peter Stone, David McAllester, Michael L. Littman, and János A. Csirik. Modeling auction price uncertainty using boosting-based conditional density estimation. In *Proceedings of the Nineteenth International Conference on Machine Learning*, 2002. To appear. Available at http://www.cs.cmu.edu/~pstone/papers.html.
18. Peter Stone. *Layered Learning in Multiagent Systems: A Winning Approach to Robotic Soccer*. MIT Press, 2000.
19. Peter Stone, Tucker Balch, and Gerhard Kraetszchmar, editors. *RoboCup-2000: Robot Soccer World Cup IV*. Lecture Notes in Artificial Intelligence 2019. Springer Verlag, Berlin, 2001.
20. Peter Stone and Amy Greenwald. The first international trading agent competition: Autonomous bidding agents. *Electronic Commerce Research*, 2002. To appear.
21. Peter Stone, Michael L. Littman, Satinder Singh, and Michael Kearns. ATTac-2000: An adaptive autonomous bidding agent. *Journal of Artificial Intelligence Research*, 15:189–206, June 2001.
22. Peter Stone, Patrick Riley, and Manuela Veloso. The CMUnited-99 champion simulator team. In M. Veloso, E. Pagello, and H. Kitano, editors, *RoboCup-99: Robot Soccer World Cup III*, pages 35–48. Springer Verlag, Berlin, 2000.
23. Manuela Veloso, Enrico Pagello, and Hiroaki Kitano, editors. *RoboCup-99: Robot Soccer World Cup III*. Springer Verlag, Berlin, 2000.
24. Manuela Veloso, William Uther, Masahiro Fujita, Minoru Asada, and Hiroaki Kitano. Playing soccer with legged robots. In *Proceedings of IROS-98, Intelligent Robots and Systems Conference*, Victoria, Canada, October 1998.
25. Michael Wellman. Personal correspondence, March 1999.
26. Michael P. Wellman, Peter R. Wurman, Kevin O'Malley, Roshan Bangera, Shou-de Lin, Daniel Reeves, and William E. Walsh. A trading agent competition. *IEEE Internet Computing*, 5(2):43–51, March/April 2001.

RoboCupJunior:
Learning with Educational Robotics

Elizabeth Sklar[1], Amy Eguchi[2], and Jeffrey Johnson[3]

[1] Dept. of Computer Science, Columbia University
1214 Amsterdam Ave
New York, NY 10027, USA
sklar@cs.columbia.edu
[2] School of Education, University of Cambridge
17 Trumpington Street
Cambridge, CB2 1QA, UK
eae24@hermes.cam.ac.uk
[3] Dept. of Design and Innovation
The Open University
Milton Keynes, MK17 8QH, UK
j.h.johnson@open.ac.uk

Abstract. The RoboCupJunior division of RoboCup is now entering its third year of international participation and is growing rapidly in size and popularity. This paper first outlines the history of the Junior league, since it was demonstrated in Paris at RoboCup 1998, and describes how it has evolved into the international sensation it is today. While the popularity of the event is self-evident, we are working to identify and quantify the educational benefits of the initiative. The remainder of the paper focuses on describing our efforts to encapsulate these qualities, highlighting results from a pilot study conducted at RoboCupJunior 2000 and presenting new data from a subsequent study of RoboCupJunior 2001.

1 Introduction

In 1998, Lund and Pagliarini demonstrated the idea of a children's league for RoboCup, using robots constructed and programmed with the LEGO Mindstorms kit to play soccer [8]. Since then, RoboCupJunior has evolved into an international event where teams of young students build robots to compete in one of three challenges: *soccer*, *rescue* and *dance* [6, 9, 18]. While the atmosphere at these events is electric, from an intellectual standpoint one asks: "what are the students learning from these activities?"

It would be too easy to say that because the students are interacting with technology they are learning something worthwhile. However, this appeared to be the conventional wisdom as children began using computers in the early days — from the 1970's into the 1990's. Today researchers are questioning this stance. For example, Healy suggests that no more than 10% of the available

G.A. Kaminka, P.U. Lima, and R. Rojas (Eds.): RoboCup 2002, LNAI 2752, pp. 238–253, 2003.

software for children has any educational value [5]. Reeves reminds us that "fifty years of media and technology comparison studies have indicated no significant differences in most instances" [17]. And Snyder warns that we are becoming "blinded by science" [19].

In our work, we are questioning the same "obvious" relationship between robotics and educational outcomes. Rather than focus just on the technology itself, we are examining the overall learning environment that results when groups of students participate in team robotic activities. We begin by outlining the history of RoboCupJunior, illustrating its growing popularity on an international scale. Second, we discuss results of a pilot study conducted at the RoboCupJunior tournament held in Melbourne in 2000 [18]. Based on this study, we make several observations about factors that we believe contributed to the success of the event. Third, we present results from a subsequent study conducted at RoboCupJunior 2001 held in Seattle. Finally, a comparison of the two studies is made, some conclusions are drawn and future directions are described.

2   History

RoboCupJunior began as a research project in Lund's LEGO lab at the University of Aarhus in Denmark. The idea was to explore the use of the LEGO Mindstorms platform for robotic soccer. The initial growth of the initiative in 1999 and early 2000, exclusively at Lund's lab, expanded the breadth of the project and increased the number of different activities offered. The focus was on continued exploration of the educational possibilities of robotics, particularly in terms of teaching young students about Artificial Life.

2.1   First Steps: 2000

At RoboCup Euro 2000 in Amsterdam, Kröse and others used the Interactive LEGO Football (ILF) software and robot design developed by Lund and Pagliarini to hold a one-day RoboCupJunior workshop [6]. Fifty children, ages 13-16, from 8 schools formed 12 teams to play one-on-one soccer. In the morning, each team was given a robot and taught how to use the ILF software. In the afternoon, there was a tournament with prizes given out at the end of the day.

Simultaneously during 2000, preparation was getting underway in Melbourne, Australia, in advance of the RoboCup 2000 conference. A committee comprised of local school teachers and representatives from universities and industry developed a blueprint for RoboCupJunior competitions involving a curriculum based, student driven approach. Three challenges were devised, each requiring a different level of sophistication.

- A **dance** challenge was designed for primary school children (up to age 12). Students would build robots that would move to music for up to two minutes. Creativity was emphasized. From a technical standpoint, this was presented as an entry-level event, since it was possible to participate using simple robots that only employ motors and no sensors. The event itself was exciting and innovative. Some children even dressed in costume themselves and performed alongside their robots (see figure 1a).

- A **sumo** challenge was designed for middle school children (ages 12-15). Two robots followed wiggly black lines and competed for possession of a central circular region on the playing field. This was presented as a middle-level event; only one robot was needed for each team and the environment was essentially static. The only dynamic elements were the two robots; they had limited interaction and did not need to respond to each other, only to changes in their own location on the playing field. (see figure 1c).
- A **soccer** challenge, inspired by Lund's project and videotapes of the senior RoboCup leagues, was designed by and for secondary school students (ages 12-18). Two teams of two robots each played on a special field, 150cm × 75cm in size. The floor of the field used a greyscale mat and the ball was an electronic device that emitted infra-red (IR) light [9]. The rules of play were developed from the RoboCup F-180 League rules (see figure 1b).

2.2   The Next Phase: 2001

During 2001, several regional events were organized around the world. In April, a workshop was offered at CHI-Camp, an activity-centered child-care program

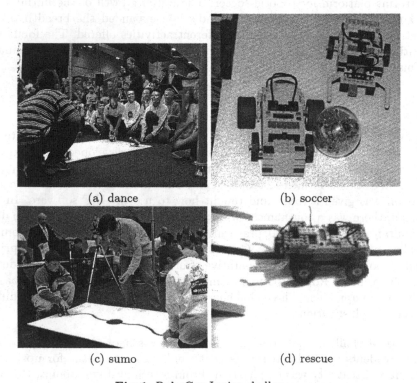

(a) dance   (b) soccer

(c) sumo   (d) rescue

Fig. 1. RoboCupJunior challenges.

for children of attendees to the annual CHI (Computer Human Interaction) conference, held in Seattle. In June, a mini RoboCupJunior tournament was held at the Autonomous Agents conference in Montréal. Six teams entered the one-day tournament, from four middle and high schools, involving six teachers, three parents and 53 students. Also in June, a RoboCupJunior tournament was incorporated into the German Open in Paderborn.

At the Japan Open 2001, Nomura and others organized a RoboCupJunior event in which 84 children participated. Most were from Fukuoka City; one team came from Tokyo and ten students came from Busan, Korea. About half of the participants were elementary school students (ages 9-12) and the other half were junior high school students (ages 13-15). Six activities were defined within several courses, and participants chose a course based on their interest and experience levels. Separate workshops focused on robot assembly and programming. Only soccer was offered (two-on-two). Some of the rules were outside the bounds of the official RoboCupJunior rules. For example, one track allowed remote controlled robots. The autonomous track used a visible light ball and a special field designed and produced by EK Japan. This field used beacons to indicate the positions of the goals and to help the robot locate itself within the field, instead of the greyscale floor mat used on the fields at RoboCupJunior 2000.

In August 2001, the second international RoboCupJunior tournament was held in Seattle at RoboCup 2001. Twenty-five teams from four countries participated: Australia, Germany, the UK and the USA. There were 104 participants (students and mentors). Again, three challenges were offered. The most significant differences from RoboCupJunior 2000 were that there were no age restrictions on challenges, tertiary (undergraduate) teams were permitted and the sumo/line-following challenge was replaced by a rescue event:

- A **rescue** challenge was designed as middle-level event. This was a timed event where one robot competed at a time. The background of the field was white, and the robot was required to follow a black line through a simulated disaster scenario. This was presented as a middle-level challenge. Again, only one robot was needed for each team. There were no dynamic elements, but accurate control of the robot based on light sensor readings is essential and surprisingly difficult. As well, the uneven terrain with a change in pitch where the robot reached a ramp and a bump in the path between the flat field and the ramp made the course even more challenging (see figure 1d).

The rules for soccer and dance were similar to RoboCupJunior 2000. The soccer field was enlarged to 122 cm by 183 cm, a factor of nearly double. This was done to accommodate increased maximum size for the robots, to allow kits other than the LEGO Mindstorms; for example, the FischerTechnik Mobile robot, where the basic building block that houses the microprocessor is considerably larger than the equivalent LEGO component.

In September 2001, the Australian National RoboCupJunior championship was held in Melbourne in association with Interact 2001 [21]. During the months preceding the tournament, five states conducted eliminations. In all, over 200 teams and 500 students participated. The finals were conducted in an auditorium with hundreds of spectators joining in to create an exciting atmosphere. This event received acclaim from industry representatives and VIP guests, to the extent that organizers were officially congratulated during a sitting of Victorian State Parliament.

3   Studies

3.1   Related Work

The notion of using robotics as a tool for education is relatively new. The recent availability of off-the-shelf robotic kits such as LEGO Mindstorms, FischerTechnik Mobile Robot and Elekit SoccerRobo have made it technically feasible and affordable for secondary and even primary schools to integrate robotics in the classroom. Most studies of this phenomenon focus on curricular ideas — explanations of what subject areas could be enhanced through robotics and methodologies for how to use the robots [10, 1, 11].

Other work has focused on outcomes. One such study was conducted at a large public university in Indiana where most of the students work full-time while trying to complete a technical degree [16]. Students take an introductory technology, engineering and computer science course in their first year (ETCS 101). A pilot version of the course, revolving around a team-based robot project using LEGO kits, was first offered in Fall 1999 and introduced into the regular curriculum in Fall 2000. The course focuses on teamwork as well as technical aspects. Students are assigned specific roles within their teams, such as material specialist and webmaster. The primary objective is to improve retention of engineering students in later subjects and ultimately to graduation. Statistical results show that the goal has been met thus far. Students who took the introductory course prior to inclusion of the robotics project had a 37% chance of leaving the ETCS program, while after inclusion of the robotics project, there is only a 5% likelihood of students leaving the program.

A comprehensive study was conducted by Wagner [24], examining the effects of robotics in primary classrooms (ages 8-12). The overriding question in her study was to determine if use of robotics in science curriculum had a greater effect on children's performance on science achievement tests than use of battery powered (non-robotic) manipulatives. The study found that use of robotics did not significantly improve general science achievement, though the use of robotics did improve programming problem solving (though not general problem solving). The study also highlighted that there are many mitigating factors when conducting a study of this sort. For example, students participating in the study are aware that they are subjects and may act differently if they were not being observed. Wagner also notes that the study opened up more questions than it answered.

Verner recognized the educational value inherent in the senior leagues of RoboCup [22], noting that RoboCup embodies project-based education, a pedagogy currently very popular in engineering curricula. He identified various components of project-based learning, e.g., motivation, problem solving, teamwork and cooperation, and administered a questionnaire to participants at RoboCup 1997 focusing on these aspects. He reported statistics on composition of team membership, length of participation in RoboCup, motivational factors and curricular subjects (for the upcoming RoboCup summer school). The study revealed that the most important motivational factor for all participants was "to apply and test [their] ideas". The study also revealed that a low motivational factor was "prospective career opportunities". The most popular curricular summer school subject was a simulator building workshop.

In the next year, Verner performed a follow-up study [23], using similar methodologies, but performing a more comprehensive analysis of the results. He broke down statistics according to role in order to analyze differences between professors and students. Motivational aspects were examined as well as applicability of general science and engineering subjects such as computer vision and multi-agent collaboration. The curricular statistics are not surprising, for example 100% of simulation league team members say that they are concerned with multi-agent collaboration, while none of them are concerned with control circuits. The motivational results reveal that professors view RoboCup as slightly more motivating than students in terms of attitude towards the subject matter and practical issues, while students view the fun of the robot soccer game as more motivating than professors.

In Verner's results, it is interesting to note the contrast between *intrinsic* and *extrinsic* motivational aspects. These factors have been studied by psychologists in basic terms such as rewarding birds for pressing levers, and more recently in relation to education [7]. *Intrinsic* rewards are those felt internally by a person achieving a task, simply out of satisfaction for having performed the task. *Extrinsic* rewards are those offered by outsiders, either verbally or materially (e.g., trophies), often having no obvious relation to the task being performed. In general, it has been found that extrinsic rewards can harm a person's natural intrinsic motivation to perform a task if the reward is given at one time and then taken away. For example, children who like to draw in their free time and are subsequently rewarded for drawing are afterward less likely to draw in their free time when the reward is no longer offered.

Verner's results show that the intrinsic rewards offered for participation in RoboCup are far more significant than the extrinsic rewards. Namely intrinsic factors: "a positive attitude towards the subject, the method and the framework for research and education suggested by the program" and "opportunity to apply your ideas and reinforce practical and teaching/learning skills" were considered highly motivating by 71% of respondents. Whereas the extrinsic factor: "ambition to cope with the RoboCup challenges and win a reward at this prestigious professional contest and forum" was considered highly motivating by only 35% of respondants.

3.2   The RoboCupJunior Challenge

The work presented here attempts to bring these various issues to bear within the RoboCupJunior arena. Two pilot studies were conducted, in 2000 and 2001, and the results of both are presented in this section. While the methodology for collecting data is similar to those above (i.e., in the form of surveys and questionnaires), the challenge of extracting valid and useful results is difficult for two reasons. First, the subjects are children who may not be able to measure accurately various motivational factors on a 5-point scale (e.g.). Second, the international composition of RoboCupJunior brings forth language and cultural issues more than in the senior leagues, since young students are less likely to be able to factor out cultural issues than adults.

3.3   Pilot Study: RoboCupJunior 2000

RoboCupJunior 2000 involved about 40 teams of children, 8 to 19 years old; one team was from the USA, one was from Germany and the remaining 38 teams were from Australia. We conducted interviews with twelve of the teachers who entered teams in the tournament, with the general stated goal of investigating the educational value of RoboCupJunior.

The interviews were conducted in two parts. First, background information was gathered on paper. Then interviews were video-recorded for subsequent analysis. The background questions were used to establish the experience level of the teacher and the specifics of the school environment, e.g., age groups, genders and subjects taught. The interview questions were divided into two parts. The first section focused on how each teacher used RoboCupJunior in their curriculum. The second section concentrated on comparing RoboCupJunior with other types of projects and activities, like science fairs, school plays, math team, etc. The questions asked about the influence of RoboCupJunior on students' behavior and motivation, with respect to schoolwork and teamwork.

The selection of the teachers to be interviewed was quite opportunistic. During the two days of the tournament, we approached teachers when they were not busy with their teams and asked them to be interviewed. The interviews took about forty minutes each. Our subjects may not represent all the teachers at the competition fully. However, it is worth noting that teachers from 9 out of the 13 schools whose teams participating in the soccer challenge were interviewed.

The analysis is based on notes taken during the interviews as well as transcripts of the videotapes. We acknowledge that the sample size is small and that the sample is biased — the respondents were teachers who believed in the initiative because they chose to enter in the first place. Additionally, we feel that the group sampled is technically more advanced than the average population of all teachers — most teach science and/or technology curriculum; several have degrees in engineering.

Our pilot study revealed remarkable consensus of opinion amongst the teachers. RoboCupJunior fits in with existing robotics curriculum; is highly motivating for participants; advances both academic and personal development skills; teaches teamwork and tolerance of others; and may attract girls into robotics as well as boys. If these attributes generalize to other teachers in other school systems, it could be seen that RoboCupJunior is a very positive educational initiative. We note that in subsequent investigations in countries other than Australia, we have found the inclusion of robotics in school curricula is unusual, as school systems vary greatly from one nation to another and even from one region to another within a single nation, depending on the government organization of school systems within a given country.

In addition, we relate several observations in terms of motivation, transfer and gender issues. All of the teachers reported that the RoboCupJunior competition itself was a motivating factor, particularly because: it is an international event, it imposes an absolute deadline (i.e., the date of the conference is fixed) and it gives children an entry-level role in the complex and stimulating field of robotics research. Several teachers commented that the context of RoboCupJunior — the fact that the young entrants participated alongside the senior competitors, some of the top robotic scientists and engineers in world — was a tremendous motivating factor for them and their students.

About half of the teachers thought the children who participated behaved better during their preparation for the competition than they did during other classroom activities. Most teachers thought RoboCupJunior was helpful in other areas of their students' schooling, although some related concern expressed by a few parents and other teachers about time taken away from other lessons in order to prepare for RoboCupJunior.

Less than ten percent of the participating children were girls, but most teachers surmised that expansion of the dance challenge may encourage girls in future (the dance challenge was limited to age 12 at RoboCupJunior 2000). In Melbourne, most of the participants were boys; indeed, less than ten percent of participants were girls. No girls attended the robot soccer or sumo tournament, though a few did help teams prepare at school but were unable to attend the tournament. Girls did participate in the dance challenge, which was restricted to primary age children (12 years and under). This increased participation could either be due to the creative nature of the dance challenge, the younger age group, or both.

3.4   Second Study: RoboCupJunior 2001

At RoboCupJunior 2001, we surveyed not only mentors, but also the students. We present the results of both surveys in this section, starting with the mentors. All participants were requested to participate in the paper-and-pencil survey. In addition, students participated in a 20-30 minute videotaped interview. The results presented here are based on the paper surveys and some notes from the videotaped interviews.

Mentors. Out of 25 mentors, 16 completed the survey (64%). Among the mentors, there are seven classroom teachers, eight parents (including one classroom teacher and two club leaders), one camp counselor, and one former RoboCupJunior student. Six of the teachers work at the middle and high school level; one is from a university. Their students ranged in age from 11 to 24.

Although most of the mentors' teaching experiences are focused in technical areas (math, physics and technology), teachers from other areas were also involved. These included biology, social studies and theology.

Among the teachers who responded to the survey, one teacher was from the US, two teachers were from Australia and four were from Germany. Only two teachers responded that they have robotics activities included in their curriculum — one from Germany and one from Australia. Both teach in public (government funded) schools. Overall, 62.5% of the mentors indicated that their students attend public schools, while 12.5% attend private (students/families pay fees for them to attend)[1].

Our research is centered around trying to identify what the students are learning from their RoboCupJunior activities. We asked both mentors and students to consider 13 specific skills and indicate whether they felt their involvement in RoboCupJunior had helped or hurt each of these skills, or if there was no effect. The selection of the specific skills listed was based on transcripts of the video interviews conducted at RoboCupJunior 2000 [18].

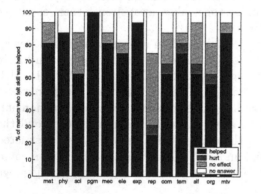

Fig. 2. Effects on various skills, according to mentors (2001).

The results are shown in figure 2. The bars illustrate the number of mentors who indicated whether each skill was helped, hurt, etc. For example, 80% of the mentors indicated that they thought their students' math skills were helped through their preparation for RoboCupJunior; approximately 12% of the mentors indicated that they thought that the RoboCupJunior preparation had no effect on their students' math skills; and 8% of mentors did not respond to the question. The overall consensus is that all the skills named were helped more than they were hurt; indeed those who felt that all skills were either helped or not affected far outnumbered those who indicated that any given skill was hurt.

One notable exception is in regard to reporting skills. Mentors ranked reporting skills as being helped less than other skills (students also ranked reporting skills low, as described in the section below). This could be due to the lack

---

[1] 25% of the mentors did not respond to the question of whether their students attend public or private school.

of activities such as keeping journals and writing lab reports, because perhaps mentors might not expect that work in robotics can help such skills — however, these types of activities are extremely important in scientific research, since researchers must be able to communicate their discoveries. Teams were encouraged to give presentations at a RoboCupJunior workshop, after the tournament was over, describing their preparation. All of the teams were invited to submit papers to the informal Junior workshop, but none of them did. Further emphasis on reporting as part of the tournament itself will help promote development of this skill set.

Students. Out of 82 students, 43 completed the surveys (52%). First, we focus on the demographic information, examining the number of students who participated in the event and the number of students who completed the survey, grouped according to country. Table 1 shows breakdowns both on an individual basis, as well as by team. These figures are relevant as the subsequent data is presented on an individual basis or team-wise, depending on which reporting mechanism is appropriate given the data being presented. In either case, it may be helpful to refer back to these tables.

Table 1. Participation, by country (2001).

	number of event participants		number of surveys completed		individual completion rate	number of teams at event		number of teams in survey		team completion rate
Australia	23	(28%)	12	(28%)	52%	10	(40%)	8	(44%)	80%
Germany	13	(16%)	12	(28%)	92%	5	(20%)	4	(22%)	80%
UK	3	(4%)	2	(5%)	66%	2	(8%)	1	(6%)	50%
USA	43	(52%)	17	(40%)	40%	8	(32%)	5	(28%)	63%
total	82		43		52%	25		18		52%

The gender gap was narrowed in 2001. Overall, 11% of participants were female. The German teams were all-male, but the other nations had mixed teams. The Americans had more females altogether; there were three all-female teams (one American, two Australian).

Next, we look at the age distribution, as shown in figure 3. Most participants are in high school, between the ages of 16 and 18.

Several questions in the survey focused on the teams' preparation, asking what was the span of preparation time, how frequently the teams met and how long each meeting lasted. Figure 4 shows these data graphically. Each mark on the plot represents one of the teams who completed the survey. The position of each mark indicates the average number of hours of preparation made by each team, per week. There are no patterns here, except to note that 77% of the teams spent at least 2 hours per week preparing. Some teams spent very little time, preparing everything at the last minute. Other teams spent up to a year preparing, meeting regularly after or during school.

We also asked questions about the type of adult supervision and help received by the teams while they prepared (figures 2(a) and 2(b)). Although these

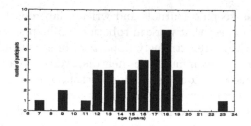

Fig. 3. Distribution of ages amongst participants (all participants, 2001).

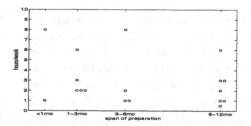

Fig. 4. Comparison of preparation times (2001).

Table 2. Adult supervision and help (2001).

number of adults helping	teams
0	3 (17%)
1	8 (44%)
2	2 (11%)
3	1 (6%)
4	2 (11%)
5	2 (11%)

(a)

level of adult assistance	teams
almost none	6 (33%)
a lot in the beginning	4 (22%)
a lot throughout	1 (6%)
mixed	7 (39%)

(b)

questions were asked on an individual basis, the figure contains an average for each team, since it is more appropriate to analyze these data on a per team basis. For the most part, there was consensus amongst team members. A few teams had wide discrepancy, but that is likely due to the fact that on many teams, members joined at different times, so those who were participants early on might have received more help from mentors than those who joined after the team had been working for a while. Some students commented that they (the mentors) were only needed to give the students the keys to the closet where the robots were stored or to go out for pizza. Others, particularly the younger students, said that they received "a lot of help throughout" their preparation.

At RoboCupJunior 2000, all teams used the LEGO Mindstorms platform. Some teams used LEGO without modifying it in any way, others made considerable mechanical and electronic developments of their own, including spinning mechanisms for kicking and non-standard sensors. In 2001, other platforms were used, namely the Fischer-Technik mobile robot (16% of teams) and the Tetrixx kit (4% of teams) developed at Gerhard Kraetzschmar's lab at the University of Ülm [4]. The LEGO Mindstorms kit was used by 80% of the teams.

All of the teams that did not use LEGO were German teams. One of the German teams that participated in RoboCupJunior 2000 using LEGO, progressed to the Tetrixx platform for 2001. Typically, the choice of which robot kit to use depends on the local culture and which platform is most familiar to the students and/or mentor. For example, at the Japan Open in 2001, almost all the teams used the Elekit Soccer Robot kit produced by EK Japan; only one team used LEGO Mindstorms. Since RoboCupJunior 2002 is being held in Japan, it is expected that there will be more diversity in platforms including LEGO, Fischer-Technik, Tetrixx and Elekit.

The heart of the survey asked the students to consider whether any of a list of skills had been affected by their participation in RoboCupJunior. They were asked to rank 13 skills as having been either helped, hurt or not affected by their participation. The answers, based on individuals' data, are shown in figure 5. Most students felt that their programming, mechanical and electronics skills had been improved.

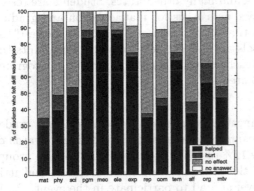 

Fig. 5. Effects on various skills, according to students (2001).

4   Analysis

Methodology. It is interesting to contrast the results of the studies from both years (2000 and 2001), although a statistical comparison cannot be made since the survey methodology differed from one year to the next. The 2000 study used open-ended questions. Subjects were prompted only when necessary (quite infrequently). The 2001 study built upon the previous year's results, consisting of a combination of open-ended and closed-ended (i.e., multiple choice) questions. The problem with open-ended questions is that the results are often difficult to tally, particularly to calculate any statistical significance due to slight variations in responses. The problem with closed-ended questions is that the respondents are often influenced by the answers already supplied (i.e., the multiple choices) and rarely provide in-depth information about their experiences or thoughts. Our compromise was to design the closed-ended questions based on data collected in 2000, while also including some open-ended questions in order to highlight differences between the two years' events. Future studies will build on results from both years.

Mentors. One large difference between RoboCupJunior 2000 and RoboCupJunior 2001 was in the number of classroom teachers who acted as mentors. In 2000, almost all of the mentors were teachers; in 2001, a smaller fraction of them were teachers. This is due to several factors. First, the timing of the event (August) was such that schools were closed, and teachers and students were involved with holidays, summer camp, etc. Still, most teams (91%) were organized through some type of institution — school, summer camp or community group. This statistic is similar to that of 2000, though in that year a larger percentage of mentors were classroom teachers and had robotics included in their curriculum.

The second factor is a political issue. A recent trend in US education is toward standardized testing. This is the case in Washington state, as well as California, Massachusetts, New York and many other states. Students are tested several times during their K-12 years, as a basis for matriculation and graduation. Teachers are forced to narrow their curriculum and "teach to the test", as the performance of individual schools are being tracked closely. This limits the amount of curricular freedom the teachers have, hence more creative programs such as robotics are typically eliminated.

Age of Students. In 2000, the dance challenge was limited to primary grades (ages 12 and under), and several teams were class efforts involving upwards of 20 students per team. In 2001, only 12% of the students were in this age group. This might be because about half the students were from overseas, and it is difficult for younger students to travel abroad to participate in the event. Or, it could be because there is still a myth among educators and parents that robotics is too difficult for young children. We should encourage younger generation and promote robotics activities since such children have more potential to develop various skills through robotics activities.

Skills. It is especially interesting to compare the 2001 mentors and students ratings for how the various skills were effected (see figures 2 and 5). Overall, more of the mentors consider that RoboCupJunior has positive effects than the students, as highlighted by figure 6. It could be considered that it is more difficult for students to assess the effects objectively than it is for mentors. Moreover it is harder for students to assess abstract skills, such as communication, self-esteem and organization, than it is for them to evaluate concrete skills, such as mathematics, physics and programming. In future studies, we will re-examine the survey to come up with more effective ways of asking students about abstract skills.

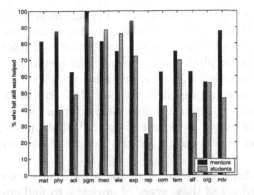

mat	math
phy	physics
sci	general science
pgm	computer programming
mec	mechanical engineering
ele	electronics
exp	experimental skills
rep	reporting
com	communication
tem	teamwork
slf	self-esteem
org	organization
mtv	motivation

Fig. 6. Variation in skill ratings between mentors and students (2001).

Future Participation. About 70% of both students (65%) and mentors (75%) expressed their willingness to participate in the RoboCupJunior international event again next year. Moreover, 75% of mentors are willing to participate in RoboCupJunior locally and nationally. This suggests that RoboCupJunior is so appealing and challenging that the participants become enthusiastic enough to continue working on it. This also shows that RoboCupJunior has great potential to grow to be an effective educational activity to enhance students learning in various ways. In order to make this happen, our future work involves continued promotion of RoboCupJunior activities, development of effective curriculum and clear assessment the effectiveness of RoboCupJunior activities in order to provide better educational environments for participants.

5 Future Directions

The motivational aspects of computer games, which have great attraction for children [20], are also found in robotic soccer. Among the 25 teams who participated in 2001, most of them spent more than one hour, and three fifths of the teams spent more than two hours, for one preparation meeting. This suggests that robotics activities are challenging and attractive enough to make students focus on their work for long periods of time. It also implies that, in order to merge this activity into regular curricula, teachers need to make effective plans to adjust the length of an activity into the regular class period without distracting students' motivation or to extend the class period to give their students enough time to explore ideas.

The emphasis on teamwork in RoboCupJunior allows students with a variety of interests and abilities an opportunity to pick their own challenges while contributing to the progress of the whole, an experience which nurtures the varied and multiple intelligences of each participant [2]. One way of applying this philosophy would be for teams in the same location to use a variety of platforms. Note that to date, all teams which have more than one robot have used the same platform for all their robots. This is not a requirement, so it will be interesting to see if this changes in the future as the teams' approaches become more sophisticated and advanced; or as teachers seek ways to challenge teams comprised of members with varying levels of experience with robotics and RoboCupJunior.

The expense to obtain new and varied platforms may hinder the accumulation of a diverse inventory. For the promotion of RoboCupJunior activities, it is important that we continue to include and highlight various platforms so that students and mentors are able to learn about the options that exist and are able to select those that are best for the team. Demonstrations at RoboCupJunior events can help make students and mentors aware of the variety of platforms available on the market today.

Although the results presented here are preliminary, the work fulfills a need in the community to examine the effects of these types of projects, to find standard and effective ways of evaluating them, and to define curricula that fosters and takes advantage of the positive elements identified. RoboCupJunior is an on-going, "plan-do-see" research program that provides effective educational activities to children of all ages, all around the world.

Acknowledgements

We are ever grateful to Brian Thomas for his tireless efforts behind the scenes of RoboCupJunior, in Australia and internationally. We thank all the students, mentors and organizers who have given of themselves and their time to prepare for and participate in RoboCupJunior events around the world.

References

1. Coradeschi S. and Malec J., How to make a challenging AI course enjoyable using the RoboCup soccer simulation system. In RoboCup-98: Robot Soccer World Cup II, Lecture Notes in Artificial Intelligence (LNAI) vol. 1604, Springer Verlag, 1998.
2. Gardner, H., Frames of Mind: The Theory of Multiple Intelligences, 1983.
3. Gonzalez, A., Digital divide closes - but schools aren't ready, USA Today, April 26, 2000.
4. http://www.tetrixx.de
5. Healy, J., Failure to connect: how computers affect our children's minds, New York: Simon & Schuster, 1998.
6. Kröse, B., Bogged, R., and Hietbrink, N., Programming robots is fun: RoboCup Jr. 2000. In Proceedings of Belgium-Netherlands AI Conference 2000, 2000.
7. Lepper, M. and Henderlong, J., Turning "play" into "work" and "work" into "play": 25 years of research on intrinsic versus extrinsic motivation. In Intrinsic and extrinsic motivation: The search for optimal motivation and performance, Academic Press, 2000.
8. Lund, H.H. and Pagliarini, L., Robot Soccer with LEGO Mindstorms. In RoboCup-98: Robot Soccer World Cup II, Lecture Notes in Artificial Intelligence (LNAI) vol. 1604, Springer Verlag, 1998.
9. Lund, H.H. and Pagliarini, L., RoboCup Jr. with LEGO Mindstorms. In Proceedings of ICRA2000, New Jersey: IEEE Press, 2000.

10. Martin, F.G., Ideal and Real Systems — A Study of Notions of Control in Under-graduates Who Design Robots. In Constructionism in Practice: Designing, Thinking, and Learning in a Digital World, Y. Kafai and M. Resnick (eds.), 1996.
11. Miglino, O., Lund, H.H. and Cardaci, M., Robotics as an Educational Tool. Journal of Interactive Learning Research, 10:1, 1999.
12. Nomura, T., personal communication (email), December 17, 2001.
13. Papert, S., Mindstorms: Children, Computers and Powerful Ideas, New York: BasicBooks, 1980.
14. Papert, S., The Children's Machine, New York: BasicBooks. 1991.
15. Piaget, J. To Understand Is To Invent, New York: The Viking Press, Inc., 1972.
16. Pomalaza-Ráez, C. and Groff, B.H. Retention 101: Where Robots Go... Students Follow, In Proceedings of the 2002 American Society for Engineering Education Annual Conference and Exposition, 2002.
17. Reeves, T. A Research Agenda for Interactive Learning in the New Millenium. In Proceedings of the World Conference on Educational Multimedia, Hypermedia & Telecommunications (EdMedia99), 1999.
18. Sklar, E.I., Johnson, J.H. and Lund, H.H. Children Learning from Team Robotics: RoboCup Junior 2000 Educational Research Report, Technical Report, The Open University, Milton Keynes, UK, 2000.
19. Snyder, T., Blinded By Science, The Executive Educator, 1994.
20. Soloway, E., How the Nintendo Generation Learns, Communications of the ACM, 34(9), 1991.
21. Thomas, B., personal communication (email), January 8, 2002.
22. Verner, I.M. The Value of Project-Based Education in Robotics. In RoboCup-97: Robot Soccer World Cup I, Lecture Notes in Artificial Intelligence (LNAI) vol. 1395, Springer Verlag, 1997.
23. Verner, I.M. The Survey of RoboCup '98: Who, How and Why. In RoboCup-98: Robot Soccer World Cup II, Lecture Notes in Artificial Intelligence (LNAI) vol. 1604, Springer Verlag, 1998.
24. Wagner, S.P. Robotics and Children: Science Achievement and Problem Solving. Journal of Computing in Childhood Education, 9:2, 1999.

A Rescue Robot Control Architecture
Ensuring Safe Semi-autonomous Operation

Andreas Birk and Holger Kenn

International University Bremen (IUB)
School of Engineering and Science
{a.birk,h.kenn}@iu-bremen.de

Abstract. The rescue robots developed at the International University
Bremen (IUB) are semi-autonomous mobile robots providing streams of
video and other essential data via wireless connections to human operated basestations, supplemented by various basic and optional behaviors
on board of the robots. Due to the limitations of wireless connections
and the complexity of rescue operations, the full operation of a robot
can not be constantly supervised by a human operator, i.e., the robots
have to be semi-autonomous. This paper describes how the main challenge of safe operation under semi-autonomous control can in general
be solved. The key elements are a special software architecture and a
scheduling framework that ensure Quality of Service (QoS) and Fail-Safe
Guarantees (FSG) despite the unpredictable performance of standard
Internet/Intranet-technologies, especially when wireless components are
involved.

1 Introduction

Rescue robots have a large potential as demonstrated for the first time on a larger
scale in the efforts with helping in the World Trade Center disaster [Sny01]. For
an overview of potential tasks of rescue robots and the related research in general
see for example [RMH01].

One of the main challenges in using robots in search and rescue missions is
to find a good tradeoff between completely remotely operated devices and full
autonomy. The complexity of search and rescue operations makes it difficult if
not impossible to use fully autonomous devices. On the other hand, the amount
of data and the drawbacks of limited communication possibilities make it undesirable if not unfeasible to put the full control of the robot into the hands of a
human operator. This paper introduces a control architecture that allows safe
semi-autonomous operation. The major challenges in this are to ensure Quality of Service (QoS) and Fail-Safe Guarantees (FSG) despite the unpredictable
performance of standard Internet/Intranet-technologies, especially when wireless
components are involved.

The rest of this paper is structured as follows. In section two, the software
architecture of the IUB rescue robots is described. In doing so, there is a special
emphasis on the main challenges from the telematics viewpoint, namely, how

G.A. Kaminka, P.U. Lima, and R. Rojas (Eds.): RoboCup 2002, LNAI 2752, pp. 254–262, 2003.
© Springer-Verlag Berlin Heidelberg 2003

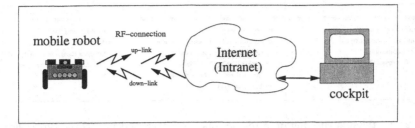

Fig. 1. The IUB rescue robots are teleoperated from a so-called cockpit by a human operator. Despite the human in the loop, they need quite some autonomous functionality ensuring FSG and QoS as the network performance is unknown and can even break completely down, especially as wireless components are involved.

Quality of Service (QoS) and Fail-Safe Guarantees (FSG) can be ensured when an unreliable wireless network connection is a major part of the control loop. The third section presents the hardware and the low-level software environment with which the system is implemented. Section four concludes the paper.

2   The Software Architecture

The IUB rescue robots are teleoperated by humans via standard network technologies (figure 1). The human in the loop ideally feels like being in full control of the system. But the unpredictable performance of networks, in terms of bandwidth, latency, and even reliability, makes it necessary to implement quite some autonomy on the mobile devices. In doing so, there are two major issues, namely ensuring FSG and QoS. FSG must never be violated at any cost. For a mobile robot, this means for example that major obstacles and gaps in the ground must be avoided or that the base must be stopped to avoid serious damages. QoS in contrast defines constraints which maximize utility as long as they are not violated. A timely response to requests from the operator for example ensures that the mobile robot moves along its path as desired. If these constraints are occasionally violated, they should at most cause some slight inconveniences to the operator, but they never must put the whole device or mission at risk.

The main challenge is to find a software architecture which supports these different types of processes. For our rescue robots, we use following approach (figure 2). The run-time system consists of three cyclic master threads T0, T1, and T2 running in timeslots in a 125 Hz major cycle. T0 includes everything dealing with FSQ. It establishes a hard realtime control-system. It is run to completion and its components are scheduled offline. T0 covers the motor- and basic motion-control as well as odometry and positioning.

The sub-threads of the master-thread T1 are so-called behaviors. Following the field of behavior-oriented robotics (see e.g. [Bro86,Ste91,Ste94] for an overview), reactive control schemes are used to establish close, dynamic couplings between sensors and motors (see [Bro86,Ste91]) which are computed in

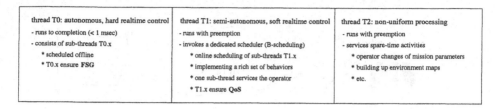

thread T0: autonomous, hard realtime control	thread T1: semi-autonomous, soft realtime control	thread T2: non-uniform processing
- runs to completion (< 1 msec)	- runs with preemption	- runs with preemption
- consists of sub-threads T0.x	- invokes a dedicated scheduler (B-scheduling)	- services spare-time activities
* scheduled offline	* online scheduling of sub-threads T1.x	* operator changes of mission parameters
* T0.x ensure **FSG**	* implementing a rich set of behaviors	* building up environment maps
	* one sub-thread services the operator	* etc.
	* T1.x ensure **QoS**	

Fig. 2. All threads running on a rescue robot are classified into three types. For each type, a respective master-tread handles the invocation of its related sub-thread. This scheme allows the combined usage of hard realtime, soft realtime, and non-uniform processing.

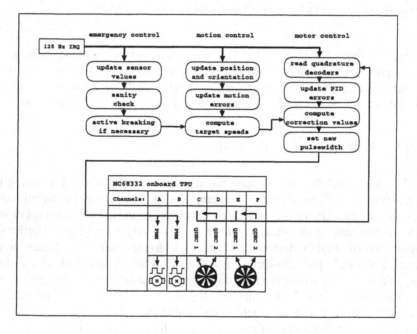

Fig. 3. The tasks for realtime control are cyclic processes running at a fixed frequency. Their target-values are asynchronously set by higher level behaviors.

pseudo-parallel. Behaviors can be used to keep the robot on a trajectory, to avoid obstacles, to approach a target, to autonomously scan for victims, and so on. The steering commands from the operator are serviced in a dedicated behavior. They are transformed to motion commands and fused with the motion commands from all other behaviors.

For the behaviors, soft realtime constraints are the only possible way to go. The "ideal" deadline until when a behaviors has to be handled is in most cases not known as it depends on unpredictable or simply too many conditions. The behaviors are scheduled online by a special so-called B-scheduler (see [BK00]) which is invoked by T1. Note that this scheduler as well as the behaviors are pre-empted by the master-scheduler. The B-scheduler guarantees a idle-free, optimally balanced execution of the behaviors, thus optimizing QoS.

Spare time activities, i.e., processes which neither contribute to the FSG nor the QoS, are handled in the master-thread T2. They can include the occasional change of mission parameters by the operator, the construction of environment maps, and so on.

2.1   The Hard Realtime Control

The T0 layer interacts with the higher layers via a shared memory buffer that is written by a thread from a higher layer and is read by the lower-layer T0 thread. The write operation is made atomic by delaying the execution of the T0 thread during write operations. So, target-values in the motion-controller can be asynchronously set by higher level behaviors.

The motion-controller so-to-say transforms the target-values on basis of odometric data to appropriate target-values for the motor-control. The motion- and motor-control layers are based on generic software modules for differential drive robots, featuring

- PID-control of wheel speed
- odometric position- and orientation-tracking
- rotational and translational trajectory control
- emergency breaking

As mentioned before, all of the involved subthreads T0.x are scheduled off-line to achieve a hard real-time control. This allows especially to include an emergency-module which ensures that the robot is stopped if it is for example extremely close to a gap in the ground. This subthread uses active breaking to get the base to a fast, but uncontrolled stop. Hence, the base will be protected in such circumstances from damage, but valuable positioning and trajectory information will be necessarily lost as this harsh breaking will include slipping motions.

The option of this subthread is hence explicitly for guaranteeing failure-safety, which only kicks in on extremely rare occasions. Normal obstacle avoidance, including controlled stops which are autonomously activated by the base, are handled on the layer of T1.

2.2   The Soft Realtime Control via Behaviors

The hard realtime is needed to ensure FSG. But for tele-operated devices in general, network performance, especially for wireless solutions, can usually not be predicted. Hence, hard realtime conditions are not an option for complete control of the device. Furthermore, hard realtime software is difficult to maintain and to extent.

The major trick in our software architecture is that a soft realtime scheduler for behaviors is run as part of the hard realtime schedule. In behavior-oriented

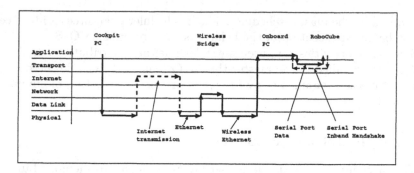

Fig. 4. The flow of the control data from the cockpit to a mobile robot. For certain parts, the time can not be predicted.

robotics, the control of a system is distributed over various processes or behaviors running in virtual parallel. The different behaviors, like controlled obstacle avoidance, ensure a smooth performance of the base.

A core behavior, especially from the viewpoint of a teleoperated device, is operator communication, i.e., the transmission of control states from the operator's console or so-called cockpit to the control hardware (figure 4). To ensure a low-latency operation over the Internet link, a protocol based on UDP packets has been implemented. The protocol is completely stateless. The packets are formed at the cockpit by synchronous evaluation of the control state and transmission to the onboard PC of the mobile platform via Internet. Here, they are received and transmitted to the RoboCube via the serial port. The communication behavior parses the packets and makes its content available to other behaviors via shared memory. Operator command-data for motion is simply fused with the data of other autonomous behaviors.

To ensure low-latency-operation, there is no retransmission on lost packets although UDP does not guarantee successful delivery of packets. However, since packets are transmitted synchronously and are only containing state information, there is no need to resend a lost packet since the following packet will contain updated state information. By exploiting this property of the protocol, low-latency operation can be assumed.

The communication between the RoboCube and the onboard PC uses inband handshaking to prevent buffer overruns in the RoboCube software. The communication layer software in the RoboCube confirms every packet with a 0x40 control code. Only if this control code has been received, the onboard PC communication layer software transmits the next packet. If the RoboCube communication layer software did not yet confirm a packet when a new packet arrives from the Internet transport layer, this packet is discarded so that the control layer software only receives recent packets, again ensuring low-latency operation.

Moreover, the communication layer measures the time between two packets. Whenever it becomes too large, the command information in the last packet is discarded and the base is transfered into a safe state depending on sensor information, i.e. stopped with the motor controller actively holding the last position.

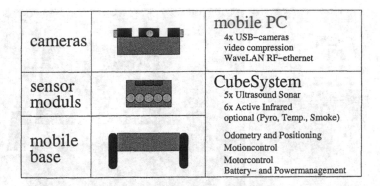

cameras		**mobile PC** 4x USB–cameras video compression WaveLAN RF–ethernet
sensor moduls		**CubeSystem** 5x Ultrasound Sonar 6x Active Infrared optional (Pyro, Temp., Smoke)
mobile base		Odometry and Positioning Motioncontrol Motorcontrol Battery– and Powermanagement

Fig. 5. A schematic overview of the different components of a rescue robot.

Plausibility checks on the same layer can be used to discard packets or to modify the implications of the information they contain. This is done in a rule-based module. This functionality is optional and allows a convenient incorporation of background knowledge about particular application domains.

2.3   The OS Support

The control software relies on the RoboCube controller platform, which is shortly described below, and on it's CubeOS operating system to implement the control application. The CubeOS nanokernel contains real-time multi-threading, abstract communication interfaces and thread control primitives. On top of the nanocore, a set of software drivers provides an application programming interface to the RoboCube's hardware.

3   The Hardware Implementation of the System

The implementation of the rescue robots is based on the so-called CubeSystem, a kind of construction kit for robotic systems. The center of the CubeSystem is the so-called RoboCube controller hardware (figure 6) based on the MC68332 processor. The compact physical shape of RoboCube is achieved through several techniques. First, board-area is minimized by using SMD-components. Second, three boards are stacked on each other leading to cubic design, hence its name Robo*Cube*.

RoboCube has a open bus architecture which allows to add "infinitely" many sensor/motor-interfaces (at the price of bandwidth). But for most applications the standard set of interfaces should be more than enough. RoboCube's basic set of ports consists of

- 24 analog/digital (A/D) converter,
- 6 digital/analog (D/A) converter,
- 16 binary Input/Output (binI/O),

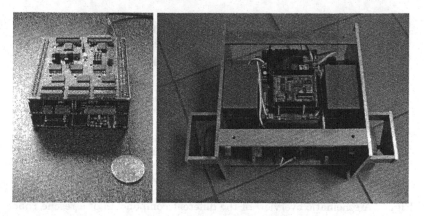

Fig. 6. Left: The RoboCube, an extremely compact embedded computer for robot control. Right: The prototype mobile base of the IUB rescue robots. It is completely constructed from CubeSystem components including the RoboCube as controller, the motor- and sensor-modules, as well as the battery-management hardware.

Fig. 7. The new mobile base with six actively driven wheels.

- 5 binary Inputs,
- 7 timer channels (TPC), and
- 3 DC-motor controller with quadrature-encoding (QDEC).

The RoboCube is described in more detail in [BKW00,BKW98].

In addition to its central component, the RoboCube as controller hardware, the CubeSystem provides additional hardware, including electronics and mechanics, and software components. In a first prototype, a midsized differential drive was used which is part of the standard CubeSystem componts (figure 6). For the more challenging locomotion tasks that are needed for rescue robots, a new base was developed that features six actively driven wheels (figure 7).

The CubeSystem features a special operating system, the CubeOS (see [Ken00]), which ranges from a micro-kernel over drivers to special high-level languages like the process description language PDL (see [Ste92]). The CubeSystem is used in basic and applied research, industrial projects and academic education. Therefore, a wide range of sensor- and motor-components exists. The CubeSystem also includes dedicated RF-network components. For compatibility reasons, radio-ethernet serviced via a mobile PC is used for our rescue robots. This PC is also used to compute the video-compression. All control and service related data going to and coming from the cockpit is directly relayed from the RF-connection to the RoboCube which handles all service and control related tasks on the rescue robot.

4 Conclusion

The paper described the IUB rescue robots. On its hardware side, the implementation of the robots is based on the CubeSystem, a kind of construction kit for robotic systems. Its use in the design of the rescue robots is shortly presented in this paper.

The main focus of this paper is on the general problem of ensuring secure but convenient control of a tele-operated device. We presented a special software architecture which incorporates Quality of Service (QoS) and Fail-Safe Guarantees (FSG). The main idea of the architecture is to find a suited way to combine hard and soft realtime scheduling.

Concretely, we use an hierarchical scheduling structure as follows. On the highest layer, there are only three threads T0, T1, T2 running in time-slots in a fixed frequency master cycle. T0 is run to completion and its subthreads T0.x establish a hard realtime control, ensuring FSG. The thread T1, which can be preempted, invokes a further soft-realtime scheduler for behaviors, which provide QoS. The behaviors establish close, dynamic couplings between sensors and motors computed in pseudo-parallel. This includes the steering-commands from the human in the loop, which are simply fused with the autonomous functionalities. The third thread T2 allows optional non-uniform processing, e.g., for operator changes of mission parameters.

References

[BK00]   Andreas Birk and Holger Kenn. Programming with behavior-processes. In *8th International Symposium on Intelligent Robotic Systems, SIRS'00*, 2000.

[BKW98] Andreas Birk, Holger Kenn, and Thomas Walle. Robocube: an "universal" "special-purpose" hardware for the robocup small robots league. In *4th International Symposium on Distributed Autonomous Robotic Systems*. Springer, 1998.

[BKW00] Andreas Birk, Holger Kenn, and Thomas Walle. On-board control in the robocup small robots league. *Advanced Robotics Journal*, 14(1):27 – 36, 2000.

[Bro86]   Rodney Brooks. Achieving artificial intelligence through building robots. Technical Report AI memo 899, MIT AI-lab, 1986.

[Ken00]   Holger Kenn. Cubeos, the manual. Technical Report MEMO 00-04, Vrije Universiteit Brussel, AI-Laboratory, 2000.

[RMH01]   M. Micire R. Murphy, J. Casper and J. Hyams. Potential tasks and research issues for mobile robots in robocup rescue. In Tucker Balch Peter Stone and Gerhard Kraetszchmar, editors, *RoboCup-2000: Robot Soccer World Cup IV*, Lecture Notes in Artificial Intelligence 2019. Springer Verlag, 2001.

[Sny01]   Rosalyn Graham Snyder. Robots assist in search and rescue efforts at wtc. *IEEE Robotics and Automation Magazine*, 8(4):26–28, December 2001.

[Ste91]   Luc Steels. Towards a theory of emergent functionality. In Jean-Arcady Meyer and Steward W. Wilson, editors, *From Animals to Animats. Proc. of the First International Conference on Simulation of Adaptive Behavior*. The MIT Press/Bradford Books, Cambridge, 1991.

[Ste92]   Luc Steels. The pdl reference manual. Technical Report MEMO 92-05, Vrije Universiteit Brussel, AI-Laboratory, 1992.

[Ste94]   Luc Steels. The artificial life roots of artificial intelligence. *Artificial Life Journal*, 1(1), 1994.

A Framework for Learning from Observation Using Primitives

Darrin C. Bentivegna[1,2] and Christopher G. Atkeson[1,3]

[1] ATR, Human Information Science Laboratories Department 3, Kyoto, Japan
[2] College of Computing, Georgia Institute of Technology, Atlanta, GA
[3] Robotics Institute, Carnegie Mellon University, Pittsburgh, PA

Abstract. This paper describes a method to learn task primitives from observation. A framework has been developed that allows an agent to use observed data to initially learn a predefined set of task primitives and the conditions under which they are used. A method is also included for the agent to increase its performance while operating in the environment. Data that is collected while a human performs a task is parsed into small parts of the task called primitives. Modules are created for each primitive that encode the movements required during the performance of the primitive, and when and where the primitives are performed.

1 Introduction

Learning without any prior knowledge in environments that contain large or continuous state spaces is a daunting task. For agents that operate in the real world, learning must occur in a reasonable amount of time. It is essential for an agent to have domain knowledge is if it to learn in the time scales needed [14]. Providing an agent with domain knowledge and also with the ability to use observation data for learning can greatly increase its learning rate. This paper describes a framework in which to conduct research that explores the use of primitives in learning from observation.

Virtual and hardware environments of air hockey and a marble maze game, figures 1 and 2, have been created as platforms in which to conduct this research. The virtual environments were first created and provided an invaluable tool in which to test algorithms that will be run on the hardware version. For this reason the physics of the virtual environments are programmed to match those of the hardware versions as much as possible. In all these environments the position data can be collected as a human operates in the environment. The architecture and current playing strategy of these environments will be described.

1.1 Primitives

Robots typically must generate commands to all their actuators at regular intervals. The analog controllers for our 30-degree of freedom humanoid robot are given desired torques for each joint at 420Hz. Thus, a task with a one second duration is parameterized with $30 * 420 = 12600$ parameters. Learning in this high

G.A. Kaminka, P.U. Lima, and R. Rojas (Eds.): RoboCup 2002, LNAI 2752, pp. 263–270, 2003.

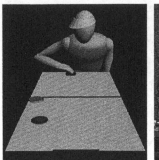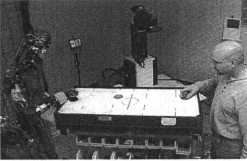

Fig. 1. The virtual air hockey environment on the left and the hardware version on the right.

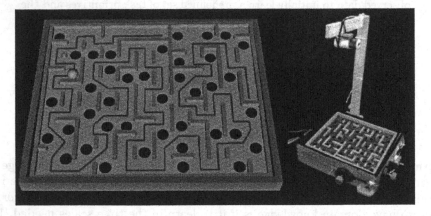

Fig. 2. The virtual marble maze game on the left modeled after the hardware version on the right.

dimensional space can be quite slow or can fail totally. Random search in such a space is hopeless. In addition, since robot movements take place in real time, learning approaches that require more than hundreds of practice movements are often not feasible. Special purpose techniques have been developed to deal with this problem, such as trajectory learning [2], learning from observation [4, 5, 9, 13, 6, 8, 10, 11], postural primitives [17], and other techniques that decompose complex tasks or movements into smaller parts [3, 7, 15].

It is our hope that primitives can be used to reduce the dimensionality of the learning problem [3, 16]. Primitives are solutions to small parts of a task that can be combined to complete the task. A solution to a task may be made up of many primitives. In the air hockey environment, for example, there may be primitives for hitting the puck, capturing the puck, and defending the goal. In this research a task expert predefines the set of primitives to be used for a given environment and algorithms are created to find the primitives in the captured data.

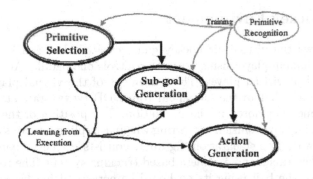

Fig. 3. Our view of a primitive.

1.2   Perceiving the Primitives

Since the observed data is continuous it must first be segmented into primitives. To accomplish this, critical events are used. Critical events are easily observable occurrences. Examples of critical events for the puck include collisions, in which the ball speed and direction are rapidly changed, and the ball traveling in a straight line with decreasing velocity. Algorithms have been created that find the primitives within the data by searching for the proper sequence of critical events.

1.3   Strategy for Primitive Use

Figure 3 shows our view of a primitive. Currently, a human, using domain knowledge, designs the candidate primitives that are to be used. The primitive recognition module segments the observed behavior into the chosen primitives. This segmented data is then used to provide the encoding for the primitive selection, sub-goal generation, and action generation modules.

The primitive selection module will provide the agent with the primitive to use for the observed state of the environment. After it has been decided which primitive to use, the desired outcome, or goal, of that primitive is specified by the sub-goal generation module. Lastly the actuators must be moved to obtain the desired outcome. The action generation module finds the actuator commands needed to execute the chosen primitive type with the current goal.

After the agent has obtained initial training from observing human performance, it should then increase its skill at that task through practice. Up to this point the agent's only high-level goal is to perform like the teacher. Its only encoding of the goal of the entire task is in the implicit encoding in the primitives performed. The learning from practice module contains the information needed to evaluate the performance of each of the modules toward obtaining a high-level task objective. This information can then be used to update the modules and improve performance beyond the teacher.

2   Air Hockey Environment

Figure 1 shows the virtual air hockey game created that can be played on a computer. A human player using a mouse controls one paddle. At the other end is a simulated or virtual player. The movement of the virtual player has been limited to match that of the humanoid robot DB (www.erato.atr.co.jp/DB/). Spin of the puck is ignored in the simulation. The position of the two paddles and the puck, and any collisions occurring within sampling intervals are recorded.

The hardware implementation, figure 1, consists of the humanoid robot, a small air hockey table, and a camera based tracking system. The robot observes the position of the ball using its on board cameras and hardware designed to supply the position of colored objects in the image. The humanoid's torso is moved during play to extend the reach of the robot. The head is moved so that the playing field is always within view.

The full list of primitives currently being explored in the air hockey environment is:

- Left Hit: the player hits the puck and it hits the left wall and then travels toward the opponent's goal.
- Straight Hit: the player hits the puck and it travels toward the opponent's goal without hitting the side walls.
- Right Hit: the player hits the puck and it hits the right wall and then travels toward the opponent's goal.
- Block: the player deliberately does not hit the puck but instead moves into a blocking position to prevent the puck from entering their goal.
- Prepare: movements made while the puck is on the opposite side from the player. The player is either preparing to setup for a shot, or preparing to defend their goal.
- Multi-Shot: movements made after a shot is attempted, but while the puck is still on the player's side. If the puck is not quickly moving toward the opponent's side, they will have the opportunity to hit it again.

3   Marble Maze Environment

In the marble maze game a player controls a marble through a maze by tilting the board that the marble is rolling on. The hardware board is tilted using two knobs and the virtual board is controlled with the mouse, figure 2. There are obstacles, in the form of holes, that the marble may fall into, and walls. In both versions the time and the board and ball positions are recorded as a human plays the game. The virtual game models the movement of the marble and treats collisions with the wall aesthetically with a significant loss of energy. The human controls the board on the hardware version by using knobs connected to encoders. The motor command generated by the encoder system is read by the computer and sent to the motors. The position of the ball is obtained using a Newtonlabs Cognacrome vision system [1]. The computer can also generate its own commands and send them to the motors.

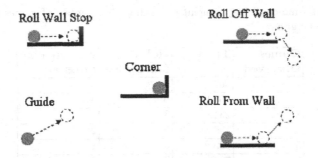

Fig. 4. Primitives used in the marble maze environment.

The primitives for the marble maze game are designed to give the agent the skills it will need to perform the task. The following primitives are currently being explored and are shown in figure 4:

- Roll Wall Stop: The ball rolls along a wall and stops when it hits another wall.
- Roll Off Wall: The ball rolls along a wall and then rolls off the end.
- Guide: The ball is moved without touching a wall.
- Roll From Wall: The ball hits, or is on, a wall and then is maneuvered off it.
- Corner: The ball is in a corner and the board is being positioned to move the marble from the corner.

4   Selecting the Appropriate Primitive and Sub-goal

As discussed in the strategy above, it is the responsibility of the primitive selection module to choose the type of primitive, based on the current state and prior observations of primitives being executed. In our implementation, the context or state in which the human has performed each primitive is extracted from the observed data, and is used by a nearest neighbor lookup process to find the past primitive executions whose context is most similar to the current context. For example the puck's position and velocity when it crosses a pre-specified line is often used as the index for a lookup. In the air hockey environment the primitives are selected and then run to completion, before the next primitive is selected and executed. In the marble maze environment a primitive can be interrupted if it is not making progress or causes the marble to fall into a hole.

The sub-goals for the primitive provide the parameters needed to perform the action. The sub-goals for the hit primitives, for example, are the desired hit location, the puck's desired post-hit velocity, and the target location. In air hockey these sub-goals are returned along with the single nearest neighbor as part of the selected primitive. The sub-goals in the marble maze game are obtained by interpolating between parameters of multiple previously executed primitives close of the selected type.

Table 1. Performance of player agent observing the number of games specified and then playing one game.

Games Observed	Time	Holes fallen into	Not making progress
1	367.3	6	5
2	257.9	6	3
3	234.6	3	3
4	189.8	5	2
5	129.9	4	1
6	72.2	3	0
7	123.4	3	1
8	73.2	4	0
9	231.0	3	3
10	243.0	3	3

5   Results

In the virtual game of air hockey an agent used data collected while observing a human to initially learn how to perform air hockey primitives and went on to increase it performance of shot primitives through practice. Agents in both the hardware and software versions have used the observed data to learn how to choose a primitive and parameters when operating in the environment. An agent in the virtual marble maze game learned how to perform primitives and an initial primitive selection strategy from observing a human. An agent also went on to increase its performance through practice. Initial research in the hardware marble maze has shown that better sensing and controlling devices are needed and a new version is currently being constructed for further research.

Table 1 shows the performance of a marble maze agent after it has observed a various number of games performed by a skilled human player. This agent only used the observed data and is not learning from practice. The observed player performed the task in about 55 seconds and never fell into a hole or was penalized for not making progress. There is an improvement in time to complete the maze up until six games are observed. But for holes fallen into, is not clear that observing more then three games has proven to be of benefit.

Since this agent is not using the learning from practice module, when it runs through the maze multiple times, it has approximately the same performance on each run. Any difference is due to noise that is purposely introduced into the simulation. A common error is for the agent to choose a primitive that has been performed on just the other side of the wall from where it is. This would create a sub-goal position that is out of reach of the marble from the current location. In this situation the marble would mostly just sit in a corner or fall in a hole that is nearby. Another frequently observed error is the agent choosing a primitive that it can not perform from the current state of the environment.

From observing the performance of this agent it can be seen that it must also have the ability to learn beyond the observation. As mentioned above, the agent computes an action using the observed data and then goes on to perform that action. To change its performance the agent must have knowledge of the overall task objective and some way to evaluate its performance toward the accomplishment of the task. It must also have a way to change its behavior as it practices to increase its performance toward completing the task.

6   Increasing Performance through Practice

There are a number of things the agent can learn to increase its performance while operating in the environment. At the primitive level it can improve the policy to become more proficient at primitive performance. The virtual air hockey player observed its own performance and collected data while practicing. This data was then used separately in a neural network and a kernel regression model to improve the hit performance of the agent. Many other methods can be used by an agent to learn a primitive through practice such as those used by Schaal and Atkeson [5] in pole balancing and of Kamon et. al. [12] in learning to grasp objects.

Agents can also learn to select more appropriate primitives and parameters. Without the learning from practice module the agent's only goal is to act like the teacher with no knowledge of a higher goal or task objectives. It is the job of the learning from practice module to provide this information so the agent's performance can be increased. The algorithms and performance of this module are currently being tested and will be presented in future research.

7   Conclusions

Agents must learn quickly if they are to operate in high dimension environments. Providing an agent with domain knowledge and the ability to learn from observation can greatly improve its learning rate. The presented framework provides much flexibility in conducting learning from observation research using primitives. The current research using this framework demonstrates its ability and future research will focus on improving the performance of the individual modules.

Acknowledgments

Support for both investigators was provided by ATR, Human Information Science Laboratories Department 3 and by National Science Foundation Award IIS-9711770. This research was supported in part by the Communications Research Laboratory (CRL).

References

1. Newton research labs homepage. http://www.newtonlabs.com.
2. C. H. An, C. G. Atkeson, and J. M. Hollerbach. *Model-Based Control of a Robot Manipulator*. MIT Press, Cambridge, MA, 1988.

3. R. C. Arkin. *Behavior-Based Robotics.* MIT Press, Cambridge, MA, 1998.
4. C. G. Atkeson and S. Schaal. Learning tasks from a single demonstration. In *Proceedings of the 1997 IEEE International Conference on Robotics and Automation (ICRA97)*, pages 1706–1712, 1997.
5. C. G. Atkeson and S. Schaal. Robot learning from demonstration. In J. D. H. Fisher, editor, *Proceedings of the 1997 International Conference on Machine Learning (ICML97)*, pages 12–20. Morgan Kaufmann, 1997.
6. P. Bakker and Y. Kuniyoshi. Robot see, robot do: An overview of robot imitation. In *AISB96 Workshop on Learning in Robots and Animals*, pages 3–11, 1996.
7. D. C. Bentivegna and C. G. Atkeson. Using primitives in learning from observation. In *First IEEE-RAS International Conference on Humanoid Robotics (Humanoids-2000)*, 2000.
8. R. Dillmann, H. Friedrich, M. Kaiser, and A. Ude. Integration of symbolic and subsymbolic learning to support robot programming by human demonstration. In G. Giralt and G. Hirzinger, editors, *Robotics Research: The Seventh International Symposium*, pages 296–307. Springer, NY, 1996.
9. G. Hayes and J. Demiris. A robot controller using learning by imitation. In *A. Borkowski and J. L. Crowley (Eds.), Proceedings of the 2nd International Symposium on Intelligent Robotic Systems*, pages 198–204, 1994.
10. G. Hirzinger. Learning and skill acquisition. In G. Giralt and G. Hirzinger, editors, *Robotics Research: The Seventh International Symposium*, pages 277–278. Springer, NY, 1996.
11. K. Ikeuchi, J. Miura, T. Suehiro, and S. Conanto. Designing skills with visual feedback for APO. In G. Giralt and G. Hirzinger, editors, *Robotics Research: The Seventh International Symposium*, pages 308–320. Springer, NY, 1996.
12. I. Kamon, T. Flash, and S. Edelman. Learning visually guided grasping: A test case in sensorimotor learning. In *IEEE Transactions on System, Man and Cybernetics*, volume 28(3), pages 266–276, 1998.
13. Y. Kuniyoshi, M. Inaba, and H. Inoue. Learning by watching: Extracting reusable task knowledge from visual observation of human performance. In *IEEE Transactions on Robotics and Automation*, pages 799–822, 1994.
14. L.-J. Lin. Hierarchical learning of robot skills by reinforcement. In *Proceedings of the 1993 International Joint Conference on Neural Networks*, pages 181–186, 1993.
15. M. J. Mataric, M. Williamson, J. Demiris, and A. Mohan. Behavior-based primitives for articulated control. In *Fifth International Conference on Simulation of Adaptive Behavior (SAB-98)*, pages 165–170. MIT Press, 1998.
16. R. A. Schmidt. *Motor Learning and Control.* Human Kinetics Publishers, Champaign, IL, 1988.
17. M. Williamson. Postural primitives: Interactive behavior for a humanoid robot arm. In *Fourth International Conference on Simulation of Adaptive Behavior*, pages 124–131, Cape Cod, MA, 1996. MIT Press.

Robosoccer-RU Open Simulation League: Principles and Algorithms

D.E. Okhotsimsky[1], V.E. Pavlovsky[1], A.N. Touganov[1], A.G. Plakhov[1],
V.V. Pavlovsky[1], S.S. Stepanov[2], and A.Yu. Zaslavsky[2]

[1] Keldysh Institute of Applied Mathematics of RAS (KIAM)
Moscow State University, Moscow, Russia
vlpavl@spp.keldysh.ru
[2] N-th.com Research, Dnepropetrovsk, Ukraine
robocup@n-th.com
http://n-th.com/

Abstract. In this paper we outline basic principles and competition rules used in a Computer soccer Simulation contest held in Eastern European countries (Robosoccer-RU League). The programming environment of this tournament ("Virtual Soccer" Software package) is described, as well as base algorithms that are implemented for powering team agents. A comparison is given between the reviewed approach and the one used in the RoboCup Simulation League, and directions for future convergence are drafted.

1 Introduction

Last decade has revealed an increasing interest within the computer science community to the research into autonomous intelligent agents and adjacent fields. These investigations cover a wide spectrum of fields, including Distributed Artificial Intelligence Systems, Artificial Life, Distributed Problem Solution and a number of others. One of the most appropriate test-benches for the relevant methods and algorithms is the computer simulation of the game of soccer. The RoboCup Simulation League has been holding the worldwide computer soccer tournaments for several years [1–7].

A closely related initiative was started in 2001 in Eastern European countries (mainly the former republics of the Soviet Union), when the first competition within the so called Robosoccer-RU League was organized. In this paper, we review basic principles and rules that underlie this contest, and describe in some details the game models, programming environment and algorithms used for autonomous software agents. A *qualitative* comparison with the RoboCup simulator is given, the design of the present implementation does not allow to carry out a direct match between correponding algorithms.

2 The Basic Principles of Robosoccer-RU Simulation

The main principle of the simulation model used by the Robosoccer-RU computer soccer League is the priority of the core algorithms forming the base for

G.A. Kaminka, P.U. Lima, and R. Rojas (Eds.): RoboCup 2002, LNAI 2752, pp. 271–278, 2003.

intelligent behavior of an agent. To put it differently, all the technical aspects related to agent-server interaction, obtaining of visual information by agent, and similar tasks, are simplified to the maximal extent. Therefore, the teams that take part in the competition are able to focus their efforts directly on developing the optimal strategy for players in the multi-agent environment.

Another significant difference is that in Robosoccer-RU League this is the strategy of *a team of robots* that is the object of research. This approach imposes serious restrictions upon several of the key parameters of the simulation system, and the Robosoccer-RU server cannot thus be considered as a simplified version of the model used in the RoboCup. Among other things, the number of players per team can vary and currently the typical values lie within the 3–5 range.

The following list enumerates the most important differences between the RoboCup [1] and Robosoccer-RU simulation models:

1. All the data from server is sent to client in structured binary form, which makes the parsing of textual messages unnecessary.
2. Full information about all movable objects (i.e. their positions and velocities) is known at any moment, up to an error communicated by the server. Thus, there is no need to analyze the visual information based on flags, lines and other markers. Consequently, players have no heads and the notion of a visible angle is not introduced.
3. There is no delay between receiving information and deciding on the next move. At every simulation step the agent possesses the current information (full or with a certain error), which it uses to decide on what changes to apply to its state.
4. The notion of stamina is not introduced.

The Robosoccer-RU competitions are carried out in real-time. There is, however, a possibility of running the server at an increased speed (limited only by the power of underlying hardware). Therefore, a very effective way exists to gather vast amounts of data for testing and optimizing the game algorithms.

3   The Physical Model and Rules of the Game

The game is played, alike RoboCup [1], in two dimensions. All the objects on the field are round and have predefined sizes and masses. A player is 2.5 times as big as the ball, and consequently six times heavier. Interactions between them are governed by a quite realistic physical model, which describes the collisions as quasi-inelastic with dissipation of energy. The degree of inelasticity is controlled by a configurable parameter. Currently, the value of this parameter corresponds to almost elastic collision; the reason for such choice is the fact that the players hit the ball with their bodies.

There are two controlling parameters that allow player to change its state: linear acceleration dV and angular velocity of player's rotation $d\alpha$ (corresponding to the Robocup's commands dash and turn). To receive information, agent used the set of functions provided by the SDK. For instance, the function GetX(short

ObjectNr) returns the value of x-coordinate of the object with the number ObjectNr, GetdY(short ObjectNr) returns the y-component of its velocity, and so on. Upon gathering all the necessary information, player sets new values for the controlling variables $(dV, d\alpha)$. There are, of course, certain limits imposed on the values of the acceleration and velocity, so that players' motion is inertial.

At present, there is no dedicated goalie in the team; every player can defend the goal, but it has no special means (like catch command) for this purpose.

The rules of the game are also simplified. In their today's form they correspond rather to the rules of mini-football (futsal). All the objects (players and ball) reflect from the edges of the field, that is corners, off-sides, outs and other standard situations are absent from the game.

4   The "Virtual Soccer" Software Package

The game simulation model is as follows [8]. The programming environment was developed for different platforms, including the MS Windows OS; all those programs implement identical mechanical models, while the algorithms controlling the players' behavior are realized as loadable modules and can be changed. All the implementations are compatible on the configuration file level, and use the same mechanism for loading team modules. The main goal of the simulation is optimization of the algorithm parameters and selection of the most effective one. Algorithms of the competing teams can belong to the same class, or to different ones.

The simulation program is composed of the three principal parts, the server and two loadable modules, modeling the behavior of the two teams. The server contains the core of the system and glues all the modules together. The implementation of loading varies from platform to platform, under Windows the DLL protocol is used. The game process is modeled using timer ticks; the simulator steps can correspond to the real (astronomic) time, or their length can be decreased and the game will be played at a high speed.

At every simulator step the server calls the team modules, Team1 and Team2 in that order. Every team module is called so many times per one step, as many players per team were defined (this number may vary, as noted above). The team module must return to the server the controlling parameters for every player in the team. While performing the calculation of the parameters, the module can access the API-functions of the server and receive the current state (position and velocity) of any object on the field. In this way the visual input of information into the system controlling the players is implemented. At the end of simulation step the server calculates next positions and velocities for all objects using the commands received from teams and internal mechanical model. Dynamics of the players' and ball's motion and their collisions are modeled. The current state of the game is determined (including goal and other situations), and if necessary, the server transfers the game into one of the predefined states, e.g. into state "before kick-off" after a goal is scored.

The present version of the server software implements a model of the game with complete information, when above the field a host-camera is placed that monitors all the events on the ground (or one such camera for each team, with identical information), and the players are controlled by two host-computers. However, if need be, it is possible for team modules to model an autonomous control system of a separate player.

A screen-shot of a match played within the "Virtual Soccer" simulation environment is shown in Fig. 1. This figure also illustrates some elements of the program interface.

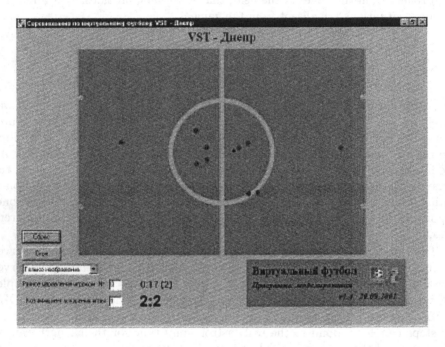

Fig. 1. A screen-shot of the soccer match played in "Virtual Soccer" simulation package.

As was mentioned above, several versions of the modeling server and tools for developing team modules are available for different computer platforms. Server can be run under operating systems MS DOS, MS Windows and Linux, and seven most widely used application development environments are supported for such languages as C/C++ and Pascal (for DOS and Windows) and GNU C/C++ compiler (for Linux).

5   An Example of Algorithm for Team Control

In the course of performed experiments a number of heuristic algorithms for controlling soccer-playing robots were investigated [9–11]. Here we outline, as an example, the algorithm developed by the team of the Keldysh Institute of Applied Mathematics of RAS (KIAM) for the Robosoccer-RU simulator, and used during the latest championship.

These algorithms, while differing by the values of characteristic parameters and the methods by which the control functions are calculated, all belong to the same class which can be defined as follows. Every player is assigned a rectangular area on the field (zone of responsibility), which can possibly be the whole field. The player must remain within the boundaries of this zone, with the only exception being that it can leave it as a result of inertial motion. In the latter case player should try to return to its zone as soon as possible.

At every simulation cycle player determines the current aim-point on the field, i.e. the spot it is moving to. We will call these spots special; the special points of a player are plotted in Fig. 2.

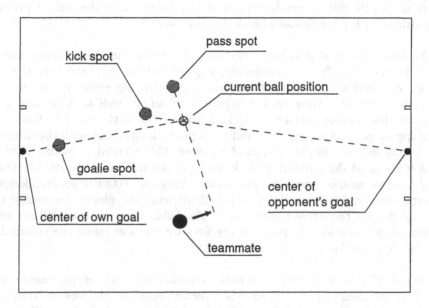

Fig. 2. The special spots (aim points) of a player are plotted, which are used for making decision on the next action.

There are several kinds of special points, namely the kick spot (from which it is possible to score a goal), the goalie spot (moving there player would defend the own goal) and the pass spot. Positions of all these points depend on the complete information about positions and velocities of all players and ball, and change quickly with time.

Let us now describe the geometric properties of the special points. The *kick spot* lies on the continuation of the ray extending from the center of the opponent's goal through the center of the ball. The distance from this point to the ball is one of the adjustment parameters of the algorithm. The *goalie spot* is the point on the line joining the center of the own goal with the ball. In different algorithms, either the distance player–goal, or the distance player–ball, are used as parameters. In the latter case, the responsibility zone for the goalie is chosen close to the goal to ensure that the goalkeeper does not follow the ball too far from the goal. Finally, the *pass spot* lies on the line joining the forecast position of the teammate (the point of interception where it would meet the ball after pass) with the ball's position.

Every algorithm is characterized by a set of parameters, which determine the priorities of different special points. The special points for all players are calculated by the team controlling module by means of position forecast functions for the objects on the field. Agent chooses the current aim among the calculated special points differently for different algorithms: by minimizing the time to reach the spot (algorithms with short forecast), by maximizing the strategic game effect (algorithms with full forecast), or by choosing the one with the highest priority (algorithms with priorities as adjustable parameters).

All the algorithms that were used can be broken into three main classes. The first one ("hard", or deterministic, algorithms) use only the special spots scheme outlined above. The second class (extended algorithms) adds models of arrangement of players on the opponent's half, as well as a tactical task (defense) that sets high priority to kicking the ball out of the own half-field. One more special point is introduced, similar to the kick spot, but with the distance player–ball shorter than the radius of a player. This allowed to realize effective dribbling, and at the same time block the kicks toward the own goal. The third class includes models where the players are assigned certain roles (goalkeeper, forward, defenseman, midfielder, etc), and allowing the players to change the role based upon the current situation on the field. These role algorithms were chosen as the base for carrying out the first tournament using the simulation package "Virtual Soccer".

To sum all this up, the parameters of the reviewed model are: the characteristics of robots, their responsibility zones, forecast depth and the ways used to pick it, geometrical parameters and priorities of special points, class of algorithm, and methods of assigning roles to players. These parameters were optimized by means of repeatedly running the game at increased speed. In the course of the research the "machine evolution" method was used among others, and best-playing teams were selected and optimal values of the parameters (and sets of parameters) were determined. In addition, the programs controlling goalie agents were "trained" separately, for in the real game there was not enough work for the goalkeepers to reliably test relevant algorithms.

As a separate stage of the investigation, a number of experiments were conducted where some of the agents were controlled by a human operator. The main aim was to obtain an extra measure of the model effectiveness. It was shown that fully automatic teams as a rule win the matches against human-aided sides.

6   Short History and Future Directions

At the conference Artificial Intelligence '2000 held in Katsyvely (Crimea, Ukraine) a group of researches representing the Keldysh Institute of Applied Mathematics of RAS and Moscow State University (Russia) put forward the idea to organize a competition similar to the RoboCup, but with simplified rules oriented to facilitate soccer robots simulation and control. Simulation software was developed, including the server and SDK for team modules programming, for operating systems MS Windows and Linux. In October, 2001 at the conference Artificial Intelligence '2001, the preliminary matches were played by the designed rules.

In December of 2001 within the framework of the annual scientific Workshop and Festival Mobile Robots'2001 held in Moscow University, the first official championship of the Robosoccer-RU League took place. Among the participants there were 10 teams from Russia and Ukraine.

These competitions showed that the main principles used for designing the rules of the Robosoccer-RU League were well-grounded. The simplification of the technical tasks, including agent–server communication, allowed the participants of the project to concentrate their efforts on the important problems of controlling the agent's behavior and game strategy.

At present, a possibility is considered of modifying the rules used in Robosoccer-RU to make them more compatible with the RoboCup [1], while keeping intact the basic principles of information retrieval by the autonomous agents.

The following changes are suggested:

1. Increasing inelasticity of collisions between objects. This can be achieved by modifying the relevant parameter, while keeping the implemented dynamical model unchanged.
2. Introducing new control parameters allowing agents to kick ball with given power and in a given direction. Agents will thus have four commands available to them, corresponding to the RoboCup's commands `dash`, `turn` and `kick`. The boundary conditions (objects reflecting off the field edge) will most probably be left in place.
3. Introducing uncertainty into the information communicated by server to agents. To this end, all returned parameters will be accompanied by a standard deviation σ, which gives the estimate of possible error in the corresponding value. Therefore, agents will only know with a certain degree of confidence that the value of a parameter lies within some interval. For different objects and at different time the value of σ can vary. It would grow for the objects that are out of the player's sight, i.e. situated behind or too far away from it. This would allow for a smooth transition from the model with complete information to the one with incomplete data, without adding the resource-consuming stage of visual information analysis.

7 Conclusion

The Robosoccer-RU League is an open competition that can be attended by researchers from countries all over the world. At the present stage of its development, the main goal is to provide the test field for improving strategic algorithms for control and interaction between autonomous agents. The outcome of this research can be applied to modeling complicated multi-agent environments, as well as used to enhance the core algorithms controlling the RoboCup Simulation League teams [1]. The results obtained so far during experiments and tournaments proved the effectiveness of the main modeling principles.

Further development of the simulation model is underway, which is intended to bring in more functional compatibility with the RoboCup Simulation League and with other RoboCup Leagues. Among other things, this will allow to directly compare algorithms developed within these two frameworks. The planned adjustments to the server program will allow to simulate the peculiarities of different RoboCup Leagues.

References

1. Mao Chen, Ehsan Foroughi, Fredrik Heintz, ZhanXiang Huang, Spiros Kapetanakis, Kostas Kostiadis, Johan Kummeneje, Itsuki Noda, Oliver Obst, Pat Riley, Timo Steffens, Yi Wang, and Xiang Yin: RoboCup SoccerServer User Manual (http://www.robocup.org/resource/ and links within).
2. Hiroaki Kitano, Yasuo Kuniyoshi, Itsuki Noda, Minoru Asada, Hitoshi Matsubara, and Ei-Ichi Osawa: Robocup: A challenge problem for AI. AI Magazine 18 (1997) 73–85
3. I.Noda, H.Matsubara, K.Hiraki, I.Frank: Soccer Server: a tool for research on multiagent systems. Appl. Artif. Intell. (AAI) Journal (USA) 12 (1998) 233–250
4. Tonaka-Ishii Kumiko, Frank Ian, Arai Katsuto: Trying to understand RoboCup. AI Magazine 21 (2000) 19–24.
5. Manuela Veloso, Peter Stone, Kwun Han, and Sorin Achim: CMUnited: A team of robotic soccer agents collaborating in an adversarial environment. Proc. of the First International Workshop on RoboCup, Nagoya, Japan, August, 1997.
6. Peter Stone and Manuela Veloso: A layered approach to learning client behaviours in the robocup soccer server. Appl. Artif. Intell. (AAI) Journal (USA) 12 (1998) 165–188.
7. Hugel Vincent, Bonnin Patrick, Blazevic Pierre: Using reactive and adaptive behaviours to play soccer. AI Magazine 21 (2000) 53–59.
8. D.E.Okhotsimsky, V.E.Pavlovsky, A.G.Plakhov, A.N.Touganov: Simulation of game of soccer robots and basic algorithms to control those robots. Artificial Intelligence (Ukrainian-Russian Journal) 3 (2000) 534–540 (in Russian)
9. D.E.Okhotsimsky, V.E.Pavlovsky, A.G.Plakhov, A.N.Touganov: Towards the CLAWAR robots soccer playing - simulation of robotic soccer. Proc. of 4-th Int. Conf. on Climbing and Walking Robots CLAWAR'2001. Karlsruhe, Germany, 24-26 September 2001, pp.451–456.
10. D.E.Okhotsimsky, V.E.Pavlovsky, A.G.Plakhov, A.N.Touganov, V.V.Pavlovsky: Simulation of game of soccer robots in the environment of 'Virtual Soccer' software package. Mechatronics, 2002. (in Russian, to be printed).
11. S.S. Stepanov, N.I. Stepanova: Turing—fifty years later. Artificial Intelligence (Ukrainian-Russian Journal) 3 (2000) 100–110 (in Russian).

An Interactive Software Environment for Gait Generation and Control Design of Sony Legged Robots

Dragos Golubovic and Huosheng Hu

Department of Computer Science
University of Essex, Colchester C04 3SQ, UK
{dgolub,hhu}@essex.ac.uk

Abstract. This paper presents a modular approach to the development of an interactive software environment for gait generation and control design of Sony legged robots. A number of modules have been developed for monitoring robot states, gait generation, control design and image processing. A dynamic model of the leg and wheel-like motion are proposed to combine both wheeled and legged properties to produce smooth quadruped motion and high flexibility. Experimental results are presented to show the feasibility of the system

1 Introduction

Increased complexity and sophistication of advanced walking robots has led to continuing progress in building software environments to aid in the development of robust functionality. This is true not only because the physical construction of these robots is time consuming and expensive, but also because the evaluation and control of their gaits often requires prolonged training and frequent reconfiguration. To speed up the development cycle and decrease the design cost and time required for gaits generation, many software environments have been developed [2], [3]. The benefit of developing a suitable software environment includes the ability to record precise and voluminous data. Indeed, a flexible software environment plays an important role in many aspects of robotics research.

The main focus of this paper is the development of an interactive software environment for the design of a real-time control algorithm of AIBO football playing robots [4]. To make design and development of gaits easier, an interactive software environment has been developed at Essex. The software environment consists of three modules (state reflector, gait generation and vision) and gives a variety of useful features for the gait generation and development. By using a mouse or keyboard commands, an operator is able to record a sequence of movements that can be replayed in a sequence. It is also a very useful tool for debugging and evaluating quadruped gaits [5].

The rest of this paper is organized as follows. Section 2 describes the construction of an interactive software environment for the control design and gait generation of Sony AIBO robots. In section 3, the control design of Sony Legged

G.A. Kaminka, P.U. Lima, and R. Rojas (Eds.): RoboCup 2002, LNAI 2752, pp. 279–287, 2003.

robots is presented, which includes the control system structure, a dynamic model of the leg and wheel-like motion. The experiment results are given in Section 4 to show the feasibility of the system. Finally, a brief conclusion and future work are presented in Section 5.

2   Building a Software Environment

The software architecture is a crucial aspect of Sony walking robots. The control software is ultimately responsible for managing the safe operation of the robot. In other words, the control software for a Sony walking robot must be carefully planned and constructed so that the derived gaits, however complex, conform to safety and efficiency specifications.

2.1   Modular Implementation

Since Sony AIBO robots have a large number of input and output parameters, their control design is complex. Therefore a modular approach is adopted here [1]. As shown in Figure 1, high-level control is conducted in a desktop PC (Pentium II 266) that is connected to the robot through a serial port (19200 baud). There are three main modules in it: a state reflector, a gait generator and an image interpreter. On the robot side a debug box has been mounted on the robot's back and connected to the PC via a cable. The next section describes these modules in more detail. Changes in any of these modules don't affect other modules, enabling users to split application development on several parts that can be carried out independently.

2.2   Module Description

Modular architecture gives provision for reconfiguration and extension, allowing the system to evolve with time, this is described in this section.

☐ **State reflector** – An internal state reflector has been incorporated to mirror the robot's state on the host computer, which is an abstract view of the actual robot's internal state, such as sensor information from the robot and control commands from the host computer. The state reflector is a set of data structures which allow the client to examine sensor information and control the robot by setting its values. In Table 1, CSensor holds basic sensor information sent from the robot and CPastReadings holds information about current and past sonar returns. The control commands for robot motions are listed in Table 2.

☐ **Communication routines** – The designed controller communicates with the robot using a handshake mechanism, and sends an appropriate command to the robot. The program executed on the robot waits for the command (Table 2) and executes it when the command has been received. After execution, the robot returns the result along with confirmation that data has been sent.

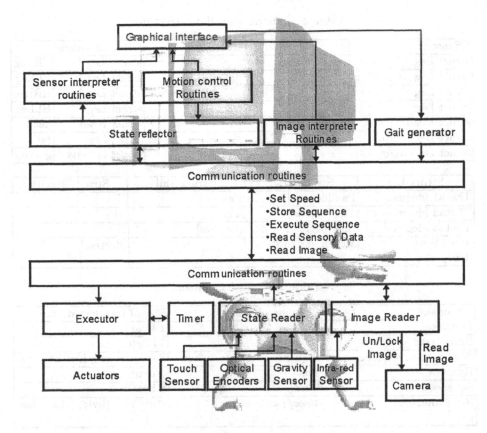

Fig. 1. Configuration of the proposed software environment

The amount of data transferred from the user's application to the robot and the other way around varies from one command to the other. A 19200-baud channel has been used.

☐ **Gait generator** – The gait generator communicates with the robot by passing a sequence of arrays that are transformed into a sequence of robot movements. It creates different gaits in a form of a sequence of arrays. In this software environment, users can move all robots' joints at the same time and record its movements in an array sequence, which can then be repeated and tested. Therefore users can create gaits and test various motions necessary for robot's mobility.

☐ **Image reader** – Gathering image snapshots and processing images can be done completely independently from the rest of the application. The size of a captured image is 144 × 76 pixels and each pixel has three bytes for colour information. Since transferring whole image through a 19200baud connection takes 45 second, an adjustable scale factor is added to reduce transfer time if necessary. A locking mechanism has been adopted to allow the transfer of the current image to be safely completed before the new snapshot image can be grabbed.

Table 1. State reflector data structure

CSensor			CPastReadings	
struct Leg	FRLeg		struct Leg *	FRLeg
struct Leg	FLLeg		struct Leg *	FLLeg
struct Leg	BRLeg		struct Leg *	BRLeg
struct Leg	BLLeg		struct Leg *	BLLeg
struct Head	head		struct Head*	head
struct Leg	tail		struct Leg*	tail
struct Gravity	gravity		struct Gravity *	gravity

Struct Leg	Struct Head	Struct Tail	Struct Gravity
Theta1 [degrees]	Pan [degrees]	Pan	X
Theta2 [degrees]	Tilt [degrees]	Tilt	Y
Theta3 [degrees]	Roll [degrees]	[degrees]	Z
TouchSen [true/false]	Mouth [degrees]		[degrees]

Table 2. Control commands

Command	Communication time	Size of transferred data
Motor on	10ms	1 byte
Read Data	100ms	74 byte
Send motion sequence	Sequence length × 100ms	Sequence length × 74 byte
Execute	10ms	1 byte
Set speed	50ms	8 byte
Read image	45sec/{scale factor}	76× 144 (byte/{scale factor}

3   Control Design

The key concept in this paper is based on movements of a four-wheeled car. Each leg tip is moving in a rectangle trajectory. Front and rear legs from the opposite sides are in the same phase and the other two legs are opposite. Projection of the mass of the robot to the ground is on the line that connects to legs, which are in touch with the ground. The centre of paw rotation is initially at the same inverse kinematic coordinate for both front legs and both rear legs. This prevents the robot from falling to the side and stabilizes the camera. Gravity sensors have been used to obtain information on body position.

3.1   Control System Structure

The control system structure consists of both kinematics and dynamics levels (Figure 2). The kinematics level involves two sub-levels: a pattern generator and a leg trajectory generator. Each leg has its own trajectory generator that determines the course of the leg endpoint. When a timing signal has been received, the leg must begin its swing/stance cycles. In order to emulate the accurate foot placement the trajectory generator plans a trajectory in foot position coordinates and then converts them to joint positions using inverse kinematics.

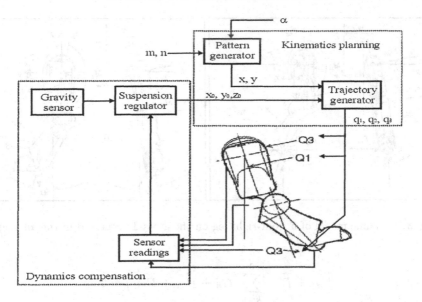

Fig. 2. Gait generation mechanism

The pattern generator provides repetitive motion of a leg and synchronization of movements with the other three legs. Gait planning depends on the velocity and heading of the robot. The time and space coordination of the motion involves a decision regarding which leg should be lifted or placed. It must be made in terms of the condition of terrain, stability requirements, speed requirements, mobility requirements and power consumption.

3.2 Dynamic Model of the Leg

Figure 3 shows the single robot's joint with its three motorized rotational axes. Forces applied to the leg differ whether the leg is on the ground or not. The set of 3 generalized coordinates $q[q1, q2, q3]$ is used to determine the mechanism position.

Each coordinate corresponds to one degree of freedom (DOF). There are two rotational segments upper limb (S1) and lower limb (S2). Angle θi is the relative rotation of the $i-th$ segment with respect to the $(i-1)-th$ segment around the axis. The dynamics equations are derived on the basis of D'Ambler's principle [6]. For the $k-th$ segment, we assume that $\vec{G_k}$ is its gravity force vector; $\vec{F_{kE}}$ is the resultant of other external forces acting on it; $\vec{M_{kE}}$ is the resultant of other external moments acting on it; $\vec{F_{k1}}$ is the resultant of the internal forces on it; $\vec{M_{k1}}$ is the resultant of the internal moments on it; $\vec{P_i}$ is the vector of the drive in the joint $Si-1$; $\vec{r}_{ij}=\vec{S_iC_j}$. In contrast, Cj is the centre of gravity of the j-th segment; if D'Ambler's principal of inertial forces is applied, we have

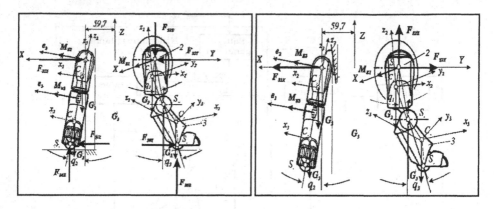

Fig. 3. Dynamic model of a front-right leg on the ground (left) and in the air (right)

$$\vec{F}_{Sj} + \vec{P}_i + \sum_{k=1}^{3} \left(\vec{G}_k + \vec{F}_{k1} + \vec{F}_{kE}\right) = 0 \qquad (1)$$

If D'Ambler's principal is applied to the inertial moment relative to the $Si - 1$, then

$$\vec{M}_{Sj} + \vec{P}_i + \sum_{k=1}^{3} \left[\vec{M}_{k1} + \vec{r}_{i-1,k} \times \left(\vec{G}_k + \vec{F}_{k1} + \vec{F}_{kE}\right) + \vec{M}_{kE}\right] = 0 \qquad (2)$$

The system equations (1) and (2) can be transformed into the matrix form (3)

$$W(q)\ddot{q} = P + U(q, \dot{q}) \qquad (3)$$

P presents the column vector of driving forces and torques in the mechanism joints. The matrix W depends on the generalized coordinates q, and U depends on q and generalized velocity. The algorithm for computing W and U is derived from general theorems of dynamics and these matrices also depend on the configuration.

3.3   Generation of Wheel-Like Motion

A trajectory refers to both the path of the tip's movement of a limb (paw), and the velocity along the path. Thus, a trajectory has both spatial and temporal aspects. The spatial aspect is the sequence of the locations of the endpoint from the start of the movement to the goal, and the temporal aspect is the time dependence along the path.

Six posture parameters used for designing the gait, m, n, Xo, Yo, Zo and α, are common parameters for each leg; but they can differ between front and rear legs. If posture parameters for the front and rear legs are not identical, the top plane of the body will make δ angle with the ground. X, Y and Z coordinates of the paw are determined by the angular targets of a leg.

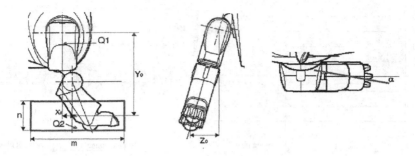

Fig. 4. Pawn trajectory

$$\Theta_2 = \arcsin\left(Z/\sqrt{x^2 + y^2 + Z^2}\right) \tag{4}$$

$$\Theta_3 = 2\arccos\left(\sqrt{x^2 + y^2 + Z^2}/2l\cos\Theta_2\right) \tag{5}$$

$$\Theta_1 = arctg(y/x) - \arccos\left(\sqrt{x^2 + y^2 + Z^2}/2l\cos\Theta_2\right) \tag{6}$$

The body velocity depends upon the width of the elliptical paw trajectory (m), the duty factor χ and the cycle period.

$$V = m/x^T \tag{7}$$

An ideal duty factor can reach the value of 0.5 (when only two legs are on the ground at the same time). The maximum value of duty factor is 1. Equation 5 shows that the increase of the body velocity can be achieved by either increasing m or decreasing T. However, the excessive increase of m factor can lead to the increase of χ, because the duty factor depends on many parameters, which lead to poor performance.

A new suspension mechanism is adopted to adjust the height of a foot to terrain with vertical elevation. Suspension mechanism can prevent a leg's up and down motion during walking. That is, when a leg is up for swing forward, a suspension mechanism should stretch to its limit, and make the vertical stroke of a leg shorter.

4   Experimental Results

To evaluate gaits with different parameters (m, n, $X0$, $Y0$, $Z0$, α) and usefulness of the developed software environment, we tested a Sony AIBO robot on both a rough and a flat terrain. During its walk the robot has been connected to the PC running applications through a debug box via a PC's serial port. After several test runs, the following values of gait parameters achieved the best stability and the fastest speed: $M = 4$; $n = 3$; $\alpha = 15$; $X_0 = 0$; $Y_0 = 110$, $Z_0 = 20$. Each walking gait is tested separately to check the validity of parameters used.

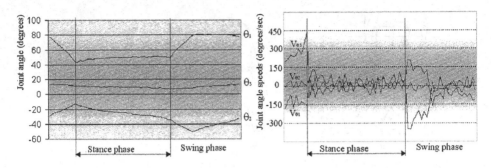

Fig. 5. Joint angles (left) and speeds (right) during a sequence of step cycles

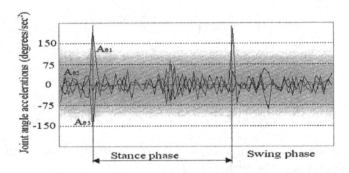

Fig. 6. Joint accelerations during a sequence of step cycles

The walking motion was obtained on flat ground and the readings from the optical encoders of the robot's joints at each step cycle. As can been seen in figures 5 and 6, targeted and achieved angles differ by an average value of 2.743 degrees. Difference is greater during a stance phase, which is understandable because during this phase the joints have to cope with the body weight of the robot and the reaction force from the ground. The average difference during stance phase is 3.56 degrees.

The effect of the suspension control was checked under dynamic walking. The robot runs over irregular terrain and the shoulder's height was sampled from gravity sensors, as shown in Fig. 7. Without the suspension mechanism the angle of the robot's top plane toward the ground becomes larger in accordance with terrain irregularity and duty factor while the suspension-controlled case is still small.

5   Conclusion and Future Work

A modular approach is adopted for the development of a useful software tool for gait generation and control design of Sony AIBO quadruped robots, which makes future improvement easy. A model of quadruped robot's gait is presented. Implementing wheel-like motions for legs reduces the mechanical complexity

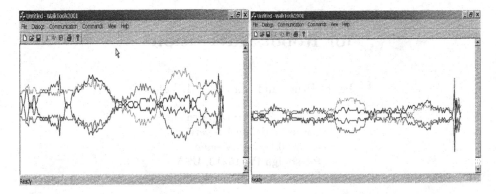

Fig. 7. Variations in shoulder's height without (left) and with (right) suspension respectively

intrinsic legged systems whist maintaining attractive performance. The designed gaits showed good results in speed, maneuverability and stability. Special care was given to maintaining stability. This allows the successful implementation of behaviours that rely on camera readings and is therefore important.

Current efforts are focused on the replacement of the analytical part of the suspension mechanism with neural networks. This allows shoulder height for each leg to be modified via trained neural networks in order to make AIBO robots more adaptive to ground roughness and improve the robot's stability.

Acknowledgements

Thanks to Prof. Pierre Blazevic and his L.R.P research team for providing the code of the earlier version of their software environment application.

References

1. P. Israel Doerchuk, W. Simon, V. Nguyen, "A Modular Approach to Intelligent Control of Simulated Joint Leg", IEEE Robotics & Automation Magazine, June 1998, pp. 12-20.
2. J. Reichler, F. Delcomyn, "Dynamics Simulation and Controller Interfacing for Legged Robots?", Int. J. of Robotics Research, Vol. 19, No. 1, 2000, page 42-58.
3. M. Maza, J. Fontaine, M. Armada, P. Gonzalez, "Wheel+Legs- A New Solution For Traction Enhancement Without Additive Soil Compaction", IEEE Robotics and Automation Magazine, June 1998, pages 26-32.
4. M. Fujita and K. Kageyama, "Development of an Autonomous Quadruped Robot for Robot Entertainment", Journal of Autonomous Robots, Vol. 5, pages 1-14, 1999.
5. R. Reeve and J. Hallam, "Control of Walking by Central Pattern Generators", Journal of Intelligent Autonomous Systems, 1995, pages 695-701.
6. M. Vukobratovic and V. Potkonjak, "Dynamics of Manipulation Robots. Theory and Applicaton", Communication and Control Engineering Series, Springer-Verlag, 1982.

Real-Time Randomized Path Planning
for Robot Navigation*

James Bruce and Manuela M. Veloso

Computer Science Department
Carnegie Mellon University
5000 Forbes Avenue
Pittsburgh PA 15213, USA
{jbruce,mmv}@cs.cmu.edu

Abstract. Mobile robots often find themselves in a situation where they must find a trajectory to another position in their environment, subject to constraints posed by obstacles and the robot's capabilities. This poses the problem of planning a path through a continuous domain. Several approaches have been used to address this problem each with some limitations, including state discretizations, planning efficiency, and lack of interleaved execution. Rapidly-exploring random trees (RRTs) are a recently developed algorithm on which fast continuous domain path planners can be based. In this work, we build a path planning system based on RRTs that interleaves planning and execution, first evaluating it in simulation and then applying it to physical robots. Our algorithm, ERRT (execution extended RRT), introduces two novel extensions of previous RRT work, the waypoint cache and adaptive cost search, which improve replanning efficiency and the quality of generated paths. ERRT is successfully applied to a multi-robot system. Results demonstrate that ERRT is improves efficiency and performs competitively with existing heuristic and reactive real-time path planning approaches. ERRT has shown to offer a major step with great potential for path planning in challenging continuous, highly dynamic domains.

Introduction

The path-planning problem is as old as mobile robots, but is not one that has found a universal solution. Specifically, in complicated, fast evolving environments such as RoboCup [3], currently popular approaches have their strengths, but still leave much to be desired. A recently developed tool that may help tackle the problem of real-time path planning are Rapidly-exploring random trees (RRTs) [7]. RRTs employ randomization to explore large state spaces

---

* This research was sponsored by Grants Nos. DABT63-99-1-0013, F30602-98-2-0135 and F30602-97-2-0250. The information in this publication does not necessarily reflect the position of the funding agencies and no official endorsement should be inferred.

G.A. Kaminka, P.U. Lima, and R. Rojas (Eds.): RoboCup 2002, LNAI 2752, pp. 288–295, 2003.

efficiently without tiling, and can form the basis for a probabilistically complete though non-optimal kinodynamic path planner [8]. They can efficiently find plans in high dimensional spaces because they avoid the state explosion that discretization faces. Furthermore, due to their incremental nature, they can maintain complicated kinematic constraints if necessary.

Most current robot systems that have been developed to date are controlled by heuristic or potential field methods at the lowest level, and many extend this upward to the level of path navigation [5]. Since the time to respond must be bounded, *reactive* methods are used to build constant or bounded time heuristics for making progress toward the goal. One reactive method that has proved quite popular is motor schemas [1]. Although they meet the need for action under time constraints, most of these methods suffer from the lack of lookahead, which can lead to highly non-optimal paths and problems with oscillation. RRTs, as used in our work and presented in this paper, should provide a good compliment for very simple control heuristics, and take much of the complexity out of composing them to form a navigation system. Specifically, local minima can be reduced substantially through lookahead.

While not as popular as heuristic methods, non-reactive planning methods for interleaved planning and execution have been developed, with promising results. Among these are agent-centered A* search methods [4] and the D* variant of A* search [9]. However, using these planners requires discretization or tiling of the world in order to operate in continuous domains. This leads to a tradeoff between a higher resolution, with is higher memory and time requirements, and a low resolution with non-optimality due to discretization. Most of the features of agent-centered search methods do not rely on A* as a basis, however, so we can achieve many of their benefits using an RRT based planner which fits more naturally into domains with continuous state spaces. In addition, the base RRT system is relatively easy to extend to environments with moving obstacles, higher dimensional state spaces, and kinematic constraints. No other planners we are currently aware of offer these possible enhancements at the simplicity and speed of an RRT-based solution. As a step in that direction, this work appears to be the first successful application of an RRT planner to a real mobile robot [6].

In order to make online planning efficient enough to be practical, we introduce two novel additions to the planner, specifically the waypoint cache for replanning and adaptive cost penalty search. The second section of this paper defines the basic RRT algorithm. The next section introduces our ERRT contribution, followed by implementation results. The final sections offers concluding remarks.

RRT Planning

Basic RRT Algorithm

In essence, an RRT planner searches for a path from an initial state to a goal state by iteratively expanding a search tree. For its search, it requires the following three domain-specific function primitives:

Function *Extend* (env:environment,current:state,
                target:state):state
Function *Distance* (current:state,target:state):real
Function *RandomState* ():state

The *Extend* function calculates a new state that can be reached from the target state by some incremental distance (usually a constant distance or time), which in general makes progress toward the goal. If a collision with an obstacle in the environment would occur by moving to that new state, EmptyState is returned. In general, any heuristic methods suitable for control of the robot can be used here, provided there is a reasonably accurate model of the results of performing its actions. The heuristic does not need to be very complicated, and does not even need to avoid obstacles (just detect when a state would hit them). However, the better the heuristic, the fewer nodes the planner will need to expand on average, since it will not need to rely as much on random exploration.

Table 1 shows the complete basic RRT planner with its stochastic decision between the search options:

- with probability p, it expands towards the goal minimizing the objective function *Distance*,
- with probability $1 - p$, it does random exploration by generating a *Random-State*.

The function *Distance* needs to provide an estimate of the time or distance (or any other objective that the algorithm is trying to minimize) that estimates how long repeated application of *Extend* would take to reach the goal. For a simple example, a holonomic point robot with no acceleration constraints can implement *Extend* simply as a step along the line from the current state to the target, and *Distance* as the Euclidean distance between the two states. Next, the function *Nearest* uses the distance function implemented for the domain to find the nearest point in the tree to some target point outside of it. The function *RandomState* simply returns a state drawn uniformly from the state space of the environment.

Finally, *ChooseTarget* chooses the goal part of the time as a directed search, and otherwise chooses a target taken uniformly from the domain as an exploration step. The main planning procedure uses these functions to iteratively pick a stochastic target and grow the nearest part of the tree towards that target. The algorithm terminates when a threshold distance to the goal has been reached, though it is also common to limit the total number of nodes that can be expanded to bound execution time.

Extended RRT Algorithm – ERRT

Some optimizations over the basic described in existing work are bidirectional search to speed planning, and encoding the tree's points in an efficient spatial data structure [2]. In this work, a KD-tree was used to speed nearest neighbor

Table 1. The basic RRT planner stochastically expands its search tree to the goal or to a random state.

```
function RRTPlan (env:environment,initial:state,
                              goal:state):rrt-tree
    var nearest,extended,target:state;
    var tree:rrt-tree;
    nearest := initial;
    rrt-tree := initial;
    while(Distance (nearest,goal) < threshold)
        target = ChooseTarget (goal);
        nearest = Nearest (tree,target);
        extended = Extend (env,nearest,target);
        if extended ≠ EmptyState then
            AddNode (tree,extended);
    return tree;

function ChooseTarget (goal:state):state
    var p:real;
    p = UniformRandom in [0.0 .. 1.0];
    if 0 < p < GoalProb then
        return goal;
    else if GoalProb < p < 1 then
        return RandomState();

function Nearest (tree:rrt-tree,target:state):state
    var nearest:state;
    nearest := EmptyState;
    foreach state s in current-tree
        if Distance (s,target) <
        Distance (nearest,target) then
            nearest := s;
    return nearest;
```

lookup, but bidirectional search was not used because it decreases the generality of the goal state specification (it must then be a specific state, and not a region of states). Additional possible optimizations include a more general biased distribution, which was explored in this work in the form of a waypoint cache. If a plan was found in a previous iteration, it is likely to yield insights into how a plan might be found at a later time when planning again; The world has changed but usually not by much, so the history from previous plans can be a guide. The waypoint cache was implemented by keeping a constant size array of states, and whenever a plan was found, all the states in the plan were placed into the cache with random replacement. This stores the knowledge of where a plan might again be found in the near future. To take advantage of this for planning, Table 2 shows the modifications to the function *ChooseTarget*.

Now, there are three probabilities in the distribution of target states. With probability $P[goal]$, the goal is chosen as the target; With probability

Table 2. The extended RRT planner stochastically expands its search tree to the goal; to a random state; or to a waypoint cache.

```
function ChooseTarget'(goal:state):state
    var p:real;
    var i:integer;
    p = UniformRandom in [0.0 .. 1.0];
    i = UniformRandom in [0 .. NumWayPoints-1];
    if 0 < p < GoalProb then
        return goal;
    else if GoalProb < p < GoalProb+WayPointProb
    then
        return WayPointCache[i];
    else if GoalProb+WayPointProb < p < 1 then
        return RandomState();
```

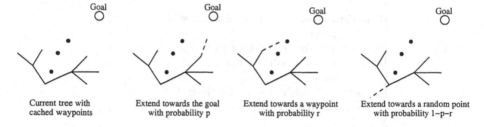

| Current tree with cached waypoints | Extend towards the goal with probability p | Extend towards a waypoint with probability r | Extend towards a random point with probability 1-p-r |

Fig. 1. Extended RRT with a waypoint cache for efficient replanning.

$P[waypoint]$, a random waypoint is chosen, and with the remaining probability a uniform state is chosen as before. The way the extended algorithm progresses is illustrated in Figure 1. Typical values used in this work were $P[goal] = 0.1$ and $P[waypoint] = 0.6$. Finally, A simple RRT planner is building a greedy approximate spanning tree, and thus ignores the path lengths from the initial state (the root node in the tree). The distance metric can be modified to include not only the distance from the tree to a target state, but also the cost to reach that state. A higher value of the multiplier on that history cost (beta) results in shorter paths from the root to the leaves, but also decreases the amount of exploration of the state space, biasing it to near the initial state in a "bushy" tree. A value of 1 for beta will always extend from the root node for any Euclidean metric in a continuous domain, while a value of 0 is equivalent to the original algorithm. The best value seems to vary with domain and even problem instance, and appears to be a steep tradeoff between finding an shorter plan and not finding one at all. To address this we implemented an adaptive mechanism that appears to work quite well. When the planner starts, beta is set to 0. Then on successive replans, if the previous run found a plan, beta is incremented, and decremented otherwise. In addition the value is clipped to between 0 and 0.65. This adaptive bias schedule reflects the idea that a bad plan is better than no plan initially, and once a plan is in the cache and search is biased toward the

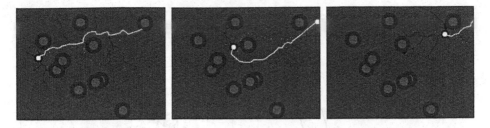

Fig. 2. An example from the simulation-based RRT planner, shown at three times during a run. The initial state (agent) is in blue, while the fixed target state is shown in red. The best plan (the one that gets closest to the goal) is shown in white.

waypoints, nudges the system to try to shorten the plan helping to improve it over successive runs.

Domain Implementations and Results

RoboCup F180 Robot Control

We tested our RRT system in simulation and then applied it so the control of real robots. In both, planning and execution are interleaved equally; A plan is created for each step taken. Three snapshots from our simulator can be seen in Figure 2. In this simple domain, the waypoints seemed to help qualitatively in that the robot didn't tend to get stuck as long in local minima. This effect of waypoints on performance was evaluated numerically, and the results are shown in in Figure 3. Since the curves diverge at moderate difficulty, it appears that waypoints help speed planning by offering "hints" from previous solutions. When the problem becomes impossible or nearly impossible, neither performs well.

For physical robot control, the system must take input from a global vision system at 30Hz, reporting the position of all field objects detected from a fixed overhead camera, and send the output to a radio server which sends velocity commands to the robots that are being controlled. The path planning problem is to navigate quickly among other robots, while they also more around executing their own behaviors. As a simplification, we examined the more simple problem of running from one end of the field to the other, with static robots acting as obstacles in the field. The extension metric we used was hen became a model of a simple heuristic "goto-point" that had already been implemented for the robot. The motivation for this heuristic approach was that executing a bad plan immediately is often better than sitting still looking for a better one that models the robot more correctly. To increase system performance, after a path had been determined, it is post processed, replacing the head of the plan with the longest obstacle-free straight path. Not only does this smooth out the resulting plan, but the robot tends to go straight at the first "restricted" point, always trying to aim at the free space. This allowed the robot to navigate at

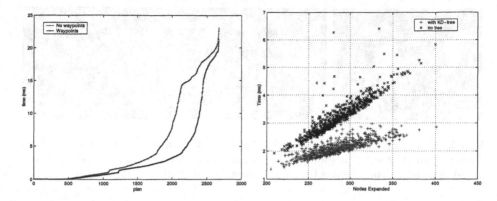

Fig. 3. The left side shows the effect of waypoints. The lines shows the sorted planning times for 2670 plans with and without waypoints, sorted by time to show the cumulative performance distribution. The curve with waypoints is significantly lower for intermediate planning times. The right side shows the plot of planning times vs. the nodes expanded. KD-trees hold a reasonable advantage even at small numbers of nodes.

up to $1.7m/s$, performing better than any previous system we have used on our robots. Videos of the current system are available at the following address: *ftp://sponge.coral.cs.cmu.edu/pub/movies/F180-RRT*

The best combination of parameters that we were able to find, trading off physical performance and success with execution time was the following: 500 nodes, 200 waypoints, $P[goal] = 0.1$, $P[waypoint] = 0.7$, and a step size of 1/15sec. To examine the efficiency gain from using a KD-tree, we ran the system with and without a KD-tree. The results are shown in Figure 3. Not only does the tree have better scalability to higher numbers of nodes due to its algorithmic advantage, but it provides an absolute performance advantage even with as few as 100 nodes. The planner was able to perform on average in 2.1ms, with the time rarely going above 3ms. This makes the system fast enough to use in our production RoboCup team, as it will allow 5 robots to be controlled from a reasonably powerful machine while leaving some time left over for higher level action selection and strategy.

Conclusion

In this work a robot control system was developed that used an RRT path planner to turn a simple reactive scheme into a high performance path planning system. The novel mechanisms of the waypoint cache and adaptive cost search were introduced, with the waypoint cache providing much improved performance on difficult but possible path planning problems. The real robot was able to perform better than previous fully reactive schemes, traveling 40% faster while avoiding obstacles, and drastically reducing oscillation and local minima problems that the reactive scheme had. This is also the first application of which we are aware using an RRT-based path planner on a real mobile robot.

Several important lessons can be drawn from this work in the context of real-time path planning in highly dynamic domains:

- A heuristic may perform better than a correct model when planning time is critical. In other words, a better model may not improve the entire system even if it makes the generated plans better.
- A plan generated from an incorrect model requires post-processing for optimal performance. The system worked without post processing, but not nearly as well as when the local metric could apply its accurate model over a longer range of the plan and thus remove most of its inaccuracies over that period of the plan.
- Pre-existing reactive control methods can easily be adapted to be RRT extension and distance metrics. It can build on these to help eliminate oscillation and local minima through its lookahead mechanism. Since many existing robots already have reactive navigation systems, and the RRT core code is highly generic, We expect this to be a common adaptation in the future.

This work could not have been conducted without the many people in our group who support our RoboCup F180 small robot team. We would specifically like to thank Brett Browning and Mike Bowling, without whom we wouldn't have a team or robots with which interesting research projects could be done.

References

1. R. C. Arkin. Motor schema-based mobile robot navigation. *International Journal of Robotics Research, August 1989*, 8(4):92–112, 1989.
2. A. Atramentov and S. M. LaValle. Efficient nearest neighbor searching for motion planning. In *submitted to 2002 IEEE International Conference on Robotics and Automation*, 2002.
3. H. Kitano, M. Asada, Y. Kuniyoshi, I. Noda, and E. Osawa. Robocup: The robot world cup initiative. In *Proceedings of the IJCAI-95 Workshop on Entertainment and AI/ALife*, 1995.
4. S. Koenig. Agent-centered search. *Artificial Intelligence*, 2002, in print.
5. J.-C. Latombe. *Robot Motion Planning*. Kluwer, 1991.
6. S. M. LaValle. Rapidly-exploring random trees (http://msl.cs.uiuc.edu/rrt/).
7. S. M. LaValle. Rapidly-exploring random trees: A new tool for path planning. In *Technical Report No. 98-11*, October 1998.
8. S. M. LaValle and J. James J. Kuffner. Randomized kinodynamic planning. In *International Journal of Robotics Research, Vol. 20, No. 5*, pages 378–400, May 2001.
9. A. Stentz. Optimal and efficient path planning for unknown and dynamic environments. In *International Journal of Robotics and Automation, Vol. 10, No. 3*, 1995.

Towards an Optimal Scoring Policy
for Simulated Soccer Agents

Jelle Kok, Remco de Boer, Nikos Vlassis, and Frans C.A. Groen

Intelligent Autonomous Systems Group, Informatics Institute
Faculty of Science, University of Amsterdam
Kruislaan 403, 1098 SJ Amsterdam, The Netherlands
{jellekok,remdboer,vlassis,groen}@science.uva.nl

Abstract. This paper describes the scoring policy which is used by the agents of the *UvA Trilearn* simulation team. In a given situation this policy enables an agent to determine the best shooting point in the goal, together with an associated probability of scoring when the ball is shot to this point. Our policy is based on an approximate method for learning the relevant statistics of the ball motion which can be regarded as a geometrically constrained continuous-time Markov process.

1 Introduction

The RoboCup Simulation League is based on a soccer simulation system called the *RoboCup Soccer Server* [2]. The *soccer server* provides a realistic multi-agent environment. Various forms of uncertainty have been added into the simulation such as sensor and actuator noise, limited perception and noise in object movement. Since the main purpose of a soccer game is to score goals, it is important for a robotic soccer agent to have a clear policy about whether he should attempt to score in a given situation, and if so, which point in the goal he should aim for. This paper describes the scoring policy that is used by the agents of the *UvA Trilearn* soccer simulation team. In a given situation this policy enables an agent to find the best shooting point in the goal, together with an associated probability of scoring. Using this scoring policy we reached 4th place at *RoboCup-2001* and won the *German Open 2002* with a total score of 110-1 over 10 matches.

2 The Optimal Scoring Problem

The *optimal scoring problem* can be stated as follows: find the point in the goal where the probability of scoring is the highest when the ball is shot to this point in a given situation. A key observation for solving *the optimal scoring problem* is that it can be decomposed into two independent subproblems:

1. Determining the probability that the ball will enter the goal when shot to a specific point in the goal from a given position.
2. Determining the probability of passing the goalkeeper in a given situation.

Since the subproblems are independent, the probability of scoring when shooting at a certain point in the goal is equal to the *product* of the two probabilities.

G.A. Kaminka, P.U. Lima, and R. Rojas (Eds.): RoboCup 2002, LNAI 2752, pp. 296–303, 2003.

2.1   Probability That the Ball Enters the Goal

In this section we will show how one can determine the probability that the ball will end up *somewhere* inside the goal when shot at a *specific* goal point. To this end we first need to compute the deviation of the ball from the aiming point. This deviation is caused by the noise which is added to the ball velocity vector in each simulation cycle[1]. Note that the ball motion can be regarded as a *diffusion* process since the position of the ball in each time step diffuses over time. We can treat it as a Markov process because the future development is completely determined by the present state. Finding an analytical solution of the corresponding diffusion process is difficult for two reasons:

- The motion noise which is added by the server is by construction non-white since it depends on the speed of the ball in the previous cycle.
- The process is geometrically constrained since the ball must enter the goal.

This makes an analytical computation of the process statistics non trivial. Therefore, we propose to *learn* the ball motion statistics from experiments. This gives an approximate solution to the problem of computing the statistical properties of a geometrically constrained continuous-time Markov process and we believe that this relatively simple alternative, can be useful in other applications as well[2].

Our solution thus amounts to estimating the *cumulative* noise directly from experiments. To this end, we calculated the deviation of the ball perpendicular to the shooting direction as a function of the distance that the ball had traveled. This function was learned by repeating an experiment in which the ball was placed at even distances between 0 and 32 metres in front of the center of the goal (zero y-coordinate) with a player directly behind it. The player then shot the ball 1,000 times from each distance with maximum power towards the center of the goal. For each instance we recorded the y-coordinate where the ball entered the goal and used these values to compute the sample standard deviation σ of the ball. To a good approximation this function could be represented by

$$\sigma(d) = -1.88 \cdot \ln(1 - d/45) \tag{1}$$

The next step is to compute the distribution of the ball when it reaches the goal line. For this we use a fundamental result from probability theory called the *Central Limit Theorem*. This theorem states that under certain conditions the distribution of the sum of N random variables x_i will be Gaussian as N goes to infinity [1]. This Gaussian g must have a zero mean and a standard deviation $\sigma = \sigma(d)$ from (1). Using this model, we can compute the probability that the ball will end up inside the goal when shot from an arbitrary position on the field perpendicularly to the goal line. This probability equals the area that lies

---

[1] In the current version of the *soccer server* the ball velocity in cycle $t + 1$ is equal to $(v_x^{t+1}, v_y^{t+1}) = 0.94 \cdot (v_x^t, v_y^t) + (\tilde{r}_1, \tilde{r}_2)$ where $\tilde{r}_1$ and $\tilde{r}_2$ are random numbers uniformly distributed over the interval $[-\text{rmax} .. \text{rmax}]$ with $\text{rmax} = 0.05 \cdot \|(v_x^t, v_y^t)\|$.

[2] e.g Brownian motion problems. The term *Brownian motion* is used to describe the movement of a particle in a liquid, subjected to collisions and other forces.

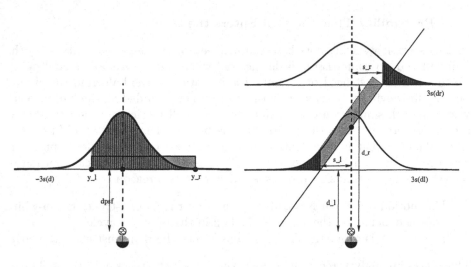

(a) Shooting straight to the goal.   (b) Shooting at an angle to the goal.

Fig. 1. Two situations of shooting to the goal (light gray) together with distributions.

under the respective Gaussian density function in between the two goalposts as is shown in Figure 1(a). When the y-coordinates of the left and right goalposts are denoted by y_l and y_r with $y_l < y_r$, this can be computed as follows:

$$P(\text{goal}) = \int_{-\infty}^{y_r} g(y;\sigma)\,dy - \int_{-\infty}^{y_l} g(y;\sigma)\,dy = G(y_r;\sigma) - G(y_l;\sigma) \qquad (2)$$

where $G(y;\sigma)$ equals the cumulative distribution function of the Gaussian $g(y;\sigma)$.

Finally, we have to compute the probability that the ball enters the goal when shot at an angle to the goal line (see Figure 1(b)). This case is somewhat more involved than the previous one due to the fact that the noise can cause the ball to travel different distances before it reaches the goal. Since different traveled distances imply different deviations according to (1), the ball distribution along the goal line is no longer Gaussian and this makes an exact calculation of the total probability difficult. However, the key observation is that we want to compute probability *masses* and that for equal masses the particular shape of the distribution that produces these masses is irrelevant and we can compute the probability mass from the identity

$$P(\text{goal}) = 1 - P(\text{not goal}) = 1 - P(\text{out from left}) - P(\text{out from right}) \qquad (3)$$

where $P(\text{not goal})$ denotes the probability that the ball misses the goal, either going out from the left or right goalpost. This probability mass is easier to compute, to a good approximation, from the tails of the Gaussian distributions corresponding to the goalposts. This is shown in Figure 1(b): when the ball reaches the left goalpost it has *effectively* traveled distance d_l and its corresponding distribution perpendicular to the shooting line is Gaussian with deviation $\sigma(d_l)$

from (1). The probability that the ball misses the goal going out from the left goalpost is approximately[3] equal to the shaded area on the left in Figure 1(b):

$$P(\text{out from left}) \approx \int_{-\infty}^{-s_l} g(y; \sigma(d_l)) \, dy \qquad (4)$$

where the integration runs up to $-s_l$ which denotes the (negative) shortest distance from the left goalpost to the shooting line. The situation that the ball misses the goal going out from the right post is analogous.

2.2   The Probability of Passing the Goalkeeper

The second subproblem can be stated as follows: given a shooting point in the goal, determine the probability that the goalkeeper intercepts the ball before it reaches the goal line. We propose an empirical method for learning this probability from examples of successful and unsuccessful scoring attempts. In our experiments we have used the goalkeeper of *RoboCup-2000* winner *FC Portugal 2000*, since it appeared to be one of the best available goalkeepers at that time.

To cast the problem into a proper mathematical framework, we note that ball interception can be regarded as a two-class classification problem: given the shooting point in the goal together with the positions of the goalkeeper and the ball (input feature vector), predict which class (intercepting or not) is most probable. Moreover, we are interested in the *posterior* probability associated with the prediction of each class. We performed an experiment in which a player repeatedly shot the ball from a fixed position straight to the goal, while the goalkeeper was placed randomly in different positions relative to the ball. A data set was formed by recording 10,000 scoring attempts, together with a boolean indicating whether the goalkeeper had intercepted the ball. An analysis of the resulting data revealed that the relevant features for classification were the following[4]:

- The absolute angle a between the goalkeeper and the shooting point
- The distance d between the ball and the goalkeeper

These two values form a two-dimensional feature vector on which the classification has been based. The recorded data set is depicted in Figure 2(a) which shows that there is an almost linear discriminant function between the two classes. We determined this discriminant function via linear regression on the boolean class indicator. This procedure is known to give the optimal *Fisher's Linear Discriminant* which has the property that it maximizes the ratio of the *between-group variance* and the *within-group variance* for the two classes [3]. The resulting discriminant function is characterized by the equation

$$u = (a - 26.1) * 0.043 + (d - 9.0) * 0.09 - 0.2 \qquad (5)$$

---

[3] There is a small probability that the ball ends up to the right of the left goalpost after travelling an 'illegal' trajectory outside the field. The ball thus actually went out from the left in this case but we neglect this probability in (4).

[4] Principled methods for automatic feature extraction are described in [3].

for distance values d between 3 and 15. This can be interpreted as follows: for a new angle-distance pair (a, d), the sample mean $(26.1, 9.0)$ is subtracted after which the inner product with the vector $(0.043, 0.09)$ is computed. The resulting vector is perpendicular to the discriminant boundary which is shifted by the offset -0.2. The pairs (a, d) for which (5) equals zero form the boundary between the two classes. This is plotted by a dotted line in Figure 2(a).

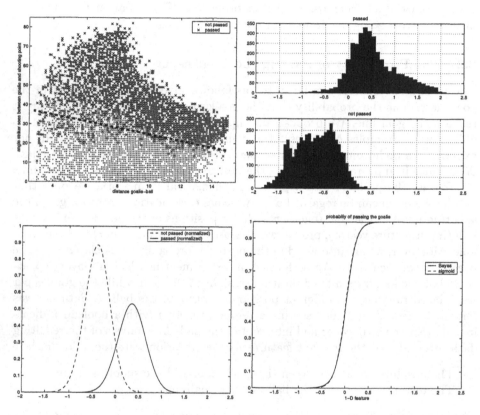

Fig. 2. Data set for goalkeeper interception experiment together with derived statistics.

Projecting all the (a_i, d_i) pairs perpendicularly to the discriminant line via (5) gives a set of one-dimensional points u_i that, to a good approximation, describe the two classes. The histogram class distributions of these points are plotted in Figure 2(b). Instead of trying to model these two distributions parametrically, we note that the relevant range for classification is only where the two histograms *overlap*. It is easy to see that the posterior probability of non-interception will be zero for approximately $u \leq -0.5$, one for $u > 0.5$ and will increase smoothly from zero to one in the interval in between. The posterior probability can thus be represented by a sigmoid function. In the region where the class distributions for interception and non-interception overlap, we fit a univariate Gaussian function on each class as shown in Figure 2(c). For each class C this gives us a Gaussian model for the class-conditional density function $P(u|C)$. With this model we can compute the posterior probability $P(C|u)$ for a class C using the Bayes rule

$$P(C|u) = \frac{P(u|C)\,P(C)}{P(u|C)\,P(C) + P(u|\bar{C})\,P(\bar{C})} \tag{6}$$

which is a sigmoid-like function. Since this is a simple two-class classification problem, $\bar{C}$ refers to the 'other' class in this case, while the prior probability $P(C)$ for a class C is computed as the proportion of points u_i in the data set which belong to C. In Figure 2(d) we have plotted the posterior probability for the non-interception class, together with the sigmoid approximation

$$P(\text{pass goalkeeper} \mid u) = \frac{1}{1 + \exp(-9.5u)} \tag{7}$$

which allows for an easy implementation.

2.3 Determining the Best Scoring Point

Having computed the probability that the ball will end up inside the goal (3) and the probability that the goalkeeper will not intercept it (7), the assumption of independence gives the total probability of scoring in a given situation as the product of these two values. This total probability is a bell-shaped function which represents the probability that the ball will enter the goal and which has a valley around the position of the goalkeeper. This curve will always have two local maxima which correspond to the left and right starting point of the valley, which can be located using a simple *hill-climbing* algorithm [4]. The highest one denotes the global maximum and is selected as the best scoring point.

3 Implementation and Demonstration

We have incorporated our scoring policy into the agent's decision loop as follows. When the agent has control of the ball, he first checks whether the probability of scoring is larger than a certain threshold[5]. If the total scoring probability exceeds this threshold then the agent tries to score by shooting the ball with maximum power towards the best scoring point. Otherwise he considers different options, such as dribbling, which he performs when the predicted success rate is high enough. However, when all possible alternatives fail and the agent stands at a close distance to the goal, he decides to shoot to the best scoring point anyhow.

Figure 3 shows two successive situations which were taken from a real match played by *UvA Trilearn*. In Figure 3(a) the player with the ball stands to the left of the goal which is covered well by the opponent goalkeeper. The scoring probability curve which corresponds to this situation is shown in Figure 3(c). The total scoring probability (solid line) is very low for all the points on the goal

---

[5] 90% in our current implementation.

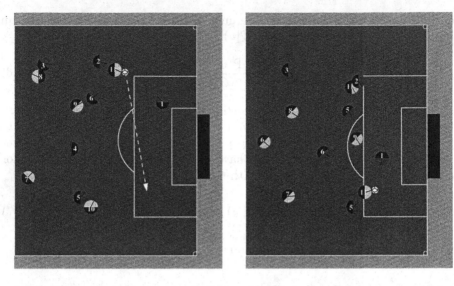

(a) Goalkeeper covers his goal well. A through pass is given.

(b) Goalkeeper has been outplayed. Good chance to score.

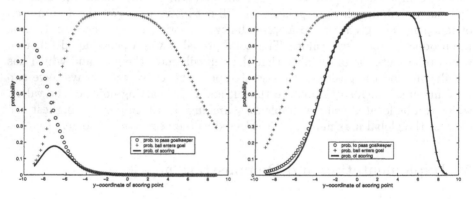

(c) Low scoring probability for all goal points. No shot is attempted.

(d) High scoring probability in right half of goal. Shot is attempted.

Fig. 3. Two successive match situations with associated scoring probability curves.

line[6] and the player with the ball thus rightly decides not to shoot to the goal. However, several cycles later the situation is completely different. The right wing attacker now has a high probability of scoring in the right half of the goal.

---

[6] Note that the noise in the ball movement causes a non-zero scoring probability when the ball is shot to a point just outside the goal. In our implementation these points are never selected however, since we only consider points on the goal line for which the single probability of entering the goal is more than 0.7 (=*EnterGoalThr*).

4 Conclusion

In this paper we have described a methodology that allows a simulated soccer agent to determine the probability of scoring when he shoots the ball to a specific point in the goal in a given situation. The single probability that the ball enters the goal (first subproblem) depends on the values of various parameters which control the movement noise of the ball, the size of the goal, etc. The approach is general in the sense that it enables one to 'learn' this probability even when these parameter values change. However, the single probability of passing the goalkeeper (second subproblem) depends on the opponent goalkeeper and different goalkeepers exhibit different behaviors. In our current implementation we have based this probability entirely on the goalkeeper of *FC Portugal*. Since this is a good goalkeeper, the approach is useful against other goalkeepers as well[7].

Ideally however, the probability of passing the goalkeeper should be *adaptive* and the model should incorporate information about the current opponent goalkeeper instead of using that of a particular team. The desired case would be to let the model adapt itself during the game, using little prior information about the current goalkeeper. This is a difficult problem because learning must be based on only a few scoring attempts. It is therefore important to extract the most relevant features and to parametrize the intercepting behavior of the opponent goalkeeper in a compact manner that permits on-line learning.

Acknowledgements

This research is/was supported by PROGRESS, the embedded systems research program of the Dutch organisation for Scientific Research NWO, the Dutch Ministry of Economic Affairs and the Technology Foundation STW.

References

1. W. Feller. *An Introduction to Probability Theory and Its Applications*, volume 1. John Wiley & Sons, Inc., New York, 1957.
2. Ehsan Foroughi, Fredrik Heintz, Spiros Kapetanakis, Kostas Kostiadis, Johan Kummeneje, Itsuki Noda, Oliver Obst, Pat Riley, and Timo Steffens. RoboCup Soccer Server User Manual: for Soccer Server version 7.06 and later, 2001. At http://sourceforge.net/projects/sserver.
3. B.D. Ripley. *Pattern Recognition and Neural Networks*. Cambridge University Press, Cambridge, U.K., 1996.
4. Stuart J. Russell and Peter Norvig. *Artificial Intelligence: A Modern Approach*. Prentice Hall, Englewood Cliffs, NJ, 1995.
5. Peter Stone, Patrick Riley, and Manuela Veloso. Defining and Using Ideal Teammate and Opponent Agent Models. In *Twelfth Innovative Applications of AI Conference (IAAI-2000)*, 2000.

---

[7] A different approach is to base the probability on the *ideal* goalkeeper performance using the known model of the world dynamics [5]. But in this case it is not straightforward to create a continuous probability function for all different situations.

Decision-Making and Tactical Behavior with Potential Fields

Jens Meyer, Robert Adolph, Daniel Stephan,
Andreas Daniel, Matthias Seekamp, Volker Weinert, and Ubbo Visser

Department for Mathematics and Computer Science
University of Bremen
Postfach 33 04 40
D-28334 Bremen, Germany
jens@informatik.uni-bremen.de

Abstract. Using potential-fields is a seldomly used technique in RoboCup scenarios. The existing approaches mainly concentrate on world state representation on single actions such as a kick. In this paper we will show how to apply potential fields to assist fast and precise decisions in an easy and intuitive way. We go beyond the existing approaches in using potential fields to determine all possible player actions, basic and advanced tactics an also general player behaviors. To ensure fast computing we mainly use basic mathematical computation for potential field related calculations. This gives us the advantage of both determining and understanding player actions. Therefore, integrating future features such as a complex online coach and progressive localization methods will be easier. We implemented the approach in our team **B**remen **U**niversity **G**oal **S**eekers (BUGS) and tested it in numerous games against other simulation league teams. The results show that CPU-time of making a decision per team has been decreased significantly. This is a crucial improvement for calculations in time-critical environments.

1 Introduction

The idea to use potential fields is based on retrieving knowledge for the best possible place for an agent to act on. These actions are kick, dribble and dash. Due to this it can easily be adapted to all RoboCup-leagues. We are able to represent all possible game situations by taking all necessary information from the already existing worldmodel of CMU-99 and interpreting them as objects in the potential fields. The decision for an action is made by a heuristic based on the determination of the distance to this point. Having a large distance will imply kicking the ball to it. With a short distance to it we will dribble to this point. If we don't have the ball we dash to the target.

There have previously been approaches with regard to potential fields. Similar to electric fields by [Johannson and Saffiotti, 2001] and similar to approaches as described in [Latombe, 1991] we use potential fields to represent world model states. In comparison to the mentioned approaches we focus on the fastest possible decision-making and general usability. This means that we use potential fields

G.A. Kaminka, P.U. Lima, and R. Rojas (Eds.): RoboCup 2002, LNAI 2752, pp. 304–311, 2003.

to derive any decision that has to be made by an agent. [Nagasaka et al., 2000] use potential fields for actions like a single kick. Our general usability approach goes further. [Johansson, 2001] combines decision-making and navigation in using potential fields. Our approach is similar, however, the difference is the environment: it is real-time, dynamic and more flexible. Therefore, the processes are more difficult.

2   Using Potential Fields in BUGS

For better understanding of the more complex associations discussed later in this paper we have a closer look towards potential fields and show their flexibility and hidden complexity.

2.1   Basic Use of Potential Fields

For building a potential field it is necessary to lay a grid upon the soccer field. The grid resolution, although it is customizable, used in the BUGS-client is 60*40, which means $\approx 2m^2$ per grid field. Based on information about all visible moving objects, the game situation and extra knowledge about own tactic and formation, numeric entries (only integer) in all grid fields are made. The relations between the different aspects are controlled by 15 changeable parameters (which are meant to be on-line manipulated by the coach, depending on various game statistics).

The point about the speed of our algorithm results from various simplifications in calculations and design of potential fields. One is that we dont have functions which will interpolate the resulting potential fields. These interpolations are unnecessary because of the predefined areas of effect of each world object (this works like *stamps* with integer values). Another one is the using of a grid instead of the soccerserver coordinates.

Every agent, including the coach, will call a potential field based on his own world model every few cycles (2-8). Timing depends on game situation and distribution of CPU-power. Although we have enough of CPU power, while still running all clients on one computer, we tend to keep it well balanced to absolutely guarantee complete decisions for all agents. One starting point only allows the next soonest potential field calculation every other turn, starting with half the agents on an even and the other half on an odd cycle. Situation-based timing is obvious: a ball-leading agent should do calculations every other cycle; a position-holding or adjusting agent, with the ball 60m away, will do so again in about 20 cycles or earlier if the ball comes closer to him.

To decide which action is next the complete field and some more information (e.g. ball possession and position, own position) are necessary. The best value within the grid always means the best position for the next action. Again, these actions are dashing, kicking and dribbling. Using only these simple player-actions, the whole space of soccer-behavior can be emulated. How far this goes and how it exceeds the obvious will be discussed next.

2.2   Advanced Use of Potential Fields

In order to understand the complexity level and the possibilities of potential fields, it is necessary to know their gradual structure. This is the point where a concrete view can be won on later possibilities and implicit conversions of advanced tactics. In fact the BUGS-potential field-method includes some ten-

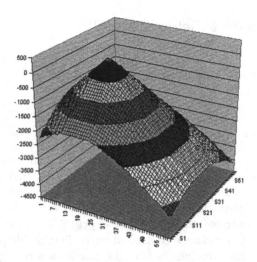

Fig. 1. A typical potential field

dencies towards planning algorithms. Like a superior plan all clients have a similar basic potential which leads towards the opponent's goal. Each individual action, which is decided, contains the adherence to these basic guidelines, thus the rough superordinate plan. While following a global intention will not make a planning algorithm, viewing all generated potential fields in parallel as one unit means a large step towards a global plan. We need to show the interaction between single potential fields. There are two reasons for the fields to interact with each other. The first reason is rather trivial. Each single field contains its player position such as offense, left middle field, etc.. We get tactical formations due to tuning this positions and possibly adjusting them to recognized opponent positions (see section 2.4). The second reason seems to be trivial too, but has non-obvious consequences: every potential field is quite similar to the fields generated by neighbor agents, thus based on (nearly) the same inputs which generates similar results. These results are only altered by their own positions and the individual noise transmitted by the soccer server. Suppose all agents building potential fields at the same time, each with its own view of the same situation, permanently influencing each other with their decisions. While one player holds the ball the others take position to be passable. This behavior results in building a complete way for the ball into the opponent's goal for most of the time while in ball possession. However, this scenario will not work most of the time due to interceptions, thus, alternatives are created at any time. This is the point of similarity to planning algorithms: based on the current situation we determine sets of actions, which hopefully results in a goal. This might be dangerous because our algorithm has not really a similarity with any planning algorithms from the implementation point of view but the rudimentary behavior is the same in some way, especially for the RoboCup simulation league where world model states and conditions for decision-making are changing fast.

2.3 Example for Advance Use

As we described above, we can assign special values to areas in the grid to gain a special behaviour. The following example shows how it works and gives some views on other tactics which we can evoke by assigning values to the grid.

Offside. A very important tactic in soccer is the use of the offside rule against the other team. Many teams use this tactic to gain freekicks and to interrupt opponents offense easily. Many teams have problems either by setting an offside trap or by recognizing the opponents offside trap. With an potential field we can assign negative potentials to either the own offside area or the opponents offside area. If we assign these potentials to the own offside area we achieve that we build up a offside trap. Due to the negative potential in this area, no field player will move into this area on his own. The major exception to this rule is the ball interception after the ball enters this area. Similar happens on the opponents offside area. We assign bad values to this area and achieve that no agent stays in or moves into this area if he don't have the ball or if the ball is already in this area.

Further Examples. The method described in the last section can be used on all possible tactical areas. To build up an offensive strategy on the field edges we can simply assign positive potentials in these particular regions. If we want an agent to stay in a specific area (eg. its position in the team), we can assign negative values to areas outside its tactical area or assigning positve values to his tactical area.

We added some additional points of possibilities for assigning values to this section. This is just a small list, which should show the power of assigning values to the grid within the potential fields:

- The own penalty area is an area where the ball shouldn't stay that long. By assigning a negative value to this area we can achieve, that the ball is kicked outside this area quickly, if an agent has the ball. Because of the negative value in this area, his target point automatically is set outside this area.
- assigning positive values to the opponents penalty area and goal, the attraction to this points is high enough to let the attacking agents move to and kick to this specific area.

A very important aspect to the value assigning is the online coach which we plan to use. With his clear view onto the game he can gain statistics about the game. So he can easily assign basic values to specific areas for all, some and even single agents. We developed a coachlanguage where we can encode data for assigning values to the agents. The coach is able to get informations from his statistics which tells him, what areas of the field is mostly used by the opponents. By assigning positive values to this areas, the agents will be able to intercept the ball or the opponents agents earlier.

2.4   Influence of the Tactical Online Coach

We develop a tactical online coach, whose purpose is the statistic evaluation of both our own team and the opponents team. In addition, it will log frequency points of positions of all moving objects. Both will be used for game evaluation, which is necessary to re-distribute player-resources, change tactics, and re-arrange player formations. These statistics are ball losses, percentile ball possession, percentile ball position per team section (defense, mid-field, offense), number of wrongly passed balls, gaining of ground and some other variables. These numbers will show the quality of each team section and in addition its' relative efficiency. Based on these values we will modify various player settings, including player type, position, relations between objects in the potential field or tactic for a single agent, and additionally player formation for a team section or the whole team. All of these changes have an influence on the potential fields, changing tactics for example may tilt the whole field (as described above), formations will simply set new orientation points for the agents, which center the agent's preferred area of action. Special regards should be considered to the changes of object relations in the potential field, because this is the most subtle way to change behavior, although it could have the greatest effects. Here is an example: While raising ball priority will probably do nothing because it is already very high, raising team mate priority slightly may result in passing the ball for a little more percentage rather than dribbling with it. A medium change in opponent priority can change the whole game. Raising it will give an evasive play, lowering may result in nearly ignoring (as long it's possible) while in ball position. Sometimes a change in relations has unforeseen consequences, which makes this way of influence as dangerous as powerful. But this is the reason why we change them, great shifts in behavior might imply great improvements in play.

3   Evaluation and Results

Probably the hardest work was the adjustment of the priorities for the evaluation algorithm as described above. For this we developed a tool which shows the calculated potential fields of all agents. We are also able to locate errors in priorities and to bring the real potential fields towards our original intentions. Our agents were running on a Pentium II 400 Mhz Processor with 128 MB of RAM located in the computer pool of the Department of Mathematics and Computer Science. The operating system on this machines is RedHat Linux 7.2. Table 1 shows our performance test based on a tool called *gprof*. This GNU-tool produces an execution profile of C or C++ programms. All values in the table refers to a complete game. The first column describes percentage of the total running time of the program used by this function. The second column describes the number of seconds accounted for by this function alone. The third column describes the total number of calls. The last colums contains the functions' names. Both rows are the most evoked functions of our agent. The function named *estimate_future_pos(...)* is a CMU-function mostly used by the worldmodel itself. The function in the second row is the function which is used to generate potential fields. The result shows that our complete potential field generation uses less than 9% of the time. Until now these numbers aren't really expressive for the RoboCup-scenario, because of their lack of comparison. Comparison of our evaluation algorithm with similar decision algorithms of other teams is difficult because we can't isolate their decision module. The only thing we can compare is the used CPU-time and the amount of memory. The used memory is less interesting, because there is enough memory available in a tournament. For extracting these results we simply used **top** (Unix-command) while playing a normal game. Both teams and the soccer server were each running on different computers (the type mentioned above). We repeated each game 15 times and took average values. Karlsruhe-Brainstormers and Mainz-Rolling-Brains were run with the old soccer server v. 7.x, our team and FC-Portugal on soccer server v. 8.x. The use of different soccer servers should not make any difference for the results. The BUGS-team appears twice in the table because of two different grid resolutions to show the relation between resolution and performance. We choose FC-Portugal because it is also based on the CMU-99 sources. Karlsruhe Brainstormers01 was chosen because of it's good performance in Seattle and Mainz-Rolling-Brains completes the list of reference teams. Results are given in table 2. We can see that our team BUGS has the best performance with regard to the maximum CPU time used with a grid-resolution of 60*40. It uses only between 40 - 64% of the time that FC Portugal needs and is twice as fast as K. Brainstormers, again, with a grid-resolution of 60*40. Similar relations can be seen in the column 'minimum used CPU' where the BUGS team uses less than 0.1%. Here, the team from Mainz has the highest values with 1.5%. As far as memory is concerned we can note that Karlsruhe Brainstormers always use the same amount of memory. This is probably due to the fact that they are completely based on artificial neural networks. The same relation between maximum and minimum memory used one can see with our team BUGS. It remains constant at a low rate. Only the team from FC Portugal has a difference in the memory. This indicates that they use various techniques for decision-making. Although we used more than twice the original field size, we are still well performing.

Our team has been accepted for the RoboCup 2002 in Fukuoka with the following qualification results: Karlsruhe Brainstormers 2001 - BUGS : 8 - 0; RoboLog - BUGS : 7 - 0. Although we lacked in offensive capabilities and we were still at the beginning at the date of qualifications, we can say due to this results, that our approach seems promising.

Table 1. potential field generation based on time and evocation

% time	self seconds	# calls	name
20.62	0.60	288024	estimate_future_pos(...)
8.59	0.25	1526	getEvaluatedAction(...)

Table 2. Best performance test based on a time evaluation relation for the algorithm

Team	Max CPU	Min CPU	Min Memory	Max Memory
FC Portugal 00	12.0%	0.3%	0.5%	1.0
BUGS(90*60)	7.6%	< 0.1%	0.7%	0.8%
BUGS(60*40)	4.6%	< 0.1%	0.6%	0.7%
K. Brainstormers 00	9.8%	0.1%	2.0%	2.1%
Mainz Rolling Brains 00	5.1%	1.5%	1.1%	1.1%

4   Conclusion

We used the potential-fields to represent all game situations. But in addition to [Nagasaka et al., 2000] we use it for all possible actions, not only for a kick. We used it to decide which action we make and what the situation is. Our method is intuitive and fast at the same time. The main advantage is, that we are able to use a single algorithm to determine the agents action ("One algorithm to fit them all"). The waiving of complex rules and algorithms is another advantage.

We are able to use the Potential-field for finding a teammate to pass the ball to as we are able to find a position a teammate will pass to. Using an online coach, makes the decision even better. With a coach we are able to give simple advises to the playing agents. Additionally we can give single agents different positions, which makes the potential-field even exacter. We use the potential-field approach in our own team in the simulation league scenario. Because of this new way of decision finding, we don't want to make any statement about the quality of this decision. But we have shown that the decision we determined is done due to an easy and especially fast algorithm. The CPU-time used by an agent is very low and the used memory also. The qualification for RC-02 in Fukuoka is a first step towards a successful team.

Acknowledgement

We thank the Carnegie Mellon team for letting us use their basic client sources.

References

[Johannson and Saffiotti, 2001] Johannson, S. J. and Saffiotti, A. (2001). Using the electric field approach in the robocup domain. In Birk, A., Coradeschi, S., and Tadokoro, S., editors, *The RoboCup 2001 International Symposium*, Lecture Notes in Artificial Intelligence, Seattle, WA. Springer. in print.

[Johansson, 2001] Johansson, S. J. (2001). An electric field approach - a strategy for sony four-legged robot. M.sc.thesis mse-2001-03, Blekinge Institute of Technology, Sweden.

[Latombe, 1991] Latombe, J. C. (1991). *Robot Motion Planning*. Kluwer Academic Publishers, Boston, USA.

[Nagasaka et al., 2000] Nagasaka, Y., Murakami, K., Naruse, T., Takahashi, T., and Mori, Y. (2000). Potential field approach to short term action planning in robocup f180 league. In Stone, P., Balch, T., and Kraetschmar, G., editors, *RoboCup Symposium 2000, Robot Soccer World Cup IV*, volume 2019 of *Lecture Notes in Artificial Intelligence*, pages 345–350, Melbourne, Australia. Springer.

Localization of Robots in F180 League Using Projective Geometry

Jerome Douret[1], Ryad Benosman[2], Salah Bouzar[1], and Jean Devars[2]

[1] Citilog
5 avenue d'Italie 75013 Paris, France
jdouret@citilog.com, bouzar@citilog.fr
http://www.citilog.fr
[2] Laboratoire des Instruments et Systemes d'Ile de France
Université Pierre et Marie Curie
4 place Jussieu 75252 PARIS Cedex 05
Boite 164, France
rbo@lis.jussieu.fr, devars@ccr.jussieu.fr
http://www.lis.jussieu.fr

Abstract. The F180 RoboCup league relies on a single camera mounted on top of the field. It is of great importance to use an adapted calibration method to locate robots. Most of the methods used are developed for specific application where 3D is required. This paper presents a new calibration method specially developped for the F180 league geometry, allowing the determination of the camera pose parameters and the correction of the parallax in the image due to different heights of observed robots. This method needs one calibration plane that also could be used for correcting optical distortions introduced by the lens.

1   Introduction

The determination of the robot location on the field is of great importance in the RoboCup contest. The camera calibration determines the intrinsics parameters of the camera and its position according to the field. A high number of calibration methods can be found in the litterature. Camera calibration has seen great improvement since the beginning of the 90's. The main drawbacks of these methods is that in most cases they were developed for special applications, sometimes using complicated formulations that are not necessary in the case of the F180 calibration problem. Projective geometry is most of the times unavoidable each time camera calibration is needed. Giving a closer look to the main task to be solved, we find out that most of the features of the calibration are points lying on planes. In this case the use of homographies is by far the most approriate tool to solve the problem. The method proposed here relies on the computation of a single homography determined between the image plane and the field plane. This homography can be used to switch from one plane to the other. Compared to [1] the developped method needs one plane of calibration at a single height, then by introducing the intrinsics parameters one can retreive any homography

G.A. Kaminka, P.U. Lima, and R. Rojas (Eds.): RoboCup 2002, LNAI 2752, pp. 312–318, 2003.
© Springer-Verlag Berlin Heidelberg 2003

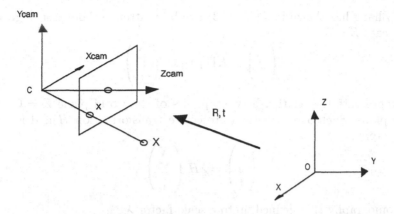

Fig. 1. Rotation and translation between world and camera coordinate frames

for a specific height. The method can be applied to any world plane but, in F180 context, we only need it for planes at different heights. The determination of the intrinsics parameters can be computed by different approaches, for a better overview the reader should refer to [3][2] where several methods are exposed.

2   The Projective Camera

A general camera can be modelized according to the pinhole model by a 3×4 projection matrix P. It represents the transformation between a world point expressed by a homogeneous 4-vector $\mathbf{X} = [X\,Y\,Z\,1]^T$, and an image point expressed by a homogeneous 3-vector $\mathbf{x} = [x\,y\,1]^T$:

$$\mathbf{x} = P\mathbf{X}\,. \tag{1}$$

The matrix P can be decomposed in blocks in the following way:

$$P = K[R\,\mathbf{t}]\,, \tag{2}$$

where, K is a upper-triangular 3×3 matrix and represents the intrinsic camera parameters, R is a 3×3 rotation matrix and $\mathbf{t}$ is a translation vector. $\{R, \mathbf{t}\}$ relates the camera orientation and position with the world coordinate system (fig. 1).

More information on the projection matrix P can be found in [3], [4].

3   Projection Matrix and World Plane at $Z = 0$

The relation (2) can be expressed as:

$$\begin{pmatrix} x \\ y \\ 1 \end{pmatrix} = K[\mathbf{r_1}\,\mathbf{r_2}\,\mathbf{r_3}\,\mathbf{t}] \begin{pmatrix} X \\ Y \\ Z \\ 1 \end{pmatrix}\,, \tag{3}$$

with $\mathbf{r_1}$, $\mathbf{r_2}$, $\mathbf{r_3}$, the three column vectors of the rotation matrix R.

Z. Zhang has shown in [5] that (3) can be written without lost of generality in the case $Z = 0$:

$$\begin{pmatrix} x \\ y \\ 1 \end{pmatrix} = K[\mathbf{r_1}\ \mathbf{r_2}\ \mathbf{t}] \begin{pmatrix} X \\ Y \\ 1 \end{pmatrix} . \tag{4}$$

This represents the relation between points of the world plane $Z = 0$ and the image plane. Such a relation is a projective transformation H and is called a homography:

$$\begin{pmatrix} x \\ y \\ 1 \end{pmatrix} = \lambda H \begin{pmatrix} X \\ Y \\ 1 \end{pmatrix} . \tag{5}$$

The homography H is defined up to a scale factor λ.

From (4) and (5), we deduce that:

$$\lambda H = K[\mathbf{r_1}\ \mathbf{r_2}\ \mathbf{t}] \tag{6}$$

$$\lambda[\mathbf{h_1}\ \mathbf{h_2}\ \mathbf{h_3}] = K[\mathbf{r_1}\ \mathbf{r_2}\ \mathbf{t}] \tag{7}$$

4   Pose Determination from a World Plane at $Z = 0$

We start with the hypothesis that the homography H has been computed from world points ($Z = 0$) and image points correspondances [3], [1]. Then, the pose $\{R, \mathbf{t}\}$ of the camera can be determined from (6) [5]:

$$[\mathbf{r_1}\ \mathbf{r_2}\ \mathbf{t}] = \frac{1}{\|K^{-1}\mathbf{h_1}\|}K^{-1}H . \tag{8}$$

As R is a rotation matrix we easily deduce $\mathbf{r_3}$ from:

$$\mathbf{r_3} = \mathbf{r_1} \times \mathbf{r_2} . \tag{9}$$

5   Homography of a World Plane in General Position

In this section we will explain the method to determine the homography H_π corresponding to a world plane π wich as been translated from a distance d on the Z axis above the the plane $Z = 0$ (cf. fig. 2). The reader should be aware that once $H_{Z=0}$ has been determined, it is possible to retrieve H_π for any plane of the 3D-space.

A plane in 3-space can be written in homogeneous representation as:

$$\pi = \begin{pmatrix} \mathbf{n} \\ d \end{pmatrix} , \tag{10}$$

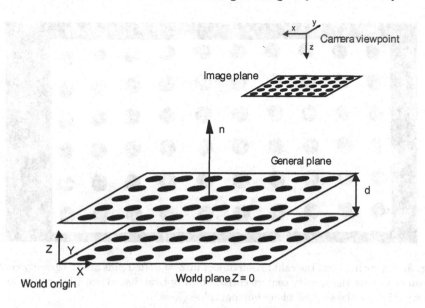

Fig. 2. Camera pose determination and homography of a general plane

with $\mathbf{n}$ a 3-vector representing the plane normal, and d a scalar representing the plane distance from the world origin.

Points $\mathbf{X}_\pi$ on a plane π verify the dot product:

$$\pi^T \mathbf{X}_\pi = 0 . \tag{11}$$

X_π can be decomposed in two blocks:

$$\mathbf{X}_\pi = \begin{pmatrix} \tilde{\mathbf{X}}_\pi \\ T \end{pmatrix} , \tag{12}$$

where $\tilde{\mathbf{X}}_\pi$ is the euclidean coordinates and T is the homogeneous term.

From (10), (11) and (12) we have:

$$\mathbf{n}^T \tilde{\mathbf{X}}_\pi + dT = 0 , \tag{13}$$

$$T = -\frac{\mathbf{n}^T \tilde{\mathbf{X}}_\pi}{d} . \tag{14}$$

Then, from (1) with $\mathbf{X} = \mathbf{X}_\pi$ and (12):

$$\mathbf{x} = K[R\,\mathbf{t}] \begin{pmatrix} \tilde{\mathbf{X}}_\pi \\ -\frac{\mathbf{n}^T \tilde{\mathbf{X}}_\pi}{d} \end{pmatrix} , \tag{15}$$

thus

$$\mathbf{x} = K \left(R - \frac{\mathbf{t}\mathbf{n}^T}{d} \right) \tilde{\mathbf{X}}_\pi , \tag{16}$$

we then have

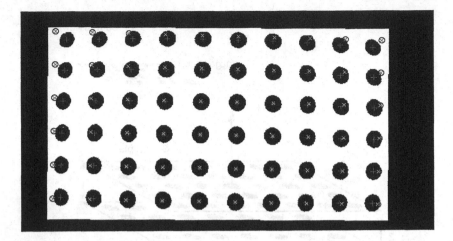

Fig. 3. Binary image of the calibration object in $Z = 0$. Red plus are the gravity centers. Green crosses are the gravity centers corrected in optical distortion. Blue circles are the reprojection by the ground plane homographie ($Z = 0$)

$$\mathbf{x} = H_\pi \tilde{\mathbf{X}}_\pi \,, \tag{17}$$

where

$$H_\pi = K \left(R - \frac{\mathbf{t}\mathbf{n}^T}{d} \right) \tag{18}$$

We have seen that all our development supposes that we know the matrix K of the intrinsic parameters. Different techniques can be found in the literature such as in [3], [5] or [2].

6   Experiments

The matrix K and the distortion parameters have been previously computed using an iterative Faugeras-Tauscani method [2][4]. The calibrated camera is placed above the plane $Z = 0$. Not necessarily in front. A known grid has been placed on this plane. After extraction of the circles gravity centers and correction of the optical distortion, we can compute the homography $H_{Z=0}$ that relates the world points of the grids with the corresponding image points (cf. fig. 3):

$$H_{Z=0} = \begin{pmatrix} 2.1606 & -0.0394 & 28.0646 \\ 0.0710 & 2.1464 & 8.8549 \\ 0.0001 & -0.0000 & 1.0000 \end{pmatrix} . \tag{19}$$

The pose of the camera is evaluated as explained in Section 4. Then we can compute the homography for a plane. We have chose a plane placed at 20 cm above the ground ($Z = -20cm$). It is supposed to be the hight of a robot. More

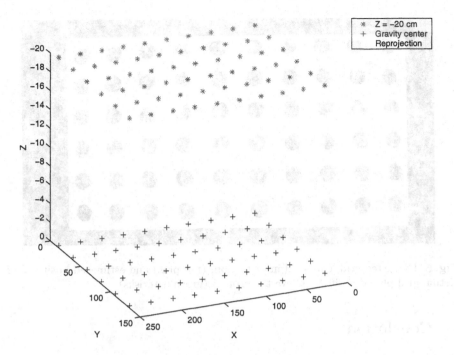

Fig. 4. 3D representation of the extracted gravity center (red plus) on the plane $Z = 0$ and the estimated position on a plane at $Z = -20cm$ (green asterisks)

Table 1. Residual errors for $H_{Z=0}$ and $H_{Z=-20cm}$. The images points have been corrected in opical distortion before the homography estimation. We can see the hight precision of the localization

Homography	Ground error	Image error
$H_{(Z=0)}$	0.12646 cm	0.26687 pixel
$H_{(Z=-20cm)}$	0.29487 cm	0.38189 pixel

precisely the hight of the color code identifying it. The position is determined by the gravity center of the color code (cf. fig. 4 and 5):

$$H_{(Z=-20cm)} = \begin{pmatrix} 618.8987 & -12.1651 & -101.5083 \\ 19.5795 & 621.2943 & 108.5343 \\ 0.0238 & 0.0075 & -13.3978 \end{pmatrix} . \tag{20}$$

For error evaluation, the calibration object has been translated by 20 cm up. Gravity centers are extracted and optical distorsion is removed. Then points positions are compared with those obteined by the method explained above. Results are presented in table 1.

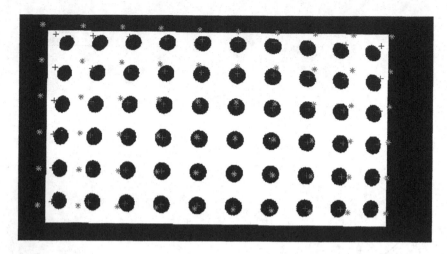

Fig. 5. Extracted grid, corrected in distortion, (red plus) and estimated positions of a virtual grid placed at 20 cm above the ground (green asterisks)

7   Conclusion

We have there proposed a simple and efficient method that deals with parallax for the F180 robots localization. It requires only a single calibration pattern on the ground flour and the camera can be posed in general position. From this one it is now possible to determine robots locations with quite a good precision. The user only needs to compute one homography per robot's hight. The experimental results have shown that the object can be localized with good accuracy at any level from the ground floor.

References

1. R. Benosman, J. Douret, and J. Devars. A simple fast an accurate calibration method for the f180 league. In *The Robocup 2001 Symposium*. LNCA Springer Verlag, New York, 2002.
2. O. D. Faugeras and G. Toscani. The calibration problem for stereo. In *Proceedings of the IEEE International Conference on ComputeVision and Pattern Recognition*, pages 15–20, 1986.
3. R. Hartley and A. Zisserman. *Multiple view geometry in computer vision*. Cambridge University Press, New York, 2000.
4. R. Horaud and O. Monga. *Vision par ordinateur, outils fondamentaux.*, chapter 5: Geometrie et calibration des cameras. Editions Herm'es, Paris, 1993.
5. Zhengyou Zhang. A flexible new technique for camera calibration. *IEEE Transactions on Pattern Analysis and Machine Intelligence*, 22(11):1330–1334, 2000.

Reinforcement Learning in Large State Spaces
Simulated Robotic Soccer as a Testbed

Karl Tuyls, Sam Maes, and Bernard Manderick

Computational Modeling Lab (COMO)
Department of Computer Science
Vrije Universiteit Brussel
Belgium
{ktuyls,sammaes}@vub.ac.be, bernard@arti.vub.ac.be
http://como.vub.ac.be

Abstract. Large state spaces and incomplete information are two problems that stand out in learning in multi-agent systems. In this paper we tackle them both by using a combination of decision trees and Bayesian networks (BNs) to model the environment and the Q-function. Simulated robotic soccer is used as a testbed, since there agents are faced with both large state spaces and incomplete information. The long-term goal of this research is to define generic techniques that allow agents to learn in large-scaled multi-agent systems.

1 Introduction

In this paper we address 2 important problems that occur when learning in multi-agent systems (MAS). The first is a problem of large state spaces. Existing formalisms such as the Markov game model[Hu99][Lit94] suffer from combinatorial explosion, since they learn values for combinations of actions. We suggest to use a combination of decision trees and Bayesian networks (BNs)[Rus94]to avoid this problem of tractability. We will discuss the problem of modeling the environment and other agents acting in the environment in the context of Markov Games. The Markov game model is defined by a set of states S, and a collection of action sets $A_1, ..., A_n$ (one set for every agent). The state transition function $S \times A_1 \times ... \times A_n \to P(S)$ maps a state and an action from every agent to a probability on S. Each agent has an associated reward function R_i :

$$S \times A_1 \times ... \times A_n \to \Re \tag{1}$$

where $S \times A_1 \times ... \times A_n$ constitutes a product space. The reward function for an agent A_i calculates a value which indicates how desired the state S and the actions of the agents $A_1, ..., A_n$ are for agent A_i.

In this model learning is done in a product space and when the number of agents increases this model becomes prohibitively Agent 1 observes the environment and all other n agents. A table represents the accumulated reward over time according to each possible situation. We represent the environment by a

G.A. Kaminka, P.U. Lima, and R. Rojas (Eds.): RoboCup 2002, LNAI 2752, pp. 319–326, 2003.
© Springer-Verlag Berlin Heidelberg 2003

set S of possible states, and each agent has a set A_i of possible actions. So we have $|S| \times |A_1| \times, ..., \times |A_n|$ possible situations, which need to be stored in a table with a matching reward value. Now if the number of agents increases and the environment becomes more complex this table becomes intractable. This is what we call the large state space problem.

Nowe and Verbeeck [Now00] avoid this problem by forcing an agent to model only the agents that are relevant to him. A similar approach is adopted in [Def01].

The second problem is one of incomplete information. Often an agent is not given all information about the environment and the other agents. For instance we don't always know what action each agent is taking, where the other agents and the ball are at every timestep. We suggest to use Bayesian networks to handle this problem of incompleteness. Bayesian networks are a compact representation of a joint probability distribution, which allows us to make estimates about certain variables, given values of other variables. We believe that BNs can contribute a great deal to this problem.

These two problems that emerge in the setting described above, will be dealt with in the context of simulated robotic soccer, and we will suggest solutions for them.

1.1   Simulated Robotic Soccer as a Testbed

We decided to use simulated robotic soccer as the test bed for our research, because it is particularly well suited for testing the specific problems we are interested in.

- Large state space, it is obvious that 23 objects on a field can be in a massive amount of states, especially if we take into account the speed, the acceleration, the direction of these objects next to their position on the field.
- Incomplete information, each agent has only a limited and noisy view of the environment.

Both the presence of these characteristics and the competitive aspect of RoboCup make it a challenging domain to work in.

In section 2 we will discuss our general solution to the problems stated in this introduction. Section 3 will discuss the methodology we will follow to test the presented ideas and section 4 will present some results. Finally we will end this paper with a conclusion.

2   Modeling the Environment and Other Agents

In this section we will present our solutions to the problems described in the introduction. We start with a small introduction on Q-learning, the form of learning under study.

2.1   Q-learning

We use a variation of reinforcement learning called single agent Q-learning. In this form of learning the Q-function maps state-action pairs to values. Let $Q^*(s, a)$ be the expected discounted reinforcement of taking action a in state s, then continuing by choosing the optimal actions. We can estimate this function by the following Q-learning rule

$$Q(s_t, a_t) = Q(s_t, a_t) + \alpha[r_{t+1} + \gamma max_a Q(s_{t+1}, a) - Q(s_t, a_t)] \qquad (2)$$

where γ is a discount factor and where α is the learning rate. r_{t+1} represents the immediate reward at time $t+1$. If each action is executed in each state an infinite number of times on an infinite run and α is decayed properly, the Q-values will converge with probability 1 to Q^*.

We will use this form of learning for learning individual skills in the simulated robotic soccer, like for instance learning to go to the ball, or learning to shoot at goal. When we come in a more challenging situation with other agents present (for example in a 2-2 situation), this Q-learning rule has to be converted to a multi-agent Q-learning rule, looking like

$$Q(s_t, a_t^1, ..., a_t^n) = Q(s_t, a_t^1, ..., a_t^n)$$
$$+ \alpha[r_{t+1} + \gamma max_{a^1, ..., a^n} Q(s_{t+1}, a^1, ..., a^n) - Q(s_t, a_t^1, ..., a_t^n)]$$

where $a_t^1, ..., a_t^n$ present the actions of agent 1 to n at time t.

2.2   Bayesian Nets for Large State Spaces

We propose to use Bayesian nets (BNs) for modeling the other agents acting in the environment and the environment itself. A Bayesian net [Rus94] is a graphical knowledge representation of a joint probability distribution. A Bayesian net has one type of node, more precisely a random node which is associated with a random variable. This random variable represents the agent's possibly uncertain beliefs about the world. The links between the nodes summarize their dependence relationships. BNs can represent a certain domain in a compact manner and this representation is equivalent to the joint probability distribution.

Our idea is to use such Bayesian nets for each agent to model the other agents in the domain. The resulting model must describe how the different agents influence each other and how they influence the reward the agent receives.

Every node of a BN has an associated conditional probability table (CPT), which quantizes the direct influence of the parents on the child node. In figure 1 we give an example BN of a situation with 4 agents and 5 state variables representing the environment. This network represents the view of agent 1, and every other agent has an analogous network representing his view. Without independence relations in the domain, the network would be fully connected. As you can see, every node has a direct influence on the accumulated reward Q.

In figure 2 you can see the associated CPT for node Q. Again this table can become very large, depending on the number of links with Q. So we still have

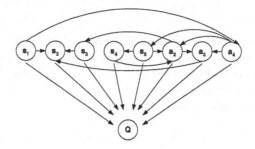

Fig. 1. Large state space solution: BN of a domain with 4 agents and 5 state variables.

s_1	s_2	s_3	s_4	a_2	a_3	a_4	Q for a_1
1	1	1	1	1	1	1	Q
1	1	1	1	1	1	2	Q
1	1	1	1	1	1	3	Q
$\vdots$							
n_{s1}	n_{s2}	n_{s3}	n_{s4}	n_{a2}	n_{a3}	n_{a4}	Q

Fig. 2. The CPT of node Q from figure 1.

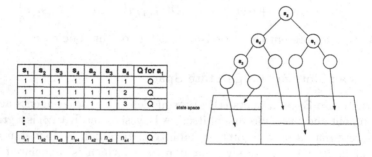

s_1	s_2	s_3	s_4	a_2	a_3	a_4	Q for a_1
1	1	1	1	1	1	1	Q
1	1	1	1	1	1	2	Q
1	1	1	1	1	1	3	Q
$\vdots$							
n_{s1}	n_{s2}	n_{s3}	n_{s4}	n_{a2}	n_{a3}	n_{a4}	Q

Fig. 3. The CPT of node Q converted to a decision tree.

a large state space problem. We suggest to use decision trees to overcome this problem. This is illustrated in figure 3 where we convert a CPT to a decision tree. On the left you see the classic table lookup with constant resolution and on the right you see a decision tree with varying levels of resolution.

Note that the tree is constructed online, and that it is continuously refined during the Q-learning process. In this way the attention of the agent can be shifted to other areas, by refining the resolution at some point in the state space. For more details on the approximating algorithm we refer to [Pye98].

2.3   Bayesian Nets for Incomplete Information

The second problem that we intend to solve in this paper is that of an agent being faced with incomplete information about the environment. In multi-agent systems in general and especially in those where a large number of agents are involved, it is common that at any given moment a specific agent can only directly observe a part of the environment and a subset of the agents.

Our solution consists of learning a Bayesian network over the domain. As we have mentioned before a BN is a concise representation of the joint probability distribution of the domain. This means that, given a subset of variables, the BN can be queried to calculate beliefs for the unknown variables. A belief for a variable consists of a probability for each possible state of the variable. In other words, a BN can be used to calculate the most probable value for an unknown variable and that information can then be used to do Q-learning.

For the moment we concentrate our effort at investigating whether the use of a Bayesian network can help agents to have a more realistic and up-to-date view of the environment and of the other agents. Until now we assume that the Bayesian network of the domain is given beforehand, learning a BN online is part of the future work.

3 Methodology

In this section we clarify where we want to go with our research, how we want to get there and also where we stand today.

The ultimate goal of our research is to define generic techniques that allows agents to learn in large-scaled multi-agent systems. To achieve this, two problems stand out. Firstly, large state and action spaces, and secondly agents being faced with incomplete information about the domain and the other agents.

We want to reach this goal by the following distinct steps. Step 1: Using single agent reinforcement learning to learn an agent simple moves, such as controlling the ball, giving a pass, dribbling, etc. using only low-level actions. All this in a setting where the agents can cope with a large state and action space and with incomplete information. This has already been done by other people [Kos99,Sto00] but is indispensable for the rest of our approach.

Step 2: Using multi-agent RL on small groups of agents to learn them skills such as scoring a goal in a situation with 2 attackers vs. 1 defender and a goalkeeper, learning to defend in the same situation, etc.

An example of incomplete information at this point could be that an agent doesn't exactly know where his teammate is, because he isn't facing in that direction. Then the agent uses the information in his Bayesian network to calculate the most probable position of the agent, given the last known position of the agent and all the other agents he can see.

To reduce the complexity of this task, we want to avoid the action selection module of the agent to manipulate low-level actions directly. Instead we want it to make use of the basic skills learned in step 1.

Step 3: Using multi-agent RL on larger groups of agents (entire teams), using Bayesian networks to help the agents in modelling the domain. Additionally we want the BNs to make use of the local structure in the conditional probability distributions (CPDs) that quantify these BNs. To clarify: our approach must take advantage of the following type of information: an attacker is independent of a defender if they are far from each other, but if they are together on the midfield they are clearly dependent. One way to do this is to insert local structure in the conditional probability distributions of the BNs [Bou96].

Again, to reduce complexity we want to use as much as possible the moves learned in step 2, instead of using basic low-level actions and moves learned during step 1.

At this point in time we are finishing step 1, and starting to tackle the problems associated with step 2. In the next section we will elaborate on what we have achieved so far.

4   Experiments

This section describes some of the experiments that we have conducted.

4.1   Learning to Run to the Ball

The first experiment conducted is an agent who learns to run to the ball. In the learning process he will explore his action set and try to exploit this knowledge to find the optimal policy, namely running to the ball via the shortest path. The experimental settings are as follows : the agent and the ball are put on the field in a random place. Every 1000 steps the ball will be randomly moved to different coordinates.

This simple example illustrates how complicated and large the state space can become. We used Q-learning to learn this skill and the state of the environment is represented by the distance to the ball and the angle of the body with the ball. We considered 2 possible actions for the agent in this situation, *turn* and *dash*. If you discretize the parameters of both actions in 10 intervals, you have alltogether 20 actions. With the default dimensions of the field[1] a player can be at most 125 meter from the ball. If we assume that the distance and the angle are discretized respectively to 1 meter and 1 degree, this makes a total of $125*360*20 = 900.000$ situations for which Q-values have to be learned. So learning with the classical table lookup method can demand quite some resources, even for simple player skills.

As explained in section 2.2 we take advantage of the fact that a lot of these situations are quite similar and that in some cases a Q-value can be associated with a set of situations instead of one situation. In figure 4 you can see a soccer field that is divided in planes with only one Q-value for each plane.

4.2   Learning to Dribble

This section describes an experiment where the goal was to learn the agent to go to the ball and to run with the ball.

---

[1] 68 * 105 meters

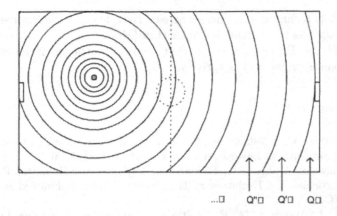

Fig. 4. An example of how a decision tree approach would split the field in regions with an equal Q-value.

We used the same variables to represent the state of the environment as in the previous experiment, but in this case an agent is capable of doing 3 actions: *turn*, *dash* and *kick*. We had to extend the reward function used in the previous experiment so that an agent is not only rewarded when he is close to the ball, but also when he performs a run with the ball.

5   Conclusion

In this paper we introduced a generic solution for learning in multi-agent systems that is able to cope with two important problems in MAS. Firstly, that of learning in large state and action spaces. Secondly, that of an agent being faced with incomplete information about the environment and other agents.

We propose to use Bayesian networks with the conditional probability distributions represented by decision trees instead of classical table lookup to solve the first problem. This reduces the size and complexity of the state and action space, because it causes Q-values to be associated with regions in the state space instead of having to learn a Q-value for every single point in the state space.

For the second problem, we propose to keep a model of the environment in a concise manner. Again we use a Bayesian network to do this, since it is a compact representation of the joint probability distribution over the environment. In this way estimates can be calculated for variables representing a part of the environment that hasn't been observed in recent timesteps.

In our experiments we prove that the learning approach is feasible for an agent running to the ball and dribbling the ball.

6   Future Work

- Allow pruning in the decision tree, so that an agent can also decrease his attention for a specific area of the state space.

- Use other techniques as decisiontrees that learn an adaptive-resolution model, such as the Parti-game algorithm [Moo95].
- Learning the Bayesian network that represents the environment and the other agents online and adaptively.

References

[Bou96]   Boutilier, C., Friedman, N., Goldszmidt, M., and Koller, D. Context-specific independence in Bayesian networks. In Proc. UAI, 1996.

[Def01]   Defaweux, A., Lenaerts, T., Maes, S., Tuyls, K., van Remortel, P., Verbeeck, K., Niching and Evolutionary Transitions in MAS. Submitted at ECOMAS-GECCO 2001.

[Hu99]   Hu, J., Wellman, M. P., Multiagent reinforcement learning in stochastic games. Submitted for publication, 1999.

[Kos99]   Kostiadis, K., Hu, H., Reinforcement Learning and Co-operation in a Simulated Multi-agent System. Proc. of IEEE/RJS IROS'99, Korea. 1999.

[Lit94]   Litmann M.L., Markov games as a framework for multi-agent reinforcement learning. Proceedings of the Eleventh International Conference on Machine Learning, pages 157–163, 1994.

[Moo95]   Moore, A. W., and Atkeson, C. The Parti-game Algorithm for Variable Resolution Reinforcement Learning in Multidimensional State Space. Machine Learning Journal, 21, 1995.

[Nod98]   Noda, I., Matsubara, H., Hiraki, K., and Frank, I., Soccer Server: A Tool for Research om Multiagent Systems. Applied Artificial Intelligence, 12:233-250, 1998.

[Now00]   Nowe, A., Verbeeck, K., Learning Automata and Pareto Optimality for Coordination in MAS. Technical report, COMO, Vrije Universiteit Brussel, 2000.

[Pea88]   Pearl, J., Probabilistic Reasoning in Intelligent Systems: Networks of Plausible Inference. Morgan Kaufmann, San Mateo, CA, 1988.

[Pye98]   Pyeatt, L.D., Howe, A.E., Decision Tree Function Approximation in Reinforcement Learning. Technical Report CS-98-112, Colorado State University, 1998.

[Rus94]   Russell, S., Norvig, P., Artificial Intelligence: a Modern Approach. Prentice Hall Series in Artificial Intelligence. Englewood Cliffs, New Jersey, 1995.

[Sto00]   Stone, P., Layered Learning in Multiagent Systems. A Winning Approach to Robotic Soccer. MIT Press, 2000.

[Sut98]   Sutton, R.S., Barto, A.G., Reinforcement Learning: An Introduction, Cambridge, MA: MIT Press, 1998.

Co-evolution of Morphology and Controller
for Biped Humanoid Robot

Ken Endo[1,2], Funinori Yamasaki[1,3], Takashi Maeno[2], and Hiroaki Kitano[4,1]

[1] Kitano Symbiotic Systems Project, ERATO, JST, Corp.
6-31-15 Jingumae, M31 Suite 6A, Shibuya-ku, Tokyo, Japan
{endo,yamasaki,kitano}@symbio.jst.go.jp
http://www.symbio.jst.go.jp
[2] Keio University
3-14-1 Hiyosi, Kohoku-ku, Yokohama, Japan
maeno@mech.keio.ac.jp
http://www.maeno.mech.keio.ac.jp
[3] Osaka University
[4] Sony Computer Science Laboratories

Abstract. In this paper, we present a method for co-evolving structures and control circuits of bi-ped humanoid robots. Currently, bi-ped walking humanoid robots are designed manually on trial-and-error basis. Although certain control theory exists, such as zero moment point (ZMP) compensation, these theories does not constrain design space of humanoid robot morphology or detailed control. Thus, engineers has to design control program for apriori designed morphology, neither of them shown to be optimal within a large design space. We propose evolutionary approaches that enables: (1) automated design of control program for a given humanoid morphology, and (2) co-evolution of morphology and control. An evolved controller has been applied to a humanoid PINO, and attained more stable walking than human designed controller. Co-evolution was achieved in a precision dynamics simulator, and discovered unexpected optimal solutions. This indicate that a complex design task of bi-ped humanoid can be performed automatically using evolution-based approach, thus varieties of humanoid robots can be design in speedy manner. This is a major importance to the emerging robotics industries.

1 Introduction

Traditionally, robotics systems has been used dominantly in factories for high-precision routine operations. In recent years, there are increasing interest in robotics systems for non-traditional use, as represented by Sony's AIBO, several prototype attempts for home robotics, rescue robots, etc. Among various possible robot shapes, human-like robots, humanoids, are of particular interests because of its visual appeal and less need to modify environment since robots has same degree of freedom to fit into the operational space. Numbers of humanoid robots have been developed aiming at possible deployment of humanoid for office and

G.A. Kaminka, P.U. Lima, and R. Rojas (Eds.): RoboCup 2002, LNAI 2752, pp. 327–341, 2003.

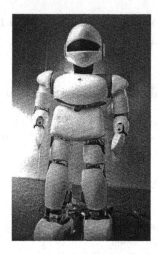 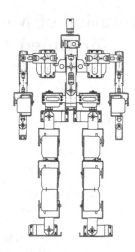

Fig. 1. Humanoid Robot PINO

home [1],[2]. However, all of them requires expensive components and extensive time to design and construct elaborate humanoids.

For humanoid to share a serious proportion of robotics industry, however, low-cost and faster design cycle is required. Research for low-cost and easy-to-design humanoid is essential for industrial exploration. To promote this avenue of research, a humanoid robot PINO [3] was developed with well designed exterior as shown Fig. 1, and using off-the-shelf components. In addition, all technical information for PINO was disclosed under GNU General Public License, as OpenPINO (http://www.openpino.org/), to facilitates open evolution.

There are several interesting issues that have emerged. First, one of the challenges is to identify methods to control such robots to walk and behave in a stable manner by overcoming lack of torque and non-trivial backrush, because cheap servomotor for radio-controlled toys are used to lower the cost. Assuming the current structural design of PINO, the use of traditional ZMP-compensation method did not fits well as it requires sufficient torque and precision to stably control the robot[4]. A new control method needs to be discovered to control it to walk in a stable manner.

Second, a current structural design is not proven to be optimal, and it will never be proven to be optimal because control methods are generally designed assuming specific hardware is given. What we wish to attain is to optimize both morphology and control at the same time, so that it is optimized for the walking behavior, instead of optimizing walking behavior for the given hardware. This is important for open evolution of robotics system, such as OpenPINO.

Our position is that we can learn from evolution of living systems on how they have developed morphology and control systems at the same time. What we should learn from the living creatures is not the structures and components themselves but how they have emerged during evolution. Optimum structures of robots can be designed only when the suitable components and locomotions for the robots are selected appropriately through evolution. Design of the robots, by the robots, for the robots, should be achieved using evolutionary method, whereas designers of the robots should only set up an environmental constraint condition for the robots.

Artificial life is one of the approaches. Sims [5] generated robots that can walk, jump and swim in computer simulation. He also generated virtual creatures which compete each other to obtain one resource [6]. Ventrella [7] presented evolutionary emergence of morphology and locomotion behavior of animated characters. Kikuchi and Hara [8] studied a method of evolutionary design of robots having tree structure that change their morphology in order to adapt themselves to the environmental conditions. However, all of them do not consider how to make practical robots.

On the other hand, evolutionary method has been tried to apply to the practical robots. Kitamura [9] used Genetic Programming, GP [10], to emerge the simple linked-locomotive robot in virtual space. Lipson [11] adopted the rapid prototyping to produce the creatures that were generated in three-dimensional virtual space. However, all of the are far from practical robots.

Until now, we have developed the method for designing the morphology and neural systems of multi-linked locomotive robots [12][13]. Both the morphology and neural systems are represented as a simple large tree structure and both of them are optimized simultaneously using evolutionary computation. This thought can be applied to development of the humanoid robot. In this paper, we propose two evolutionary approaches. At first, an evolved controller has been applied to a humanoid PINO, and attained more stable walking than human designed controller. Secondly, co-evolution were achieved in a precision dynamics simulator.

2   Humanoid Robot PINO

Humanoid robot PINO has been developed to be a platform of humanoid robot research used in many fields of studies such as interaction, artificial intelligence and so on. PINO is composed of such cheap of-the-shelf components as servomotors used in radio control car and so on. Fig. 2 shows the whole system of PINO.

Here, only the control program is generated with Genetic Algorithm. PINO has 6 DOFs for each leg, 5 for each arm, 2 for the trunk, and 2 for the head. 10 DOFs of legs are used for walking and the others are kept staying. Each joint is control to follow the desired trajectory which is given with

$$\dot{\theta}_i = \alpha_i \sin\left(\omega t + \theta_{1i}\right) + \beta_i \cos\left(\omega t + \theta_{2i}\right) \tag{1}$$

Where α_i and β_i denote the gain, and θ_{1i} and θ_{2i} denote the phase difference of sinusoidal and cosine waveform respectively. Also, ω represents the angular velocity. These parameters are generated with GA. we use the evaluate function as follow:

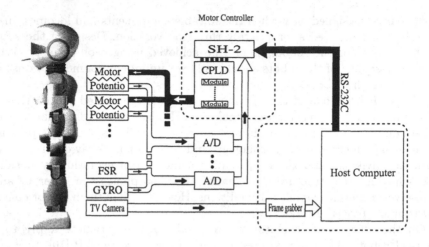

Fig. 2. system of PINO

$$fitness = 800 - 1000 \times height_{foot}$$
$$-5.0 \times energy_{max}$$
$$-0.1 \times energy_{sum}$$
$$-0.8 \times neckangle_{max}$$
$$+5.0 \times time \qquad (2)$$

where $height_{foot}$ is the max height of lifted leg, $energy_{max}$ is the max energy of robot, $energy_{sum}$ is the sum of energy of robot, $neckangle$ is the max angle of neck toward absolute axis and $time$ is the time for which PINO can walk in the dynamic simulation. After 10 second dynamic simulation, all robots are evaluated with this function. The parameters of GA is shown in Table 1.

Table 1. GA parameters

population size	100
generation	300
crossover ratio	0.9
mutation ratio	0.02

As the result, the walking pattern shown in Fig. 3 is generated. However the structure of robot is given before the simulation and control method is a simple oscillatory circuits. We cannot say that this is the optimal robot which has optimal structure and control program. In order to generate the optimal robot, the structure have also to be considered as well as control program. From the next section, we propose the method for co-evolution of morphology and controller of bi-ped humanoid robot.

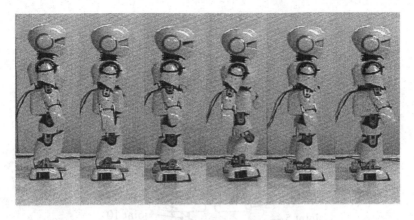

Fig. 3. walking pattern of PINO

3   Model of Robot

3.1   Morphology

Humanoid robots are composed of large numbers of components such as sensors, actuators and so on that it is difficult to consider optimal choice for all of them simultaneously. In order to develop the basic method for generating the both of morphology and locomotion, at first, the models which are easy to simulate in computers for short time are needed. Therefore The multi-link model of robot as shown in Fig. 4 is used here. This three-dimensional robot is composed of 10 links for body and legs and two plates for each foot. The length of five links for upper body, upper limbs and lower limbs change during the evolution though the total length of all links is constant. Joints are numbered as joint 1 to 10 as shown in Fig. 4. Driving torque of each joint can be change from -30kgfcm to 30kgfcm reflecting the real robots that may be constructed in the future study. The joints 3 and 8 have the range of motions between 0 and $\pi/2$ and other joints have between $-\pi/2$ and $\pi/2$ respectively. Densities of the links of leg and upper body are 0.314kg/m and 4.557kg/m, respectively and the length of one leg is 0.28 m. These parameters are based on PINO so as to improve the structure of PINO in the future study. These parameters are constant though the lengths of upper body, upper and lower limbs of the robot change in the process of GA.

3.2   Controller

A lot of researches about generating the locomotion of artificial life or robots with neural network and evolutionary computation have been conducted[14][15]. However the size of chromosomes becomes too large to effeciently generate the valid solution when the both morphology and locomotion are evolved simultaneously. Moreover we have to take the velocity of all joints and external force from the ground in account in order to control the robots. In the biomechanics,

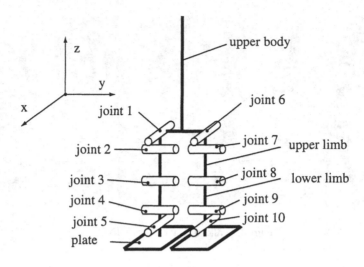

Fig. 4. model of robot

pattern generators are often used for generating the walking pattern of human because the bi-ped walking the periodical and symmetrical motion, that is to say, the structure of the control system can be decided in advance. Until now, many studies of neural oscillators have been conducted. The control system composed of neural oscillators can generate the rhythm for the bi-ped walking. Unlike the recurrent neural network, not so large length of chromosome is needed. However any application for the real robots has not been accomplished. Our goal is designing method that can generate detail structure and locomotion of bi-ped humanoid robot. Therefore we can make the difference between the real world and computer simulation minimal with our method.

The structure of control system is decided according to the basic locomotion of bi-ped walking as shown in fig. 5. Hf and He are neurons for the hip joints. Kf and Ke are neuron for knees. The action of each neuron is expressed as follow.

$$T_i \dot{u}_i = -ui - \sum_{ij} w_{ij} y(u_j) - \beta y(v_i) + U_0$$

$$+ \sum_k FB_k \tag{3}$$

$$T_i' \dot{v} = -v_i - y_i \tag{4}$$

$$y(x_i) = \frac{1}{1 + e^{-\tau(x_i)}} \tag{5}$$

where FB_k is a feedback signal from the body of robot such as the angle of each joint or external force of the feet, u_i is the inner state of the ith neuron, v_i is a variable representing the degree of the adaptation or self-inhibition effect of the ith neuron, U_0 is an external input with a constant rate, w is a connecting weight, and T_i and T_i' are time constants of the inner state and the adaptation

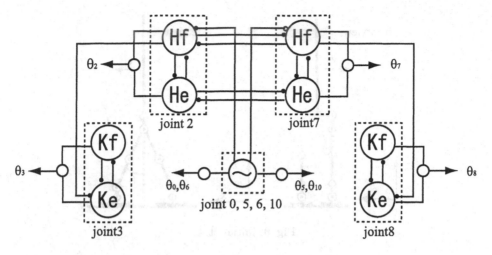

Fig. 5. structure of control system

effect, respectively. The neuron which is in top of Fig. 5 is for joint 0, 5, 6, and 10 that generates only sine signal. In the white circle in Fig. 5, the desired trajectory of each joint is given with following,

$$\theta_k = p_k(y(u_{k1}) - y(u_{k2})) \tag{6}$$

where, θ_k is the desired trajectory and p_k is the gain for the joint k. The desired trajectory of joint is given from the output of neurons. Thus the driving torque of each joint is given with controlling the angle of joints to desired trajectory with PD control. However the maximum driving torque is ±30kgfcm and each gain for PD control are decided in advance. This value is decided based on the PINO. The plates of feet are kept parallel to the ground. This method is often used for bi-ped humanoid robot in order to make the problem simple.

4   Method

4.1   Simulation

The environment which robots walk on is the flat ground. When the dynamic simulation starts, the posture of the robot is in the state of the initial position as show in Fig. 6. Initial angle of θ_i and velocity v_x, v_y are decoded from chromosomes. When the dynamic simulation begin, the control system starts to work and driving torque is generated at the each joint, that is, the robots begin to walk. The only robots with neural systems that can generate the rhythm for walking get periodical and stable bi-ped walking. On the contrary, the robot with bad control system falls down immediately. If the knee, hip and other parts of body of robots gets contact with the ground or the motion of robot continue staying the same place for 0.5sec, simulation is over and next one begin in order to avoid wasting the time.

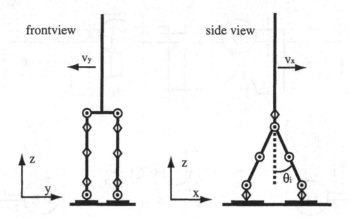

Fig. 6. initial state

Dynamic simulation is conducted to calculate for 5 sec per a robot. the movement of robots resulting from their interaction with the environment. Motions of the robot are calculated by the fourth order Runge-Kutta method. One time step is 0.2 msec. Contact response with ground of the links is accomplished by a hybrid model using both spring and damper under the influence of friction and gravity. The friction is so large that robots never slip during walking.

4.2   Evolutionary Computation

GA is the method for optimization based on the evolution of creature. GA has been used for many complex problems[16]. In this paper, a fixed length genetic algorithm is used to evolve the controllers and morphologies. Each chromosome includes the information of initial angle, velocity, length of each link and weights of each neuron in control systems. Here, we use the GA which deal with real number from 0 to 1. Robots with low-fitness are eliminated by selection, and new robots are produced using crossover and mutation. Then their morphologies and control systems are generated from generation to generation. Finally converge to a reasonably optimal solution.

Crossover is the operation to create new children in the next generation from parents selected due to their fitness. Here, BLX-α [17] is used as the crossover for real number GA. BLX-α is useful to generating the walking pattern because this crossover can explore the best solution more certainly in the middle or latter of calculation, that is to say, this method can adjust the walking pattern in detail. Each factor in the chromosomes is decided as follow:

$$c_{1i,2i} = u(min(p_{1i}, p_{2i}) - \alpha I_i,$$
$$max(p_{1i}, p_{2i}) + \alpha I_i) \tag{7}$$
$$I_i = |p_{1i} - p_{2i}| \tag{8}$$

where $p_1 = (p_{11} \cdots p_{1n})$, $p_2 = (p_{21} \cdots p_{2n})$ are parents, $c_1 = (c_{11} \cdots c_{1n})$, $c_2 = (c_{21} \cdots c_{2n})$ are children, and $u(x, y)$ is the uniform deviates2 from x to

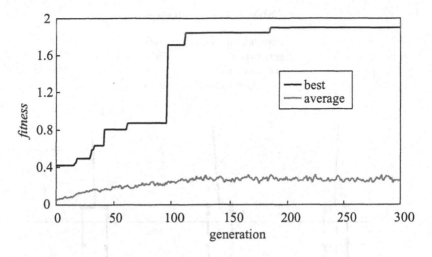

Fig. 7. change of fitness

y. Here α is set to 0.05. In this way, the length of total chromosomes does not change. Selection is operated due to finesses of the robots. The larger the fitness is, the easier the robot is selected. Mutation is the operation to change the part of some chromosomes of robots selected randomly. When mutation occurred to c_i, the new factor c_n is given as follow:

$$c_n = c_i + \frac{rand_g}{10} \tag{9}$$

where $rand_g$ donates the gaussian diates. This operation also works without changing the total length of chromosomes. With these operations, the only robots with large fitness can survive.

During the evolution, walking distance of all robots are evaluated. As the evaluate function,

$$fitness = l_g \tag{10}$$

is used, where l_g is distance of the center of gravity of robots from the initial point. That is to say, robots are evaluated just the moving distance. This condition emerges just bi-ped walking locomotion that robots lift one leg up, at first, brings it forward, and lifts another leg up when the swing leg get contact with the ground.

The parameters of GA is as shown in Table 2. Moreover we use the elite preservation strategy at the same time.

5   Results and Discussions

Calculation using GA is conducted for the model mentioned above. The best fitness and average of all is shown in Fig. 7. At first, all robots can move only

Table 2. GA parameters

population size	100
generation	300
crossover ratio	0.8
mutation ratio	0.05

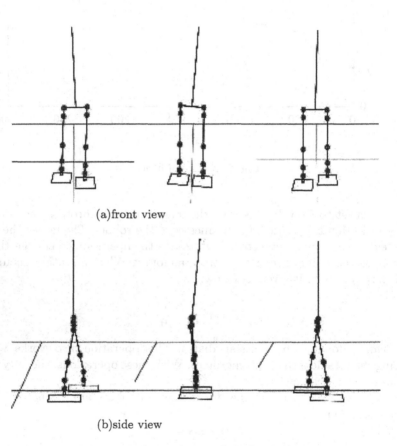

(a)front view

(b)side view

Fig. 8. walking pattern of the best robot

a little bit and the fitnesses are low. Gradually, the robots that can walk are emerged and their moving distance increase. Finally, some robots keep walking till the end of dynamic simulation.

The walking pattern of the best robot at the final generation is shown in Fig. 8, and angle of each joint during walking is shown if Fig. 9. This robot has 0.667m of upper body, 0.1309m of upper limbs and 0.0726m of lower limbs. When the real robot is constructed, these parameters can be more useful than intuition.

After the calculation, the basic walking pattern is emerged that robot lifts one leg up, bring forward and lifts another leg up when the swing leg gets contact

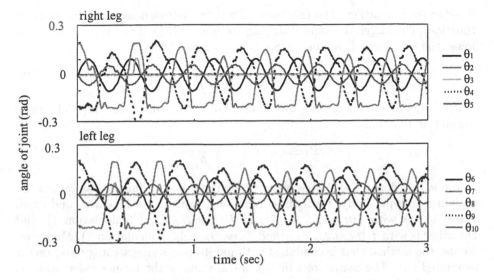

Fig. 9. angle of joint during walking

with the ground. Note that this robot walk with both of joint of knees $\theta_{3,8}$ kept straight. There are three possible reasons. First, robot has low compliance at all joints because of PD controller. Human has the compliant joints and make use of this compliance to walk passively. Therefore, human walks efficiently with swing leg bended. Secondly, this robot walks only on the flat ground in the evolution. In order to walk on the ground which has some slope, or of which shape is not regular, robot cannot walk with this walking pattern. This is the problem about the evaluation and environment robot walk on in the dynamic simulation. Finally, the other evaluations such as efficiency of walking and so on are not considered during the evolution. Here, we pay attention to the establishment of basic method for co-evolution of morphology and controller. In the next section, the design of bi-ped humanoid robot is taken as multi optimal problem and the both the walking distance, efficiency of walking and stability are evaluated.

6   Multi Optimal Problem

In the former calculation, the only one evaluation function is used which is the distance between the center of mass of the robot and initial point. In this section, the design of the robot is taken as the multi optimal problem, MOP, in which two evaluate functions are considered. Moreover two calculations are conducted in order to discuss the influence for the walking pattern of each evaluation.

A distance of walking is often used for emergence of the ability of walking robot because it is easy to be handled and understood. Therefore we define one of the fitness as,

$$fitness_{movability} = l_g \tag{11}$$

like former simulation. The efficiency of walking is taken as a second evaluate function. The larger the sum of driving torque of all joints of the robot is, the lower the efficiency of walking is. So as the second fitness,

$$fitness_{efficiency} = \frac{1}{1 + \int_t \Sigma_i |\tau_i| dt} \tag{12}$$

is defined, where, τ_i is driving torque of joint i per a unit time step. The third evaluation function is

$$fitness_{stability} = \frac{1}{\int |\dot{\theta}_{upper}|} \tag{13}$$

where $\dot{\theta}_{upper}$ donates the angle velocity of upper body. This fitness means the stability of upper body. With these functions, two calculations are conducted, which one is with $fitness_{movability}$ and $fitness_{efficiency}$ (calculation 1), and the other is with $fitness_{movability}$ and $fitness_{stability}$ (calculation 2). Moreover, we use the method that is combined with pareto preserving strategy and vector evaluated GA. The parameters of GA is the same as the former calculation as shown in Table 2.

7   Results and Disccusions

After the calculation, pareto optimal solution, 73 for calculation 1 and 19 for calculation 2, are emerged at the final generaion as shown in Fig. 10. However all of them walk with the leg kept straight like the robot in Fig. 8. The value of $fitness_{movability}$ means just the point which the robot falls down in the calculation 1. In fact, the robot which falls down as soon as the dynamic simulation begins can get high $fitness_{efficiency}$. This robot can survive if other efficient walking pattern dose not exist. This means that the efficiency of walking has no relationship with the way to walk like this. In the calculation 2, the robot which just stand without walking can get high $fitness_{stability}$ if other stable walking pattern dose not exist because upper body does not move. Therefore we can say that this gait is the best solution under the condition which robot with this controller walk on the flat ground.

8   Future Works

In this paper, the walking distance, efficiency of walking and stability of upper body are evaluated for just walking. However we can use many other evaluation functions for other tasks. Secondly, we use the simple multi-link model. More detail structure have to be used in order to improve PINO or make the other real robot. Finally, the movement of upper body such as arm can be considered for walking or the other tasks. The size of chromosomes of our method is so small that all of them are possible to be conducted.

The resulting walking patterns are nowhere near human walking pattern. It it an interesting future subject of study that what constraints give emergence to human like walking patterns.

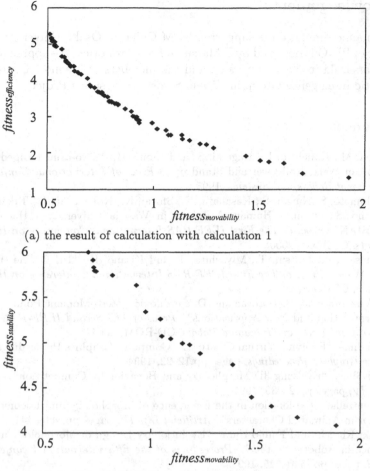

(a) the result of calculation with calculation 1

(b) the result of calculation with calculation 2

Fig. 10. pareto optimal solutions of final generation

9   Conclusions

In this paper, we present a method for co-evolving structures and control circuits of bi-ped humanoid robots. We propose evolutionary approaches that enables: (1) automated design of control program for a given humanoid morphology, and (2) co-evolution of morphology and control. An evolved controller has been applied to a humanoid PINO, and attained more stable walking than human designed controller. Moreover, Co-evolution were achieved in a precision dynamics simulator, and discovered unexpected optimal solutions which walk with knees kept straight with the small size of chromosome.

Acknowledgements

The dynamic simulation is supported by M Ogino in Osaka University and the exterior of PINO is designed by T Matsui in flower-robotics. We appreciate them, Prof. Yamazaki in Keio University, and the members of Maeno laboratory and Symbiotic Intelligence Group in Kitano Symbiotic Systems Project

References

1. Inaba, M., Kanehiro, F., Kagami, S. and Inoue, H. "Two-armed Bipedal Robot that can Walk, Roll Over and Stand up". *Proc. of International Conference on Intelligent Robots and Systems*, 1995.
2. Hashimoto, S. Narita, S., Kasahara, K., Shirai, K., Kobayashi, T., Takanishi, A., Sugano, S., et. al. "Humanoid Robots in Waseda University – Hadaly-2 and WABIAN". *Proc. of The First IEEE-RAS International Conference on Humanoid Robots*, CDROM, 2000.
3. Yamasaki, F., Matsui, T., Miyashita, T. and Kitano, H. "PINO The Humanoid that Walk". *Proc. of The First IEEE-RAS International Conference on Humanoid Robots*, CDROM, 2000.
4. M. Vukobratović, B. Borovac and D. Šurdilović. "Zero-Moment Point – Propoer Interpretation and New Apprications". *Proc. of The Second IEEE-RAS International Conference on Humanoid Robots*, CD-ROM, 2001.
5. Karl Sims. "Evolving Virtual Creatures", Computer Graphics Proceedings". *Computer Graphics Proceedings*, pages pp.12–22, 1994.
6. Karl Sims. "Evolving 3D Morphology and Behavior by Competition". *Artificial Life IV*, pages pp.28–39, 1994.
7. J. Ventrella. "Exploration in the Emergence of Morphology and Locomotion Behavior in Animated Characters". *Artificial Life IV*, pages pp. 436–441, 1994.
8. Kohki Kikuchi and Fumio Hara. "Evolutionary Design of Morphology and Intelligence in Robotic System". *Proceedings of the fifth international conference on SAB*, pages pp. 540–545, 1998.
9. Shinzo Kitamura, Yuzuru Kakuda, Hajime Murao, Jun Gotoh and Masaya Koyabu. "A Design Method as Inverse Problems and Application of Emergent Computations". *SICE*, Vol.36(No.1):pp. 90–97, 2000.
10. J. Koza. *"Genetic Programming II"*. MIT Press, 1994.
11. H. Lipson and J. B. Plollack. "Automatic design and manufacture of robotic lifeforms". *Nature*, Vol.406(No.6799):pp. 974–978, 2000.
12. Ken Endo, Takashi Maeno. "Simultaneous Generation of Morphology of Body and Neural System of Multi-Linked Locomotive Robot using Evolutionary Computation". *Proceedings of the 32nd International Symposium on Robotics*, CDROM, 2001.
13. Ken Endo, Takashi Maeno. "Simultaneous Design of Morphology of Body, Neural Systems and Adaptability to Environment of Multi-Link-Type Locomotive Robots using Genetic Programming". *Proc. IEEE/RSJ International Conference on Intelligent Robots and Systems*, pages pp.2282–2287, 2001.
14. Fukuda, T., Komata, Y., Arakawa, T. "Stabilization Control of Biped Locomotion Robot based learning with GAs having Self-adaptive Mutation and Recurrent Neural Networks". *Proc. of the International Conference on Robotics and Automation*, pages pp.217–222, 1997.

15. Cao, M., Kawamura, A. "A Design Method of Neural Oscillatory Networks for Generation of Humanoid Biped walking Patterns". *Proc. of the International Conference on Robotics and Automation*, pages pp.2357–2362, 1998.
16. Kitano, H. "Designing neural networks using genetic algorithms with graph generation system". *Complex System*, pages pp.454–461, 1990.
17. Eshleman, L. J. and Schaffer, J. D. "Real-Coded Genetic Algorithms and Interval-Schemata". *Foundations of Genetic Algorithms 2*, pages pp.187–202, 1993.

Towards Real-Time Strategic Teamwork: A RoboCup Case Study

Kenichi Yoshimura[1], Nick Barnes[1], Ralph Rönnquist[3], and Liz Sonenberg[2]

[1] Department of Computer Science and Software Engineering
The University of Melbourne, Parkville, VIC, Australia
{kyosh,nmb}@cs.mu.oz.au
[2] Department of Information Systems
The University of Melbourne, Parkville, VIC, Australia
l.sonenberg@dis.unimelb.edu.au
[3] Agent-Oriented Software Pty. Ltd. 221 Bouverie St. Carlton, VIC Australia
ralph.ronnquist@agent-software.com.au

Abstract. RooBots competed in the F180 League of the RoboCup 2001 competition in Seattle, USA. In this article, we present an architectural overview of our system involving an integration of an agent-oriented programming framework to support strategic decisions, with various low-level perception and control elements. Our AI Module includes a novel mechanism to facilitate dynamic formation change by an individual agent and we report a preliminary evaluation of the approach drawn from performance in the 2001 competition.

1 Introduction

Two University of Melbourne RoboCup teams, MU-Cows 2000 [4] and RooBots 2001 [8], have participated in the F180 League. In 2000 the emphasis was on hardware and software issues at the individual robot level of action. A major advance for 2001, and the focus of this article, was the addition of an AI Module enabling the coding, and rapid modification, of high level strategies.

In this paper we motivate an agent-oriented approach to robotic soccer for hardware leagues, and address the following questions associated with the implementation of the AI Module.

1. How can one take advantage of the high-level abstractions supported by the agent-oriented approach for specifying strategic teamwork within the constraints of a real-time domain and the realities of low level robot control? (Sections 2 and 3)
2. How can one facilitate tactically appropriate, dynamic restructuring of team formations (Sections 4 and 5)?

2 Architectural Overview

Our base system SmHost has a modular architecture, with interactions among the modules specified by interface definitions. The architecture proved highly

G.A. Kaminka, P.U. Lima, and R. Rojas (Eds.): RoboCup 2002, LNAI 2752, pp. 342–350, 2003.
© Springer-Verlag Berlin Heidelberg 2003

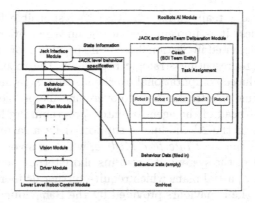

Fig. 1. Architectural Overview of SmHost and AI Module.

successful in facilitating modification of the base system: easy customisation for different hardware configurations (eg. a new path planner for omnidirectional robots), reusing existing components (eg. the vision system), and development of new modules (eg. the AI module). The resulting system used in 2001 is illustrated in Figure 1.

In the F180 League a camera is mounted above the field, enabling teams to perceive most required information with each frame. Objects are identified by their colours, and positions of the objects are calculated using camera calibration with associated uncertainty.

The *Behaviour Module* interacts with the *Path Planning Module* to implement basic skills such as kicking, dribbling, marking of an opposition robot, moving to a point, and goalkeeper behaviour. The behaviours are robust in the face of failures. For example, once it commits to a particular behaviour, a robot pursues a given goal until a new behaviour is selected. We use a method that combines deliberative and reactive path planning to plan a collision-free path. The *Behaviour Module* specifies a destination anywhere within the field and the robot moves to it efficiently without collisions.

3   The AI Module

The behaviour of an agent depends on its role. We used two distinctive roles for field players – a defensive and an offensive role – and the specialised goalkeeper. Role assignment occurs by manual setting based on formations (Section 3.3) but can be overridden by other run-time considerations (Section 4). Behaviour specification occurs at a strategic level (Section 3.4) both for individual agent behaviour, and team-level coordination.

3.1   Module Overview

The module has two major components – the *Deliberation Module* and the *Jack Interface Module*. The *Deliberation Module* comprises agents representing individual robots and a team entity (the Coach) responsible for coordination of individual activities. It is implemented using an agent-oriented programming environment, as discussed in Section 3.2. While providing programming abstractions suitable for representing strategic behaviour, the relatively low speed of this module introduced computational overheads that were unacceptable for the high-speed, real-time robotic domain. To overcome the problem of the inherited computational overhead of the agent-oriented programming framework, the deliberation process of the AI Module is supported by a faster, short-term goal selection module – the *Jack Interface Module*, which is invoked at the same frequency as the rest of the system. It performs short-term goal selection based on the instructions, ie. partial plans which require further deliberation before being mapped to one of the behaviours provided by the Behaviour Module.

3.2   The Agent-Oriented Programming Environment

JACK Intelligent Agents has been developed by Agent Oriented Software Pty. Ltd. [1] to provide general-purpose agent-oriented extensions to the Java programming language. The theoretical Belief Desire Intention (BDI) model of artificial intelligence was used as a foundation of the JACK framework. JACK agents are autonomous software components that have explicit goals to achieve or events to handle (desires). Each agent holds a plan library, i.e. a collection of plans that provide sequences of instructions to achieve a goal or handle a given event. Plans can be abstract, or partial, requiring completion at run-time. The agent pursues its given goals, adopting the appropriate plans (intentions) according to its current set of data (beliefs) about the state of the world.

SimpleTeam [3, 9] is a plug-in extension of JACK Intelligent Agents. It provides an abstraction that separates the specification of team-level strategies and the specification of individual agents' activities. This was achieved by the introduction of a new software entity, a *team instance*. A team instance is the software representative for a team, and it exists to coordinate behaviour and facilitate agent communication.

In SimpleTeam, a system is modelled in terms of participating agents (teams). A programmer can specify a particular type of team instance by declaring what constitutes a team in terms of roles, eg. an attacking team consists of left wing role and right wing role. Furthermore, a role only specifies the requirements to take on the role, rather than specifying the actual teams (agents). That is, team members can be selected dynamically at run-time depending on the availabilities of the agents. The instance of the team is used to monitor team progress, and coordinate activities among the team members as required.

Team instances can also be compared with the so-called facilitators used in multi-agent systems (see, for instance, Open Agent Architecture [2]). However, while facilitators normally provide only a communications and brokering facility, team instances actually perform all reasoning related to coordination and distribution of activity among members, which provides facilities for specification of teams with coordination of joint activities among the team members.

3.3   Formations, Roles, and Zone-Based Distribution of Tasks

We started our design and implementation by using the previously studied notion of *formations*, *roles* and *zones* to develop our team [6]. A *formation* is a representation of overall team strategy, summarising the number of defenders and attackers. A *role* is an explanation of responsibilities of an individual player (ie. one of `defender`, `attacker` or `goalkeeper`). For example, a player taking on a role attacker aims to score a goal while considering the best course of action to make the contributions to the team. A *zone* is a portion of the field for which a player is responsible or allowed to reallocate itself freely. A different team formation can be selected from the graphical user interface of the system.

3.4   High Level Behaviours

The AI Module consists of: the Jack Interface Module that connects the high-level (strategy) with appropriate low-level behaviours (motion) (Section 2); five agents, each an ordinary BDI agent that determines the behaviour of an individual robot based on its current role, as determined by the initial formation (Section 3.3) or other factors (Section 4); and a SimpleTeam team entity (the Coach), responsible for role assignments and coordination of individual agent activities. The Coach performs a role assignment depending on the current team's formation and availability of the agents in the system (ie. a robot can be removed from the field due to hardware problems or being penalised by the referee). The Coach posts an appropriate event to the individual agent in the system when new state information arrives (eg. defender event for a defensive agent).

An individual agent decides what to do depending on its current role, which in turn is specified by various TeamPlans of the Coach team entity. An example is shown in the following statements of the TeamPlan perform role assignments. The first statement posts a defensive event to robot 1, and the second statement posts an offensive event to robot 2. A different combination of those specifications allows a designer to develop a new team strategy without having to specify low level behaviours.

```
@team_achieve(coach.robot1,
    coach.robot1.cooperative_defence_event());
@team_achieve(coach.robot2,
    coach.robot2.cooperative_offence_event());
```

This modular separation of high-level and lower-level behaviours allowed rapid modification of the team-level strategy (by modification of TeamPlans for Coach team entity), and modifications of the individual agent behaviours (by modification of Plans for the individual BDI agent).

A new team strategy can be integrated into the system by writing a TeamPlan for the Coach team entity (ie. invoking a different combination of behaviours by the individual agent). The new plan can be added to the plan library of the Coach team entity without modifying any other components of the system.

Below is a selection of the partial plans available to the deliberation components (*JACK-level behaviours*). For example, the Attacker Behaviour involves deliberation to pass the ball to a team member when the agent is not in a position to take a direct shot at the opponent goal. An identification of a pass receiver is done in the Jack Interface Module as the location of the receiver is constantly changing.

- **DEFENCE CLEAR BALL BEHAVIOUR**: The robot attempts to clear the ball from the team's defence zone. It attempts to pass the ball to the closest attacker (a robot located in the opponent defence zone) or kick the ball towards opponent goal. If the ball is located too close to the own goal, it dribbles the ball away from the goal before it attempts to kick the ball.
- **ATTACKER BEHAVIOUR**: Behaviour of forward player. If it has possession of the ball, it attempts to shoot a goal, pass the ball to team members, or dribble to a better position, depending on the distance between the current location and the opponent goal. If it does not have ball possession, it attempts to move to an open space and wait for a pass from team members.

4   Dynamic Restructuring of Formations

Stone and his colleague achieved flexibility by switching the team's formation dynamically using globally accessible information such as a time remaining and a current score difference. The triggering conditions for a dynamic formation change was specified in *Locker-room agreements* [6]. We adapted Parker's idea of *motivation* [5] for the RoboCup domain to introduce a different form of flexibility to the formation, role and zone based approach. In Parker's work, an individual robot takes its progress (ie. relative performance of the task), and the progress of other robots, into account when it makes a decision regarding to which task the robot should commit. Rather than modelling the motivation using relative performance, which seems impossible to obtain meaningfully in this domain, we modelled the *urgency* of the situation.

The urgency motivations utilise information such as number of team members in defence and offence zone, distance between player and ball, impatience, and defensiveness and offensiveness factors. The approach proved to be useful in the domain as it allowed dynamic restructuring of the current formation, in which an individual agent decides to disobey the current formation and role specifications, and participate in an activity that requires an immediate attention. The defensiveness and offensiveness factors express how much risk the team is willing to take in order to gain potential benefits (eg. when the offensiveness is set to zero, the team is not offensive at all. Consequently, a defensive agent would never consider participating in an offensive activity). Those values can be modified through the graphical user interface of the AI Module.

In summary, there were two distinctive roles within the system: a defensive role and an offensive role. Depending on the role an agent is playing, the contribution made by the agent differs. In principle, the formation specification assigns a role to an individual agent. Depending on a result of an individual agent's urgency calculation, it can either decide to play the specified role, or another role that appears more urgent. Although the urgency calculation allows an individual agent to decide whether or not to obey its primary role specification (ie. specified by a current formation), the agent *remembers* its primary role even if it decides to disobey the role temporarily. That is, once an *urgent* situation ends, the agent returns to its primary role. Hence, the current formation of the team and the results of the urgency calculations by the individual agents determine the number of agents playing a particular role.

5   Evaluation

The key question we would like to answer is: can (relatively abstract) strategic behaviours be specified in the deliberation component (as a combination of individual and team behaviours) in a way that robust and effective team play occurs, when the strategy is elaborated in context at run-time, and then mapped to low level behaviours. A thorough evaluation of the effectiveness of the combination of the various elements integrated into our system would require extensive empirical work, in both 'set plays' and real game situations.

In the following evaluations, we explore the added flexibility in dynamic restructuring that may be offered by allowing the urgency calculations to override the manual assignment to attacker or defender roles. Further analysis and evaluation of the system is reported in [10].

For the purpose of this analysis, we used videos of footage taken from the overhead game camera. The output of the videos can be fed into the system in the same way as the real game setting, and the system is able to perform analysis of the current situation in the same way except it cannot actually control the robots, ie. the system assumes video output is the actual image taken from the overhead camera, and performs analysis to prepare instructions for the robots. Although it does not allow evaluation of every individual aspect of the system in every possible scenario, it does allow us to see how the system really performs given the situations that arise in the tournament.

The video can also be used to identify and comment on the strengths of particular aspects of performance against a real competitor. This is in some ways better than just setting up own experiments as it shows fitness for purpose to an external goal, rather than just in a contrived situation.

Although the game against RoGi ended as a scoreless draw, it is an interesting game for post-game analysis because the RooBots did not create enough opportunities to score goals during the game. There were number of occasions when additional robots in the offensive activities could have increased the chance of scoring goals against them because RoGi was playing very defensively. Figure 2 illustrates a typical situation which was observed frequently during the game.

Figure 3 illustrates the motivation of defensive agent D_1 during the game against the RoGi Team. The result suggests there were several occasions in

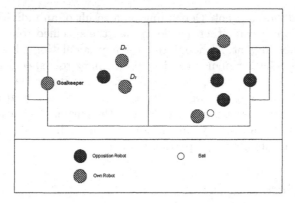

Fig. 2. RoGi Team's very defensive strategy made RooBots offensive robots to score a goal very difficult.

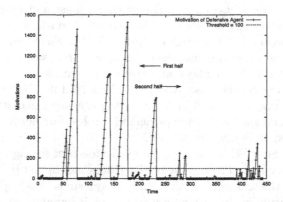

Fig. 3. Motivation of defensive agent D_1 during the game against RoGi illustrating threshold-dependent potential role shifts.

which the agent could have been eager to participate in the offensive activity, ie. the value of motivation exceeded the threshold value.

A comparison of the motivation in the first half and the second half suggests RoGi changed their strategy in the second half of the game, because the increase in the agent's motivation was much greater in the first half (maximum value of 1500) while the value was much less in the second half (maximum value of 340). The comparison also suggests it was a more dynamic game in the second half because urgent situations are resolved much faster - hence the maximum value of the motivation was less.

Post-game analysis of the game against RoGi revealed the most opportunities for the urgency calculation to have an impact. However the post-game analysis of the game against Cornell also deserves comment. Both Cornell and RooBots had reliable and fast omnidirectional robots, and demonstrated a number of strategic plays. Of particular note is the cooperative defensive strategy of the

RooBots' team, discussed further in [10]. The defensive robots were marking the opposition robots cooperatively, which minimised the efficiency of Cornell's passing game, and kept direct shots on goal to a minimum. The defensive agents switched their activities flexibly among themselves, for example, they identified unmarked opposition players to mark, and demonstrated emergent cooperative strategic placement to minimise goal scoring (eg the second robot places itself behind the defensive robot located closest to the ball). Cornell Big Red scored most of their goals when the RooBots' team was penalised near the goal.

6   Discussion

Roobots played competitively in the 2001 competition. The AI Module was developed using a general-purpose, agent-oriented programming environment that facilitated specification, and rapid modification of strategic behaviours at an abstract level that was elaborated, in context, at run-time. To manage real-time operation while allowing adequate time for deliberation, timing issues were handled by coding at an intermediate level and by adopting a rapid computation to guide role switching and team restructuring.

Preliminary evaluation of the addition to the AI module of the local computation of heuristics to facilitate timely role changes, has demonstrated the viability of the approach to impact on the play of the game, even though this approach was not able to be tested in live games. Our ability to encode and rapidly adapt *both* individual and team behaviour at the strategic level during the competition was a clear demonstration of the value of high-level, agent oriented, programming. Areas of attention for future work include: additional knowledge engineering to encode a richer range of behaviours; and further exploration of ways to enhance dynamic role allocation and team restructuring.

Acknowledgments

The authors would like to acknowledge the effort and involvement of the RooBots 2001 team. In particular, we would like to express our appreciation to Andrew Howard, now at ISI, for configuring the simulation for our experiments. We are especially grateful for the significant financial support provided by the Advanced Engineering Centre for Manufacturing, a joint activity of the University of Melbourne and RMIT University.

References

1. P. Busetta, R. Rönnquist, A. Hodgson, A. Lucas: JACK Intelligent Agents - Components for Intelligent Agents in Java. Proceedings of the International Conference on Autonomous Agents (2001)
2. P. R. Cohen, A. Cheyer, M. Wang, S. C. Baeg: An open agent architecture. Proceedings of the AAAI Spring Symposium on Software Agents. (1994)

3. A. Hodgson, R. Rönnquist, P. Busetta Specification of Coordinated Agent Behaviour (the SimpleTeam Approach). Technical Report, Agent Oriented Software Pty. Ltd. (2001)
4. A. Howard: MuCows. RoboCup-00: Robot Soccer World Cup IV Springer LNCS Vol. 2019 (2001)
5. L. E. Parker: Heterogeneous Multi-Robot Cooperation PhD thesis. Department of Electrical Engineering and Computer Science, Massachusetts Institute of Technology (1994)
6. P. Stone, M. Veloso: Task decomposition, dynamic role assignment, and low-bandwidth communication for real-time strategic teamwork. Artificial Intelligence, volume 100, number 2, (June, 1999)
7. D. Pynadath, M. Tambe: An automated teamwork infrastructure for heterogeneous software agents and humans. Journal of Autonomous Agents and Multi-agent Systems (2001)
8. J. Thomas, K. Yoshimura, A. Peel: RooBots. RoboCup-01: Robot Soccer World Cup V (2002)
9. K. Yoshimura, R. Rönnquist, E. Sonenberg: An approach to specifying coordinated agent behaviour. Proceedings of the Third Pacific Rim International Workshop on Multi-Agents (2000)
10. K. Yoshimura: Towards real-time strategic teamwork in robotic soccer. Master Thesis. The University of Melbourne (2002).
   http://www.cs.mu.oz.au/~kyosh/thesis/thesis.html

MUREA: A MUlti-Resolution Evidence Accumulation Method for Robot Localization in Known Environments

Marcello Restelli[1], Domenico G. Sorrenti[2], and Fabio M. Marchese[3]

[1] Politecnico di Milano
Dept. Elettronica e Informazione
Piazza Leonardo da Vinci 32, 20135 Milano, Italy
restelli@elet.polimi.it
[2] Università degli Studi di Milano - Bicocca
Dept. Informatica, Sistemistica e Comunicazione
Via Bicocca degli Arcimboldi 8, 20126 Milano, Italy
sorrenti@disco.unimib.it
[3] Università degli Studi di Milano - Bicocca
Dept. Informatica, Sistemistica e Comunicazione
Via Bicocca degli Arcimboldi 8, 20126 Milano, Italy
marchese@disco.unimib.it

Abstract. We present MUREA (MUlti-Resolution Evidence Accumulation): a mobile robot localization method for known 2D environments. It is an evidence accumulation method where the complexity is reduced by means of a multi-resolution scheme. The added value of the contribution, in the authors opinion, are 1) the method per sé; 2) the capability of the system to accept both raw sensor data as well as independently generated localization estimates; 3) the capability of the system to give out a (less) accurate estimate whenever asked to do so (e.g. before its regular completion), which could be called *any-time localization*.

Our experience in robotic research (specifically RoboCup competitions) allows us to assert that a localization system cannot rely on a reduced set of workspace features. It often happens that some of the features, expected to be detectable, are not perceived. The reasons for this can range from occlusion, to noise on the sensors, to imperfect algorithms processing the sensor data. Although we use omnidirectional vision as the main sensing, we do feel the convenience of a localization algorithm independent from a specific sensory system. Moreover, we wanted a system capable to accept raw sensor data, without any intermediate interpretation.

We aimed also at what we call *any-time localization*, i.e. the capability of the system to provide its best estimate whenever a timeout expires. This results very useful in a realistic real-time robot system; on the other hand, the usual behavior of other known robot localization algorithms is not to have an available output until their completion.

The remainder of the paper is organized as follows: in section 1 we very briefly review a very reduced set of localization approaches, the ones more related to

G.A. Kaminka, P.U. Lima, and R. Rojas (Eds.): RoboCup 2002, LNAI 2752, pp. 351–358, 2003.

our approach. In section 2 we describe our proposal. Some results are presented and discussed in section 3, while in section 4 we draw some conclusions.

1 Localization Methods

The approaches more related to the one here presented are all based on the use of sensors which provide dense data. They accomplish a match between dense sensor scans and the map of the environment without the need for extracting landmark features. Most of them base on probabilistic approaches.

Scan matching techniques [1] use *Kalman Filtering* and assume that both the movement and measurements are affected by White Gaussian Noise. These techniques being local methods, cannot recover from bad matches and/or errors in the model. *Grid-based Markov Localization* [2] operates on raw sensor measurements. This approach, when applied to fine-grained grids, could turn into a very expensive computation. In order to overcome the huge search-space, these techniques use to include several optimizations [3]; the most frequent being to update only the data in a small area around the robot. Recently, *Monte Carlo Localization* [4] gained increasing interest. This approach bases on randomly generating localization hypotheses. In contrast with Kalman filtering techniques, these methods can globally localize a robot; with respect to grid-based Markov localization, the Monte Carlo methods require less memory and are more accurate. Another interesting method is due to Olson [5]; in order to match the map generated by the robot sensors with the a priori known map of the environment, the method bases on a maximum-likelihood similarity measure. In order to find the pose with the best match, it imposes a grid decomposition of the search-space and applies a branch-and-bound technique to limit the travel. The main drawback of this approach is the high computational cost required to compare the maps.

2 System Architecture and Localization Algorithm

The system has three main components: the map of the environment, the perceptions and the localization engine. The environment is represented by a 2D geometrical map that can be inserted in the system "manually" (i.e. through a configuration file) or can be built by an automatic system, as e.g. in [6]. The map is made up of simple geometrical primitives, i.e. points, lines, circles, etc., that we call *types*. For each primitive a list of attributes must be specified, which describe its main characteristics. Moreover, for each map element we have to specify the sensors able to sense it.

On the other hand, we have sensor data and, possibly, other localization applications. Both produce perceptions, intended to be everything that provides information (even partial) about the the robot pose. Each perception is characterized by type, attributes, and the sensor that perceived it; these data are useful in order to reduce the number of comparisons between perceptions and map elements, as shown later in section 2.2.

The localization engine takes in input the map of the environment as well as the perceptions, and outputs the estimated pose(s) of the robot (if the environment and/or the perceptions have inherent ambiguities).

As mentioned above, we want an evidence accumulation method, where the difficulty is in accumulating the evidence while working at high resolution in order to get an accurate estimate. We divide the search-space in subregions (hereafter cells, section 2.1), to which we associate a counter, as usual in evidence accumulation methods. Since we deal with a localization problem for a mobile robot in 2D, the search-space is a 3D space, i.e. (X, Y, Θ), the coordinates of the robot pose.

Each perception increases the counter associated to a cell if some cell point is compatible with both the perception and the model (see section 2.2 for compatibility). Then, on the basis of the votes collected by each cell, the system selects (section 2.3) the ones which are more likely to contain the correct robot pose. This process is further iterated on the selected cells (section 2.4) until at least one termination condition is matched (section 2.5).

2.1   The Cells

The localization task is to find the point (x, y, θ) in the 3D search space (X, Y, Θ) that gives the best fit between the perceptions and the world model. In order to achieve this goal, the search-space is divided into cells. We currently define a cell as a convex connected subregion of the search space. In particular, unlike other approaches, we decided to use cylindrical cells, characterized by a circle in the plane (X, Y) and a segment on the Θ axis. The reason for this is the simplification in the subsequent section 2.2, on the voting phase.

The use of cylindrical cells implies that we have to cope with the overlapping of adjacent cells, in the (X, Y) subspace. We distributed the elements (circles in (X, Y)) of our decomposition as if we had an hexagonal tessellation (see Figure 1 on the right). This choice, with respect to other 2D tessellations, allows for a minimum overlapping between the elements of our decomposition. Each circle is therefore centered on an hexagon and its radius is equal to the length of an edge of it.

2.2   The Voting Phase

The system determines, for each cell, how many perceptions are compatible with both the map and a robot pose inside the cell. We define a function Γ that, given a perception, a map element and a pose returns *true* if, in that pose, the specified map element can generate that perception, otherwise it returns *false*:

$$\Gamma : P \times M \times L^n \to \{true, false\} \qquad (1)$$

where P, M and L^n are respectively the set of all the possible perceptions, the set of all the map elements and the n-dimensional space of the robot pose.

We say that a perception p *votes* a cell C iff exists a map element m so that: $Attrib(p) \subseteq Attrib(m)$, $Sensor(p) \subseteq Sensor(m)$ and $\exists\, \bar{l} \in C \mid \Gamma(p, m, \bar{l})$,

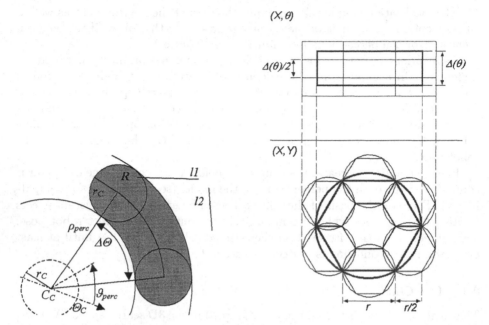

Fig. 1. On the left: Verification of the compatibility between a perception and a cell. On the right: The generation of the refined hypotheses

where *Attrib* returns the attributes of its argument and *Sensor* returns the sensor(s) associated to its argument.

In other words, the attributes of the perception must be one of those associated to the map element, the map element must be perceivable by the sensor that has produced the perception, and a pose inside the cell must exists that is *compatible* with both the perception and the map element. It is worth noting that Γ is in charge of checking whether a perception, e.g. a point perception, can be an observation of a certain map element for the pose associated to the cell, e.g. a line. The possible lack of homogeneity of the two items, i.e. perception and map-element, is therefore confined inside Γ.

See Figure 1 on the left for an example of what happens in this phase. Here we have to evaluate whether the point perception $(\rho_{perc}, \vartheta_{perc})$ votes the cell $C \equiv (C_C, \Theta_C, r_C, \Delta\Theta)$, where we called: C_C the point (X_C, Y_C), Θ_C the central value of the robot orientation interval for the cell, r_C the radius of the cell in the (X, Y) plane and $\Delta\Theta$ is the robot orientation interval.

In order to get the vote, a map element should be found inside the depicted region **R**. In the example we have two map elements, of type *line*; this type is obviously compatible with a *point* perception. In this case, the cell C gets the vote because the map element $l1$ intersects the region **R**, not because of the map element $l2$.

The more the votes of a cell, the more reliable is the match between the perceived world and its representation, and the more are the chances that the robot pose falls inside that cell.

2.3   The Selection Phase

After the voting phase, we select the most promising cells, which will be subdivided and considered in the next voting phase. By most promising we mean most compatible with the input sensor data, where the compatibility is as described above. Therefore the aim is now to search for the maxima in the vote accumulator. It should be now clear that a selection takes place at each level of resolution, which increases at each iteration of the whole process. At the each level we look for the absolute maximum, and we select all the cells which took more votes than a given percentage of the absolute maximum.

2.4   The Generation of the Refined Hypotheses

Given a cell C (father) of radius r and height $\Delta(\theta)$ its refinement consists in producing 21 cells (sons) with radius $r/2$ and height $\Delta(\theta)/2$, disposed as shown in Figure 1 on the right. In practice, we create a son with halved dimensions with respect to the father and put it at the center of the father. Then we surround it with other cells of the same size by respecting an hexagonal distribution of our tessellation elements (circles) in the (X, Y) plane. The union of the sons is a region larger than the region occupied by the father. The reason for this choice (different from those used in similar approaches) is in what we call *the phase problem*, i.e. in the misalignment of tessellation boundaries and the correct localization. Actually, if the correct pose falls near a border of a cell, because of the noise affecting the sensor data, some votes could scatter among contiguous cells.

2.5   The Termination Condition

The process sketched above terminates when any of the following condition holds.

1. The size of the cells gets smaller than the precision required by the application. This is the most favorable situation, since in this case the noise is not perceivable, at the precision required by the application.
2. The size of the cells gets so small that the noise on the sensor data creates a vote dispersion. This is an unfavorable situation because, due to the noise, the process comes to a stop before reaching the required precision.
3. The most voted cell did not receive more than a given percentage of the available votes. This is an even worse situation, because the support from the sensor data is really low.
4. A timeout expires. In this situation the precision of the solution is not relevant.

2.6   The Selection of the Solution

When one of the termination condition takes place, the system has to provide its currently best solution(s). In order to accomplish this task we cluster the adjacent cells in the vote accumulator as long as voted cells are encountered. Then we compute the barycenter of the cluster as the weighted average of the cell centers. The weights are the votes received by each cell. This is the output of the system. It is supplied with an associated estimate of its precision. This estimate is based upon the size of the cluster, which is useful for discriminating the case in which the solution has been required too early (e.g. for a timeout) or when there is not enough support from the data. Moreover, the solution is output with an associated reliability, which is correlated to the received votes.

3   Localization Experiments

We made some experiments with a robot equipped with an omnidirectional vision system, based on a multi-part mirror [7]. This mirror allows the vision system to have a resolution of about 40 mm, for distances under 6 m. We put the robot into a partially built RoboCup F2000 field. In the experiments we did not use either the flag-posts nor the poles that should surround the field, so the experiments are quite general. We defined three map elements of type line and attribute "blue" to describe the blue goal, seven lines and one circle with attribute "white" to describe the borders of the field. We also specified that every map element can be perceived by the vision sensor. The vision sensor produces just two types of perceptions: white point perception and blue direction perception. Since the goals are not flat objects, some of the green-blue transitions generates blue point perceptions which are affected by large radial errors; therefore we used only the direction for the blue perceptions.

We placed the robot inside the field at known positions and then we ran the localization procedure. The required accuracy was set to 100 mm and 1°; the system will stop when the cell size will be smaller than the setting. The reference system is located in the center of the field, with the x axis directed toward the blue goal. The computation ran on a PC Pentium III 800 MHz under Linux Mandrake 8.1.

In order to clarify the functioning of the localization process, in the following we show how the number of selected cells changes at each step of the process. Two experiments are reported in Figure 2 and in table 1.

The data in the tables are organized as follows: each row is associated to a level, i.e. a set of cells that have the same size, and contains the data for the selected cells. In the first two columns there are the dimensions of the cells, expressed by their radius and height. The third column contains the ratio between the number of cells that has been selected and the number of cells tested for compatibility, while the last column contains the percentage of votes (with respect to the maximum number of votes available) obtained by the most voted cell.

In the first experiment 58 perceptions were collected by the vision system. The real robot pose, manually measured, was $x = 20.5$ cm, $y = -150$ cm, $\theta = 0°$. The localization process returned the pose $\widehat{x} = 17.07$ cm, $\widehat{y} = -146.19$ cm, $\widehat{\theta} = 1.04°$. The whole process took 367 ms.

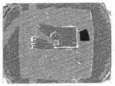

Fig. 2. Experiments: the first couple of images is related to experiment 1, while the second one is related to experiment 2

Table 1. Experiment 1 on the left, Experiment 2 on the right; data of the cells which have been selected

$\rho(cm)$	$\Delta(\theta)(°)$	cells	% max votes
320	90.00	4/4	100%
160	45.00	22/56	100%
80	22.50	28/209	100%
40	11.25	7/305	99%
20	5.63	3/64	91%
10	2.81	1/43	81%
5	1.41	2/21	67%

$\rho(cm)$	$\Delta(\theta)(°)$	cells	% max votes
320	90.00	4/4	100%
160	45.00	23/56	100%
80	22.50	17/207	100%
40	11.25	5/229	95%
20	5.63	3/62	90%
10	2.81	2/49	83%
5	1.41	3/35	71%

In the second experiment 163 perceptions were collected by the vision system. The real robot pose, manually measured, was $x = 350\ cm$, $y = -150\ cm$, $\theta = 0°$. The localization process returned the pose $\widehat{x} = 345.87\ cm$, $\widehat{y} = -154.81\ cm$, $\widehat{\theta} = -1.38°$. The whole process took $483\ ms$.

Including the results from other experiments, the evaluation of the errors are summarized in the following: average position error $= 5.63\ cm$, maximum position error $= 9.32\ cm$, average orientation error $= 0.72°$, maximum orientation error $= 1.41°$.

We have not yet introduced any optimization to the code, neither on the algorithmic side neither on the compiling. Especially for the first reason, we are confident to be able to drastically reduce computation.

We can draw some preliminary considerations from these experiments. By using the hierarchical search technique, the system had to test 702 cells in the first experiment and 642 in the second one. If we had used an a priori grid made up of cells with radius $= 5\ cm$ and height $= 1.4°$, we should have had to test about 10^6 cells. This would have implied several minutes of computation before returning any solution.

The data in table 1 show the typical evolution of the search process: at the beginning we have large cells that collect several votes and there are a number of maxima, then, as long as the cell size decreases, we can notice a reduction in the votes and in the number of the selected cells.

4   Conclusions

We presented a mobile robot localization method for known 2D environments. We claim that evidence accumulation methods provide robustness against noisy data; henceforth we devised a grid-based method where the complexity is reduced by means of a multi-resolution scheme. The added values of the contribution are its multi-resolution scheme, the capability to deal both with raw sensor data as well as other localization estimates, and what we call *any-time localization*, which is the capability of the system to give out a pose estimate whenever asked to do so. We designed the system in order to have it independent from the geometric primitives used in the model definition as well as from the sensory system.

The experimentation confirm the ideas behind the approach, even though no code optimization has been carried out, that allows to expect large speedups.

References

1. Gutmann, J., Burgard, W., Fox, D., Konolige, K.: An experimental comparison of localization methods. In: proceedings of the IEEE/RSJ International Conference on Intelligent Robots and Systems (IROS98). (1998)
2. Burgard, W., Fox, D., Hennig, D., Schmidt, T.: Estimating the absolute position of a mobile robot using position probability grids. In: AAAI/IAAI, Vol. 2. (1996) 896–901
3. Burgard, W., Derr, A., Fox, D., Cremers, A.: Integrating global position estimation and position tracking for mobile robots: the dynamic markov localization approach. In: proceedings of IEEE/RSJ International Conference on Intelligent Robots and Systems (IROS). (1998)
4. Dellaert, F., Fox, D., Burgard, W., Thrun, S.: Monte carlo localization for mobile robots. In: proceedings of the IEEE International Conference on Robotics and Automation (ICRA99). (1999)
5. Olson, C.F.: Probabilistic self-localization for mobile robots. IEEE Transactions on Robotics and Automation **16** (2000) 55–66
6. Lu, F., Milios, E.: Globally consistent range scan alignment for environment mapping. Autonomous Robots **4** (1997) 333–349
7. Marchese, F.M., Sorrenti, D.G.: Omni-directional vision with a multi-part mirror. In: proceedings of the International Workshop on RoboCup. (2000) 289–298

Direct Reward and Indirect Reward
in Multi-agent Reinforcement Learning

Masayuki Ohta

Cyber Assist Research Center
National Institution of Advanced Industrial Science and Technology
AIST Tokyo Waterfront 2-41-6 Aomi Koto-ku Tokyo 135-0064, Japan
ohta@carc.aist.go.jp

Abstract. When we apply reinforcement learning onto multi-agent environment, credit assignment problem will occur, because it is sometimes difficult to define which agents are the real contributors. If we praise all agents, when a group of cooperative agents get reward, some agents which did not contribute it will also reinforce their policies. On the other hand, if we praise obvious contributors only, indirect contribution will not be reinforced. For the first step to reduce this dilemma, we propose a classification of reward, and then investigate the feature of it. We treat a positioning task on SoccerServer for the experiments. The empirical results show that direct reward takes effect faster and helps obtaining individuality. On the contrary, indirect reward takes effect slower, but agents tend to form a group and obtain another effective positioning.

1 Introduction

When we apply reinforcement learning[5] onto multi-agent environment, problems peculiar to multi-agent environment arise. The problem that maximizing reward of individual agents does not guarantee maximizing the reward of the whole cooperative group of agents is one of them. We focus on this problem and are going to solve this by deciding whom to reward. Supposing the environment that many robots, which is unfamiliar to each other, are learning cooperative tasks without communication, we put the following constraints to the experiment environment. Supposing the environment that many robots meet the first time each other, we did our experiment under the constraints that agents learn simultaneously without communication in noisy environment. There are some researches which deal with similar environment. Sen et.al [8] showed that normal Q-learning[3] can acquire the optimal policy without sharing information by block pushing problem, and Arai[2] reported effectiveness of Profit-Sharing[4] in noisy multi-agent environment without communication, using pursuit Game. However, both of them are such kind of problem that maximizing reward of each agent lead to maximizing the reward as a whole automatically. In this paper we treat a positioning problem on simulated soccer, in which indirect helps are significant contribution as well as actions that achieves a goal directly.

G.A. Kaminka, P.U. Lima, and R. Rojas (Eds.): RoboCup 2002, LNAI 2752, pp. 359–366, 2003.
© Springer-Verlag Berlin Heidelberg 2003

The outline of this paper is as following. In section 2, we introduce a problem of reinforcement learning on multi-agent environment, and define a classification of reward as this problem. In section 3, we show the details of our agents and the learning algorithm. In section 4, we show the result of experiments to investigate the feature of each kind of reward. And, in section 5, the related works are shown.

2   Problem of Multi-agent Reinforcement Learning

2.1   Reinforcement Learning in Multi-agent Environment

Reinforcement learning is a learning method that agents change their policies so as to maximize rewards given by the environment. We can apply this to a problem whose optimal action is not known, but we have to reward agents in proper condition. When a group of agents learns cooperative behaviors with reinforcement learning, the way to distribute the reward is one of the most important problems, which is called credit assignment problem. This is because indirect assists will be important factors as well as direct actions result in rewards. But it is sometimes difficult to define whose assists are worth rewarding, especially without sharing information, so a method that praise the whole agents is sometimes taken. Further, there is a following dilemma of whether to praise direct contributions or to praise all agents.

- If some agents which contributed directly only are praised, reinforced actions are relevant to the reward. But, all agents are going to achieve the goal only by itself, and after all, the group of agents will not maximize the sum of whole agents' reward. This is just like struggling for the reward with themselves.
- If all cooperative agents are praised when they achieved their goal, the combination of the agents' actions will be reinforced. But, because not all agents are relevant to the reward, some agents (such as agents just doing exploration) may reinforce bad policies.

It seems useful to use mixture of them in proper ratio, therefore, we have to investigate the feature of these reward beforehand.

2.2   Direct Reward and Indirect Reward

To distinguish between reward for direct contribution and reward for indirect contribution in multi-agent reinforcement learning, we call them "direct reward" and "indirect reward" respectively. The definitions are as followings.

- Direct Reward:
  The reward that was not provided if actions of other agents were not changed and only oneself selected other action.
- Indirect Reward:
  The reward that was provided even if actions of other agents were not changed and only oneself selected other action.

For example, in robotic soccer, direct reward is given to the player who succeeded in shooting a goal or simply kicked the ball, and indirect reward is given to the teammates who guarded opponents or defended their goal. Here, the point we should pay attention to is that the reward for the agent which passed the ball to the shooter is direct reward (even if it is called "assist"). This is because they could not shoot a goal without this action, obviously. The word of "direct reward" and "indirect reward" is used by Miyazaki[6] also. Their definitions are very similar to our definition, but different to some extent. In their definition, using an example of "Pursuit Game", direct reward is given to the agent which did the last action to catch the pray, and indirect reward is given to the other agents. But reward given to these surrounding agents is direct reward in my definition, because their last action is also necessary to catch the pray.

3   Details of Learning Agents

3.1   Learning Positioning on SoccerServer

As a testing-ground, we use SoccerServer[7] which is a simulator of robotic soccer. It realized abstracted real-world problem, and has been used for a lot of researchs. We investigated the feature of direct reward and indirect reward by experiment on learning effective positioning policy on SoccerServer. In soccer, positioning policy is closely related to the strength, and position for indirect contribution is very important as well as position for direct contribution. We consider an evolution of learning team against fixed positioning team, in which they completely have the same ability besides positioning. The effectiveness is measured by the score of the learning team. Both learning and fixed positioning agents are hand-coded, and behave as following.

- if (lost sight of the ball) look for the ball
- else if(ball is in kickable area) shoot or pass or clear (hand-coded)
- else if(nearest from the ball) chase the ball
- else go back to the base position and trace the ball

Each agent belongs to the learning team decides its base position with its own neural network. They divide the soccer field into a grid, then the neural network calculate the expected discounted reward in the case that their base position is at the center of the cell. The cell with the highest expected score in the neighborhood is selected as the next base position. The inputs of the neural network are "distance from the closest teammate", "distance from the closest opponent", "x-coordinate", and "y-coordinate" of the cell. Layout of players on the field is the state $s \in S$ of that time, and distance from teammates and opponents is the value that reflect the state. Also, the x-coordinate and y-coordinate can be treated as the next action $a \in A$ of the agent. Thus, the neural network is a function approximation of the action-value function $Q(s, a)$. The agents improve this function approximation in order to find an effective positioning.

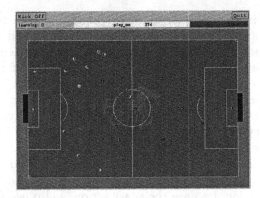

Fig. 1. A screen-shot: just after the learning experiment began. Learning team (left) against fixed positioning team (right)

3.2   Learning Algorithm

The purpose of the agent which belongs to the learning team is to find the optimal policy π, which is defined as the following.

$$Q^*(s,a) = \max_{\pi} Q^{\pi}(s,a) \quad (\forall s \in S, \forall a \in A(s))$$

where S = All possible combination of all players' position
$$A = \langle (0,0), (0,1)...(max\_x - 1, max\_y - 1) \rangle$$

In this research, we adopt Monte Carlo method which is a kind of nonbootstrapping method to estimate $Q^{\pi}(s,a)$, because of its robustness against violations of the Markov property [10]. The expected return (because the memory is limited, we use the expected return in N steps) starting from s, taking the action a and thereafter following policy π is defined as

$$Q^{\pi}(s,a) \approx E_{\pi} \left\{ \sum_{k=0}^{N-1} \gamma^k r_{t+k+1} \mid s_t = s, a_t = a \right\}$$

where $0 \leq \gamma < 1$ is a discount-rate parameter, and r_x is the reward at time x.

Neural network of an agent, which approximate $Q^{\pi}(s,a)$, has random weight at first. Fig.1 shows a screen shot of the early stage of learning. In this figure, all players are putting position toward the edge of the field. Begin with this random policy, agents learn with algorithm shown in Fig.2. In the experiment using the SoccerServer, because it takes long time to change the base position, we execute 1. for each step, and from 2. to 5. for every 50 steps, indeed. And it is also an important point that, at the step 2. in the algorithm, the neural network is recalculated with the weights at that time before doing back propagation. Because of this, agents do not have to save the condition of the neural network in each step.

Initialize,

   initialize the neural network
   Histry ← empty list
   Reward_Sum ← empty list
   (Both size of History and size of Reward_Sum are N)

In each step,

1. If (get reward r_t)
   From the bottom to the top $Reward\_Sum(n) \leftarrow Reward\_Sum(n) + \gamma^{n-1} \cdot r_t$
   where $Reward\_Sum(n)$ is the nth element of the Reward_Sum from the bottom, and $0 \leq \gamma < 1$ is a discount-rate parameter.

2. Take out the top element of History(N) and Reward_Sum(N), then reinforce as the following equation using back propagation.

$$Q(History(N)) \leftarrow (1 - \alpha)Q(History(N)) + \alpha \cdot Reward\_Sum(N)$$

   where $0 \leq \alpha < 1$ is a learning rate factor.

3. Shift all elements of the History and Reward_Sum to the top direction.

4. Recalculate the best action.
$$\begin{cases} probability\ 1 - \epsilon & a_t \leftarrow \max_a Q^{\pi_t}(s, a) \\ otherwise & a_t \leftarrow random\ a \in A \end{cases}$$
   where $0 < \epsilon \leq 1$ is probability of exploration

5. Add the current state-action pair to the bottom of the History.
   History(1) ← (s_t, a_t)
   Reward_Sum(1) ← 0

Fig. 2. Learning algorism in this experiment

4 Experiments

In order to examine a difference of the feature between direct reward and indirect reward, we did learning test with each reward separately. In each experiment, we continue executing the soccer simulation of learning team and fixed position team, and the effectiveness is measured by the score of the learning team in a unit time. The difference between the learning team by direct reward and the learning team by indirect reward is only the condition of reward. In both case, we use discount-rate $\gamma = 0.9$, learning rate $\alpha = 0.5$, and probability of exploration $\epsilon = 0.1$.

4.1 Learning with Direct Reward

In the first experiment, agents learn a policy which is effective against a fixed position team, with direct reward only. We gave agents the direct reward when

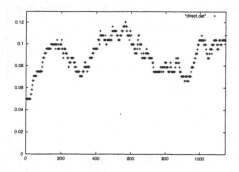
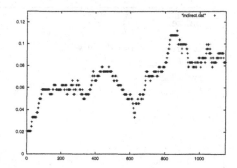

Fig. 3. Score of the learning team reinforced only by direct reward against a team with fixed policy

Fig. 4. Score of the learning team reinforced only by indirect reward against a team with fixed policy

they kick the ball by themselves. Fig.3 shows the learning curve in which x-axis indicates the time scale by a minute (= 600 step), and y-axis indicates the score of learning team in a minute. The score is the average value in one hour. Because of the randomness produced by the simulator, the learning curve is not stabilized, but we can see the agent could learn effective positioning. In this experiment, all agents expected to take close position each other where they can kick the ball frequently, but the experiment shows that agents took relatively distributed positioning. This is because only one agent can kick the ball in the same time and therefore learned having individuality. A typical pattern which is acquired by the learning team is like Fig.5.

4.2   Learning with Indirect Reward

Second, we did just the same experiment as the first one, except for the reward. In this experiment, agents get reward only when they see a teammate kicking the ball. The result of this experiment is shown in Fig.4, and a typical positioning pattern is like Fig.6. The learning went much slower than the experiment with the direct reward, but at last, agents shows almost the same efficiency. In this case, agents acquired a positioning policy that all agents tend to form a group, and moves together. Even if this indirect reward teaches that "one player is enough to chase the ball", the result shows the opposite outcome. This is only because of the feature of the SoccerServer on which agents can not discriminate teammates if they are away from each other. With this feature, because some agents chase the ball and others follow them, this learning team changes its position by the position of the ball.

4.3   Discussion

In the above two experiments, we can see the following results.

– Direct reward affects learning very quickly, and indirect reward affects learning relatively slow.

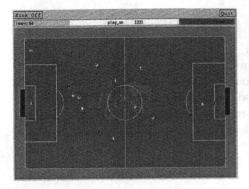 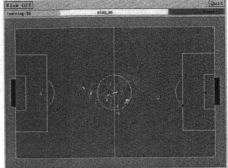

Fig. 5. Typical positioning acquired by direct reward

Fig. 6. Typical positioning acquired by indirect reward

- Both agents showed the same effectivity finally, but they acquired totally different policy.
- Agents learned with direct reward took distributed formation, and the agents learned with indirect reward took crowd formation.

In multi-agent environment individuality is very important factor, because that is related to distribute the role. But, in this experiment, the other acquired policy also had the similar effectivity, even if they are totally different. Therefore, mixture of these two kind of rewards is worth testing. Especially, if "direct reward" is used in a big ratio at first, and if it is reduced along the time we can expect that the score during the learning can be improved.

5   Related Works

Observational Reinforcement Learning[1] solved the problem that exploration causes bad effect on the other agents' learning in multi-agent environment. They also treat a positioning task on SoccerServer. Their solution is to use a reward which reinforce the position where the agents think it is good, by their perception information. Using this rewarding agents can have almost the same effect as the exploration, even if it reduce their exploration rate. This method is very useful, but it is a kind of supervised learning, and agents need to know some candidate answers beforehand. It is also interesting that, the agents reinforced by observational reward have similar feature to the agents reinforced by indirect reward.

Miyazaki[6] also classify the reward for reinforcement learning into direct reward and indirect reward. But as we already pointed out, the definition is different from ours. They showed necessary and sufficient condition of direct and indirect reward ratio to preserve the rationality. In their research, they are interested in the fixed ratio, but in this paper we focused on the change along the time.

6   Conclusion

We proposed a classification of reward, direct reward and indirect reward, in reinforcement learning. The direct reward affects quickly, and indirect reward affects slowly. Individuality is acquired using direct reward, but crowd formation acquired with indirect reward also showed the similar effectivity. We could see the trade-off between these reward, therefore, changing the mixture ratio of direct reward and indirect reward during the learning can be a future work.

References

1. T. Andou. Andhill-98: A robocup team which reinforces positioning with observation. In M. Asada and H. Kitano, editors, *RoboCup-98: Robot Soccer World Cup II*, pages 338–345. Springer Verlag, 1998.
2. S. Arai and K. Sycara. Effective learning approach for planning and scheduling in multi-agent domain. In *Proceedings of the 6th International Conference on Simulation of Adaptive Behavior*, pages 507–516, 2000.
3. C.J.C.H.Watkins. *Learning from Delayed Rewards*. PhD thesis, Cambridge University, Cambridge, England, 1989.
4. J. J. Grefenstette. Credit assignment in rule discovery systems based on genetic algorithms. In *Machine Learning*, volume 3, pages 225–245, 1988.
5. L. P. Kaelbling, M. L. Littman, and A. W. Moore. Reinforcement learning: A survey. *Journal of Artificial Intelligence Research*, 4:237–285, 1996.
6. K. Miyazaki and S. Kobayashi. Rationality of reward sharing in multi-agent reinforcement learning. In *Second Pacific Rim International Workshop on Multi-Agents*, pages 111–125, 1999.
7. I. Noda, H. Matsubara, K. Hiraki, and I. Frank. Soccer server: A tool for research on multiagent systems. In *Applied Artificial Intelligence*, volume 12, pages 233–250, 1998.
8. S. Sen, M. Sekaran, and J. Hale. Proceedings of the 12th national conference on artificial intelligence. In *Learning to Coordinate without Sharing Information*, pages 426–431, 1994.
9. P. Stone and D. McAllester. An Architecture for Action Selection in Robotic Soccer. In *Proceedings of the Fifth International Conference on Autonomous Agents*, 2001.
10. R. S. Sutton and A. G. Barto. *Reinforcement Learning: An Introduction*. MIT Press, 1998.

Relating the Entropy of Joint Beliefs
to Multi-agent Coordination

Mikhail Prokopenko and Peter Wang

Intelligent Interactive Technology
CSIRO Mathematical and Information Sciences
Locked Bag 17, North Ryde, NSW 1670, Australia
{mikhail.prokopenko,peter.wang}@csiro.au

Abstract. Current approaches to activity coordination in multi-agent systems (teams) range from strictly top down (plan-based coordination) to purely emergent (reactive coordination), with many hybrid variants, each having its specific advantages and disadvantages. It appears to be extremely difficult to rigorously compare various hybrid approaches to multi-agent coordination (and communication), given the lack of a generic semantics or some guidelines. In this paper, we studied some intuitive inter-agent communication policies and characterised them in terms of generic information-theoretic properties. In particular, the relative entropy of joint beliefs was suggested as an indicator of teams coordination potential. Our novel behaviour-based agent architecture (based on the Deep Behaviour Projection framework) enabled consistent reasoning about belief change, including beliefs about other agents. This allowed us to examine some of the identified communication policies empirically. The obtained results confirmed that there are certain interesting invariants – in particular, a change in team coordination (and overall performance) was shown to be within the boundaries indicated by the relative information entropy.

1 On Entropy and Multi-agent Agreements

The primary objective of this work is a formal characterisation of certain classes of multi-agent agreements. In achieving this goal, we tried to make as few assumptions as possible about the choice of inter-agent communication variables and periods of team synchronisation (extensively analysed by Stone and Veloso [8]). In particular, we studied *selfish* agreements covering "selfish" agents that communicate data about themselves only, *transitively-selfish* agreements ensuring that each "cooperative" agent always communicates the data about some other agent, and *mixed* agreements, where a team composition parameter determines the precise split between selfish and cooperative agents.

In order to capture the agreements in a formal information-theoretic setting we analysed the joint "output" of inter-agent communication after each period of team synchronisation. Then we estimated the *relative entropy* as a precise measure of the amount of freedom of choice (the degree of randomness) [7]

G.A. Kaminka, P.U. Lima, and R. Rojas (Eds.): RoboCup 2002, LNAI 2752, pp. 367–374, 2003.

contained in the resultant joint beliefs. Our intention was to use the relative entropy of joint beliefs in multi-agent teams as a generic indicator of the team coordination potential. Clearly, the team following an agreement with near-zero entropy (almost no "misunderstanding" in joint beliefs) has a higher coordination potential than the team adherent to an agreement with near-maximal entropy (joint beliefs are almost random).

We start our analysis with a simple protocol $\mathcal{P}_1$ that allows an agent to communicate data about only one agent precisely. In other words, each agent is able to encode either the data about itself or about the other agent. Without loss of generality, we may assume that the protocol $\mathcal{P}_1$ has enough symbols to encode n distinguishable objects and a single-object capacity for each communication message. We introduce a binary relation $S(a_i, a_j)$ to denote that the agent a_i *sends* a message containing the object a_j. Let S^* denote the transitive closure of the relation S. Arguably, on of the most intuitive agreements is an agreement among selfish agents – since the data about themselves is, arguably, more readily available, the selfish agents choose this data as their content. In fact, we may assume for our analysis that each agent is always "self-aware". Formally, $K(a_i, a_i) = true$ for a Boolean (belief-)function K defined for each agent pair. Generally, we propose the following definition.

Definition 1. *A locker-room agreement is called* selfish *if and only if* $S(a_i, a_i)$ *for all agents* a_i, $1 \le i \le n$.
A locker-room agreement is called transitively-selfish *if and only if* $S^*(a_i, a_i)$ *for all agents* a_i, $1 \le i \le n$.
A non transitively-selfish agreement is called mixed.

One might argue that the transitively-selfish agreement is an agreement among more "cooperative" agents choosing to communicate the data about the other agent (when available). Notice, however, that (given a successful team synchronisation) everyone is in the "loop". Of course, by definition, a selfish locker-room agreement is always transitively-selfish. In a mixed agreement, there are (αn) agents such that $S(a_i, a_i)$, and $(1 - \alpha)n$ agents such that $S(a_i, a_j)$ where $i \ne j$. Basically, the value of α determines the team composition (and we sometimes refer to α as the team composition parameter).

In order to formally capture the distinction among selfish, transitively-selfish and mixed agreements, we consider the joint "output" of inter-agent communication at the end of each period of team synchronisation. More precisely, we analyse joint beliefs represented by the sequence of individual beliefs $K_t = K(a_1, a_1), \ldots, K(a_i, a_j), \ldots, K(a_n, a_n)$, where $1 \le i \le n$ and $1 \le j \le n$, at the time t. In other words, rather than compute the amount of information contained in each message we attempt to estimate how much information is contained in the whole *team* after a period of team synchronisation.

In the simplest cases, the amount of information can be measured by the logarithm (to the base 2) of the number of available choices. The *entropy* is a precise measure of the amount of freedom of choice (or of the degree of randomness) contained in the object – an object with many possible states has high entropy. Formally, the entropy of a probability distribution $P = \{p_1; p_2; \ldots; p_m\}$ is defined by

$$H(P) = \sum_{i=1}^{m} p_i * \log(1/p_i).$$

Having calculated the entropy $H(P)$ of a certain information source (such as a joint result of inter-agent communication) with the probability distribution P, one can compare this to the maximum value H_{max} this entropy could have, assuming that the source employs the same symbols. The ratio of the actual to the maximum entropy is called the *relative entropy* of the source [7]. Therefore, if we calculate the relative entropy H_r of K_{t+p} we can characterise the multi-agent agreement employed between t and $t + p$. The following representation results were obtained[1].

Theorem 1. *Selfish agreements attain minimal entropy.*

Transitively-selfish agreements without the selfish agents attain maximal entropy asymptotically when the number of agents $n \to \infty$.

The trajectory of the relative entropy in multi-agent teams $(n > 2)$ following mixed agreements does not have a fixed-point as a function $H_r(\alpha)$ of the team composition parameter: $H_r(\alpha) \neq \alpha$.

This theorem basically states that whenever team agents agree to communicate the data about themselves only, they eventually leave nothing to choice. In other words, they always maximise their joint beliefs upon successful synchronisations. The obvious drawback is that while using single channels this saturation of joint beliefs requires that every agent takes turns in communication according to some schedule, and hence, large teams may take a while to minimise the entropy. The clear benefit, on the other hand, is that this minimisation is shown to be theoretically possible.

On the other hand, the "organisation" or "order" brought about by the transitively-selfish agreements is not sufficient to combat the entropy. Intuitively, the pair-wise "ignorance" of agents grows faster than the transitively-selfish agreement can cope with. Clearly, with the number of agents approaching infinity (and the entropy reaching its maximum asymptotically) the time to synchronise the team becomes infinite as well.

Obviously, the entropy of joint beliefs in multi-agent systems following mixed agreements exhibits some properties of both selfish and transitively-selfish configurations. We might expect that the selfish agents will bring in some order (as the compensation for potentially redundant information about themselves), while the cooperative (transitively-selfish) agents will lead to a higher degree of randomness (providing sometimes potentially non-trivial information about other agents). Formally, the relative entropy produced by mixed agreements asymptotically approaches 1 with growth in the number of agents. In other words, the selfish agents "loose" the battle for order (asymptotically) when the number of agents is infinitely large. Interestingly, however, the lower limit is not

---

[1] The proofs are omitted due to the lack of space.

zero, meaning that absolute order is never achievable regardless of the team split or the number of agents. In fact, our results showed that the joint beliefs obtainable in multi-agent teams with mixed agreements exhibit information-theoretic *complexity* in terms of the team composition. It has been recently pointed out in the literature (eg., by Suzudo [9]) that the entropy trajectory is a useful descriptor for a variety of self-organised patterns: eg., non-complex cellular automata (CA) have a fixed-point entropy trajectory and converge quickly to either very low or very high values. It should be noted that Suzudo considered the entropy of CA associated with the temporal pattern, while our analysis is focused on entropy of joint beliefs associated with the team composition parameter.

Our analysis was carried out for the protocol $\mathcal{P}_1$. However, it can be easily shown that protocols with higher capacities can be analysed in already presented terms. For example, consider the protocol $\mathcal{P}_2$ allowing an agent to communicate data about precisely two agents (including the data about itself). In other words, in the case of n agents the protocol $\mathcal{P}_2$ has enough symbols to encode n agents and two-objects capacity for each communication message. It is, nevertheless, possible to consider every message $S(a_i, a_j + a_k)$, where $+$ denotes the concatenation of the symbols corresponding to two objects, as two consecutive separate messages $S(a_i, a_j)$ and $S(a_i, a_k)$. This decomposition can be applied if $i = j$ or $i = k$ as well. Therefore, in order to analyse resultant joint beliefs one can double the synchronisation period in length and consider as a result the union of two sets of joint beliefs – the first set obtained after all messages with the first object are communicated, and the second set obtained after all messages with the second object are communicated. In other words, the decomposition allows to reduce the analysis of the protocol $\mathcal{P}_2$ (or any k-object capacity protocol $\mathcal{P}_k$) to that of the protocol $\mathcal{P}_1$ – simply because each divided message conforms to $\mathcal{P}_1$. That is, the resultant joint beliefs will be a combination of beliefs obtained by some selfish, transitively-selfish or mixed agreement in $\mathcal{P}_1$.

Another interesting reduction can be obtained in cases when agents intend to communicate the data about other objects in the environments (eg., the ball vectors in the RoboCup environment). In this case we just consider the ball to be a silent agent in the $(n+1)$-agent team. More precisely, denoting by b the ball object, the messages $S(a_i, a_j + \ldots + b)$ would be possible while $S(b, a_j + \ldots + b)$ would be ruled out, again reducing the consideration to the protocol $\mathcal{P}_1$.

In summary, the advantage of higher-capacity protocols is in the shorter periods of required synchronisation but not in some exceptional information-theoretic properties of resultant joint beliefs.

2   Agents Situated in Time and Relativity of Behaviours

The strength of the presented analysis, we believe, is in its generic nature. The results lay down some general guidelines in terms of team composition and suggest definite boundaries on the team coordination potential.

In this section we focus on the agents ability to dynamically change their beliefs under different scenaria. We assumed previously that (during any synchronisation period) joint and individual beliefs can only expand, while obviously some of them should be discarded with time and some should be reconciled with new observations. At this stage, we shall describe some design and implementation details required to verify maximal and minimal limits of the entropy contained in the agents' dynamic beliefs.

In general, the agent's capability to maintain dynamic beliefs is based on another very important cognitive skill – the ability to remove itself from the current context. This ability is sometimes informally referred to as "possession of a reality simulator" [2]. Running a reality simulator or "imagining" allows the agent to reflect on past behaviour and project the outcome of future behaviour. For example, Joordens [2] makes a conjecture that higher mental states emerge as a result of a reality simulator: "an animal with no reality simulator basically lives in the present tense, and sees the world through only its eyes, at all times", while "the possession of a reality simulator may also allow an organism to experience many of the high-level cognitive processes that we identify with being human". Moreover, there is a possibility that an organism with a reality simulator is more likely to engage in cooperative behaviour because of its ability to conceptualise rewards to others, and long-term rewards to itself.

We maintain that "world model" should appear in the architecture incrementally. In our previous work [4–6] we described the Deep Behaviour Projection (DBP) hierarchical framework. The DBP framework formally represents *increasing* levels of agent reasoning abilities, where every new level can be projected onto a deeper (more basic) behaviour. Put simply, a DBP behaviour can be present in the architecture in two forms: implicit (emergent) and explicit (embedded).

It is interesting at this stage to compare such behaviour duplication in DBP with the distinction between *automatic processes* and *controlled processes* in cognitive psychology. It is well-known that certain processes become highly automatic through repetition and are unconsciously triggered in the presence of certain stimuli, while controlled processes are mostly goal-oriented rather than reactive. With time and/or practice newly learned behaviours often shift from being controlled to automatic.

What the DBP approach suggests in addition, is that *the reactive/cognitive distinction is always relative* in a hierarchical architecture. The behaviour produced by the level l_k may appear reactive with respect to the level l_{k+1} but, at the same time, may look deliberate with respect to the level l_{k-1}. Let us exemplify this with the following three levels of the DBP agents:

- tropistic behaviour: Sensors → Effectors
- hysteretic behaviour: Sensors & Memory → Effectors
- tactical behaviour: Sensors & Memory & Task → Effectors.

The hysteretic behaviour is definitely more reactive when compared with the tactical behaviour, because the latter uses the task states in choosing the effectors. However, contrasted with a very basic tropistic behaviour, the hysteresis provided by (internal) memory states ensures a *degree* of cognition. More precisely, the hysteretic behaviour addresses some lagging of an effect behind its cause, providing a (temporary) resistance to change that occurred previously.

For instance, in order to intercept a fast moving ball the agent needs to observe the shift in the ball positions and estimate its velocity before activating the effectors. Thus, the hysteretic behaviour is slightly more deliberate than the tropistic one (exemplified by a simple chase after the ball) – it better situates the agent in time (not only in space) and allows it to better respond to changes. Continuing with the example we re-iterate that the hysteretic intercept is a behaviour embedded explicitly, while the tropistic intercept is only possible as an emergent result of the recurring chase.

Thus, a reality simulator appears *incrementally* – starting from a basic ability to detect a change (eg., in direction) and moving towards a more and more comprehensive incorporation of the temporal asymmetry or "time's arrow" (eg., from direction-sensitive cells to a measurement of a shift in observed positions, to the notion of velocity emerging after a series of measurements, etc.). This means that an emergence of essentially new behavioural patterns always indicates a need for new elements in the agent architecture. At some stage, increasing levels of reasoning about change require an ability to consistently maintain the agent's beliefs – expand, contract or revise them according to some rational principles, such as the principle of minimal change (information economy) [1].

In order to address this requirement, we explicitly introduced a domain model into the DBP architecture, resulting in the following hierarchy (a refinement of the architecture reported in [6]):

$$\langle S, E, \quad tropistic\_behaviour : S \to E,$$
$$I, \quad hysteretic\_behaviour : I \times S \to E, \qquad update : I \times S \to I,$$
$$T, \quad tactical\_behaviour : I \times S \times T \to E,$$
$$tactics : I \times S \times T \to 2^T, \qquad decision : I \times S \times T \to T,$$
$$D, \quad domain\_update : I \times S \times D \to D,$$
$$domain\_revision : I \times S \times D \to D,$$
$$domain\_projection : I \times S \times D \to S \, \rangle$$

where S is a set of agent sensory states, E is a set of agent effectors, I is a set of internal agent states, T is a set of agent task states, and D is a set of domain model states. The DBP agents extrapolate their domain model each simulation cycle with the *domain_update* function, and revise it with the *domain_revise* function whenever new information becomes available. The partition between update and revision corresponds to the well-known distinction between belief update and belief revision [3]. In particular, the belief *update* is appropriate when the world has changed and the agents need to accommodate this change into the previously correct beliefs. The belief *revision* should be used to incorporate new information about the same state of the world, in order to correct potential inconsistencies.

In the absence of new observations, the updated domain model $d^* = domain\_update\,(i, s, d)$ is the best approximation of the domain. In these cases, the domain model d^* is transformed by the *domain_projection* function into the agent's sensory state $s^* = domain\_projection(i, s, d^*)$. Very importantly, all the choices made by the agent based on s^* are not distinguishable from the choices it could have made if the same sensory state s^* was a result of the direct sensory input. Intuitively, the *domain_projection* function projects the results of the reality simulator and the agent *imagines* that these results have been observed directly. The projection function is needed only in the absence of new observations, and should not be invoked at other times – the imaginative side of the agent is not needed when "live" information is available anyway.

3 Experimental Results and Conclusion

In order to support our analysis of boundaries on the team coordination potential, we varied communication policies while leaving all other factors (agents skills and tactics) unchanged. The factors beyond our control (eg., a possible change in the opponent strategy) were minimised by repeated runs. This focused the experiment on the dependency (if any) between communication policies (and therefore, resultant joint beliefs) and the team coordination potential.

Our benchmark opponent was selected from the top five teams of the RoboCup-2001 championship. The baseline test team ("Full Communications") was our team running with standard communication messages (512 symbols $\approx$ 100-objects capacity) – we used the protocol of the Soccer Server 7.10. This enabled the full use of the benchmark as well. Then we investigated three communication policies with the protocol $\mathcal{P}_1$. The first policy ("Ball") was to communicate only the ball object, if the data were accurate enough. This mixed variant is quite similar to the transitively-selfish agreement, with high relative entropy and very local coordination, enabling a pressing aggressive game (simply because the players close to the ball might be unaware of each other). The second policy ("Ball | Self") allowed, in addition, each agent to communicate the data about itself according to a schedule, but possibly at times when some other agent communicated the ball object. This mix is much closer to the selfish agreement, with low relative entropy and very global coordination, enabling a passing non-aggressive game (now the players within the ball neighbourhood are often aware of each other, and in addition more team-mates can be considered for a pass). The third policy ("Ball | Self | Wait") prevented self-messages when a team-mate was likely to say ball. This implicit synchronisation is aimed at some mixture of local and global coordination, balancing predominantly pressing game with some passing chances – truly a mixed agreement with (anticipated) bounded relative entropy. The results are presented in the table below.

Table 1. Results against the benchmark after 100 games for each test.

Team	Goals For	Goals Against	Wins	Draws	Losses	Points
Full Communications	111	101	38	29	33	143
Ball	123	125	34	31	35	133
Ball	Self	102	124	26	27	47	105
Ball	Self	Wait	114	112	35	27	38	132

All the tests have performed, as expected, worse than the baseline. The "Ball" policy achieved almost a parity with the benchmark, while the "Ball | Self" policy was clearly worse. Obviously, this just indicates that the pressing game (emerging as a result of the high entropy of joint beliefs and the ensuing local coordination) is more suitable against this particular benchmark. This conjecture was supported by performance of the "Ball | Self | Wait" policy, achieving an equality against the benchmark as well. Apparently, the information contained in the self-messages and communicated fairly infrequently was not enough to create statistically significant passing chances, and therefore, the emergent coordination was more local than global. Importantly, the third (mixed) policy was *within the boundaries* marked by the first two variants (and closer to the first one), as suggested by the relative entropy of joint beliefs. Similar encouraging results were obtained for extensions of all three policies to the protocol $\mathcal{P}_2$.

These empirical results illustrate the dependency between communication policies, the information entropy of joint beliefs and the team coordination potential. Identification of this relation is a main contribution of the presented analysis, opening a new general perspective on reasoning about belief dynamics in multi-agent scenaria.

Acknowledgements

The authors are grateful to Marc Butler, Thomas Howard and Ryszard Kowalczyk for their exceptionally valuable prior contributions to our RoboCup Simulation efforts and studies of multi-agent systems.

References

1. Peter Gärdenfors. *Knowledge in Flux: Modeling the Dynamics of Epistemic States.* Bradford Books, MIT Press, Cambridge Massachusetts, 1988.
2. Steve Joordens. Project Cetacea: A Study of High-Level Cognition In Toothed Whales. http://www.psych.utoronto.ca/~joordens/courses/PsyD58/Cetacea.html.
3. Pavlos Peppas, Abhaya Nayak, Maurice Pagnucco, Norman Foo, Rex Kwok and Mikhail Prokopenko. Revision vs. Update: Taking a Closer Look. In Proceedings of the 12th European Conference on Artificial Intelligence, 1996.
4. Mikhail Prokopenko and Marc Butler. Tactical Reasoning in Synthetic Multi-Agent Systems: a Case Study. In Proceedings of the IJCAI-99 Workshop on Nonmonotonic Reasoning, Action and Change, Stockholm, 1999.
5. Mikhail Prokopenko, Marc Butler and Thomas Howard. On Emergence of Scalable Tactical and Strategic Behaviour. In RoboCup-2000: Robot Soccer World Cup IV, Springer, 2000.
6. Mikhail Prokopenko, Peter Wang and Thomas Howard. Cyberoos'2001: 'Deep Behaviour Projection' Agent Architecture. In RoboCup-2001: Robot Soccer World Cup V, Springer, 2001.
7. Claude E. Shannon and Warren Weaver. *The Mathematical Theory of Communication.* University of Illinois Press, 1949.
8. Peter Stone and Manuela Veloso. Task Decomposition, Dynamic Role Assignment, and Low-Bandwidth Communication for Real-Time Strategic Teamwork. In Artificial Intelligence, volume 100, number 2, June 1999.
9. Tomoaki Suzudo. The entropy trajectory: A perspective to classify complex systems. In Proceedings of the International Symposium on Frontier of Time Series Modeling, Tokyo, 2000.

Real-Time Decision Making under Uncertainty of Self-localization Results

Takeshi Fukase, Yuichi Kobayashi, Ryuichi Ueda,
Takanobu Kawabe, and Tamio Arai

The University of Tokyo, 7-3-1 Hongo, Bunkyo-ku, Tokyo 113-8656, Japan
{fukase,kobayasi,ueda,kawabe,arai}@prince.pe.u-tokyo.ac.jp
http://www.arai.pe.u-tokyo.ac.jp/

Abstract. In this paper, we present a real-time decision making method for a quadruped robot whose sensor and locomotion have large errors. We make a State-Action Map by off-line planning considering the uncertainty of the robot's location with Dynamic Programming (DP). Using this map, the robot can immediately decide optimal action that minimizes the time to reach a target state at any state. The number of observation is also minimized. We compress this map for implementation with Vector Quantization (VQ). Using the differences of the values between the optimal action and others as distortion measure of VQ minimizes the total loss of optimality.

Keywords: Dynamic Programming, Vector Quantization, Planning under Uncertainty, Real-time Decision Making

1 Introduction

In Sony Four-Legged Robot League, self-localization with insufficient sensor information and unreliable locomotion is an big problem. Moreover, to localize itself, the robot must swing its head to look for landmarks because the robot's camera has a narrow visual field. It is required to keep the frequency of this "off-ball" observation behavior as small as possible. As a result, the robot is required to judge whether it should execute landmarks observation action or walking action. The simplest criterion for the judgment is to adapt a fixed threshold of the location's uncertainty [2], however, there are many situations in which the robot can decide its action without precise self-localization results.

Mitsunaga *et al.* proposed a decision making tree that gives consideration to the observational strategy based on information criterion [3]. The tree is made from the large experimental teaching data, which contains the information of the motion planning and the probability distribution models of sensing and locomotion. In order to apply larger problems, however, the decision making architecture should once analyze these two kinds of information separately.

Our approach to the real-time decision making method deals with:

- modeling uncertainty in the robot's locomotion and observations,
- adopting Dynamic Programming (DP) [4] to motion planning,

G.A. Kaminka, P.U. Lima, and R. Rojas (Eds.): RoboCup 2002, LNAI 2752, pp. 375–383, 2003.

– enlarging the state space of planning (configuration space) so as to include the uncertainty parameters,
– compressing the off-line calculated information using Vector Quantization.

The robot's locomotion models and observation models are taken into consideration respectively in the process of DP, which guarantees the optimality. By the expansion of the state space to include uncertainty parameters, the observational cost can be computed in the framework of DP.

From another point of view, an effective design of reflective behavior has been proposed by Hugel et al.[5]. But it needs highly sophisticated designer's empirical intuition. Our framework realizes the similar behavior as [2, 3, 5], but is based on the automatic design. So the idea can be applied to the larger problems more easily.

In section 2, the task in the Legged Robot League is specified. Section 3 outlines the proposed real-time motion decision method. In Section 4,5, and 6, the implementation of the method to the task is described. In Section 7, the proposed method is evaluated in the simulation and the experiment.

2   Task and Assumption

The robot's task is to approach the ball from the proper direction so as not to attack the own goal. The followings are the assumptions for the later discussion.

– there are eight discrete walking actions and one observation action,
– the walking actions yield large odometry errors,
– the six unique landmarks are placed around the field,
– the measurement of distance to the landmark contains large errors,
– the robot does not look away from the ball while walking towards it,
– the robot swings its head horizontally for self-localization at the observation action.

The state of the robot and the ball are represented by the next five variables (x, y, θ, r, ϕ), which are shown in Fig.5. (x, y, θ) is the robot's pose on the field. r and ϕ are the distance and orientation of the ball from the robot.

3   Real-Time Decision Making

From the above-mentioned discussion, real-time decision making methods are required to meet following properties: 1) automatic design which can discuss optimality, 2) low computational cost, and 3) ability to express the observational cost and the uncertainty of localization.

To meet the first characteristic, we adopt DP, which is widely used to solve the optimal control problems. The low computational property means that the robot ERS-2100 has 32MB RAM and its calculation speed is equivalent to the 200MHz PC. The volume of DP result is too large to implement on the robot. In order to compress it, we apply Vector Quantization (VQ) [6].

The aspects of uncertainty and observational costs are important in this paper. The uncertainty can be considered as variables of the state space [7].

3.1 Motion Planning with Dynamic Programming

Let $x \in \mathcal{X} \subset R^n$ denote the state vector and $u \in \mathcal{U} \subset R^m$ denote the control input vector. The system dynamics in discrete time is expressed as:

$$x_{k+1} = f[x_k, u_k]. \tag{1}$$

The deterministic control policy is given by $u_k = \pi(x_k)$. The purpose of the optimal control problem is to find the optimal policy $\pi^*(x)$ that maximizes

$$S = \sum_{k=1}^{T} R[x_k, u_k], \tag{2}$$

where $R[x_k, u_k]$ is the immediate evaluation function of each state and control input pair and T is the time step until the task ends.

We substitute discrete s and a for x and u, respectively. Here, $\mathcal{S}$ and $\mathcal{A}$ are the set of discrete states and actions. Bellman equation in discrete time and space (without the discount factor) can be formulated as follows:

$$V^*(s) = \max_a \sum_{s'} \mathcal{P}_{ss'}^a [\mathcal{R}_{ss'}^a + V^*(s')], \tag{3}$$

$$Q^*(s, a) = \max_a \sum_{s'} \mathcal{P}_{ss'}^a [\mathcal{R}_{ss'}^a + \max_{a'} Q^*(s', a')], \tag{4}$$

where $\mathcal{P}_{ss'}^a$ denotes the transition probability from state s to s' by taking action a, and $\mathcal{R}_{ss'}^a$ denotes the immediate evaluation given to the state transition from s to s' by taking action a. The optimal state-value function $V^*(s)$ denotes the expected evaluation which is given by taking actions at state s under the optimal policy π^*. The optimal action-value function $Q^*(s, a)$ denotes the expected evaluation after taking action a at state s, in the same way. We call π^* State-Action Map in this paper.

3.2 Planning Optimal Behavior under Uncertainty

When the motions are planned, the variance of pose estimation and the observational cost should be taken into consideration. Fig.1 shows an example where the variance of the posture estimation enlarges when the robot executes a walking action. Fig.2 shows an example where the variance decreases when the robot takes observation. These factors can be formulated as:

$$(x_{k+1}, \psi_{k+1}) = f'[(x_k, \psi_k), (u_k, \omega_k)], \tag{5}$$

where ψ denotes the state variance vector and ω denotes the observational control vector. Thus, the optimal control problem can be solved in the expanded state space $\{x, \psi | x \in \mathcal{X}, \psi \in \ominus\}$. Fig.3 shows the abstraction of the state transition in the expanded state space. The increase of the variance in the original state space can be expressed as the transition along the ψ axis.

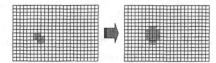

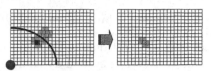

Fig. 1. A state's transition on the occasion of the robot's movement.

Fig. 2. A state's transition on the occasion of a landmark observation.

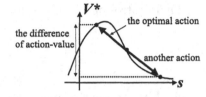

Fig. 3. The state transition in the expanded state space.

Fig. 4. The differences between the optimal action and another.

3.3 Compression of State-Action Map with Vector Quantization

The map should be compressed in order to implement on the limited amount of robot's memory. We apply Vector Quantization as a data compression method. The map is distorted through compression, and the optimality of action data is lost. We should pay attention not to maximize the decode rate but to minimize the increase of the time to reach the target. Hence, we calculate the differences between the optimal action and others based on the value function as Fig.4, and utilize it as a distortion measure.

4 Implementation 1: Dynamic Programming

4.1 Symbols Definition

Firstly, we quantize (x, y, θ, ϕ) as $100[\text{mm}] \times 100[\text{mm}] \times 15[\text{deg}] \times 100[\text{mm}]$ (Fig.5). We divide r into 12 intervals. Each have different width since the qantized interval does not need to be shorted when the ball is far from the robot. The shortest interval width is 100[mm] and the widest interval width is infinite. Moreover, we add one more parameter ψ which denotes the shape of region in which the robot exists with high probability. ψ is represented to a combination of some $s_{\text{p}i_x i_y i_\theta}$s, which are cuboids in the $xy\theta$-space (Fig.6). The area which the robot exists with high probability is represented as $s_{\text{r}i_x i_y i_\theta i_\psi}$. We restrict the number of ψs to 811 in a lot of combinations of cuboids so as to save the amount of calculation. We define i_ψ as the larger i_ψ becomes, the more the number of ψ's cuboids increases. Eventually, we let a state $\forall s \in S$ have six indexes as $s_{i_x i_y i_\theta i_r i_\phi i_\psi}$. Hereafter, we often describe $s_{i_x i_y i_\theta i_r i_\phi i_\psi}$, $s_{\text{r}i_x i_y i_\theta i_\psi}$ and $s_{\text{b}i_r i_\phi}$ as s_i, s_{ri} and s_{bi}, respectively.

Secondly, we define some symbols on actions. The robot has nine fixed actions as Table 1. Each action has the following attributes:

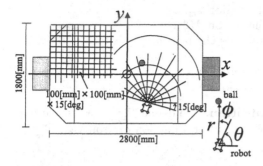

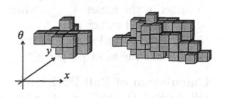

Fig. 5. The robot's position is divided into three-dimensional grids, and the ball's position is divided into two-dimensional grids.

Fig. 6. A quantized ψ consist of three-dimensional cuboids in (x, y, θ) space. When the robot's position is estimated precisely, the number of cuboids in ψ is small.

Table 1. Actions and Parameters of them.

Action a_i	$M_p^{a_i}$ [mm],[deg] $(p = (0,0,0))$	$\mathcal{R}^{a_i}$ [msec]
1:forward	$(70 \pm 30, 0 \pm 15, 0 \pm 6)$	-768
2:backword	$(-40 \pm 40, 0 \pm 15, 0 \pm 6)$	-768
3:rightside	$(0 \pm 20, -60 \pm 30, 4 \pm 4)$	-896
4:leftside	$(0 \pm 20, 60 \pm 30, -4 \pm 4)$	-896
5:rightforward	$(10 \pm 10, 37.5 \pm 17.5, -14.5 \pm 6.5)$	-832
6:leftforward	$(10 \pm 10, -37.5 \pm 17.5, 14.5 \pm 6.5)$	-832
7:rollright	$(35 \pm 15, -35 \pm 15, 11.5 \pm 6.5)$	-832
8:rollleft	$(35 \pm 15, 35 \pm 15, -11.5 \pm 6.5)$	-832
9:observation	$(0 \pm 0, 0 \pm 0, 0 \pm 0)$	-2800

- Time consumption : $\mathcal{R}^{a_i}(< 0)$. We regard a action's time consumption as negative reward. We assume that $\forall \mathcal{R}^{a_i}$ is independent of $\forall s \in \mathcal{S}$.
- Capable region of the robot's pose after an action a_i which is caused at a pose $p : M_p^{a_i}$. For brief calculation, we assume that the robot moves to a random pose in $M_p^{a_i}$ with the uniform probability, and that the shape of $M_p^{a_i}$ is a cuboid.

Finally we assume that the optimal policy $\pi^*(s)$ is deterministic, i.e. $\pi^*(s)$ chooses one action when a state s is designated.

4.2 Calculation of Probability and Execution of DP Algorithm

We use the value iteration algorithm [4] to obtain the optimal policy π^* with the equation (3). We should refer to the calculation algorithm of $\mathcal{P}_{s_i s_j}^{a_k}$ to execute the value iteration algorithm. We calculate $\mathcal{P}_{s_i s_j}^{a_k}$ with the next two algorithms.

Calculation of Pose's Transition. We do not treat stochastically the renewal of s_{ri} after an action a_k (we represent it as $s_{ri}^{a_k}$) since s_{ri} and $s_{ri}^{a_k}$ are already stochastic in themselves. We choose the most proper $s_{ri}^{a_k}$ with the following way;

1. Choose a pose p randomly from the region s_{ri}.
2. Choose a pose q randomly from the region $M_p^{a_k}$.
3. Record the region $s_{j_x j_y j_\theta}$ which contains the pose q.
4. Iterate 1-3 sufficiently.
5. Bind all recorded regions and make a region $\hat{s}_{ri}^{a_k}$.
6. Choose the most proper $s_{ri}^{a_k}$ to approximate $\hat{s}_{ri}^{a_k}$.

Calculation of Ball Position's Transition. We define $\mathcal{P}_{s_{bi}s_{bj}}^{a_k}$ as the probability which the ball's position becomes s_{bj} after an action a_k from s_{bi}. $\mathcal{P}_{s_{bi}s_{bj}}^{a_k}$ is calculated with the following way;

1. Assume that the robot's pose is p.
2. Choose a pose q randomly from the region $M_p^{a_k}$.
3. Choose a ball posistion b randomly from the region s_{bi}.
4. Calculate the new ball position b' from p, q and b.
5. Record the region s_{bj} which includes the position b'.
6. Iterate 1-5 sufficiently.
7. Calculate $\mathcal{P}_{s_{bi}s_{bj}}^{a_k}$ from the frequency that s_{bj} is recorded.

If $s_{ri}^{a_k} = s_{rj}$, the value of $\mathcal{P}_{s_i s_j}^{a_k}$ is the same as that of $\mathcal{P}_{s_{bi}s_{bj}}^{a_k}$, if not, $\mathcal{P}_{s_i s_j}^{a_k}$ becomes zero.

5   Implementation 2: Compression of State-Action Map

We use Vector Quantization (VQ) [6] so as to compress the State-Action Map π^*, since the data amount of π^* is 588 MB and the robot does not have such a huge amount of RAM. The maximum volume of data that can be transferred to the robot is 16MB. We use Pairwise Nearest Neighbor (PNN) algorithm to choose initial codebooks, and Generalized Lloyd Algorithm (GLA) to refine them [8].

5.1   Definition of Vector

We explain the way with which representative vectors are made. At first, we divide the map since the State-Action Map is too large to be executed VQ all at once. We divide the map $\mathcal{S}$ into Γ_j ($j = 1, 2, \ldots, N_{\Gamma_j}$). Γ_j has all states whose indexes of ψ are $2j - 1$ or $2j$. VQ is executed in each Γ_j independently. Furthermore, we divide each Γ_j into six dimensional cuboids Ω_{jk} ($k = 1, 2, \ldots, N_\Omega$). Any two cuboids in the same Γ must be congruence. We arrange all states of a Ω_{jk} in a order, and we define $v_{jk} = (\pi^*(s_1^{(jk)}), \pi^*(s_2^{(jk)}), \ldots, \pi^*(s_{N_e}^{(jk)}))$ as a vector which is used in VQ.

Each edge's width of each Ω_{jk} should be decided that the same vectors are produced in Γ_j as much as possible, since it is favorable for VQ. We decide them to minimize the next entropy function:

$$H = -\sum_{k=1}^{N_\Omega} \frac{1}{N_\Omega} \log \frac{N_s(v_{jk})}{N_\Omega}, \tag{6}$$

where $N_s(v_{jk})$ means the number of the same vectors with v_{jk} (it counts (v_{jk})).

5.2   Definition of Distorsion

Next, we must define distorsion of any two vectors for VQ. We define the distorsion between two vectors, v and w as

$$D[v, w] = \sum_{\ell=1}^{N_e} D[v_\ell, w_\ell], \tag{7}$$

where $v_\ell, w_\ell \in \mathcal{A}$ are the ℓth elements of v and w respectively. We must define the distorsion $D[a_m, a_n]$ about $\forall m, n$. $D[a_m, a_n]$ is calculated from the optimal action-value function (4) as

$$D[a_m, a_n] = \frac{\sum_{k=1}^{N_\Omega} \sum_{\ell=1}^{N_e} \delta_{\pi^*(s_\ell^{(jk)}), a_m} \{Q^*(s_\ell^{(jk)}, a_m) - Q^*(s_\ell^{(jk)}, a_n)\}}{\sum_{k=1}^{N_\Omega} \sum_{\ell=1}^{N_e} \delta_{\pi^*(s_\ell^{(jk)}), a_m}}, \tag{8}$$

where, $\delta_{\alpha, \beta}$ is Kronecker delta.

To execute PNN and GLA based on this distorsion, we can obtain the compressed State-Action Map. For the calculation of DP and VQ, we spend three days on a Pentium III 866 MHz PC.

6   Implementation 3: The On-Line Algorithm

The tasks of the on-line part are to recognize the current state of the robot and to search an optimal action from the compressed map. We use Uniform Monte Carlo Localization (Uniform MCL) [1] for self-localization, and for modeling of state transitions which are caused by the landmark observation action. Simulations of Section 7 use this state transition models. In experiments of Section 7, the robot specifies the current state of the robot with Uniform MCL results.

7   Simulation and Experiment

7.1   Purpose and Conditions of Simulation

We inspect the efficiency of our method by simulation. We compare the results of following two methods in order to verify the effectiveness to consider the self-localization's uncertainty.

1. Referring map method: utilizes the compressed map for all the decision making including the judgment of observation.
2. Threshold method: uses the compressed map without variance for making choice of walking actions. The robot observes landmarks when the width of the probability distribution is over a fixed threshold, which is $(x_{th}, y_{th}, \theta_{th}) = (600[\text{mm}], 500[\text{mm}], 60[\text{deg}])$.

Other conditions are settled as follows.

Table 2. The results of the simulations.

Condition	Time[sec]	# of obs.	Success rate
	Referring map method		
1	31.4	2.6	10/10
2	37.6	3.6	10/10
3	35.9	2.8	10/10
	Threshold method		
1	34.4	4.0	10/10
2	41.5	4.6	8/10
3	38.6	3.6	9/10

Table 3. The results of the experiment.

Condition	Time[sec]	# of obs.	Success rate
1	27.5	1.4	9/10
2	42.0	3.0	6/10
3	41.1	2.3	8/10

Table 4. Initial positions.

Condition	r[mm]	ϕ[deg]	x[mm]	y[mm]	θ[deg]
1	2100	30	-1000	-600	0
2	1800	0	1000	0	180
3	2100	60	1000	-600	90

- Table 4 shows initial conditions. The robot knows the initial positions.
- The robot's real pose is updated with random errors. The robot updates its estimating state according to the transition probability.
- The robot acquires the relative position to landmarks with random errors.
- In referring the map case, the task is terminated when the robot's estimating state belongs to the terminative states. In using threshold case, it is terminated when the robot's estimating pose belongs to the terminative states.
- Success cases are that the robot actually reaches a target position.

7.2 Results and Discussion of Simulation

We simulated 10 times on each case and initial conditions. The results are shown in Table 2. In the referring the map case, the robot succeeded to reach the target position at all trials. This indicates that the calculation of DP converged and the distortion of the compressed map was small. In the using the thresholds case, there were some failures. In the referring the map case, both the average number of observation and the time to reach the target were smaller than using thresholds case. These results indicate that the robot observed more effectively as a result of the off-line planning.

Fig. 7. An example of experiments.

7.3 Experiment

We implemented the described method and evaluated it with experiments. The initial conditions are settled exactly the same as the simulation. We judged a trial to be success if the robot touched the ball at first time from proper direction. The results of the experiments are shown in Table 3. The total success rate was about 75%. The failure cases were that the robot touched the ball unintentionally. These were due to the measurement error of the ball, which was not assumed in our model.

8   Conclusion

We took the uncertainty of the robot's pose into account by expanding the state space and designed a State-Action Map with DP by off-line calculation. The map was compressed with VQ in order to implement on the limited amount of robot's memory. We also defined the distortion between any two actions based on the action-value function. The total distortion of the map through compression was minimized as a result. By the simulations and experiments, it was verified that the robot observes the landmarks more efficiently than the fixed threshold case.

References

1. R. Ueda, T. Fukase, Y. Kobayashi, T. Arai, H. Yuasa and J. Ota: "Uniform Monte Carlo Localization – Fast and Robust Self-localization Method for Mobile Robots," Proc. of ICRA-2002, to appear.
2. E. Winner and M. Veloso: "Multi-Fidelity Robotic Behaviors: Acting With Variable State Information," Proc. of the Seventeenth National Conference on Artificial Intelligence, Austin, August 2000.
3. N. Mitsunaga and M. Asada: "Observation strategy for decision making based on information criterion," Proc. of IROS-2000, pp.1211-1216, 2000.
4. R. S. Sutton and A. G. Barto: "Reinforcement Learning: An Introduction," The MIT Press, 1998.
5. V. Hugel, P. Bonnin and P. Blazevic: "Reactive and Adaptive Control Architecture Designed for the Sony Legged Robots League in RoboCup 1999," Proc. of IROS-2000, pp.1032-1037, 2000.
6. A. Gersho and R. M. Gray: "Vector Quantization and Signal Compression," Kluwer Academic Publishers, 1992.
7. S. M. LaValle: "Roboto Motion Planning: A Game–Theoretic Foundation," Algorithmica, Vol. 26, pp.430-465, 2000.
8. W. H. Equitz: "A new vector quantization picture coding," IEEE Trans. Acoust. Speech Signal Process., pp. 1568-1575, October 1989.

KiRo – An Autonomous Table Soccer Player

Thilo Weigel and Bernhard Nebel

Institut für Informatik
Universität Freiburg
79110 Freiburg, Germany
{weigel,nebel}@informatik.uni-freiburg.de

Abstract. This paper presents KiRo – a system capable of playing table soccer on a competitive level and in a fully autonomous way. It can serve a human both as a teammate and an opponent but also allows for matches between two artificial players. KiRo introduces the table soccer game as a new domain for the research in the fields of robotics and artificial intelligence.

1 Introduction

The vision of the RoboCup research community is to build a robotic soccer team capable of beating the human world champion – by 2050 [3]. However, the games of the past RoboCup competitions show, that there is a long way to go before we even can think about playing against a human team. It would be clearly helpful if one could define tasks related to RoboCup that allow for a competition against humans without being forced to implement everything necessary to play real soccer. For example, one could define a mixed human/machine game for the simulation league. In fact, there have been such games already.

Even more interesting would be a game that is already well known and played by a lot of people. Such a game is *table soccer*[1]. This game is a popular pastime in bars and amusement arcades similar to billiards, but also a sport in its own right with competitions and even world championships. Due to the rather simple environment and the restricted skills required for playing it, it seemed realistic to us to develop an autonomous table soccer player capable of beating ordinary human players and to face the challenge of beating the human world champion before the year 2050.

Based on our experience of developing the *CS Freiburg* robotic soccer team [2, 4–6], we started to design and construct an autonomous table soccer player, which we called *KiRo*[2]. The table soccer game raises research questions similar to the ones addressed in the RoboCup context. However, as the sensor and motor problems are easier to solve, table soccer allows one to focus on high-level research issues as in the simulation league. Nevertheless, it presents the

---

[1] Table soccer is also commonly known as "Bar Football" or "Foosball".
[2] *KiRo* stands for *Kicker-Roboter*, which is the german expression for "table soccer robot".

G.A. Kaminka, P.U. Lima, and R. Rojas (Eds.): RoboCup 2002, LNAI 2752, pp. 384–392, 2003.
© Springer-Verlag Berlin Heidelberg 2003

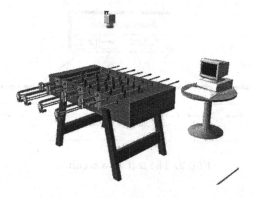

Fig. 1. The hardware setup

challenge of constructing an integrated system and has the fascination of a real robot league. Among other things, it seems feasible to successfully apply learning techniques in a real world scenario and it seems worthwhile to explore how the behavior of the opponent can be modeled in order to refine the player's strategy.

An autonomous table soccer player has the potential of fascinating people watching or playing against it. It joins entertainment and research and thus may be attractive for various purposes. Maybe there will be a "table soccer league" in the future?

The rest of the paper is structured as follows. We start with a description of the general system architecture in section 2. Section 3 presents details of the hardware we developed to control the rotational and translational movements of a player's rod. Section 4 describes how we gain a model of the world from the camera data. Section 5 presents KiRo's basic actions and how they are selected. Section 6 reports results from matches KiRo played in the public. In section 7 we conclude and give an outlook on our future work.

2   General Architecture

An important criterion in the design of KiRo was to modify the natural environment only as much as absolutely necessary. Therefore we bought a commercially available table soccer and attached the units for controlling the rods to the outside of the table. Each unit is individually mountable and controls one rod of a player. The only sensors used are absolute position encoders of the motors and a color camera overlooking the table[3]. A standard personal computer connects to the camera and control unit and handles all the information processing during a game. Figure 1 gives a sketch of the setup.

Figure 2 shows the structure of the control software we developed. From the camera data the position of the ball and the positions of the players are

---

[3] We discarded the idea of mounting a grid of photo sensors just above the playing surface for ball recognition, because this would have meant a considerable modification of the soccer table.

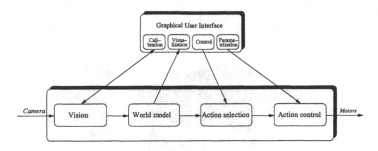

Fig. 2. The software architecture

estimated. These estimates are integrated into a world model where the direction of motion and the velocity of an object are calculated. In addition, the world model generates information which helps to locate the ball if not visible. The encoders are used to detect if the ball is locked between a figure and the floor. This information is very helpful if a player wants to stop and control the ball, e.g. for a pass to a figure of the same rod.

Based on the world model the action selection modules decides which behavior from a set of basic skills is the most appropriate one for the given situation. The execution of the selected action is then monitored by the action control module which sends the suitable commands to the motors.

Table soccer can be a very fast game where the ball may move at velocities of up to 10 m/s. This means that even at a frame rate of 50 Hz the ball possibly travels as far as 200 mm between two consecutive frames. In order to cope with these demanding conditions we attempt to minimize the delay between a change in the environment and an action being taken in response. By synchronizing the vision and action selection processes we achieve that an action is selected and executed as soon as a new camera image is available. This reduces the delay to the amount of time needed for digitizing the camera's analogue signal (approximately 20ms at a very high shutter speed) plus the time needed for processing the new information and communicating with the motor controllers (currently approximately 11 ms). In order to cope with this delay, we date back by 20ms the timestamp which is assigned to a newly arrived image and estimate the positions of all objects 11 ms ahead of the current time. Of course, this increases the uncertainty of an object's position estimate, but decreases the effects of the delay.

But reactiveness isn't everything anyway: Interestingly, professional players affirmed, that very often their strategy envisions just *not* to react to the movements or posture of the ball or the opponent figures. At an advanced level of play one would be fooled by an opponent's trick too easily and it is therefore advisable to concentrate on an elaborate and constantly changing positioning scheme. What distinguishes a professional player is rather his strategical play and his motoric skills to manipulate the ball than his fast reaction time.

Fig. 3. A control unit

3   Hardware

Because in Germany *Löwen* soccer tables are commonly used both for competitions and recreation we decided to use their *Home Soccer* model[4] for our purposes. The table provides a playing field of the size 1200mm x 680mm and has four rods on each side. There are figures attached to each rod (1 for the goal keeper, 2 for the defender, 5 for the mid field and 3 for the attacker), which can be used to manipulate the ball. We designed the units for controlling the rotational and translational movements of a player's rod in such a way that they are easily mountable to other manufacturer's tables as well. Figure 3 shows a model of a control unit with a player's rod attached to it. Coupled to a belt drive, the slide glides on a spline shaft when the belt is moved by a motor. A second motor and belt drive cause the spline shaft, and thus the belt pulleys of the slide, to rotate. As the player's rod is attached to the upper belt pulley of the slide, any desired translational and rotational movement of a player can be achieved by controlling the corresponding motors appropriately.

The *Faulhaber* servo motors and motor controllers we use are addressable via an RS232 link in a comfortable way. To control eight motors (2 for each unit) at the same time we equipped the PC *AMD Athlon, 700 MHz, 256 MB Ram* with a *Stallion Easy I/O* multi-port serial adapter.

Even though more specialized sensors could be used, we preferred to rely mainly on the position encoders of the motors and on one color camera. The vision system we employ consists of a *Phytec VCAM-110* camera and a *Phytec pciGRABBER-4* frame grabber, providing PAL images in YUV format. Because we analyze each half frame individually, we achieve an effective frame rate of 50 Hz with an image resolution of 384x288 pixels. In addition, a safety light grid is used to guarantee that nobody will be harmed when putting a hand between the player rods.

4   Vision and World Modeling

Using the very efficient CMVision library [1] for color segmentation we are able to extract the positions of the players and the position of the ball at a frame

---

[4] http://www.loewen.de/produkte/soccer/homesocc.htm

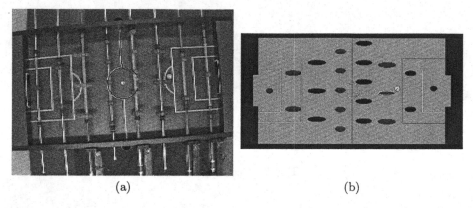

(a)   (b)

Fig. 4. An image from the overhead camera (a) and the world model derived from it (b). In the image the calibration circle and line are plotted black. In the world model the ball is marked as a white circle and the ball owner is marked by a white frame

rate of 50 Hz. Since the position of the table relative to the camera may change during a game, we have developed a simple but effective calibrating mechanism which allows us to re-calibrate the system every few seconds. The transformation matrix from image coordinates to real world coordinates is determined by examining the field lines and finding both the center circle and the center lines using a simple template matching method. First, starting with default values, the position and the size of a circle template is varied systematically until the correlation with the camera image reaches a maxima. As in the succesive cycle the previously determined circle center, circle position and line orientation are taken as starting values, the described method usually finds the relevant field lines within a few milliseconds – if the soccer table doesn't move considerably. The circle's center then yields the position of the table, the angle of the straight lines its orientation and the circle radius the zoom factor. Figure 4 (a) shows an image from the overhead camera. It can be seen that the calibration routine recognized the center circle and line.

A player's rod has only two degrees of freedom and both its position and the distance between its figures are known. Thus, individually detecting the positions of all the figures of a rod creates redundant information. This means that we can improve the estimates of the figures' inclination and position by averaging over all figures of that rod. The *a priori* knowledge also permits us to improve the estimates for an individual player because different blobs belonging to the same figure can be associated reliably.

The angle of a figure is estimated by comparing the width of its bounding box with the minimum and maximum possible values. Due to the limited resolution of the camera image only a rough and ambiguous estimate is possible. For instance, one cannot really tell if a figure is pointing right towards the table or in the opposite direction. However, by examining to which side of a rod a figure's bounding box further extends, it can usually be detected towards which side the figure is inclined. Knowing towards which side of a rod a figure is "up" and assuming that a figure is "down", when the bounding box and thus the figure's angle is small, is sufficient for our purposes at the moment.

Currently we use a yellow ball in order to simplify the perception problem. Since there is no other yellow object on the field, all yellow blobs can be used to calculate an overall bounding box. Usually its center corresponds to the center of the ball on the field, but there might be considerable inaccuracies if the ball is partially covered by a rod's figure. However, knowing the expected size of the ball, the bounding box can be reconstructed taking into consideration the covering figure.

Quite often the ball cannot be identified in the camera image. This happens either because a goal was scored or - more frequently - because the ball is obscured completely by a figure. In order to ensure an appropriate behavior even in these situations, we mark a figure as the "ball owner" if the visible ball is close enough to it. The knowledge, which figure was the ball owner before the camera lost track of the ball permits us to assume that the ball is located right underneath this figure, even if this figure is moving.

Figure 4 (b) shows a screenshot of the world model constructed from the camera image. Note, that even though not plotted in the world model, it is known, towards which side of a rod a figure is inclined.

5   Action Selection and Action Control

In the first prototype version of KiRo we employ a simple decision-tree like action selection mechanism. It considers the current game situation and chooses one of the following basic actions for execution:

- *DefaultAction* move and turn rod to default home position
- *KickBall*: rotate the rod by 90° to kick the ball forward
- *BlockBall*: move the rod so that a figure intercepts the ball
- *ClearBall*: move to the same position as *BlockBall* but turn the rod in order to let the ball pass from behind
- *BlockAtPos*: move the rod so that a figure prevents the ball passing at a specific position
- *ClearAtPos*: move the rod to a specific position and turn the rod in order to let the ball pass from behind

Figure 5 shows the decision tree used to select an action for the rod of a player. Only a few predicates are used and the actions are selected in a straightforward way. All the rods are treated in the same way, except that the positions for *BlockAtPos* and *BlockBall* are calculated individually.

Every figure of a player's rod can move within a certain range. Usually the ranges of two figures overlap and consequently there may be situations with two figures as candidate for moving to a specific target position. In these cases we select the figure with the best trade-off between its distance to the target position and the distance from its range limits to the target position. To avoid oscillation, e.g. when blocking the moving ball, we additionally prefer the figure that was selected in the last cycle already.

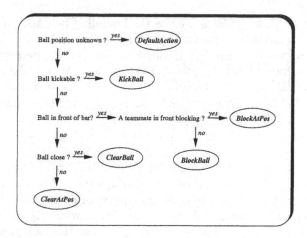

Fig. 5. The decision tree for selecting an action

The exact target position where a figure tries to block the ball depends on the position, direction and velocity of the ball. If the ball is moving very fast, the position where the ball is anticipated to pass the rod is taken. However, if the ball is moving very slowly, the target position is set in the way of the expected kicking direction of the opponent: it is assumed that the figures of an offensive rod always aim at the goal and that other figures usually try to kick the ball just forward. In order to achieve smooth transitions between the anticipated and the expected position, the target positions for intermediate ball velocities are calculated by interpolating between the two positions.

To avoid unnecessary "hectic" behavior the velocity at which a rod is moved is determined by considering how urgent it is to reach a given target position. If the ball is far away and it is moving only slowly there is no need for a fast reaction. But the closer and the faster the ball gets, the higher is the speed assigned to the rods.

The currently available basic actions and the manner of selecting them lead to a very "agile" and effective behavior. The well organized team line up and the reliable ball blocking skill make it quite difficult for an opponent to bring the ball forward. In turn, the fact that the ball is kicked forward as soon as possible makes it hard for opponents to react fast enough to block it. Test games have shown, that even with a simple strategy like the one presented here, beginners and amateurs can be beaten by the autonomous table soccer player.

6   Results

At the RoboCup German Open '02 in Paderborn and the Hannover Industrial Fair '02 KiRo played during nine days for a total of about 22 hours against human players. Mostly men, but also a lot of women were queuing up, curious to play table soccer player against a machine. In the same way kids, adolescents

Table 1. Game results

	Games won : Games lost	Goals shot : Goals received
Beginners	17 : 0	154 : 28
Amateurs	56 : 11	501 : 284
Advanced Players	3 : 11	75 : 117
Professionals	0 : 4	7 : 40
Total	**76 : 26**	**737 : 469**

and adults were fascinated by KiRo, ambitious to win and obviously having fun when playing. We were surprised by the fact, that most of the "test players" had considerable experience and were already playing at a high standard.

Altogether we recorded 102 matches KiRo played against human opponents, ignoring a lot of "trial games", where people gave up very early or just wanted a quick impression of how it is like to play against a machine. Always two players were playing as a team against KiRo. For all the games we recorded the team's playing standard, which we assessed by observing the players' skills and their strategical behavior, distinguishing between the following categories:

- A *beginner* has hardly ever played and has neither special skills nor a strategical understanding for the game.
- An *amateur* plays once in a while, has fundamental skills and a strategical understanding of the game.
- An *advanced player* is playing regularly and consciously improving his skills and strategy while playing
- A *professional* is explicitly practicing special shots or tricks, plays with an elaborate strategy and competes at tournaments

Table 1 shows the results of the games. Of course, only a rough and subjective assessment of the teams' playing standard was possible. KiRo won about 75% of all the games and proofed to be a challenge for beginners and amateurs. Even against two professional players (one of them the runner up at the European Championships in 1998), KiRo managed to score some lucky goals until they got used to its playing style. Nevertheless, like the audience and all the other players they appreciated KiRo and offered to contribute their experience and knowledge for improving KiRo's strategy.

7   Conclusion and Future Work

We presented a system capable of playing table soccer in a fully autonomous way. In its first prototype version it plays with a simple but effective strategy and is able to win against beginners and amateurs. People playing against KiRo were obviously having fun and with respect to the entertaining aspect (not the social aspect, though) of the game they saw little difference to playing against a human player.

The first positive feedback from human test players allows us to be optimistic regarding the acceptance of KiRo to the wider public. But the existing prototype is more than just a toy: it also represents a robust basis for research in the fields of robotics and artificial intelligence. In competitions against human players or other artificial players research can be evaluated in an attractive way in the real world.

Our future work includes improving the hardware and extending the vision system to enable playing with a white ball. In addition, we plan to focus on designing a new action selection mechanism which incorporates new skills, allows for different playing styles and adapts itself to the characteristics and capabilities of the opponent player. For tuning the parameters of the basic skills we attempt to apply learning techniques in the real environment.

Acknowledgments

This work has been partially supported by *Deutsche Forschungsgemeinschaft* (DFG), by *SICK AG*, and by *Faulhaber GMBH & CO.KG*. The authors would also like to thank *Joachim Koschikowski* for the technical drawings of the control units.

References

1. James Bruce, Tucker Balch, and Manuela M. Veloso. Fast and inexpensive color image segmentation for interactive robots. In *Proc. of the 2000 IEEE/RSJ International Conference on Intelligent Robots and Systems (IROS '00)*, volume 3, pages 2061 – 2066, October 2000.
2. Jens-Steffen Gutmann, Wolfgang Hatzack, Immanuel Herrmann, Bernhard Nebel, Frank Rittinger, Augustinus Topor, Thilo Weigel, and Bruno Welsch. The CS Freiburg robotic soccer team: Reliable self-localization, multirobot sensor integration, and basic soccer skills. In M. Asada and H. Kitano, editors, *RoboCup-98: Robot Soccer World Cup II*, Lecture Notes in Artificial Intelligence, pages 93–108. Springer-Verlag, 1999.
3. Hiroaki Kitano, Minoru Asada, Yasuo Kuniyoshi, Itsuki Noda, Eiichi Osawa, and Hitoshi Matsubara. RoboCup: A challenge problem for AI. *AI Magazine*, 18(1):73–85, 1997.
4. Bernhard Nebel, Jens-Steffen Gutmann, and Wolfgang Hatzack. The CS Freiburg '99 team. In M. Veloso, E. Pagello, and H. Kitano, editors, *RoboCup-99: Robot Soccer World Cup III*, Lecture Notes in Artificial Intelligence, pages 703–706. Springer-Verlag, 2000.
5. Thilo Weigel, Willi Auerbach, Markus Dietl, Burhard Dümler, Jens-Steffen Gutmann, Kornel Marko, Klaus Müller, Bernhard Nebel, Boris Szerbakowski, and Maximiliam Thiel. CS Freiburg: Doing the right thing in a group. In P. Stone, G. Kraetzschmar, T. Balch, and H. Kitano, editors, *RoboCup-2000: Robot Soccer World Cup IV*, Lecture Notes in Artificial Intelligence. Springer-Verlag, 2001.
6. Thilo Weigel, Alexander Kleiner, Florian Diesch, Markus Dietl, Jens-Steffen Gutmann, Bernhard Nebel, Patrick Stiegeler, and Boris Szerbakowski. CS Freiburg 2001. In P. Stone, G. Kraetzschmar, T. Balch, and H. Kitano, editors, *RoboCup-2001: Robot Soccer World Cup V*, Lecture Notes in Artificial Intelligence. Springer-Verlag, 2002.

Adaptive Methods to Improve Self-localization in Robot Soccer

Ingo Dahm[1] and Jens Ziegler[2]

[1] Computer Engineering Institute
University of Dortmund, D-44227 Dortmund, Germany
ingo.dahm@uni-dortmund.de
[2] Dept. of Computer Science
University of Dortmund, D-44227 Dortmund, Germany
jens.ziegler@uni-dortmund.de

Abstract. This paper shows adaptive strategies to improve the reliability and performance of self-localization in robot soccer with legged robots. Adaptiveness is the common feature of the presented algorithms and has proved essential to enhance the quality of localization by a new classification technique, essential to increase the confidence level of internal information about the environment by extracting reliability information and by communicating them via parameterizable acoustic communication, and essential to circumvent manual implementations of walking patterns by evolving them automatically.

1 Introduction

The autonomous mobile robot teams in the different leagues of RoboCup face very special requirements. One of the most important problems that these teams have to solve are navigation and self-localization. Therefore, algorithms are needed that in fast changing, dynamical environments give reliable information about the actual state. Cooperation in teams of robots is a topic of recent research, indicating that reliable and fast communication is crucial for successful control.

In order to improve the quality of navigation, it is necessary to increase the performance of the process that extracts information from the sensory input. Here, an approach is presented that adds a meta level of information to the sensor data: a reliability factor is calculated from visual information that represents the accuracy of the data. The internal representation of the actual state of the game – called *world model* – of each robot is then communicated to other team robots via acoustic communication in order to enhance the local reliability information.

If the robots' localization module depends on odometry data, which is the fact with the robots of our part of the German United Team, it is crucial for them to have robust locomotion modules. Robustness is used here in terms of returning reliable information about the effective covered distance during a given time with a given walking pattern. Robustness, speed and reliability are all facets of the overall quality of a walking pattern and are used within an Evolutionary

G.A. Kaminka, P.U. Lima, and R. Rojas (Eds.): RoboCup 2002, LNAI 2752, pp. 393–408, 2003.

Algorithm to automatically develop well performing walking programs in the above mentioned sense.

The rest of the paper is organized as follows. In Section 2, we describe how reliability information can be extracted during classification. The principle of improving accuracy and speed of the robots' walking patterns is illustrated in Section 3. Thereafter, we briefly present a robust method of acoustical communication. This is followed by a discussion, how the suggested methods improve the accuracy of self-localization.

2   Vision-Based Navigation

Each legged robot is equipped with a camera. The hardware-based vision processor provides a robust eight-color differentiation [29]. Since main objects are characterized by color [26], a basic object classification can be done by using that module. Nevertheless, observed objects have more properties that can be used for classification. Some of them (e.g. shape, size) can be estimated efficiently or are extracted during image processing anyway [6, 23]. Thus, additional features can be included in the classification process with negligible increase of processing time.

Robots' actions are mainly affected by the observed dynamic environment. Accidentally false classified objects can impair the robots' behavior dramatically. Thus, enhancements in classification can improve the overall robots' performance. To improve the accuracy of object detection under the aspects of the real-time limits, we suggest a technique that classifies objects with M properties and assigns a reliability information to every decision. This reliability information can be used for further optimizations in navigation as shown in Section 5.

2.1   Object Classification by Signal Space Detection (SSD)

For that, all extracted M properties of an object are used to determine the classifiers output. Without noisy components, these properties can be viewed as coordinates of fixed points in a M-dimensional signal space (Fig. 1 for $M = 2$). Each of these so-called admissible signal points is associated with a fixed classification. In Fig. 1, an admissible signal point $\underline{c}_i$ is associated with the class i. Given this constellation, the signal space can be partitioned so that decision regions are formed which are bounded by hyperplanes (so-called decision planes).

In typical implementations, the properties of objects cannot be identified ideally. A set of inexactly estimated properties can also be represented as a point in signal space. The classification is determined by the position of this so-called observed signal point $\underline{r}_j$ relative to the bounding hyperplanes. In Fig. 1, $\underline{r}_0$ is associated with class 2 and $\underline{r}_1$ is associated with class 1.

If inexact property estimation can be modeled as exact values disturbed by average white gaussian noise, then the decision planes are easy to estimate. For that, the signal space must be partitioned into Voronoi Regions to get classifications of highest accuracy [28].

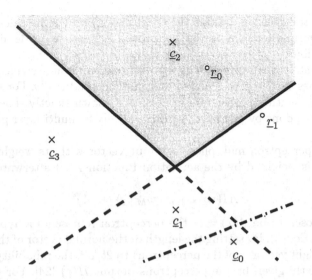

Fig. 1. Illustrated concept of object classification using the Signal Space Detection approach for $M = 2$.

For colored noise, the euklidic distance is not a good measure to estimate the correct class of an observed object. In some cases, the signal space can be transformed into a white-noise domain [14, 13]. Besides, the hyperplanes can be set using a neural network approach. In the next section, we show how reliability information can be extracted using conventional networks like multilayer perceptrons (MLP) [1, 16].

2.2 Extracting Reliability Information

In [24], a method to extract reliability information using a special SSD detector was introduced. An observed signal point, which is positioned close to an admissible signal point, represents a very confident decision (e.g. r_0 in Fig. 1). On the other hand, an observed signal point which lies close to a decision plane marks an unreliable decision (e.g. r_1 in Fig. 1). That is, the distance from an observed signal point to the admissible signal points and to the decision planes is a measure for the reliability of the classification. The consideration of these distances allows the calculation of the individual probabilities for the possible detector outputs: to be member of a certain class ($r \in C$) or not ($r \notin C$).

Assuming that the observed signal point is r, the soft-output for the classification i, which is called $L(i)$, can be calculated with the so-called log-likelihood ratio after [15]:

$$L(i) = ln\frac{P(i = C|r)}{P(i \neq C|r)} \tag{1}$$

Note, that a positive value $L(i)$ indicates r is classified to belong to C, a negative value means r is classified *not* to belong to C. The absolute value of $L(i)$ is the reliability of the decision. In [24], the exact procedure for the calculation of this reliability information using the SSD approach is presented in detail for practical implementations.

Unfortunately, that approach uses predefined admissible signal points. Thus, decision planes can be precalculated and implemented easily. For typical object classifications, neither properties nor noise are known exactly. Therefore, classification is often done by neural networks, typically by multi-layer perceptrons [1, 16].

A single perceptron multiplies the input vector with its weight vector. The dot-product is weighted by the activation function $A(x)$ afterwards as done in Eq. (2) [1].

$$A\left((w_1, w_2, \ldots w_{M+1}) \cdot (\underline{r}, 1)\right) \tag{2}$$

If $A(x)$ is chosen to be $A(x) = x$, the perceptron represents a hyperplane H as illustrated in Eq. (3). By setting the length of the normal vector of the hyperplane (resp. the weight vector $\underline{w}$ of the perceptron) to $2b/\sigma^2$, the reliability information of $\underline{r}$ is implicitly given by the perceptrons output $H(\underline{r})$ [24]. For that, b is the distance from the admissible signal point to the plane and σ^2 represents the noise variance [24].

$$H : \begin{pmatrix} w_1 \\ w_2 \\ \ldots \\ w_M \end{pmatrix} \underline{r} + w_{M+1} = 0. \tag{3}$$

Since the variance typically changes for different sensor data, it must be measured at run-time or approximated by an estimate of typical channel characteristics. The admissible signal point can be approximated by the center of all observed signal points that are classified to be a member of the same class. This can be done efficiently after the training phase.

Unfortunately, due to simplified learning rules, typically a sigmoid activation function (see Eq. (4)) is used in common neural networks [16]. Thus, the distance from H to $\underline{r}$ cannot be calculated directly using conventional perceptrons. To extract the reliability information, the inverse function $A^{-1}(x)$ after Eq. (5) must be applied.

$$A : x \to \frac{1}{1 + e^{c(t-x)}} \tag{4}$$

$$A^{-1} : x \to t - \frac{1}{c} \cdot ln\left(\frac{1}{x} - 1\right) \tag{5}$$

2.3   Implementation Issues

In the signal space, the decision regions are typically bounded by a set of several hyperplanes. Not all planes contribute to the determination of the reliability information. Thus, we have to choose the appropriate bounding hyperplane for calculating the soft information. In Fig. 1 for example, the hyperplane, which is visualized by the dash-dot line, is obviously not decisive for $\underline{r}_0$. Therefore, we have to define a set of decisive hyperplanes for each output vector. That k-dimensional vector gives the position of the observed signal point relatively to all decision planes. The classification can be done by assigning a class to every possible output vector. This can be implemented using the MLP network approach. On the other hand, the algebraic sign of the extracted reliability can be used with a boolean algebra for classification. This approach is very efficient, especially under run-time constraints.

An implementation of the supposed methodology is very similar to conventional neural networks: M property extraction units (e.g. sensors) are connected with k perceptrons. These perceptrons represent the decision planes. After the training phase, the weights must normalized so that $|(w_1, w_2, \ldots w_M)| = 2b/\sigma^2$. To calculate the reliability (resp. the distance of $\underline{r}$ to the closest decision plane), the outputs of the perceptrons must be weighted by A^{-1}.

This calculated additional information leads to a significantly increased accuracy of self-localization. The way how reliability information improves the localization process is presented in Section 5. Nevertheless, the performance of this approach crucially depends on the accuracy of sensory information.

3   Movement

A reliable estimation of the actual robot position even with insufficient sensor data can be done only with high-quality odometry data. Therefore, the development of robust walking is necessary, with robustness describing not only fast and stable walking but also less slipping for precise self-localization based on dead reckoning.

3.1   Evolution of Walking

The progress in the development of faster, more robust and computationally more powerful robots is mirrored in the Sony Legged League: this young league of the RoboCup federation has now reached the second generation of four-legged robots and the challenging edutainment robot market is expanding with increasing speed which will have a great influence on the future development of the Legged League robots. A major drawback of this tendency is that with almost every new robot architecture a re-implementation of the walking program is necessary, leading to complete new design whenever the robot platform is changed. Programming and control of walking robots is difficult, because of the high dimensionality of the movements and the complex sensory and motor limitations, let alone the various uncertainties that arise during the operation. Even if the original walking program proves satisfactory, parameter changes of the hardware (e.g. a slight change of the position of the center of mass of the robot, changes in maximum acceleration or speed of joints, or changes in weight or length of limbs) may cause unwanted defects in terms of stability, robustness against slackness or speed. In order to avoid this effects and to circumvent additional and expensive work, adaptive methods should be used that automatically generate programs for walking.

The evolution of robot control programs has been the topic of recent publications [20, 2, 3, 12, 22, 21, 27] and especially the field of walking robots becomes more and more important [17, 7]. Gait patterns of stick insects have been analyzed to gain more detailed information on natural gait coordination algorithms [10]. Many researchers have often been inspired by biology to build legged robots. An overview can be found in [19]. Nevertheless, the above-mentioned approaches deal with a special instance of an autonomous robot (or walking agent), on which the architecture of the developed control system heavily depends.

It was one of the main goals of this work to make the evolution of robot controllers as independent as possible from morphology specific information. So morphology-related information, although available, will not be used. If, for example, a joint looses the ability to reach certain positions, the outcome of an inverse transformation, which depends on the correct working joint, will be useless. Additionally, the algorithm for the inverse transformation is correct only for a single robot. A machine-learning algorithm, however, should be able to cope with changing hardware and environmental conditions.

A first step towards control of movements of a legged robot is to move the single legs according to a desired trajectory. This trajectory depends on the desired behavior and requires very well coordinated synchronous movements of all joints involved. Thus, describing a movement of a robot requires to give the time dependent values of the acting forces for each involved joint during the motion. The next sections shall now explain the experimental setup and preliminary results from the evolution of walking with Genetic Programming.

3.2   The Evolutionary Algorithm

A first step toward control of movements of a legged robot is to move single joints according to a desired movement of more complex parts of the robot, e.g. a limb. Coordinating the movement results in the necessity to give a time series of motive forces or nominal angles for each joint of the robot, which sums up to 3 joints for a single leg and an overall of 12 joints for the whole four-legged robot at each discrete time step t during the motion. This sequence has to be coordinated in time to achieve the desired movement in sufficient quality. The Evolutionary Algorithm now has to fulfill certain requirements:

- The structure of the individual has to be interpreted as a robot control program.
- Therefore it is necessary to have operations in the global operator set that allow to control motors.
- The quality of the executed individual has to be measured and fed back into the algorithm.
- Better individuals must have a higher probability to spread their genetic information into the next generation.
- The genetic information must be varied to get an evolutionary drift towards better and better walking programs.

Table 1. Koza tableau with parameter settings for the Evolutionary Algorithm.

Parameters	Values
Objective:	Evolve parameter set that makes the robot walk
Terminal set	Real numbers
Selection scheme	Roulette wheel selection
Population size	20
Crossover probability	0.3
Mutation probability	0.1
Random replacement probability	0.09
Termination criterion	No. of generations
Maximum size of individual	4 14-dimensional vectors
Initialization method	Random

Representation. An individual in the current setting is a set of vectors

$$I = \{i_1, i_2, i_3, i_4\} \tag{6}$$

with each i_k being a vector.

$$i_k = (x_1, x_2, \ldots, x_{12}, b, t). \tag{7}$$

The values $x_1, \ldots, x_{12}$ represent motor angles for all 12 motors of the legs of the robot, the value b is a boolean variable indicating whether the movement of the joints to the nominal values x_k shall be a linear movement or a free point-to-point movement. The value t gives the time after which all motors $m_k, k \in \{1, \ldots, 12\}$ have to have reached the desired position x_k. Walking is a cyclic movement and here one loop is separated into different phases. The robot is supposed to be in the first phase i_1 at the beginning of the walking. After a certain time given by t_1, the next phase starts and the motors move to the positions given in i_2. After time t_2, the desired positions are reached and the next phase starts. After reaching the positions in phase i_4, the next phase is again phase i_1, so that the walking is divided into four phases. This rotation scheme continues as long as the robot walks. The evolutionary algorithm now has $4 \times 14 = 56$ degrees of freedom and several additional parameters which are given in Table 1.

In other experiments a different representation was implemented. To avoid possible erratic movements, a variable walking pattern was used that could be adjusted with a set of ten parameters which are variables for a mathematical model of a set of superimposed oscillations that are used to calculate the leg movements. Preliminary experiments used this representation with reduced complexity (see Section 3.2).

Measuring Fitness. There are two ways of measuring the fitness of an individual in the current algorithm. The first one is an realization of an interactive evolutionary process: two individuals are executed on a robot and a human observer has to manually decide which of both individuals has a higher quality. This approach circumvents numerical values as the fitness criterion, and the experimenter is relieved of implementing a fitness function that includes 'soft' criteria such as smoothness, grip, and elegance of movements, criteria which can easily be observed and rated by any human experimenter. On the other hand, a comparison of individuals from different generations is difficult because of the lack of objective numerical data. This has led to the implementation of an automatic fitness evaluation module which uses a camera to track the robot during the motion. The distance between start and end point divided by the time used gives the speed of the movement. This setting has some disadvantages that makes it difficult to use, e.g. a robot falling over is probably considered as a fast forward moving robot.

The main problem of both approaches is the time consuming evaluation of individuals, because each individual of each generation has to be down-loaded to the robot, executed and evaluated. Due to the fact that evolution is a 'blind watchmaker', movements are likely to emerge that make the robot stumble and fall, which has the effect that a human experimenter is needed to observe the evaluations *all the time*.

New approaches are currently investigated that try to learn from the user's decisions to develop a heuristic function that can be used instead of the time consuming evaluation with real robots[1]. Artificial Neural Networks will be trained with pairs of individuals along with the observers decision which of them represents the better walking. Once this heuristic is established in sufficient quality, it will be used to evaluate individuals *offline*. The potential effect is less long lasting experiments and a better quality of the resulting programs.

Selection Scheme. Individuals are compared pairwise and assigned a static fitness value. This method is known as tournament selection [3], but in this special case, a tournament is only needed to discriminate between good and poor performing individuals. The better individual is assigned a better—and static—fitness value that in turn is used in subsequent steps. After all individuals are evaluated, a fitness proportional selection takes place (called roulette-wheel-selection). Selected individuals are either mutated, recombined with other individuals or replaced by randomly initialized new individuals.

Mutation. One of the 56 parameters of an individual is randomly selected and mutated by adding a standard (0,1)-Gaussian distributed random variable.

Crossover. Two individuals are recombined by randomly exchanging single parameters or sequences of parameters. The special parameters b, t are recombined separately due to their different domains.

---

[1] The execution of evolved walking programs during long lasting experiments is a strenuous process for both experimenter and robot hardware. It is thus desirable to increase the speed of the evolutionary process (and therewith to decrease the total number of evaluations) in order to minimize the wear-out of expensive hardware.

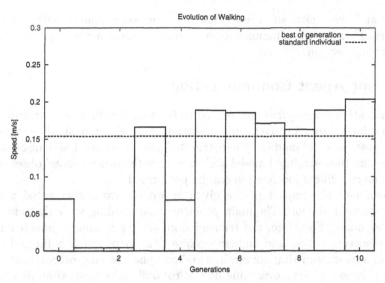

Fig. 2. Development of the speed of the fastest individual per generation. The horizontal line indicates the speed of the standard walking used for soccer.

Results. Fig. 2 shows preliminary results of a preliminary experiment with reduced complexity and a smaller population. The representation is now a 10-dimensional vector parameterizing a mathematical model of walking. The model describes the trajectory (position and orientation) of the center of mass of the whole robot and the parameters are responsible for the speed, frequency and radius of leg movements. We used this simplified model in our first experiments in order to increase the convergence speed of the evolution by decreasing the size of the search space. The speed of the robot using the standard parameter setting (describing the gait pattern that is used as the default walking by the German United Team) is shown as the horizontal line at $0.154\frac{m}{s}$ in Fig. 2. The fitness of the best individual of every generation is shown. It is astounding that, even with a very small population size of four individuals, an increase of maximum speed of nearly 30% could be observed. The only fitness criterion was linear speed of the movement. Neither robustness nor smoothness of the walking pattern were taken into account for fitness calculation. Deviations to both sides during the walking, stumbling or crawling were frequently observed phenomena. This leads to the assumption that additional criteria must be taken into account for fitness evaluation, resulting in a multi-objective optimization [11]. Multiple criteria can be adopted easily in our Evolutionary Algorithm by varying the decision criterion of the tournaments. This leads to a selection pressure on the individuals that is proportional to the frequency of the corresponding criteria. This experiments are promising and indicate that the objective function needs to be defined very carefully in order to yield optimal results.

Having improved odometry data gained from robust walking and reliable vision-based self-localization, the robot's position can then be estimated more exactly, and even more so, if individual information is shared with other team members. Therefore, a communication channel is implemented and presented in the following section.

4   Robot Agent Communication

Communication is treated as an enabling technology for efficient distributed work in multi robot teams. A robust communication channel can be used to replace the robots' internal world models by a distributed global model. This can be done be broadcasting the calculated model and to receive the other robots' observations. Thus, a more reliable localization can be performed.

To evaluate the impact of the given approach, we implemented a robust acoustic communication. The main problem when dealing with that channel is the heavy noise. Therefore, the transmission quality is mainly affected by the audience speech, echos, and ambience noise. The bandwidth is limited due to quality of sensors, run-time constraints and complicated channel features. As the channel parameters vary over time due to robots' movement, time dependency of noise, and echos, the communication must be adapted to the actual channel parameters.

The second complicated constraint is the run-time limited processing time. Since world models use to age very fast and the transmitted data is very error-sensitive, the data transmission must be effective and almost error free. Therefore, a fast error correction code (ECC) must be established. The two most common approaches for error correction are the use of Block Codes (e.g. so-called Reed Solomon Codes [18, 30]), and the utilization of convolutional codes as for so-called Turbo Codes [8]. Due to the real-time constraints it is impossible to use a complex code for error detection in robot communication. Such codes are characterized by a time intensive decoding phase. Thus, a specialized parity check code is used for communication by our team.

The relevant information is stored symbolically in a $M \times M$-matrix. Every row and every column is protected by a parity check bit [25]. We use even parity, that means the number of ones in each row and column including the parity bit is even. This is illustrated in Fig. 3. If one bit error inside the $M \times M$ array occurs, the parity check of the corresponding row and column fails. Thus, the error position is easy to detect as the intersection of the erroneous row and column. The error value is given implicitly, since we handle boolean information.

The situation changes, if more errors occur or if parity bits become corrupted. To solve this problem, we use an n-dimensional parity check, for $n = 3$ a parity cube. Note, that n is the dimension of a hypercube that contains M^n bits. When all parity checks fail (for $n = 3$, column, row, depth), the erroneous check lines intersect at the bit, that is most likely corrupted. If the checks of only two parities fail, the probable error position can be estimated at the intersection of the corresponding row and column. Nevertheless, it is not sure if this bit is really a corrupted one or not: for example, two erroneous bits in a line cause a successful parity check for the corrupted bits, two corrupted parity bits cause unwanted corruption of a correct bit.

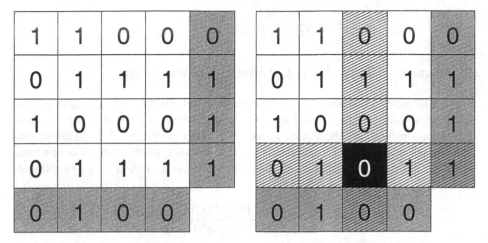

Fig. 3. Parity check code using a two-dimensional concept. Received parities (gray regions) are compared with calculated information. Intersection of defect line and row points to erroneous position (black).

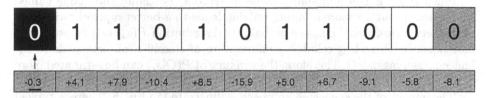

Fig. 4. Enhanced parity check code using soft information to estimate possible error position by examining single bit reliabilities. The parity bit is shaded gray, the erroneous bit is marked black.

To improve the error correction capability, the soft information about every bit is very useful. To extract the reliability of a bit, we perform a discrete Fast Fourier Transform (FFT) [9, 5]. The FFT data is then classified using the method given in Section 2. If the reliability of a possible erroneous bit is low, then it becomes inverted. This idea is illustrated in Fig. 4. There, 10 bits are parity checked. The error position cannot be calculated. Since reliability information about every bit is calculated, the symbol with the lowest soft information becomes corrected. The calculation of soft information leads to enhancements in error correction capability. Furthermore, we use soft information as a measure of overall channel quality. So we are able to trade code rate resp. bandwidth against error correction capability. The code rate can be adjusted to the actual channel capacity.

The suggested method is very fast, because it uses bitwise operations. This can be done parallel on the robots, because multi-bit operations are possible with our architecture. With that ECC, the code rate $c(n)$ for an n-dimensional hypercube that contains M^n bits is given in Eq. (8). The code rate can be increased by larger side length M, error correction capability rises with dimensionality n.

$$c(n) = \frac{M^n}{M^n + nM^{(n-1)}} = 1 - \frac{1}{\frac{1}{n}M + 1} \tag{8}$$

5   Bayesian Based Probabilistic Localization

The additional information about the decision reliability leads to an improved localization and navigation concept. The playing field is separated into discrete grid locations. We create a state-space with these positions. A position in this state space is called s_i. Observations O of landmarks, goals, and walls are combined with a priori information of the actual state and of the robots' movement. To do this, we use Bayes' Theorem [4]

$$P(s_i|O) = \frac{P(s_i)P(O|s_i)}{\Sigma_j P(s_j)P(O|s_j)} \tag{9}$$

where $P(s_i)$ is the a priori probability that the robot is in state s_i. $P(s_i|O)$ is the posterior probability that the robot is in state s_i given that it has just observed O and $P(O|s_i)$ is the probability of observing O in state s_i.

Since $P(s_i)$ is the probability to be in state s_i (without knowledge gained from visual input), a more accurate walking leads to a better a priori estimation of the actual position. Thus, the probability distribution $P(s_i)$ can be estimated more exactly. Providing reliability information of classified objects leads to enhanced observations O. Therefore, the variance of $P(O|s_i)$ can be estimated more exactly. Consequently, $P(s_i|O)$ provides more information with higher reliability.

The impact of the suggested approach is illustrated in Fig. 5. There, a typical scene is shown: The keeper stands inside the opponents goal. Since it hides the right border of the goal, the width of the goal dx is estimated incorrectly at t_0. As distance is calculated by applying intercept theorems, this leads to an incorrect self localization $s_i^{t_0}$ based on the observed situation (bold line in Fig. 5, A^{t_0}). At t_1, both robots have moved. The observation O now shows the goal in its full width. With the conventional approach, the a priori probability of being in one of the states $s_i^{t_1}$ (bold line in Fig. 5, A^{t_1}) is relatively high. A move to the posterior correct position (marked by a cross in Fig. 5, A^{t_1}) seems rather unlikely due to odometry data.

Using reliability information, the observation at t_0 and thus a calculated possible position $s_i^{t_0}$ is marked as low reliable[2] (grey area in Fig. 5, B^{t_0}). In contrast, the reliable observation O at t_1 gives a posterior position $s_i^{t_1}$ (grey circle in Fig. 5, B^{t_1}) with high reliability. Reliable odometry data supports this calculated decision.

The acoustic communication can be used to further increase the precision of the robots' world model. Therefore, every robot broadcasts its observed data, especially the estimated positions of ball and robots. For each robot, the received data is synchronized with its internal world model. This approach is demonstrated in Fig. 6: Since its disadvantageous position, robot 2 cannot localize

---

[2] As shape is used to classify objects, the non-rectangular shape of the goal at t_0 indicates a low reliability.

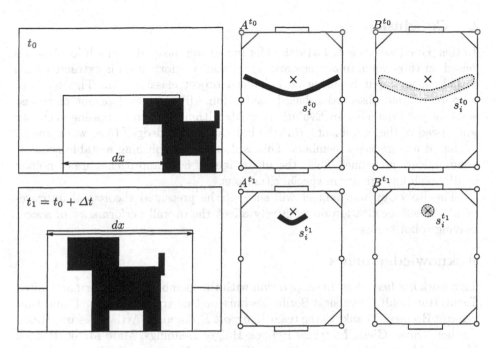

Fig. 5. A robots observation of a keeper standing inside the goal. Object borders are partially hidden. The estimated position of the observer using the conventional approach is shown in the middle. The position calculated with our method is illustrated right.

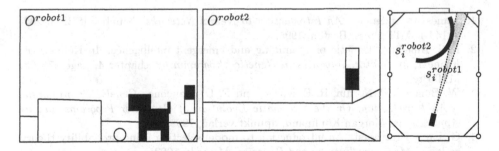

Fig. 6. Observations of two cooperative robots. The left illustration presents the observation of robot 1, that leads to a accurate self localization. The sketch in the middle shows the observation of robot 2. Due to its awkward viewpoint, robot 2 is unable to localize itself accurately. On the right, the combination of both observations leads to an improved localization of robot 2.

itself exactly (bold line in Fig. 6). Robot 1 observes the second robot under a certain angle (gray area in Fig. 6). The observations of both robots are combined. Thus, the position of robot 2 can be estimated with significantly improved accuracy.

6 Conclusion

In this paper, we presented a method for increasing the quality of self-localization based on three main improvements: (i) reliability information is extracted from visual sensor input by using an enhanced object classification. This leads to a more reliable observation-based navigation. (ii) the development of robust walking patterns with an Evolutionary Algorithm leads to increasing accuracy and speed of the movements. (iii) the individual knowledge of the world model is shared among team members. This is done by establishing a stable acoustic communication channel. Thus, the advantages of both approaches are combined to diminish uncertainty in special situations.

The RoboCup tournament will show if the presented theoretical improvements in self-localization do positively affect the overall performance of soccer playing robot teams.

Acknowledgements

This work has been done in cooperation with the members of the German United Team: Humboldt Universität Berlin, Technische Universität Darmstadt and Universität Bremen. Thanks to the team *Ruhrpott Hellhounds*: Arthur Cesarz, Simon Fischer, Oliver Giese, Matthias Hebbel, Holger Hennings, Marc Malik, Patrick Matters, Markus Meier, Ingo Mierswa, Christian Neumann, Denis Piepenstock, Lars Schley, and Jens Rentmeister. Jens Ziegler has been supported by the Deutsche Forschungsgemeinschaft (DFG) under grant Ba 1042/6-2.

References

1. James A. Anderson. *An Introduction to Neural Networks*. Number ISBN 0-262-01144-1. MIT Press. Boston, 1995.
2. P. J. Angeline. Genetic programming and emergent intelligence. In Kenneth E. Kinnear, Jr., editor, *Advances in Genetic Programming*, chapter 4, pages 75–98. MIT Press, 1994.
3. W. Banzhaf, P. Nordin, R. E. Keller, and F. D. Francone. *Genetic Programming – An Introduction; On the Automatic Evolution of Computer Programs and its Applications*. Morgan Kaufmann, dpunkt.verlag, 1998.
4. G. Larry Bretthorst. An introduction to model selection using probability theory as logic. *Maximum Entropy and Bayesian Methods*, 1993.
5. E. Oren Brigham. *The Fast Fourier Transform and Its Applications*. Prentice Hall, 1st edition, October 1997.
6. J. Bruce, Tucker Balch, and Maria Manuela Veloso. Fast and inexpensive color image segmentation for interactive robots. In *Proceedings of the 2000 IEEE/RSJ International Conference on Intelligent Robots and Systems (IROS '00)*, volume 3, pages 2061 – 2066, October 2000.
7. J. Busch, J. Ziegler, C. Aue, A. Ross, D. Sawitzki, and Wolfgang Banzhaf. Automatic generation of control programs for walking robots using genetic programming. In J. A. Foster, E. Lutton, J. Miller, C. Ryan, and A. G. B. Tettamanzi, editors, *Proceedings of the 5th European Conference on Genetic Programming*, volume 2278 of *Lecture Notes in Computer Science*, pages 258–268. Springer, New York, 2002.

8. C.Berrou, A.Glavieux, and P.Thitimajshima. Near shannon limit error correcting coding and decoding: Turbo-codes (1). In *International Conference on on Communications*, pages 1064–1070, Geneva, Switzerland, 1993.
9. J.W. Cooley and J.W.Tukey. An algorithm for the machine calculation of complex fourier series. *Mathematics of Computation*, 19(90):297–301, 1965.
10. H. Cruse. Coordination of leg movement in walking animals. In J.-A. Meyer and S.W. Wilson, editors, *From animals to animats. Intl. Conf. on Simulation of Adaptive Behavior*, pages 105–119. MIT Press, Cambridge, MA, 1991.
11. Kalyanmoy Deb. Multi-objective genetic algorithms: Problem difficulties and construction of test problems. Technical Report of the Collaborative Research Center 531 *Computational Intelligence* CI–49/98, University of Dortmund, October 1998.
12. P. Dittrich, A. Bürgel, and W. Banzhaf. Learning to control a robot with random morphology. In P. Husbands and J.-A. Meyer, editors, *Proceedings First European Workshop on Evolutionary Robotics*, pages 165–178. Springer, Berlin, 1998.
13. G.Stromberg. *Signal Space Detection with Application to Magnetic Recording*. PhD thesis, University of Dortmund, September 2000.
14. G.Stromberg, M.Hassner, and U.Schwiegelshohn. Signal Space Detection in Colored Noise. *IEEE Transactions on Magnetics*, 36(3):604–612, May 2000.
15. J. Hagenauer, E. Offer, and L. Papke. Iterative decoding of binary block and convolutional codes. IT-42:429–445, March 1996.
16. Simon Haykin. *Neural Networks: A Comprehensive Foundation*. Number ISBN 0-02-352761-7. Macmillan College Publishing Company Inc., 1994.
17. G. S. Hornby, M. Fujita, S. Takamura, T. Yamamoto, and O. Hanagata. Autonomous evolution of gaits with the sony quadruped robot. In Wolfgang Banzhaf, Jason Daida, Agoston E. Eiben, Max H. Garzon, Vasant Honavar, Mark Jakiela, and Robert E. Smith, editors, *Proceedings of the Genetic and Evolutionary Computation Conference*, volume 2, pages 1297–1304, Orlando, Florida, USA, 13-17 1999. Morgan Kaufmann.
18. I.S.Reed and G.Solomon. Polynomial Codes over certain Finite Fields. *J Soc.Indust.Appl.Math.*, 8(2), June 1960.
19. K. Kleiner. Look to the insect. *New Scientist, No. 1951, 12 Nov. 1994*, 144:27–29, 1994.
20. J. R. Koza. *Genetic Programming*. MIT Press, Cambridge, MA, 1992.
21. M. A. Lewis, A. H. Fagg, and A. Solidum. Genetic programming approach to the construction of a neural network control of a walking robot. In *Proceedings of the 1992 IEEE InternationalConference on Robotics and Automation*, pages 2618–2623, Nice, France, 1992. Electronica Bks.
22. M. Olmer, W. Banzhaf, and P. Nordin. Evolving real-time behavior modules for a real robot with genetic programming. In M. Jamshidi, F. Pin, and P. Dauchez, editors, *Proceedings of the International Symposium on Robotics and Manufacturing (ISRAM-96)*, Robotics and Manufacturing, pages 675 – 680. Asme Press, New York, 1996.
23. Francis Quek. An algorithm for the rapid computation of boundaries of run-length encoded regions. *Pattern Recognition Journal*, 33:1637–1649, 2000.
24. S. Schmermbeck and G. Stromberg. Soft-output signal space detectors (S^3D). Technical Report 0102, Computer Engineering Institute (CEI), University of Dortmund, 2002.
25. F. J. MacWilliams, N. J. A. Sloane. *The Theory of Error–Correcting Codes*. North-Holland, Amsterdam, 1977.
26. SONY. *Sony Four Legged Robot Football League Rule Book*. SONY, 2nd edition, 2000.

27. Graham F. Spencer. Automatic generation of programs for crawling and walking. In Kenneth E. Kinnear, Jr., editor, *Advances in Genetic Programming*, chapter 15, pages 335–353. MIT Press, 1994.
28. T.Jeon and J.Moon. A Systematic Approach to Signal Space Detection. *IEEE Transactions on Magnetics*, 33(5):2737–2739, September 1997.
29. Manuela Veloso, William Uther, Masahiro Fujita, Minoru Asada, and Hiroaki Kitano. Playing soccer with legged robots. In *Intl. Conference on Intelligent Robots and Systems IEEE/RSJ*, pages 437–442, October 1998.
30. W.Blanz, C.E.Cox, G.Fettweis, M.Hassner, and U.Schwiegelshohn. A Key Equation Solver for variable Block Reed-Solomon Decoders. *IBM Technical Bulletin*, 1995.

Team Coordination
among Robotic Soccer Players

Matthijs T.J. Spaan and Frans C.A. Groen

Intelligent Autonomous Systems group, Informatics Institute
Faculty of Science, University of Amsterdam, the Netherlands
{mtjspaan,groen}@science.uva.nl

Abstract. We present an approach for coordinating a team of soccer
playing robots, used by Clockwork Orange in the RoboCup middle-size
league. It is based on the idea of dynamically distributing roles among
the team members and adds the notion of a global team strategy (attack,
defend and intercept). Utility functions are used for estimating how well
suited a robot is for a certain role. They are not only based on the time
the robot expects to need to reach the ball but also on the robot's position
in the field. Empirical results from the RoboCup 2001 tournament are
presented demonstrating the value of extending role distribution with a
team strategy.

1 Introduction

An interesting research topic in RoboCup is the problem of coordinating a team
of agents, whether it be software agents or real world agents. Middle-size league
teams traditionally focus on issues like robot control, real-time image processing, self localization and fusion of sensor data but in the last years actively
coordinating the multi-agent system has come into reach. We present an approach for coordinating a team of middle-size robots which uses a global team
strategy. This approach was used in Clockwork Orange, the Dutch RoboSoccer
Team [5] at the RoboCup 2001 tournament. The team is a collaboration effort
of the Delft University of Technology, the Utrecht University and the University
of Amsterdam.

First we will shortly discuss related approaches used by some other teams.
Next we describe our role-based team coordination mechanism and how it influences action selection. We finish with results obtained at RoboCup 2001 and
draw some conclusions.

2 Related Work

We view RoboCup middle-size league as an application in which intentional cooperation is the preferred choice for a cooperation model as opposed to the swarm
model, a distinction made by Parker [3]. Swarm cooperation focuses on the emergent cooperative behavior in large groups of robots, each of which individually

G.A. Kaminka, P.U. Lima, and R. Rojas (Eds.): RoboCup 2002, LNAI 2752, pp. 409–416, 2003.

has limited capabilities. When robots achieve purposeful cooperation built on their individual higher level capabilities the cooperation is called intentional.

We opt for intentional cooperation since in the RoboCup domain several tasks such as defending and attacking are required, the number of robots is very limited, timing is crucial for success and the robots can be heterogeneous in their hardware and capabilities. Other teams consider a deliberative approach to the team strategy acquisition useless in such a dynamic and hostile environment [7].

A common approach for intentional cooperation is a system based on the distribution of roles among the field players. The players of CS Freiburg distribute roles amongst themselves, namely an active, support and strategic role [9]. Each robot determines its utility to pursue a certain role and informs its teammates. Based on these utilities a robot chooses his role. Roles are also distributed among the players of ART [1]. The roles they define are a main attacker which demands ball possession, a supporting attacker and a defender. The protocol for distribution of the roles among the players is based on utility functions.

Dynamic role assignment based on utility functions seems a flexible way for achieving cooperation, but most of the standard role distributing schemes as designed by other middle-size league teams seem to employ just one team strategy: *attack*. However if one defines ball possession as a prerequisite for being able to attack one can see that in a typical middle-size league only a limited amount of time is spent attacking. It usually takes a lot of time to find and obtain the ball. Therefore we have extended this model with two more team strategies: *defend* and *intercept*. The team strategy determines what roles have to be assigned among the team members. It extends formations as defined in [6] by assigning priorities to the roles to cope with a variable number of participating agents.

3   Team Coordination

We have divided the soccer game in three states: either your team has the ball and attacks, the other team has the ball and your team defends, or nobody has ball possession and your team tries to obtain it. For simplicity we assume the game is characterized by ball possession alone, knowledge regarding the status of the ball is provided by our shared world model [2]. A problem of such a finite state machine could be that it is prone to oscillations between the team states. To prevent such an unfortunate situation the protocol for deciding on team strategy and distributing roles "locks" the team strategy during a cycle of the coordination process.

We define a team strategy as a distribution of certain roles over the available field players, where a role is defined as a mapping of situations to individual robot actions. The team strategy poses limitations on the possible mapping of roles to robots. Note that only three roles are associated with each team strategy as the goalkeeper does not actively participate in team play: it has its fixed role of goalkeeper and has fundamentally different hardware.

We have assigned priorities to each role in a certain team strategy, since during a game not all three field players may be in play but some roles are more

Table 1. Distribution of roles associated with each team strategy.

Team strategy	Role #1	Role #2	Role #3
Attack	AttackWithBall	PassiveDefend	AttackWithoutBall
Defend	ActiveDefend	PassiveDefend	ActiveDefend
Intercept	InterceptBall	PassiveDefend	InterceptBall

important than others. Table 1 shows the roles for each team strategy, with #1 being the most and #3 being the least important role. If there is one field player available only role #1 will be assigned, with two field players active roles #1 and #2 will assigned etc. Role #1 is always a ball oriented role: with only one field player ready for duty you want it to go after the ball. This is also the case when communication fails, the robot will assume it is the only player in the team and fulfill role#1.

A robot in role PassiveDefend (PD) waits in front of its own goal for the opponent team to attack. Role InterceptBall (IB) chases the ball trying to obtain control over it. Role ActiveDefend (AD) is a defensive variant of the previous role. When a robot controls the ball it assumes role AttackWithBall (AWB), which usually means dribbling with it toward the enemy goal followed by a shot. Role AttackWithoutBall (AWoB) describes an auxiliary attacker moving toward the enemy goal together with the main attacker.

The role distribution approaches already in use at RoboCup usually have three roles: an attacker, a supporting attacker and a defender. These can be respectively identified with AttackWithBall, AttackWithoutBall and PassiveDefend. Adding team strategies suggests we also have to differentiate the existing roles. The added roles InterceptBall and ActiveDefend seem necessary in our view, but one could easily argue a different set of roles is necessary and sufficient to play a decent game of robot soccer.

Utility Functions

To decide which robot should be assigned which role a mechanism based on utility functions is used. Each role is associated with a utility function which tries to measure how well suited a robot is for this role in the current state of the world. For an attacking role it is easy to define a useful utility function. This is more complicated for a defending role, since an attacker only has to focus on the ball while a defender should assume a good position waiting for things to come.

We propose to compose the utility functions for each role on two measures: first one is the time a robot expects it needs to reach the ball. This time is based on the shortest angle the robot has to turn to face the ball and the Euclidean distance between them. This is important for roles that want to chase after the ball: ActiveDefend, InterceptBall and AttackWithBall. For the last role we also take into account whether or not a robot controls the ball.

Second measure is how well the position of a robot is suited for the role. We added an evaluation mechanism for this purpose based on attracting and repelling areas on the field [4]. This measure is needed for the non ball oriented roles PassiveDefend and AttackWithoutBall, but it is also relevant for the ball oriented roles to fall back upon when the position of the ball is unknown.

Assignment of Roles

Clockwork Orange's shared world model [2] simplifies the task of assigning roles to robots. When a robot notices a change in ball possession it alerts its teammates by telling them the new team strategy. The robot continues by calculating its own utility for each of the roles in the new team strategy (see table 1) and transmits this information to its teammates. Upon receiving the new team strategy they do the same. While waiting for a certain time on the utility scores of teammates each robot calculates these scores based on its own world model. Utility scores coming in from a teammate have preference however, which introduces a level of redundancy.

After receiving utility scores of each teammate or when a timeout occurred, each robot selects its role by comparing the utility scores each team member has for each role available, starting with the most important role. We try to limit the impact of oscillations between team strategies by letting the robot ignore all incoming new team strategies while still busy waiting for utility scores from teammates.

Impact of Role on Action Selection

Assigning roles to robots only makes sense if the robot takes its role (and possibly those of its teammates) into account when selecting the next action it should take. It should execute the next action which benefits the team the most, and its role provides the robot with a description of what the team expects of it. Without going into too much detail we will shortly describe the use of roles in our action planning [4].

Action planning is modeled using Markov decision processes, similar to Tambe's approach used in the simulation league[8]). A robot's role determines its action space and influences its reward function. In order to be able to find a good solution to the Markov decision problem we discretize the action space (instead of the state space which remains continuous), which means a robot considers only a finite set of actions at a time. Actions are defined as having a certain type like move or dribble and certain parameters like target positions, whose number is potentially infinite. As a solution to this problem we only consider a finite number of target positions. The size of the set of actions lies in the order of magnitude of 50. The role of a robot determines the contents of this set: a defensive role will lead to more move actions than shoot or dribble actions while role AttackWithBall for instance will contribute more shoot and dribble actions than plain move actions.

Our reward function is designed as follows: estimate the desirability of the current world state by looking at several soccer heuristics, simulate the action on this world to obtain a new world state, estimate the desirability of this new world state, and the difference between the two estimates is the reward. The soccer heuristics are about whether the ball is in one of the goals, ball possession, strategic positioning and how well the location of the robot is suited for its role. So to what extent an action is considered beneficiary to the team partially depends on the robot's role.

4   Results

Clockwork Orange successfully participated in the RoboCup 2001 tournament in Seattle, USA reaching the quarterfinals. In total seven games were played, resulting in three victories, one draw and three losses. At the German Open 2002 tournament Clockwork Orange became fourth. Results regarding team coordination will be presented from the last four and a half[1] last games from RoboCup 2001. We will start with the outcomes of these matches: Clockwork Orange vs. Trackies 0-8, Fun2maS 5-0, Artisti Veneti 3-0, GMD 1-4, CS Freiburg 0-4.

Next we will discuss a 30 second fragment from the match against GMD, shown in figure 1. This fragment gives an example of how our coordination mechanism works under good conditions: the world model is consistent at an acceptable degree. The robots in our team are called Caspar, Ronald and Nomada.

At the start of the fragment Caspar has control over the ball and each robot believes the team strategy is *attack*, as they should. The team has correctly assigned the AttackWithBall role to Caspar and the AttackWithoutBall role to Ronald while Nomada is standing close to the own goal area in role PassiveDefend. Then Caspar loses the ball, the team switches to team strategy *intercept* and the two attacking robots switch to role InterceptBall. Between $t = 115$ and $t = 118$ there is some confusion whether or not the opponent controls the ball which leads to oscillations between team strategies *intercept* and *defend*.

At about the same time as Ronald gains possession of the ball Nomada is neatly shut down and removed from the game. This means the team has lost its defender and one of the other two should fill the gap. Ronald does so by switching to role PassiveDefend at $t = 124$, after having been in error for a short while: it was at the same time as Caspar in role AttackWithBall although it was really Caspar which controlled the ball.

Table 2 visualizes the distribution of team strategies for the games listed above. It shows team strategy *intercept* is the most common in all but one match. The exception is the game against Fun2maS in which *attack* is dominant. This seems consistent with the outcome of the match.

The distribution of roles over robots can be found in table 3. It shows that the AttackWithoutBall role has been assigned only a small amount of time. It

---

[1] During the half-time interval of the third game the team coordination implementation was frozen for the rest of the tournament.

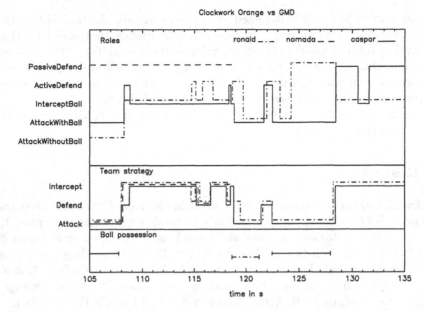

Fig. 1. Visualization of team strategy, role distribution and ball possession during a 30 second period of the RoboCup 2001 game against GMD. The x-axis displays the wall clock time in seconds since the start of the game. The robots involved are Ronald, Caspar and Nomada (removed from the game 118.88 seconds after game start). Their role and team strategy are shown on the y-axis. When one of them has ball possession a line is drawn in the bottom part of the graph.

Table 2. The portion of time the team spent in each team strategy. The surface area of the circles is proportional to the amount of time spent in each team strategy or role relative to the total time. Right columns show these total times in seconds.

	Attack	Defend	Intercept	Total
Trackies	·	·	●	1170.30
Fun2maS	●	·	●	2539.04
Artisti Veneti	·	·	●	2811.09
GMD	·	·	●	2588.36
CS Freiburg	·	·	●	3147.06

is the least important role of team strategy *attack* which means it will only be used if there are three field players active, each accurately knows its position and one of them has ball possession.

To see the influence of a robot's role on its action selection we have included table 4. It shows what type of actions have been chosen while the robot was in a certain role. The data is a summary of all robots during the last four and

Table 3. The portion of time each robot spent in each role.

	PD	AD	IB	AWB	AWoB	Total
Trackies	•	·	●	·	·	1050.45
Fun2maS	●	·	•	●	·	2256.67
Artisti Veneti	•	·	●	·	·	2638.13
GMD	•	·	●	•	·	2467.76
CS Freiburg	●	·	●	•	··	2843.96

Table 4. The portion of time spent executing an action of a certain type while in a certain role. Data is from all field player robots during the four and a half last games of RoboCup 2001.

	Turn	Move	Dribble	Shoot	Seek	Chase	Total
PD	•	●	·	·	•	•	3529.41
AD	·	•		·	·	●	1325.78
IB	·	•	·		•	●	4238.73
AWB	·	·	•	·	·	●	1812.27
AWoB	•	●	·		·	•	326.89

a half games of RoboCup 2001 which lasts just over three hours. The table demonstrates that a robot's role influences the kind of actions it takes. Chase actions, whose purpose it is to obtain the ball, are not used as much in roles PassiveDefend and AttackWithoutBall as in the other roles, which one would expect given their nature.

5   Discussion

Figure 1 shows the good performance of our team coordination mechanism under good conditions, but even then inconsistencies sometimes occur. For instance at $t = 131$ Caspar briefly switches to role InterceptBall when it shouldn't. The reason is that Caspar's world model has not received a position update from Ronald's world model for a while, as Ronald has no estimate of its own position that is accurate enough to communicate. From Caspar's point of view it is the only active member of the team and it should thus fulfill the most important role in team strategy *intercept*: InterceptBall. These kind of problems are common and should be properly dealt with.

As table 2 shows the total amount of time spent in team strategy *attack* is rather low, only 28% of time (almost three and a half hours). This would seem to confirm our intuition that extending role-based approaches with a global team strategy makes sense, although we do not have the resources (two complete teams) to confirm this. In RoboCup simulation league however these lines of reasoning are common.

The team strategy sub-tables also show that most of the time (53%) is spent in *intercept*, resulting from the fact that it is hard to detect whether the other team controls the ball. This would call for a more sophisticated way of determining the applicable team strategy than just looking at ball possession alone. Ball possession is a good first indication but other concepts like ball position on the field or the relative distances of teammates and opponents can be added. This would also reduce the number of oscillations caused by the possibly rapid changes in ball possession.

Acknowledgements

We would like to express our gratitude to Nikos Vlassis for his support. This research is supported by PROGRESS, the embedded systems research program of the Dutch organisation for Scientific Research NWO, the Dutch Ministry of Economic Affairs and the Technology Foundation STW.

References

1. C. Castelpietra, L. Iocchi, M. Piaggio, A. Scalzo, and A. Sgorbissa. Communication and coordination among heterogeneous mid-size players: ART99. In P. Stone, T. Balch, and G. Kraetzschmar, editors, *RoboCup 2000: Robot Soccer World Cup IV*. Springer-Verlag, 2001.
2. F.C.A. Groen, J. Roodhart, M. Spaan, R. Donkervoort, and N. Vlassis. A distributed world model for robot soccer that supports the development of team skills. In *Proceedings of the 13th Belgian-Dutch Conference on Artificial Intelligence (BNAIC'01)*, Amsterdam, 2001.
3. L. E. Parker. *Heterogeneous Multi-Robot Cooperation*. PhD thesis, Massachusetts Institute of Technology, 1994.
4. M. T. J. Spaan. Team play among soccer robots. Master's thesis, University of Amsterdam, 2002. http://www.science.uva.nl/research/ias.
5. M. T. J. Spaan, M. Wiering, R. Bartelds, R. Donkervoort, P. Jonker, and F. Groen. Clockwork Orange: The Dutch RoboSoccer Team. In A. Birk, S. Coradeschi, and S. Tadokoro, editors, *RoboCup 2001*. Springer-Verlag, to appear.
6. P. Stone and M. Veloso. Task decomposition, dynamic role assignment, and low-bandwidth communication for real-time strategic teamwork. *Artificial Intelligence*, 110, 1999.
7. Y. Takahashi, S. Ikenoue, S. Inui, K. Hikita, and M. Asada. Osaka University "Trackies 2001". In A. Birk, S. Coradeschi, and S. Tadokoro, editors, *RoboCup 2001*. Springer-Verlag, to appear.
8. M. Tambe and W. Zhang. Towards flexible teamwork in persistent teams: Extended report. *Journal of Autonomous Agents and Multi-Agent Systems*, 3(2):159–183, 2000.
9. Th. Weigel, W. Auerbach, M. Dietl, B. Dümler, J. Gutmann, K. Marko, K. Müller, B. Nebel, B. Szerbakowski, and M. Thiel. CS Freiburg: Doing the right thing in a group. In P. Stone, T. Balch, and G. Kraetzschmar, editors, *RoboCup 2000: Robot Soccer World Cup IV*. Springer-Verlag, 2001.

An Architecture for a National RoboCup Team

Thomas Röfer

Center for Computing Technology (TZI), FB3
Universität Bremen
Postfach 330440, 28334 Bremen, Germany
roefer@tzi.de

Abstract. This paper describes the architecture used by the German-Team 2002 in the Sony Legged Robot League. It focuses on the special needs of a national team, i.e. a "team of teams" from different universities in one country that compete against each other in national contests, but that will jointly line up at the international RoboCup championship. In addition, the tools developed by the GermanTeam will be presented, e.g. the first 3-D simulation used in the Sony Legged Robot League.

1 Introduction

All RoboCup leagues share the problem that there are more teams that want to participate in the world championship than a normal contest schedule can integrate. Therefore, each league has its own approach to limit the number of participants to a certain amount. For instance, teams in the simulation league have to qualify by submitting a team description and two log files, one of a game against a strong opponent, the other of a game against an average one. Based on this material, a committee selects the teams for the championship. In contrast, participants in the Sony Legged Robot League only qualify by submitting a description of their scientific goals - before they have even worked with the robots. Each year, the Sony Legged League grows a little bit, e.g. from 16 to 19 teams from 2001 to 2002. So far, teams that were once accepted in the league were allowed to stay during the following years without a further qualification, amongst other reasons because of their investment in the robots. Thus, only a few new teams have the chance to join the league.

Currently, it is discussed how to provide to chance to participate in the league to more research groups. One solution would be to set up *national teams*, as the GermanTeam that was founded in 2001 [1]. The GermanTeam currently consists of students and researchers at five universities: the Humboldt-Universität zu Berlin, the Universität Bremen, the Technische Universität Darmstadt, the Universität Dortmund, and the Freie Universität Berlin. The members of the GermanTeam are allowed to participate as separate teams in national contests, but will jointly line up at the international RoboCup championship as a single team.

The other solution would be to install national leagues, of which the winning team will get the ticket to participate in the international contest. On the one

G.A. Kaminka, P.U. Lima, and R. Rojas (Eds.): RoboCup 2002, LNAI 2752, pp. 417–425, 2003.

hand, this approach would enforce the competition, but on the other hand, the goal of the RoboCup initiative is to promote research, and competing teams do not work together very well. Therefore, it may be a good compromise to support collaboration on the lower, national level, while stressing the element of competition on the international level.

The GermanTeam is an example of a national team. The members will participate as separate teams in the German Open 2002, but will form a single team at Fukuoka. Obviously, the results of the team would not be very good if the members will develop separately until the middle of April, and then try to integrate their code to a single team in only two months. Therefore, an architecture for robot control programs was developed that allows to implement different solutions for the tasks involved in playing robot soccer. The solutions are exchangeable, compatible to each other, and they can even be distributed over a varying number of concurrent processes. The approach will be described in section 2. Finally, in section 3, the tools that were implemented to support the development of the robot control programs are presented.

2   Multi-team Support

The major goal of the architecture presented in this paper is them ability to support the collaboration between the university-teams in the German national team. Some tasks may be solved only once for the whole team, so any team can use them. Others will be implemented differently by each team, e.g. the behavior control. A specific solution for a certain task is called a *module*. To be able to share modules, interfaces were defined for all tasks that could be identified for playing robot soccer in the Sony Legged League. These tasks will be summarized in the next section. To be able to easily compare the performance of different solutions for same task, it is possible to switch between them at runtime. The mechanism that support this kind of development are descibed in section 2.2. However, a common software interface cannot hide the fact that some implementations will need more processing time that others. To compensate for these differences, each team can use its own *process layout*, i.e. they can group together modules to processes that are running concurrently (cf. section 2.2)

2.1   Tasks

Figure 1 depicts the tasks that were identified by the GermanTeam for playing soccer in the Sony Legged Robot League. They can be structured into five levels:

Sensor Data Processing. On this level, the data received from the sensors is preprocessed. For instance, the image delivered by the camera is segmented, and then it is converted into a set of blobs, i.e. image regions of the same color class. The current states of the joints are analyzed to determine the direction the camera is looking at. In addition, further sensors can be employed to determine whether the robot has been picked up, or whether it fell down.

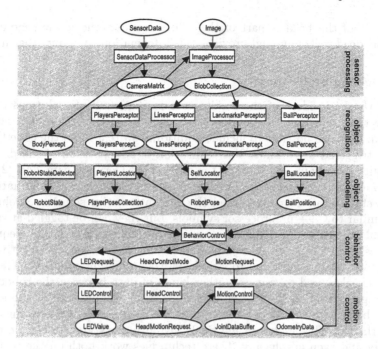

Fig. 1. The modules implemented by the German Team 2002

Object Recognition. On this level, the information provided by the previous level is searched to find objects that are known to exist on the field, i.e. landmarks (goals and flags), field lines, other players, and the ball. The sensor readings that were associated to objects that are called *percepts*.

Object Modeling. Percepts immediately result from the current sensor readings. However, most objects are not continuously visible, and noise in the sensor readings may even result in a misrecognition of an object. Therefore, the positions of the dynamic objects on the field have to modeled, i.e. the location of the robot itself, the poses (i.e. the (x, y, θ) positions on the field) of the other robots, and the position of the ball. The result of this level is the estimated *world state*.

Behavior Control. Based on the world state and the role of the robot, the fourth level generates the behavior of the robot. This can either be performed very reactively, or deliberative components may be involved. The behavior level sends requests to the fifth level to perform the selected motions.

Motion Control. The final level performs the motions requested by the behavior level. It distinguishes between motions of the head and of the body (i.e. walking). When walking or standing, the head is controlled autonomously, e.g., to find the ball or to look for landmarks, but when a kick is performed, the movement of the head is part of the whole motion. The motion module also performs dead reckoning and provides this information to many other modules.

2.2   Debugging Support

One of the basic ideas of the architecture is that multiple solutions exist for a single task, and that the developer can switch between them at runtime. In addition, it is also possible to include additional switches into the code that can also be triggered at runtime. The realization is an extension of the debugging techniques already implemented in the code of the GermanTeam 2001 [2]: *debug requests* and *solution requests*. The system manages two sets of information, the current state of all *debug keys*, and the currently active solutions. Debug keys work similar to C++ preprocessor symbols, but they can be toggled at runtime. A special infrastructure called *debug queues* is employed to transmit requests to all processes on a robot to change thisinformation at runtime, i.e. to activate and to deactivate debug keys and to switch between different solutions. The debug queues are also used to transmit other kinds of data between the robot(s) and the debugging tool on the PC (cf. section 3). For example, motion requests can directly be sent to the robot, images, text messages, and even drawings can be sent to the PC. This allows, to effectively visualize the state of a certain module, textually and even graphically. These techniques work both on the real robots and on the simulated ones (cf. section 3.1).

2.3   Process-Layouts

As already mentioned, each team can group its modules together to processes of their own choice. Such an arrangement is called a process layout. The German-Team 2002 has developed its own model for processes and the communication between them:

Communication between Processes. In the robot control program developed by the GermanTeam 2001 for the championship in Seattle, the different processes exchanged their data through a shared memory [2], i.e., a blackboard architecture [3] was employed. This approach lacked of a simple concept how to exchange data in a safe and coordinated way. The locking mechanism employed wasted a lot of computing power and it only guaranteed consistency during a single access, but the entries in the shared memory could still change from one access to the other. Therefore, an additional scheme had to be implemented, as, e.g., making copies of all entries in the shared memory at the beginning of a certain calculation step to keep them consistent. In addition, the use of a shared memory is not compatible to the new ability of the Sony Aibo robots to exchange data between processes via a wireless network.

The communication scheme introduced in GT2002 addresses these issues. It uses standard operating system mechanisms to communicate between processes, and therefore it also works via the wireless network. In the approach, no difference exists between inter-process communication and exchanging data with the

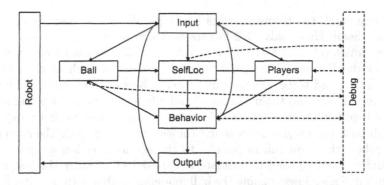

Fig. 2. Process layout of the Bremen Byters. The broken lines indicate the debugging part

operating system. A single line of code is sufficient to establish a communication link. A predefined scheme separates the processing time into a communication phase and a calculation phase.

The inter-object communication is performed by *senders* and *receivers* exchanging *packages*. A sender contains a single instance of a package. After it was directed to send the package, it will automatically transfer it to all receivers as soon as they have requested the package. Each receiver also contains an instance of a package. The communication scheme is performed by continuously repeating three phases for each process:

1. All receivers of a process receive all packages that are currently available.
2. The process performs its normal calculations, e.g. image processing, planning, etc. During this, packages can already be sent.
3. All senders that were directed to transmit their package and have not done it yet will send it to the corresponding receivers, if they are ready to accept it.

Note that the communication does not involve any queuing. A process can miss to receive a certain package if it is too slow, i.e., its computation in phase 2 takes too much time. In this aspect, the communication scheme resembles the shared memory approach. Whenever a process enters phase 2, it is equipped with the most current data available.

The whole communication is performed automatically; only the connections between senders and receivers have to be specified. In fact, the command to send a package is the only one that has to be called explicitly. This significantly eases the implementation of new processes.

Different Layouts. The figures 2 and 3 show two different layouts. Both contain a debug process that is connected to all other processes via debug queues. Note that debug queues are transmitted as normal packages, i.e. a package contains a whole queue. Comparing the two process layouts, it can be recognized that on the one hand, the Bremen Byters try to parallelize as much as possible; on the other hand, Humboldt 2002 focuses on using only a few processes, i.e. the first four levels (cf. Fig. 1) are all integrated into the process *Cognition*. In the layout of the Bremen Byters, one process is used for each of the levels one, four, and five, and three processes implement parts of the levels two and three, i.e. the recognition and the modeling of individual aspects of the world state are grouped together. Odometry is used to decompose information that is dependent: although both the *players* process and the *ball* process require the current pose of the robot, they can run in parallel to the self-localization process, because the odometry can be used to estimate the spatial offset since the last absolute localization. This allows running the ball modeling with a high priority, resulting in a fast update rate, while the self-localization can run as a background process to perform a computationally expensive probabilistic method as, e.g., the one described in [4] or the method used by the GermanTeam 2001 [2].

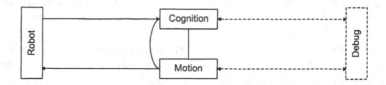

Fig. 3. Process layout of Humboldt 2002. The broken lines indicate the debugging part

Currently, it is not known which process layout will be the more successful one. The Darmstadt Dribbling Dackels are using a third approach that is a compromise between the two discussed here, and all three will compete against each other at the German Open. So the best can be used for the world championship.

3   Development Tools on the PC

Two tools were implemented on the PC to ease the development of the robot control programs. The first is a 3-D simulator, and the second is a general tool that provides nearly any support imaginable, even the simulator is integrated.

3.1   SimRobot

SimRobot is a kinematic robotics simulator that was developed in the author's group [1]. It is written in C++ and is distributed in public domain [6]. It consists of a portable simulation kernel and platform specific graphical user interfaces. Implementations exist for the *X Window System*, *Microsoft Windows 3.1/95/98/ME/NT/2000/XP*, and *IBM OS/2*. Currently, only the development for the 32 bit versions of Microsoft Windows is continued.

A simulation in SimRobot consists of three parts: the simulation kernel, the graphical user interface, and a controller that is provided by the user. The GermanTeam 2002 has implemented the whole simulation of up to eight robots including the inter-process communication described in section 2.3 as such a controller, providing the same environment to robot control programs as they will find on the real robots. In addition, an object called the oracle provides information to the robot control programs that is not available on the real robots, i.e. the robots own location on the field, the poses of the teammates and the opponents, and the position of the ball. On the one hand, this allows implementing functionality that relies on such information before the corresponding modules that determine it are completely implemented. On the other hand, it can be used by the implementators of such modules to compare their results with the correct ones.

3.2   RobotControl

RobotControl is the successor of *DogControl*, the debugging tool used by the GermanTeam in 2001 [2]. Its purpose is to integrate all functionality that is required during the development of the control programs for the Sony Aibo robots.

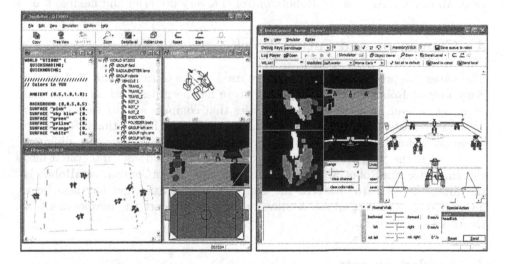

Fig. 4. a) SimRobot simulating the GermanTeam 2002 (left). b) RobotControl: color tool, simulation, message viewer, and motion tester (right)

Running Robot Controllers. First of all, RobotControl has the ability to run the process-layouts that make up the robot control programs. The simulation kernel of SimRobot is integrated into RobotControl, but in contrast to SimRobot, the robot controller cannot only be provided with simulated inputs. It is also possible to connect it to real robots via the wireless network, and, as a third possibility, the inputs can be generated by replaying log files.

Log Files can either be recorded with a robot, storing them on a memory stick, or the data can be transferred from the robot via the wireless network to RobotControl, and then it will be recorded to a file on the harddisk of the PC. As the same robot controller code runs in all environments, even a simulated robot can produce log files. Log files can contain sensor data and intermediate data as, e.g., blob collections. RobotControl is able to replay log files in real-time or step by step. As RobotControl can run under a debugger, all normal debugging features are available (setting breakpoints, inspecting variables, etc.).

Extensibility. The main purpose of RobotControl is to function as the user interface of the Aibo robots. Therefore, it provides the infrastructure to easily add new toolbars and dialogs. The window layout of RobotControl is always stored and restored on restart. Figure 4b shows a screenshot of RobotControl, in which several toolbars and dialogs can be seen. Toolbars control the replay of log files, they control running the simulation, they allow sending debug keys to real or simulated robots, provide the ability of switching solutions and configuring the wireless network, etc. Dialogs allow generating color tables (for image segmentation, shown in Fig. 4b left), display the simulator scene (Fig. 4b right.), control the motions of the robot (Fig. 4b lower left pane) and debug drawings (Fig. 4b center). As a result, RobotControl is a very powerful and flexible tool.

4   Conclusion and Future Work

The paper has presented the architecture used by the GermanTeam 2002 in the Sony Legged Robot League. The architecture has been designed for a national team, i.e. a team from different universities that compete against each other in national contests, but that will form a single team at the international RoboCup world championship. The architecture is currently implemented on two different systems, i.e. the Sony Aibo robots and on Microsoft Windows - integrated into the simulator SimRobot and the control software RobotControl. SimRobot is the first 3-D simulator used in the Sony Legged League, and has also been integrated into RobotControl, a universal tool to support the development of the robot soccer team.

Acknowledgements

Although the author contributed to the architecture presented in this paper, namely by realizing the communication scheme and the simulation, the architecture itself is the result of the work of many people in the GermanTeam. From the author's point of view, the main "architects" of the team are Mattias Jüngel, Martin Loetzsch (both Humboldt Universität zu Berlin), and Max Riesler (Technische Universität Darmstadt). The author wants to thank them and also all the other members of the team, who are filling the architecture with life.

The author also thanks the Sony Corporation for their professional support, the Deutsche Forschungsgemeinschaft (DFG) for funding parts of the project through the priority program "Cooperating teams of mobile robots in dynamic environments".

References

1. Burkhard, H.-D., Düffert, U., Jüngel, M., Lötzsch, M., Koschmieder, N., Laue, T., Röfer, T., Spiess, K., Sztybryc, A., Brunn, R., Risler, M., v. Stryk, O.: German-Team 2001. Technical report. Only available online: http://www.tzi.de/kogrob/papers/GermanTeam2001report.pdf (2001).
2. Brunn, R., Düffert, U., Jüngel, M., Laue, T., Lötzsch, M., Petters, S., Risler, M., Röfer, T., Spiess, K., Sztybryc, A.: GermanTeam 2001. In RoboCup 2001. Lecture Notes in Artificial Intelligence. Springer (2001), to appear.
3. Jagannathan, V., Dodhiawala, R., Baum, L.: Blackboard Architectures and Applications. Academic Press, Inc. (1989).
4. Lenser, S., Veloso, M.: Sensor resetting localization for poorly modeled mobile robots. In Proc. of the IEEE International Conference on Robotics and Automation (2000).
5. Röfer, T.: Strategies for Using a Simulation in the Development of the Bremen Autonomous Wheelchair. In Zobel, R., Moeller, D. (Eds.): Simulation-Past, Present and Future. Society for Computer Simulation International (1998) 460-464.
6. SimRobot homepage. http://www.tzi.de/simrobot.

Probabilistic Vision-Based Opponent Tracking in Robot Soccer

Thorsten Schmitt, Robert Hanek, Sebastian Buck, and Michael Beetz

TU München, Institut für Informatik, 80290 München, Germany
{schmittt,hanek,buck,beetzm}@in.tum.de
http://www9.in.tum.de/agilo

Abstract. Good soccer players must keep their eyes on their opponents in order to make the right plays and moves. The same holds for soccer robots, too. In this paper, we apply probabilistic multiple object tracking to the continual estimation of the positions of opponent players in autonomous robot soccer. We extend MHT [3], an existing tracking algorithm, to handle multiple mobile sensors with uncertain positions, discuss the specification of probabilistic models needed by the algorithm, and describe the required vision-interpretation algorithms. The tracking algorithm enables robots to estimate the positions and motions of fast moving robots both accurately and robustly. We have applied the multiple object tracking algorithm throughout the RoboCup 2001 world championship. Empirical results show the applicability of multiple hypotheses tracking to vision-based opponent tracking and demonstrates the advantages for crowded environments.

1 Introduction

Good soccer players must keep their eyes on their opponents in order to make the right plays and moves. The same holds for soccer robots, too [2]. Unfortunately, object tracking systems are difficult to realize. Observations of the robots are inaccurate and incomplete. Sometimes the sensors hallucinate objects. Often the robots cannot perceptually distinguish the individual objects in their environments. To reliably estimate the positions and motions of the objects despite these perturbations, researchers have proposed object tracking algorithms that are capable of tracking multiple objects. Tracking algorithms use motion models of the objects and sequences of observation to distinguish real object observations from clutter and can thereby keep track of object positions both more reliably and more accurately.

Multiple object tracking is particular difficult for autonomous robot soccer, where the state is to be estimated by multiple mobile sensors with uncertain positions, the soccer field is only partly visible for each sensor, occlusion of robots is a problem, the robots change their direction and speed very abruptly, and the models of the dynamic states of the robots of the other team are very crude and uncertain.

G.A. Kaminka, P.U. Lima, and R. Rojas (Eds.): RoboCup 2002, LNAI 2752, pp. 426–434, 2003.
© Springer-Verlag Berlin Heidelberg 2003

Many robots employ probabilistic state estimation algorithms for keeping track of the moving objects in their environments [12], such as Multiple Hypothesis Tracking (MHT) [8, 3] and Joint Probabilistic Data Association Filter (JPDAF) [1, 11]. Using probabilistic motion and sensing models these algorithms maintain probabilistic estimates of the objects' positions and update these estimates with each new observation. Probabilistic tracking algorithms are attractive because they are concise, elegant, well understood, and remarkably robust.

In this paper we show how the MHT algorithm can be applied to opponent tracking in autonomous robot soccer. This application requires programmers to equip the robots with sophisticated mechanisms for observing the required information, and to provide probabilistic domain descriptions that the algorithm needs for successful operation. These probabilistic descriptions include motion models and sensing models, such as the probability of the robot detecting an object within sensor range. We show that such mechanisms enable the MHT to reliably and accurately estimate the positions of opponent robots using passive vision-based perception where the cameras have a very restricted field of view. In addition, we will show that the cooperation between robots provides the robots with a more complete estimate of the world state, a substantial speed up in the detection of motions, and more accurate position estimates.

In the remainder of the paper we proceed as follows. The next section describes the MHT algorithm. In the subsequent section we provide a detailed account of how to apply the MHT to autonomous robot soccer. We conclude with empirical results and a discussion of related work.

2 Multiple Hypothesis Tracking

Multiple hypothesis tracking considers the following state estimation problem. The world is populated with a set of stationary and moving objects. The number of objects may vary and they might be occluded and out of sensor range. Robots are equipped with sensing routines that are capable of detecting objects within sensor range, of estimating the positions of the detected objects, and of assessing the accuracy of their estimate.

The objective of the MHT algorithm is to keep a set of object hypotheses, each describing a unique real object and its position, to maintain the set of hypotheses over time, and to estimate the likelihood of the individual hypotheses.

The basic data structure used by the MHT algorithm is the object hypothesis. An object hypothesis consists of an estimated position, orientation, and velocity of an object, a measure of uncertainty associated with the estimation, and a second measure that represents the degree of belief that this hypothesis accurately reflects an existing object. Because the number of objects might vary new hypotheses might have to be added and old ones might have to be deleted.

Before we dive into the details of the MHT algorithm let us first get an intuition of how it works. The MHT algorithm maintains a forest of object hypotheses, that is a set of trees. The nodes in the forest are object hypotheses and represent the association of an observed object with an existing object hy-

---

algorithm MULTIPLEHYPOTHESISTRACKING()

```
1   let Ĥᵏ = {ĥ₁ᵏ,...,ĥₘₖᵏ}  % predicted hyps.
2     Z(k) = {z₁(k),...,zₙₖ(k)}   % observed features
3     Hᵏ = {h₁ᵏ,...,hₒₖᵏ}  % new hyps.
4     Xᵏ⁻ᴺ  % world state at time step k-N.
5   do for k ← 1 to ∞
6     do Z(k) ← INTERPRETSENSORDATA(GETSENSORDATA());
7        Ĥᵏ ← APPLYMOTIONMODEL(Hᵏ⁻¹, M);
8        for i ← 1 to nₖ
9        do for j ← 1 to mₖ
10           do hᵢⱼᵏ ← ASSOCIATE(ĥⱼᵏ, zᵢ(k));
11              COMPUTE(P(hᵢⱼᵏ|Z(k)))
12           for j ← 1 to nₖ
13           do Hᵏ ← Hᵏ ∪ {GENERATENEWHYP(zⱼ(k))};
14           PRUNEHYPOTHESES(Hᵏ);
15           Xᵏ⁻ᴺ ← {x₁ᵏ⁻ᴺ,...,xₒₖ₋ₙᵏ⁻ᴺ}
```

Fig. 1. The multiple hypothesis tracking algorithm.

pothesis. Each hypothesis has an association probability, which indicates the likelihood that observed object and object hypothesis refer to the same object. In order to determine this probability the motion model is applied to the object hypothesis of the previous iteration, in order to predict where the object will be now. Then the association probability is computed by weighing the distance between the predicted and the observed object position. Thus in every iteration of the algorithm each observation is associated with each existing object hypothesis.

Our MHT algorithm is an extension of Reid's algorithm [8]. It extends Reid's version in that it can handle multiple mobile sensors with uncertain positions. The computational structure of the algorithm is shown in Fig. 1. An iteration begins with the set of hypotheses of object states $H^k = \{h_1^k,\ldots,h_m^k\}$ from the previous iteration k. Each h_i^k is a random variable ranging over the state space of a single object and represents a different assignment of measurements to objects, which was performed in the past. The algorithm maintains a Kalman filter for each hypothesis.

With the arrival of new sensor data (6), $Z(k+1) = \{z_1(k+1),\ldots,z_{n_{k+1}}(k+1)\}$, the motion model (7) is applied to each hypothesis and intermediate hypotheses $\hat{h}_i^{k+1}$ are predicted. Assignments of measurements to objects (10) are accomplished on the basis of a statistical distance measurement, such as the Mahalanobis distance. Each subsequent child hypothesis represents one possible interpretation of the set of observed objects and, together with its parent hypothesis, represents one possible interpretation of all past observations. With every iteration of the MHT probabilities (11) describing the validity of an hypothesis are calculated. Furthermore for every observed object an new hypothesis with associated probability is created (13). The equations used for the computation of these probabilities can be found in [9].

In order to constrain the growth of the hypothesis trees the algorithm prunes improbable branches (14). Pruning is based on a combination of ratio pruning, i.e. a simple lower limit on the ratio of the probabilities of the current and best hypotheses, and the N-scan-back algorithm [8]. This algorithm assumes that any ambiguity at time k is resolved by time $k + N$. Consequently if at time k hypothesis h_i^{k-1} has m children, the sum of the probabilities of the leaf notes of each branch is calculated. The branch with the greatest probability is retained and the others are discarded. After pruning the world state of X^{k-N} can be extracted (15). Please note that this world state is always N steps delayed behind the latest observations. However, this delay can be overcome by N observers performing observations in parallel.

3   Applying MHT to Autonomous Robot Soccer

Autonomous robot soccer confronts object tracking mechanisms with challenging research problems. The camera system with an opening angle of 90° and pointed to the front gives an individual robot only a very restricted view of the game situation. Therefore, the robot needs to cooperate to get a more complete picture of the game situation. Vibrations of the camera, spot light effects, and poor lighting conditions cause substantial inaccuracies. Even small vibrations that cause jumps of only a few pixel lines cause deviations of more than half a meter in the depth estimation, if the objects are several meters away. The opponent robots change their speed and moving directions very quickly and therefore an iteration of the tracking algorithm has to be very fast such that the inaccuracies of the motion model does not have such a huge effect.

The information needed for object tracking is provided by the perception system and includes the following kinds of information: (1) partial state estimates broadcasted by other robots, (2) feature maps extracted from captured images, and (3) odometric information. The estimates broadcasted by the team mates comprise the respective robot's location and the locations of the opponents. From the captured camera images the feature detectors extract problem-specific feature maps that correspond to (1) static objects in the environment including the goal, the borders of the field, and the lines on the field, (2) a color blob corresponding to the ball, and (3) the visual features of the opponents.

The working horse of the perception component are a color classification and segmentation algorithm that is used to segment a captured image into colored regions and blobs (see Fig. 2b). The color segmented image is then processed by a feature extraction algorithm (see Fig. 3) that estimates the 2D positions and the covariances of the objects of interest. At present it is assumed that the objects are colored black and have approximately circular shape. Object detection is performed on the basis of blob analysis. The position of an object is estimated on the basis of a pinhole camera model. Due to rotations and radial distortions of the lenses this model is highly non-linear. The uncertainty estima-

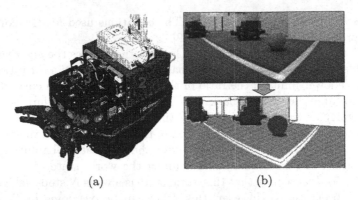

(a)   (b)

Fig. 2. An AGILO soccer robot (a) and an image captured by the robot and the feature map that is computed for self, ball, and opponent localization (b).

---

algorithm INTERPRETSENSORDATA($\widehat{\Phi}, \widehat{C}_\phi$)

1   $\underline{let}\,\widehat{\Phi}$ % robot pose
2   I % image data
3   $R = \{r_1, \ldots, r_{n_k}\}$ % set of regions
4   ω % augmented mean
5   C_ω % augmented covariance
6   $Z(k) = \{z_1(k), \ldots, z_{n_k}(k)\}$ % observed feat.
7   $\underline{do}\,I \leftarrow$ GETSENSORDATA();
8       $R \leftarrow$ EXTRACTBLACKREGIONS(I);
9       $R \leftarrow$ CHECKCONSTRAINTS(R);
10      $R \leftarrow$ EXTRACTCASCADEDROBOTS(R);
11      $\underline{for}\,i \leftarrow 1\,\underline{to}\,|R|$
12      $\underline{do}\,(row, col, width) \leftarrow$ EXTRACTFEATURES(r_i);
13          $\omega \leftarrow \left[\widehat{\Phi}, row, col, width\right]^T$;
14          $C_\omega \leftarrow \begin{pmatrix} \widehat{C}_\phi & 0 & 0 & 0 \\ 0 & \sigma_{row} & 0 & 0 \\ 0 & 0 & \sigma_{col} & 0 \\ 0 & 0 & 0 & \sigma_{width} \end{pmatrix}$;
15          $z_i(k) \leftarrow$ UNSCENTEDTRANSFORM(ω, C_ω, opp);

Fig. 3. The Algorithm used for feature extraction and uncertainty estimation.

tion process is based on the unscented transformation [7]. This allows the use of non-linear measurement equations, the incorporation of parameters describing the measurement uncertainty of the sensor at hand as well as an efficient way of propagating the uncertainty of the observing robots pose. A detailed description of the feature extraction algorithm and uncertainty estimation process can be found in [10].

4   Empirical Investigation

The multiple object tracking algorithm described in this paper has been employed by our AGILO robot soccer team in the fifth robot soccer world championship in Seattle (2001). Our RoboCup team consists of four Pioneer I robots
(see Fig. 2a). The robot is equipped with a single on board linux computer (2), a
wireless Ethernet (1) for communication, and several sonar sensors (4) for collision avoidance. A color CCD camera with an opening angle of 90° (3) is mounted
fix on the robot. The robot also has a dribbling (5) and a kicking device (6) that
enable the robot to dribble and shoot the ball. In Seattle the team has played
six games for a total of about 120 minutes and advanced to the quarter finals.

Unfortunately, in midsize robot soccer there is no external sensing device
which records a global view of the game and can be used as the ground truth for
experiments. Thus for the experimental results in this section we can only use
the subjective information of our robots and argue for the plausibility of their
behavior and belief states. To do so, we have written log files and recorded the
games using video cameras in order to evaluate our algorithm. The analysis of
the log files from RoboCup 2001, revealed that an average MHT update takes
between 6 to 7 msecs. This allows our implementation to process all observations
of all robots (max. frame rate: 25Hz) in real time. The minimum and maximum
iteration times were measured to be 1.1 msecs and 86 msecs respectively. On
average the MHT tracked 3.2 opponents. This is a reasonable number since
there are maximal 4 opponent players and players can be send off or have to be
rebooted off field. In breaks of the games (when people get on to the field) or
when there are crowds of robots the MHT successfully tracked up to 11 objects.

A typical result of the AGILO game state estimator is shown in Fig. 3.
The upper picture shows the positions of the AGILO players of the own team,
computed through vision-based self localization [10, 5]. The middle picture shows
the individual observations of the opponent robots. The opponent observations
performed by the AGILO robots are indicated with circles, crosses, diamonds,
and triangles. In the lower picture the tracks as they were resolved by the MHT
are displayed. They are divided into subsections. The number of the robot that
contributed the most observations to this part of the track is denoted next to
the track.

Qualitatively, we can estimate the accuracy of the game state estimation by
looking for the jumps in the tracked lines. The tracks of the opponents look very
reasonable. They are less accurate and sometimes only partial. This is due to the
high inaccuracy and incompleteness of the sensory data. However, it is observable
that several tracks resulted from merging the observations of different robots. In
addition, the merging of the different observations results in fewer hallucinated
obstacles and therefore allows for more efficient navigation paths. Several wrong
opponent observations made by the goal keeper (1) were correctly omitted by the
MHT and not assigned to a track. We have cross checked the tracks computed
by the algorithm using video sequences recorded during the matches. The tracks
are qualitatively correct and seem to be accurate. A more thorough evaluation
is only possibly based on the ground truth for the situations. We are currently

implementing tracking software for a camera mounted above the field that allows us to compute the ground truth for the next RoboCup championship.

The cooperation of the different robots increases both, the completeness and the accuracy of state estimation. Accuracy can be substantially increased by fusing the observations of different robots because the depth estimate of positions are much more inaccurate than the lateral positions in the image. This can be accomplished through the Kalman filter's property to optimally fuse observations from different robots into global hypotheses with smaller covariances. The completeness of state estimation can be increased because all the robots can see only parts of the field and can be complemented with observations of the team mates. The other effect we observed was that cooperation allowed to maintain the identity of opponent players over an extended period of time, even though the field of view of the observing robots is limited. This point is well illustrated in Fig. 3. The three opponent field players were tracked successfully over a period of 30 seconds.

5   Related Work

Related work comprises work done on object tracking in the robot soccer domain and probabilistic and vision-based tracking of moving targets. To the best of our knowledge no probabilistic state estimation method has been proposed for tracking the opponent robots in robot soccer or similar application domains. Dietl et al. [4] estimate the positions of the opponents and store them in the team world model but they solve the correspondence problem on a rather coarse level. Probabilistic tracking of multiple moving objects has been proposed by Schulz et al. [11]. They apply sample-based JPDAF estimation to the tracking of moving people with a moving robot using laser range data. The required computational power for the particle filters is opposed by the heuristic based pruning strategies of the MHT algorithm. Hue et al.[6] are also tracking multiple objects with particle filters. In their work data association is performed on the basis of the Gibbs sampler. Our approach to multiple hypothesis tracking is most closely related to the one proposed by Cox and Miller [3]. We extend their work on multiple hypothesis tracking in that we apply the method to a much more challenging application domain where we have multiple moving observers with uncertain positions. In addition, we perform object tracking at an object rather than on a feature level.

6   Conclusions

In this paper, we have extended and analyzed a probabilistic object tracking algorithm for a team of vision-based autonomously moving robots. Our results suggest that purely image-based probabilistic estimation of complex game states is feasible in real time even in complex and fast changing environments. We have also seen that maintaining trees of possible tracks is particularly useful for estimating a global state based on multiple mobile sensors with position uncertainty.

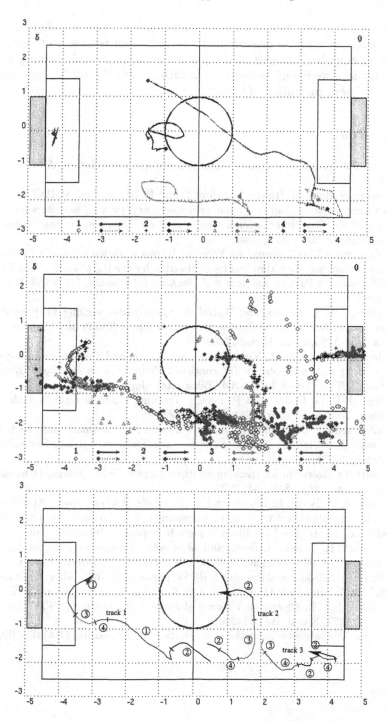

Fig. 4. Opponent observations and resolved tracks.

Finally, we have seen how the state estimation modules of individual robots can cooperate in order to produce more accurate and reliable state estimation. Besides an empirical analysis of the parameter settings and learning accurate sensing models, we intend to compare in future work the MHT algorithm with the JPDAF implementation of [11].

References

1. Y. Bar-Shalom and T. Fortmann. Tracking and data association. Academic Press., 1988.
2. M. Beetz, S. Buck, R. Hanek, T. Schmitt, and B. Radig. The AGILO autonomous robot soccer team: Computational principles, experiences, and perspectives. In *Procs. of the First International Conference on Autonomous Agents and Multiagent Systems*, 2002. to appear.
3. I.J. Cox and S.L. Hingorani. An Efficient Implementation of Reid's Multiple Hypothesis Tracking Algorithm and Its Evaluation for the Purpose of Visual Tracking. *IEEE Trans. on Pattern Analysis and Machine Intelligence*, 18(2):138–150, February 1996.
4. M. Dietl, J.-S. Gutmann, and B. Nebel. Cooperative sensing in dynamic environments. In *International Conference on Intelligent Robots and Systems (IROS)*, pages 1706–1713, Maui, Hawaii, 2001.
5. R. Hanek and T. Schmitt. Vision-based localization and data fusion in a system of cooperating mobile robots. In *International Conference on Intelligent Robots and Systems (IROS)*, pages 1199–1204, Takamatsu, Japan, 2000.
6. C. Hue, J.-P. Le Cadre, and P. Perez. Tracking multiple objects with particle filtering. Technical Report 1361, IRISA, 2000.
7. S. Julier and J. Uhlmann. A new extension of the kalman filter to nonlinear systems. The 11th Int. Symp. on Aerospace/Defence Sensing, Simulation and Controls., 1997.
8. D. Reid. An algorithm for tracking multiple targets. IEEE Transactions on Automatic Control, 24(6):843–854, 1979.
9. T. Schmitt, M. Beetz, R. Hanek, and S. Buck. Watch their moves: Applying probabilistic multiple object tracking to autonomous robot soccer. In *AAAI National Conference on Artificial Intelligence*, page to appear, Edmonton, Canada, 2002.
10. T. Schmitt, R. Hanek, S. Buck, and M. Beetz. Cooperative probabilistic state estimation for vision-based autonomous mobile robots. In *International Conference on Intelligent Robots and Systems (IROS)*, pages 1630–1638, Maui, Hawaii, 2001.
11. D. Schulz, W. Burgard, D. Fox, and A.B. Cremers. Multiple object tracking with a mobile robot. In *Computer Vision and Pattern Recognition (CVPR)*, volume 1, pages 371–377, Kauai, Hawaii, 2001.
12. S. Thrun. Probabilistic algorithms in robotics. *AI Magazine*, 21(4):93–109, 2000.

Behavior Acquisition Based on Multi-module Learning System in Multi-agent Environment

Yasutake Takahashi, Kazuhiro Edazawa, and Minoru Asada

Emergent Robotics Area, Dept. of Adaptive Machine Systems
Graduate School of Engineering, Osaka University
Yamadaoka 2-1, Suita, Osaka 565-0871, Japan
{yasutake,asada}@ams.eng.osaka-u.ac.jp
eda@er.ams.eng.osaka-u.ac.jp

Abstract. The conventional reinforcement learning approaches have difficulties to handle the policy alternation of the opponents because it may cause dynamic changes of state transition probabilities of which stability is necessary for the learning to converge. This paper presents a method of multi-module reinforcement learning in a multiagent environment, by which the learning agent can adapt itself to the policy changes of the opponents. We show a preliminary result of a simple soccer situation in the context of RoboCup.

1 Introduction

There have been an increasing number of approaches to robot behavior acquisition based on the reinforcement learning methods. The conventional approaches need an assumption that the environment is almost fixed or changing slowly so that the learning agent can regard the state transition probabilities are consistent during its learning. Therefore, it seems difficult to apply the reinforcement learning method to a multiagent system because a policy alternation of the other agents may occur, which dynamically changes the state transition probabilities from the viewpoint of the learning agent. RoboCup provides such a typical one, that is, a highly dynamic, hostile environment, in which an agent has to obtain purposive behaviors.

There are a number of papers on reinforcement learning system in a multiagent environment. Asada et al. [1] proposed a method which estimates the state vectors representing the relationship between the learner's behavior and those of other agents in the environment using a technique from system identification, then the reinforcement learning based on the estimated state vectors is applied to obtain the optimal behavior policy. However, this method requires re-learning or adjustment of learning agent's policy whenever the other agents change their policies, even if they switch their policies back which the learning agent has already adjusted before. This problem happens because one learning module can maintain only one policy.

A multiple learning module approach would provide one solution for this problem. If we can assign multiple learning modules to different situations in

G.A. Kaminka, P.U. Lima, and R. Rojas (Eds.): RoboCup 2002, LNAI 2752, pp. 435–442, 2003.

which each module can regard the state transition probabilities are consistent, then the system would provide reasonable performance. There are a number of works on the multi-learning module systems.

Singh [2, 3] has proposed compositional Q-learning in which an agent learns multiple sequential decision tasks with multi learning modules. Each module learns its own elemental task while the system has a gating module for the sequential task, and this module learns to select one of the elemental task modules. Takahashi and Asada [4] proposed a method by which a hierarchical structure for behavior learning is self-organized. The modules in the lower networks are organized as experts to move to different categories of sensor value regions and learn lower level behaviors using motor commands. In the meantime, the modules in the higher networks are organized as experts which learn higher level behaviors using lower modules. Each module assigns its own goal state by itself. However, there is no such measure to identify the situation that the agent can change modules corresponding to the current situation.

Sutton [5] has proposed DYNA-architecture which integrate world model learning and execution-time planning. Singh [6] has proposed a method of learning a hierarchy of models of the DYNA-architectures. The world model is not for the identification of the situations, but only for improving the scalability of reinforcement learning algorithms.

Doya et al. [7] have proposed MOdular Selection and Identification for Control (MOSAIC), which is a modular reinforcement learning architecture for nonlinear, non-stationary control tasks. The basic idea is to decompose a complex task into multiple domains in space and time based on the predictability of the environmental dynamics. Each module has a state prediction model and a reinforcement learning controller. The models have limited capabilities of state prediction as linear predictors, therefore the multiple prediction models are required for the non-linear task. A domain is specified as a region in which one linear predictor can estimate sensor outputs based on its own prediction capability. The responsibility signal is defined by a function of the prediction errors, and the signals of the modules define the outputs of the reinforcement learning controllers. Haruno et al. [8, 9] have proposed another implementation of MOSAIC based on multiple modules of forward and inverse models.

In this paper, we propose a method by which multiple modules are assigned to different situations and learn purposive behaviors for the specified situations as results of the other agent's behaviors. We show a preliminary result of a simple soccer situation in the context of RoboCup.

2   A Basic Idea and an Assumption

The basic idea is that the learning agent could assign one reinforcement learning module to each situation if it can distinguish a number of situations in which the state transition probabilities are consistent. We introduce a multiple learning module approach to realize this idea. A module consists of a learning component which models the world and an execution-time planning one. The whole system will follow these procedure simultaneously.

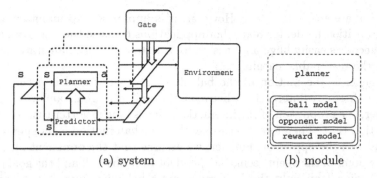

(a) system   (b) module

Fig. 1. A multi-module learning system and an architecture of a module

- find a model which represents the best estimation among the modules,
- update the model, and
- calculate action values to accomplish a given task based on dynamic programming (DP).

As a preliminary experiment, we prepare a case of ball chasing behavior with collision avoidance in the context of RoboCup. The problem here is to find the model which can most accurately describe the opponent's behavior from the view point of the learning agent. It may take a time to distinguish the situation, then, we put an assumption.

- The policy of the opponent might change match by match but is fixed during one match.

3   A Multi-module Learning System

Fig.1(a) shows a basic architecture of the proposed system, that is, a multi-module reinforcement learning one. Each module has a forward model (predictor) which represents the state transition model and a behavior learner (policy planner) which estimates the state-action value function based on the forward model in the reinforcement learning manner. This idea of combination of a forward model and a reinforcement learning system is similar to the H-DYNA architecture [6] or MOSAIC [7–9]. In other words, we extend such architectures to an application of behavior acquisition in the multi-agent environment.

The system selects one module which has the best estimation of the state transition sequence by activating a gate signal corresponding to a module and by deactivating the goal signals of other modules, and the selected module sends action commands based on its policy.

3.1   Predictor

In this experiment, the agent recognizes a ball, a goal, and the opponent in the environment. The state space of the planner consists of features of all objects in order to calculate state values (discounted sum of the reward received over time) for each state and action pair. However, it is impractical to maintain a full size state transition model for real robot applications because the size of state-action space becomes easily huge and it is really rare to experience all state transitions within the reasonable learning time.

In general, the motion of the ball depends on the goal and the opponent because there are interactions between the ball, the goal, and the opponent. However, the proportion of the interaction time is much shorter than that of non-interaction time. Therefore, we assume that the ball motion is independent from the goal and the opponent. Further, we assume that the opponent motion from the viewpoint of the agent seems independent from the ball and the goal positions and to depend on only the learning agent's behavior even if the opponent's decision may depend on the ball and/or the goal positions. If the system has maintain the forward models of the ball, the goal, and the opponent separately, the each model can be much more compact and it is easy to experience most state transition within reasonable learning time.

Fig.1 (b) shows an architecture of one module in our system. As mentioned above, the module has three forward models for the ball, the goal, and the opponent. We estimate the state transition probability $\hat{\mathcal{P}}^a_{ss'}$ for the triplet of state s, action a, and next state s' using the following equation:

$$\hat{\mathcal{P}}^a_{ss'} = \hat{\mathcal{P}}^a_{b_s b_{s'}} \cdot \hat{\mathcal{P}}^a_{g_s g_{s'}} \cdot \hat{\mathcal{P}}^a_{o_s o_{s'}} , \tag{1}$$

where a state $s \in S$ is a combination of three states in the ball state space $b_s \in {}^bS$, the goal state space $g_s \in {}^gS$, and the opponent state space $o_s \in {}^oS$. The system has not only the state transition model but also a reward model $\hat{\mathcal{R}}^a_{ss'}$.

We simply store all experiences (state-action-next state sequences) to estimate these models. According to the assumption mentioned in **2**, we share the state transition models of the ball and the goal and the reward model among the modules, and each module has its own opponent model. This leads to further compact model representation.

3.2 Planner

Now we have the estimated state transition probabilities $\hat{\mathcal{P}}^a_{ss'}$ and the expected rewards $\hat{\mathcal{R}}^a_{ss'}$, then, an approximated state-action value function $Q(s,a)$ for a state action pair (s, a) is given by

$$Q(s,a) = \sum_{s'} \hat{\mathcal{P}}^a_{ss'} \left[\hat{\mathcal{R}}^a_{ss'} + \gamma \max_{a'} Q(s',a') \right] , \tag{2}$$

where $\hat{\mathcal{P}}^a_{ss'}$ and $\hat{\mathcal{R}}^a_{ss'}$ are the state-transition probabilities and expected rewards, respectively, and the γ is the discount rate.

3.3 Gating Signals

The basic idea of gating signals is similar to Tani and Nolfi's work [10] and the MOSAIC architecture [7–9]. The gating signal of the module becomes larger if

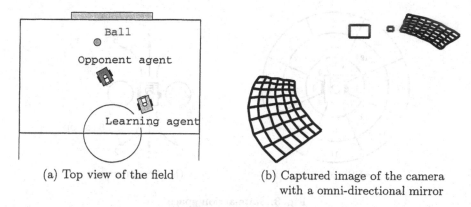

(a) Top view of the field

(b) Captured image of the camera with a omni-directional mirror

Fig. 2. Simulation Environment

the module performs better state transition prediction during a certain period, else smaller. We assume that the module which performs best state transition prediction has the best policy against the current situation because the planner of the module is based on the model which describes the situation best. In our proposed architecture, the gating signal is used for the gating the action outputs from modules. We calculate the gating signals g_i of the module i as follows:

$$g_i = \prod_{t=-T+1}^{0} \frac{e^{\lambda p_i^t}}{\sum_j e^{\lambda p_j^t}}$$

where p_i is the occurrence probability of the state transition from the previous $(t-1)$ state to the current (t) one according to the model i, and the λ is a scaling factor.

4 Experiments

We have studied the preliminary experiments so far. The task of the learning agent is to catch the ball while it avoids the collision with an opponent.

4.1 Setting

We apply the proposed system to a mobile robot which participates in the RoboCup middle size league. The robot has an omni-directional camera system. A simple color image processing is applied to detect an ball area and an opponent one in the image in real-time (every 33ms). The driving mechanism is a PWS (Power Wheeled System); the vehicle is fitted with two differential wheels. The wheels are driven independently by separated DC motors, and two extra free wheels ensure the static stability. Figure 2 (a) shows one of situations in which the learning agent encounters and Figure 2 (b) shows the simulated captured image of the camera with the omni-directional mirror mounted on the robots. The larger box indicates the opponent and the smaller one indicates the ball.

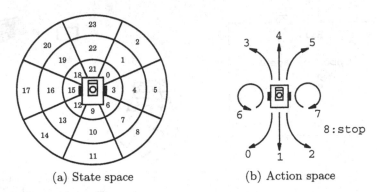

(a) State space   (b) Action space

Fig. 3. State-action space

Table 1. Comparison of the success rates between the agent with multi-module system and one with one-module system

system	success rate
multi-module	61 %
one-module	50 %

The state space is constructed in terms of the centroids of the ball and the opponent on the image (Figure 3 (a)). The action space is constructed in terms of two torque values to be sent to two motors corresponding to two wheels (Figure 3 (b)). These parameters of the robot system are unknown to the robot, and it tries to estimate the mapping from sensory information to appropriate motor commands by the method.

The opponent has a number of behaviors such as "stop", "move left", and "move right", and switches them randomly after a fixed period. The learning agent has models to those behaviors of the opponents. The learning agent behaves randomly while it gathers the data of the ball and the opponent image positions and builds up the models of them.

4.2   Simulation Result

We have applied the method to a learning agent and compared the other agent which has only one learning modules. Table 1 shows the success rate of these two system after the learning. The success indicates that the learning agent successfully catches the ball with collision avoidance while the opponent moves randomly. The success rate indicates the number of successes in the one hundred trials. The multi-module system shows better performance than the one-module system. Figure 4 shows an example sequence of the behavior when the agent executes its learned policy and the opponent behaves randomly after a fixed period. Figure 5 shows the sequence of the gating signal (the opponent's behavior estimation) during the behavior. The arrows and alphabet indexes at the bottom correspond to the indexes of the figure 4. The agent seems to fail to estimate the

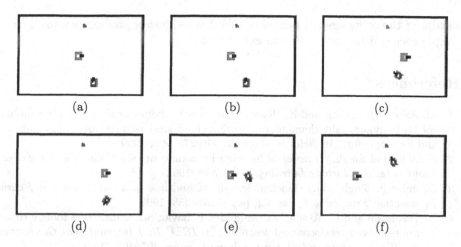

Fig. 4. A sequence of a chasing behavior

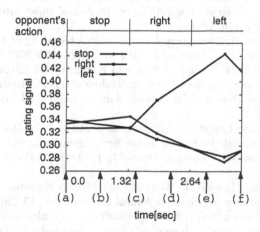

Fig. 5. A sequence of gating signal while the agent executes its learned policy

opponent's behavior at the beginning and end periods, however, it accomplishes the given task. This mean that even if the agent fails to estimates the other agent's behavior, there is no problem in some situations where the learning agents policy does not depends on the other agent's behavior. For example, the opponent's behavior does not depend on the agent's behavior when the ball is near and the opponent is far from the agent. In such a case, the agent does not have to estimate the other's behaviors correctly.

5   Conclusion

In this paper, we proposed a method by which multiple modules are assigned to different situations and learn purposive behaviors for the specified situations as results of the other agent's behaviors. We have shown a preliminary result of a simple soccer situation in the context of RoboCup.

References

1. M. Asada, E. Uchibe, and K. Hosoda. Cooperative behavior acquisition for mobile robots in dynamically changing real worlds via vision-based reinforcement learning and development. *Artificial Intelligence*, 110:275–292, 1999.
2. Satinder Pal Singh. Transfer of learning by composing solutions of elemental sequential tasks. *Machine Learning*, 8:323–339, 1992.
3. Satinder P. Singh. The effeicient learnig of multiple task sequences. In *Neural Information Processing Systems 4*, pages 251–258, 1992.
4. Y. Takahashi and M. Asada. Vision-guided behavior acquisition of a mobile robot by multi-layered reinforcement learning. In *IEEE/RSJ International Conference on Intelligent Robots and Systems*, volume 1, pages 395–402, 2000.
5. Richard S. Sutton. Integrated modeling and control based on reinforcement learning and dynamic programming. *Advances in Neural Information Processing Systems 3*, pages 471–478, 1991.
6. Satinder P. Singh. Reinforcement learning with a hierarchy of abstract models. In *National Conference on Artificial Intelligence*, pages 202–207, 1992.
7. Kenji Doya, Kazuyuki Samejima, Ken ichi Katagiri, and Mitsuo Kawato. Multiple model-based reinforcement learning. Technical report, Kawato Dynamic Brain Project Technical Report, KDB-TR-08, Japan Science and Technology Corporation, June 2000.
8. Masahiko Haruno, Daniel M. Wolpert, and Mitsuo Kawato. Multiple paired forward-inverse models for human motor learning and control. *Advances in Neural Information Processing Systems*, 11:31–37, 1999. MIT Press, Cambridge, Massachusetts.
9. Masahiko Haruno, Daniel M. Wolpert, and Mitsuo Kawato. Mosaic model for sensorimotor learning and control. *Neural Computation*, 13:2201–2220, 2001.
10. Jun Tani and Stefano Nolfi. Self-organization of modules and their hierarchy in robot learning problems: A dynamical systems approach. Technical report, Technical Report: SCSL-TR-97-008, 1997.

Simulation League – League Summary

Oliver Obst

University of Koblenz, Germany

1 Simulation League

In the simulation league the RoboCup soccer server provides a standard platform for simulated soccer teams to play against each other over a local network. Each team connects 11 player programs and possibly a coach client to the server, which simulates the 2D soccer field and distributes the sensory information to the clients. Besides the team clients the RoboCup soccer monitor or other visualization and debug tools can be connected as a client to the server to provide 2D or 3D visual information or information like game statistics and analysis for the spectators.

Fig. 1. Soccer Simulation Participants

1.1 Introduction

The simulation league forms a counterpart to the hardware leagues which have to create or program robots that actually operate in the real world. In the hardware leagues it is necessary to provide a minimal basis that allows the robots to function in the real world, like, e.g. image processing, the identification of objects, motor control, orientation and localization, before any aspect of strategy or multiagent cooperation can be addressed.

In the simulated world, however, it is possible to detach oneself as far as one desires from the complexities that arise when embedding an autonomous agent in an environment. The environment can be made (at least in principle) fully reproducible and, if required, fully observable and controllable. In addition, in simulation it is possible to quickly and automatically reenact a much larger number of experiments than would be possible with real-world robots. One has accurate control over which models are used for the sensory perception,

G.A. Kaminka, P.U. Lima, and R. Rojas (Eds.): RoboCup 2002, LNAI 2752, pp. 443–452, 2003.

how exactly the synchronization of visual perception and actuators looks like, how precisely agent actuations are translated into the physical reality of the simulation.

The perception/actuation models used in the simulation league are much simpler than the mappings one finds in real-world scenarios; also, presently, the simulation model does not attempt to mimic realistic sensors and actuators though it does include noise and distortion models. However, this simplicity, on the other hand, opens up qualitatively new dimensions. It allows to concentrate to new levels of the pertinent problem, namely learning, teamwork, coordination and cooperation which, at the present time, are still very difficult to address in the hardware leagues. It is this element where the relevance of the simulation league derives from and by which it complements the other leagues of RoboCup. Sensomotoric coordination has still to be incorporated into the model, but forms only a side-issue which has to be integrated into the larger perspective of single- and multiagent learning, coordination and cooperation.

In all these respects, the simulation league goes beyond the implementation of artificial, shallow theoretically defined toy tasks and offers a deep and multi-faceted scenario serving as a challenge to develop AI methods.

1.2   Teams and Tournament

Overview. In the 2002 simulation tournament 42 teams participated, with the traditionally strongly represented countries Japan, Germany and Iran each having seven or more teams in the tournament. Other teams came from China, Australia, USA, the Netherlands, Russia, Poland, Belgium and – for the first time – India. The tournament was organized into a two-round, round-robin stage followed by a double elimination round for the eight strongest teams (quarter-final level). In the first round, the groups had 5-6 members, the first two being seeded according to their performance in RoboCup 2001 and other official tournaments since then. The best three of each group proceeded into the second round, where each group had 6 members. Only the best two teams from each group in the second round proceeded into the double elimination. This configuration enabled most teams to have a large number of encounters and was to make sure that no strong team would be eliminated early on. The success of this concept was indeed corroborated by the strong performance of the eight teams surviving to the elimination round.

The overall playing strength of the teams in the tournament was quite impressive. The playing level of the tournament showed increased and consistent improvement as compared to last year's tournament. More professional and scholarly approaches are being used by a wider number of teams. Modern techniques of AI and machine learning (e.g. particle swarm localization and explicit experimental statistics for certain standard configurations [4] – team Trilearn from the University of Amsterdam (Netherlands) – or Reinforcement Learning – like that used by the Brainstormers) have become a standard approach whose use is not anymore restricted to specialized teams, but has entered the domain of general know-how.

Table 1. Countries represented in the simulation league (soccer tournament)

Country	No. Teams
Japan	11
Iran	9
Germany	8
Australia	3
China	3
Belgium	1
Canada	1
India	1
Netherlands	1
Poland	1
Portugal	1
Russia	1
USA	1

The format of the games has remained the same, with some modifications in details. The evaluation has been replaced by an evaluation challenge; its goal is to probe new features that have been introduced into the simulation environment and to test their influence on the performance of the teams. The idea was to move away from the purely evaluative element which, it was felt, could be achieved with much higher significance and better statistical quality under laboratory conditions. Instead, the goal was to move towards an explorative instrument which would allow to estimate the influence of simulator changes a year before they are bindingly introduced as official tournament features. One of the motivations for this change of policy was this year's milestone discussion (see Sec. 1.3) and the desire to move to a strategy for future simulator development which would be both more long-term and more committed.

Agent Strategies. The tournament was won by the champion of 2001, Tsinghuaeolus, from Tsinghua University in Beijing (China), who, even more clearly than last year, dominated the tournament. Tsinghuaeolus possessed skills, especially ball handling, of a very high quality. Precise passing and quick and effective positioning were the immediately visible capabilities of the team [3].

Motivated by the case-based approach of AT Humboldt [10], the Q formalism is used to create a table that makes a 1-step prediction of which kick achieves which ball displacement. Since this is independent of position, it is sufficient to consider a pure $Q(a)$ table (where a is the action selected and $Q(a)$ its value) instead of a much larger $Q(s, a)$ space usually used. These single-step optimizations are then used to search an optimal kick strategy in the the feasible action space. This allows an intelligent selection of acceptable kick actions, e.g. taking into account to prevent interception of the ball by an opponent or other aspects. It combines the advantages of the Dynamic Programming view of action selection with the possibility to filter actions that do not fulfill minimum requirements.

Table 2. Matches and results of the 8 finalists

Final match	
Tsinghuaeolus	7:0
Everest	

Double Elimination – Winners Round

FC Portugal	1:0	FC Portugal				
Wright Eagle			0:7	Tsinghuaeolus		
Tsinghuaeolus	2:0	Tsinghuaeolus			1:0	
TIT HELIOS						
Brainstormers	3:0	Brainstormers				
rUNSWift II			1:2	Everest		
Everest	3:2	Everest				
UvA Trilearn						

Double Elimination – Losers Round

Wright Eagle	2:0	Wright Eagle	1:2	Brainstormers		Brainstormers	
rUNSWift II		Brainstormers			2:1		0:4
TIT HELIOS	0:4	UvA Trilearn	1:0	UvA Trilearn		Everest	
UvA Trilearn		FC Portugal					

Tsinghuaeolus' dribbling mechanism is hand-coded and puts high priority on making sure that the ball is kept kickable at all times and that the ball is kept out of all opponents kickable areas. Moving forward to the desired direction carries only a second priority in this model.

Another aspect which is tackled by Tsinghuaeolus is the creation of a globally coherent strategy from individual local observations [11]. The decentralization of the typical RoboCup scenario and the very limited bandwidth creates a pressure on the agent teams to make decisions individually for each agent while, in the same time trying to improve the situation for the whole team. For this purpose, Tsinghuaeolus uses a task decomposition mechanism. It decomposes the global task into subtasks that can each be executed by a single agent. The individual tasks are then allocated to that agent that is able to carry them out, creating so-called *pairs of arrangements*. These arrangements are evaluated to attain a measure for the performance of the complete task. A branch-and-bound search is performed on the set of arrangements to find the set of arrangements achieving the highest score (see also [3]).

A *mutex* mechanism is applied that allows to treat actions which are mutually exclusive as compared to actions which can be combined. In addition a mixture term for the joint influence of actions is included in the calculation. A specific element of the Tsinghuaeolus design is the mediator which is an architectural unit responsible for resolving wasteful or mutually exclusive action selection. In ambiguous cases, the system relies on the natural dynamics of the robot soccer environment to break the symmetry and to resolve the decisions. It turns out that the mechanism, together with the selected utility functions, is sufficiently robust to work also when the agents differ in what they perceive (as is the case for the RoboCup scenario).

Second in the tournament was the team *Everest* [9] from the Beijing Institute of Technology. Their code was based on Tsinghuaeolus 2001 and their playing style was similar, though they were clearly inferior to the champion while superior to a large number of strong teams. Team Brainstormers from the Universities Karlsruhe and Dortmund (Germany) achieved the 3rd place and thereby maintaining their consistent top-class performance displayed over the tournaments of the last years. An increasing number of the Brainstormers capabilities have been trained via Reinforcement Learning in the last years, this year adding a learned behavior for selecting the best pass receiver to the repertoire [8]. Another element learned by Brainstormers using Reinforcement Learning techniques are attack situations which, up to now, used to have been hand-coded by the Brainstormers team. Thus, the Brainstormers model acts as paradigm that proves that it is indeed possible to actually learn significant aspects of a soccer player strategy [7].

The fourth place in the tournament was achieved by UvA Amsterdam. This team applied several principled approaches to develop useful strategies. It used particle filters for self- and ball localization as a specific instantiation of a Bayesian filtering approach [4] which improves over earlier approaches to Bayesian filtering [2].

Another aspect which has been tackled in a principled way by UvA Amsterdam is the scoring. They devise experiments in which scoring attempts are undertaken under controlled conditions. This yields a probability distribution for the success of goal shots. Then, a probability is derived that a ball is successfully intercepted by the goalkeeper and feature detection mechanisms as well as discriminant analysis is used to separate the successful from the unsuccessful cases. This results in a powerful and principled way of analyzing whether a goal kick is going to be successful or not. It allows the UvA players to indeed realize a goal-kicking situation with a high probability when the opportunity arises. Such an approach is closely related to minimax distributed dynamic programming approaches which become increasingly popular.

These minimax approaches are relatively fragile with respect to the selection and stability of their strategies. To overcome this problem and to extend the strategy horizon of their agents, Baltic Lübeck provides its players with explicit micro-strategies [1]. These are applied in situations where the player do not need to react immediately, but have a certain degree of freedom to prepare longer-termed moves. These micro-strategies can be seen as puzzle pieces that may be used to describe possible movements of players. These pieces are then adapted into the players' current situation context whenever they fulfill certain properties. They can prepare a flank or provide movement patterns to escape marking. Also, they serve to encourage or exclude certain pass patterns.

The problem of specifying the behavior of multiagent teams was tackled in an approach by RoboLog Koblenz. The team behavior is specified with UML statecharts and can be translated into running Prolog code for each agent [5]. An agent processes one transition of the statechart in a simulation step for atomic actions, it can execute parallel transitions for actions that can be performed simultaneously.

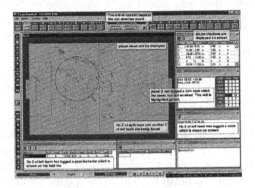

Fig. 2. SBCe "Team Assistant"

Presentation Tools. This year's presentation tournament was won by the SBCe "Team Assistant" [6] from Shahid Beheshti University (Iran) which was, rather than the favorites in earlier tournaments not a visualization tool that would create an appealing visual presentation of the simulation games, but a debugging software to allow team developers to accurately control and analyze the player behaviors in specific game situations.

Fig. 3. Wright Eagle "Magic Box"

1.3   Milestone Discussion

An important issue of this year's event was the high-profile discussion of the further development of the simulation league. In the past years the development of the simulator has seen important innovations, amongst other things a neck, heterogeneous players and a complex coaching language. However, these developments have been taking place in principle on a year-to-year basis. It has then been increasingly felt that the simulation league should adopt an explicit long-term perspective that will, at some point, integrate with the other leagues to the ultimate goal of RoboCup 2050. At the same time, one would desire to develop the simulator in such a way as to allow teams to expand upon their techniques and capabilities while not disrupting achieved capabilities without good reason.

Therefore, a milestone map was conceived and discussed in a panel presentation during the RoboCup Symposium. One of the most important questions concerning the future of the simulation league is whether it should remain on a relatively high level where one focuses on the multiagent aspect or whether it should become increasingly concrete and close to real robot simulations. To tackle this problem, it was suggested to support the high-level simulation for the next decades while at some point initiating the development of realistic simulators. After a certain phase of overlap, the focus would then shift to the more realistic simulations and the high level view would begin to phase out.

A central aspect to simulator development has been the pressure to extend the present 2D scenario to 3D which introduces a new level of complexity. While this idea has been discussed in the past years without materializing into action, in this year the simulation league has committed to elevate this aspect to the rank of a central milestone. It is hoped that preliminary 3D competitions can be held already during RoboCup 2003 in parallel to the 'classical' 2D competition. Further milestones suggested were the introduction of nonlinear and historic noise types, an abstract leg dynamics (which would create a link between the high level and the realistic simulation) and concepts to allow large scale statistical evaluations. In addition, the milestones included the introduction of realistic dynamics, collision models together with event-based simulation that would no longer be implemented as a pseudo-synchronous perception/actuation cycle, but would capture the spirit of realistic situations with no true synchronization. Long-term milestones for the "realistic simulator" branch included the development of humanoid simulators.

All these changes require a systematic reorganization and a strongly improved modularization of the present simulator. Following the milestone discussions at RoboCup 2002, the simulation maintenance team has committed itself vigorously to address this situation. At the present time, it is actively and decisively pursuing the required refactoring of the simulator and the implementation of the central 3D milestone. A version is expected to be available in RoboCup 2003 and to form part of next year's evaluation challenge as the first official platform at which innovations to the simulation model are being presented to the public.

1.4 After the Competitions

To further have the possibility of testing teams and in order to provide a competition-like setting all year long the Simulated Soccer Internet League has been established after RoboCup 2002 was over. Developers install their teams on the competition machines, hosted at the University of Koblenz, via the Internet. The server and teams are started automatically, but other than during the RoboCup competitions a slowed down server is used to keep the number of required machines low. Each time an Internet league round is over, developers can download the recorded log files and use them for analysis of their team's behavior.

Last but not least a further novelty is the availability of the RoboCup competition matches in Flash file format, so that RoboCup 2002 Simulation League matches can be replayed with simply a web browser using a flash plug-in. The game files are available from the results section on
http://www.uni-koblenz.de/~fruit/orga/rc02/

2   Results and Teams

Table 3. Top 8 teams, team competition

1	TsinghuAeolus	China
2	Everest	China
3	Brainstormers	Germany
4	UvA Trilearn	Netherlands
5	Wright Eagle	China
5	FC Portugal 2002	Portugal
7	TIT HELIOS	Japan
7	rUNSWift	Australia

Table 4. Winners, coach competition

1	FC Portugal	Portugal
2	Helli-Respina 2002	Iran

Table 5. Winner, presentation competition

1	SBCe	Iran

Table 6. Qualified presentation teams (6 teams from 5 countries)

Wright Eagle	Univ. of Sci. & Tech. of China	China
RoboLog Koblenz 2002	Universität Koblenz-Landau	Germany
SBC++	Shahid Beheshti University	Iran
SBCE	Shahid Beheshti University	Iran
YowAI2002	The University of Electro-Communications	Japan
FC Portugal 2002	University of Porto and University of Aveiro	Portugal

Table 7. Qualified teams for coach competition (9 teams from 5 countries)

Wright Eagle	Univ. of Sci. & Tech. of China	China
RoboLog Koblenz 2002	Universität Koblenz-Landau	Germany
Mainz Rolling Brains	University of Mainz	Germany
The Dirty Dozen	University of Osnabrück	Germany
Helli-Respina 2002	Allameh Helli High School	Iran
Pasargad	AmirKabir University of Technology	Iran
Sharif Arvand	Sharif University of Technology	Iran
FC Portugal 2002	University of Aveiro and University of Porto	Portugal
ATTUnited-2002	AT&T Labs - Research	USA

Table 8. Team Competition (45 teams from 14 countries)

Cyberoos2002	CSIRO	Australia
rUNSWift	University of New South Wales	Australia
CrocaRoos 2002	University of Queensland	Australia
Cow'n'Action	ULB	Belgium
UBCDynamo02	University of British Columbia	Canada
Everest	Beijing Institute of Technology	China
SHU2002	Shanghai University	China
Tsinghuaeolus	State Key Lab of	China
	Intelligent Technology and Systems	
Wright Eagle	Univ. of Sci. & Tech. of China	China
AT Humboldt 2002	Humboldt University Berlin	Germany
RoboLog Koblenz 2002	Universität Koblenz-Landau	Germany
BUGS	University of Bremen	Germany
Virtual Werder 2002/A	University of Bremen	Germany
Brainstormers	University of Karlsruhe	Germany
Baltic Luebeck	University of Lübeck	Germany
Mainz Rolling Brains	University of Mainz	Germany
The Dirty Dozen	University of Osnabrück	Germany
IITKanpur	Indian Institute of Technology Kanpur	India
Helli-Respina 2002	Allameh Helli High School	Iran
PolyteCS	AmirKabir University of Technology	Iran
Iranians	Iran University of Science And Technology	Iran
Persepolis	JavanFarhangsara	Iran
AVAN	Qazvin Islamic Azad University	Iran
Sharif Arvand	Sharif University of Technology	Iran
Thunder	Tehran University	Iran
Matrix	University of Shahid Beheshti	Iran
UTUtd	University ofTehran	Iran
chagamma	AIST/JAIST	Japan
Puppets	Fukui University	Japan
RaiC02	Fukui University	Japan
Harmony	Hokkaido University	Japan
Toricolor Diamonds	Kanazawa Institute of Technology	Japan
YAMAKASA	Kyushu University	Japan
Gemini	National Institute of Advanced	Japan
	Industrial Science and Technology	
Hana	Osaka Prefecture University	Japan
YowAI2002	The University of Electro-Communications	Japan
TIT HELIOS	Tokyo Institute of Technology	Japan
TUT-ChoNaSo	Toyohashi University of Technology	Japan
UvA Trilearn	University of Amsterdam	Netherlands
WROCLAW2002	Wroclaw University ofTechnology	Poland
FC Portugal 2002	University of Aveiro and University of Porto	Portugal
ERA-Polytech	New ERA Company &	Russia
	St.Petersburg Technical University	
n-th.com	Company n-th.com	Ukraine
ATTUnited-2002	AT&T Labs - Research	USA
Wahoo Wunderkind	University of Virginia	USA

References

1. Martin Haker, André Meyer, Behboud Kalantary, Daniel Polani, and Thomas Martinetz. Team description for baltic lübeck 2002. In Gal A. Kaminka, Pedro U. Lima, and Raul Rojas, editors, *RoboCup 2002: Robot Soccer World Cup VI, Fukuoka, Japan*, 2002. Pre-Proceedings.
2. Martin Haker, André Meyer, Daniel Polani, and Thomas Martinetz. A method for incorporation of new evidence to improve world state estimation. In A. Birk, S. Coradeschi, and S. Tadokoro, editors, *RoboCup-2001: Robot Soccer World Cup V*, Berlin, 2002. Springer.
3. Yao Jinyi and Cai Yunpeng. Team description of TsinghuAeolus. In Gal A. Kaminka, Pedro U. Lima, and Raul Rojas, editors, *RoboCup 2002: Robot Soccer World Cup VI*, Fukuoka, Japan, 2002. Pre-Proceedings.
4. Jelle Kok, Remco de Boer, Nikos Vlassis, and Frans Groen. UvA Trilearn 2002 team description. In Gal A. Kaminka, Pedro U. Lima, and Raul Rojas, editors, *RoboCup 2002: Robot Soccer World Cup VI*, Fukuoka, Japan, 2002. Pre-Proceedings.
5. Jan Murray, Oliver Obst, and Frieder Stolzenburg. RoboLog Koblenz 2002 – team description. In Gal A. Kaminka, Pedro U. Lima, and Raul Rojas, editors, *RoboCup 2002: Robot Soccer World Cup VI*, Fukuoka, Japan, 2002. Pre-Proceedings.
6. Eslam Nazemi, Amir Reza Zareian, Reza Samimi, and Foruhar Ali Shiva. Team assistant. In Gal A. Kaminka, Pedro U. Lima, and Raul Rojas, editors, *RoboCup 2002: Robot Soccer World Cup VI*, Fukuoka, Japan, 2002. Pre-Proceedings.
7. Martin Riedmiller and Artur Merke. Using machine learning techniques in complex multi-agent domains. In I. Stamatescu, W. Menzel, M. Richter, and U. Ratsch, editors, *Perspectives on Adaptivity and Learning*, LNCS. Springer, 2002.
8. Martin Riedmiller, Artur Merke, Andreas Hoffmann, Manuel Nickschas, D. Withopf, and F. Zacharias. Brainstormers 2002 – team description. In Gal A. Kaminka, Pedro U. Lima, and Raul Rojas, editors, *RoboCup 2002: Robot Soccer World Cup VI*, Fukuoka, Japan, 2002. Pre-Proceedings.
9. Gu Yang, Liu Junfeng, Cui Lihui, and Pan Feng. Everest 2002 team description. In Gal A. Kaminka, Pedro U. Lima, and Raul Rojas, editors, *RoboCup 2002: Robot Soccer World Cup VI*, Fukuoka, Japan, 2002. Pre-Proceedings.
10. Jinyi Yao, Jiang Chen, and Zengqi Sun. An application in robocup combining q-learning with adversarial planning. In *RoboCup 2002*, 2002.
11. Cai Yunpeng, Chen Jiang, Yao Jinyi, and Li Shi. Global planning from local eyeshot: An implementation of observation-based plan coordination in robocup simulation games. In A. Birk, S. Coradeschi, and S. Tadokoro, editors, *RoboCup-2001: Robot Soccer World Cup V*, Berlin, 2002. Springer.

RoboCup 2002 Small-Size League Review

Brett Browning

School of Computer Science
Carnegie Mellon University
Pittsburgh PA 15213, USA
brettb@cs.cmu.edu
http://www.cs.cmu.edu/~brettb/

1   Introduction

The RoboCup challenge, to build soccer playing robots able to compete against the best human soccer players, is a goal well beyond our current levels of robot technology. Our current competition structure, with its various leagues, aims to step towards this goal by focusing on different aspects of the RoboCup problem. In the small-size league, global perception allows us to focus primarily on single and multi-robot control and multi-robot teamwork.

RoboCup 2002 showcased the significant level of progress made in the small-size league over the last few years. Indeed, the small-size league has to be amongst the most exciting competitions at RoboCup. Significant advancements in robot design, control, and team coordination lead to the incredible 2002 small-size grand final between former two-time champions Big Red (Cornell University, US) and FU-Fighters (Free University of Berlin, Germany). Spectators and competitors alike, were truly in awe of the sheer speed of activity in the final game. Indeed, never in the history of RoboCup has a robot soccer final been played with such speed and control.

In many ways, RoboCup 2002 was a watershed year for the small-size league. We have made many changes to our competition, ranging from the qualification process through to challenge events and the way individual games are run, in order to push research developments within the competition to the next level. Some of the changes that we have begun will not be completed until RoboCup 2003 and beyond. We believe and hope that these changes will continue to make the small-size league a hotbed of robot intelligence development in the future.

In the following sections we will review the new changes that were wrought for the small-size league in 2002, as well as reviewing the main competition itself. We will finish our review of the small-size league with a projection of the changes we hope to finalize for RoboCup 2003 and where the future of this very exciting league is headed.

2   New Features for 2002

To reach the lofty goals of RoboCup, our competition must constantly evolve in synchronicity with the research developments by competition teams. If the competition fails to evolve, research developments will stagnate into over-engineered

G.A. Kaminka, P.U. Lima, and R. Rojas (Eds.): RoboCup 2002, LNAI 2752, pp. 453–459, 2003.
© Springer-Verlag Berlin Heidelberg 2003

solutions that have no general applicability. For RoboCup 2002, we undertook a series of changes to our competition, some of which will not be complete until 2003 and beyond, that we hope will continue to push research developments in the coming years. In particular, our changes focused on the following goals:

1. Complete autonomy for the duration of the game
2. Large size field with no walls, with 11 vs 11 competitions
3. Regional competitions
4. Challenge events
5. FIFA compatible rules
6. Logging of each individual game for later analysis

Each of these changes has the goal of promoting research. Continuing the small-size tradition, the field was once again modified this year. A wider and longer field, along with a wider goal mouth, was used to help promote more interesting team game play. Our rule format has changed to be FIFA compliant, to help keep the competition in-line with the eventual goal of RoboCup. We have begun a process of moving towards using regional competitions, of which there is an ever growing number, to operate as qualification mechanisms for RoboCup. Using regional competitions in this way will help RoboCup grow beyond the constrained limitations of one event, and will continue to ensure that the RoboCup event maintains its status as the World Championships of robot soccer. To promote research in opponent modeling and associated opponent-customized strategic planning, we have begun the first steps to log each and every game from a global perception perspective. These video logs will be available for teams to process after the competition. We hope that for RoboCup 2003, we will have on-line logging that teams will be able to access after each game of the competition.

2.1   Challenge Events

Perhaps the largest changes to the competition have been the introduction of Challenge events and the move to full autonomy for the entire duration of each game. Challenge events have been a regular item in the Sony legged league and Simulator leagues for a while now. Essentially, they promote quantitative evaluations of particular aspects of the robot technology that is developed to play robot soccer. In Fukuoka, we introduced three challenges for the first small-size Challenge competition. The three challenges range in difficulty and are designed to quantitatively compare each team as well as to challenge the state-of-the-art. The first two challenges fit well within any team's capabilities, while the third challenges the abilities of every team. The three challenges are:

– **Challenge 1: The navigation challenge.** One robot must navigate from defense box to defense box through an unknown, static, robot-sized obstacle field. The robot must complete five laps, where each lap consists of traveling from the start defense box to the opposite defense box and back. A penalties of 10s is added for each collision, no matter how small, between the robot and the obstacles.

- **Challenge 2: The shooting challenge.** One robot must score as many goals as possible within 2 minutes. Each time the robot scores, a ball is released on the halfway line on top of the 45 degree sidewall causing the ball to roll into the middle of the field with some variation. At the same time the scoring ball is removed from the field.

- **Challenge 3: The passing challenge.** Two robots, each restricted to one half of the field, must pass the ball back and forth. Each complete alternate pass is counted. An alternate pass is one where robot A passes to robot B and then robot B passes back to A on the opposite side of the circle from the original pass. As with challenge 2, the robots have 2 minutes to complete as many alternate passes as possible.

As expected, the first two challenges were easily completed by all teams while challenge three proved difficult for all but except Cornell Big Red (indeed most teams did not participate). RoboDragons (Aichi Prefectural University, Japan) in their first RoboCup competition were the surprise team by defeating defending champions LuckyStar (Ngee Ann Polytechnic, Singapore) in the goal scoring challenge. The final results for the top four placings were:

Rank	Challenge 1		Challenge 2		Challenge 3	
1	Luckystar	24.9	RoboDragons	23	Cornell	10
2	FUFighters	27.2	LuckyStar	22	Roobots	1
3	Cornell	28.8	Fufighters	19	CMDragons02	1/2
4	CMDragons02	28.7+1hit	Roobots	14		

2.2 Complete Full Game Autonomy

While our robot systems are autonomous, until this competition, all the referee commands were translated to the robot teams via human operators from each development team. Previously, robots were physically moved into game restart positions such as free kicks, penalties, and kick offs, and system autonomy was started and stopped via computer commands activated by a human operator from each team (ie. robots would be halted during game stoppages). Such a game structure often lead to boring sections where a human would take a significant amount of time to micro-position a robot to take a kick, often to no great effect. Secondly, teams could gain milliseconds of advantage by guessing their system latency to activate their system earlier than the referee's whistle thereby guaranteeing their robots would move first. Given the powerful kicking mechanisms that some robots possess, starting milliseconds ahead of the other team can make a substantial difference in the state of the game. Finally, RoboCup is aimed towards developing intelligent *autonomous* robots. Thus, having *completely autonomous* robots for the entire duration of each game is in-line with the goals of RoboCup..

To address these concerns, the organization committee for 2002 developed the Referee Box. In essence, the referee box translates the referee's directives into computer usable signals thereby removing the human operators from the loop. Although the current referee box implementation translates all the referee's commands, only start and stop commands were compulsory for 2002. Nearly all the teams were able to start and stop autonomously. Some teams, were able to operate completely autonomously for nearly the entire game (eg. CMDragons02 (Carnegie Mellon, USA)), which certainly made the robot handler's job easier! For teams that could not operate autonomously with the start and stop signals, a penalty was incurred. A neutral human operator was required to restart the penalized team at the referee's command thereby incurring significant restart latency. For RoboCup 2003, the small-size league will move to complete autonomy for the duration of the game. Thus, no human operator will be allowed to touch a robot or computer while the game is in progress except during time-outs and half-time breaks.

The current implementation of the referee box is a computer program with a Graphical User Interface (GUI) that runs on a laptop. The laptop is connected to each team computer via a spilt RS-232 serial cable running at 9600bps with no parity, 8 data bits, and 1 stop bit. The assistant referee, who previously had time-keeping duties, operates the referee box by clicking on the appropriate button in accordance with the referee's commands.

The full details of the 2002 referee box implementation are available online at *http://www.cs.cmu.edu/~brettb/robocup/referee.html*. The referee box is available for operation in both Microsoft Windows environments, and Linux environments. The source code is freely available in both cases. Each program maintains a running clock, the game score, the time-out clocks and available time-outs, and translates each referee command into a single ASCII character that is sent to each team via the serial cable. The protocol is simple to ensure that all teams are able to use it properly, although we expect to extend and modify the protocol when required. Currently, the referee box does not log any information, although we expect to include this operation in the next release.

On the whole, the referee box was a wonderful success. One cannot imagine how the final, where both teams were capable of very high accelerations, would have been manageable without its use. We hope that for RoboCup 2003, *no* team will require human intervention during the game.

3   Main Competition

The main competition demonstrated clear advancements in the level of technology. Clearly, the leading teams have progressed a long way. More interestingly, the main body of the competition has steadily improved as well. Most teams had working robots capable of playing a game of soccer that would be competitive at previous RoboCups. Indeed, the improvements within the league were evident early on during the qualification process.

Teams were required to submit their team description paper and video footage of their team playing soccer as part of the qualification process. The organization committee ranked the teams, based in part on the video footage and prior team performance, and selected the top 20 teams for the main competition. Due to the limitations on time and space, only 20 teams could be accommodated at RoboCup. Thus, from the 31 teams that submitted the qualification material, only 20 could participate. We hope that in the future regional competitions will take the place of the qualification process, and will also provide an avenue for RoboCup to grow beyond the finite limitations of the one event. As part of the qualification process, the top eight teams were given a ranking based on prior performance and allocated to one of the four groups. The remaining teams were allocated to groups randomly. Within each group, a round-robin tournament was held during the first three days of competition with the top two teams from each group entering the elimination rounds.

There were a number of surprises during the round-robin phase. The RoboDragons, a first-time RoboCup team, followed up on their challenge winning performance by reaching the quarter finals. Along the way they defeated the RoboRoos (University of Queensland, Australia) in a very close game. They met their match in the quarter final, however, in the form of the FU-Fighters. The FU-Fighters introduced specially designed omnidirectional wheels that enabled their robots to accelerate at incredible speeds. Exact figures were not available, but accelerations figures of close to $5m.s^{-1}$ would not be surprising. Big Red, demonstrated a similar high-speed approach where four wheels were the key to acceleration rather than special wheels. Big Red also unveiled another innovation: a super high-speed dribbler. With their new dribbler, the Big Red robots were able to drag the ball around the field at will. This tactic, a turnaround from their passing approach in 2001, formed a significant part of their game strategy that produced results. CMDragons02, another quarter final team, demonstrated a unique software innovation: an autonomous play-based strategy engine that adapted on-line to the weaknesses of the opponent. Although Carnegie Mellon has previously demonstrated adaptive role-switching and on-line planning [1], to the author's knowledge this is the first use of adaptive strategy in any of the real-robot leagues.

The full list of quarter finalists includes LuckyStar, Field Rangers (Singapore Polytechnic, Singapore), FU-Fighters, RoboDragons, Roobots (University of Melbourne, Australia), CMDragons'02 (Carnegie Mellon, USA), Big Red, and newcomers IUT Flash (Isfahan University of Technology, Iran). Of these teams, Big Red, FU-Fighters, LuckyStar, and Roobots, went on to the semi-finals. Here, defending champions LuckyStar came up short in the game of speed against FU-Fighters. It now seems that the FU-Fighters have become the informal speed-kings of RoboCup and heir apparent to LuckStar. LuckyStar went on to beat Roobots, who lost to BigRed in the other semi-final, for third.

The grand-final between FU-Fighters and eventual champions Big Red, proved to be the climactic event of the competition. These two teams have played on numerous occasions in previous competitions dating back to RoboCup'99. Both teams have very aggressive strategies. The resulting game was a spectators delight. Big Red used their fast acceleration and powerful dribbler to move the ball around the field. Meanwhile FU-Fighters used their incredible speed and chip-kicker to attack, attack, attack. In two 10 minute halves no less than 10 goals were scored. Indeed, the first two goals (the first to Big Red, the second to FU-Fighters) came within the first minute of the game, which is certainly a small-size grand-final record. Once the dust had settled, Big Red had reasserted their dominance in the small-size league winning for the third time and it was once again the end of another exciting RoboCup competition.One wonders what new wonders will be in store for RoboCup 2003.

For interested readers, the following web-links are relevant:

- RoboCup 2002 scores: *http://www.robocup2002.org*.
- Small-size 2002 web-site: *http://www.cs.cmu.edu/~brettb/robocup*.
- RoboCup main web-site: *http://www.robocup.org/*.

4   Summary of 2002, the Future and Results

In these few pages, we have tried to highlight many of the competition changes, and technological innovations that made RoboCup 2002 small-size such a wonderful competition. This is an ever-evolving competition where cutting edge research is being performed and that research is evaluated in the hardest possible way. The most notable achievements, research-wise, are the movements to full autonomy and the advances in high-speed control and adaptable strategy.

The stage is now set for RoboCup 2003 to be a very exciting year. The changes that have been wrought in the competition will continue to evolve. In particular, RoboCup 2003 will present the first robot league with autonomy for the entire game. Additionally, much work is in progress to broaden the research impact of the league. Collaborative efforts between teams are currently underway to develop and release an open source simulator, and an open source vision system. Likewise, efforts are currently underway in some camps to completely release RoboCup 2002 source code. Such open source approaches will further improve the research impact of our competition and help reduce the start up work required by new teams. The future for small-size is bright indeed.

References

1. Veloso, M., Bowling, M., Achim, S., Han, K., and Stone, P., "The CMUnited-98 champion small robot team", In Asada, M., and Kitano, H., (eds), RoboCup-98: Robot Soccer World Cup II, pages 77-92. Springer Verlag, Berlin, 1999.

Appendix: Results

Table 1. Qualified f-180 Small Size Teams

Lucky Star	Ngee Ann Polytechnic	Singapore
5DPO	Universidade do Porto	Portugal
All Botz	University of Auckland	New Zealand
CM Dragons 02	Carnegie Mellon University	USA
Team Canuck	University of Alberta	Canada
Cornell Big Red	Cornell University	USA
FU-Fighters	Freie Universität Berlin	Germany
Field Rangers	Singapore Polytechnic	Singapore
IUB Team 2002	International University Bremen	Germany
IUT Flash	Isfahan University of Technology	Iran
KU-Boxes 2002	Kinki University	Japan
OMNI	Osaka University	Japan
Owaribito-CU	Chubu University	Japan
RobBobcats	Ohio University	USA
RoboDragon	Aichi Prefectural University	Japan
RoboRoos	University of Queensland	Australia
ROGI Team	Universidad de Girona	Spain
Roobots	University of Melbourne	Australia
Sharif CESR	Sharif University of Technology	Iran
RoboSix Team	University Pierre and Marie Curie	France

Table 2. Results: f-180 Small Size League

1	Big Red	Cornell University	USA
2	FU-Fighters	Free University of Berlin	Germany
3	Lucky Star	Ngee Ann Polytechnic	Singapore

Medium Size League:
2002 Assessment and Achievements

Andrea Bonarini

Department of Electronics and Information
Politecnico di Milano
Milan, Italy
bonarini@elet.polimi.it

Abstract. Robots in the Robocup Middle Size League (MSL) have dimensions comparable with robots that could be used in other real world applications. MSL provides a framework to test these robots in a challenging environment where actions should be decided in real-time. In many cases, the achievements shown in this competition are important also for real world applications, and have been exported there. Some other results put in evidence what can be done by focusing on specific issues with the aim of producing more interesting and effective entertainment by autonomous robots.

1 Introduction

Most of the present Medium Size League (MSL) robots are fully autonomous: they can take decisions by the on-board computational capabilities, using data that come from on-board sensors and radio communication devices linking the robots of a team. These achievements involve research and technology issues in fields ranging from mechanics to electronics, from sensors to actuators, from low-level control to team strategy and learning. We first discuss the main achievements in each area, then we summarize the most relevant aspects emerged during the 2002 competition. Finally, we present the future directions for the league.

2 Where Are We Now in MSL?

In this section, we discuss the main achievements for each technological area involved in the development of MSL robots, and we put in evidence the driving forces that lead us to this point.

2.1 Mechanics

he majority of MSL robots is based on the common kinematics consisting of two independent traction wheels, but an increasing number of teams have developed either omnidirectional robots, or robots with steerable wheels. In general, it has been noticed that these robots are more agile, and can produce a more

G.A. Kaminka, P.U. Lima, and R. Rojas (Eds.): RoboCup 2002, LNAI 2752, pp. 460–468, 2003.
© Springer-Verlag Berlin Heidelberg 2003

interesting game, but also that this is not enough to be successful. At present, no omnidirectional base is commercially available for MSL, so all omnidirectional robots should be developed from scratch. Some teams use commercial bases having the more common kinematics, thus saving at least some of the efforts required to build mechanical stuff. MSL robots may change their configuration to kick or try to get the ball. According to the rules, they should occupy at most a square 50 cm by 50 cm, for the majority of time; for short periods they may extend up to 60 cm by 60 cm. These dimension boundaries have been selected to have a significant portion of the field free from robot bodies, and, at the same time, allow robots to bring on board the needed computational power, usually a full size PC board, or a portable computer, or a PC104 board. Almost all MSL robots have some kicking device, able to kick the ball up to 5-6 meters per second. Kicking devices are implemented by all sort of mechanical arrangements, from charged springs, to compressed air pistons. A couple of teams have also implemented devices that, while leaving the ball rolling as stated by the rules, can maintain the ball in contact with the robot body even when this is turning (Philips team) or it is going back (Muratec FC team). The last version of the rules allow robots moving back with the ball for at most 50 centimeters, so to avoid undesired situations that may make the game less interesting.

2.2   Electronics, Communication and On-board Computing

As mentioned above, almost all the teams perform on-board the computation needed to play. Some teams still send images to an off-line station that elaborates them and send back information to control the robots. Some other teams use external computational power to fuse the sensor information coming from the teammates and build a team plan. Electronics on board include power control for engines and kickers. In some cases it is implemented by the teams, otherwise it is taken from the market. This is one of the main sources for malfunctioning, and it is critical for the reliability of robots. Up to now, the most successful teams have also been those able to bring the majority of their robots through the whole set of matches up to the finals. Even brilliant teams have lost finals or semi-finals also due to HW problems with their robots. This issue is also relevant from a general application point of view: reliability is needed to go to the market. On the other side, presently available commercial robots usually do not run in the extreme conditions where MSL robots should operate, including sudden acceleration changes, fast speed, collisions with other robots or field elements. Communication in MSL is mainly concerned with wireless LAN: the rules explicitly state that robots can communicate only using the 2.4 GHz band, pos- sibly using the IEEE 802.11b standard. All the communication devices used in MSL are commercially available, and many teams had problems during games, only in part reduced by the introduction of access points on the fields; these are devices aimed at partitioning the wireless LAN and providing good coverage in limited environments. Also the communication issue has relevance for real-world applications, but no research is done in this area within MSL. In some cases the problem is in part reduced by adopting emerging behaviors that do not need communication (e.g., [6], or coordination architectures robust with respect to communication degradation (e.g., [3]).

2.3 Sensors and Vision

Sensor and vision systems are used both for (self-)localization, and to detect elements of the environment to interact with.

Vision is implemented either by single front cameras, single mobile cam- eras (e.g., Osaka Trackies), multiple cameras (e.g., Philips), or panoramic sensors (e.g., [5], Artisti Veneti, and Osaka Trackies). External cameras are not allowed. Panoramic sensors have been adopted by many teams, since in the time needed to elaborate a frame image it is possible to collect information all around the robot. Some teams (e.g., Osaka Trackies) use commercial sensors, while others have developed special purpose sensors, including multi-part mirrors and isometric mirrors [5] that do not introduce deformation at the ground level; these teams have developed mirror design algorithms, calibration methods, and interpretation algorithms ad hoc, contributing to the scientific progress in the area.

The main vision activities concern recognizing objects in the field, and localizing them. Object recognition is mainly done by color analysis, since the MSL rules associate different colors to the different elements in the environment: the ball is red, the field green, the goals respectively blue and yellow, robots and peo- ple in the field black, markers on robots cyan and magenta for the two teams. One of the main issues each team has to face is color calibration, which also depends on light intensity. The present rules limit the acceptable range of light intensity in each part of the field (shadows included), but most of the teams have been able to cope with variations due to settings that couldn't be modified. Color calibration is done either manually, or by all sort of algorithms, including neural networks. Color interpretation models go from the simpler "sliced pizza", to irregular patchwork, to neural networks. Robustness with respect to light variation is still seen as an important challenge to be faced. Once the elements of the environment have been recognized and localized, they may be used for self localization. This is not a trivial task, due to the MSL setting. All the fixed elements of the field can be (partially) covered at each time by other robots; moreover, some positions on the field with respect to landmarks do not satisfy the applicability conditions for standard localization algorithms. Some teams have developed innovative self-localization algorithms (e.g., [8]).

The only other significant sensors used in MSL are laser range finders (LRF), which have been one of the keys of success for some teams in the past [8]. In 2002, the wall on the field borders has been removed, thus making the LRF task more difficult, and the research in this area even more challenging.

2.4 Control

Control issues in MSL concern different aspects, from motor control to behaviors. The typical control architecture for a MSL robot includes low level controllers able to reach and eventually maintain set points for the engines. In most cases these controllers are commercial or standard ones. Someone has implemented fuzzy controllers to face this task [2]. Set points to motors are provided by higher level controllers either implemented as behaviors (in some cases fuzzy behaviors [2]), or as standard programs (such as planners, e.g., [8]) or even as interacting dynamical systems [4]. Behaviors are usually considered as control models triggered by some conditions, and issuing some action to the lower level controllers. The relationship with the original behaviors and the subsumption architecture proposed by Rodney Brooks in the eighties is usually weak. The input to higher level controllers is given by sensors, eventually filtered by a world modeler that can fuse data coming from different sensors and from other teammates in a reliable situation description (e.g., [8] [7]). The world modelling activity is done by most teams on each robot, while others adopt a centralized world modeler integrating information from all the robots once for all.

2.5   Multi-robot Cooperation

Multi-robot cooperation is an important issue not fully exploited, yet, mainly due to the physical limitations of the robots. Up to now, robots are able to share their knowledge and to cooperate to select the best action (for instance to decide which one has to go to the ball). There have been also some demonstrations about the possibility to substitute a robot no longer able to perform its task or drive a robot no longer able to perceive directly the environment due to sensor malfunctioning. Some interesting collaboration forms may emerge from interaction without communication as seen, among the others, in games where Freiburg CS and the Artisti Veneti teams played, still in 2001. More complex collaboration has not been fully developed, yet. One of the current challenges is ball passing, up to now successfully seen in an official game only once, giving the impression that it was not so effective. The problems seem to concern the reliability and effectiveness of this kind of concerted actions, more than the difficulty in coordination. More complex forms of cooperation have been announced (e.g., [3]) but not yet seen in official matches.

2.6   Learning

Learning in MSL have to face the problem of scarce information flow. Usually, in a game, a robot is involved in a small number of actions, compared with the quantity needed by most of the present learning algorithms. At least one team is using reinforcement learning to develop off-line both single behaviors, and cooperating behaviors [9]. Another team claim to be able to adapt on-line the behavior of the team to that of the opponents [1], but it has not been demonstrated in an official match, yet.

3   The 2002 Games

The Robocup 2002 games have been held in the Fukuoka Dome, a baseball stadium. The location had some potential problems, successfully faced by most of the teams.

There was a strong illumination source external to the fields (the one used for baseball matches in the Dome), producing undesired shadows, and biasing the light color temperature. Illumination conditions were different among the different fields, but most teams were able to play after a relatively short calibration activity. Nobody seemed to have on-line calibration, but this also seemed to be unnecessary.

Fields were closed by black and white pole ranges, one every 40 centimeters, 1 meter away from the border lines. On the sides behind the poles, there were advertisement panels, about 120 cm long and 50 cm high, placed in a way similar to those on real soccer field. One advertisement range was also put at the last moment on 40 cm boxes to make them visible from the camera positioned on the opposite side. Public could go all around the field. This arrangement was compatible with the rules designed to have some security border around the field, but at the same time to allow unexpected situations outside the field that may cause problems to standard vision systems. Some teams asked to people wearing blue shirts or orange caps to move away from the field, but most teams had no particular problems. Such kind of requests will be strongly discouraged from the next tournament.

The ball provided by the organization was different from that of the previous year, more yellowish, and much more bright. Many teams complained not to be able to distinguish it either from the yellow goal (which was reddish) or from white lines, but this did not seem to be a big problem during matches. The field was 2 meters shorter than expected (8 meters instead of 10), and seemed a little bit too crowded.

Despite these potential problems, most teams were able to play interesting matches, after a couple of days of set up, dedicated, as usual, to recover HW problems and to tune SW. Most teams had some HW problems in many matches, thus bringing in evidence once more that the reliability of our machines is not yet high enough for the market or a live TV show.

The fields were equipped by access points having directional antennas to improve communication reliability. Only three channels were assigned to the league, two for playing and 1 for practicing. Many teams had problems to use the access points, so the matches were played both by teams using the access points provided by the organization, and teams using their own access point or directly broadcasting on wireless LANs. This also put in evidence one of the major problems of the league, not faced by any research effort: the reliability of communication devices in the Robocup environment, where wireless LANs should support intensive band occupation.

At the game start, according to the rules, only teams whose robots were able to reach autonomously their initial position could take a preferred position in the field, the others had to place their robots on fixed points. Almost no teams were able to leave robots to reach reliably their starting positions. Precise self-localization and self-positioning are still problems to be solved.

The absence of walls on the borders of the field, introduced this year for the first time, came up to be quite easy to manage, also because rules did not include any sanction against teams kicking the ball off the field. Most of the teams did not care to keep the ball in, but referees were always ready to put the ball in again, at their own risk. Some referees have been injured by robots and this opened a discussion about the inclusion of at least the first Asimov's robotic law[1] in our robot control programs. MSL robots can be dangerous if badly programmed, and this should be taken into account on the way to the match with human players in 2050 (the long-term Robocup goal). Notice also that this law is not included in any commercial or industrial robot, yet.

Some teams were able at least to show the intention to keep the ball inside the field. This is a challenging control problem, if you consider also that manoeuvering space is small in a MSL field, and that robots can move faster than 1 meter per second. There have been many situations where robots continuously kicked off the ball, when operating in 1 meter from the corner pole. This was one of the undesired game slow down. Another one was due to the strategy of some teams to place more than one robot on the ball, thus creating a corner, or a sort of wall, hard to be passed.

Most of the teams shown a good obstacle avoidance behavior, and charging, which was quite strictly sanctioned according to the rules, was common only in the first games.

The game has not improved a lot with respect to the previous year. Some teams were able to plan a trajectory to (try to) keep the ball inside the field. Some teams had strategies to have robot cooperating in managing difficult situations; we have seen a robot leaving the possible trajectory of a teammate that was bearing the ball, another robot helped by a teammate (or substituted by it) when the ball was stuck.

3.1   Challenges

A MSL competition parallel to soccer matches concerned scientific challenges.

The first one consisted of dribbling the ball between a couple of black poles from the home area to the opposite goal. The aim was to push teams to face ball control problems. Very few teams have been able to show interesting behaviors and a lot of work should still be done. The winner was GMD-Musashi whose robot matched a pole by few millimeters, and scored the goal in about 10 seconds. The suspicion among spectators was that the whole task had been performed in open-loop, without any feedback from sensors. Probably, next challenges will have obstacles in positions a priori unknown.

The second challenge consisted of a free demonstration of collaboration among robots. This gave also an idea of what the teams thought was possible to show in this area. Four teams tried to pass the ball (only one succeeded, but with a quite frontal dash). The robot of another team provided to a blind teammate the position of the ball and the blind one was able to reach it. The

---

[1] A robot may not injure a human being, or, through inaction, allow a human being to come to harm, unless this would violate a higher order law". This law, first appeared in the short story "Runaround" published by Isaac Asimov in 1942.

robot of the Artisti Veneti team was able to take autonomously the role of the goal keeper when this was turned off, so dynamically changing its role. This last had the highest score from the jury composed by team leaders of all the other teams and technical committee members.

3.2   Mixed Teams Match

The third MSL event was the match done by two teams made up with robots belonging to different teams, excluded from the tournament after round robin. The participants had only few hours to set up the teams. It turned out that robots were not able to communicate with each other, due to the different communication modes and types of messages; anyway, both teams could perform a quite exciting game ended 3-2, including a goal scored in the home goal by a strong kick bounced on a well-positioned opponent goal keeper.

This experience put in evidence some interesting questions. Communication is not needed to have an amusing game, since robots can be arranged to play reasonably also without exchanging information. It would be interesting to compare the performance of teams adopting communication to coordinate the robots, and teams adopting emergent behaviors. To exploit communication, a common background is needed: this question has not been faced in this league, yet. It has been decided to set up a research effort to define a common language to exchange information, studying what it is actually needed to exchange.

Finally, this experience demonstrated that a team can be set up in few hours, starting from running robots, and this is an encouraging result.

4   Conclusion and Future Directions

In conclusion, we are far away from the long term goal of playing against human players, but we are on the way. Our robots can show complex behaviors, interesting enough to keep excited spectators around the field for the whole match.

Many teams have applied their scientific results outside Robocup, by using their localization algorithms, their world modelers, or their sensors in service robotics, and even space robotics. Robocup seems to play the role of catalyst for research efforts that have a recognized importance for the society and the scientific community in the large, as shown by the large number of Robocup-related papers published in international conferences and journals.

The next steps MSL will take are in large part directed towards the destructuration of the playing environment. In the next years we aim to be able to play with natural light, possibly changing during the day, with a regular FIFA ball (no longer red, but multi-colored), with nets in the the goals instead of colored panels. The size of the field will also be enlarged, to make it possible more interesting actions, possibly coordinated. More ball control will be achieved to have robots able to really dribble the opponents, and to keep the ball inside the field. The teams will also be more coordinated, with robots able to understand the situation and possibly to decide what to do without any explicit exchange of information. In the short term also a "referee box" sending to the robots the decisions of the referee will be implemented, so making the robots aware of the referee decisions and enabling them to behave accordingly. This is on the way of having robots able to understand the FIFA referee signals, as needed to play against human champions.

The qualified teams and the results aregiven in the following tables:

Table 1. Qualified f-2000 Middle Size Teams

Agilo RoboCuppers	Munich University of Technology	Germany
Artisti Veneti	University of Padua	Italy
Eigen	Keio University	Japan
FU-Fighters 2002	Freie Universität Berlin	Germany
Fusion	Kyushu University, Hitachi Information and Control Systems, Fukuoka University	Japan
KIRC	Kyushu Institute of Technology	Japan
MINE	Mie University	Japan
Muratec FC	Murata Machinery LTD	Japan
Osaka University Trackies 2002	Osaka University	Japan
Philips Cyber Football Team	Philips Centre for Industrial Technology	The Netherlands
RFC Uppsala	Uppsala University	Sweden
Sharif CE	Sharif University of Technology	Iran
UTTORI United	Utsunomiya University	Japan
WinKIT	Kanazawa Institute of Technology, Yumekobo	Japan
GMD-Musashi	Fraunhofer Institute AIS, GMD-JRL, Kyushu Institute of Technology, University of Kytakyushu, University of Lecce	Germany, Japan

Table 2. Results: f-2000 Middle Size Robot League

1	EIGEN	Keio University	Japan
2	WinKIT	Kanazawa Institute of Technology	Japan
3	Trackies 2002	Osaka University	Japan

References

1. A. Bonarini. Evolutionary learning, reinforcement learning, and fuzzy rules for knowledge acquisition in agent-based systems. *Proceedings of the IEEE*, 89(9):1334-1346, 2001.
2. A. Bonarini, G. Invernizzi, F. Marchese, M. Matteucci, M. Restelli, and D. Sorrenti. Fun2mas: the milan robocup team. In S. Takodoro A. Birk, S. Coradeschi, editor, *RoboCup 2001-Robot Soccer World Cup V*, volume 2377, pages 639-642, Berlin, D, 2002. Springer Verlag.

3. A. Bonarini and M. Restelli. An architecture to implement agents co-operating in dynamic environments. In *Proceedings of AAMAS 2002 - Autonomous Agents and Multi-Agent Systems*, pages 1143-1144, New York, NY, 2002. ACM Press.
4. A. Bredenfeld, V. Becanovic, T. Christaller, H. Günter, G. Indiveri, H-U. Kobialka, P-G. Plöger, and P. Schöll. Gmd-robots. In *RoboCup 2001-Robot Soccer World Cup V (Cit.)*, pages 648-652.
5. P. Lima, A. Bonarini, C. Machado, F.M. Marchese, C. Marques, F. Ribeiro, and D.G. Sorrenti. Omni-directional catadioptric vision for soccer robots. *International Journal of Robotics and Autonomous Systems*, 36(2-3):87-102, 2001.
6. E. Pagello, A. D'angelo, and E. Menegatti. Artisti veneti 2002, evolving an heterogeneous robot team for the middle-size league. In *this volume*, 2003.
7. D. G. Sorrenti, M. Restelli, and F. M. Marchese. A robot localization method based on evidence accumulation and multi-resolution. In *Proceedings of the IEEE/RSJ International Conference on Intelligent Robots and Systems (IROS'02)*, pages 415-420, Piscataway, NJ, 2002. IEEE Press.
8. T. Weigel, A. Kleiner, F. Diesch, M. Dietl, J-S. Gutmann, B. Nebel, P. Stiegeler, and B. Szerbakowski. Cs freiburg 2001. In *RoboCup 2001-Robot Soccer World Cup V (Cit.)*, pages 26-38.
9. E. Uchibeand M. Yanase and M. Asada. Evolutionary behavior selection with activation/termination constraints. In *RoboCup 2001-Robot Soccer World Cup V (Cit.)*, pages 234-243.

Sony Four Legged Robot League
at RoboCup 2002

Masahiro Fujita

Sony Corporation
6-7-35 Kitashinagawa
Shinagawa-ku, Tokyo 141-0001, Japan

Abstract. We report research activities in the Sony Four Legged Robot League at RoboCup 2002. 19 teams including 3 new teams participated in the league. We revised some rules and setup specifications such as a larger field and 4 robots for each team. In addition wireless LAN system were employed for inter-robot communication. These revisions encouraged the participants to develop team play behaviors.

1 Introduction

We started the Sony Four Legged Robot League at RoboCup-98 in Paris [Fujita00] as an exhibition match with three teams, which were from Carnegie Mellon University (USA), Laboratory of Robotics of Paris (France), and Osaka University (Japan). Since then, we have been increasing the number of teams, and in 2002 we have the Four Legged Robot league by 19 teams from 18 countries.

The significant features of this league are:

- All teams must use the same robot platform (Figure 1) without any modification. This means that it is a software competition but participants have to use physical robots, unlike Simulation League.
- The robot platform is a legged robot, which needs to walk. The robot sometimes falls down accidentally, and need to recover. This feature is unique to the Four Legged Robot League expect for the Humanoid League, which started at RoboCup-02 as an exhibition match.
- There is no global vision sensor. This is the same situation as in the Middle Size Robot League.

Especially, the same robot platform allows to reuse software among participants. Therefore, accumulation of technologies has been done in this league, and the technology level has become rapidly very high In this article, we focus on the description of research activities in the Four Legged Robot League at RoboCup-02.

2 Revised Rule and Field

From 1998 to 2001, the field size was about 2 by 3 meters and the number of players of each team was 3 including a goalie. This size and the number of players

G.A. Kaminka, P.U. Lima, and R. Rojas (Eds.): RoboCup 2002, LNAI 2752, pp. 469–476, 2003.

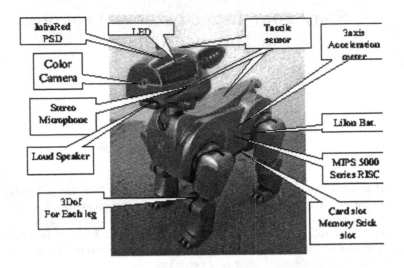

Fig. 1. The robot platform used in RoboCup-02 (ERS-210)

were a good balance for the robot platform and the average level of technologies of the participants. However, we felt, the field was so small that many robots gathered around the ball, which caused a game to become stack quite often. In addition, we felt that the number of players, 3, was also so small such that it is difficult to develop team play with two robots excluding the goalie. Therefore, we decided to enlarge the size of the field and the number of robots for RoboCup-02. The size of the field is now about 3 by 4 meters, and the number of robots is 4 for each team including the goalie. The color specification of the field is the same as before. Figure2 shows the field used in RoboCup-02.

In order to encourage teams to develop team play, we introduced a wireless LAN system (IEEE 812.11b), which allows robots to communicate between each other. The robot can send its position and its perception results such as a position of the ball and goals. This cooperative perception capability is very important because the resolution of the on-board vision system of robot does not allow to recognize the ball from a far distance. In addition, in order to pass the ball to other robots, the position information of the players are crucial. Color stickers are attached to the body of the robots, which allow to estimate the position of an other robot, however, it is difficult to detect the team and opponent team robots by the color detector. Furthermore, it is difficult to estimate the position of the other robots. Thus, the wireless LAN system helps sharing the self localization results among the team robots.

Communication is achieved through a host PC. Namely we assign an IP address to each robot, and each robot send the information to the host PC, which then forward the information to the other robots. We decided that the PC should not be used for remote computation but only for the purpose of communication.

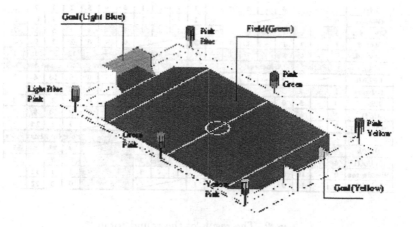

Fig. 2. The field used in RoboCup-02

In addition to the communication purpose among the robots, the wireless LAN system is used to control the game by the referee. A game controller software running on the host PC sends some pre-defined commands at proper timings by the referee. For example, a game start signal is sent to all robots such that the robots can start the game without human intereference. When a goal is scored, a message can be sent to all robots such that the scoring team can display some happy behaviors.

Regarding the details of the rule and the setup, please refer to [Rules].

3   Result of Championship Tournament

We divided the all teams into 4 groups (A,B,C,D group), each of which is formed by 5 teams except for the D group. The semifinalists of RoboCup-01 are allocated in different groups, and new participants, which were Georgia Institute of Technology (USA), University of Newcastle (Australia), and Tecnologico de Monterrey (Mexico), were allocated in different groups. The result of the round robin is shown in Figure 3.

The top two teams from each group can participate in a championship tournament. The result of the tournament is shown in Figure 4. The champion of RoboCup-02 is Carnegie Mellon University (CMU, USA), the second place is University of New South Wales (UNSW, Australia), and the third place is University of Newcastle (UNC, Australia). The final game was a very exciting one. First, CMU scored 2 goals, and then UNSW made 2 goals to be the even score. Then, UNSW made a goal to lead 3 by 2, but CMU finally made a goal to be even. Finally, a penalty kick (PK) match was carried out, and CMU won and became the champion. The semifinal also ended in a draw and a PK was carried out, which UNC won for recording the third prize. It should be noted here that 3

	LRV	OSAKA	SWEDEN	McGill	Newcastle	Point	Goal	Lost	Place
LRV		0 - 0	0 - 1	1 - 1	0 - 5	2	1	7	3
OSAKA	0 - 0		0 - 2	1 - 1	1 - 8	2	2	11	5
SWEDEN	1 - 0	2 - 0		3 - 0	0 - 3	9	6	3	2
McGill	1 - 1	1 - 1	0 - 3		0 - 4	2	2	9	4
Newcastle	5 - 0	8 - 1	3 - 0	4 - 0		12	20	1	1

C	UPENN	Melbourne	ESSEX	USTC	Monterrey	Point	Goal	Lost	Place
UPENN		0 - 1	5 - 0	1 - 3	8 - 0	6	14	4	3
Melbourne	1 - 0		6 - 0	4 - 1	11 - 1	12	22	2	1
ESSEX	0 - 5	0 - 6		1 - 2	1 - 0	3	2	13	4
USTC	3 - 1	1 - 4	2 - 1		4 - 0	9	10	6	2
Monterrey	0 - 8	1 - 11	0 - 1	0 - 4		0	1	24	5

D	UNSW	KYUSHU	Washington	BALKAN	Point	Goal	Lost	Place
UNSW		7 - 0	10 - 0	16 - 0	9	33	0	1
KYUSHU	0 - 7		2 - 0	5 - 0	6	7	7	2
Washington	0 - 10	0 - 2		1 - 0	3	1	12	3
BALKAN	0 - 16	0 - 5	0 - 1		0	0	22	4

Fig. 3. The result of the round robin

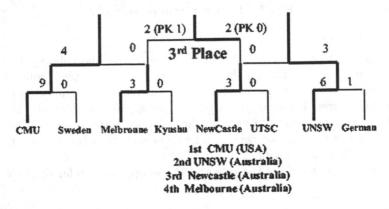

1st CMU (USA)
2nd UNSW (Australia)
3rd Newcastle (Australia)
4th Melbourne (Australia)

Fig. 4. The result of the championship tournament

of the top 4 teams are from Australia, including the new participant, University of Newcastle. The photos of a game in this league is shownin Figure 5.

4 Summary of Advanced Technologies

As we described in the previous section, some teams utilize a strategy of assigning robots to regional positions, such as a left winger, a right winger, a sweeper, and a goalie. Each robot computes its position by a localization algorithm employing for example a probabilistic approach (Monte-Carlo localization or Grid-based Markov localization), and tries to act in the pre-assigned area during a game. In addition, the robots share their position information using the wireless LAN system, and avoid the situation of no robot going to the ball. There are two ways for roll assignment, a static roll assignment and a dynamic roll assignment. CMU, the champion team of RoboCup-02, utilizes a dynamic roll assignment, by which efficient team formation is achieved depending on the current situations.

Fig. 5. Exciting Game in ihe Four Legged Robot League

Cooperative perception is achieved in the team formation strategy. Namely, the ball position and the robots' position are shared among the robots, therefore even if the ball is too far from some robots to perceive, if one robot perceives the ball position with its vision system, the position information is shared among all teammates.

In order to achieve a cooperative play as described above, many basic skills for each robot have to be implemented. Vision, walking, and ball manipulation system are examples. World modeling and behavior selection are also necessary. These basic skills have been developed in the Four Legged Robot League since 1998. The technology accumulation and sharing have been efficiently done in this league, such that many teams could benefit from the results of other teams in the previous years and performed very well at RoboCup-02.

5 RoboCup Challenges

The aim of RoboCup is not just to win a game. The scientific approaches are encouraged in order to develop an autonomous robot functioning in the realworld and in realtime. Therefore, we have been defining some technical routines, named RoboCup Challenges, every year. In RoboCup-02 we defined three RoboCup challenges, which were a Pattern Analysis Challenge, a Collaboration Challenge (version 2002), and a Ball Collection Challenge.

5.1 Pattern Analysis Challenge

One of the important challenges in RoboCup is not to use color information. Since 1998 we have been using color information to identify important items in the soccer domain such as the ball and the goals. However, we need to spend a lot of time to tune color parameters for the identification, and need to keep constant lighting conditions around field during the whole event as much as possible. An aim of the Pattern Analysis Challenge is to replace color painted items by black-and-white pattern items, so that we can carry out RoboCup in a more natural environment.

We selected 5 different shapes with black-and-white cross stripes. Two examples are shown in Figure 6. There are different sizes for each pattern. We selected 3 patterns among them and put them in random rotation at three positions; two corners of the field and the top of the goal. The participants had not known the selected patterns, the sizes, and the rotation angles before the challenge started. After submitting their programs with memory media (Memory Stick), we announced the selected patterns and the sizes and the rotation angles. Then, within 3 minutes, a robot had to visit the positions and generates sounds corresponding to the patterns.

Any teams could not identify all three patterns within 3 minutes at RoboCup 2002. However, three teams, CMU, UNSW, and University of Washington, could identify two of the three patterns.

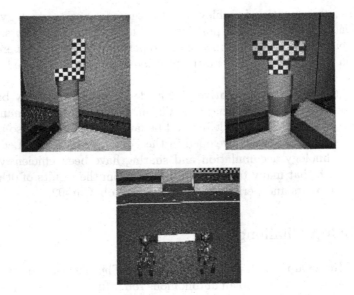

Fig. 6. Top two: Patterns used in Pattern Analysis Challenge. Bottom: Collaboration Challenge 2002

5.2   Collaboration Challenge 2002

The second challenge is to move a bar by two robots in a collaborative way. First, the two robots have to rotate the bar, and second, they have to push the bar in the same direction, for placing it into the penalty area. Thus, two robots have to share information about timing; when to rotate and when to push. Figure.6 shows the bar used in this challenge.

Three teams, UNSW, CMU, and UTSC, were able to complete the collaboration task within 3 minutes.

5.3 Ball Collection Challenge

The third challenge is to confirm basic skills, to search for a ball, to go close to it, and push it into one of the goals. However, in this challenge, 10 balls and two robots are in the field. Therefore, it is better to handle different balls by each robot. Only one team, UNSW, was able to score all 10 goals in this challenge. It should be noted here that the top 4 teams, UNSW, CMU, University of New castle, and University of Melbourne, are also the top 4 teams in this challenge.

6 Future of the Four Legged Robot League

There will be significant changes in the Four Legged Robot League in RoboCup-03. First, Sony released the OPEN-R SDK [OPEN-R SDK], by which any user can program the AIBO ERS-210(A). This means that in RoboCup-03, this league will become open entry league. Then, we hope that many new teams will join the league to accelerate the activity of the accumulation of technologies. Second, the Four Legged Robot League is going to be operated by selected committees from the universities. Until RoboCup-02, the operation was done by members of Sony Digital Creatures Laboratory, however, we have already selected technical committees and organizing committees, defining the rules and challenges for RoboCup-03 as of writing this article.

Technically, our targets is to remove well defined environment conditions, such as a uniform and consistent lighting conditions, and the existence of field walls surrounding the field. We define proper challenges so that we can perform feasibility studies to achieve our technical target. We hope that within 5 years, we will be able to enjoy watching RoboCup Four Legged Robot League in every country without any need of special setups.

7 Summary

In this article, we reported technical aspects of the RoboCup Four Legged Robot League in 2002. The wider field and the increase of the number of robots resulted in the development of team play behaviors. The wireless LAN system plays an important role to achieve good team behaviors. Now, the technology levels of the participants go up, and we can enjoy watching exciting soccer games. The next target is to have local competitions in the world, and to increase the sharing information in order to accumulate the developed technologies.

The following tables conveniently summarize the various teams and the outcome of the competition:

Table 1. Qualified Four-Legged Teams

rUNSWift	University of New South Wales	Australia
CM-Pack'02	Carnegie Mellon University	USA
UPennalizers	University of Pennsylvania	USA
Les 3 Mousquetaires	Laboratoire de Robotique de Versailles	France
Baby Tigers	Osaka University	Japan
SPQR	University of Rome	Italy
ASURA	Kyushu Institute of Technology, Fukuoka Institute of Technology	Japan
Wright Eagle 2002	University of Science and Technology of China	China
German Team	HU Berlin, University of Bremen, TU Darmstadt, University of Dortmund	Germany
ARAIBO	University of Tokyo	Japan
McGill Red Dogs	McGill University	Canada
Essex Rovers	University of Eseex	UK
UW Huskies	University of Washington	USA
Team Sweden	Orebro University	Sweden
Cerberus	Bogazici University, Technical University of Sofia	Bulgaria
RoboMutts++	University of Melbourne	Australia
NUBots	University of Newcastle	UK
Borregos Salvajes	TEC de Monterrey	Mexico
Yellow Jackets	Georgia Tech	USA

Table 2. Results: Four-Legged Robot League

1	CM Pack'02	Carnegie Mellon University	USA
2	rUNSWift	University of New South Wales	Australia
3	NUbot	The University of Newcastle	Australia

Acknowledgement

We thank all participants of the Four Legged Robot League in RoboCup-02. In addition, we also thank Sony ERC for their sponsoring our league, and members of Sony Digital Creatures Laboratory for their technical and operational support.

References

[Fujita00] Fujita M., et. al. : Vision, Strategy, and Localization Using the Sony Legged Robots at RoboCup-98. AI Magazine, Vol.21, No.1, pp.45–56
[Rules] https://www.openr.org/page1_2003/index.html
[OPEN-R SDK] http://www.aibo.com/openr

RoboCupRescue Simulation League

Tomoichi Takahashi

Meijo University, Department of Information Sciences
1-501 Shiogamaguchi , Tenpaku-ku, Nagoya, 468-8502 Japan
ttaka@ccmfs.meijo-u.ac.jp

1 Introduction

This paper overviews all results of RoboCupRescue simulation league at 2002.

RoboCupRescue simulation has a lot in common with RoboCupSoccer simulation. It handles distributed, multiagent domains and agents do their tasks with limited communication and sensing abilities. The distinctions between rescue and soccer are scales of domain, multiple hierarchies in agents and interactions with various disaster simulations [1]. The agents are firefighters, police workers, ambulance workers and their control centers.

The basis of RoboCupRescue is a disaster rescue scenario in which the rescue agents attempt to minimize damages to civilians and buildings after an earthquake. Agents in a competing rescue team do rescue operations in a disaster world, and cooperate each other to save buried ones, to extinguish fires, to repair roads, etc. The teams do not compete against each other directly like games in RoboCupSoccer. They operate independently in the copies of a disaster world and compare their performance.

It provides not only a platform for Multi-Agent System research domain but also a prototype system for decision support system at public offices.

2 Improvements Rescue Simulation and Changes in Rules

After 2001 competition , several proposals were done and they were discussed over RoboCupResuce mailing list (r-resc@ISI.edu). The following four proposals were adopted.

1. GIS file of a virtual city map,
2. Tools to change parameters that specify magnitudes of earthquakes,
3. Civilian agent modules which actions can be specified as rules,
4. A new traffic simulator that runs stably.

Evaluatin Rule: Rescue operations are themselves multi-purpose activities to save human lives. Their performance is evaluated by a composite metric of human lives, building damages and etc. The followings are metrics used in 2001 and 2002:

$$V_{2001} = L + 1 - \frac{H}{Hint} \times \frac{B}{Bmax}$$

$$V_{2002} = (P + \frac{H}{Hint}) \times \sqrt{\frac{B}{Bmax}}$$

G.A. Kaminka, P.U. Lima, and R. Rojas (Eds.): RoboCup 2002, LNAI 2752, pp. 477–481, 2003.

where L is the number of dead persons, P = the number of agents $-L$ is the number of live persons, H is the amount of HP(health point) values of all agents and the ratio to the initial time, $H/Hint$, shows the efficiency of operations, B is the area of houses that are not burnt, and $Bmax$ is the area of all houses. At 2002, the metric was changed to represent the rescue agent's operations more directly than 2001, because their direct contribution in V_{2001} was less than 1.0.

Disaster Setting: Earthquakes may occur anyplace in the world. Rescue operations will be done in unexpected or unfamiliar situations. Teams are supposed to do rescue operations equally well at two cities, Kobe city and a virtual city (Fig. 1) under various disasters. Following files sets disasters.

map of city file contains the network of road and properties of buildings. Using different maps is equal to be in different cities.

gis_initial file specifies the number of agents - rescue agents and civilians - and their initial locations. The population or locations of civilians are different from morning to night. The parameters in this file represent such situations.

dis_initial file describes the magnitudes of earthquake and how much damages are at where.

At 2002, teams are requires to submit gis_initial and dis_initial files before competition. The files were used for games to create various situations, because teams do not know the content of other team's gis_initial and dis_initial files. This situation stresses planning under real-time constraints are required more than last year.

Fig. 1. Rescue simulation - performance display (left), virtual city map (middle), Kobe city map (right) -

Communication Model: A rescue team is composed of heterogeneous agents - fire brigades, ambulances, polices and their center agents. Center agents can communicate with agents under their commands at remote locations, while the communications among other agents are limited within a specified range (30m). The center agents can collect data from distributed agents under their commands and control them to rescue efficiently. Table 1 shows the range of agents' number that is specified in the gis_initial file. The agents are required to work cooperatively at two conditions - with center agents and with no center agents.

Table 1. Number of agents and ignition points

numbers	min.	max.	numbers	min.	max.
Fire Brigade	10	15	Fire Brigade Center	0	1
Police Force	10	15	Police Force Center	0	1
Ambulance	5	8	Ambulance Center	0	1
Civilian	70	90	Refuges	1	5
ignition points	2	8			

Table 2. List of participating teams

team	country	affiliation
Arian	Iran	Sharif University of Technology
Gemini	Japan	National Institute of Advanced Industrial Science and Technology (AIST)
Kures2002	Japan	Kansai University
NITRescue02	Japan	Nagoya Institute of Technology
RoboAkut	Turkey	Bogazici University
Team WaGuMi	Japan	JAIST/AIST
YowAI2002	Japan	The University of Electro-Communications
Rescue team for Rescue	Japan	Future University-Hakodate

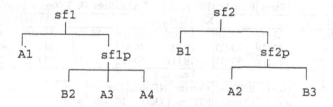

Fig. 2. semi-final games

Civilian Agent as Environment: Civilian agents play important roles in disasters. They may walk to refuges, say at homes, ask for help, or work for helping other civilians. A new framework to describe such civilian's behaviors was proposed and civilian agents implemented by the frame were used [2].

3 Final Results and Awards

Eight teams from three countries (15 teams from 6 countries at pre-registered time) participated this year. Rescue team for Rescue was a system that speaks comments on rescue operations [3]. At team meeting before competition, it was decided that Rescue team for Rescue commented all games using Kobe city map.

The rest seven teams were divided into groups A and B. They got points according to V_{2002} metric. The numbers in tables are V_{2002} metric values and the numbers in parenthesis show the points. The total points in the preliminary games ranked them and decided their positions at semi-final games (Fig. 2).

Table 3. Scores of Preliminary Games

Group A

gis_i f. dis_i f.	YowAl. NITRes.	NITRes. RoboAk.	RoboAk. Kures.	Kures. YowAl	YowAl. NITRes.	NITRes. RoboAk.	RoboAk. Kures.	Kures. YowAl	total points	rank
Map	Kobe City				Virtual City					
YowAl.	79 (3)	94 (3)	90 (3)	73 (3)	95 (3)	94 (3)	46 (3)	86 (3)	24	A1
NITRes.	43 (2)	81 (2)	20 (1)	62 (2)	49 (0)	89 (2)	39 (2)	78 (2)	13	A2
RoboAk.	31 (0)	30 (0)	18 (0)	23 (0)	66 (2)	49 (0)	35 (0)	62 (1)	3	A4
Kures.	38 (1)	36 (1)	23 (2)	47 (1)	56 (1)	54 (1)	38 (1)	62 (0)	8	A3

Group B

gis_i f. dis_i f.	Arian Gemini	Gemini TWagumi	TWagumi Arian	Arian Gemini	Gemini TWagumi	TWagumi Arian	total points	rank
Map	Kobe City			Virtual City				
Arian	21 (2)	68 (2)	58 (2)	96 (2)	90 (2)	62 (1)	11	B1
Gemini	12 (0)	26 (0)	17 (0)	41 (0)	64 (0)	49 (0)	0	B3
T.Wagumi	13 (1)	31 (1)	22 (1)	60 (1)	69 (1)	63 (2)	7	B2

Table 4. Scores of semi-final leagues

League 1

gis_i f. dis_i f.	TWagumi Kures.	Kures. RoboAk.	RoboAk. TWagumi	TWagumi Kures.	Kures. RoboAk.	RoboAk. TWagumi	total points
Map	Kobe City			Virtual City			
T.Wagumi	23 (0)	28 (0)	17 (0)	47 (1)	55 (0)	51 (0)	1
Kures.	27 (2)	39 (2)	29 (2)	46 (0)	65 (2)	53 (1)	*9
RoboAk.	24 (1)	35 (1)	18 (1)	50 (2)	64 (1)	54 (2)	8

League 2

gis_i f. dis_i f.	NITRes. Gemini	Gemini NITRes.	NITRes. Gemini	Gemini NITRes.	total points
Map	Kobe City		Virtual City		
NITRes.	76 (1)	67 (1)	89 (1)	84 (1)	*4
Gemini	31 (0)	33 (0)	49 (0)	59 (0)	0

Semi-final games

	sf1						sf2				
gis_i f. dis_i f.	YowAl. Arian	Kures. Arian	YowAl. Arian	Kures. Arian	total points		Arian YowAl.	NITRes. YowAl.	Arian YowAl.	NITRes. YowAl.	total points
Map	Kobe City		Virtual City				Kobe City		Virtual City		
YowAl.	57 (1)	70 (1)	86 (1)	78 (1)	*4	Arian	69 (1)	76 (1)	86 (1)	53 (0)	*3
Kures.	36 (0)	40 (0)	58 (0)	59 (0)	0	NITRes.	23 (0)	67 (0)	55 (0)	88 (1)	1

* marked teams proceed to next stages.

Winner was Arian, YowAI2002 was the second place and the third place was NITrescue02. It was interesting that the top two teams employed different communication models to cooperate their agents. Arian made the most of communications among agents, while YowAI2002 restricted communications. The difference comes from their images or experiences of disasters. Arian from Iran considers that communication such as PDAs, or cellular phones should be used at disaster areas, while YowAI2002 from Japan thinks communication lines will be damaged by earthquakes and not be used as usual at such time.

Table 5. Scores of final and 3rd-place games

Final game				3rd-place final game	
Map gis_i f. dis_i f.	Kobe City YowAI2002 RoboAkut	result		Kobe City Team Wagui NITrescue02	result
YowAI2002 Arian	87.9 90.5	2nd place winner	Kures2002 NITrescue02	34.7 46.5	 3rd place

Table 6. Results: Rescue Simulation League

1	Arian	Sharif University of Technology	Iran
2	YowAI2002	The University of Electro-Communications	Japan
3	NITrescue02	Nagoya Institute of Technology	Japan

SICE (The Society of Instrument and Control Engineers) award was given the new traffic simulator developers, Takeshi Morimoto and Tesuhiko Koto.

4   Discussions and Futures Developments

Disaster rescue is one of the most serious social issues that involve very large numbers of heterogeneous agents in the hostile environment. The difference in Arian and YowAI2002's approaches spotlights how the communication model between rescue agents should be. The communication is not only one of key issues of multi-agent systems but also interoperability among rescue teams from various countries in real disaster situations. They are very important from both research and application viewpoints, and will be taken into considerations to rules setting and competition styles.

Others topics that were discussed to be considered in future are evacuation from skyscrapers or underground shopping centers, disaster models at various countries and regions - brick houses or wooden houses - , and the size of a city.

I acknowledge all teams for their contributions and technical stuffs for their support during competitions.

References

1. T. Takahashi, S. Tadokoro, M. Ohta, N. Ito; *Agent Based Approach in Disaster Rescue Simulation - From Test-Bed of Multiagent System to Practical Application -*, RoboCup2001: RobotSoccer World Cup V, pp.102-111, Springer (LNAI 2377), 2002
2. K. Shinoda. I. Noda, M. Ohta; *Behavior Design of Civilian Agent for Rescue Simulation* , Proc. of Challenges in Open Agent Systems / AAMAS02, pp.135-138, 2002, 7
3. T. Morishita, I. Frank, *et al.*; *Simulating Inter-agent Communication in Disaster Relief Scenarios - An Initial Implementation of Rescue-MIKE -*, Proc. SCIE Annual Conference 2002 in Osaka, MM15-4

RoboCupRescue Robot League
A Short Summary

Satoshi Tadokoro

Dept. of Computer & Systems Engineering
Kobe University, Rokkodai, Nada, Kobe 657-8501 Japan
tadokoro@cs.kobe-u.ac.jp

Results

Ten teams from five countries participated in the RoboCupRescue RobotLeague in 2002 as shown in Table 1. Most robots are remotely teleoperated and have limited autonomy. Because of the complexity of the problem, fully autonomous robots cannot be practical. Adjusted autonomy, shared autonomy, and autonomy for human interface are suitable to apply AI to the real disaster problems.

Table 1. Participants of the RoboCupRescue Robot League

Team Name	Affiliation	Characteristics
COMPETITION		
HANIF Rescue Robot Team	YSC (Iran)	Crawler type, large
IUB Team 2002	Intl. Univ. Bremen (Germany)	Buggy type, balloon camera
KAVOSH	Javan Robotics Club (Iran)	2 Crawler types, periscope camera
Kingston Fire Brigade	Univ. Auckland (New Zealand)	Tire type, autonomous, small
MARR	Tokyo Inst. Tech. (Japan)	2 Crawler types, fast
SCARABS	New Roads School (USA)	Tire type, wired, high school team
Sharif Rescue Robot	Sharif Univ. Tech. (Iran)	2 Crawler types, crawler mechanism
UVS-IV	Kobe Univ. (Japan)	2 Crawler types, mapping
DEMONSTRATION		
MINORI 2002	Nippon Inst. Tech. (Japan)	Crawler type
ZMP Sensorbot	ZMP Inc. (Japan)	Crawler type, wired

Observations

Three fields of earthquake disaster were created by Yuki Nakagawa (National Museum of Emergent Science) following a standard proposed by Adam Jacoff (NIST). A Japanese-house field was developed as the orange zone. Type of disasters depends on countries and regions because local situations such as houses,

G.A. Kaminka, P.U. Lima, and R. Rojas (Eds.): RoboCup 2002, LNAI 2752, pp. 482–484, 2003.

Fig. 1. MARR, the 2nd position winner of the RoboCupRescue Robot League 2002

streets and styles of habitation are different. For example, pan-cake crush was typical in Turkey, but first-floor crush was widely observed at Kobe Earthquake in Japan. Futon mats made serious trouble in search and rescue operations in Japan. It is important to evaluate robots and systems under wide variety of realistic situations according to the local needs. The rubble-pile field simulated debris that was completely destroyed where voids are so small that large robots could not enter.

Thirty victim dummies were distributed in the fields (on the surface, lightly trapped, in a void, or entombed). Babies and adults were painted gray simulating dirt and could not be easily recognized by robot cameras. They emit living signals such as heat of bodies, sound of shouting, CO_2, motion of body parts, although they do not react to robots interactively.

Table 2. Results: Rescue Robot League

1	KAVOSH	Javan Robotics Club	Iran
2	MARR	Tokyo Institute of Technology	Japan

Score is calculated by a formula evaluating number of victims found, positional accuracy, quality of maps generated. Number of robots and number of operators are also considered in order to promote research of multi-agent autonomous robots. When an operator declares that he/she found a victim, referees check the validity on site.

The following problems were observed as lessons of the competition.

- Ropes, strings, news papers, towels, and futon mat obstructed motion of robots. They are sometimes caught by the crawler mechanisms, and caused the robot to be stuck and to derail.
- Wireless communication sometimes made serious problems. When camera image is jammed, operators could not move robots. IP connection was sometimes cut under the unstable wireless environment.

- Localization was an important problem. Robots sometimes lost their ways. They could not identify unique victims and found the same victims several times.
- Reliability was important. Robots had damage at the transportation.
- Human interface had a major effect on performance. Practice and operators' skill were also important.

Target of RoboCupRescue is not limited to this field setup. Wide variety of disasters happen and robots are expected to deploy in any situation. For example, humanitarian demining is an important issue in robotics, and RoboCup should contribute the promotion of technology of this purpose. Continuous participation of teams to the competition will lead advance of necessary technology as in the football leagues.

Lessons Learned
from Fukuoka 2002 Humanoid League

Thomas Christaller

Fraunhofer Institute Autonomous intelligent Systems
Sankt Augustin, Germany
GMD-Japan Research Laboratory
Kitakyushu, Japan

1 Rules

1.1 Performance Factors

We would like to trigger developments towards fully autonomous self-build humanoid robots. Therefore we took so-called performance factors for the different dimensions with regard to autonomy (external power cord, computer outside robot, remote control). Each were to be 1.2 and if more then one is applicable then they are multiplied (1.2, 1.44, 1.728, 2.0736). These factors were either used as penalty factor (e.g. in the walking the time was multiplied by them) or as handicap (in penalty kicking the score was divided by them). I think that they are working quite well (with regard to the above stated intention) and will certainly prefer the more autonomous robots but will also allow for semi-autonomous ones if their performance is much better then that of the autonomous ones. No changes needed.

1.2 Changing Rules

Because it was the first time we had the humanoid league it was accepted that we changed the rules in accordance with the affordances of the challenges and the problems we experienced there. But at Padua we should have a meeting in the beginning with all team leaders and find out with what exact set of rules everybody has to live with during the competition. We should avoid changing the rules as much as possible.

2 Challenges

2.1 Stand on One Leg

This is definitely no problem for most of the humanoid robots or it shouldn't be one while it is one for humans! It is a wonderful entry if the audience is also involved in this. It was done in Fukuoka by asking everybody in the audience to perform this challenge together with the robots.

G.A. Kaminka, P.U. Lima, and R. Rojas (Eds.): RoboCup 2002, LNAI 2752, pp. 485–488, 2003.
© Springer-Verlag Berlin Heidelberg 2003

2.2 Walking

We developed partially the rules during the team leader meetings in consensus. Roughly they have a tendency to prefer those robots which have a good ratio between weight, power, and gait width. It is up to now fair to the different physical heights of the robots because the lenght of way is 5 times its physical height. Every touch of a human during the walking gives a penalty which is linearly increasing: 20 sec/1st touch, 40 sec/2nd touch, 60 sec/3rd touch etc. The suggestion from participants is to ask for a proof for each robot that it is capable to walk at least the 1st sector in the walking competition as a prerequisite for taking part in the competition.

2.3 Penalty Kick

Again the physical height of the striking robot was used to determine the distance between ball and striker while the measurements of the goals were only available for the two categories (40 cm and 80 cm height). We had to change the roles how the movements of the goalie and the striker are related to each another, first, to give the striker a realistic chance we introduced a 5 sec latency after the starting whistle before the goalie may start to walk towards the ball to reduce the angle which could be used to score a goal. Second, the line of the goal area was used a astrict demarcation line so that striker and goalie do not touch each another. We had some problems with the ball and the field. The ball was big enough but it was so light that it often went astray due to small uneven parts in the field.

2.4 Free Style

This turned out to be very entertaining and also very demanding for the teams.

3 Scheduling and Dissemination of Information

All in all for walking, penalty kick, and free style the time schedule turned out to be overly optimistic with regard to the set-uptime needed. While the teams in charge were very busy, everybody else including the audience had to be entertained. This was this year done perfectly by Hajime Asama and a professional moderator in Japanese. To ease this job, a suggestion could be that every team sends in a CAD-animation in which the construction of the robot is explained and a video on which the performance of the robot in the laboratory is demonstrated. Both could be demonstrated during set-up time and one of the team members may serve as an interview partner. In any case the live moderation made it interesting and we shouldn't give it up instead of the videos but integrate them. They can perfectly go together. It was also good, when the robots were brought as close as possible to the audience so that they could get a closer look - and better photos, before the robots start in a challenge.

4   Environment for Challenges

There is the proposal to synchronize the constraints for the environment (colours used, floor, lighting, etc) with another league namely the 4-legged robot league. I will get in contact with those in charge for the small-size league. It was also requested by the participants to have an extra space for rehearsal and practicing. The stage itself was always occupied by Asimo or by those teams in an actual challenge. The booths were for most of the teams OK but there was absolutely no space for rehearsal.

5   Organisation

As far as I have observed all the teams were highly satisfied with the local support and their booths. Many thanks has to go for Junichi Itakura who was acting in a very competent, most friendly, and calm way. We have to ensure that in Padua we will have a similar competent and responsible person.

The Technical Committe is in the process to be set up. Minoru Asada already stated some names. I will contact all of them during this week.

The **IEEE-RAS** International Conference on Humanoid Robots is taking place biannual in autumn. Last one was at Waseda University[1]. The next will be in 2003 in Karlsruhe and Munich (Germany). General chair is Alois Knoll (TU München) and local chair is Rüdiger Dillmann (Karlsruhe). I will talk with both to make them aware of the Humanoid League in RoboCup and find a way how to collaborate. E.g. the participants in the humanoid league should be willing to submit a co-authored paper for this conference to present the humanoid league as well as advertising the RoboCup event.

There was a suggestion of participants with regard to register a humanoid for RoboCup, namely to ask for more specific technical data e.g. length of legs, corpse, head, arms, foot print, weight, time for set-up, life time of battery. This may help us to make much better suited distinctions between the classes and fine tune the rules etc for the next RoboCup. So, this is in addition to the list, Minoru Asada already distributed in his last mail.

We should also try to attract all research groups working on humanoid robots and "modules" (like humanoid arms, hands, legs, or vision) to come to RoboCup and exhibit their systems even if the do not take part in the competitions. So, let me ask you to spread the information about the Humanoid League at Padua.

---

[1] check http://www.humanoid.waseda.ac.jp/Humanoids2001/

Appendix: Results

Table 1. Best Humanoid Award

1	NAGARA	Gifu Industries Association	Japan

Table 2. Results: Humanoid Walk

1	NAGARA	Gifu Industries' Association	Japan
2	Robo-Erectus	Singapore Polytechnic	Singapore
3	Foots-Prints	individual	Japan

Table 3. Results: H-40 Class Penalty shoot

1	Foots-Prints	individual	Japan
2	Tao-Pie-Pie	University of Auckland	New Zealand

Table 4. Results: H-80 Class Penalty shoot

1	NAGARA	Gifu Industries Association	Japan
2	Osaka Univ. Senchans	Osaka University	Japan

Table 5. Results: Free Style

1	Southern Denmark	The Maersk Mc-Kinney Moller Institute for Production Technology	Denmark
2	NAGARA	Gifu Industries Association	Japan
3	Tao-Pie-Pie	University of Auckland	New Zealand

RoboCupJunior 2002: The State of the League

Elizabeth Sklar

Dept of Computer Science, Columbia University
1214 Amsterdam Ave
New York, NY 10027, USA
sklar@cs.columbia.edu

Abstract. The RoboCupJunior division of RoboCup has just completed its third year of international participation and is growing rapidly in size and popularity. This paper describes the state of the league and looks closely at three components: participants, challenge events and educational value. We discuss the technical and educational progress of the league, identify problems and outline plans for future directions.

1 Introduction

The third international RoboCupJunior tournament was held at RoboCup 2002. As indicated by the number and range of registrations, the initiative has exploded in popularity. Fifty-nine teams from twelve countries participated (see table 1). For the first time, the event attracted teams from a wide geographical region.

Table 1. Countries represented

country	number of teams	country	number of teams
Australia	8	Korea	5
Canada	1	Macao	2
Denmark	1	Norway	1
Finland	1	Slovakia	1
Germany	5	Thailand	4
Japan	29	USA	1

This paper outlines the state of the league. It is divided as follows: participants (section 2); challenge events (section 3); educational value (section 4); and issues (section 5). We discuss the league from both technical and educational standpoints, identify problems within the league, discuss a variety of issues associated with expansion and close by outlining plans for the future.

G.A. Kaminka, P.U. Lima, and R. Rojas (Eds.): RoboCup 2002, LNAI 2752, pp. 489–495, 2003.

a. Social event.   b. Volunteers.   c. Teammates.

Fig. 1. Participants

2 Participants

The event in 2002 faced new challenges in terms of the number of participants, language and cultural issues, as well as differences in attitude regarding the meaning and mission of the Junior initiative.

In total, 236 students and mentors were involved. Table 2 lists each team and indicates which teams participated in which challenges — dance, one-on-one soccer and two-on-two soccer. The challenges themselves are discussed in the next section. Students ranged in age from 9 to 18 years of age. The participation rate of females increased to 16.5%, up from 10% in 2000. All events were conducted in both English and Japanese.

The tournament took place over a two-day period. During the first day, a round-robin was held for all the soccer teams. Most round-robins consisted of 5 teams, so every team played at least 4 games. During the second day, the finals for all the soccer teams took place. In addition, on the second day, friendship games for the soccer teams not participating in the finals occurred; and the dance event was held.

A social event was held on the evening between the two days of competition. This was a party put together by the local sponsors (Fukuoka City) and included many aspects of Japanese culture, including food, origami, music and dancing. Attendance was excellent, by both students and mentors.

Most teams were chosen to come to the international tournament through local selection events. These events seemed to vary greatly in size and scope from one region to another. All teams were asked to submit an application for participation at the international level, since it was anticipated that more teams would want to come than would be feasible in the venue. Some regional organizers submitted "placeholder" applications because their selection tournaments were not scheduled to take place until after the application deadline. The application included a short essay describing the team. Below are a few excerpts from the team essays:

- *We are the only girl robotic team of our school. We have two robots, snow and white. Snow is the field player and white our goalie. We hope that we will be selected ... so that the other girls of our school will see how exciting science can be.*

Table 2. Team statistics

dance	1-on-1 soccer	primary 2-on-2 soccer	secondary 2-on-2 soccer	number of members	team name	country
			X	3	3Peace!!	Japan
	X			3	AC IOI bot	Thailand
			X	3	AC119	Thailand
X				3	AHIMO	Japan
			X	3	ALEX	Japan
X				5	beautiful sky	Japan
			X	5	BIG WAVE	Japan
X				4	Blood Hound Monkeys	Australia
X			X	6	CanadA.I. (as in A.I.)	Canada
X				3	Choukou Dance Robo	Japan
X				4	Da Piratin' Penguins	USA
			X	5	E-Strikers	Australia
			X	3	HARRY	Japan
			X	4	ILI	Australia
			X	3	K-five	Japan
		X		5	LEGOFriends	Japan
		X		3	Lion	Republic of Korea
			X	5	LITTLE BY LITTLE	Japan
			X	4	Macao United Team A	China
			X	4	Macao United Team B	China
			X	4	Mount Soboku	Australia
			X	3	Norway	Norway
			X	4	Page 1 of 2	Australia
			X	5	Pilatoren	Germany
		X		3	P-K	Republic of Korea
			X	4	psychos	Germany
		X		3	PUKKABORO	Japan
		X		3	Red devil	Republic of Korea
			X	5	red of the dragons	Japan
			X	5	Robotic Atom Junior	Japan
			X	5	Saarland Mind Over Matter	Germany
			X	5	Saarland Omniwheelers	Germany
X				8	SAKURA	Japan
		X		3	Samurai-damashii	Japan
		X		5	Schole Asoka A	Japan
		X		5	Schole Asoka B	Japan
			X	4	SG-1 [Martin]	Thailand
	X			4	SG-2 [George]	Thailand
	X			3	Slovakia	Slovakia
X			X	4	snowwhite	Germany
			X	3	SPIRIT OF SUE	Japan
	X			3	Team Denmark	Denmark
	X			3	Team Finland	Finland
X				6	Team Hori-Hori	Japan
			X	4	Team TROUSSIER	Japan
X				3	The Groove	Australia
X				5	The Samurai	Japan
			X	4	Thunder From Down UNder	Australia
		X		3	Tiger	Republic of Korea
		X		5	Tokai 1	Japan
			X	3	Tokai 2	Japan
X			X	3	Victory	Japan
		X		4	Victory friends3 SUGOIZO!	Japan
			X	4	Waggles	Australia
		X		3	Windows	Republic of Korea
		X		4	winning3	Japan
			X	3	W-wing	Japan
			X	3	YAMAKASA	Japan
			X	5	YOSHIZUKA	Japan
12	5	13	32	236	← TOTALS	

– We [are from] Genkaijima Island, ... a small island located off Hakata bay, about 30 minutes from Hakatapier by ferry. We are all buddies, born and grown up together on the island. Our junior high school has been promoting activities in the community, learning something through information and deepening international understanding through exchanging programs under the catchphrase "Let's launch out into the sea for the future with the Genkaijima Island spirit."

– "Little by little," is our team name. It comes from the Aesop's Fables, "The Hare and the Tortoise." ... Our big plan is that, with the steadfast endeavor, our robot will outdo the hare and come out on top.

- *We will have truly valuable experiences learning a lot through teamwork and exchange with many children from overseas.*

- *The motto of our robots ... is "Simple is Best".*

- *Our team uses original parts (not a commercial kit) and assembled ourselves. We used half or more of our efforts to make more sophisticated program to control robot.*

- *In the dance competition..., you get to use creativity as well as programming skills so it's more fun than doing soccer or rescue.*

3   Challenge Events

Teams entered one of two soccer challenges (one-on-one or two-on-two) or the dance event. Three teams participated in both soccer and dance: CanadA.I. (Canada), Snowwhite (Germany) and Victory (Japan).

In the soccer event, a one-on-one competition was tried for the first time at the international tournament. A relatively small number of teams entered (5 for one-on-one compared to 45 for two-on-two). While this event allows teams with only one robot to participate, the game itself may be somewhat limiting since the field is small (1/2 the size of the two-on-two field) and there are no teamwork issues to address. Nonetheless, there is a strong sentiment, particularly in European countries, to retain the one-on-one challenge.

A new *friendship game* was introduced this year as an exhibition event. Teams were paired, each team supplying one robot, and the pairs participated in two-on-two games. In this way, teams that brought either one or two robots were able not only to experience the added complexity of the two-on-two game, but also to interact with other teams in a shared project. The teams that did not reach the finals participated in the friendship games while the finals were taking place.

Perhaps the group as a whole that showed the most progress this year was the dance event. Twelve teams participated, each demonstrating unique and creative ways of combining technology with art and music. Some teams' routines told stories. Many teams shared their country's culture through traditional dances, music and costumes — worn by both robots and students. Several teams built robots out of wood, like puppets, dressed and decorated for the occasion.

Another advancement was in the expansion of robot platforms, by both soccer and dance teams. In 2000, all teams used LEGO Mindstorms (see figure 3a). In 2002, teams used a variety of other off-the-shelf kits, including the Fischertechnik Mobile Robot (figure 3b), the Elekit SoccerRobo (figure 3c) and the Tetrixx robot. This year, a non-trivial number of teams built their own robots from basic components, rather than using off-the-shelf kits. Many of these were the dance robots, as described above.

Fig. 2. Soccer and dance teams

a. LEGO   b. Fischertechnik   c. Elekit

Fig. 3. Robot kits

4   Educational Value

As in past years [1, 2], mentors and students participated in a study examining the educational value of RoboCupJunior. This year, participants completed both paper-and-pencil surveys as well as video-taped interviews (of students only). 57% of teams completed the surveys, totalling 104 responses. Preliminary results from the students' surveys are shown below.

In the survey, students were presented with multiple questions about each of nine skills[1]: math (mat), physics (phy), computer programming (pgm), mechanical engineering (mec), electronics (ele), general science (sci), communication (com), teamwork (tem) and personal development (pdv), which includes aspects of self-esteem, organization and motivation. They were asked, on a skill-by-skill basis, did RoboCupJunior and/or your robotics experience have a positive effect? Responses were given on a 5-point Likert scale. The results are shown in figure 4.

It is interesting to note that 60% of the students indicated that they did not feel their math skills were affected by their participation in RoboCupJunior or their experience with robotics. This result concurs with the prior studies and points out that while students recognize the obvious relationship between robotics and engineering (mec and ele) and programming skills (pgm), work is needed at the curricular level to connect math skills to proficiency in robotics.

---

[1] The abbreviations in parenthesis correspond to the labels along the horizontal axis of figure 4.

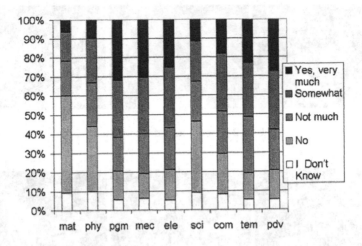

Fig. 4. Perceived effects on various skills, according to students

This is important because, as any robotics researcher will agree, strong knowledge of mathematics is required for success in technological fields; and students must be cognizant of the connection.

5   Issues

Issues relating to the competitive nature of the games were extremely prevalent throughout the tournament this year, much to the dismay of the organizers — and indeed, many of the students. Much of the tension surrounding the competition seemed to stem from mentors and parents.

There was an attempt to mix teams based on geographical region; however this was thwarted due to complaints from local teachers. The difficulty lay in the fact that the international teams were in the secondary school age group, while most of the local teams were in the primary school age group. Thus, a division of teams based on age would mean that the local primary age teams would play with each other — just as they had in their local selection tournaments — while the international teams would mostly play with other international teams and have limited opportunity to mix with the local teams. However, the notion of unfairness in the competition due to matching teams of disparate ages prevailed over the desire to create a friendly atmosphere in which teams from different cultures could share experiences with technology.

There was a disappointing relationship between students' attention to the survey described in section 4 and their performance in the competition. Students whose teams did well were happy to complete the survey and ranked their experience highly. Students whose robots did not win games were less positive about their experience. The contention is that the educational value is preserved regardless of competition performance. To mitigate this situation, perhaps future studies will be conducted outside of the competition event. In addition, perhaps more awards are needed in order that students whose robots lose games still receive rewards for their participation and for their learning experience.

The rapid expansion of the league presents many challenges for the future. If all countries are required to send their "national champions", then how do new countries with little or no national following get involved? In a geographically large country, is it practical to hold a national championship? Finally, emphasis on the competitive aspects go against the RoboCupJunior mission, so how can teams be chosen to go a selective event without using competition to decide who gets to go? This problem seems inherent in the initiative, and so must be addressed at a high level in the organization with agreement of all active members from participating countries.

6   Summary

This paper has given a brief overview of the current state of the RoboCupJunior league. Topics regarding participation, challenge events and research were presented. Issues relating to the rapid expansion of the league, as well as the increased competitiveness amongst participants, were discussed.

The mission of RoboCupJunior is to create a learning environment for today and to foster understanding among humans and technology for tomorrow. It is hoped, as the league continues to expand in terms of the number of participants, the span of countries involved and the range of challenges, that the more contentious issues surrounding the competition can be left behind in favor of the more positive aspects relating to education and exchange of cultural traditions and technical ideas.

References

1. Sklar, E.I., Johnson, J.H. and Lund, H.H., Children Learning from Team Robotics: RoboCup Junior 2000 Educational Research Report, Technical Report, The Open University, Milton Keynes, UK, 2000.
2. Sklar, E.I., Eguchi, A. and Johnson, J.H., RoboCupJunior: learning with educational robotics, in Proceedings of RoboCup-2002.

Author Index

Lecture Notes in Artificial Intelligence (LNAI)

Lecture Notes in Computer Science